America Online Official Internet Guide

SECOND EDITION

America Online Official Internet Guide

SECOND EDITION

David Peal

Osborne/**McGraw-Hill**

Berkeley New York St. Louis San Francisco
Auckland Bogotá Hamburg London Madrid
Mexico City Milan Montreal New Delhi Panama City
Paris São Paulo Singapore Sydney
Tokyo Toronto

Osborne/**McGraw-Hill**
2600 Tenth Street
Berkeley, California 94710
U.S.A.

For information on translations or book distributors outside the U.S.A., or to arrange bulk purchase discounts for sales promotions, premiums, or fund-raisers, please contact Osborne/**McGraw-Hill** at the above address.

America Online Official Internet Guide, Second Edition

Screenshot Credits:

Page 346: Reprinted with permission. Infoseek, Infoseek Ultra, Ultrasmart, Ultraseek, Ultraseek Server, Infoseek Desktop, iSeek, QuickSeek, ImageSeek, Ultrashop, the Infoseek logo and the tag line, "Once you know, you know" are trademarks of Infoseek Corporation which may be registered in certain jurisdictions. Other trademarks shown are trademarks of their respective owners. Copyright © 1994–1998 Infoseek Corporation. All rights reserved.

Page 361: Reprinted with permission from C/NET: The Computer Network, copyright © 1996.

Page 436: Copyright 1998 Internet Society. All rights reserved. Internet Society, ISOC, and the Internet Society logo are registered trademarks of the Internet Society and may not be reproduced without the prior consent of the Internet Society.

Page 476: Reproduced with permission from CCH Business Owner's Toolkit published and copyrighted by CCH INCORPORATED, 2700 Lake Cook Road, Riverwoods, Illinois, 60015 (www. Toolkit.cch.com).

890 AGM AGM 90198765432109

ISBN 0-07-882516-4
ISBN 0-07-882517-2

Publisher
Brandon A. Nordin

Editor-in-Chief
Scott Rogers

Acquisitions Editor
Megg Bonar

Project Editor
Nancy McLauglin

Editorial Assistant
Stephane Thomas

Technical Editor
Jeff Borsecnik

Copy Editor
Sally Engelfried

Proofreader
Tim Loughman

Indexer
Valerie Robbins

Computer Designer
Jani P. Beckwith

Illustrator
Lance Ravella

Series Designer
Roberta Steele

**Dedicated to the memory of
my father and to my mother,
who always encouraged me to explore.**

About the Author...

David Peal brings his ten years of editorial, technical writing, and publishing experience to the second edition of the *America Online Official Internet Guide*. He is the author of *Access the Internet* (Sybex, 1997) and editor of the *Small Business Guide to the Web* (Lycos/McMillan, 1997). For AOL Press, he has edited the *Students' Guide to the Internet* (1998) and the forthcoming second edition of *You've Got Pictures* (1999). He is also the former editorial manager of the Internet Connection channel at AOL, where he worked to develop several "personality forums" for the Internet Connection areas (including AnswerMan and Pro's Corner). Peal was the developer and writer for the *Commercial Users Guide to the Internet* (Thompson Publishing Group, 1994), one of the first business publications about the Internet.

CONTENTS AT A GLANCE

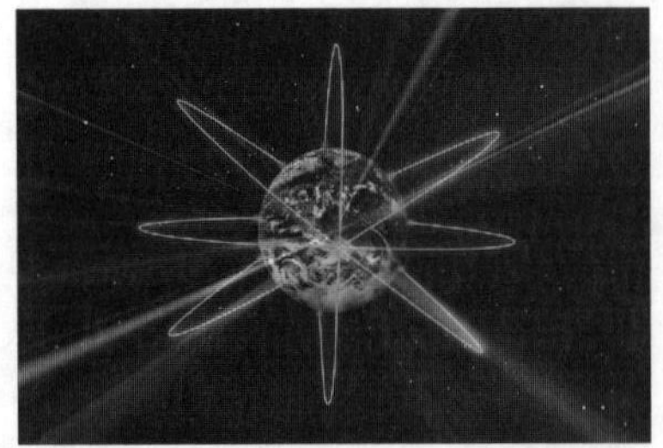

CONTENTS

FOREWORD

The reasons why people use America Online are as varied and diverse as our millions of members, but I believe if there's one common factor that contributes to their loyalty, it's the welcoming sense of community we bring to an online service. AOL became a pioneer of sorts with our efforts to humanize and simplify the online experience—previously unheard-of concepts for a medium that in its early days was a little alienating and difficult to use.

Today's Internet presents many of the same possibilities and drawbacks that once typified online services—there's an exciting world of information and services out there, but wandering through this vast territory without the proper maps can be somewhat bewildering. By contrast, exploring the Internet with America Online is a rich, fascinating experience—I liken it to traveling first class, with the best tour guides and excellent accommodations. Our customized navigational tools and resources make the Internet accessible and easy to use, with all the support and community you've come to expect from AOL. And this is your guidebook for your AOL Internet travels.

Many of our members appreciate AOL as a simple, affordable way to connect to the Internet, but, as this book proves, we're really much more than a cybergateway.

The *America Online Official Internet Guide* shows you how to use AOL to make the most of your Internet explorations. David Peal draws on his years of working with AOL to share insider tips that can turn your Internet experience into something truly extraordinary. His entertaining chapters not only reveal how to use AOL's Internet tools, they also show how AOL adds value to the Internet with our special programming and services.

In the same way that America Online has carved out a reputation as the leading provider of online services, publisher Osborne/McGraw-Hill has a tradition of serving its customers with unsurpassed quality. Readers turn to Osborne for their high-end computer and Internet books written by first-rate authors. Our collaboration on the *America Online Official Internet Guide* brings together Osborne's expertise in computer book publishing with what I believe is the best, most enjoyable way to explore the Internet. I hope you enjoy the results of our efforts, both throughout the pages of this book and on the Internet itself.

—Steve Case, Chairman and CEO of America Online

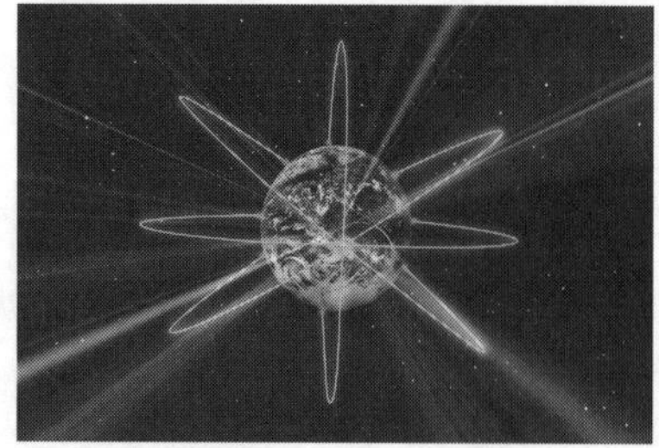

ACKNOWLEDGMENTS

In the first place I would like to thank Steve Case for his generous foreword and for doing more than anyone to open the Internet to everyone. Only America Online has delivered on the promise of making the Internet easy, fun, and truly useful.

Many people at America Online supported this book through months of hard work, and I would especially like to thank Brad Schepp, Judy Karpinski, and John Dyn. Adam Bartlett, product manager for AOL 4.0 for Windows, helped address my countless questions for well over a year. Steve Dennett, product manager for AOL 4.0 for the Macintosh, worked with me in creating the new appendix. John Tierney, product manager for Personal Publisher, made pre-release software available, thus making it possible for me to write Chapter 7. The AOL 4.0 software team, especially Ken Folsom and Steve Hunt, provided expert advice on many occasions.

Authors and technical editors often compete. Not in this case. Jeff Borsecnik was the ideal technical editor. He scrutinized every detail and tried out every procedure, while always reading from the beginner's perspective. He was a pleasure to work with, and he did much to improve this book.

Marie Cloutier-Tuberosa, a witty writer and sometime realtor, did the hard work of revising Chapter 11 despite a cantankerous computer.

In the first edition I benefited from the expertise of several folks who work behind the scenes at AOL, including David O'Donnell and Bob Hirsh. Many details in the second edition still reflect their influence. Carmel Hazard helped out with some newsgroup details in the second edition.

Osborne/McGraw-Hill once again was a pleasure to work with. In particular I want to thank Brandon Nordin, Publisher; Scott Rogers, Editor-in-Chief; Megg Bonar, Acquisitions Editor Extraordinaire; and Bernadette Jurich, Business Development Manager. Stephane Thomas did a great job coordinating this complicated project and keeping everyone in good spirits. Many people at Osborne helped make the physical book. Claire Splan started as Project Editor, and her successors, Madhu Prasher and Nancy McLaughlin, were the consummate professionals. Sally Engelfried, Copy Editor, once again made me painfully aware of my occasional awkwardness and illogic as a writer. Jani Beckwith, Designer, did an extraordinary job laying out this book and incorporating the extensive reprint updates, and Tim Loughman proofread it in record time.

On the home front, Carol, Gabriel, and Ella once again provided inspiration, love, company, and distraction, as well as more encouragement than I deserved. Once again, they put everything in perspective.

In the year since the publication of the first edition of this book, several years in "Web time" have passed. Today you'll find countless new places to visit and millions of new people putting down roots in cyberspace. Unlike other famous frontiers in history, the Internet shows no signs of closing, but it does show signs of becoming more civilized. Cities and highways are replacing the dirt trails of the early Net. Traveling this new and much-expanded territory has gotten dramatically easier. For kids, in particular, the Net's gotten to be a safer place to play, thanks in good part to the efforts of America Online.

This new edition introduces version AOL 4.0, which makes the entire Internet experience more manageable than it has ever been—on AOL or elsewhere. This book shows you how to make AOL your home port for all your online adventures.

HOW THIS BOOK IS ORGANIZED

Chapter 1 introduces the Internet, and Chapter 2 introduces AOL's Internet features. If you're new to the Internet and AOL, you'll want to spend time with these chapters.

Each of the next six chapters looks at the major Internet "tools," and you can read them in any order, depending on what you want to do. In Chapters 3 through 5, you'll learn about AOL's tools for communicating with people on the Internet (electronic mail, mailing lists, and newsgroups). Then, in Chapters 6 through 8, you'll find out how to use AOL's tools for browsing the Web, publishing on the Web, and downloading files.

The Internet is getting so big that just about everyone needs to become familiar with the many ways of finding information and people. Chapter 9 shows you how to find anything and anyone on AOL and the Net. Chapter 10 shows you how to go beyond AOL's built-in Internet features and use popular software such as Netscape Navigator (for exploring the World Wide Web), Internet Relay Chat (for chatting on the Internet), and Telnet (for taking part in interactive virtual communities).

Chapter 11 suggests several hundred awesome Web sites to use as starting points for your Internet adventures.

SOFTWARE COVERED IN THIS BOOK

This is a book about AOL 4.0, which comes in three versions: Windows (that is, Windows 3.1); Windows 95 and 98; and Macintosh. The book focuses on the Windows 95/98 version and shows illustrations of that version, but it does call attention to the minor differences between the two Windows versions when appropriate. AOL 4.0 for the Macintosh is indistinguishable in most ways from AOL 4.0 for Windows 95. The remaining differences are spelled out in a new appendix, which also highlights special AOL resources for members who use a Macintosh.

WHAT'S NEW IN AOL 4.0?

AOL 4.0 represents the largest software upgrade AOL has ever made and the most ambitious effort yet to integrate the Internet thoroughly into the online service. AOL was listening to what Internet users wanted, and the result is AOL 4.0. Here's what you'll find in AOL 4.0:

Easier to get online AOL 4.0 gives you the option of storing your password, so you don't have to enter it every time you sign on. Here's another new feature to speed up the sign-on process: you can redial an access number automatically. It's also easier to set up and use "locations," for using AOL on the road. Once online with AOL 4.0, you can switch to another screen name without first signing off. Read all about improved access in Appendix A.

Easier to get around AOL sports a classy new customizable toolbar (those little pictures at the top of your display, which you click to get around AOL and the Net). Use the toolbar's new Mail Center menu to get direct access to all AOL features related to e-mail. Use the Internet menu to go directly to the Web and other Internet features. You can make the toolbar smaller (to see more on your screen), and you can add your own buttons to the toolbar, so you can go directly to your local weather forecast, your stock portfolio, or anything else, including your favorite Web site. The Welcome screen has been revamped and now takes you directly to essential places such as Parental Controls, AOL's expanded Web site, the latest news, and Member Services. Read about AOL's new look in Chapter 2.

Easier to keep track of where you've been A new navigation bar lets you enter AOL keywords and Internet addresses at any time, from any place. You can even leave off the messy *http://* part of Web addresses. AOL's "History Trail" automatically keeps track of what you do on both AOL and the Internet, making it easier to return to places you've recently visited. For those Net and AOL destinations you really like, you can keep track of your "Favorite Places." With AOL 4.0 you can even put links to your Favorite places into Instant Messages. Read all about the improved navigation in Chapter 2 and Favorite Places in Chapter 6.

Awesome e-mail E-mail is the center of life for millions on the Internet, and AOL has made substantial improvements in everything mail-related. All three of your mailboxes (New Mail, Sent Mail, Old Mail) are available in one window. No more poking through the Mail menu looking for a copy of that message you sent yesterday! You can now automatically spell-check the messages you send. Also new, you can attach multiple files to a single message. The Address Book is now genuinely useful, and you can automatically add names and addresses to it. It is alphabetized, fully editable, and can be used to store free-form information about your contacts as well as digitized images of them. Read all about mail improvements in Chapter 3.

Better browsing Microsoft's Internet Explorer is your "default" (built-in) browser, and it has become even more secure. This means it's even safer to buy stuff on the Web. AOL 4.0 comes with several "plug ins," including RealAudio and Shockwave, so seeing and hearing sound and video on the Web are automatic. No more "helper applications"! A new AOL Web site, Multimedia Showcase, takes you to the places that show off the new multimedia features of your AOL browser. Thanks to the new navigation bar, the browser doesn't have its own buttons for stopping, going back, and so on. The result is a cleaner browser window with more room for actually seeing stuff on the Web. Read all about browser enhancements in Chapter 6.

Easier to work offline Flash Sessions (for reading and writing your e-mail and newsgroup messages while offline) have been renamed Automatic AOL and received a facelift. Your downloaded e-mail messages and newsgroup postings are stored in your Personal Filing Cabinet, which has been redesigned for quicker access, easier searching, and password-protection. While offline you can view and edit any images you have saved on your hard drive, using AOL 4.0's new Picture Gallery, always available from the File menu. Read all about offline features in Chapter 5 (Automatic AOL) and Chapter 6 (Personal Filing Cabinet).

More great content! Also new is the entire lineup of AOL channels, those universes of content devoted to both familiar AOL channel themes (like Sports and News) and new ones (Families, Influence, and WorkPlace). Channels now have a consistent look and a common way to find information. Most AOL channels now have relationships with major information providers such as Barnes & Noble, ParentSoup, AutoVantage, and CBS, who supply a stream of new content every day.

Too much content? Whether you're searching AOL or the Net, start with the new Find button on the navigation bar. For searching AOL, AOL Find has been revamped for searching within and between channels. AOL NetFind is the perfect place to start whenever you want to find something or someone on the Internet. Finally, if you ever get lost, AOL's Help areas have been expanded in scope. Help of all types is available from both the Help menu (offline) and *keyword: Help* (online).

Read all about it in Chapter 1 (Help), Chapter 2 (channel lineup and AOL Find), and Chapter 9 (AOL NetFind).

WHAT DO YOU THINK?

Your comments and suggestions can help me improve this book. What do you think? What's not correct? What's missing? What would you like to see more of? Less of? For future editions I'd also like to find out in what ways the Internet has become indispensable for you. Please send your suggestions, comments, and stories in an e-mail message to me at **dpeal**. If you've never sent an e-mail message, what are you waiting for? Chapter 3 contains everything you need to know to send and receive electronic mail.

Chapter 1

America Online: Your Gateway to the Internet

To newcomers, the Internet can seem intimidating, even scary. Folks with even a little experience, however, have a different story to tell. They experience the Internet not as a network of cables and computers but as a community—actually, a collection of many thousands of small communities. On the Internet, as in any community, it's the people who count. Here you will find people from all over the country and the world who share your hobbies, passions, and preoccupations.

The Internet, or Net, is also a staggeringly large source of information, but, unlike other information resources, anyone can use the Internet, and anyone can contribute to it. On America Online it's easy to do both. On your travels you will find that the communities and information resources of AOL and the Net complement each other. What you don't find on one, you're likely to find on the other. When you have questions about finding information or locating people on the Internet, AOL can help in many ways, as you'll see later in this chapter.

The Internet is an immense enterprise, whether it's measured by the amount of information or the number of people or by the rate of growth of both. America Online makes the Internet a manageable and seamless extension of the AOL community, and its e-mail software lets you communicate with millions on the Net. AOL also provides the behind-the-scenes technologies to give you the most reliable and enjoyable experience on the Internet. Finally, AOL, with its large and helpful community, never leaves you alone on the Net. Think of AOL as your home and safe haven on the Internet.

If you want to learn to navigate the Net's rich resources and take part in the creation of new electronic communities, this book is for you! Read it to find out how America Online can make your Internet experience as fun, useful, and easy as possible. This chapter gives you an overview of:

- How the Internet and AOL can be indispensable in your daily life
- How America Online differs from other Internet Service Providers (ISPs)
- How the Internet came to be what it is today

You don't have to *do* anything in this chapter, though you're welcome to check out some of the Web sites and AOL areas, or *forums*, if you'd like. In the rest of the book you will find the nitty-gritty how-to material, and in Chapter 11 you'll find a directory of hundreds of worthwhile Internet sites. If you're brand new at all this, Appendix B has a glossary of essential Internet terms.

ONLINE, INDISPENSABLE

I can still recall the excitement of discovering, in early 1994, the "first elementary school with a site on the World Wide Web": Mr. Marshall's fifth grade class in Grand River, Michigan. Recently, at the start of a new school year, I needed the phone numbers for my kids' public elementary schools in Maryland. I didn't think twice about how to get the information; I used America Online to go onto the World Wide Web, the multimedia part of the Internet. Within minutes I found just what I needed. Even better, I saved the cost of a phone call and avoided the bother of getting put on hold or playing phone tag. Thousands of schools are giving kids the chance to do research, take part in collaborative school projects, and publish their work for others to see. The Web66 site shown in Figure 1-1 can take you to the more than 10,000 schools worldwide that have a Web presence.

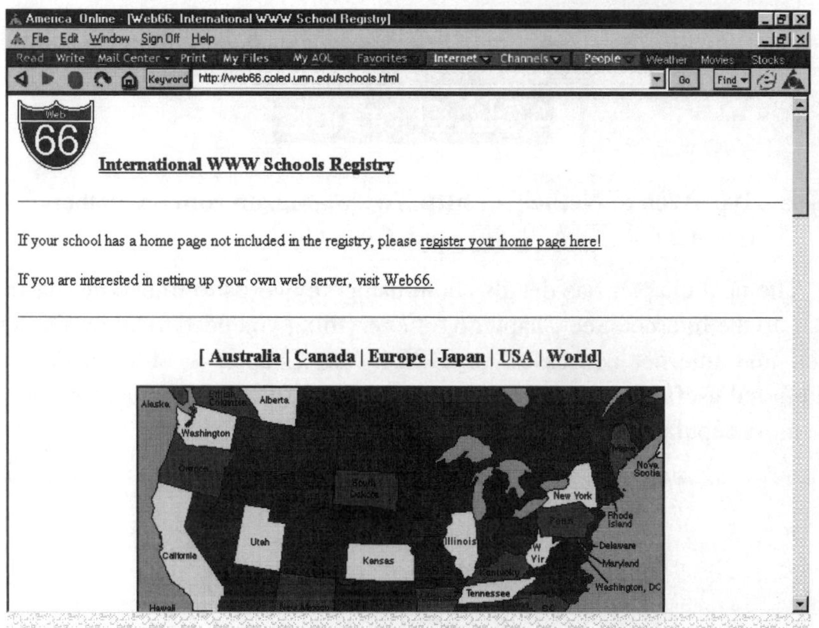

FIGURE 1-1 More than 10,000 schools around the world have Web sites; you can find them all here

What follows are a few indispensable sites you'll find on both the Web and AOL. There's a lot more to the Internet than the Web, but chances are that you'll be spending a good deal of your time on the Internet visiting useful sites like these (see "The Heart of the Net" later in this chapter). To keep up with the best and most indispensable sites on the Web, start at AOL's Web site. From the Welcome screen, just click Go to the Web.

Keywords

You can use *keywords* to get anywhere on AOL or the Net. In AOL 4.0, you can type a keyword or Internet address directly into the AOL toolbar. On AOL, the best Web sites have their own keywords, so instead of typing **http://www.aol.com**, for instance, you can just type in **Web**. For any Web site, you can leave off *http://* when using the Address box (but not when using the old Keyword window).

In this book, *keyword: Such-and-such* is shorthand for the following:

1. Use your mouse to select whatever's currently displayed in the AOL address box on the main screen:

2. Type **Web** or **Nethelp** or **http://www.amazon.com** or another Internet URL or AOL keyword. Click Go.

The next chapter has details about using keywords to transport you from AOL to the Internet. See Chapter 6 for everything you need to know about the Web and Internet addresses, or URLs. See Chapter 11 for hundreds of additional useful Internet resources, plus a list of the keywords available for the most popular Web sites.

Planning a Vacation or an Outing?

Last year, while planning a family vacation on the Delaware beach, I used the World Wide Web to find a place to stay. This summer, a neighbor of mine rented a cottage in Maine using the Internet. The Web's **CityNet** is an excellent way to learn about new places anywhere in the world. Closer to home, I have planned many a weekend outing with the help of Web resources such as the superb, up-to-date, and always free **National Park Service** Web site, **ParkNet**. Before leaving the house for local trips I routinely fetch the weather reports at *keyword: Weather*, where the diligent can also download satellite maps and find out what the weather's like in Juneau and Phoenix.

How do you get to that new place you learned about on the Internet? **MapQuest**, shown in Figure 1-2, provides street maps for any address in the U.S. I use MapQuest

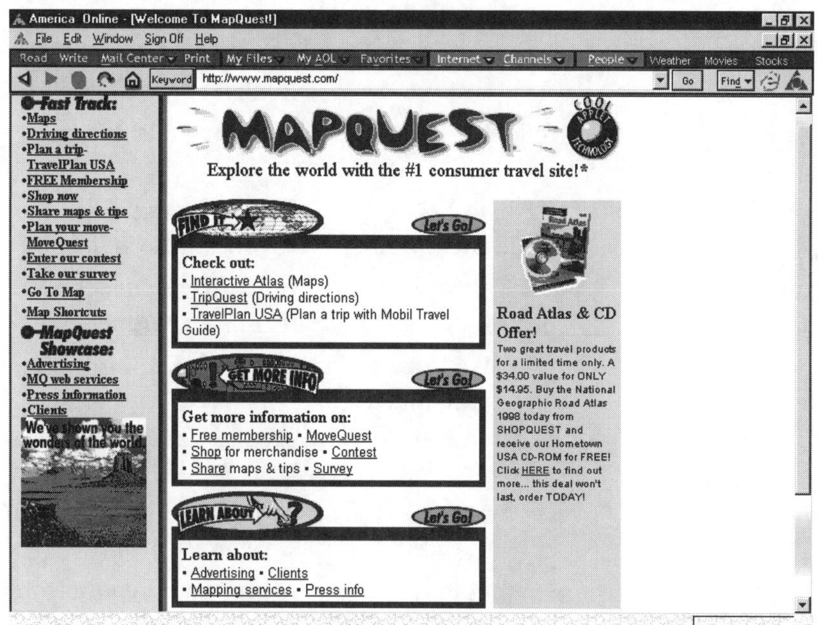

FIGURE 1-2 MapQuest helps you pinpoint any location in the U.S.—and get turn-by-turn driving directions

all the time to find new places in the confusing welter of streets where I make my home. After finding a street map with a destination (down to the block), I "zoom out" to see the larger framework of roads and highways, so I can plan the car trip. I print a series of maps to show both the street location and the larger gridwork.

Note *Internet addresses for all three of these excellent trip-planning resources (CityNet, ParkNet, and MapQuest) are listed in Table 1.1, along with other essential resources. Chapter 9 introduces a series of other sites for finding local addresses, street maps, business locations, Zip codes, and other community information.*

Subject	Site	Address (URL)
Books, purchasing	Amazon.com Barnes and Noble AOL Store	**http://www.amazon.com/** *keyword: Barnes* *keyword: AOLstore*, click Books
Cars, pricing old and new ones	Kelley's Blue Book	**http://www.kbb.com/**
CDs, purchasing	CDNow Music Boulevard	**http://www.cdnow.com/** *keyword: Music Boulevard*
Computers, getting information about	CNET ZDNet	**http://www.cnet.com/** **http://www.zdnet.com/**
Encyclopedias	Columbia Concise, Grolier Multimedia, and Compton's Living Encyclopedias	*keyword: Encyclopedias*
Entertainment	Asylum	**http://www.asylum.com/** *keyword: Asylum*
Health	Health A to Z	**http://www.healthatoz.com/**
Home, buying one	HomeFair	**http://www.homefair.com/**

TABLE 1-1 A sampling of indispensable Web sites. Many more sites can be found in Chapter 11

Subject	Site	Address (URL)
Jobs, finding one	Monster Board America's Job Board	**http://www.monster.com/** **http://www.ajb.dni.us/**
Maps of any place in the U.S.	MapQuest	**http://www.mapquest.com/**
Money, yours	American Express: Be Your Own Financial Advisor	**http://www.americanexpress.com/advisors/assess/**
News, the world's	Crayon (Create Your Own Newspaper)	**http://crayon.net/**
	Editor & Publisher	**http://www.mediainfo.com/emedia/**
Parks, U.S.	ParkNet	**http://www.nps.gov/**
People, finding them	AOL NetFind	*keyword: NetFind*
Places, learning about them	CityNet	**http://city.net/**
Quotes	Bartlett's Quotations	**http://www.columbia.edu/acis/bartleby/bartlett/**
Schools, Web sites of	Web66 (a registry of schools with Web sites) (Figure 1-1)	**http://web66.coled.umn.edu/schools.html**
Shakespeare	Shakespeare	**http://the-tech.mit.edu/Shakespeare/works.html**
Taxes	Internal Revenue Service	**http://www.irs.ustreas.gov/**

TABLE 1-1 A sampling of indispensable Web sites. Many more sites can be found in Chapter 11 (*continued*)

The Heart of the Net

The Internet used to be a place where all you could do was read. It was inhabited primarily by scientists and other academics. With the rise of the World Wide Web, things have changed. Many people think of the World Wide Web as the *graphical* part of the Internet, and more and more sites feature video, animation, and other multimedia effects as well. The Web consists of millions of *pages* of information *linked* together in a way that makes it easy to go to related information with just a mouse click. AOL's own Web site, AOL.com (*keyword: Web*), ranks as one of the most visited and most indispensable on the planet. You can read more about the Web and AOL.com in Chapter 6. Then, in Chapter 7 you'll learn how to make your own Web page using AOL's Personal Publisher.

Changing Jobs?

Chances are good that your dream company has a Web site. If not, you can still make an informed career choice using one of many Web sites, such as the **Monster Board** or **America's Job Bank**, the federal government's enormous and searchable directory. You can then apply for some jobs electronically by sending your resume in an electronic mail (e-mail) message. In Chapter 3 you can read all about getting and sending e-mail to people on the Internet. On AOL itself, the **AboutWork** forum (*keyword: Aboutwork*) helps you find a job, then dress for success even if you work out of your home and live in a bathrobe. It's part of the new **WorkPlace** channel.

AOL's Web site has a section called TimeSavers, consisting of many invaluable Internet resources, including a half dozen career-related services.

Not Enough Time to Shop?

Don't live close to a superstore that's likely to have that obscure title by Toscanini (or Hootie and the Blowfish)? **CDNow** and **Music Boulevard** are two Internet-only stores specializing in audio CDs. You can search for specific CDs, do some comparison shopping, hear sample sound clips, and, of course, purchase CDs.

These days, I go online every week or so to buy books. I love books, but they get expensive. On AOL I have a choice of ways to save money in making book purchases. *Keyword*: *BarnesandNoble* takes me to **Barnes and Noble**'s Web site (available from the AOL area shown in Figure 1-3), and *keyword: Amazon.com* (also available from the AOL Web site) takes me to **Amazon.com**, a bookstore that exists only on the Internet. Both stores offer competitive discounts on many current titles and both can ship just about anywhere, usually without your having to pay a penny in sales tax.

What else can you buy online? Chocolate, wine, flowers, tickets, software, hardware, and stocks, for starters. You can buy big things, too, or at least use the Net to make a more informed decision. You can get all the information you need to purchase a car at **Kelley's Blue Book**, and I refinanced my mortgage using a mortgage broker available on AOL, which I learned about on the Internet at the **HomeFair** site.

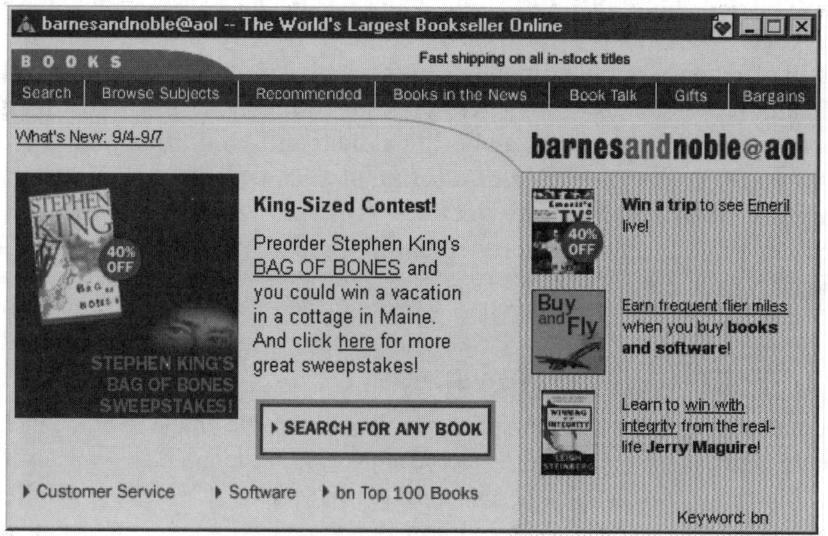

FIGURE 1-3 AOL brings the convenience of a Barnes and Noble superstore to your computer

The new version of AOL has a menu called Perks, where you can discover many of the tangible benefits of belonging to AOL.

AOL's Shopping channel makes online shopping easier than using the Yellow Pages. Apparel, books, computer equipment, toys—in short everything is available from online department stores like JC Penney, iQVC, Eddie Bauer, and Lands End. Join AOL Shoppers Advantage and get low-price guarantees and discounts, plus the very best in customer support at the AOL store (*keyword: AOLstore*).

Tip

Is it safe to purchase something on the Internet using your credit card number? The Microsoft browser built into your AOL software supports "128-bit" encryption. This level of security is as safe as anything you're likely to do in the much more menacing "real" world. Chapter 6 has more to say on the subject.

Need Medical Information?

Whether someone in your family has a particularly nasty cold or you want to reduce the risks of a heart attack, you'll find information and knowledgeable people on the Net, as well as sources of online solace and support. I have helped family members find excellent sources of information about Alzheimer's disease and autism on the Net. The **Virtual Hospital** Web site at the University of Iowa is an older site that still offers an enormous amount of authoritative information for both patients and health professionals. These days I also avail myself of the Web's **Health A to Z**, a vast collection of links and original material. You'll find other excellent health-related sites in the "Health" section of Chapter 11. On AOL itself, visit the **Better Health & Medical Network** (*keyword: Better Health*) for a vast collection of interactive features and informational resources, conveniently arranged by ailment.

No Time to Read the Newspaper?

Hundreds of magazines and newspapers are now available on the Internet, including some that are available *only* on the Net. Computers, music, politics—whatever your interest, whether mainstream or underground, it's there. **CNET** and **ZDNet**, for example, have become irreplaceable information resources for the computer industries.

For daily news of the old-fashioned kind, one estimate put the number of newspapers on the Net at the end of 1997 at 4,000! Your local newspaper may have an online edition, with up-to-date versions of your favorite features, whether it's the comic page or the job listings. I like **Editor & Publisher**'s searchable list of the world's newspapers.

For news—what's going on, right now, in your city, nation, and world—start in AOL's News channel, which gives you the latest scoop from ABC and other sources. It's the place to get breaking news about the latest plane crash or the most recent pronouncement from Washington. For other newspapers on the Net, see the "News" section in Chapter 11.

The most intriguing news sites are the ones that don't yet exist, that pop up in response to some event, such as the recent sites devoted to the reversion of Hong Kong to China, the first photos from the surface of Mars, and the death of Princess Diana. When something happens in the world, chances are a Web site will be the best way to find out about it.

Overwhelmed by information? Create your own newspaper, literally, at **Crayon**, shown in Figure 1-4. You can tailor a newspaper to your own needs and base it on bits and pieces of dozens of other newspapers.

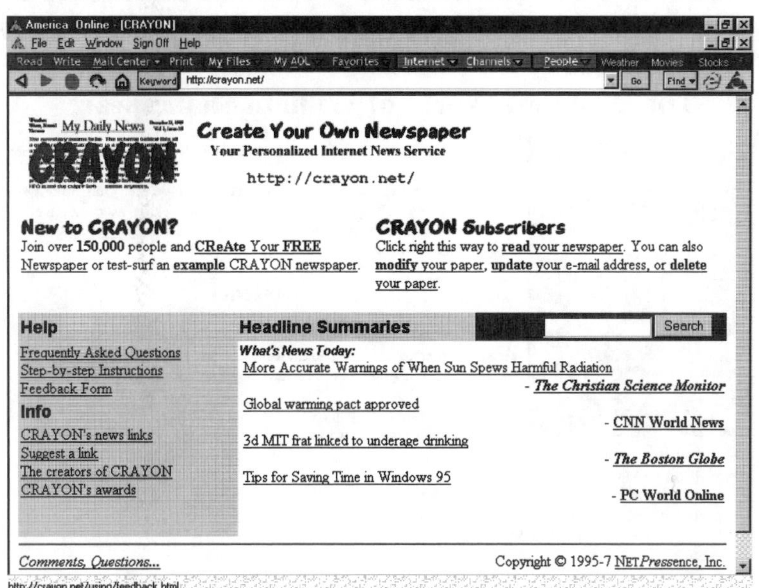

FIGURE 1-4 Create your own custom newspaper based on the information you want from your favorite newspapers

Looking for Just the Right Word?

If you ever need an apt quote, visit the **Bartlett's Quotations** site on the Web, a searchable list of thousands of notable quotations. Writers and speakers in need of a **Shakespeare** quote in particular will love MIT's searchable archive of the Bard's entire corpus (see Figure 1-5). For authoritative reference material, the **Columbia Concise Encyclopedia** is now available on AOL at *keyword: Encyclopedia*. New to AOL 4.0 are searchable versions of the Merriam-Webster Thesaurus and Collegiate Dictionary, readily available from the Edit menu.

If you're serious about writing, AOL's Writer's Club (*keyword: Writers*) will put you in touch with hundreds of other AOL members, who will share their secrets about different types of writing and provide insights into the writing business. If you want, you'll find a mentor, and if you need more information you'll find countless links to the Web's rich publishing resources. This forum can be found in the new Interests channel.

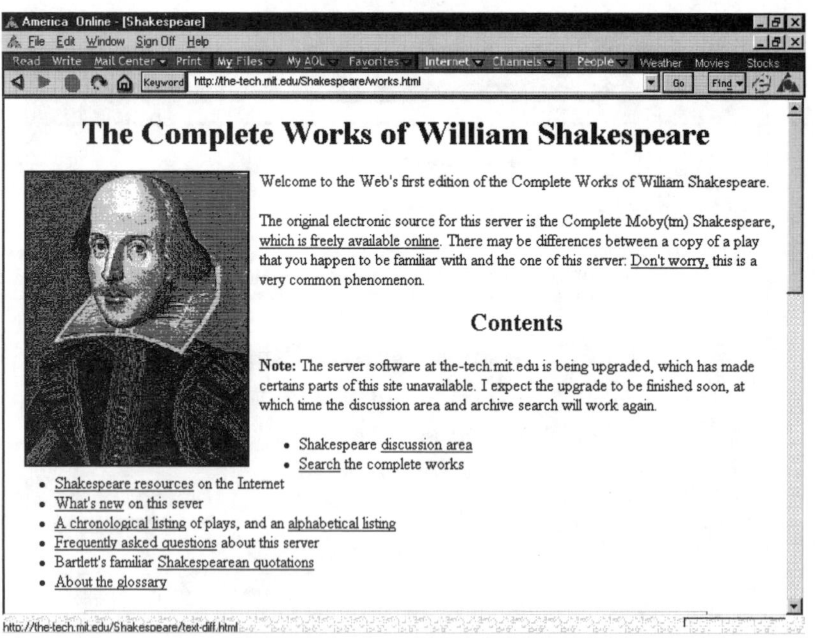

FIGURE 1-5 For salty wisdom, start with the Bard

AOL's Channels

AOL is organized in *channels*, which you can choose from the Channel menu and the Channel button of the AOL toolbar. Think of a channel as an online city, sometimes with millions of people, whose members have a passion for and collective expertise in sports, personal finance, and other large subjects. An AOL channel is a much different thing from a TV channel. For one thing, it's interactive, which means you help shape the content. Within channels you'll find dozens of communities devoted to specific topics.

In the latest version of AOL (4.0), the channels have a new look and new organization, making it easier to find what you need and to explore what you're curious about. If you're new to AOL, choose a channel and start exploring! The next chapter takes a closer look at AOL's channels, and Chapter 11 brings you hundreds of Web sites arranged by channel.

Planning Your Financial Future?

On AOL, you can access the Internet to visit hundreds of personal finance–related Web sites for up-to-the-moment information and timely authoritative advice. At the **American Express** Web site, for example, you'll find a series of online calculators you can use to figure out how much you're worth, how much you need to save in order to retire in reasonable comfort, how much you have to salt away each year to send your child to college, and other indispensable information. (See "Personal Finance" in Chapter 11 for more such sites.) From AOL you can visit the Fidelity, Schwab, and Vanguard Web sites, among others. To calculate the penalty of your prosperity, visit the all-too-informative **Internal Revenue Service** Web site.

AOL's Personal Finance channel provides just about everything you need to make an informed investment decision without leaving the comfortable confines of AOL. With this channel's services you can do the following:

- Compare related stocks and funds
- Find summaries of analysts' recommendations
- Get the latest on-target observations of the Motley Fools, AOL's resident financial wizards
- Study Morningstar's reviews of mutual funds or Hoover's profiles of American companies

Need a Break from All This Serious Stuff?

It's easier and *much* cheaper to meet celebrities on AOL than in New York or Hollywood. In AOL's Entertainment channel, you can find a movie to see or book to read, then hang out at MTV Online and Rolling Stone. Or, check out AOL's own **Asylum**, completely devoted to the world of entertainment. The AOL version (for members only) is at *keyword: Asylum*; the Web version (for the world), at http://www.asylum.com.

HOW AMERICA ONLINE DIFFERS FROM ORDINARY INTERNET SERVICE PROVIDERS

New people are continually joining the Internet community, adding their pages and postings to what is already an ocean of information. If you have just plain Internet access from an Internet Service Provider (*ISP*), the Net can seem like some strange city in a foreign country whose language is incomprehensible. In contrast, on AOL you'll get the pleasures of big-city life while avoiding the big-city frustrations of growth, congestion, and the anxieties of feeling lonely and getting lost. On AOL you'll find out what it means to experience the Internet as a community.

Any Internet SP can give you some software and hook you up to the Net, but you'll find that accessing the Internet through AOL adds layer upon layer of value to the plain Internet connection you can get anywhere else. Plus, it's just more fun. On AOL you get:

- Community: The tools for communicating with people you know, such as message boards, chat, e-mail, and Instant Messages—plus you'll find many hundreds of online areas that together form a congenial environment for making new friends.
- Selected Net resources: A careful selection of the best Internet resources throughout AOL's areas and channels, providing a clear framework for what you can do on the Internet
- Value: The best of the Net and the unique AOL experience in a single reasonably priced package
- Speed: The AOL software, servers, and networking technologies
- Safety: Both the tools to keep your kids out of trouble and the technologies to buy things securely on the Web

- Openness: Access to just about all Internet software and the ability to go anywhere and do anything on the Internet
- Help: Assistance that is available any time, in any way that works for you

I'm on AOL. Am I on the Internet?

America Online is a commercial online service that runs on a complex of powerful computers. AOL provides information from a wide variety of sources (such as magazines and news services) in a wide variety of formats (such as forums and software libraries). More and more of the content is original (that is, AOL produces it). For many people, some of the best content comes from members themselves, who can communicate with each other by e-mail, on message boards, and in chat rooms. Much of what you may like best about AOL—the chat rooms and the online versions of magazines such as *Newsweek*—is *not* available to people who aren't members.

On America Online you are always one mouse click away from the Internet.

While AOL is centralized, the Internet is decentralized. No one owns it. No one guarantees the content or is accountable for the quality of what you find. It can be difficult to navigate, mostly because there's so much of it, and there's no inherent order to the content—no Dewey decimal system.

From AOL, at no additional cost and with no additional software, you have full access to the Internet. The result is that AOL provides the benefits of both a comfortable environment that's easy to use and direct access to dynamic, globe-spanning Internet content that's growing by the hour. This access to the Internet is built right into your AOL software.

Still don't know where you are? If you're doing one of the following things, you're on the Internet:

- You're using AOL's World Wide Web "browser" (shown in Figures 1-1 through 1-5) to visit a site such as **http://www.whitehouse.gov**.
- You're sending e-mail to, or receiving e-mail from, someone whose address includes an "at" sign (@) and an "address," such as **president@whitehouse.gov**.
- You're looking at a newsgroup window, reading a newsgroup like **rec.autos.antique.** (For more on newsgroups, see Chapter 5.)

If you're in a chat room, visiting an AOL forum, using the AOL software download libraries, or writing an e-mail message, you're on AOL.

Community

What really sets AOL apart from the myriad Internet Service Providers is community. With millions of members in the U.S, Canada, and Europe, AOL offers many opportunities for you to meet people. One consequence is that on AOL you can always find someone to answer your questions about the Internet. This is especially important because people on the Internet don't always like to repeatedly answer "newbies'" questions. You can also find friends on AOL with whom you can swap Internet discoveries.

As on the Internet, community comes in two major forms on AOL:

- Communities based on live communication: *chat rooms* (for groups of AOL members), *Instant Messages* (for conversations between two people on AOL), and now *Instant Messenger* (for conversations between two people, when at least one person is on the Net). The real-world analogue to this kind of communication is the phone conversation.
- Communities based on communication that's delayed, such as electronic mail, mailing lists, and message boards. The real-world analogue in this case is the U.S. Postal Service, which is less than instantaneous but still indispensable.

Chat

AOL is famous (and also infamous) for its chat capabilities. Chat lets you communicate live with a group of people. You type your comments, press ENTER, and everyone in the chat room sees your words. Chat is one of those things you'll find only on AOL. Yes, the Internet does have something called IRC (Internet Relay Chat), which you can read about in Chapter 10, and chat rooms are coming to the Web. The difference is, on AOL chat is easy and effortless.

An AOL chat room is like a local deli, soda fountain, or tavern: you'll usually know who you can find there, and you'll likely talk the same "language." With the creation of AOL's International channel, however, the language may not be English! You'll find a list of hundreds of chat rooms in the People Connection channel.

Tip *Your Buddy List, shown in Figure 1-6, lets you know which of your AOL friends are online at the same time you're online. From the Buddy List window, you can send an Instant Message to a friend who's online, or you can invite a group of friends into a private chat room. More information about this feature is available from the People menu; choose View Buddy List. If you're unfamiliar with using menus—or haven't installed AOL yet!—Chapter 2 provides all you need to know.*

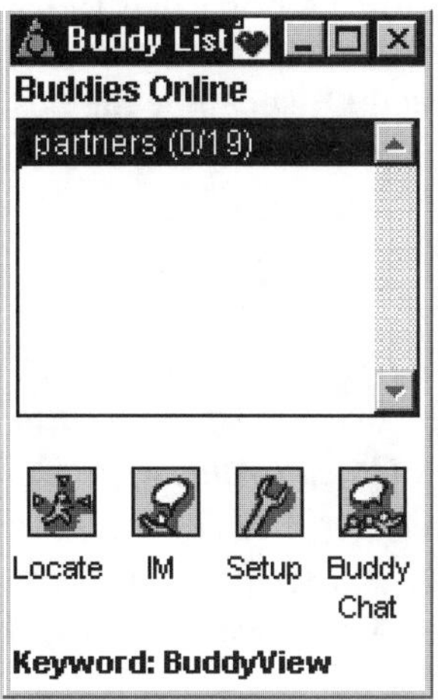

FIGURE 1-6 With Buddy Lists, you can find out who's currently online and exchange Instant Messages

Instant Messages

I love Instant Messages, or *IMs*. This form of communication, perfected by AOL, allows members to have instantaneous electronic "conversations" with other members. The conversations take place between two people (not groups), and both people must be signed on. AOL 4.0 permits members to use styled text (such as bold and italics), to vary the colors of text and backgrounds, and to insert links to Web sites and AOL areas directly into messages. No other service provides a feature this useful or flexible.

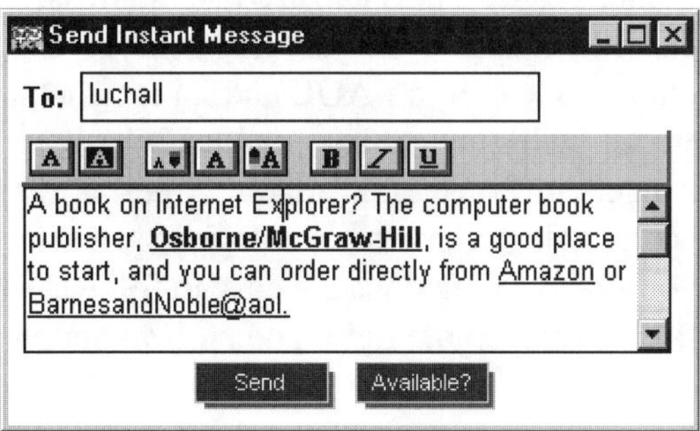

To send an Instant Message, go to the People menu and select Instant Message. Enter your friend's screen name, type a message and click Send. Your Buddy List

(Figure 1-6) is a convenient way to know when your IM buddies sign on—and off. Just select a signed-on buddy from the list, and click Instant Message. If you're ever working on a project, your Buddy List can be the best way to stay in close contact with the others. If you want, you can stay off others' Buddy Lists to avoid unwanted messages—just click Privacy Preferences.

Note *This book does not go into the details of AOL-only features such as chat rooms and Instant Messages. For help, start with the resources mentioned in the "Many Ways to Get Help" section below. In addition, I strongly recommend that you get a copy of Tom Lichty's* ***Official America Online Tour Guide*** *for a complete discussion of all the features unique to AOL. Another excellent book is* ***America Online for Busy People*** *by David Einstein (Osborne/McGraw-Hill, 1997). Both books are available through the AOL Store's Bookstore* (keyword: Bookshop).

Instant Messenger: Tête-à-tête on the Net

More and more you'll find Internet-based chat and Web-based message boards, but for now, AOL sets the standard for easy and reliable electronic communication. *Instant Messenger* is an AOL communications tool based on Instant Messages that is now available to the general Internet community. Friends or family who use the Internet but not AOL may be interested in it, and as an AOL member you'll want them to have it. Two people *not* on AOL can communicate this way, too.

Instant Messenger gives nonmembers who have friends on AOL a Buddy List plus the capability of getting member profiles and exchanging Instant Messages with those friends. If you have friends and family who have Internet accounts through other services, they can use Instant Messenger to "talk" with you. On your end, it looks and feels just like sending Instant Messages to another AOL member. If you're on AOL and an Internet friend has Instant Messenger, that person will show up in your Buddy List.

Instant Messenger software is available, free, at the AOL Web site (**http://www.aol.com**). All you have to do is download and install the software, then register; the onscreen instructions are easy to follow. The IM "interface" provides both a Buddy List (on the right) and an IM window (on the left).

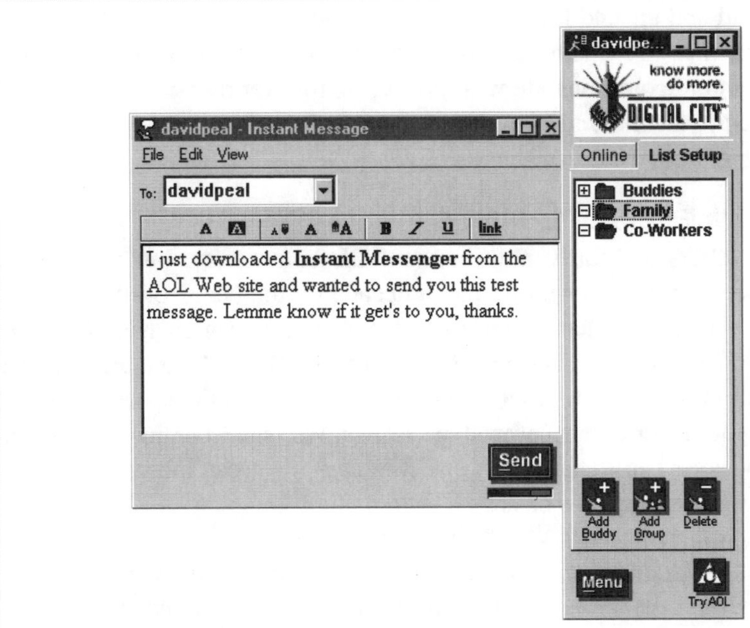

When you as an AOL member receive an Instant Messenger message, you're first notified that "An Internet user has sent you an Instant Message. Accept?" If you click OK, the message looks exactly like a regular IM. Instant Messenger also offers the familiar controls for using "styled" text—bold and italics, for example, as well as links.

Electronic Mail: Reaching Anyone, Anywhere

Electronic mail or *e-mail* (or sometimes just *mail*) is hardly unique to AOL, but AOL does offer a uniquely simple-to-use e-mail program, which has been vastly enhanced in features and usability in Version 4.0. With e-mail you can send letters (called messages) to anyone on AOL or the Internet.

Unlike chat and Instant Messages, e-mail does not take place live. Your mail will arrive in minutes (seconds if your recipient is an AOL member), but the recipient might be on vacation in Fiji and may not get around to answering you for a couple of weeks or at all. There are many benefits to this delayed communication. Messages can be composed and refined while you are offline, so you can keep a copy of every message you send and receive. With a message to AOL members, you can actually

change your mind and unsend it if it hasn't been read yet. AOL makes it easy not only to exchange messages with individuals on the Internet but also to exchange files with them and to communicate with *groups* on the Net by e-mail. Chapters 3 and 4 are devoted to the miracle of e-mail and mailing lists.

Electronic Newsletters by E-mail

Electronic newsletters are fairly new in the AOL community, but mailing list programs have been around for more than a decade on the Net. You'll find many dozens of free e-mail newsletters on AOL for channels such as Kids Only and Computing as well as for forums such as ParentSoup, the Book Report, and Hecklers Online. Each week or so these newsletters go out to subscribers' electronic mailboxes with information about forum or channel events, special tips, Web site recommendations, and more. Subscribing is easy on AOL. At *keyword: Newsletters* you can subscribe to dozens of electronic newsletters simply by clicking a button.

Note *Chapter 4 is devoted to mailing lists, one of the most informative resources on the Net. Chapter 4 also introduces interactive newsletters, which allow you to send messages to other list subscribers; distribution-only newsletters are "one-way."*

Selected Net Resources

Unlike what you find on AOL, the information on the Internet follows no standards. That doesn't mean that the miracle-diet site you just discovered is not reliable; it's just that no one guarantees that it's reliable or accurate or that it's particularly useful for your purposes. If you're changing jobs, writing a paper, researching your competition, or moving to a new city, you don't want to take chances on old or incorrect information.

Here's where AOL offers more value than the garden-variety ISP. AOL gives you clear guideposts as you start your Internet explorations. You'll find the best Internet sites integrated into channels as well as resources unavailable to nonmembers and lots of opportunities to interact with members via message boards, chat rooms, and e-mail, so you can get help and exchange Internet discoveries about shared interests. All this content—Net sites, AOL resources, and community features—is organized into some 1,500 AOL areas, or forums, about everything from tennis and politics to mutual funds and health. (You can read more about AOL areas in Chapter 2.) An AOL area can provide essential context and vastly simplify your search for people and information on the Internet.

For example, if you go to an AOL area created by a major computer vendor—Dell, Adobe, Compaq, Microsoft, Apple, Gateway, or Micron, for example—you will get instant access to AOL-only information about the company's products, plus you'll usually get a link to the company's Web site, often those specific parts of the Web sites of likely interest to you.

Value

For one reasonable monthly fee you get unlimited access to the entire Internet in addition to all of AOL's exclusive content and community (see "AOL's Billing Plans"). Other providers offer flat-rate pricing, too, but only on AOL do you get the following benefits and value:

- The pleasures of community
- Exclusive content that provides essential context to the Internet's tools and information resources
- Controls that help parents keep their kids safe in cyberspace
- Help resources in every form—human, fax, e-mail, BBS, and phone
- The sort of fun you'll never have on an ISP!

AOL's Billing Plans

AOL offers several price plans, to meet diverse needs:

- The $21.95 per month standard plan is effective April 1998 and provides unlimited use of AOL, including access to the Internet. This plan is available at an even lower rate if you pay ahead of time (see the next two items).
- For $19.95 per month you get unlimited use of AOL, including access to the Internet, if you pay in advance for one year.
- The $9.95 per month Bring Your Own Access" plan provides unlimited access to thousands of unique AOL features, including access to the Internet, if you already have an Internet connection or access through a network on your job or at school. See the section "Using AOL with a Network or Internet Service Provider" in Appendix A.

- The $4.95 per month light-usage plan provides three hours of AOL, including the Internet, with additional time priced at just $2.50 per hour. Members with this plan and the following one are notified via a small window when they go back and forth between most content (whether it's on AOL or the Internet) and free areas such as *keyword: Member services*.
- The $9.95 per month "limited" plan offers five free hours, plus additional hours at $2.95 an hour.

Finally, the Games channel now charges extra for certain areas. These premium services are explained at *keyword: Games guide*. *Keyword: Billing* has the details about the billing plans, plan switching, your account, your bill, and other good stuff.

Speed

AOL provides fast Internet access, too. Speed is especially important on the World Wide Web because sites in high demand and sites on poky Internet computers can be s-l-o-w. Chapter 6 gives you tips for making your Internet connection even faster. AOL's latest World Wide Web software was built by Microsoft and customized for the AOL service.

AOL also has the tremendous resources and technical expertise to run a huge collection of finely tuned Internet computers, or *servers*. Most ISPs these days offer very good browsers, such as Microsoft's Internet Explorer and Netscape's Navigator (Communicator), but if the computers and Internet connections of these ISPs are working slowly or not at all, even the best software doesn't do you any good. AOL offers superior software and the blazing connections required to make the Internet work for you. Both the "client" software (on your computer) and the "server" software (on AOL's computers) use a technology called *caching*—a way of storing frequently used data to significantly speed up your access to the World Wide Web and to other Internet resources.

Here's another reason AOL is fast: It uses one of the fastest networks in the communications industry, AOLnet, based on the ANS network. (In the early 1990s ANS managed the network that predated today's Internet.) Some AOLnet access numbers let you connect to AOL and the Net using 56K modems, many more support 33.6 kbps access, and research on faster cable and phone access is a priority at AOL. For now, ISDN is not supported. For the latest information, go to *keyword: Highspeed*.

Finally, AOL has helped to develop a special *compression* technology created by Johnson-Grace, an AOL company. This technology reduces the size of the graphics files you get over the World Wide Web and AOL, allowing for faster transmission and better image quality.

Safety

Every community has its darker side and shadier characters. America Online gives parents the tools and the flexibility to assert some control over what their kids see and do on the Internet. What is "unsafe" is a matter of perspective and of personal taste, of course, so AOL's policy is not to censor but to give parents the tools to make such restrictions as they see fit.

AOL gives parents powerful controls to limit kids' access to this material. These controls are available in the Parental Controls area, as shown in Figure 1-7, and Parental Controls are now available from both the AOL Welcome Screen and the new My AOL menu. In addition, whenever you create a new screen name, you'll be asked whether you want to set up Parental Controls for that name. One of the choices available allows parents to restrict a child to the Kids Only channel, where it's not possible to freely browse the Web. Appendix C is devoted to AOL's Parental Controls.

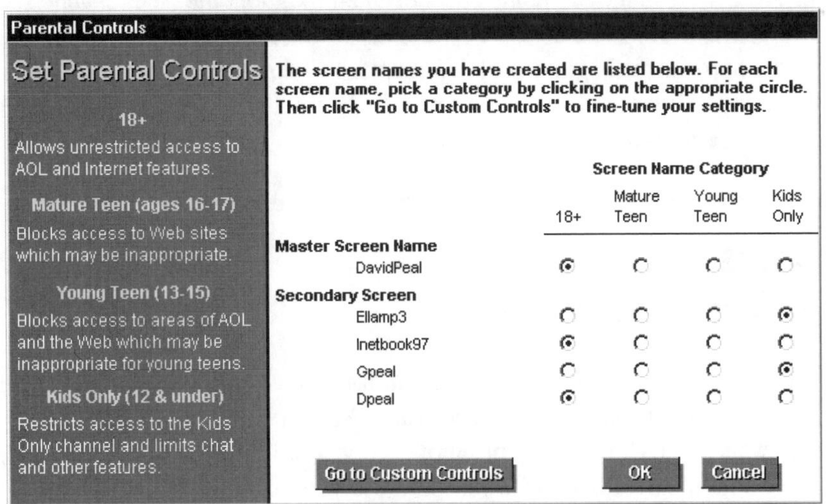

FIGURE 1-7 Parental Controls: peace of mind when your kids are on the Net

Using these tools, parents can:

- Keep kids out of chat rooms and prevent them from receiving Instant Messages
- Restrict kids' receipt of e-mail—either all e-mail or e-mail from specific e-mail addresses
- Block kids' access to specific newsgroups (or all newsgroups) and prevent them from downloading pictures from newsgroups
- Restrict kids to the Kids Only channel, with its kid-appropriate content and limited Web-browsing opportunities

Safe Transactions

There's another sense in which AOL provides for safety. Your commercial transactions on the service have always been transmitted over AOL's private network with a very high degree of security, so you can shop on AOL knowing that your financial transactions are confidential.

You can save time and money by taking advantage of the buying opportunities at the AOL Store in the Shopping channel and throughout the other channels. On the Internet as well, you can now buy directly from many sites (see "Not Enough Time to Shop?" at the beginning of this chapter). Chapter 6 looks into the question of the safety of financial transactions over the Internet and "Shopping" in Chapter 11 provides a mini-directory of Web stores.

Openness

AOL is open in two important ways.

- AOL's Internet access is open in that it is not censored. You can use AOL's built-in software to access any Web site, any mailing list, any newsgroup (with the exception of a very small number of patently illegal ones), and any other site whose address you know. *AOL doesn't censor sites in any way*, but instead gives parents the power to control what their kids do and see on the Net.

- AOL's Internet access is also open in that it gives you the choice of using other Internet software with your AOL software. AOL's built-in Internet tools are easy to use and will probably do anything you want them to do. But if you have a yen to use a different World Wide Web browser (such as Netscape Navigator) or a tool that has no built-in counterpart (an Internet Relay Chat program such as mIRC), you'll appreciate the openness enabled by AOL for Windows. Chapter 10 has all the details.

Many Ways to Get Help

Most Internet Service Providers turn the Internet into one of those holiday toys that "require assembly": you've got to find software, figure out how to use it, stumble around searching for things to do with the software, and waste time waiting on hold while you're trying to get phone help during business hours. Want to find someone with the same problem, and find out their solution to your shared troubles? Good luck.

AOL provides all the Internet help resources you're likely to want. These help resources are geared to people with different needs and different ways of learning. They are always at your disposal when you're using America Online, even when you're offline, using the Help menu. The single most useful help resource on AOL is the revamped Members Services area (*keyword: Members*), where you can get answers to your AOL and Net questions and get billing and account information.

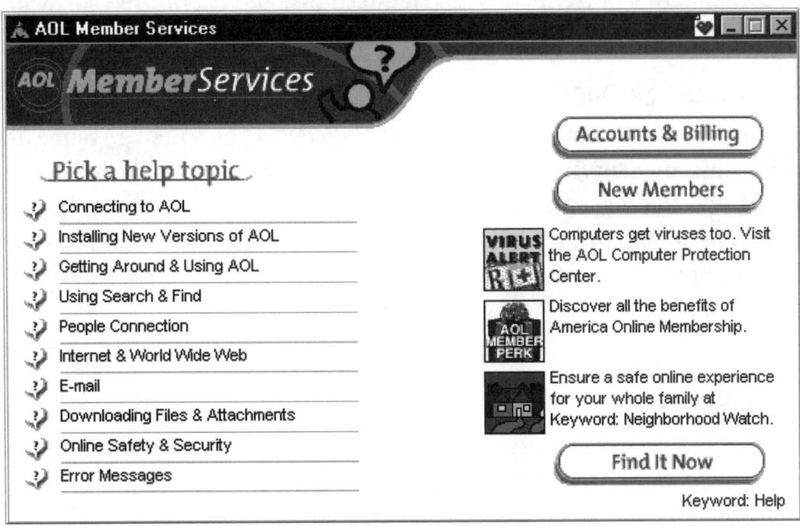

Tip *AOL lets you keep track of your favorite destinations on AOL and the Internet in your Favorite Places folder, always available when you click Favorites on the toolbar (the row of little pictures at the top of your AOL screen—see Chapter 2 for more information). When you first set up AOL, you'll find a helpful folder within your Favorite Places called About AOL, with links to some important areas on AOL for getting help.*

Teach Yourself

Some AOL features interest you more than other features. Chat rooms and online auditoriums are too public for some people; Instant Messages offer all the "immediacy" they want. Some people are download dudes; others just want useful information and actually *like* to search for information. At *keyword: Learn AOL* you can get step-by-step guides that let you teach yourself all the major AOL features, such as chat, e-mail, finding information, and using message boards. Other tutorials (such as Download 101) are available at *keyword: Help* (click Tutorials).

Learn from Others

Members helping members: that's the AOL tradition and that's what sets AOL apart from the ISPs. For many members it's the best way to both learn about the service (and the Internet) and to meet others. At *keyword: MHM*, you'll find useful message boards, compilations of frequently asked questions, and useful free software.

Ask Customer Service

At any time while you're on AOL, *keyword: Help* takes you to a huge range of online and offline customer service resources, whether you need help connecting to AOL, using AOL, or finding your way on the Net. You'll find live, interactive help, voluminous help text, information about AOL's fax-based help, and lots of phone numbers to call any time of the day or night. At the end of Appendix A you'll find a list of other phone numbers you can use to get help.

Get Internet Help

AOL's voluminous help resources are always at your fingertips. Offline, just go to the AOL Help menu, select Offline Help and use the handy searchable index. Online, go to *keyword: Help*, which is part of the new Member Services area. Click Internet & World Wide Web for how-to help with the browser, newsgroups, FTP, and other

Internet features. Or, click Error Messages for advice on responding to those occasional, pesky Internet error messages. This same information is available at AOL.com by clicking NetHelp.

Visit the Mail Center

The new Mail Center menu takes you to the Mail Center area on AOL, where you'll find e-mail tutorials, tips, and general information for making e-mail an indispensable part of your life. At *keyword: Mailing lists* you'll get the lowdown on lists, plus an AOL-only directory of several thousand of the best mailing lists. When you're using the Write Mail window (see Chapter 3), just click Help for assistance with any aspect of sending and receiving e-mail messages.

WHAT KIND OF BEAST IS THE INTERNET?

I've gotten this far without defining the Internet. Defining the Internet as a network doesn't really say much about the Internet experience. The Internet was never intended by some "inventor" to be the globe-spanning, dynamic thing it is today. Once you get the hang of the Internet, you will probably experience it as a community, not as some "network of networks." Understanding three simple facts about the Internet can make for a better experience of the Net community and a better grasp of what the Internet is about:

- All sorts of computers can communicate on the Internet.
- Using the Internet requires different programs to do different things.
- To people who use it, the Internet is not a physical network but a social one.

AOL's Stake in the Net

Across the service, you'll discover that AOL either owns key Internet technologies or has a strategic alliance with the companies that create these technologies. Some of these technologies are available to members for free or at reduced rates, such as PrimeHost (*keyword: Primehost*), a commercial Web-hosting service for businesses and organizations that want someone else to physically maintain and secure their Web sites.

In 1994–1995, AOL acquired a series of key Internet companies, including Navisoft, Booklink (makers of the first AOL browser), WAIS Inc., ANS,

Johnson-Grace, and GNN. Many of these companies' products and services, such as Johnson-Grace's compression technology, have been thoroughly integrated into AOL. Others, like ANS, which is responsible for AOL's massive data network, are (usually) invisible to you as an AOL member.

Since 1995, AOL has shifted its strategy from buying cutting-edge companies to making partnerships with the companies that lead the Internet industry. America Online's past acquisitions and current alliances with the most important players in the Internet industry—Microsoft, Netscape, Excite, and Switchboard—ensure that AOL members will always have access to the best technologies in the marketplace.

ALL SORTS OF COMPUTERS COMMUNICATE ON THE INTERNET

When you talk on the telephone, you set up what's called a *dedicated connection* between your phone and the phone you're calling. When you send someone electronic mail, the connection is *not* dedicated. Instead, the message is broken up into *packets*—little pieces of data, all the same size, with information about their sequence, origin, and destination. The packets are sent separately to their destination using the best available path, crossing many separate computer networks in the process. Packets from the same message might find different routes to their destination, where they're put back together again, as shown in Figure 1-8. Since packets contain information about the message as a whole and about the correct sequence of packets, any errors in reassembling some information cause packets to be re-sent. That's why your e-mail does not arrive as gibberish.

Here's the important point: *any* computer—whether it's based on Windows or the Mac or on bigger systems such as Unix or a mainframe—can take part in this exchange of packets if it has some software that does the work of making packets, correcting errors, and reassembling files.

Something called TCP/IP allows two-way communication. That's what the word "interactive" really means: on the Internet you produce information as well as

What It All Means

In Appendix B you will find a list of essential Internet terms, with short definitions. When you're online, the AOL Glossary (*keyword: Glossary*) gives short definitions of common AOL and Net terms.

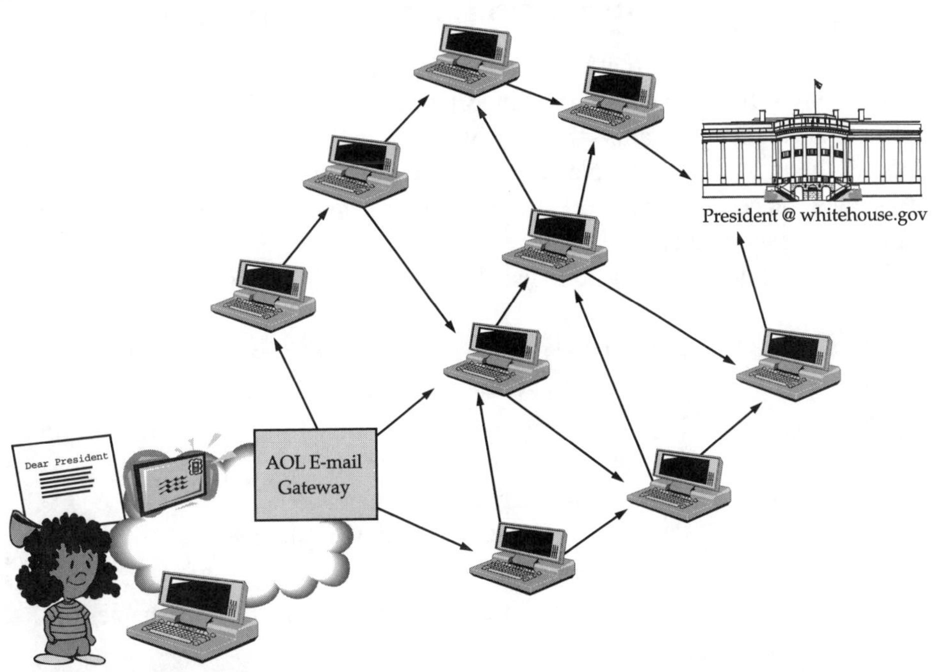

FIGURE 1-8 Packet switching at work. How that message gets to the President. Whether you get a reply is another question!

consume it. On AOL you can produce a Web site, an e-mail message, a newsgroup article, or an FTP file, and you'll find all the Internet applications you need to share information with other people.

What does all this mean for you as an AOL member?

- Packets move at different speeds, over congested networks, and through sluggish servers, all of which can explain why visiting a Web site can take longer than visiting an AOL area. A lot longer in some cases—and that's the value of AOL's investment in high-performance technology. However, you will still likely experience a difference between visiting AOL and Internet destinations.
- The diverse and autonomous computers and networks hooked up to this global network are the source of content that's overwhelming in quantity and wildly diverse in quality and appeal. AOL provides the editorial filters, the Parental Controls, and the search tools you need to find what you and your family want (see Appendix C).

DIFFERENT PROGRAMS TO DO DIFFERENT THINGS

Learning to "use the Internet" means learning to use Net software, which is like learning any software but with two important differences. First, you must learn to use several smaller programs—not one big program—to do several different tasks. Second, the tasks don't take place on a single PC, but on a network. Because the tasks take place on a network of computers, many of them enable you to communicate with others.

To use the Internet you need to use the following simple programs:

An e-mail reader	To send and receive e-mail messages with other individuals on AOL and the Internet.	(Chapter 3)
A newsgroup reader	To post messages on any of tens of thousands of international "bulletin boards," each devoted to a specific subject; anyone interested in the subject can read your messages.	(Chapter 5)
A World Wide Web browser	To browse multimedia creations of words, pictures, and sounds.	(Chapter 6)
An FTP (file transfer protocol) program	To retrieve software, images, sounds, programs, and other kinds of files from distant Internet computers, and to make these files available to others everywhere.	(Chapter 8)

Each of these programs is built into your AOL software and supported by AOL's computers. One of them, the World Wide Web browser, gives you access to several other tools. On AOL you can use your Web browser to visit FTP sites, to send an e-mail message, and to call up AOL's newsgroup reader. One day, you may be using the browser to search your hard disk! For now, however, effective use of e-mail, newsgroups, and FTP requires use of the specific programs built into the AOL software, not the browser. The browser is indispensable, but it's still best suited to just browsing the Web.

THE INTERNET AS A SOCIAL NETWORK

America Online differs from other online services in many ways. Most important, AOL is a community. No it's not always "cozy," and everyone doesn't know everyone else, but AOL members do have plenty of ways—from IMs to e-mail—to communicate with other members safely and reliably. They also have countless places, from chat rooms to forums, to meet people and make friends.

AOL's access to the Internet puts members in touch with a larger, more international community, with its own history, culture, and ways of governing itself. In fact, the Internet community can be thought of as a country of sorts. Before embarking on a visit to this new country, it's a good idea to understand something about the sort of place you're about to visit.

A Little History

The Net is the unintended result of many separate dreams and real-world developments. Nobody invented it. First, there were dreamers—early visionaries like Vannevar Bush (in the 1940s), J.C.R. Licklider (in the 1960s), Ted Nelson (since the 1960s), and Tim Berners-Lee (since the late 1980s). As a director in the government's Advanced Research Projects Agency (ARPA) in the early 1960s, Licklider had direct influence on the people who built government networks. He dreamed of a future in which interconnected computing machines would take over people's routine tasks and allow them to spend more time at creative and productive tasks. Bush, Nelson, and Berners-Lee are pioneers of a different sort. They imagined new ways of linking related knowledge in a universally available format. Their work continues to inspire the creators of today's World Wide Web, the center of today's Internet.

Who's Got the Mouse, or How Many People Are on the Internet?

At the beginning of 1998, approximately one American adult in four visits the World Wide Web more or less regularly, and ten million people (everywhere) have bought something on the Web. An influential market research firm, FIND/SVP, estimates that by the end of 1998, 75 million adults and 25 million kids in the U.S. will use the Internet. Jostling for the mouse will soon replace sibling battles for the TV channel switcher.

SOURCE:
Cyberatlas (**http://www.cyberatlas.com**) and FIND/SVP (**http://etrg.findsvp.com/timeline/trends.html**)

A Global Community

Chances are very good that most of what you do on the Internet will involve American Internet users and American Internet content. Two thirds of all *hosts* (computers directly on the Internet) are American. However, more than 200 countries have access to the Internet, and on the Internet the information about the rest of the world (and universe) is overwhelming in scope. Whether you're planning a trip to Fiji, writing a paper about ancient Mesopotamia, studying English gardens, learning about the teas of Sri Lanka, dreaming of a golf trip to Scotland, or searching for a pen pal in Italy, the Internet can make your job easier, faster, less costly, and more fun. See the "International" section of Chapter 11 for a sampling of international sites.

Behaving Like a Native of a Global Community

Through e-mail, mailing lists, and newsgroups, the Internet gives you many ways of communicating with other people around the world. Like any community, the Net has its own guidelines for how to behave. This code of *netiquette* can be boiled down to two precepts:

- Respect the people who might read anything you write and publish on the Net, because you can never predict in whose hands (or mailbox) something will end up. No one can read your mind or see your body language on the Net, so what you write in jest may be taken seriously. Also, be aware that what you send to one person or place can be forwarded to thousands of people or places.
- Respect the physical Internet itself by not wasting bandwidth and storage space with unsolicited or inappropriate messages, especially commercial postings to noncommercial places or, in general, unsolicited commercial postings. (For technical jargon like *bandwidth*, see Appendix B.)

What happens when you violate netiquette? Minor infringements can get you *flamed*—verbally criticized in a mailing list or newsgroup. It's not a particularly pleasant experience. Major infringements can get your membership revoked on AOL. In between these extremes, you may discover the existence of various blacklists that limit access to some Internet services.

1

Note *All networks expect their users to comply with rules when they use the network to explore the world; America Online is no different. AOL does not limit members' access to the Internet, but it does expect them to comply with its Rules of the Road guidelines while they're using all Internet services. You'll find more details about these rules later in this book, but all you need to know is available at* keyword: Rules of the road.

Do unto others, and do unto the network. That pretty much sums up netiquette. Chapters 4 and 5 give more details about proper behavior on mailing lists and newsgroups, the two places where netiquette matters the most.

How the Net Community Governs Itself

Netiquette goes a long way to explaining how Internet citizens control their own destiny. It's the Net's common law. The closest the Net comes to formal government is the Internet Society, an international organization made up of companies, individuals, and government agencies that work to guarantee the well-being of the Internet as a physical network.

Based in Reston, Virginia, several miles from America Online's new headquarters near Dulles Airport, the Internet Society helps set the standards with which tens of thousands of autonomous networks comply, making the Net possible. It does its work through annual meetings, regular publications, and subgroups such as the Internet Engineering Task Force and the Internet Architecture Standards Board. Neither elected by the Internet community nor appointed by the world's "real" governments, the Internet Society nonetheless effectively plans the standards required for the Internet's future growth. More and more, companies such as Microsoft, Netscape, and AOL itself are shaping the standards-making process, especially the part of the process that relates to the World Wide Web. Standards for the Web are worked out by the World Wide Web Consortium, an industry consortium based in Cambridge, Massachusetts, and operated by research labs in the U.S., France, and Japan.

The Web sites for the Internet Society and World Wide Web Consortium respectively are **http://www.isoc.org** and **http://www.w3c.org**. Visit them to learn about the key issues on the Internet today. Joining the Internet Society is an effective means to show support for the Internet community, and a very good way to stay informed about Internet developments.

Doing Business in the Net Community

Today the Net is a wide-open field for doing business. Hundreds of companies are even creating "intranets," private networks attached to the global Internet, in order to improve internal communication. "Extranets" are beginning to tie together business partners in business-to-business networks.

What do businesses do on the Internet? Smart businesses know that the Net's a great way of cutting costs in every aspect of a business: in doing competitive research, learning about markets, recruiting employees, staying in touch with partners and staff, doing targeted, Net-appropriate marketing, and providing customer support. The Internet is emerging as a phenomenal place to buy and sell stuff, too. As security technologies mature, the Net *will* become a place to make money, creating a better experience for consumers as well as companies small and large.

The Internet has a reputation for being "anti-business." This is less true with each passing month. Yes, you may find pockets of hostility to business on the Internet, and there are places where commercial postings are inappropriate. Further, many small businesses new to the Net are insensitive to the finer points of netiquette. If government made the early Net possible, however, it's business that is driving it today.

FROM HERE...

This chapter covered a lot of ground: it conveyed the benefits of the Internet, the benefits of using the Net on AOL, and a little something of the *reality* of the Internet on AOL. In the next chapter you learn how to sign onto and get around AOL, and you'll find out exactly *where* the Internet is on AOL.

Chapter 2

Navigating from AOL to the Internet

America Online offers a port of call for all your Internet explorations. For one thing, you get easy access to all things Internet, from e-mail to the World Wide Web. Also, on AOL you get directions to the best Internet resources—the best Web sites and members' favorite newsgroups. You also get abundant help and how-to resources if you ever have questions about using the software or finding resources. Finally, on AOL you're always welcome and can usually find a person to offer guidance, or provide company, or just point the way.

This chapter describes:

- Signing on (how you connect to AOL)
- The essential parts of the AOL display (what you see on your screen)
- Destinations on AOL and the Internet (where you can go when you're online)
- Doing several things at once on AOL and the Net (ways to make the most of your experience)

Note *This chapter assumes you have installed the AOL 4.0 for Windows software (use* keyword: Upgrade *if you're not yet using this version of AOL). Appendix A walks you through the process if you haven't yet installed AOL. If you are new to computers as well as to AOL, Appendix D introduces you to working with AOL 4.0 for the Macintosh.*

GETTING ONLINE

To connect with AOL, also known as *signing on*, you start your computer, make sure no one is using the phone line, flick the modem on (unless the modem is inside your computer), and follow these steps:

1. With your mouse, double-click the AOL icon, whether it's in a Windows 3.1 program window or on the Windows 95 desktop; if it's on your Windows 95 Start menu, a single click will do.

The AOL program may take a moment to display or *load*—it's a big program. When it does display, the Welcome window appears, and you are able to enter your password.

Tip *If you use Windows 95 and are using AOL 4.0, you may see an AOL icon on the Windows 95 toolbar positioned at the very bottom of your screen. A single click on the icon opens AOL.*

2. Type your password in the Enter Password box. It will appear as a series of asterisks:

Enter Password

```
********
```

3. Click the Sign On button. AOL now looks for the modem, dials the local phone number you chose during installation (covered in Appendix A), establishes a connection with the AOL network, and verifies your password. That sounds like a lot, but don't worry; you don't have to do a thing while you're connecting to AOL.

Tip *If you're the only one signing onto your account from your PC, or if you jointly use your account with people in your family or work, you can have AOL remember your password so you don't have to enter it each time you sign on. The first time you use AOL 4.0, a window comes up and asks you whether you want to save your password. If you save it, then the next time you sign on, all you have to do is click Sign On Again (assuming you use the same screen name).*

When you successfully sign onto AOL, you'll see two windows, or (in AOL-speak) *screens*: the Channels screen and then (on top of it) the Welcome screen. You may also get information about how to set up your Buddy List, a way of knowing which of your friends or colleagues are online when you're online (see "Where Am I—Online, Offline, on the Net?"). From the Welcome screen, there's a button you can click to go to the Channels screen, and from the Channels screen, there's a button that takes you back to the Welcome screen.

Note *If you're on the road or abroad, or if you find yourself at someone else's computer, you can sign on using the steps provided in Appendix A.*

Where Am I—Online, Offline, on the Net?

You're online from the time you sign onto AOL to the time you sign off. The rest of the time you're offline. Unlike other providers, AOL gives you many ways to automate routine online tasks, so you go online only when you have to (or want to). You can do such things as write e-mail, use Personal Filing Cabinet to read your e-mail (see Chapter 3), and take part in newsgroups while you are offline. Chapter 4 covers Automatic AOL, the feature that enables much of this offline access.

While you're signed onto AOL you can visit the Internet at any time and in many ways, depending on what you want to do. To use the Net, you don't have to sign off and then sign on again or use any special software or pay anything extra. The Internet is a seamless extension of AOL.

Later in this chapter you'll find a directory of the places on AOL from which you start your explorations of the Internet ("Destinations on the Internet, or: Where on AOL *Is* the Internet, Anyway?").

PLUGGING INTO A CHANNEL

The Channels screen is the first thing you see when you sign on to AOL (Figure 2-1); it displays AOL's 18 *channels*, so-called because AOL creates programs, just like the studios and networks of the TV world. AOL's channels differ from TV channels in that they are *interactive* (the experience is social) and *dynamic* (there's something new almost daily). They give you many opportunities to find essential information, take polls, offer your opinions, share your experiences, and meet other members. Also unlike TV, they're always available and you can usually find information of interest to you, so you aren't restricted to what the programming committees of network TV want you to see.

Tip *At* keyword: Click & go *you will find a slideshow providing an overview of each of AOL's channels. Slideshows are brand-new multimedia presentations that blend images and streaming sound. (What's a keyword? See the "Navigating with Keywords" box.)*

Each AOL channel is devoted to a broad subject, like entertainment, personal finance, or sports. With AOL 4.0, every channel is now arranged in a similar way, so you can easily find new areas to explore. Throughout AOL's channels you'll find

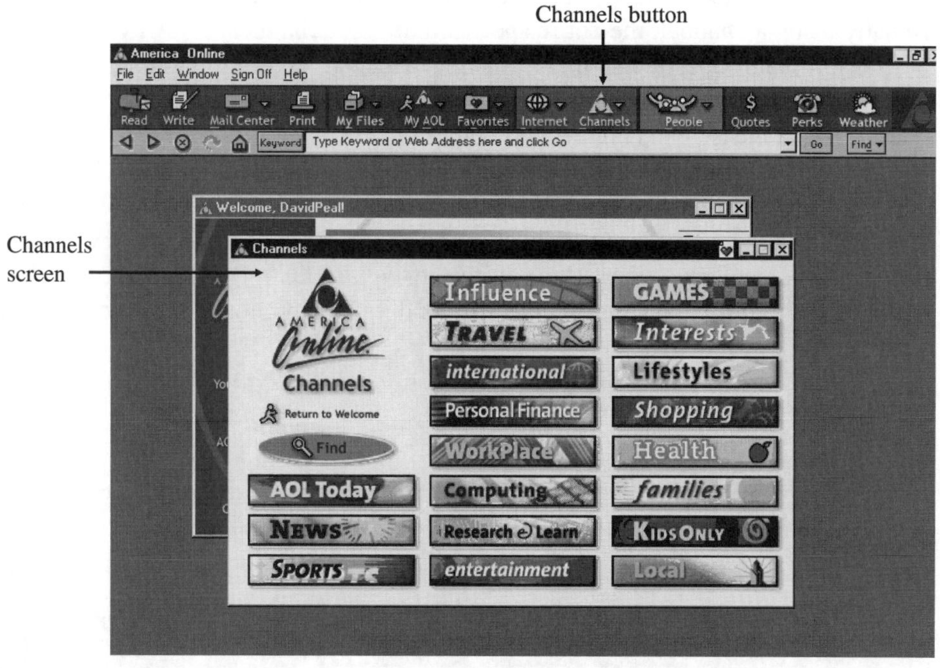

FIGURE 2-1 The easy-to-use Channels screen gives you direct access to the topics you care about

Internet content in the form of links to great Web sites and newsgroups, as well as content that is available only on AOL. (See "Anatomy of an AOL Forum.")

Tip *If you're an old-timer, you'll notice some changes to AOL's channel line-up. The **Hub** and **MusicSpace** channels, for example, have found a home in **Entertainment. Digital Cities** is now called the **Local** channel. **Reference** has morphed into **Research and Learning, Computers & Software** into **Computing**, and **Marketplace** into **Shopping**. The **Internet Connection** has been slimmed down to a window available from the new Internet menu. New channels include **WorkPlace**, **Families**, and **Lifestyle**. The biggest change is the redesign of AOL's channels according to a standard layout, which makes it much easier to explore new territory.*

Your favorite channel is always at your fingertips. The toolbar's Channels menu (discussed later in this chapter) gives you the Channels screen information in a

convenient list that's available when the channels screen is not. And whenever you're actually using a channel, the entire spectrum of other channels is always available on the left-hand side of the main channel window. Figure 2-2 shows the new **Families** channel in AOL's new channel layout.

The Welcome Screen (Figure 2-3) comes up whenever you sign onto AOL and is available throughout your entire session. It gives you fast access to AOL's most popular features, such as e-mail, People Connection, and the Internet, and to any new features or live events currently going on. With AOL 4.0, note the new buttons on the Welcome Screen that take you to the Web (AOL's home page), Member Services (help), Parental Controls (see Appendix C), and quotes (the stock market variety).

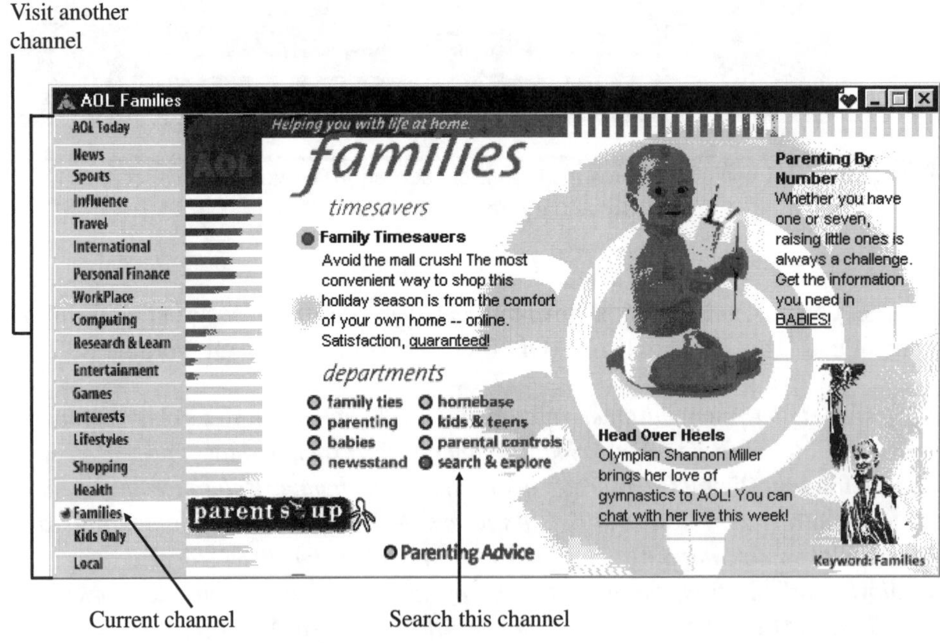

FIGURE 2-2 AOL's new channel layout—and the new **Families** channel

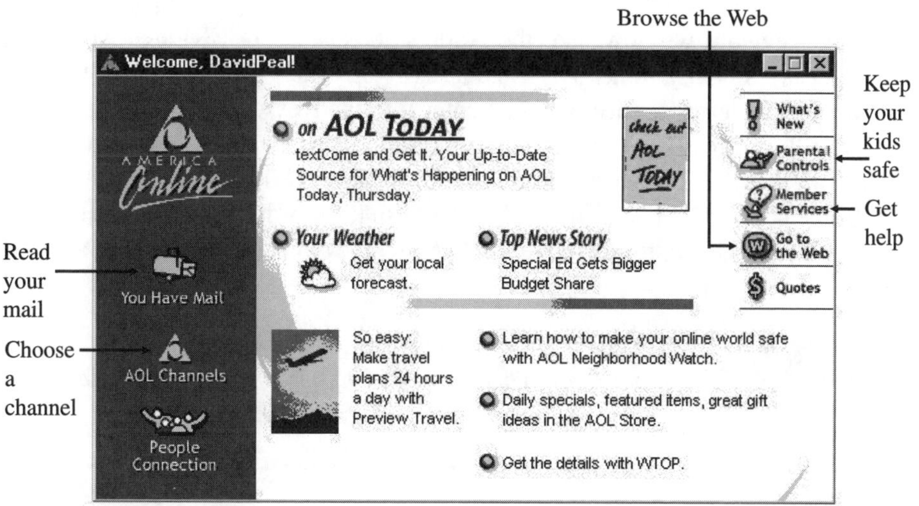

FIGURE 2-3 The Welcome Screen can take you to current AOL events as well as to your electronic mailbox, the Internet, and People Connection

Navigating with Keywords

An easy way to navigate AOL and the Internet is by using *keywords* (see Table 2-1). Think of a keyword as a shortcut. Every AOL area and feature and many of the most popular Web destinations have their own keywords—the keyword for the NetGuide area, for example, is *Netguide*. With AOL 4.0, you can retrieve the Keyword window with the navigation bar's Address box; it's also still available by pressing CTRL-K and by clicking the Keyword button on the navigation bar. Here's the Keyword window:

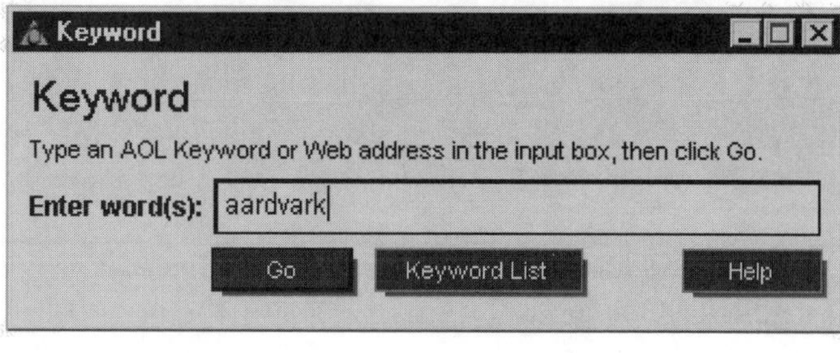

The Keyword window, like the Address box, accepts URLs as well as keywords, so if you know a URL (or Internet address), such as **http://www.microsoft.com**, you can enter it in the Keyword field, press Go, and you'll go directly to the Net site. Important Internet-related keywords are listed in Table 2-1. Chapter 6 plumbs the mysteries of URLs.

Some popular Web sites have plain-English keywords, which can be used in the place of URLs, for example: *Switchboard*, *Four11*, and *Disney.com*.

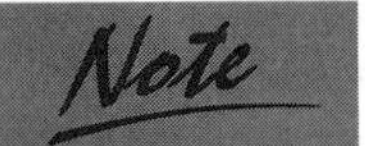

Keywords are not case sensitive: ftp, FTP, Ftp *all take you to the same area. This book will uppercase the first letter of keywords, but you don't have to follow that practice.*

Keyword	Takes you to...
Access	Information about global and domestic AOL access; includes a list of numbers and a convenient set of troubleshooting tips
Billing	Explanation of everything related to your bill, with forms for changing your billing information
Ftp	Provides access to thousands of FTP sites from which you can download millions of files
Http[URL]	To go directly to a Web site whose URL (or Internet address) you know
Internet connection	Highlights AOL's Internet offerings—direct access to the Web, AOL NetFind, FTP, Personal Publisher, and more
Keyword	What else? A master list of keywords, including keywords to take you directly to specific Web sites
Mailing list	Includes general information about joining lists, plus links to AOL's own mailing lists

TABLE 2-1 Some Essential Keywords for Using the Internet on America Online

Keyword	Takes you to...
Member services	Comprehensive AOL help
Modem	Information about AOL's current and planned high-speed access
Multimedia showcase	A Web pitstop for people who want to explore the graphical and other groovy features of AOL's Web browser
Netfind	AOL's exclusive Web site, tailored for ease of use, from which you can start all your online adventures
Newsgroups	Starting point for exploring 30,000-plus discussion groups (Chapter 5)
Personal Publisher	Make your own Web page using Personal Publisher
Screen name	Change your screen name
Telnet	Telnet software and tips for accessing remote computers (Chapter 10), such as library catalogs
Web	Go directly to AOL's Web site
Www (same as keyword: Web)	Go directly to AOL.com, AOL's Web site

TABLE 2-1 Some Essential Keywords for Using the Internet on America Online (*continued*)

SIGNING OFF

AOL gives you several ways to sign off. Which way you use depends on how you like to do things—with the mouse, from menus, or using the keyboard—and whether you want to keep AOL open (so you can sign on again later without reloading the software).

- From the Sign Off menu, choose Sign Off, move your mouse cursor to the menu at the top of your screen, click and release your mouse, slide the mouse cursor to Sign Off, and click again. This action signs you off but keeps the AOL application open, so you can easily sign on again later in the day.

- Press ALT-F4. (On your keyboard, hold down the ALT key and press the F4 key at the same time.) This action signs you off and closes the AOL application.
- In Windows 95, click once in the little box with an X in the far upper-right of the main AOL window. In Windows 3.1, double-click the little box in the far upper-*left* of the main window. This action, too, signs you off and closes the AOL application.

Switch Screen Names without Signing Off

With AOL 4.0, the AOL software lets you switch screen names without signing off. From the Sign Off menu, select Switch Screen Names. You'll be prompted first for the screen name and password to which you want to switch. Appendix A tells you how to add screen names to your account.

THE THREE ESSENTIAL PARTS OF THE AOL DISPLAY

AOL consists of three very important elements that you use to get around the service (Figure 2-4):

- The *menu bar*, at the very top of your display, lets you manage files, documents, and windows. If you're familiar with other Windows programs, you'll be familiar with the File, Edit, Window, and Help menus. In AOL Version 4.0, the menu bar has been simplified, with many AOL functions and features transferred to the toolbar.
- The *toolbar* gives you direct access to all the important AOL features, including the Internet-related features. What you used to find in the menu bar is now likely to be available in the toolbar. Most pertinent to the Net are Mail Center, Favorites, and Internet.
- New with AOL 4.0 is the *navigation bar*, which features the Address box and navigational controls. You use the navigation bar to get to the specific places you want to visit on AOL and the Net

Note *For longtime AOL users: The traditional AOL Keyword window is still available (click the Keyword button shown in Figure 2-4), but the Address box can now be used for both AOL keywords and Internet URLs.*

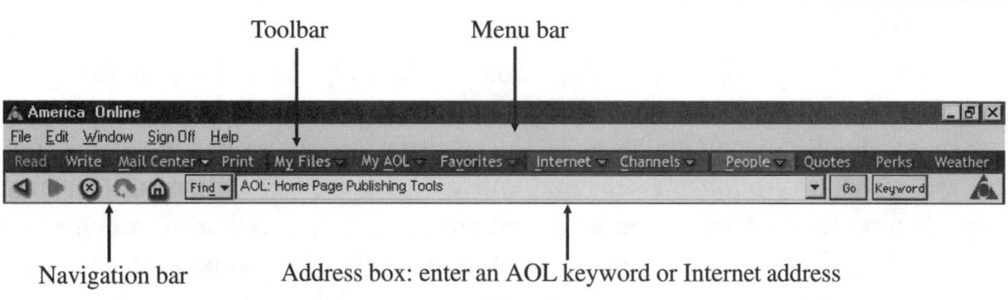

FIGURE 2-4 The entire Internet is available from the AOL toolbar

Keyboard Alternatives

For some menu items (whether they're on the menu bar or a toolbar menu), a keyboard alternative is available. This means that you can go directly to the item using the keyboard instead of selecting from the menu. Keyboard alternatives are usually listed in each menu to the right of an item. For example, in the Mail Center menu next to Write Mail, you'll see CTRL-M. This means that from anywhere on AOL, you can compose an e-mail message by holding down the Control (CTRL) key and pressing the letter *M* at the same time. Use keyboard alternatives as shortcuts to the features you use all the time.

Here are some useful keyboard alternatives:

- Writing an e-mail message (CTRL-M)
- Reading mail (CTRL-R)
- Opening a file (CTRL-O)
- Printing (CTRL-P)
- Saving a file (CTRL-S)
- Opening the Keyword window (CTRL-K)
- Sending an Instant Message (CTRL-I)
- Adding an item to your Favorite Places (CTRL-SHIFT-+)

THE AOL MENU BAR

Each menu gives you a set of related choices. The Help menu, for example, gives you all sorts of help, from tutorials to lists of access numbers to assistance with account and billing problems. To open a menu so you can see your choices, just click the menu's name. To make a selection, move the mouse arrow down the menu to the selection (or *command*) you want and click again. If you don't find what you were looking for, close the menu by keeping the mouse button pressed down and moving the mouse arrow off the menu and then releasing the mouse button.

While you're offline, you'll see five menus—File, Edit, Sign On, Window, and Help; once you sign on, the Sign On menu turns into the Sign Off menu. The basic menus may be familiar to you from other Windows programs. They're used for standard tasks:

File Edit Window Sign Off Help

- The File menu lets you open, save, and print files, whether they're images or text documents or something else. With AOL 4.0, it contains a new, AOL-only item, Open Picture Gallery, which lets you view and edit images (see Chapter 8).
- The Edit menu lets you do things *within* documents: copy text from one place and paste to another, for example, and do a spell check.
- The Window menu is a fixture of all Windows programs: it lets you fiddle with the way windows are displayed on your screen relative to each other. The most important feature of this menu is, for many people, the list of open windows. While you're online, open windows are listed and numbered at the bottom of the Window menu. Select any open window from this window to bring that window to the top of your display (so you can see it and do stuff).
- The Sign On menu has a single choice: when you're offline, it brings up the Sign On window, which you use to go online. Once online, this menu changes into the Sign Off menu, which gives you two choices: to sign off or to remain signed on but switch to another screen name.

- The Help menu provides lots of kinds of help, offline as well as online. (Some kinds of help you must use offline, if, for example, you can't sign on.) Online, the best source of help is AOL's Member Services area (*keyword: Help*). On AOL, customer service is always at your fingertips.

THE AOL TOOLBAR

The new AOL toolbar is the row of small pictures, or clickable buttons, that you see just below the menu bar. With AOL 4.0 the toolbar has a new look, including a simpler layout and drop-down menus. Whenever you see a triangle by a button, clicking the button brings up a menu, or list, to choose from.

Figure 2-5 shows what's on the toolbar. The last three items on the right can only be seen if your monitor is set at 800x600 resolution or higher. They can also be

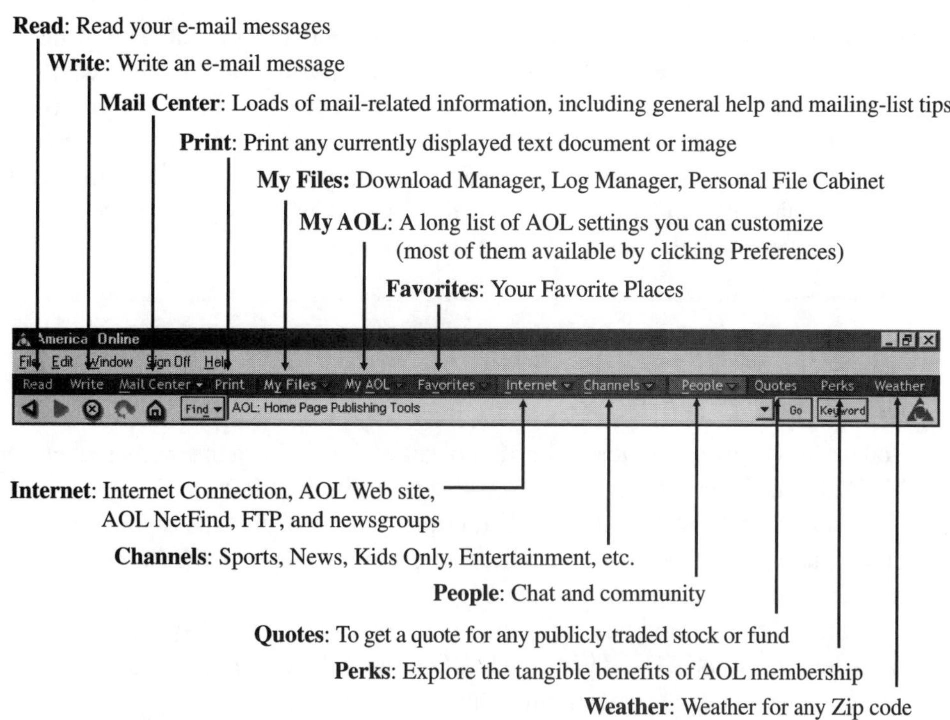

FIGURE 2-5 The toolbar gives you fast access to all AOL features; I've customized the three buttons on the far right

customized, as explained a little later in "Customizing Your Toolbar." Clicking a button once (note that you don't have to double-click) either *does* something (like printing a document when you click the Print button, or displaying the Write Mail window when you click Write) or brings up a menu of things you can do.

Here's a quick overview of the new toolbar menus. Note that the drop-down menus do much of the work that the menu bar handled in earlier AOL versions.

Tip *In order to see three toolbar items—Quotes, Perks, Weather—your screen resolution must be set at a screen resolution of 800x600 or higher. To set your resolution, use your Windows 3.1/Windows 95 Control Panel, and double-click on Display. Under Settings, change the Desktop area to at least 800x600 (pixels). You'll probably have to restart your computer to make the change take effect. Everything looks a little smaller when you change the resolution, but you see more that way!*

MAIL CENTER This menu takes you to information about electronic mail (e-mail) and gives you access to all of AOL's e-mail features (writing and reading e-mail). From the same menu you can also see lists of messages you have received (Old Mail) and messages you have sent (Sent Mail). You can also set up an Automatic AOL session (formerly know as a FlashSession) so you can download and send e-mail automatically and thus minimize the amount of time you spend online. Chapter 3 covers e-mail; Chapter 4 covers mailing lists.

On Your Own Terms: Setting Preferences on AOL and Windows

You can customize America Online in dozens of ways. From the toolbar, click My AOL and select Preferences. You'll see 14 different buttons, letting you customize features such as the toolbar, e-mail, the Web, chat, passwords, and more. Throughout this book, specific preferences are mentioned in connection with the corresponding Internet features.

Some of the general ways in which your display looks and system works can't be set within AOL. Using your Windows 3.1 or Windows 95 control panels, you can adjust (among other things) the following:

- The sounds associated with particular events such as signing on (Sounds control panel); if you don't like the sounds you hear when certain things happen, just turn them off!
- The palette used to define the colors of every window element (Display control panel).
- Your keyboard's responsiveness and the shapes your mouse cursor assumes (Keyboard and Mouse control panels, respectively).
- The monitor resolution (Display control panel)

In Windows 95, control panels are available from the Start menu (select Settings, then Control Panel); in Windows 3.1 they're available from the Program Manager.

MY AOL You can express your personal preferences in many ways on AOL: everything from specifying your home page on the World Wide Web to determining how you reply to your e-mail messages (see "On Your Own Terms: Setting Preferences on AOL and Windows"). You can also set preferences for children in your family with an important feature known as Parental Controls (see Appendix C). This is also the place to turn when you want to add a screen name to your account.

MY FILES AOL's useful programs for helping you track your private information: Download Manager (for keeping track of the files you download from various sources on AOL and the Net), Log Manager (for recording a chat session as well as any plain-text information), and Personal Filing Cabinet (for keeping copies of all the e-mail you get and send, among other things). See Chapter 3 for more information about Download Manager and Chapter 8 on the Personal Filing Cabinet.

FAVORITES Allows you to track your Favorite Places on AOL and the Net: your favorite newsgroups, Web sites, AOL forums, even your most important e-mail messages. Chapter 6 has the scoop on Favorite Places.

My Shortcuts

From the Favorites menu you get access to My Shortcuts, a popular AOL feature with a new name. Using this feature you can assign a keystroke (CTRL plus a number from 0 to 9) to up to ten AOL areas or Internet sites you visit frequently. AOL includes some keywords for you to use, but you can customize this list as you please. To add your own shortcuts:

1. While offline or online, select My Shortcuts from the Favorites menu.
2. Select Edit Shortcuts.
3. In the Edit Shortcuts window, select an existing shortcut in the Shortcut Title box and type in a new title for your shortcut (for example, **Liszt**). In the Keyword/Internet Address box to the right of the title, select the existing address and type in the new one (**http://www.liszt.com**). To the far right you'll see the keystrokes you've just assigned to your new shortcut (for example, CTRL-9).
4. Click Save Changes.

In the future, to go to your new shortcut, press CTRL-9 (or whatever). There is no faster way to visit a favorite Web site, but choose carefully, since you can set up only ten shortcuts.

INTERNET This toolbar's Internet menu gives you direct access to the Web, newsgroups, and file downloading (FTP). The first choice, Internet Connection, takes you to the new AOL Internet Connection, which takes you to the best of AOL's Internet offerings, such as Personal Publisher (Chapter 7) and AOL NetFind (Chapter 9). A box at the Internet Connection lets you type in an Internet address (URL) to go directly to any Internet address whose address you know. The Internet menu also takes you to AOL's Web site (Chapter 6). Or, go directly to AOL's Newsgroup area (Chapter 6) or Search Newsgroups (Chapter 9).

CHANNELS A drop-down list of AOL's channels, this menu does the work of the Channels screen (see Figure 2-1) when that screen's not available (or viewable). AOL Today, at the top of the menu, gives a schedule of the day's live events and where they'll take place online.

PEOPLE This menu takes you to the **People Connection** channel, AOL Live, your Buddy List, the searchable AOL Member Directory (see Chapter 9), and Instant Messages. You can even use AOL's Send a Page feature if you know someone's pager number!

THE AOL NAVIGATION BAR

Navigating the online world means getting from one "place" (or computer) to another. With AOL 4.0's navigation bar (Figure 2-6), navigating becomes simpler. You now navigate AOL and the Internet using the same set of controls for getting around (going forward, going backward, and stopping).

Note: *In AOL's online documentation you'll see* toolbar *used to refer to both the toolbar (described in the previous section) and what I'm calling the navigation bar in this section. I refer to them separately because they're different horizontal bars with different looks and different purposes.*

The navigation bar's Address box lets you enter both AOL keywords and Internet addresses (URLs). Unlike the Keyword window, the Address box keeps track of

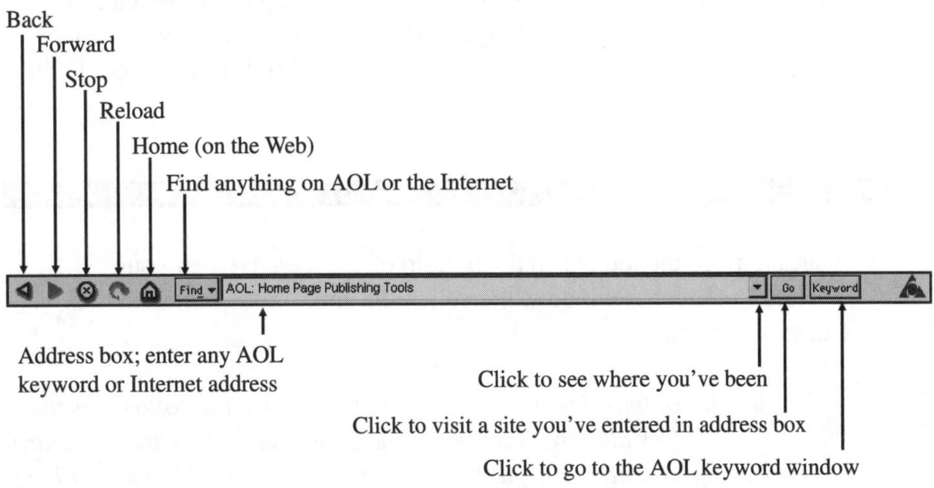

FIGURE 2-6 AOL's navigation bar

both AOL and Internet sites. Your resulting "history" is a list of the last 25 places you visited on AOL and on the Net.

Chapter 6, on the World Wide Web, discusses the navigational buttons (backward, forward, stop, etc.) in detail.

The Find button gives you the choice of finding information on AOL or on the Web. Select Find it on AOL, and you'll go to a window similar to the one shown in Figure 2-8. Select Find it on the Web to go AOL's NetFind, which you'll learn about shortly. Select AOL's Access Numbers for a handy list of phone numbers (for accessing AOL from different parts of the country), which is searchable by area code and by location.

Customizing Your Toolbar

You can customize the full AOL toolbar (the toolbar plus the navigation bar) in several ways:

- You can free up extra space by removing the buttons (pictures) on the toolbar. To do so, select My AOL | Preferences, then click Toolbar. In the Toolbar Preferences window, put a check in the Text only box under Appearance, and click OK. Only the text labels (Print, Internet, etc.) will appear on the toolbar.

- You can move the toolbar to the bottom of the screen. Open your Toolbar Preferences window, then click the appropriate button in the Location section.

Placing the toolbar (including the navigation bar) at the bottom can make your screen less cluttered and give clearer access to the window control boxes in the upper right-hand corner, as well as to the title bar and Favorite Places heart just to the left of the control boxes. Note that toolbar menus scroll up when the toolbar is at the bottom.

- If your screen resolution is 800x600 or greater, you can remove any of the last three items from your toolbar (Quotes, Perks, Weather) and replace any or all three with any Favorite Place of your choice. To remove an item, right-click it and select Remove from Toolbar. To add an item, it must be "Favorite Place-able"; that is, it must have a heart on its title bar. If it does, just drag the heart to the empty spot on the toolbar. You'll be asked to select a picture for the item from a set of images. Favorite Places are discussed in Chapter 6.

*I use my toolbar icons for local weather (*keyword: Weather, *then the weather for my Zip code) and local movies (from Digital Cities).*

DESTINATIONS ON AOL

On the Internet they're called *sites* on AOL they're called *areas* or *forums*. In either case, think of them as places to explore—the reason you go online in the first place. Figure 2-7 shows NetGuide, one of the best Web sites *about* the Internet.

FIGURE 2-7 NetGuide, the place to get information about the Internet

Anatomy of an AOL Forum

Forums draw people who share a specific interest—investing, relationships, parenting, religion, books, cars, quilting, edgy humor, whatever. Some forums have leaders; others don't.

Unlike most Web sites, most AOL forums are interactive. That means they offer ways of communicating with other people who share your interest. Some have dedicated chat rooms. Others have regular events, in which the forum leader or a guest chats with members about a specific topic. In many, you can ask the forum leaders questions and subscribe to special e-mail newsletters for people who frequent the forum. Others take polls and share the results. Most important, forums have message boards, so members can communicate directly with each other. The most important part of any forum is the people who frequent it and the content they create, mostly in message boards. Many computing-related forums have software libraries too, with programs to download.

Most forums have links to related forums and Internet sites. The Better Health and Medical Network, for example, is just the starting point for people with specific interests about everything from AIDS to Women's Health. Supporting the subforums are more than 50 message boards, free access for AOL members to Medline (the National Library of Medicine's database of articles from medical journals), links to related Internet sites, the Better Health bookstore, and regular chats about specific ailments. It's a true feast of information and a community in which everyone will find a niche, support group, or reading room. Your best guide to AOL's forums is John and Jennifer Kaufeld's, *The Official America Online Yellow Pages* (Osborne/McGraw-Hill, 1998).

Finding Forums on AOL

AOL offers you more than 1,500 forums, or areas, to choose from. How do you find the ones of likely interest to you? It's easy. Start by either clicking the Find button on the Channels screen or the Find button on the toolbar and then selecting Find it on AOL. In the window that appears (see Figure 2-8), you can either search for a specific forum or browse within channels.

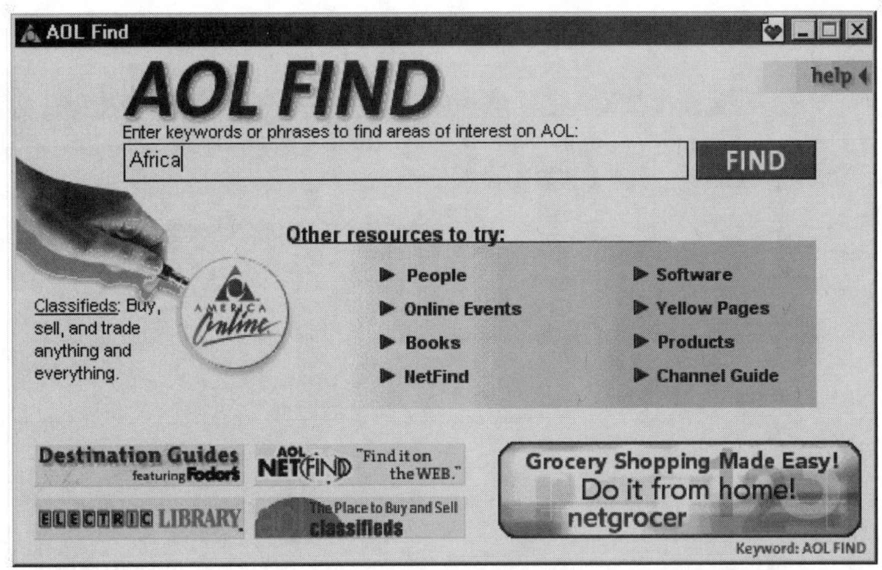

FIGURE 2-8 The new AOL Find window speeds your search for people and places

AOL Find is your hub for finding people, places, and events on AOL. Just type in any words reflecting your interest, and click Find to bring up the window shown in Figure 2-9. For searches within a channel, click Channel Guide (Figure 2-8) to browse alphabetized lists of areas for each channel (Figure 2-10). Use the Channel Guide to jump to the channel and to do targeted searches within it.

Find Central focuses on AOL searches. For Net searches, Chapter 9 presents the best search sites, with tips for selecting and using them.

Another way to match your interests to areas available on AOL is at *keyword: Quick Start*. Click Match Your Interests to bring up a list of topics (Figure 2-11), such as health and medicine, then click Show Me! Click any topic to find a selection of the best, exclusively AOL resources for that topic.

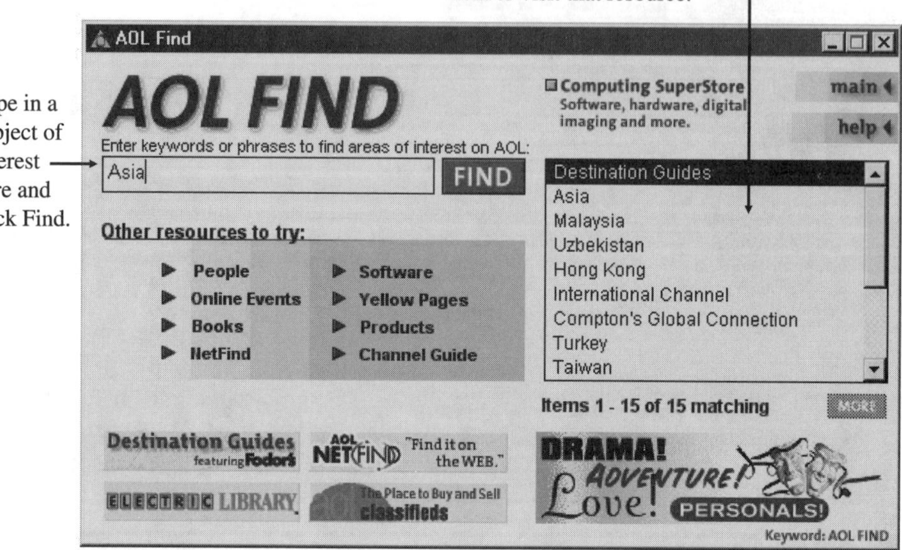

FIGURE 2-9 AOL Find lets you find areas of interest, no matter what channel they're in

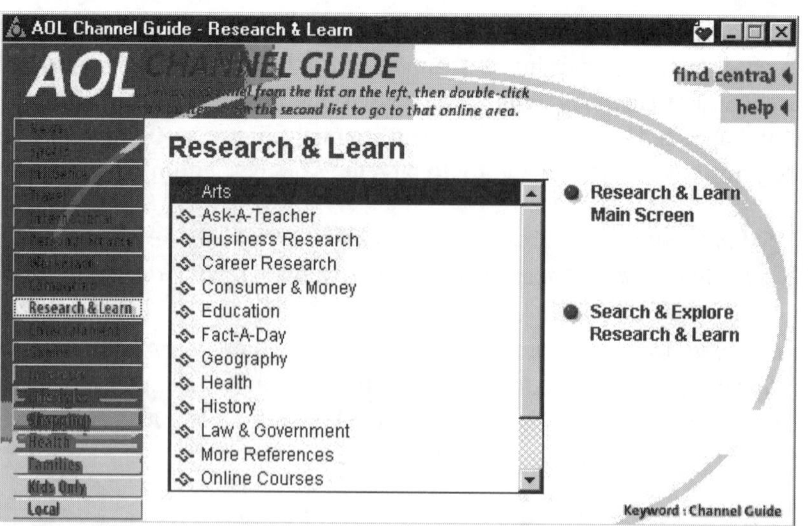

FIGURE 2-10 The AOL Channel Guide provides alphabetical listings of all AOL areas, channel by channel

FIGURE 2-11 Match Your Interests helps you find AOL areas of likely interest to you

For more extensive and detailed matches between your interests and AOL's offerings, go to *keyword: Interest Profiles* (Figure 2-12). You'll be walked through a series of screens in which you indicate your level of expertise and your favorite topics (such as computing). You're then asked to identify your favorite *sub*topics (such as home computing). When you're done, AOL sends you (by e-mail) a list of forums that are likely to interest you, based on the information you've given. I've used this feature to discover new places on AOL and was surprised by what I had been missing!

DESTINATIONS ON THE INTERNET, OR WHERE ON AOL *IS* THE INTERNET, ANYWAY?

On AOL you're always a click away from the Internet, whether you use the navigation bar to go a site of your choosing or the toolbar to go to one of AOL's many Internet-related areas.

WHERE IS THE AMERICA ONLINE WEB SITE (AOL.COM)? To visit AOL's huge new Web site (Figure 2-13), select Go to the Web from the Internet menu. The Welcome screen's Go to the Web link can take you there, too (Figure 2-3).

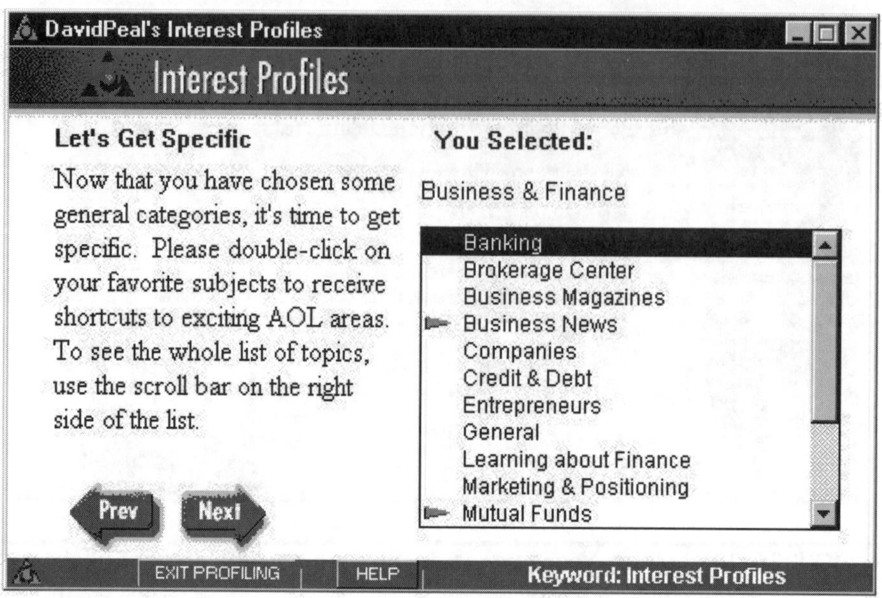

FIGURE 2-12 Interest Profiles asks you what you're *really* interested in

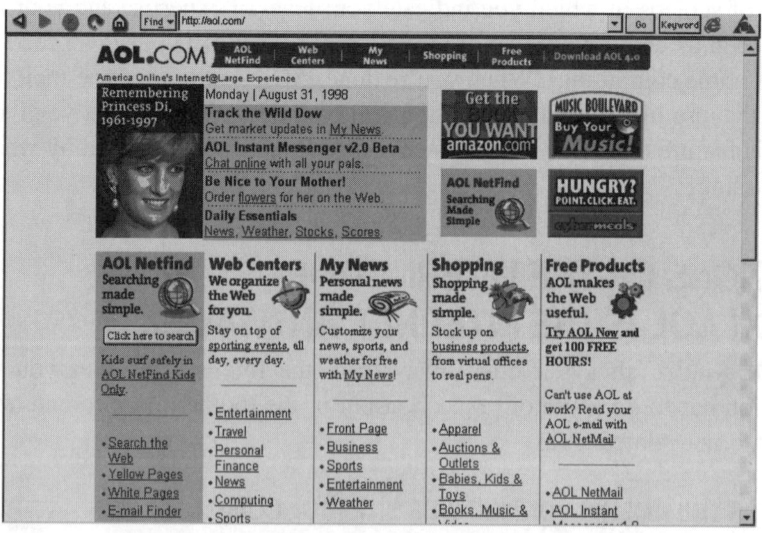

FIGURE 2-13 The America Online World Wide Web site is one of the Internet's most popular destinations

HOW DO I FIND OUT WHAT'S BEST ON THE INTERNET? The new redesigned and simplified Internet Connection (Figure 2-14) is conveniently available by selecting Internet Connection from the toolbar's Internet menu. The Internet Connection gives you the best of the Net at a glance. Click TimeSavers for the most practical sites for buying a car, planning a trip, staying healthy, and living better. A newer area is On the Net (*keyword: On the Net*), a more interactive area with links to Internet-related message boards and online classes on HTML, Web graphics, AOLPress, and other topics. From AOL.com, you have access to more than a dozen Web channels directing you to the very best Web sites.

HOW DO I GET TO A WEB PAGE OTHER THAN AOL'S? On the navigation bar, both the Address box and the Keyword button take you directly to any Web site whose address who know. You simply enter the full address (for example, **http://www.disney.com**) into the window and press Go (or ENTER). Something new in AOL 4.0 is that you can leave off the *http:*. For the really popular sites, just a keyword (*disney.com* in this case) will suffice. The Internet Connection (*keyword: Internet*), offers yet another way of entering an address and going directly to a site.

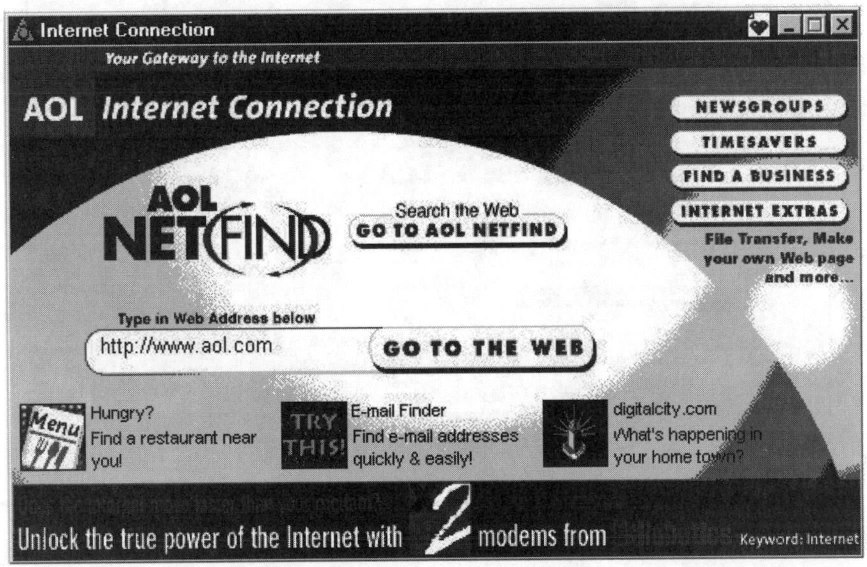

FIGURE 2-14 The Internet Connection: The Net at a glance

HOW DO I FIND SPECIFIC INFORMATION ON THE INTERNET? AOL NetFind (Figure 2-15) should be your starting point for just about any kind of Internet search. AOL NetFind is always available, and any of the following paths will whisk you there.

- Use *keyword: Netfind.*
- Type in **http://www.aol.com/netfind** in the Address box.
- Click the Find button on the navigation bar and select Find it on the Web.
- Select Internet on the toolbar and choose AOL NetFind.

Chapter 9 introduces all aspects of this truly indispensable Internet resource.

WHERE DO I GO TO CREATE MY OWN WEB PAGE? At *keyword: Personal Publisher* you will find everything you need to create your own personal page on the World Wide Web. Making your own page is a breeze on AOL, as you'll see in Chapter 7.

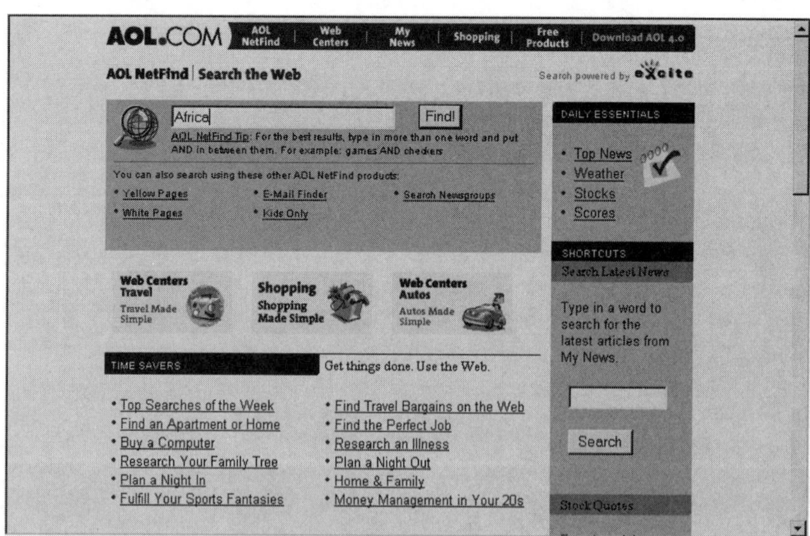

FIGURE 2-15 AOL NetFind is always available, and it's the quickest way to find specific bits of information on the Net

WHERE DO I GO TO SEND SOMEONE E-MAIL AND TO READ THE MESSAGES PEOPLE SEND ME? On AOL you can compose electronic mail messages and send them to any part of the world with Internet access. From the toolbar, you can read your mail (click Read) and send a message (click Write). Figure 2-16 shows the completely redesigned AOL mailbox, with quick access to new, old, and sent electronic mail. Chapters 3 and 4 provide all the steps and tips you need to become a great communicator—so let your mom or your accountant hear from you!

WHERE DO I GO TO TAKE PART IN A GLOBAL BULLETIN BOARD (NEWSGROUP)? Newsgroups are public Internet bulletin boards devoted to topics from scuba diving to vegetarian cooking. You can read postings from among the newsgroups AOL carries and write newsgroup postings for tens of thousands of people to see. *Keyword: Newsgroups* takes you to the Newsgroups window, shown in Figure 2-17. (Or, use the toolbar's Internet menu.) In Chapter 5, you'll get the complete scoop.

WHERE DO I GO TO GET INTERNET SOFTWARE? You don't have to go onto the Internet to get the best Internet software. AOL's software library at *keyword:*

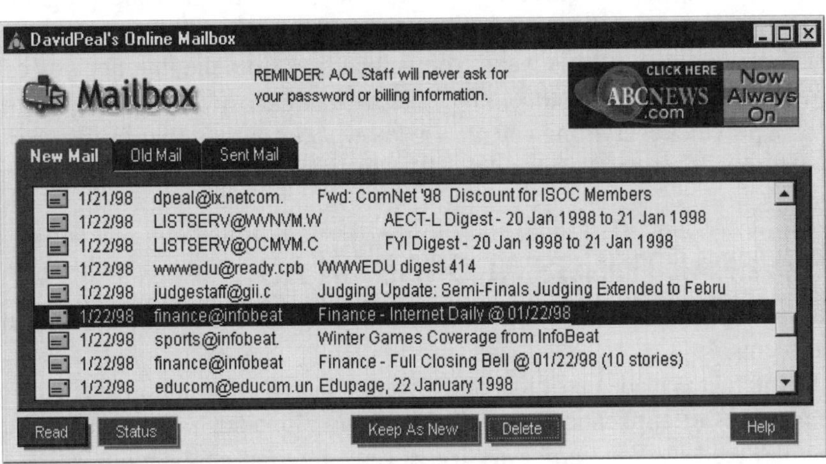

FIGURE 2-16 On AOL you get your own mailbox to manage your electronic correspondence

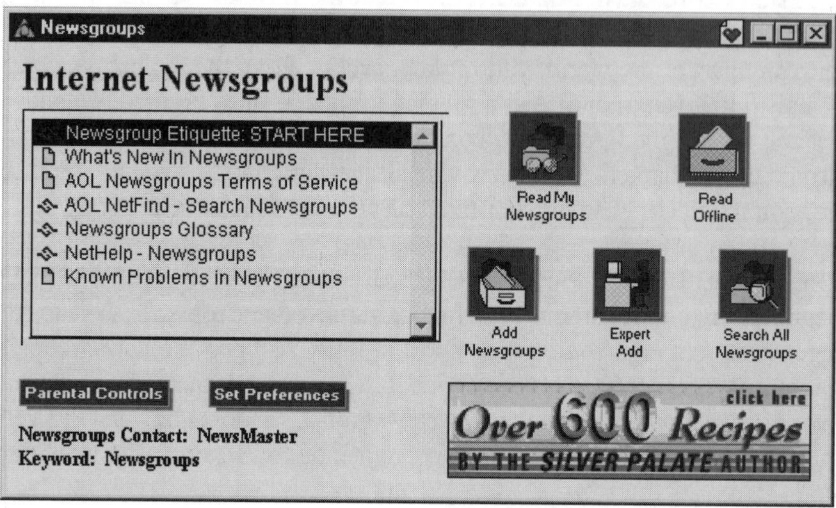

FIGURE 2-17 The main Newsgroups window on AOL: take part in a discussion group, read postings, meet new people, learn something

Filesearch has a huge archive for you to choose from—and the programs are virus-free! At *keyword: Software*, the Internet folder has excellent software as well. If you need additional files or want to download files from the Internet, you can use the Net's File Transfer Protocol (FTP), now available from the Internet menu. Chapter 8 provides everything you need to know about getting files from either AOL or the Internet. Chapter 10 provides URLs for several huge Web sites devoted to shareware.

DOING SEVERAL THINGS AT ONCE ON AOL

All those forums and sites! It might sound unmanageable, but it's all much simpler than it seems.

The Internet is made up of lots of different types of information available using different types of applications (primarily an e-mail reader, a Web browser, and a newsgroup reader). You can easily use several Internet applications at the same time—while also taking part in exclusively AOL activities such as chatting and exploring forums.

In one open window you can read your e-mail, in another you can browse the Web, in yet another you can do stock research. Of course, with two hands and limited time, you can really *do* one thing at a time, but all the windows are open at the same time.

Using Windows programs, you can readily transfer data between open windows. You can, for instance, copy a URL (Web address) from the Address box into an e-mail message and send it to someone else. Or you can paste a URL into the Address box and click Go to visit the site.

How do you do this? With Windows, you first use the mouse to select what you want to copy. Then you press CTRL-C (the C is short for copy). In Windows 95 or 98, you can also right-click and select Copy. Then switch to the window into which you want to paste the text and press CTRL-V (move).

How do you switch between open windows? Pressing CTRL-F6 allows you to view open windows one at a time ("cycle" through them). You'll also find the names of open windows listed at the bottom of the Window menu. Select a window listed in this menu to make that window active. Clicking any part of a window brings that window to the top of the pile of open windows.

Likewise, you can work with both AOL and another Windows program at the same time, copying data between them, using the word processor to write a letter about what you're doing—whatever. Just about anything you *download* (copy to your computer) will likely require another program to use: a word processing document will require a program such as Word, for example, and a spreadsheet will require a program such as Excel.

Working with multiple applications is like working with many windows within a single program. Press ALT-TAB to move from one open program to another—or, in Windows 95 or 98, you can go to the Taskbar and click on the icon of any open program to bring that program forward. To copy information between programs, you can use the CTRL-C and CTRL-V keystrokes (for copying and pasting): copy the data, switch programs, then paste the data.

FROM HERE...

Chapters 1 and 2 provide all the background you need to make full use of the Internet on AOL. The road from here can go any direction you want. I suggest that you get familiar with *all* of AOL's Internet capabilities, even if, like most people, you're most interested in e-mail and the Web. It's worth having a sense of what's possible if only because AOL makes it so simple to explore.

The next three chapters cover Internet communications: mail (Chapter 3), mailing lists (Chapter 4), and newsgroups (Chapter 5). Then the book turns to the Net's information resources: the Web in Chapters 6 and 7, followed by FTP in Chapter 8. In Chapter 9, you'll learn the secrets of searching the Net for information using *all* the tools. Chapter 10 is devoted to the non-AOL software (such as Netscape) that extends AOL as your complete online Internet provider.

Chapter 3

Communicating with E-mail

For millions of people in almost every country, *electronic mail*, or *e-mail*, or just *mail*, has become a necessity as routine and universal as the telephone and toothbrush. Thanks to the latest version of AOL (4.0), you can now manage your mail more easily: all of your old and new e-mail is available from a single window, and the brand-new Address Book makes it a breeze to keep track of the people with whom you communicate by e-mail. This chapter provides everything you need to use e-mail to communicate with people on AOL and the Internet:

- The elements of an e-mail address
- The elements of a message
- Sending and receiving messages
- Managing your incoming and outgoing mail
- Sending and receiving files attached to messages
- Sending *effective* messages

The next chapter is all about mailing lists, the myriad e-mail-based communities you can find on AOL and the Internet.

Where Is E-mail on AOL?

On AOL you are never far from your electronic mailbox. You even have a choice of ways of writing and reading e-mail messages:

- You can write e-mail by clicking the Write button on the toolbar or by selecting Write Mail from the Mail Center menu.
- You can read your new e-mail by clicking the big You Have Mail button on the Welcome screen, by clicking the Read button on the toolbar, or by selecting Read Mail from the Mail Center menu.

The Mail Center menu, available from the toolbar, is loaded with advice, tips, and troubleshooting hints. Using this menu, you can set mail preferences, access your Address Book, set up an Automatic AOL session, subscribe to any of dozens of e-mail newsletters, and more.

IT'S ALL IN THE MESSAGE

Think of an e-mail message in terms of a typical letter you get via the U.S. Postal Service. Both have a sender and a recipient, and both contain a *message* that one person wants to share with another.

E-mail differs in many ways from paper mail, however, and the differences are what make e-mail a better medium in some ways:

- The same e-mail message can go, at no extra cost, to many people at the same time. See "Sending E-Mail to More Than One Recipient."
- E-mail messages allow for a subject line that states, in the sender's words, what the e-mail message is about, such as "Urgent request" or "Six pounds, nine ounces," "New planet discovered." The subject line is a courtesy to the person receiving the message. When you receive e-mail on AOL, the Subject line can help you figure out which messages to read first (and which not to read at all). Subject lines can also help you keep track of old messages.
- E-mail messages can have useful files *attached* to them—such as a report or the latest photo of the kids. It's easier to get files via e-mail than via FTP or the Web (discussed in Chapters 6 and 8), and there's no extra charge. Now, in AOL 4.0, you can also insert photos into messages. Think of attachments as similar to the packages you get via the postal service. See "Working with Files: Sending Attachments."
- E-mail messages are usually delivered within seconds (on AOL) or minutes (on the Internet), instead of a few days. In general, e-mail is much less expensive than the paper letters sent through the U.S. Post Office.

WHAT IS AN E-MAIL ADDRESS?

How does your message get to someone else's computer? That's the purpose of the e-mail address you include when you send the message. An e-mail address has two simple parts: the user name and the domain name, separated by the "at" sign (@). Think of the *user name* as a person and the *domain name* as the computer attached to the Internet through which that person gets access.

What Is Your Internet E-Mail Address?

Anyone sending you an e-mail message over the Internet must know your e-mail address. There is a very simple way to figure out your e-mail address on the Internet. Just take your AOL screen name (the screen name you *signed on* with) and add an "at" sign (@) and **aol.com**. If your screen name is SteveCase, anyone with Internet access, anywhere in the world, can send a message to you by addressing it to **stevecase@aol.com**. It doesn't matter whether you use uppercase or lowercase letters, although lowercase is the norm on the Net. Don't know your screen name or the screen name you're currently using? Just check out the title bar of the Welcome screen!

Who You Are on the Internet: User Name

A *user name* on the Internet is the same thing as a *screen name* on AOL: it's the bit of text that identifies individual people on a specific network. On AOL, other members can get mail to you just by using your screen name (**stevecase** instead of **stevecase@aol.com**).

Usually, user names and screen names clearly refer to an actual person or are chosen so that they can be easily remembered. On the Net, it's common to use some combination of first and last names to create a user name. On AOL, there is a stronger tendency to choose personas or at least names that express some personality.

Tip *If you're going to get and receive much Internet mail, you might want to create a special screen name that clearly reflects who you are, especially if you plan to take an active part in mailing lists (Chapter 4). On the Internet you'll find AOL-style nicknames when you use Internet Relay Chat (IRC) and multi-user dimensions (MUDs), discussed in Chapter 10.*

Where You Are on the Internet: Domain Name

People use *domain names* to identify and communicate with computers connected to the Internet. Every domain name is unique. A domain name has two or more parts, proceeding from specific to general and separated by periods, pronounced "dot" when spoken. Your domain name, **aol.com**, is pronounced "a-o-l dot c-o-m."

The last part of a domain name (the *com*, for example, in *aol.com*) is considered the top-level domain, the most general part. Domains outside the U.S. *usually* have two-character top-level domains: *fi* for Finland, *dk* for Denmark, *ca* for Canada, *uk* for the United Kingdom, and so on. In the U.S., top-level domains *usually* have one of the three-letter "generic" names shown in Table 3-1.

The system works well but isn't always predictable. You'll find three-letter domains outside the U.S., and many American schools, for example, belong to the Departments of Education of their states and not to an *edu* domain. (For example, **mcps.k12.md.us** is the domain for the Montgomery County Public Schools, grades K through 12, in the state of Maryland, U.S.) Some foreign domain names have two top-level names to indicate both domain type *and* country. In the United Kingdom, for example, university (*ac*ademic) domain names sometimes end in **ac.uk** and *co*mmercial domain names in **co.uk**.

In the near future, the system is likely to be dramatically expanded through the creation of new top-level domains, some with more than three letters. A few of the new domains under consideration are *store* (for businesses that sell things on the

Domain	Example	Description
com	aol.com	Commercial domains (a huge group and the fastest-growing category)
edu	mit.edu	Educational institutions
net	commerce.net	Networks and some companies
mil	dscc.dla.mil	Branch of the U.S. armed services
gov	helix.nih.gov	Non-military domains owned and operated by the U.S. government
org	eff.org	Non-profit organizations

TABLE 3-1 Major domains

Web), *info* (for information services), *rec* (for outfits offering entertainment activities), and *web* (for companies that offer Web-related activities).

Tip: *This system, called the Domain Name System, is used throughout the Internet and is the basis of Internet addressing—not just e-mail addresses. Chapter 6 goes into Internet addresses, commonly known as URLs, short for Uniform Resource Locators.*

COMPOSING AND SENDING AN E-MAIL MESSAGE

The easiest way to compose a new message from scratch is to click the Write button on your toolbar, shown here. This brings up the Write Mail window (Figure 3-1).

Every message you compose on AOL uses the window you see in Figure 3-1. It doesn't matter whether you're composing a brand-new message or replying to or forwarding a message you've received from someone else. In each case, you use the same window.

Tip: *You don't have to sign on to write a message. You can click Write while offline, draft your message, then sign on only when you're ready to send the message. Or, click Send Later, and when you sign on, retrieve the message from your Personal Filing Cabinet, where it will be kept in the Mail Waiting To Be Sent folder (AOL will automatically ask you whether you want to send messages in that folder when you sign on). Your Personal Filing Cabinet is available from the My File menu and is discussed toward the end of this chapter.*

With AOL's mail program you ordinarily provide the following three pieces of information with every message:

- The **recipient's e-mail address** goes in the Send To field. If the recipient is on AOL, just put in the screen name; you can leave out the **@aol.com**. A recipient on the Net requires a full e-mail address—user name plus domain name.

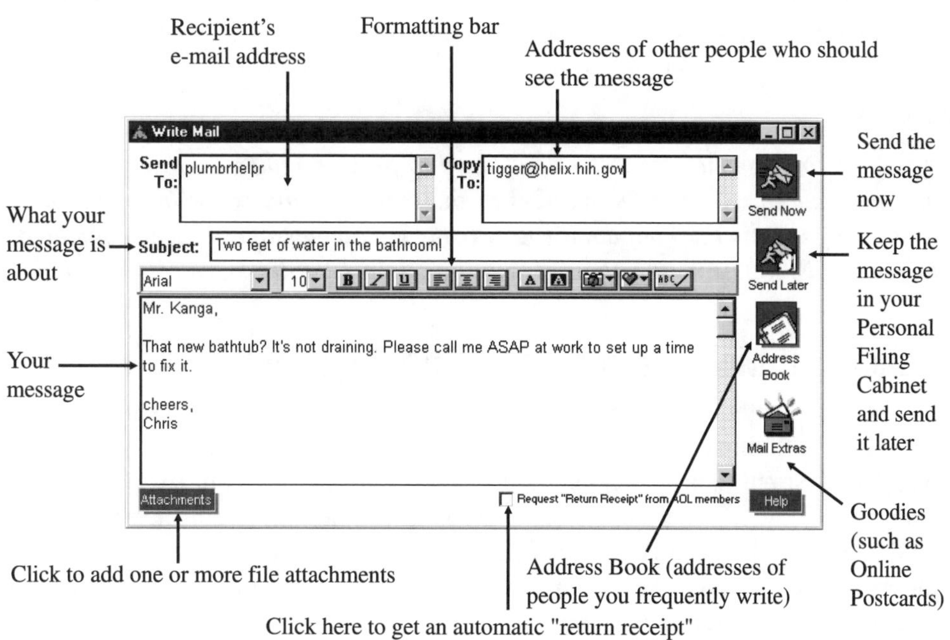

FIGURE 3-1 Compose your messages here, whether you're writing people on AOL or the Internet

Caution *E-mail addresses must be exact, in contrast to paper mail. While the U.S. Post Office might be able to discern the recipient's address if it's hard to read or partially incorrect, e-mail addresses must be just so. Just like regular letters, messages that can't be delivered over the Internet come back—they "bounce," sometimes after a few days, sometimes accompanied by a cryptic message. On AOL you'll know right away if you attempt to send a message to an AOL screen name that doesn't exist; AOL won't let you send it. However, AOL cannot check the accuracy of Internet e-mail addresses you put in the Send To or Copy To field. The bottom line: double-check your Internet addresses before clicking Send Now!*

- The message's **subject**, in the Subject line, which gives the other person some idea of what the message is about.
- The **message** itself, in the big message box (with the scroll bar to accommodate messages too long to fit in the box). As for actual content, a message can be a word or several pages; books have been written about how to write messages. "Putting Your Best Foot Forward," at the end of this chapter, has tips for writing messages that get attention.

With AOL you're not restricted to plain text in your messages. You can now use colored text, vary the font size and style, drop in pictures, and add hyperlinks. "Adding Pizzazz to Your AOL Mail" shows how to do all this.

Tip *If you're forwarding a message (that is, sending a message you received to someone else), you don't have to provide either a subject line or a message; all you need is the address of the recipient. You can read more about forwarding later in this chapter. If you're using e-mail messages to send commands to mailing list software, you can omit the subject line. Chapter 4 covers lists in detail.*

Sending E-Mail to More Than One Recipient

It's a simple matter to send mail to more than one person: just separate their e-mail addresses by commas. It doesn't matter whether the recipients are on AOL or not on AOL; you put their addresses in any order, separated by commas. If you find yourself sending messages to the same group of people over and over, you can use AOL's Address Book to create a special distribution list, so that you can send one message automatically to everyone on the list (see "Keeping an Address Book on America Online" later in this chapter).

If you use the AOL Address Book to send mail to multiple addresses, AOL adds the commas.

Differences Between AOL Mail and Internet Mail

In principle, sending e-mail over the Internet seems just like sending it to someone on AOL, but in practice there are some important differences:

- **Address.** On AOL the person to whom you send messages can be addressed by screen name alone. On the Net you must know the domain name as well. This is standard practice, by the way. If you omit the domain name, the Net's mail "protocol" assumes you're sending the mail to someone on the same domain as yourself. So, if you leave off the domain in that message to **kevin@northcoast.com**, the Kevin whose domain is **@aol.com** will get your message. This is one error that AOL is not going to catch!

- **File size.** You cannot send or receive file attachments greater than about 2 Mb over the Internet. On AOL-to-AOL mail, however, the limit is higher—about 16 Mb. See "Working with Files: Sending Attachments."
- **Ability to unsend.** Once a message has left AOL and gone to someone on the Internet, you can't change your mind and unsend it (as you can with a message sent over AOL to someone on AOL).
- **Availability of status.** Likewise, the status of a message sent over the Internet is not available, while on AOL you can find out whether someone has read your message—and even be informed automatically if someone on AOL has received a message you sent (if you put a check in the little Return Receipt box at the bottom of the Write Mail window). See "If You Change Your Mind: Unsending a Message" later in this chapter.
- **Formatting.** Since AOL 3.0, you have been able to add all kinds of formatting to your messages: add background and text colors, apply bold and italics, and insert Web links. Only AOL members will experience these effects; Internet recipients will receive plain old text. See "Adding Pizzazz to Your AOL Mail." (Note, however, that there is some Internet formatting that AOL doesn't yet support; many services allow you to write messages in HTML—just like Web pages—but when you get such messages on AOL, the HTML will be partly or completely removed.)

CCing and BCCing

You'll often want others to be apprised of messages you send. For example, in a company setting, you may want to notify your boss if you're sending a message to her boss or someone outside the department. With AOL you can send a *carbon copy* (also known as a *courtesy copy*) to people who should know of your message but aren't its main recipients.

There's often a subtle calculation involved in choosing the persons to CC. If you've prepared a long report for someone and are sending it as an attached file, CCing your boss can make your boss the true recipient. There can be a downside, too. If the message turns into a thread—a series of replies and counter-replies—

anyone initially CCed may want to take part, and the exchange can turn into a free-for-all.

Tip *If a message to many direct (Send To) and indirect (Copy To) recipients turns into a two-way discussion or becomes personal in any way, it's a good idea to prune the list of participants. This way you can turn a potential free-for-all into a true tête-à-tête. To do this, you can add and remove addresses from the Send To and Copy To fields when you make replies (covered later in this chapter).*

- To CC someone, just put his or her address in the Copy To field. For multiple people being CCed, separate their addresses by commas. These recipients can be on AOL or the Internet and in any order—although alphabetizing long lists can keep feathers from getting ruffled if certain people don't like to be listed last!

Finding Mail Help on AOL

Several areas on AOL provide online help and information as you use e-mail. The Mail Center, available from the tool bar's Mail Center menu, offers abundant help, plus tips for finding people, saving time, and staying informed. The focus of the Mail Center is on e-mail sent from one member to another. (By the way, if you've been on AOL for a while, you'll know that the Mail Center used to be called the Post Office.) You'll also find Help buttons on the Write Mail window, on your mailbox, and on every message you receive!

Unlike a regular CC, a BCC (blind carbon copy), as the name suggests, is a carbon copy that the direct (Send To) recipients *won't be aware of.* BCCs can be a little risky. Imagine that you *receive* a BCC but neglect to notice that the sender wanted to keep the BCC secret from the direct recipients. Suppose you decide to reply to the message and you send your reply to the original sender and all the direct recipients (by clicking Reply All). Some recipient(s) may be offended by the secretiveness.

An occasion where BCCs do make sense is when you don't want a long list of recipients of the same message to know of each other's existence (or e-mail address). Say you want to send a joke out to both coworkers and family or friends, and you don't want the coworkers to see the addresses of your family or friends, and vice versa. Or, you could use BCCs if you create and distribute an electronic newsletter but don't want the subscribers to know each other's individual e-mail address. You'll spare your subscribers some unsolicited mail by keeping their addresses confidential.

To send a BCC:

- In the Copy To field, place the recipient's address *in parentheses*. For multiple BCC recipients, separate the addresses-in-parentheses by commas. You can BCC people on AOL and the Net, in any order. In the Copy To field, you can use both BCCs and CCs.

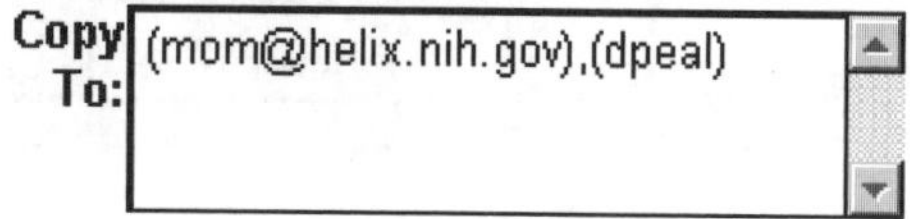

Spell Checking Your Message

Some messages are more important than others. If it's a message to your boss, you may want to make sure you haven't included a typo; if it's to your spouse, he or she is likely to be a little more tolerant. With AOL 4.0, you can now spell check your e-mail messages before sending them.

To run a spell check on your message before you send it into the ether, you first position your text cursor at the beginning of the message and then click the small ABC button on the Write Mail formatting toolbar (see Figure 3-1). If you're familiar with word processors, you won't be surprised by what happens next. AOL's spell checker compares each word and series of characters in your message to the closest-matching word in its built-in dictionary. Any words it can't identify are brought to your attention in the Check Spelling window shown in Figure 3-2. If the speller has an entry similar to your word, it will be suggested; if it doesn't, you'll be asked whether you intended to use this particular spelling.

Just because a word's not in the speller's dictionary doesn't mean it's not a word or at least meaningful to you and your readers. For every questionable word the speller catches, you have several ways to respond:

- If it's not an error, you can tell the program either to skip the particular word, phrase, or acronym by clicking Skip (or Skip All to tell the speller to ignore the word each time it occurs in the message).
- If it's not an error and you use the word all the time, you can tell the speller to learn it by adding it to the built-in dictionary (click Learn).

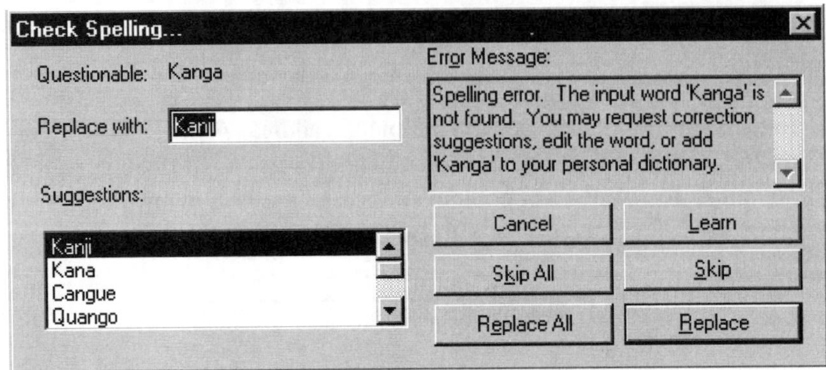

FIGURE 3-2 Spot those mail typos before they come back to bite

Note *To see the words you've had the speller learn—your personal dictionary—select My AOL | Preferences, and click on Spelling. In the Spelling Preferences window, find the Dictionaries section and click on Edit (to the right of Personal Dictionary). You'll see a list of words you've added to the speller. Currently, you can use this window to delete an entry (select it and click Delete) but not add an entry.*

- If it is a bona fide error, you can correct the mistake by either using AOL's suggestion (click Replace) or by typing one of your own into the Replace with box. If more than one suggestion appears, select one (or type in one of your own), then click Replace. You can also edit AOL's suggestion by adding or changing characters using the mouse and keyboard. Click Replace All to do a global search in the message for all instances where you misspelled the word and to replace them.
- If you've typed a word twice ("the the," for example), the speller will flag it; click Delete to remove one of the instances (where you see Replace in Figure 3-2).

Click Start to restart the search for typos if you've switched tasks for any reason. To spell check a single word as you're typing your message, double-click the word to select it and then click the ABC speller button.

Unlike some word processors, the AOL speller won't catch your typos as you make them.

A little Spell Check Complete window comes up when you've completed the spell check. Click OK, and proceed to send the message as described in the next section.

Tip *If you're a stickler for this sort of thing, or if spelling isn't your strong suit, you can run a spell check* automatically *before sending any message. On the AOL toolbar, click My AOL | Preferences, and click the Mail button. Place a check before "Perform a spell check before sending mail" and click OK.*

Sending Your Message

With the address(es) typed in, write a short and punchy Subject line that sums up what you want to say. Now type your message in the big box, as shown in Figure 3-1. At the bottom of the Write Mail window, notice the Request "Return Receipt" from AOL members box. If you click in this box, you will automatically receive an e-mail notice informing you of who read the message and at what time. Receipt of mail by someone on the Internet won't trigger an automatic message.

Tip *You can write your message before you enter any address. One reason to do this is to refine your message and proof it carefully before sending it; putting in addresses last can keep you from sending the message accidentally or prematurely. A message sent accidentally to the Internet can't be "unsent."*

Once you've composed a message, you send it on its way by clicking **Send Now**. After you click Send Now, the message closes automatically, and a little window comes up confirming that the message was sent. Click OK.

Tip *To send a message (or an Instant Message) once it's been written and addressed, use the keyboard to press* CTRL-ENTER.

Clicking Send Later places your message in a *queue* to be sent either during an Automatic AOL session (discussed in the next chapter) or when you're ready to sign off AOL. You would also click Send Later when you've written a message while offline (not signed on); when you sign on the next time, you'll be asked whether you want to send the message. Don't send the message if you want to edit it further. To edit a message marked "Send Later," open your Personal Filing Cabinet (available from the My Files menu) and look for the message in the Mail Waiting To Be Sent folder.

What happens after a message is sent? AOL gives you the choice of *not* closing the message you just sent. (See "Mail Preferences.") Not closing a message is a good way to double-check your message. If you change your mind about sending the

message, AOL gives you a way to *unsend* messages sent to other people on AOL (see "If You Change Your Mind: Unsending a Message"). Keeping a message open is also an alternative to using blind carbon copies (BCCs). For example, after you've sent a message to the direct recipient, you can change the address and send the same message to someone else.

Canceling a Message

If you decide not to send a message and you've got Windows 95, just click the little X in the upper right-hand corner. In Windows 3.1, double-click in the control box in the upper left-hand corner. If you've written anything in the message box, you'll be asked whether you want to save the message. Click Yes if you do, then navigate to a directory (folder) where you want to save your message and give it a name. With the message saved, you can later edit it with a word processor or AOL's built-in text editor. You bring up the text editor by simply going to AOL's File menu, choosing Open, and hunting for that message.

Mail Preferences

America Online lets you define several aspects of the way you use e-mail. You can:

- Confirm that messages have been sent
- Keep messages open after they've been sent
- Store your messages in your Personal Filing Cabinet
- View addresses in headers as hyperlinks (so you can click a link to send a message to the person who was CCed)
- Automatically perform a spell check of your outgoing messages
- Quote your replies in Internet fashion instead of AOL fashion

Some of these aspects will matter to you more than others; all are easy to turn on and off. The most important preferences are discussed throughout this chapter.

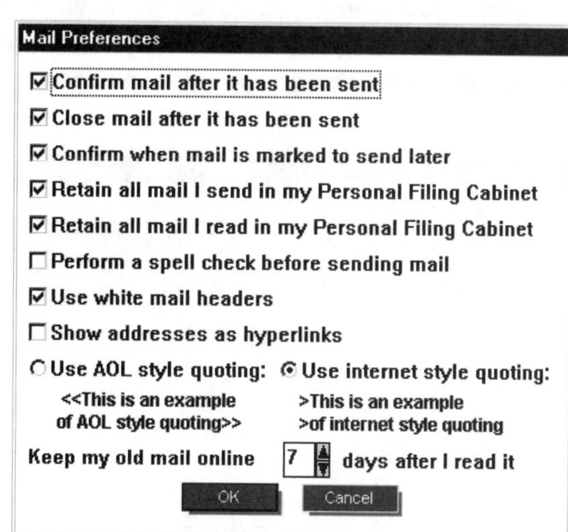

To bring up the Mail Preferences window, click the My AOL button in the toolbar, click on Preferences, then on Mail. Check or uncheck a preference by clicking inside the little box. If there are multiple screen names on your master account, you can set up mail preferences only for the screen name used to sign onto the current AOL session. Click OK when you're done.

Note that mail preferences are different from Mail Controls (available from the Mail Center menu on the toolbar), which allow you to block unsolicited mail (see "Avoiding Unwanted E-mail"). When you set Mail Controls under Parental Controls, discussed in Appendix C, you are controlling a screen name's ability (among other things) to receive mail with attachments.

If You Change Your Mind: Unsending a Message

From time to time, you may want to unsend messages. For example, sometimes when I reread my messages I find that I've been intemperate, or that I've made a typo, or that, for some reason, the file I wanted to attach didn't get attached.

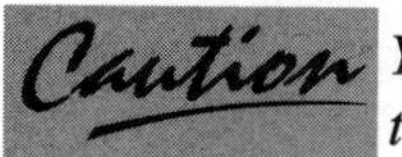

You can unsend messages to other AOL members but not to people on the Internet.

To reread a message you've sent, click Read on the toolbar. In your Online Mailbox, click Sent Mail. The last message sent will be at the top of the list.

Double-click the message. Select it and click Status to see whether it's been read by your AOL recipient. If the message has been read, the screen name of the recipient will appear alongside the time the message was opened.

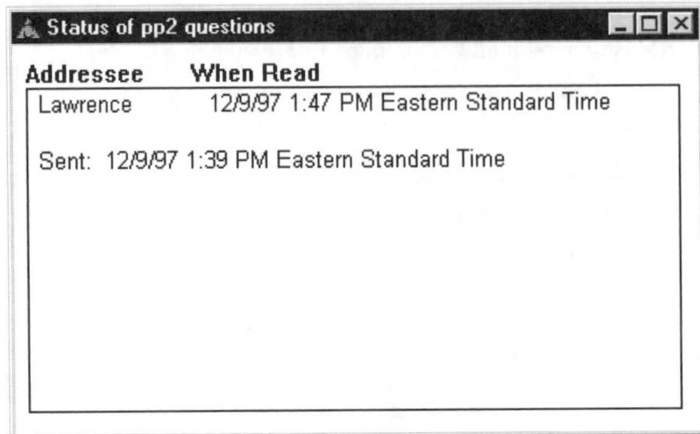

To unsend a message to an AOL member:

- If the message wasn't read, select the message and click Unsend, confirming that you don't want to keep a copy of the message. If the message went to more than one recipient and if any one of them has read the message, you can't unsend it to the others. If a message goes out to a couple of people and if one of those people is on the Internet, it can't be unsent either.

KEEPING AN ADDRESS BOOK ON AMERICA ONLINE

Your AOL Address Book lets you keep track of the addresses of all the people and groups of people you routinely correspond with. With AOL 4.0, AOL's Address Book has a whole new look, and each screen name on an account gets its own Address Book. Here are some of the new features you may find yourself using on a daily basis:

- With an open message from a friend (or enemy, or anyone), you can now automatically add that person's e-mail address to your Address Book by just clicking the new Add Address button.
- Addresses are now alphabetized and editable, so you can alphabetize by first name or last name.

- It's now possible to keep notes about your friends (such as their street address and birthday), as well as photos of them (if you have the digitized image handy).
- It's now much easier to keep small-scale mailing lists, in order to send a single message to many people at the same time.

Using your Address Book can keep your Internet mail from bouncing and vastly simplify your communication with your mail-friends, especially if group members have messy, arbitrary, or otherwise forgettable addresses.

Tip *You can add to and edit your Address Book while offline, which is useful if you compose offline messages or if you don't want to sign on just to add someone's address.*

To add an entry to your Address Book, you have a choice. With a received e-mail message open, simply click Add Address. You'll see the New Person window, with AOL's effort to transfer the name and e-mail address from the message to its Address Book. Make sure the information was correctly transferred. You can type in any of the four boxes, and copy and paste between them as required.

The second (manual) way to add an entry to your Address Book (Figure 3-3) is to select Address Book from the Mail Center menu. In the Address Book window, click New Person (in the lower left). In the New Person window, supply a first name, last name, e-mail address, and any notes about the person, as shown here.

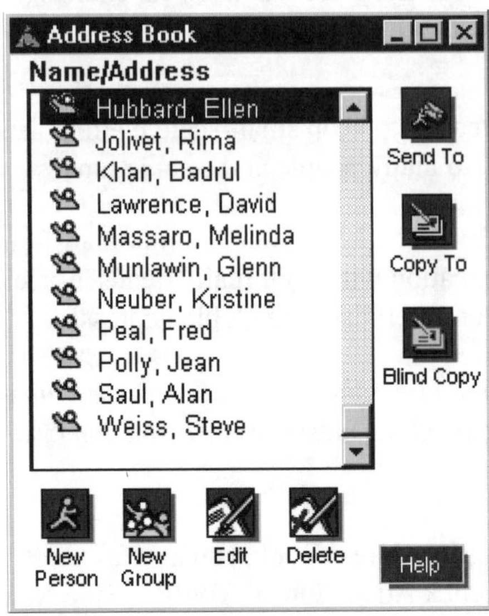

FIGURE 3-3 AOL's Address Book is a snap to update with new names and addresses

Click the Picture tab to paste in or select (click Select Picture) a digitized image of your buddy. Adding a picture is entirely optional. In fact, to create an entry for a new person, the only piece of information you must add is the e-mail address; if you leave the first and last names blank, addresses will be arranged by the e-mail address itself.

Note *The Address Book orders names in the last-name, first-name format. It is easy (as I have discovered) to wind up with names alphabetized by a combination of first names and last names, but it's also easy to make the entries consistent. Once a name has been entered, just select it and click the Edit button (Figure 3-3) and make any changes. Remember that AOL alphabetizes by whatever is in the Last Name field. To move text, select it and select Cut from the Edit menu, then position the text cursor where you want to put the text and select Paste from the Edit menu.*

To use the Address Book to create a mailing list:

1. Open your Address Book (select it from the Mail Center).

2. Click New Group.
3. In the Group Name window, type in the group name, identifying its purpose, its location, or something else, such as *Softball Team* or *Family*. What you type in this box is the phrase that appears in the main alphabetized window of the Address Book when you're done.

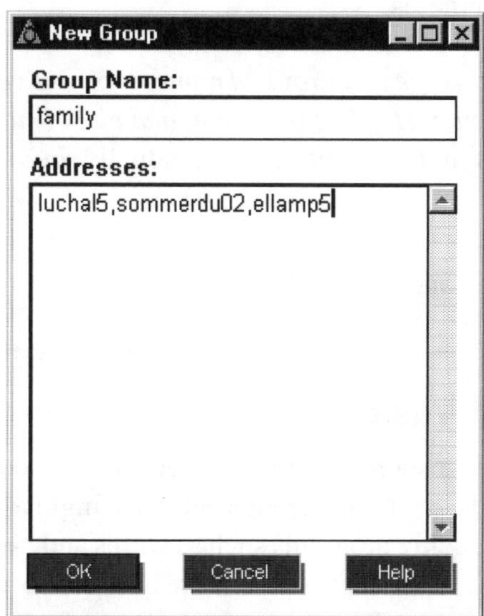

4. In the Addresses box, type in your group's e-mail addresses, separated by commas. Click OK when you're done.

Note *Using the Address Book is like having your own personal mailing list software. The Address Book automates the task of sending one message to many people, and it's easy to maintain.*

To enter addresses while composing a message:

1. With the Write Mail window open, click Address Book. (You can also start with the Address Book, select a name, and click the Send To, Copy To, or Blind Copy button; a Write Mail window comes up with the addressee you just selected.)

2. From the Address Book, select the name of the person to whom you want to send a message. Click the Send To button or the Copy To or Blind Copy button, as appropriate. The address will automatically be plugged into the field you chose. If you have multiple recipients or many people to copy, repeat this step until you're done. Multiple recipients will be automatically separated by a comma, and BCC's will be automatically placed in parentheses.

Note *To send a message to a group of names that you've entered using the New Group button, just select the group and click Send To, Copy To, or Blind Copy. The addresses will be entered* individually *into the appropriate field, separated by commas.*

3. Type and send your message!

Finding an Address

The million-dollar question is, "How do you find someone's Internet e-mail address?" A few years ago, the answer was highly involved, requiring acquaintance with prickly programs such as **whois** and **netfind** and other tools devised in the days when Internet users were likely to be academic researchers or network administrators. Today it's a lot easier to find an e-mail address. On AOL, start with the Member Directory (available from the toolbar's People menu); on the Internet, start with a service such as Four11, which is available over the World Wide Web (**http://www.four11.com**). This and other Web services are discussed in Chapter 9.

ADDING PIZZAZZ TO YOUR AOL MAIL

E-mail is ugly! Black letters against a white background, just like the typewriter I used until the early 1980s. Since AOL 3.0, AOL has given you the ability to make your messages much more interesting to look at. The catch is, these new features are available only for your messages to other AOL members who are using at least AOL 3.0, so your creations won't be appreciated on the Internet; they'll arrive as plain text.

Tip *Use the right-hand button of your mouse at any time while writing a message to get instant access to all the formatting and editing options at your disposal in AOL 4.0 for Windows.*

In your member-to-member messages you can now take your text and add flair, color, and outrageous effects such as:

- Text color
- Background color
- Font (the shape and look of the letters)
- Text size
- Style (bold, italic, underlining)
- Alignment (to align a message with the left or right margin, or to center it)
- Adding image files directly into your messages to other AOL members

Applying these features couldn't be easier. In the Write Mail window, type a message. Use your mouse to select some text. Now click each of the little buttons to see what it does (Figure 3-4). Figure 3-5 (in a few pages) shows a formatted message.

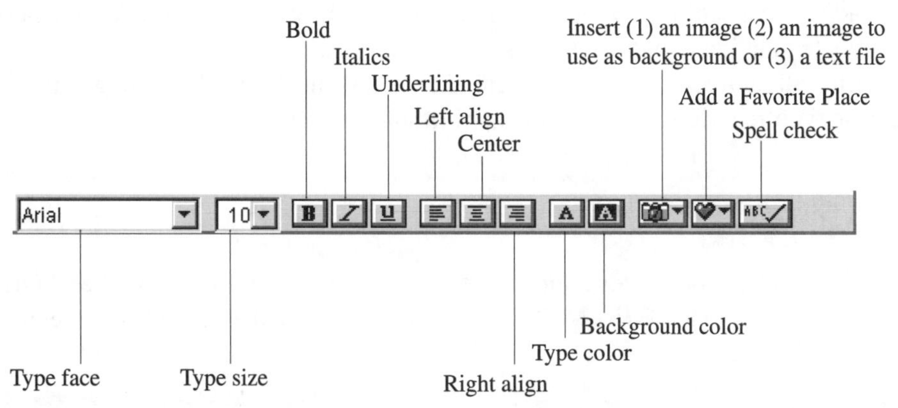

FIGURE 3-4 Formatting your e-mail message is now easy on AOL

Formatting gives you some powerful new ways to emphasize words: italics for important words, large bold text for headers, and colors for attention-getting backgrounds, for example.

AOL 4.0 for Windows gives you both global control over how messages look (to give them all the same look and feel) and local control (making each message unique). To set the font, font size, and font style of all your e-mail messages (as well as Instant Messages), select My AOL | Preferences and click on Font.

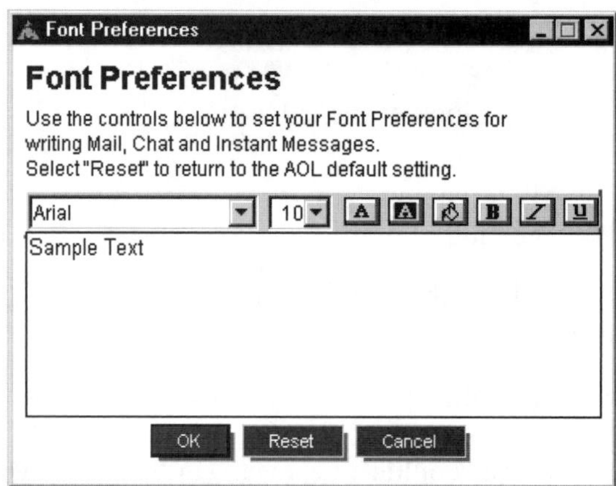

From the large drop-down box (click the triangle), choose a font; from the small drop-down box, choose a font size. Click the other buttons to set the font color, the background color, and the font style (bold, italic, underline). For each choice, you'll see a bit of sample text. Click OK when you're content. These settings will apply to every single e-mail message you write. However, to achieve specific effects, you can adjust your settings for individual messages while using the Write Mail window. To create individual masterpieces, see "Mail Extras."

Like all such effects, these mail enhancements can also be distracting, unless, of course, you're writing ransom notes or birthday invitations.

Mail Extras

AOL 4.0 lets you achieve some awesome effects in your mail to other AOL members. With the Write Mail window open (or from the Mail Center menu), select Mail Extra.

In the Mail Extras window, click Colors & Style to get a dozen custom-made pictorial effects, such as "Hello," which you can use in your own messages. Or, create your own electronic stationery, with personalized headings. Click Stationery to get a dozen designs you can use in your own messages. Figure 3-5 shows the combination of a Color & Style effect ("Hello") and stationery ("Blue-Striped Border"). Just copy and paste using the Edit menu to create your own messages, combining colors, styles, stationery, and, of course, smileys.

Tip *In your mail to AOL members, you can even add bullets, those dots you use in a word processor to list things. Here's how: with the cursor at the beginning of a line, hold down the* ALT *key and, keeping it pressed down, type* ***249*** *on your numeric keypad, then release the* ALT *key. But don't put symbols in your non-AOL mail. They won't make it through AOL's e-mail gateway to the Internet, and there's no guaranteeing what they'll look like.*

Adding Clickable Hyperlinks to Your AOL Mail

A *hyperlink* (or just *link*) is a special kind of text that, when you click it, takes you to a Web site or AOL area (jump ahead to Chapter 6 to find out more about linking). Like formatting, hyperlinks can be used only in messages sent to other AOL

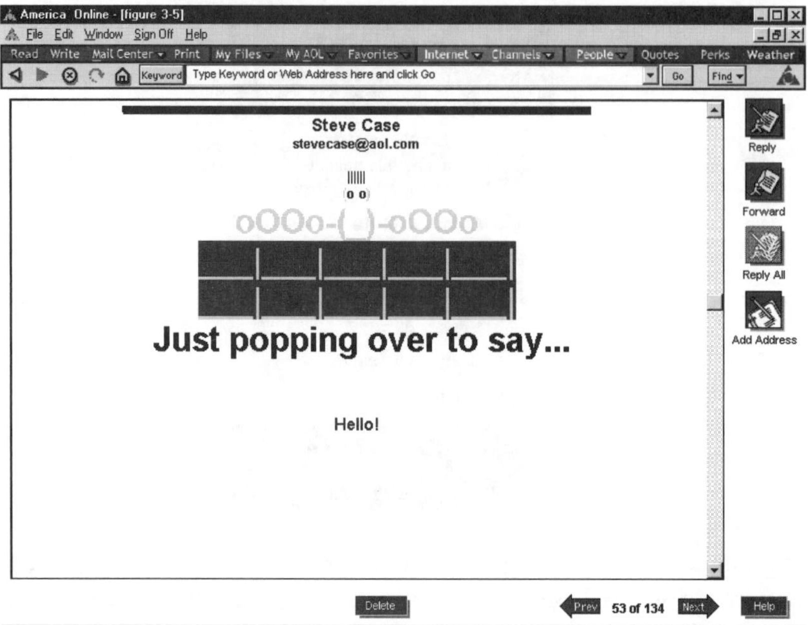

FIGURE 3-5 In your mail to other AOL members, use Mail Extras to create effects like these

members. They will usually be automatically stripped out of messages to people who aren't on AOL.

There are two ways to add hyperlinks:

- *If you know the Internet address (or URL)*: Select some text in a message you're writing in the Write Mail window. Ideally, the text should concretely describe the site—it's what gives the recipient the *incentive* to click. Right-click and select Insert a Hyperlink. In the Edit Hyperlink box, type in a Web address (which usually begins **http://**). Click OK, finish the message, and send it. Chapter 6 covers URLs. You can also right-click and enter both the text and the URL:

Edit Hyperlink

Text: Global Schoolhouse

Url: http://www.gsh.org

OK | Cancel | Launch

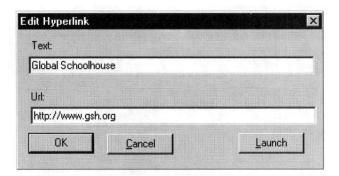

- *If the site you want to link to is in your Favorite Places folder:* From the Write Mail window, click on the heart on your mail toolbar (Figure 3-4), select a favorite, and release your mouse.

A link will be placed in your message. Finish the message and send it. Using this technique you can add hyperlinks even when you're offline. (Here's a shortcut: start *from* a Web site or AOL forum you like, click the heart in the title bar, and click the Insert in Mail button.)

Here's what recipients of the message see:

For some good ideas about integrating the Net in the classroom, a good place to start is the Global Schoolhouse. I also recommend the WWWEdu ("we do") mailing list, which you can learn about at this site.

When they click the underlined text they'll go to one of your favorite places on AOL or the Internet.

How to Send a Greeting Card by E-Mail

AOL's new Online Greetings service (available at *keyword: Online Greetings* or by clicking Mail Extras from the Write Mail window) lets you attach a "greeting card"— in the form of an image file—to an e-mail message, and then send it in place of that birthday, anniversary, thank-you, get well, or friendship card. Dozens of designs are available. It's easier, cheaper, far faster, and much more convenient than choosing a card in the drugstore.

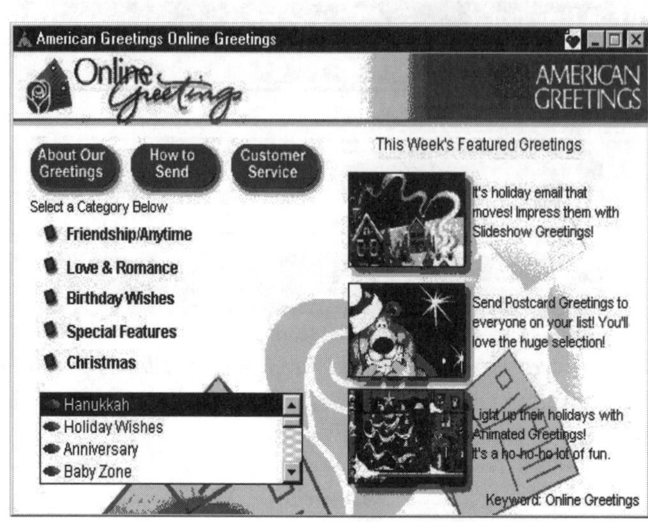

Two minor qualifications: The person to whom you're sending the card must have e-mail and be able to receive attachments, and the service is not free (but it's still a lot cheaper than the paper variety). AOL is offering the service in conjunction with American Greeting. Online postcards are also available by clicking Mail Extras.

Adding Image Files to Your AOL Mail

New to AOL 4.0 is the ability to drop a digitized photo or other image directly into a message. To do this, just click the Camera button on the Write Mail toolbar and select Insert a Picture from the menu that comes up. You'll then pick an image from your hard disk (or network or floppy or wherever). The image will appear directly in the message, after the most recently typed text.

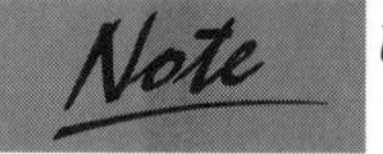

Unfortunately, it's not yet possible to wrap text around an image.

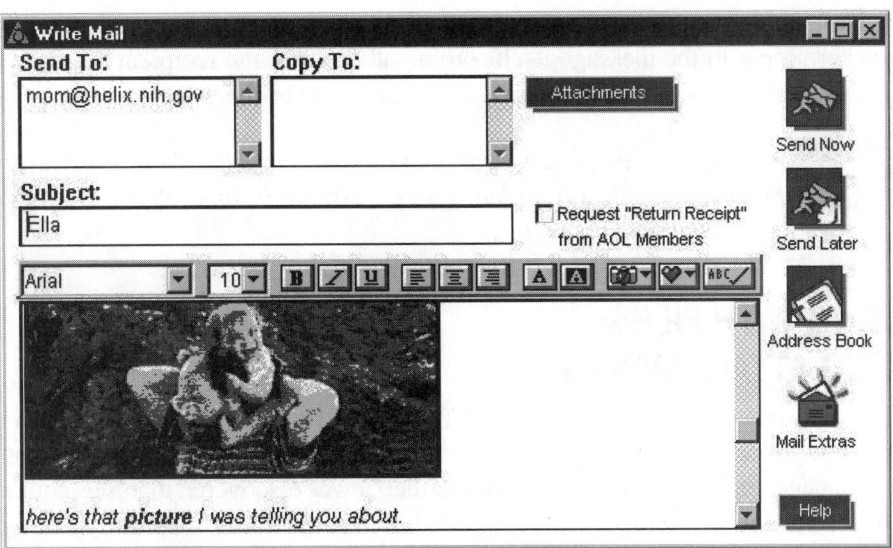

Click Send Now to *upload* the image (transfer it from your PC to an AOL computer) together with your message. Once it's been uploaded to AOL, your message and image will be available to the AOL member you've chosen to honor with the image.

Note *Your recipients on AOL can tell if an image is part of the message because, in the New Mailbox, the message has a special icon "clipped' to it. When they open the message, they get a window asking them to confirm that they know who the sender is. Only after doing so will your recipients be able to see the message with the inserted picture. Non-AOL members and members using versions earlier than AOL 4.0 can't yet receive inserted pictures. (AOL 3.0 members will get the file as an attachment.)*

If you want to send an image to someone on the Internet, you must attach it (instead of inserting it), as described in the next section, "Working with Files: Sending Attachments." In your messages to AOL members you can both attach and

insert files. The benefit to attaching a file to a message is that the recipient will get quicker access to the message itself; on the other hand, the recipient will have to take the trouble to download and save the image if he or she wants to view it.

Tip *AOL 4.0 makes photos available to you. Just click Mail Extras, click Photos, and select from butterflies, basketballs, and other images. Your recipient will get a link to the image.*

WORKING WITH FILES: SENDING ATTACHMENTS

Files are everywhere when you use a PC. You use files when you create documents with your word processor or spreadsheet, when you install AOL, and when you make a Web page. Early in the history of the Internet, it was discovered that files could be attached to e-mail messages and could thus be exchanged almost as easily as simple messages (that was before they invented FTP, the standard way of transferring files, discussed in Chapter 8).

Tip *If you use AOL at work and at home, you can use AOL to send* yourself *files—sending them from work, then receiving them at home! It's easier than carrying around a bunch of disks.*

On AOL, it's easy to attach files to messages you send. Likewise, you can receive files if they've been attached to messages sent to you. The following section is about attaching files. You can read "Retrieving a File from a Message," a little later in this chapter, if you're on the receiving end.

Note *As a rule of thumb, you can both send and receive over the Internet any file that's less than 2 megabytes (Mb), though on AOL you can exchange files much bigger than this limit. Ordinary word processing documents are rarely greater than 50K (1/40th of 2 Mb). A more realistic limit is 1 Mb, according to David O'Donnell, AOL's Postmaster. Don't know how big your file is? Using Windows 3.1's File Manager or Windows 95's Explorer, navigate to the folder (directory) with the file you want to send, and look in the Size column for the file's size in kilobytes (a Mb is 1024 kilobytes).*

Attaching a File to a Message

AOL makes it easy to attach any file you want to a message; all you need to do is specify the filename and location. With AOL 4.0, you can add several files, and they'll be automatically zipped (compressed) into a single file for easier downloading by your recipient. I used this feature regularly in writing this book for sending stuff to my editor: screen captures, chapters, drafts, outlines, and other word-processed documents.

Using AOL, you can send files both to other AOL members and to people on the Net; with multiple Send To's and Copy To's you can simultaneously send the *same* attachment to several people on AOL and the Net.

There's one hitch, but it's really just a small one. AOL's e-mail program follows a standard called MIME, the *Multipurpose Internet Mail Extension*, which was designed to simplify the transfer of files through the computer gateways that regulate the flow of messages between different e-mail systems and the Internet. I f you want to send someone a file attachment over the Internet, your recipient must also be using an e-mail program that supports the MIME format. Basically, MIME works by converting your *binary* document (a formatted word-processed file, for instance) into a *text* document, and then telling the recipient's e-mail program how to handle the attached file.

Sometimes a MIME document is received as what looks like gibberish and has to be *decoded*, but there is plenty of software available for free on AOL that will do this. The attachments you receive will ordinarily be immediately usable; only the more unusual file formats will require that you decode them.

To attach a file to your e-mail message:

1. With the Write Mail window open, type in the recipient's address, the subject, and the message, then click the Attachments button. The Attachments window comes up.

You can click the Attachments button at any time while you're composing your message.

Attachments
You can attach one or more files to this mail; multiple attached files will be compressed. For each file you want to attach click Attach, select the file, and click Open.
C:\David\ella2.jpg
Attach
Detach
OK
Cancel
Help

2. Click the Attach button, then navigate to the file you want to attach, and select the file.

   If you want to attach more than one file, repeat this step for additional files. Those files will be automatically bundled up in a zipped file whose filename is the name of the first file you selected and whose extension is ZIP. Change your mind? Select a file or files in the Attachments window and click Detach. Click OK when you've identified all the file(s) you want to attach.

3. Click Send Now or Send Later. The File Transfer box pops up (or will pop up, if the message is going to be sent later) to tell you that your file is being sent. Its "thermometer" (the blue box) measures the progress of your file as it travels from your PC to AOL. A little window tells you when your file has been sent; click OK.

After you've sent a file, you can check whether the message was read but not whether the file was downloaded. To check the message status, from the Mail Center menu select Sent Mail, select the message, and click the Status button.

If the recipient is on AOL, the zipped file can be downloaded using AOL's Download Manager (see Chapter 8 for more about this nifty feature). An Internet recipient can unzip it using a readily available program such as PKZIP or WinZip (also discussed in Chapter 8).

Tip *Sometimes, you cannot send a file that is in use by some other program. A few programs, such as Microsoft's Word, sometimes don't let go of files even after you've closed the document. If a file is either in use by another program or still in its grip (as in the case of Word), it will appear that your file is attached to your message, but it won't be sent. You'll have to completely close the application (Word, in this case), and then send the file again. To avoid embarrassment, you should probably unsend the file-less message (if your recipient's on AOL).*

Sending Spam: Don't Do It

Spam is unsolicited e-mail. Sending spam on AOL and the Internet is a taboo, but not because cyberspace denizens have delicate feelings or follow vegetarian diets. Rather, spam wastes space on people's hard disks, wastes network bandwidth, and wastes the time of many people. Take a few seconds of wasted time per person, multiply it by thousands of people, and you have an enormous waste of people's time. For most people, it's a nuisance; for some it's an invasion of privacy. For AOL, it's a serious offense and a matter for the courts.

Sending spam from AOL is an especially bad idea. Here's the official word from AOL's Community Action Team (CAT): "If you send unsolicited commercial e-mail messages to individuals on AOL or on the Internet, you run the same risk as in posting such messages to mailing lists. You may receive a TOS [AOL Terms of Service] warning, and repeated violations may lead to the termination of your AOL account."

See "Avoiding Unwanted E-mail" a little later in this chapter for tips on avoiding junk e-mail.

YOU'VE GOT MAIL! READING YOUR MAIL

You've got mail! If your PC is equipped for sound, you may have heard a genial male voice intone these words the last time you signed onto AOL. Reading your mail is easy on AOL. Just click the big You Have Mail button on the Welcome screen. You can also read your mail by clicking the Read button on your AOL toolbar or selecting New Mail from the Mail Center menu. Your online mailbox now comes up (Figure 3-6).

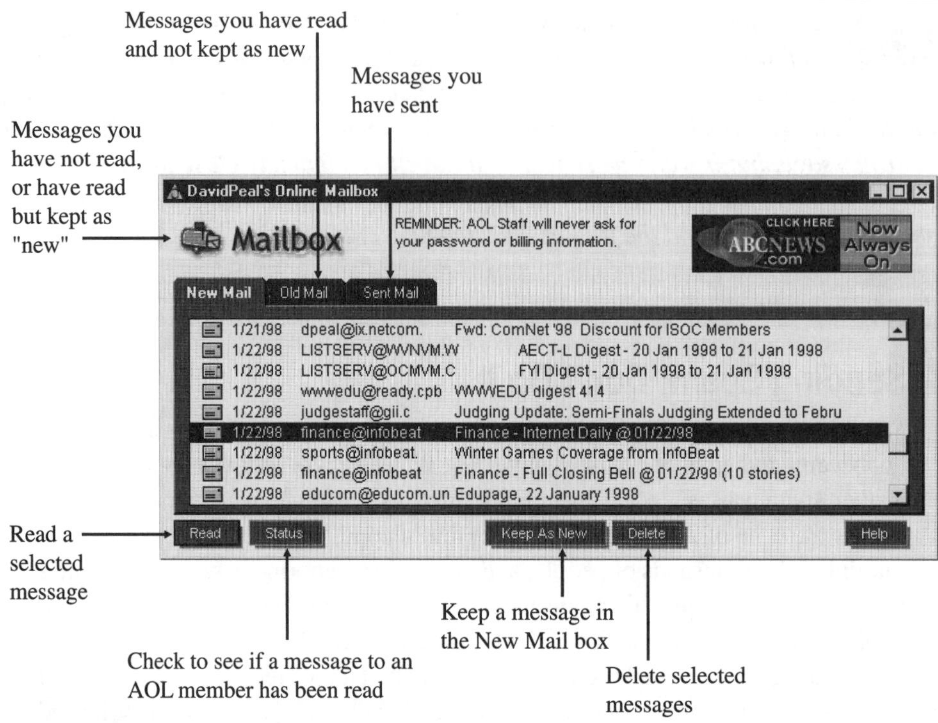

FIGURE 3-6 New mail arrives day and night on AOL

Note *New with AOL 4.0, all three of your AOL mailboxes are available in a single convenient window, called* **<your screen name>Online Mailbox** *(for example, Dilbert's Online Mailbox). Your three mailboxes are called New, Old, and Sent. "Managing Your Mail" explains the differences.*

Each line of your mailbox is devoted to a single message and has four pieces of information. You'll see the same information in all three mailboxes (New, Old, and Sent):

- Whether the message has a file attached to it. If it does, you'll see a little disk icon attached to the ordinary letter icon (see "Retrieving a File from a Message").
- Date when the message was sent. Messages are displayed from oldest (top of the New mailbox) to most recent (bottom of the New mailbox). To see your most recent mail, you have to scroll down to the end of the list.

Tip *Messages you receive after opening the New Mail window won't show up while the window's still open. Click the Read icon on the toolbar again to see whether you have new messages. The newest messages will be at the end of the list.*

- E-mail address of sender. If the message is from someone on AOL, you'll see just the screen name. If it's from someone on the Net, you'll see part of the domain name as well. If it's from a mailing list, you'll see the name of the software that sent the message, such as LISTSERV@ MAELSTROM.... Chapter 4 delves into the mysteries of mailing lists.

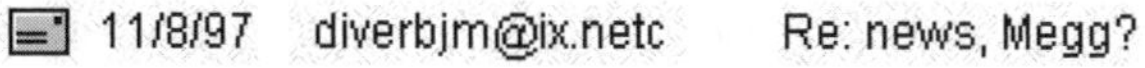

11/8/97 diverbjm@ix.netc Re: news, Megg?

- The message's Subject line, exactly as the sender typed it. If the Subject doesn't fit in the space available in the New Mail box, it will be cut off.

To open a message, just double-click on it (it's the same thing as selecting the message and clicking Read). The information in the New mailbox forms part of a message's *header*. When you open the message, you'll find more detailed header information about who sent the message, exactly when, whether a file's attached and if so how big it is, and more. At the top of the e-mail message, the more useful header information is listed, as in this header from a mailing list:

Subj: **Finance - Internet Daily @ 12/09/97**
Date: 12/10/97 2:37:07 AM Eastern Standard Time
From: finance@infobeat.com (InfoBeat)
To: davidpeal@AOL.COM

At the bottom of the message, you'll find less useful header (or footer) information, such as information showing the path of the message from its source to AOL and the unique Message ID, which can be useful to AOL's mail administrators in troubleshooting e-mail problems. Under Mail Preferences (available by selecting Preferences from the toolbar's My AOL menu, then clicking Mail), you can choose to set off the first set of headers (the human-readable stuff at the top of the message) in gray. Just uncheck the Use White Mail Headers box.

With the New Mail box open, what do you read first? I start by scanning the subjects and senders. Junk mail usually stands out because of the unknown sender, brash subject line, or both:

```
Earn millions without breaking any laws, now
```

I'm likely to delete such mail instantly and instinctively, although AOL has a new and useful way to deal with such stuff automatically (see Appendix C) so it won't even get to your mailbox in the first place.

I read personal messages first. Then I read my favorite mailing lists; they're not personal, but they do deal with subjects I care about and contain messages from people whose opinions and discoveries I want to know.

Tip *On AOL, you can use Automatic AOL (formerly called FlashSessions) to do most of your mail reading offline. This feature is especially useful if you have a high volume of mail or subscribe to many mailing lists. You can read about Automatic AOL in Chapter 4.*

Retrieving a File from a Message

You can always tell if someone's sent you a file as an attachment to their message. In the New mailbox, you'll see the following icon:

Tip *Be careful about what you download! If a message from a stranger has a file attachment, view it with suspicion. Don't download files attached to e-mail unless you know and trust the sender.*

The messages most likely to contain an attachment are from any mailing list digests to which you subscribe (a digest is a compilation of all the day's messages for the list). If the day's messages exceed about 28K (that is, 28 kilobytes, or about a dozen e-mail messages), the digest will be sent as a file attachment. Download the file and read it using the built-in Windows text processor (Notepad or, for bigger files, Wordpad).

Note *Tomorrow's digest, if it's an attachment, may have the same name as today's. You will need to make sure to save any important messages as files with a different name so they're not overwritten (replaced) by the next digest you download. Saving is discussed at the end of this chapter.*

To retrieve a file attached to a message:

1. Open the message with the attached file by double-clicking it. Before the actual message, you will see two lines of information indicating (1) the name and size of the file and (2) the estimated DL (download) time it will take for you to retrieve the file, given the speed of your modem connection and the size of the file.

   File: urls.doc (13312 bytes)
   DL Time (28800 bps): < 1 minute

   Sometimes, as when you receive a message that must be manually decoded, you will get instructions for retrieving the file or you'll be referred to the Mail Center for more information.

2. Click the Download Now button at the bottom of the message window. Click Download Later if you want to download the file later (during an Automatic AOL session or just before signing off). A link to the file will be in your Download Manager, which is always available from the toolbar's My Files menu.

3. In AOL's Download Manager window, confirm the filename (changing it, if you want) and navigate to a directory on your hard disk where you want to store it. (The default—AOL's first choice—is to download the file using its original name and to drop it into the Download subdirectory of the America Online 4.0 directory. I use the default for mailing lists and non-personal attachments, but change the name for everything else.)

Click OK to confirm either the default or the directory of your choice. If a file of the same name already exists, you'll be asked to confirm that you want to overwrite (delete) the existing one. The File Transfer box (just like the one you see when you attach and send a file) tracks the download and tells you when it's done.

Note *AOL's Download Manager, available from the My Files menu even when you're offline, is a wonderful tool for keeping track of all the files you download, whether you get them from an FTP site, a newsgroup, an e-mail message, or an AOL software library. It conveniently lets you download files in batches, and it helps you keep track of the names of your downloaded files and the directories in which you placed them. See Chapter 8 for more information about AOL's Download Manager.*

To make use of the file you've downloaded, you'll need a program to view it, play it, run it—in other words, to use it. AOL has built-in features that let you automatically play some image and sound files. In other cases, you'll need a special application that could be anything from an MPEG viewer for a video file or a word processor for a DOC file.

If you've downloaded a program, you will probably want to run the file from the Windows File Manager (Windows 3.1) or taskbar (Windows 95). Chapter 8 offers advice for using files of different formats.

Some files you download will not be usable with any program you have on your computer because they are either encoded (scrambled, to facilitate transfer as text) or compressed (reduced, for quicker download). The message with the attached file will indicate what kind of file is attached—a MIME file (.MME), UUencoded file (.UUE), or compressed (.ZIP) file, for example. In any of these cases, you'll need a special program to decode or decompress the file and make it useful. At *keyword: Filesearch* (click Shareware), you can search AOL's enormous software library for a program to help you with this. Do a search, using the file type as a keyword. Now, download the program, run it, and follow the instructions (on the screen or in the Help menu) for converting files.

Tip *Three programs I like for decoding or decompressing attached files are* ***StuffIt****, a Macintosh program now available for Windows (useful for unzipping files sent by Mac users),* ***WinZip*** *(for creating zipped files as well as unzipping them); and* ***ZRFW****, which can decode most UUE and MME files. All are available, free, on AOL at* keyword: File Search. *If these programs don't work, ask the sender to re-send the file using another format (such as text).*

Remember Birthdays with E-Mail Reminders

Do you have trouble remembering your sister's birthday or parents' anniversary? Can't keep track of Thanksgiving or Chanukah from year to year? Now you can use AOL's free e-mail Reminder Service to receive a message 14 days and (optionally) again 4 days before a major holiday or personal event. It's at *keyword: Reminder*. Just click Create Your Reminder and fill in the blanks, continue to the next page, and click Save when you're done. The Reminder service is now available from the My AOL menu as well.

Replying to and Forwarding a Message with an Attachment

When you receive mail, you will often want to reply to the person who sent the message. Less often you will want to forward the message to someone else (both of these options and others are discussed later in this chapter in "Managing Your Mail"). If someone sends you a message with an attachment and you reply to the message, the attachment *won't* be included with the reply. If someone sends you an attachment and you forward it to someone else, the attachment *will* be included. You aren't given the option of detaching the file when you forward a message.

Avoiding Unwanted E-mail

Junk e-mail—unsolicited commercial mail—is an unpleasant byproduct of the commercialization of the Internet. Such mail is usually sent out of ignorance of how the Internet works. As people learn about you or see your screen name on AOL (especially in chat rooms and message boards), you may find unsolicited mail in your mailbox. What do you do? AOL recognizes the annoying, invasive, and costly aspects of unsolicited e-mail, and the company has vigorously challenged the right to spam in court.

AOL's Mail Controls, explained in Appendix C, give you the ability to filter out all mail addressed to you from mail addresses known to send unsolicited commercial messages on the Internet. These are the messages that show up from unknown senders with Subject lines that are meant to entice and messages that usually try to separate you from your money.

Tip *If you're a parent you can use e-mail controls (as explained in Appendix C) to limit the e-mail your child can receive from strangers. For all of AOL's e-mail safety features, visit AOL Neighborhood Watch (*keyword: Neighborhood Watch*) and click E-Mail Safety.*

When you do get spam—and you probably will from time to time—it's not always a good idea to tell the spammer to buzz off or not to send you any more messages. Your response tells the spammer that you read your mail, and it also confirms your e-mail address. Just forward junk mail to TOSspam, offensive e-mail to TOSEmail1, and suspicious attached files to TOSfiles, then delete the message.

MANAGING YOUR MAIL

Every message you get can be handled in several ways. You can:

- Read it, then respond (reply) to it or forward it
- Read it, then delete it
- Read it, then keep it as new (so it remains in your New mailbox)
- Delete it without reading it

Tip *In reading several new e-mail messages, you can move to the next message simply by clicking the Next button at the bottom of the screen. To read the previous message, click Prev. You can also use the RIGHT ARROW and LEFT ARROW keys to move through your messages*

Return Mail: Replying

The easiest way to *send* a message is to reply to a message someone has already sent you. What makes it so easy? When you reply to a message by clicking Reply, some or all of the message itself (depending on what you've selected), plus the address and the subject line, automatically become part of your message. All you have to do is write your own response to the message.

Tip *In selecting some of the text of the original message, you'll want to include just the part of the original message to which you want to respond (called quoting), in order to frame and focus your response. If your message elicits a reply, you may be quoted in turn.*

Let's say you receive a message and want to reply to the person who wrote you.

1. Use your mouse to select the part of the message to which you want to respond. Select the entire message if there are numerous points you want to reply to. This selected text will appear quoted and set off by special characters in the recipient's e-mail.
2. Click reply to respond to just the person who wrote the message. Click on Reply All if you want to reach all the recipients of the message, including all the people CCed; if they were CCed on the original message, they'll be CCed on your reply. If there wasn't anyone CCed on the original, the Reply All button is dimmed, which means it can't be clicked.
3. You'll see a Write Mail window, with the Subject line in the title bar, preceded by the word *Re*, a colon, and the Subject line of the original message. If you want, edit the Send To and Copy To fields by adding and dropping names (either AOL screen names or Net addresses), separating multiple addresses by commas.
4. If you want, select the bit of automatically generated text on the first line:

and type in a more personal greeting, such as:

5. Now type in your actual reply—your comments replying to the original message. Most people put their replies after the quoted message they're replying to.

6. When you're done, click Send Now or Send Later.

Replies are tracked in your Sent mailbox, just like any message you send. As with a message you originate from scratch, a reply can be unsent, and you can keep track of its status (whether it's been read). See "If You Change Your Mind: Unsending a Message" earlier in this chapter.

Don't Quote Me on That

On AOL you have a choice in the way you "quote" in your replies. You can place "AOL-style" quote marks at the beginning and end of the quoted passage (<<...>>), or you can place "Internet-style" quotes at *the beginning of each quoted line*. In the latter, each line begins with the greater-than sign (>) and a space. I strongly prefer the Internet style, because it makes it clear what is quoted and also makes it possible to reply to different parts of the original message. The downside is that it looks ugly and there's a possibility of weird formatting when the recipient opens the message. To set your preferences, click My AOL on the main toolbar, click Preferences, click the Mail button, click in the appropriate radio button (AOL-style or Internet-style) at the bottom of the Mail Preferences window, and then click OK.

Sharing a Message: Forwarding

Forwarding a message means sending it to someone who wasn't a direct (Send To) or indirect (Copy To) recipient. As with a reply, you can choose to forward an entire message or a part of it.

To forward a message:

1. With the message displayed, select the exact part of the message to be forwarded and click Forward. *Selecting nothing will cause the entire message to be forwarded.* A Write Mail window comes up, with either part of the message quoted or nothing. (Yes, you see nothing when the *whole* message is being forwarded.)
2. Enter the address of the recipient in the Send To field, and, if you want, include additional recipients in the Copy To field. Use your Address Book to grab a frequently used e-mail address or group of addresses.
3. Edit the Subject line if you wish. (If you do nothing, it will read *Fwd*: plus the Subject line of the original message.)
4. Type any comments of your own into the message box; they'll precede the message you're forwarding. If you're forwarding *part* of a message, put your comments before or after the bit you've selected. Click Send Now or Send Later. If you're forwarding a message, you don't have to write anything, but recipients might not realize at first that the message was meant for someone else.

Tip *If you use AOL in any kind of a company or organization, forwarding can be a more effective way of taking part in a group exchange than replying. Why? Because forwarding retains the entire message as-is, without the intrusive quote marks that are used in replies. Plus, it preserves the entire thread of the message. For example, if you send a message requesting information to someone who can't help you but that person then forwards it to another person who forwards it to yet another person, the ultimate recipient will have a complete record of the exchange. The guy at the end will know who wanted the information and why, as well as who has already been approached. You're likely to get better and faster information than you would if you pursued it by phone and wound up playing phone tag with several people.*

Keeping a Message "As New"

When you read a message and then close the message and return to the New Mailbox, a check appears through it. This tells AOL to remove the message from New Mail when you close your mailbox. Next time you open that mailbox, the message won't appear, but it will be available for a few days in Old Mail. (Note that every message in the Old Mail box has a check through it, which means you've read them all and did not keep them as new.) To keep a message in New Mail, just select it and click Keep as New.

Why would you keep a message "new"? It's a good way to keep your most recent mail in one place, especially the personal messages. Why wouldn't you do this? Because it slows down the window's display when you open it, and it is redundant if you're using your Personal Filing Cabinet to keep a copy of all your messages. The wisely moderate solution is to keep your most important recent messages in your New Mail window and to get into the habit of using your Personal Filing Cabinet (which is always available offline), as explained later in this chapter.

What if you've read a message and banished it to your Old mailbox (that is, closed the New mailbox after you read it without keeping it as new)? You can bring it back to your New mailbox by selecting the message in the Old mailbox and clicking Keep As New, then closing your mailbox. It shows up again in your New mailbox next time you open it. See "Managing Your Mailboxes" for an overview of how the three mailboxes are related.

Deleting Messages

Of course, you don't have to read, reply to, or forward each message you get. You can also delete them even without reading them. Actively deleting messages from your New Mail window is a good idea, because on AOL you can keep only 550 messages in your New and Old mailboxes combined. Unceremoniously deleting unsolicited messages is a very good idea.

While deleting messages makes room for new messages, it doesn't necessarily mean you have to throw away copies of old messages. The next section, "Saving and Printing Messages," offers several techniques for saving messages.

To delete a message that's in your mailbox, select the message and click the Delete button on the mailbox window. Or, just press the DEL key on your keyboard. To delete a sequential group of messages in your mailbox, hold down the SHIFT key, click on all the messages you want to get rid of, and then click Delete (or press the DEL key). To delete messages scattered throughout your mailbox, hold down the CTRL key, click on each message you want to get rid of, and then delete them.

Tip *After you've read a message and it's still displayed, click the Delete button on the message itself to delete it. If you find you've mistakenly deleted a message, your Personal Filing Cabinet will have a copy of the message if you follow the instructions in "Saving and Printing Messages."*

Managing Your Mailboxes

On AOL every screen name gets three mailboxes. With AOL 4.0, all three mailboxes are available in a single window (refer back Figure 3-6). To switch between the mailboxes, just click the appropriate tab.

- **New Mail** Messages that you haven't yet read, plus messages you have read and decided to keep as new (by selecting them and clicking Keep as New).
- **Old Mail** Messages you've read in the past several days and haven't kept as new. Using Mail Preferences (from the My AOL menu, select Preferences and click on Mail), you can choose to make your old mail available for up to 7 days.
- **Sent Mail** Messages you've sent in the past month or so (up to 550 messages).

You cannot keep an unlimited number of e-mail messages. Every message you receive goes into your New Mail box, which can hold 550 messages. The 550 figure includes the usually small number of messages in your Old Mail box, which holds messages that you've read but did not keep as new. Your Old mailbox holds only a few days' worth of e-mail and can be quite useful if you've accidentally neglected to keep as new a message you recently read. The Sent mailbox can hold up to 550 messages, and the oldest messages will get bumped by new ones when you reach this magic number. *No new or sent message is available after about a month, no matter how many messages are in those mailboxes*. That's where your Personal Filing Cabinet comes in handy.

Tips for managing your mail:

- At the bottom of your most recent new message is a bold number like **133 of 133**, indicating how many messages are in your New Mail box. Use this number to keep track of your mail.
- Actively use your Personal Filing Cabinet, so you can keep the mail messages you've read and sent on your computer for as long as you want, as explained later in "Use Your Personal Filing Cabinet to Save Your Messages."

SAVING AND PRINTING MESSAGES

AOL gives you several ways of saving a copy of all e-mail messages that you send and receive. In any organization, you may want to keep a record of all messages for legal and archival purposes. Any particularly important individual messages (to bosses or buddies, for example) are worth storing as well. In general, saving a message can also save you time and trouble.

Any open message can be easily saved on your hard disk as a text file, that is, a file you can open in your word processor (or the text processor built into AOL). With the message displayed, go to the File menu and select Save As. Then give the file a name and find a directory to save it in. You can later read the message by selecting Open File 1 and navigating to the place where you've stored the file.

Note *Saving a message as a separate text file is the safest way to keep a copy of your message. You can even copy it to a disk for safekeeping. Unlike your Favorite Places or Personal Filing Cabinet, you can access messages saved as individual files from the word processor. The downside to saving e-mail as individual files is that it's easy to forget filenames and to clutter up your hard drive with very small files.*

NetMail: Read and Send Mail from the Web!

If you have the Bring Your Own Access plan (in other words, if you use another Internet service provider, or ISP, to access AOL as described in Appendix A), you can use AOL's new NetMail service to send and receive your e-mail *from the Web*. This means that you'll be able to read your AOL mail while at work or at other places where you don't have AOL installed.

To do so, you must be logged onto your other provider's service (WorldNet, MindSpring, Netcom, etc.), and you must *not* be signed onto AOL.

You then visit NetMail (via a link from the home page of the AOL Web site), sign on (typing your regular screen name and password when asked to do so), and read your e-mail. Your mailboxes and the Write Mail window are designed to appear on the Web just as they appear on AOL.

You can get more information about this new service, which hadn't launched when this book went to press, from AOL's Web site (click Go to the Web from the Welcome screen).

Use Your Personal Filing Cabinet to Save Your Messages

On AOL, you get three mailboxes for every screen name and up to five screen names for every account. Because AOL deletes old mail to make room for new mail when your New mailbox is full, it is a good idea to use your Personal Filing Cabinet (Figure 3-7) to keep a copy of *every* message you send and receive on your hard drive—not on AOL's computers (where your three mailboxes store messages). Here's how:

1. Select Preferences from the My AOL menu on the main toolbar. Click Mail to bring up the Mail Preferences window.
2. Make sure there's a check mark in the boxes by either (or both) of the two options: "Retain all mail I send in my Personal Filing Cabinet" and "Retain all mail I read in my Personal Filing Cabinet." Click OK.

Now messages will automatically be kept in your Personal Filing Cabinet (PFC), available to you from the My Files menu. Note that in addition to old e-mail, your PFC keeps track of newsgroup messages you've downloaded and e-mail you've composed but chosen to send later. In the Mail folder are three subfolders. Each is individually available from Mail Center | Read Offline Mail.

- Incoming/Saved Mail includes all the mail you read; if you don't read a message, it won't show up here.

Tip *You can use your Personal Filing Cabinet either offline or online. That means you can search, read, and print old messages without having to sign on first. All three folders in your PFC are available from Mail Center | Read Offline Mail.*

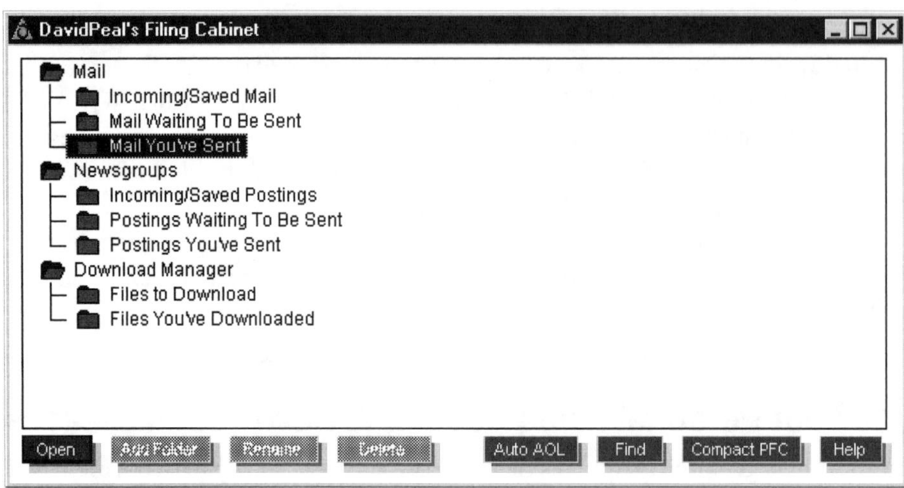

FIGURE 3-7 Use your Personal Filing Cabinet to keep a copy of all the messages you send and receive

- Mail Waiting To Be Sent includes mail you've composed offline or otherwise chosen to send later (by clicking Send Later).
- Mail You've Sent is the same as the mail in your Sent mailbox, but without the time limit.

How do you find a message saved in your Personal Filing Cabinet?

1. From the My Files menu, select Personal Filing Cabinet (PFC). Click Find to bring up the Search window.

2. Indicate whether you want to search through every folder in your PFC (click All Folders) or just the open ones (click Open Folders Only).
3. Indicate whether you want to search messages by their Subject lines (Titles Only) or by their *content* (Full Text)—words used in the actual body of old messages you've sent and received.
4. In the Find What box, type in the text you're searching. You'll enter different keywords depending on whether you're searching full text or just Subject lines.
5. Click Find Next until you find what you're seeking (if it's there!).

Since your Personal Filing Cabinet is created on your hard disk, you should manage it to keep it from getting too big. For one thing, a big Personal Filing Cabinet can take awhile to open and especially close; it can also slow the AOL program overall.

To set your Filing Cabinet preferences:

1. Click on the My AOL button on your toolbar.
2. Select Preferences and click the Personal Filing Cabinet button.

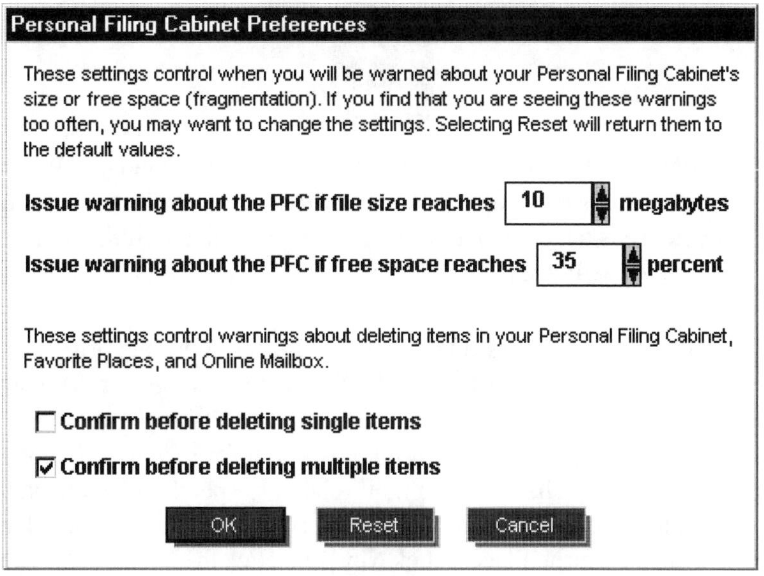
Personal Filing Cabinet Preferences
These settings control when you will be warned about your Personal Filing Cabinet's size or free space (fragmentation). If you find that you are seeing these warnings too often, you may want to change the settings. Selecting Reset will return them to the default values.
Issue warning about the PFC if file size reaches
10
megabytes
Issue warning about the PFC if free space reaches
35
percent
These settings control warnings about deleting items in your Personal Filing Cabinet, Favorite Places, and Online Mailbox.
Confirm before deleting single items
Confirm before deleting multiple items
OK
Reset
Cancel

3. Use the Preferences box to indicate how much of your computer, in megabytes or percent (or both), to devote to your Personal Filing Cabinet. When these limits are reached, you receive a warning message and will be asked whether you want to compact your PFC to make it smaller. Use Preferences, too, if you want to be asked to confirm the deletion of any PFC items.

When you're running out of disk space, you may want to reduce the size of your Personal Filing Cabinet, as follows: with the PFC open, click the Compact PFC button. You can do this offline.

Favorite Places

Your Favorite Places folder gives you a way to save your most important individual messages. Like just about any window you see on AOL, *every e-mail message window has a little heart on the title bar.* To transfer a message from a mailbox to your Favorite Places folder, click the heart. The message will be moved to the Favorite Places folder.

To read a message saved in this way:

1. Select Favorites | Favorite Places.

2. Double-click the message to read it. Note that the standard "Prev" and "Next" buttons don't appear on Favorite Place e-mail messages. Instead, all you see is a Delete button, which you can click to remove the message from Favorite Places.

Why would you save a message in Favorite Places? I use Favorite Places to save important work-related messages, plus the Welcome messages of the many mailing lists to which I belong. I have customized Favorite Places by adding folders for certain kinds of messages. While writing this book, for example, I kept a Favorite Places folder for every chapter, with mail related to specific chapters stored in the appropriate folders. (Chapter 6 goes into Favorite Places in more detail, but to add a folder, just open Favorite Places, click New, and click the New Folder radio button. Type a folder name, and click OK.)

Tip *If you're a heavy e-mail user, use both Personal Filing Cabinet and Favorite Places to keep track of e-mail messages you may want to use for a specific purpose in the future.*

Printing Messages

The reasons for printing a message are pretty straightforward: to keep a record of it in your real filing cabinet, to edit it, or to read it at your leisure.

1. Make sure you have a printer attached to your computer, and make sure it works and is turned on. (This book can't help you with printer problems, but AOL's Computing channel has special forums devoted to companies that make printers, such as Hewlett-Packard [*keyword: Companies*].)
2. Retrieve the message to print so that it's displayed. It may be in a mailbox, your Favorite Places folder, your Personal Filing Cabinet, or a text file.
3. Click the Print button on the AOL toolbar (or simply press CTRL-P), and click OK.

PUTTING YOUR BEST FOOT FORWARD

For many, e-mail is taking the place of the phone call. In both, you're communicating from a distance. There are plenty of differences between e-mail and a phone call, however. In e-mail, you can't hear the timbre of someone's voice, and you can't interrupt someone, as you can when they're talking. E-mail is also asynchronous: you can take as long as you want to respond, or not respond at all. Here are some suggestions for communicating as effectively as possible using e-mail.

Cries and Whispers—Don't Do Either in E-mail

A way of showing you really want to get attention is by *shouting*—using ALL CAPITAL LETTERS. Business spammers, the people who send out unsolicited make-money-fast mail to thousands of people, use the technique all the time. But the attention they get is mostly negative.

```
GREETINGS FRIEND. HAVE YOU BEEN DREAMING OF BECOMING YOUR OWN BOSS? DO
YOU WANT TO MAKE THOUSANDS OF DOLLARS A WEEK WITHOUT RISK? WELL...
```

The best way to emphasize individual words in messages you send to someone on AOL is to use italics, as explained in "Adding Pizzazz to Your AOL Mail." To emphasize words in messages sent over the Net, I like to use asterisks on either side of the word (to get some *attention*). Other people use underscores to get _attention_. But, ultimately, the best way to get attention on both AOL and the Net is to write concisely, clearly, and respectfully. Sounds dull, but it's true.

Whispering means using all small letters and no punctuation, and it can be contagious in organizations. It looks cool, at first—kind of like an ee cummings poem:

```
hi guys what do you think of that new design have a look at
the comps on the wall and let me know what you think come to
our team meeting today with ideas...
```

Whispering is pleasanter than shouting, but whispered messages can be even harder to read and figure out than shouted messages. Avoiding punctuation can make a message subject to misinterpretation.

Take a Deep Breath Before Clicking Send

The powerful features and flexible controls you enjoy on America Online don't always extend to the Internet, which is, after, highly decentralized. In the case of e-mail, for instance, you can't unsend a message after it's been sent. That's a good reason to avoid sending any message you might later regret. It's easy to misunderstand a message you receive because there's no body language to clarify the context, and messages are often hastily typed and sent. Be sure to double-check messages you write so that any emotional freight is clearly marked as such and not subject to misinterpretation. Counting to ten is sometimes a good idea.

Personalize Your Message

Brevity is a good thing when you're competing for attention, but excessive brevity can easily sound clipped—insultingly to-the-point and impersonal. Unless this is the message you want to convey, it's often a good idea to personalize your messages. Begin with the recipient's name on a separate line, for example. And in replies, make sure to type over the bit that begins

```
In a message dated 98-10-15 04:53:40 EDT, you write:
```


Don't be averse to saying "you" in the body of the message. As in any discussion, if you disagree strongly about something, try to find something positive in your opponent's position or some point of agreement and phrase your criticisms constructively. In e-mail it is simply too easy to take polar positions on issues that are less than profound. Keeping things personal can defuse an e-mail fight (also known as a *flame*). Finally, I like to end messages with a "thanks" and my real name. On mailing lists in particular, nothing is more annoying than not knowing the real person behind a strong opinion.

Quote Aptly

You'll save a recipient's time (multiplied by the number of recipients) if you quote only what needs to be quoted in your replies. (This is de rigueur in mailing lists, where no one wants to repeatedly see the same message over and over again.) You do this by selecting (with your mouse) the most pertinent word or words in the original message before clicking Reply or Reply All. Keep your reply to the point and, in general, devote each message to one idea.

Sometimes It's Faster in Person

Not everyone communicates effectively in writing. Some people don't like to write at all or don't answer their mail in a timely manner. If your message matters and your recipient may not be a writer or an e-mailer, talk it over in person. If you're messaging many people who work in the same place, the overhead of everyone reading and responding to your message may be greater than the trouble it takes to walk door to door to get a response. A face-to-face (*F2F*) conversation can consist of more replies, counter-replies, and nuances in a minute than an e-mail exchange can accommodate in an hour. And it's a good chance to schmooze.

Keep Track of Your Messages

With the volume of e-mail many people receive every day, it is nearly impossible to predict which messages will really matter. Print messages from your boss, your mother, or anyone who matters in your life.

Delete Messages Before AOL Deletes Them for You

Because of the limits on the number of pieces of mail you can hold in your various AOL mailboxes (New, Old, and Sent), and because of the volume of e-mail you're likely to receive, especially if you join mailing lists, keep your New mailbox as lean as possible. If you have a total of 550 pieces of mail in your New mailbox, mail sent to you will not be deliverable. AOL members will get a nice message to this effect; your friends on the Net will get the less-nice message that their message to you has bounced. If you're using your Personal Filing Cabinet, there's no reason to hold any nonessential messages in your New Mail box.

Signal Your Feelings

Words on paper can't convey intention and emotion the way a raised eyebrow or wrinkled nose can. Many *emoticons*—ways of expressing emotion through typed characters—were invented in newsgroups. It's enough to recommend that you tell people when you're kidding as well as when you're angry. At *keyword: CDN smileys*, you'll find a list of abbreviations to help you signal your feelings (for example, ROFL means "rolling on the floor laughing"). Since many people don't know what these things mean, it can be best to use smileys. Everyone's familiar with a smiley face :-). If you're not, turn your head to the left to get the effect.

Tip *Show your surprise, blow a kiss, wink knowingly. If you feel the need to express an emotion in e-mail, click Mail Extras (from the Write Mail window), and click Smileys.*

Rewrite Again and Again, Offline

A frequent reason I unsend a message is that I discover a mistake or typo. Rereading your messages before sending them can spare you both the negative consequences of an intemperate remark and the flush of embarrassment if you've made a particularly silly error in spelling. The more important the message, the greater the possible negative consequences of sending it off prematurely. (Make sure you've saved the message as pure text to avoid having weird characters appear in place of your word processor's curly quotes and other nontext characters. Weird characters don't make such a hot impression either.) A final thing to remember: if even a single recipient of your message is on the Net (i.e., does not have an AOL screen name), you will not be able to unsend the message to any AOL recipients.

RSVPs and Other Niceties

As troublesome as it seems to reply to an e-mail message, it is a lot easier than sitting down to write a response on a piece of paper, attaching a stamp to an envelope, and mailing it; it's cheaper than the phone; and it's faster than doing it face to face. Everyone gets a lot of mail today, but communication works only if it's two-way. Not answering mail, especially if it's from someone you know and a reply has been requested, can be rude. It reduces the power of a rich new communications medium. You don't, of course, have to answer obnoxious unsolicited mail or respond to a mailing list message unless you have something to say.

What's the Point of Your Message?

To make everyone's life easier, it's a good idea to put one idea, or point, in each message (and never send a message without a point). The way to tell whether you have one point in your message is if you can express that point concisely in the Subject line. The reason to avoid multiple points is that they can't easily be replied to, short of quoting the entire message. It's especially maddening if there are multiple recipients, since they will each have varying degrees of interest in the various themes of your message and the replies may turn into a messy thread. If more than one recipient is involved, the resulting threads can get all tangled up.

Make It Easy on Your Reader

Here are some mechanical devices for making it easier for your reader to read your message.

- Add a blank line between paragraphs; the white space gives people a chance to breathe.
- If you want to include items in a list form, keep each item short and make sure it has the same structure as the others. Usually, I use asterisks (*) for unnumbered lists (things whose order has no necessary sequence) and numbers (1,2,3…) for numbered lists (things whose order matters, as in a recipe or any procedure).

A Peek at the Future of E-mail on AOL...

As this book was being completed, AOL announced its plans to integrate Microsoft's Outlook Express e-mail program into the AOL software. Outlook offers everything that the AOL e-mail software offers, plus the ability to: write messages in the form of HTML, which is used to create Web pages (see Chapters 6 and 7); encrypt and digitally "sign" messages; create and name folders for your incoming, outgoing, and deleted mail; maintain complex address books, with a great deal of information about individuals and groups; and add numbered/bulleted lists and a broad range of other formatting effects to your messages.

FROM HERE...

AOL's e-mail gives you power, flexibility, and ease of use without the bother of having to install and configure complex software. Features like the Personal Filing Cabinet, Favorite Places folder, Address Book, Automatic AOL, and the informative Mail Center add more value to the mix. The next two chapters look at mailing lists and newsgroups, two different tools that allow you to engage in regular communication with groups of people about a topic of shared interest.

Chapter 4

Discovering Internet Mailing Lists

Welcome to mailing lists—e-mail on steroids. A mailing list, or just *list*, lets people anywhere in the world easily share their thoughts with each other about a common interest. The principle is simple. Think of a mailing list as a fancy version of your AOL Address Book. Using the AOL Address Book, you can send the same message to many people at the same time. You create a *group* consisting of several e-mail addresses on AOL or the Internet. Send an e-mail message to the group, and the message automatically goes into each individual's mailbox. Mailing lists all work a little differently, but the principle is the same. Currently there are more than 80,000 mailing lists on the Internet.

This chapter does the following:

- Introduces the key list types (discussion lists and newsletters; moderated and unmoderated lists)
- Shows you how to find lists that may interest you
- Provides instructions for joining any list
- Gives advice for taking part in lists and managing your list mail
- Highlights some of the best lists available to AOL members

MAILING LIST ABCs

Lists vary in a couple of ways. Some lists support active discussion, while others are informational newsletters written by one person and sent to many people. Some lists are moderated by a person who makes sure the messages are on topic. And, lists are administered by different kinds of list software, with different commands for doing basic things like joining and leaving the list (called *subscribing* and *unsubscribing* in list lingo).

The mechanical nuances of list software are spelled out in the "Reference" section at the end of this chapter.

What You Really Need to Know About Mailing Lists

Behind the variations from list to list, you'll find the same vibrant, self-regulating microcommunities of interest and passion. Lists are probably the best way to meet other people on the Internet, to get current information about any topic of personal or professional interest, and to keep up with new Internet resources about any topic. Lists are where community happens on the Internet.

Here's another thing to remember about mailing lists: all you need to use them is e-mail; the fancy list software that does all the work is located on some Internet computer that you don't need to worry about. You communicate with people on the list and with the list software by sending e-mail.

To join any list, you follow the same three simple steps:

1. *Find a list to join.* Whatever your interest, you'll learn to uncover good mailing lists in "Finding a Mailing List for You." A selection of lists is provided in "Net Newsletters…For Keeping Up with the Internet" and "A Sampler Of AOL Newsletters," which includes many easy-to-get electronic newsletters created especially for AOL members.
2. *Subscribe to the list. Subscribing* means sending a simple e-mail message to the list's administrative e-mail address, as explained in "Subscribing to a Mailing List." Subscribing to a list *isn't* like subscribing to a magazine—it doesn't cost a penny, for one thing. To *subscribe* and *unsubscribe*, you send a message to software, not a person, which handles these tasks. Once you're subscribed, there are usually all sorts of options at your disposal, such as receiving all the lists' messages in a single e-mail *digest*. The software handles these options too. For more details about the mechanics of joining and customizing lists, see the "Reference" section at the end of this chapter.

Whenever you learn about a list, make sure to get the information spelled out in the "Before You Subscribe" box later in this chapter.

3. *Take part in the list.* Taking part means reading and perhaps sending messages to the *people* on the list. Tips for making your messages to others as effective as possible are provided in "Mailing List Netiquette." To avoid getting swamped by e-mail, have a look at the guidelines for "Managing Your Mail" later in this chapter.

Discussion Lists and Distribution Lists (Newsletters)

Some mailing lists let everyone on the list talk to everyone else. I belong to a great list called **our-kids**, for example, which is a community of several hundred parents of kids with developmental disabilities. Parents share their dilemmas, offer suggestions, give support, and generally prove themselves to be good listeners. This kind of *discussion* list is genuinely interactive. There are other lists for parents with "spirited" kids, asthmatic kids, deaf kids, and kids of every other variety. You'll find thousands of other discussion lists devoted to topics such as body piercing, violin playing, Japanese animation, and Internet advertising.

The other type of mailing lists goes into your mailbox but doesn't let you take part. These *distribution* lists are really electronic newsletters, like the one shown in Figure 4-1. They can tie a community together by providing everyone with the same information at the same time. However, with electronic newsletters, you usually do not know who else is subscribing and what they think of the topics discussed in the newsletter. These electronic creations cost nothing to print, very little to distribute, and don't add to the world's garbage.

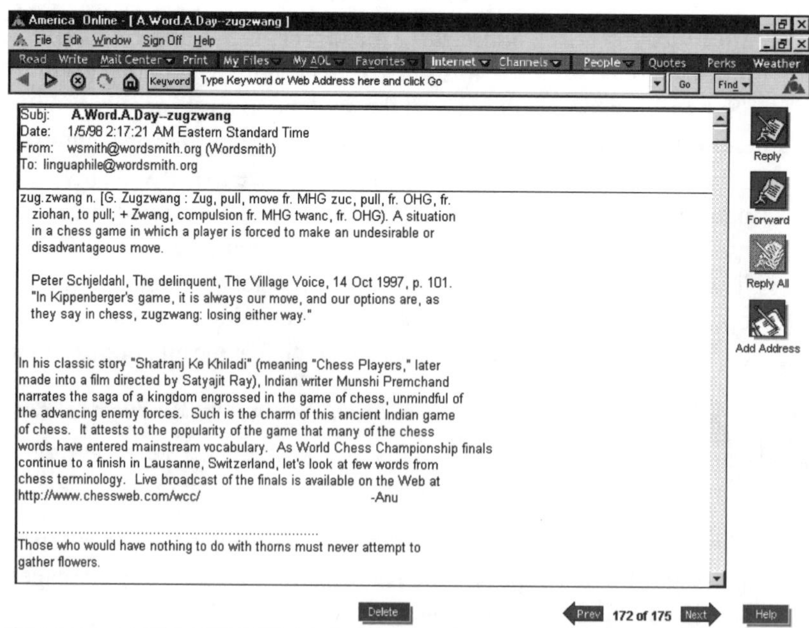

FIGURE 4-1 Excerpt from Word.A.Day, the e-mail newsletter that delivers a fresh word to your mailbox each morning

Electronic newsletters are becoming increasingly popular on the Internet as a means for a company to stay in touch with customers who express an interest in their services. You can often subscribe to such lists directly at the company's Web site, by filling in a form and clicking a button. Some Web sites that offer mailing-list newsletters with point-and-click Web subscription are Medscape (**http://www.medscape.com**), AudioNet (**http://www.audionet.com**), and the outstanding new site for seniors, Third Age (**http://www.thirdage.com**). For you, such newsletters can be a way of staying informed about additions to important Web sites. Two additional Net-related newsletters are highlighted later in "Net Newsletters...For Keeping Up With The Internet."

More and more, you'll find Web sites being created as the focal point for especially lively mailing lists. See the "A Community of Believers" box a little later in this chapter for one example. Another list-spawned "Webzine" grew out of Preemie-L, the mailing list for parents of premature babies (**http://home.vicnet.net.au/~garyh/preemie.htm**). The Word.A.Day Web site (**http://www.wordsmith.org/awad/**) grew out of the mailing list of the same name (Figure 4-1). Approximately 100,000 word lovers in more than 100 countries receive the list's daily message. The Web site gives people an easy way to subscribe and offers the list's archives to the entire Internet community.

AOL's channels and many individual AOL forums make active use of the Internet's list software to distribute forum and channel newsletters. You can read about some of them later in this chapter ("A Sampler of AOL Newsletters").

LISTS, MODERATED AND UNMODERATED

For the most part, only people who are serious about a list's topic will take the trouble to subscribe. In practice, some lists have an additional level of control to make sure the people on the list are serious about a topic or stay *on* the topic. This second level of control requires a person, or *list moderator*.

A list moderator may assume the burden of personally approving every new subscriber but usually does no more (and this is not a small job) than screening every message to the whole list in order to keep the list from drifting from its theme. This screening of people and messages can keep a list focused, but it violates some people's sense of free speech. It's also a lot of unpaid work for the moderator, so really active moderation is not common.

Moderated lists can be more informative than unmoderated lists, and moderators can prevent Internet rituals such as flaming (trashing one's opponents) from getting out of hand. A moderator can be especially welcome in large groups and groups devoted to contentious topics. But there are some moderators who define the list's

topic more narrowly than some subscribers are comfortable with—and from such tensions new lists are born. For the most part, however, lists moderate themselves collectively, with subscribers sharing a purpose and gently (or sometimes not so gently) reinforcing it, especially among newcomers.

How do you tell whether a list is moderated? One way is to read about the list before joining it. Checking out a mailing list is easy when you're using one of the resources described in the next section.

FINDING A MAILING LIST FOR YOU

If you're looking for a mailing list to join, a good place to start is *keyword: Newsletter*, where you'll find more than fifty AOL newsletters that will keep you abreast of changes and events in your favorite AOL channels and forums. Most AOL newsletters are published weekly so that your mailbox won't get choked with messages. On the Internet, many very Web large sites, like CNET, Wired, and ZDNet, let you subscribe to highly informative newsletters merely by entering your e-mail address in a box on the site.

For the wilder world of interactive discussion lists on the Internet, an excellent place to start is a resource called *Publicly Accessible Mailing Lists* (PAML), which conveniently arranges thousands of lists by name and subject. PAML is now searchable as well (**http://www.neosoft.com/internet/paml/**). Figure 4-2 shows a PAML subject search for lists dealing with the environment. Click any of the sometimes cryptic list names for a short description of the list's purpose, subscription information, and, often, a link to the list's home on the Web. This excellent, well-established Internet resource can quickly plug you into communities of people who share your specific interests.

If you're seeking additional lists, try Liszt, a searchable index of mailing lists, available (like PAML) on the World Wide Web. *Keyword: Liszt* takes you there directly. This gigantic database provides information about more than 90,000 mailing lists! (See Figure 4-3.)

Liszt gives you useful information about specific mailing lists, as well as a useful overview of other people's favorite lists (check out Liszt Select). In the case of some lists, you can subscribe directly from Liszt. Chapter 9 discusses the Liszt index in greater detail.

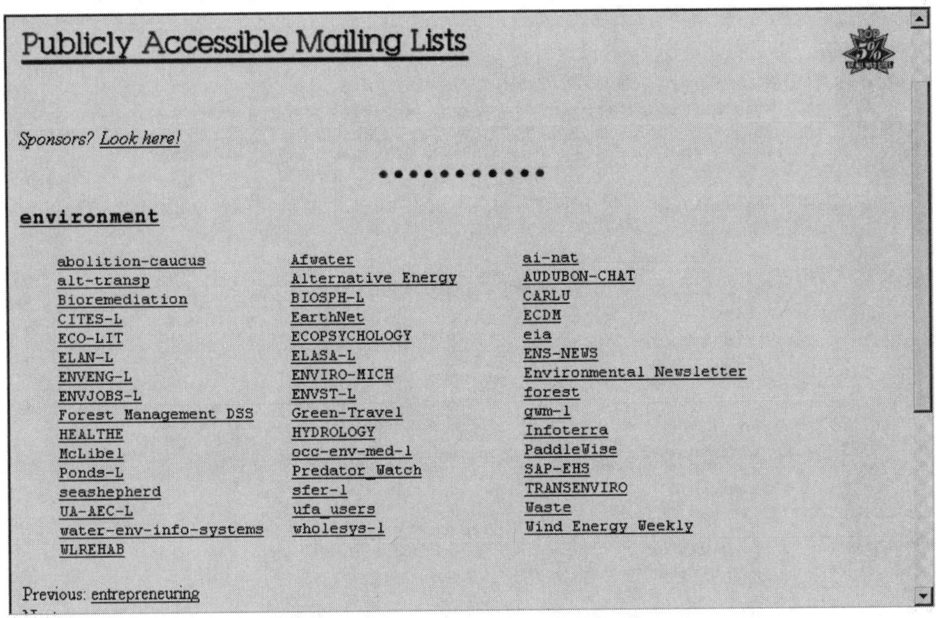

FIGURE 4-2 A subject search of Publicly Accessible Mailing Lists. These lists all pertain to the environment; click any list for more information about how to join

SUBSCRIBING TO A MAILING LIST

Lists vary in some fundamental ways, as described in the previous sections. Some are fully interactive discussion lists, while others are for distribution only (newsletters). Some are moderated, but most are pretty much self-regulating. These factors can shape your experience of belonging to a list.

There's another way in which lists vary from from one another: they are administered by different kinds of software, which you use to subscribe to (join) and unsubscribe from (leave) lists.

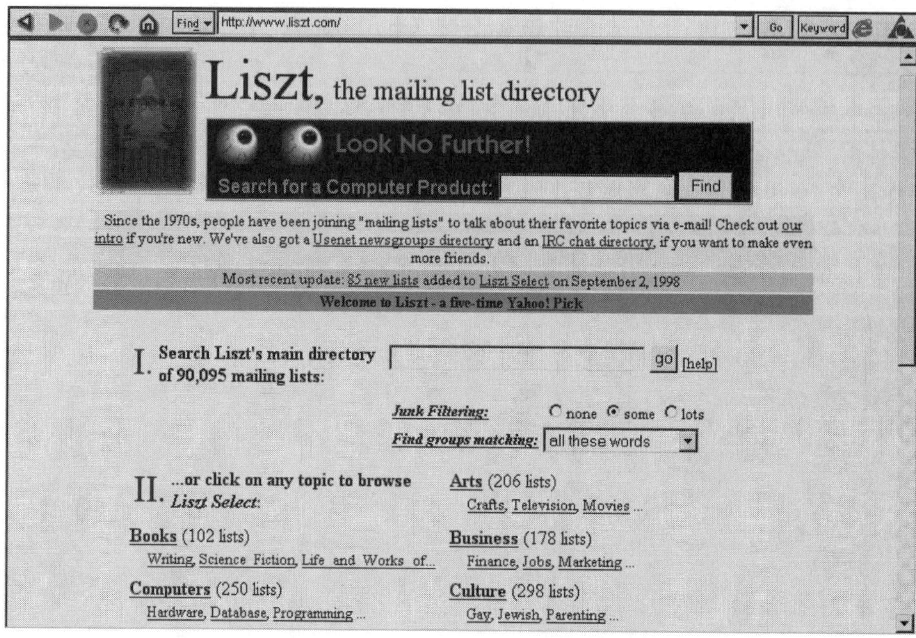

FIGURE 4-3 Liszt has become the preeminent Internet service for finding mailing lists

The oldest and most widely used list software is *LISTSERV*, invented by Eric Thomas in 1986. *LISTSERV* is the actual name of the software to which you send e-mail whenever you join or leave a LISTSERV-based list. LISTSERV is widely used because it can support very big lists and because it offers many options. It's the software of choice at America Online, so it's a good idea to learn how it works (see "LISTSERV: Joining, Leaving, and Customizing").

Note *A product called Unix Listserv (only the L is capitalized) is used to run some lists. It is not the same as the LISTSERV product in use at AOL and other sites.*

This chapter capitalizes LISTSERV to make the distinction from that product. Traditionally, you'll see LISTSERV lists and their associated commands in capital letters, but you can use lowercase when you join these lists.

Listproc is a piece of software modeled after LISTSERV and customized to run on Unix computers. Its commands are broadly similar to LISTSERV's. The third big name in mailing list software is *Majordomo*, a free package meant for smaller systems than LISTSERV.

You'll also find smaller packages such as Smartlist, Mailbase, Mailserv, and a host of improvised *reflectors,* which are simple distribution lists with primitive features that merely redistribute a message to several individuals after it is sent to a group address.

At the end of this chapter, in "Reference," you'll get the specifics of how you join and use these mailing lists.

Before You Subscribe...

For every mailing list, you'll need three pieces of information to subscribe. A resource like Liszt, described above, will provide all three bits of information.

- The **list name** (for example, Humor, the list name for the Contemporary Humor List). Sending a message to the list causes your message to be sent to all the individuals who have subscribed to the list. Many list names end in hyphen *l* (*-l*), for *list*. Note: that's the letter *l,* not the number one (*1*).
- The **administrative address**, that is, the e-mail address to which you send your subscription and unsubscription requests (in the example of the Contemporary Humor List, it is **listserv@uga.cc.uga.edu**). Most administrative addresses indicate the type of list software (*listserv*, *majordomo*, *listproc*), while a few take the list name and tack on *-request*. Traditionally, the -request lists are maintained by a person who individually approves all new subscriptions. Some LISTSERV lists use -request for messages to the list's owner.
- The **list address**, that is, the e-mail address to which you send messages to people in the group when you want to take part (for example, **humor@uga.cc.uga.edu**). Generally, the list address consists of the list name, the @ sign, and the domain name. In the case of the Humor list, special instructions for participation are provided when you subscribe. Note that the domain name (the bit after the @ sign) is usually the same for the administrative and the list address (in this case, **uga.cc.uga.edu**).

Common Mailing List Commands

The three main types of list software vary in the commands they make available, but they all offer commands for joining and leaving (subscribing and unsubscribing), and they all offer the important option of receiving a digest. The slight variations between names can be confusing, but Table 4-1 can help you keep the major commands straight.

	LISTSERV	Listproc	Majordomo
To subscribe	**subscribe** ***listname [your full name]*** or ***sub listname [your full name]***	**subscribe** ***listname your name*** or **join** ***listname your name***	**subscribe** ***listname [your.address]*** Note: *your.address* is the e-mail address at which you want to receive the list, if different from the address you're subscribing from—useful if you're using AOL's "bring your own access" service.
To get a digest	**set** ***listname digest***	**set** ***listname mail digest***	**subscribe** ***listname-digest*** Note: The list owner can choose not to set up a list as a digest. To get a digest (if there is one), you must first subscribe to the regular list. When requesting the digest, you should also send a message (it can be in the same e-mail message) simultaneously *unsubscribing* from the regular list (see below).
To unsubscribe	**signoff** ***listname***	**unsubscribe** ***listname*** or **signoff** ***listname***	**unsubscribe** ***listname*** [***your.address***] Note: Use *your.adddress* if you receive the list at a different address from the one you used to send the unsubscribe message.

TABLE 4-1 Commonly used mailing list commands

Please Note

In this chapter, whenever text is just bold, that's exactly what you type in the Write Mail window: **listserv.nodak.edu** (for example). Whenever text is bold and italics—***domain.name*** (for example)—you must type something, but what you type will depend on the name of the list, its address, domain name, or your address. Anything in square brackets—[ ]— is optional!

What do you do with these commands in Table 4-1? First, click Write, on the toolbar. In the Write Mail window, the administrative address goes in the To field, the Subject field is blank, and the actual command goes in the message box. Just click Send Now when everything's in order. See the example a little later in "Subscribing to a LISTSERV List."

Tip *You can place several commands in one message—***help** *and* ***subscribe listname****, for example. Just make sure they're on separate lines. Some commands are contingent on others, however, so you'll have to send separate messages. For example, you can't get a LISTSERV digest without first subscribing to the list. Finally, don't worry about uppercase and lowercase. Mailing list purists capitalize everything associated with LISTSERV, from list names to command names, but in fact, the software doesn't care and will accept lowercase.*

Every List Has Two Addresses

Never, ever send your administrative e-mail—messages about joining, leaving, or customizing—to the people on the list itself. They're not interested in your efforts to join the list or leave it, and they may give you a hard time if you send a subscribe message to 700 people.

- Administrative e-mail goes to **listserv**@*domain.name*... or **majordomo**@*domain.name*... or *listname-l@domain.name*.
- Real e-mail (to the other people who subscribe to the list) goes to *listname@domain.name*.

MAILING LIST NETIQUETTE

Chapter 3 modestly offered some general guidelines for communicating effectively by e-mail in the "Putting Your Best Foot Forward" section. All of those guidelines—quote aptly, stick to one subject, respect the other guy, signal your feelings, etc.—apply to mailing lists as well. In addition, mailing lists have their own set of guidelines that mostly have to do with the mechanics of lists. Sending a message to a list is a shade more anonymous than sending a message to an individual, and the netiquette requires that much more sensitivity since you'll be communicating with people you may not know personally.

Here are some things to keep in mind:

- Don't send a message to the members of a list when it should be sent to the list-management software.
- Joining a list is not like visiting a Web site or browsing a newsgroup. Make sure the list is for you before joining it.
- Read the list for several weeks before *posting*, or sending a message to the group. *Lurking* (just reading the messages) is the way to take the pulse of an e-mail microcommunity and decide whether it's for you. There's nothing wrong with continuing to lurk if you're there primarily to learn; on the Net, learning is OK! You'll find that a mailing list has a group of regulars who more or less dominate the proceedings.
- If you do take part, keep your messages to lists on topic. Messages go into the mailboxes of all subscribers, and subscribers will not appreciate junk mail.
- Remember that list owners control their lists. America Online has no control over lists or list owners. Obscenities that might not faze one moderator might be cause for a TOS violation on AOL (see *keyword: TOS*). That's why AOL offers the Mail Controls described in Appendix C.
- Save the Welcome message you automatically receive when you subscribe to a list. It contains useful information about how best to use the list, how to unsubscribe, and so on.

Tip *On some lists, you'll regularly (usually monthly) receive a FAQ—a list of frequently asked questions about the list. This FAQ will include an overview of the list's scope as well as instructions about customizing your subscription and leaving the list. Save the FAQ with the Welcome message. Sometimes the FAQ will include the same information as the Welcome message but will be more up to date.*

- If you are going to be away from your computer for some time, you can (1) leave any lists to which you subscribe or (if they're LISTSERV lists) (2) use the LISTSERV NOMAIL feature (see Table 4-2 at the end of this chapter) to temporarily suspend your subscription.
- Do not send a commercial solicitation to the list without first checking with the list's moderator or owner. The only time it's acceptable to send a commercial solicitation is when buying or selling has been explicitly approved by the list's leader or in the list's charter or FAQ document.
- If you are going to delete a screen name that is subscribed to one or more lists, or if you will be canceling your AOL account, make sure to unsubscribe from any lists to which the screen name is subscribed. Otherwise, your messages will keep coming, but they will bounce and be a nuisance for list owners. Steps for unsubscribing can be found in every list's Welcome message.
- Respect people on the list. People from different cultures and persuasions might not understand or appreciate jokes and irony. When personal comments are appropriate, send them to an individual, not the list.
- Take personal responsibility for what you write. A strong opinion will probably be taken more seriously if it's associated with a real name than if it's associated with a screen name that doesn't reveal a real first or last name. However, while it is a good idea on Internet mailing lists to let people know your true identity, it's *not* a good idea to provide contact information such as your address and phone number.

MANAGING YOUR MAIL

A single discussion list can fill up your mailbox in a few days. If that happens, messages will start bouncing—getting returned to the list. In this case, list owners are within their rights to remove you from a list. Moreover, unless you have infinite time at your disposal and a list is of grave professional importance to you, you won't want to read every message that every subscriber sends. Even the best lists have their share of off-topic messages, otherwise known as *noise*.

Here are some tips for keeping up with the traffic and avoiding a full mailbox:

- If a mailing list offers a digest, get it. LISTSERV-type lists offer digests as a rule, as do some of the newer software packages. Majordomo offers digests too, but instead of first subscribing to a list and then (via e-mail) setting it to digest mode, you must subscribe to a separate list called (for example) **majordomo-users-digest**. Listproc is like LISTSERV in that you

first subscribe to the list, then set it: **set anthro-lib mail digest**, for example. Note the addition of the word *mail* to the Listproc command. When in doubt, request **help** from the list software administering the list you want to join. Liszt (**http://www.liszt.com**) has some help resources as well.

- If you subscribe to several mailing lists, consider creating a screen name for each list or group of related lists. For every AOL account, you can have five screen names, and each can keep up to 550 pieces of mail in the New and Old mailboxes combined. (To create additional screen names for use with your account, go to *keyword: Names,* select Create a Screen Name, and follow the simple onscreen instructions.) If you do use multiple screen names, *do not delete a screen name without first unsubscribing from any mailing lists to which the screen name belonged.*
- Use Automatic AOL to download unread e-mail and send outgoing e-mail. See "Taming E-Mail with Automatic AOL" for the how-to.
- If your mailing list is also carried as a Usenet newsgroup, you should consider quitting the mailing list and participating in the newsgroup. (Chapter 5 goes into the differences between using mailing lists and using newsgroups.) Information on how to do so will be given in AOL's Internet Mailing List Directory entry for that list (available at *keyword: Mailing Lists* under the Browse the Directory button), on the list's Welcome message, or possibly in both places. The *bit.listserv.** newsgroups *mirror* more than 300 Internet mailing lists and are available at *keyword: Newsgroups* (click Add Newsgroups, then click *bit*).

Note *On the Internet, the word* mirror *refers to a site or service that carries an exact copy of another site or service in order to reduce network pressure or make a popular service more widely available. The best FTP and Web sites have FTP and Web mirrors, and AOL features a set of FTP mirrors for members' favorite sites.*

- The archives for some lists are available on the World Wide Web. They lack the interactive quality of mail-based lists but are a useful way of accessing old information. Otherwise, you may have to learn a list's *index* commands by sending the Help command to the list's administrative address. Practice varies, list by list. More than a dozen K–12 mailing lists for teachers are archived at Global SchoolNet Foundation (**http://gsn.org/majordomo/**). More and more lists can be expected to offer Web archives and Web-based subscription forms.

Taming E-Mail with Automatic AOL

Here's another feature that sets AOL apart and can reduce your connect charges and phone bills. Using Automatic AOL, you can retrieve your new unread mail automatically, either at a specified time every day or on demand, when you're online. With this feature, AOL automatically performs a series of tasks you request, such as downloading your e-mail and newsgroup messages and sending any messages you have chosen to "send later." Messages downloaded in an Automatic AOL session are stored for you in your Personal Filing Cabinet, where you can read them offline, without incurring the cost of being online or the bother of tying up the phone line.

Setting up an Automatic AOL session requires these simple steps:

1. From the Mail Center menu, select Setup Automatic AOL. A Welcome message comes up. Click Expert Setup.
2. Indicate *what* you want to do in an Automatic AOL session. From the Automatic AOL window shown in Figure 4-4, tell AOL whether you want to:
   - Send the messages you've chosen to send later
   - Get your unread mail
   - Download files attached to incoming messages

Note *The folders referred to in the Automatic AOL window are in your Personal Filing Cabinet. Mail you've downloaded is available in the* **Incoming/Saved Mail** *folder (in the main Mail folder), while mail you want to send later (during an Automatic AOL session) is kept in the* **Mail Waiting To Be Sent** *folder.*

3. Indicate *when* you want to do the tasks you've chosen. If you want to run an Automatic AOL session right now ("on demand"), just click Run Automatic AOL Now (see Figure 4-4), to bring up this window:

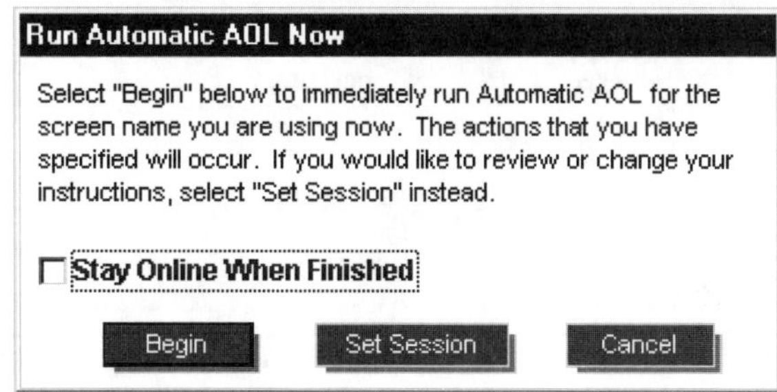

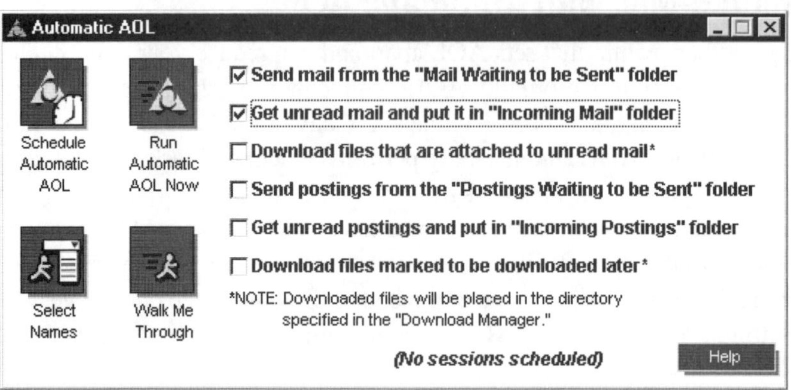

FIGURE 4-4 An Automatic AOL session lets you automatically send and retrieve batches of e-mail—a good way of taking part in a high-volume list

If you want to schedule a regular session (daily, say), click Schedule Automatic AOL to bring up the window shown in Figure 4-5. Make sure there's a check mark in the Enable Scheduler check box (click in the box if it's not already selected). Then, specify some combination of time, interval, and day of the week.

FIGURE 4-5 Tell AOL when you want it to get (or send) your e-mail

Note *If you are offline when you start a session, there must be at least one name and password specified (using Select Names), and the session will run for that screen name or names. If you are online when you start a session, you needn't specify any screen name, and it doesn't matter which ones you do specify; your Automatic AOL session is only going to download messages for the screen name with which you signed on.*

AOL's Mailing Lists

Mailing lists support thousands of communities on the Internet—but the mechanics of joining and customizing them can seem a bit unfriendly, with all those inflexible computer commands! America Online offers LISTSERV-based mailing lists throughout its channels, but you'd never know they were LISTSERV; you subscribe and unsubscribe by pointing and clicking. Figure 4-6 shows the Kids Only newsletter. *Keyword: Newsletter* has everything you need.

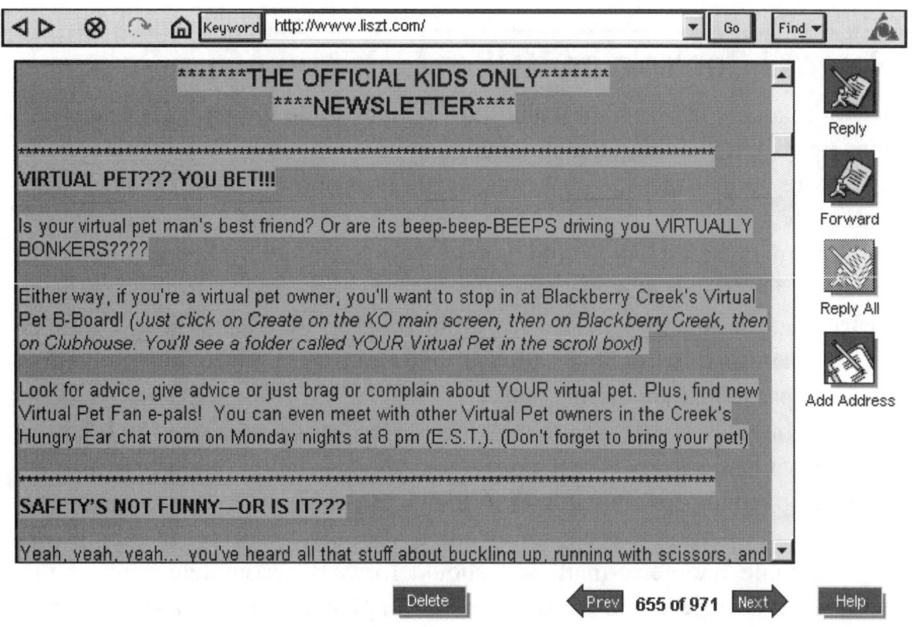

FIGURE 4-6 A channel newsletter from the folks in Kids Only

A SAMPLER OF AOL NEWSLETTERS

Once you have a taste for how easy it is to subscribe to mailing lists, it's tempting to start subscribing to lots of them right away. Where to start? *Keyword: Newsletter* takes you to a list of dozens of AOL channel and forum newsletters, a small number of which are highlighted below. Newsletters by their nature have a clear voice and are written by a single person. They can be a good way to stay informed about a subject or your favorite AOL area or Web site. Most AOL mailing lists are weekly; they won't clutter up your mailbox like an interactive mailing list. Your weekly message will in most cases include information for unsubscribing. On some you'll find text that's been enriched with background colors and formatting, as in Figure 4-6.

Tip *All of AOL's mailing lists use LISTSERV software, and all are run at* **listserv.aol.com** *(which you can abbreviate as* **list***). To unsubscribe to any AOL list, just send an e-mail message to* **listserv@listserv.aol.com** *or just* ***listserv@list****, with anything in the Subject line, and put the following in the body of the message:* **signoff** ***listname****, substituting the actual list name for* ***listname****. Instructions for unsubscribing are provided at the end of every AOL newsletter.*

Parental Controls on Mailing Lists and AOL's Policy

If you're a parent who has taught your children to be wary of strangers, you may be concerned about the strangers they can encounter on mailing lists or anywhere on the Internet. You might want to take a moment to read AOL's policy about allowing kids access to mailing lists:

"Internet mailing lists are not monitored, censored, or otherwise filtered by America Online, and America Online is not responsible for any content distributed via a mailing list. It is important for parents and guardians of minors to be aware of this fact and exercise discretion when evaluating how their children participate in mailing lists."

The Internet is similar to real life in the sense that it is possible to electronically meet people and interact with them. Minors should be cautioned to never give out personal information, such as complete real name, telephone numbers, or addresses, to any strangers. If your child receives unsolicited or objectionable Internet e-mail, you should forward a complete copy of the e-mail to AOL screen name Postmaster and explain that it was unsolicited. You should send objectionable or unsolicited mail received from America Online members to AOL screen name *TOSEmail1* or *TOSEmail2*. In general, you should apply common-sense guidelines from the non-electronic world to your child's online sessions.... If you have specific questions about Internet mailing lists, you can send e-mail to AOL screen name ListMaster."

To provide even better protection, AOL has recently introduced Mail Controls (*keyword: Mail controls*), which enable parents to restrict the mail received by their kids. See Appendix C for more information about these controls.

Top Tips

At *keyword: Newsletter,* you can sign up for any of several newsletters that deliver a tip every few days to your mailbox. Click AOL User Tips for beginners tips (such as how to forward your e-mail), as well as more advanced stuff (such as how to increase your horizontal screen "real estate").

The Newsletter for the Internet Channel: IC Hilites

To keep up with AOL's broad Internet offerings, subscribe to IC Hilites. You'll be plied with Internet insights, jargon, and tidbits, along with a sampling of oddball and notable Web sites. When AOL does something new on the Net, you'll find out in this newsletter what it means for you. Subscribe at *keyword: Newsletter* (open the Computing Tips folder).

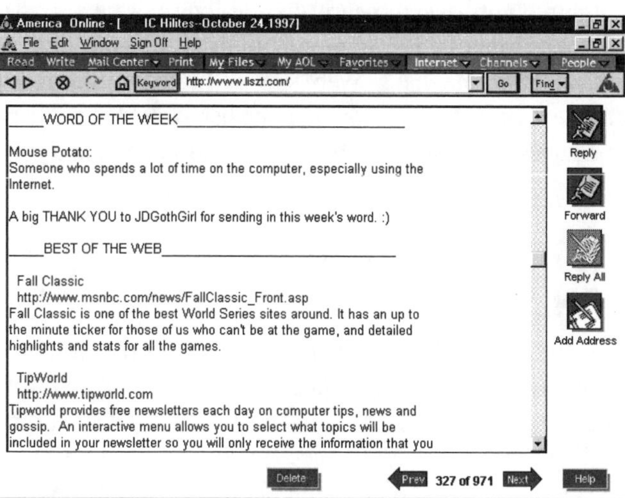

NetGirl Newsletter

The NetGirl forum, devoted to the world of online relationships, is one of AOL's most popular, and now it's part of the Love@AOL forum. This weekly newsletter brings romantically inclined AOL members selected questions and answers about cyber-relationships together with information about upcoming NetGirl events, new Web sites, and the like. You can subscribe to the newsletter at *keyword: NetGirl* (click the Table of Contents to find out how).

A Community of Believers

BELIEF-L
Subscribe To: listserv@list
Subject line: ***anything***
Body: subscribe belief-l ***your name***

David O'Donnell, AOL's "Postmaster General Emeritus," is the owner of this lively mailing list about personal ideologies. Subscribers debate everything from religious, ethical, and moral issues to abstruse points of physics—as well as more whimsical (and occasionally personal) subjects. Belief-L (jokingly referred to by its subscribers as "Elf-Bile") has developed quite a special community over its nearly decade-long existence, so it is expecially important that those interested in joining read the FAQ and Welcome message before doing so. Visit the list's Web site at **http://www.mindspring.com/~atropos/elf-bile/** to get the low-down on the list. Note that the list can at times exceed 150 messages a day, so be prepared to spend some time trying to keep up.

NET NEWSLETTERS...FOR KEEPING UP WITH THE INTERNET

The following small sampling indicates the kind of information you can have for free on the Internet. These newsletters can be a great way to stay informed about the things you're interested in. Using Liszt and the AOL Internet Mailing List Directory, you can identify lists that address your specific personal and professional interests. For a profile of a classic Internet discussion list (moderated by AOL's Postmaster), see "A Community of Believers."

Tour Bus

Subscribe To: listserv@listserv.aol.com [or **listserv@list**, if you're subscribing from AOL]
Body: ***subscribe tourbus***

Bob Rankin and Patrick Douglas Crispen write this popular newsletter (hosted at AOL), which every few days looks at new or must-see Internet resources. These Internet old-timers have much experience helping newcomers make the most of the Net, and they do a beautiful job translating technical concepts. Two things to note about this newsletter: because so many people subscribe, this newsletter accepts advertising; don't be surprised or shocked to see ads in this and other newsletters. Also, this newsletter is available, as are more and more newsletters, on the Web (**http://www.worldvillage.com/tourbus.htm**).

Scout Report

Subscribe To: listserv@cs.wisc.edu
Subject line: ***anything***
Body: ***subscribe scout-report firstname lastname***

This weekly newsletter highlighting serious new Internet resources is written by Susan Calcari and a staff of researchers. With all the emphasis on "hot" and "cool" sites elsewhere, the Scout Report is committed to discovering and sharing useful and informative sites. The Scout Report is also available on the World Wide Web (**http://www.cs.wisc.edu/scout/report/**). Recently, staffers have spun off specialized Scout Report lists for kids, as well as lists devoted to the social sciences and economics.

The newsletter itself is available in either ASCII (plain text) or HTML for reading in a World Wide Web browser (see "Using a Mailing List in HTML Format"). When you use the browser to open the Scout Report in HTML format, text is both formatted (bold, etc.) and linked to actual Web sites. The Scout Report is also available via Gopher and FTP and in Adobe Acrobat format (for more about Acrobat, see Chapter 6).

Yahoo!'s Picks of the Week

OK, you *are* interested in hot and cool sites. The folks at Yahoo have created a very big directory of Web sites, and they add to this list daily (Chapter 9 has more to say about Yahoo). Each week they post their picks at their Web site. You can find out

Using a Mailing List in HTML Format

Some Web-related mailing lists, like Scout Report, give you the option of receiving the list as simple text (which you read in a word processor) or as HTML (which you read using a browser such as AOL's). Using the HTML format lets you link directly to Internet resources. If you get such a mailing list, here's how to use an HTML message to browse the Internet:

1. **Display the message** as you would any message.
2. **Save the message as an HTM file on your hard disk**. From the File menu, select Save. Give the file a name *that includes* ***htm*** *as the extension*. For example, **thescout.htm** or **netsurf1.htm**. On Windows HTML files are shortened to HTM files to fit the old three-letter restriction on file extensions.

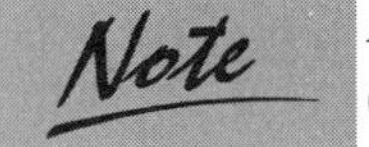

If the file arrives as an attachment because it is over 28K (which is likely), you can download it and save it as an HTM file.

3. **Open the HTM file**. From the File menu, select Open, then navigate to the directory where you saved the file, and select it. Because the file has *HTM* as its extension, it opens the AOL browser with the page displayed, including formatting and clickable links.

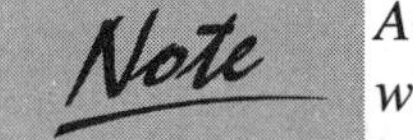

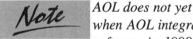

AOL does not yet support HTML in e-mail, but it will do so when AOL integrates the Microsoft Outlook Express e-mail software in 1998. HTML lets you send clickable text and messages with complex formatting to anyone on the Internet.

If the file arrives as an attachment because it is over 28K (which is likely), you can download it and save it as an HTM file.

their favorites by e-mail, too, by simply visiting **http://www.yahoo.com/picks/** and (at the bottom of the page) typing in your e-mail address and clicking a button. You unsubscribe by sending a message to **yahoo-picks-request@yahooinc.com** with anything in the Subject line and (in the body of the message) **unsubscribe** ***your.e-mail.address***.

REFERENCE: JOINING AND USING LISTSERV, LISTPROC, AND MAJORDOMO MAILING LISTS

Mailing lists are administered by different kinds of software. You communicate with this software by e-mail. All you do is send messages and receive replies. You'll find excellent discussion lists as well as distribution lists (newsletters) on all major types of mailing list software. The slight variations in software commands and capabilities is a small price to pay for the incredible community experience available with mailing lists. Just remember that it's not important to understand exactly what *ACK* and *Repro* and the like mean, as long as you know what they can do for you and how you can use them to make the most of your mailing list experience (see Table 4-2).

LISTSERV: Joining, Leaving, and Customizing

LISTSERV has more features than you want to know, so it helps to know which features are most likely to contribute to your experience with mailing lists.

If you are interested in subscribing to a particular LISTSERV-type mailing list and know the administrative address, you can usually get information about the list (what it's about and who it's for) by sending a message to **listserv@*domain.name*** and typing **info *listname*** in the body of the message. To get information about the famous Tourbus mailing list, for example, mentioned in the previous section, send a message to **listserv@listserv.aol.com** (or just **listserv@list**), write **info tourbus** in the body, and then click Send Now.

Subscribing to a LISTSERV List

When you subscribe to a LISTSERV list, you're talking (by e-mail, that is) to a piece of software called *LISTSERV*—its e-mail name is **listserv**. All your *administrative* dealings with the list go to the administrative address (**listserv@*domain***), not the actual list address (***listname@domain***). LISTSERV administrative addresses look like this:

```
listserv@peach.ease.lsoft.com
listserv@listserv.aol.com
```

To subscribe to a LISTSERV list, follow these general steps.

1. Open the Write Mail window (click Write on the toolbar). Type **listserv@*domain.name*** in the Send To field (for example, **listserv@peach.ease.lsoft.com**), leave the Copy To and Subject fields blank.

2. Put the following in the body of the message:

   ```
   subscribe listname [your real name]
   ```

   For example: **subscribe scout-report John Amann**. Whether you include your real name (separated by spaces) is optional. If this particular mailing list supports a command that lets people view a listing of subscribers, your name and e-mail address will appear on the listing.

3. Click Send Now.

Tip *When you use AOL's Internet Mailing List Directory or one of the Net's directories, such as Liszt (*keyword: Liszt), *you'll find all the information you need to join, leave, and customize individual LISTSERV mailing lists.*

If the address seems generic, it is; one piece of LISTSERV software can be used to administer any number of mailing lists on a single Internet computer. There are dozens of mailing lists at **listserv.aol.com**, for example.

Remember that it's a piece of software that's reading your message, not a person. Any human message such as:

```
hi, please sign me up for the kennel management list. thanks,
wendell poodle
```

will be read as if it were a computer command, and returned to you via another e-mail message, because the words you've typed, beginning with "hi," are not recognized commands.

You can use the special abbreviation **list** *in place of* **listserv.aol.com** *when sending mail to AOL's LISTSERV computer.*

Unless you've made a typo, you'll usually get a response by return mail saying that you have been added to the membership list. For larger LISTSERV lists, you may be asked to reply within 24 or 48 hours to the confirmation and say *OK* or something similar in your message, just to confirm your address.

Once you are added, you usually receive a message welcoming you to the list (see Figure 4-7 for an example). Some Welcome messages provide an overview of the scope of the list's topic, and some lists provide a monthly FAQ to answer administrative and substantive questions. You may also receive a message called "Output of your job," which summarizes the computer time used to process your request. You can delete this message.

Tip *The easiest way to save a Welcome message is to create a special folder for such messages in your Favorite Places folder. To do so, select Favorites | Favorite Places, click New, click Folder, and name the new folder* ***Mailing lists****. Click OK. With a new Welcome message open, just click the little heart on the title bar. The message will be removed from your New mailbox and dropped automatically into your Favorite Places folder. Open Favorite Places and drag the new Welcome message to the Mailing list folder.*

Customizing Your LISTSERV Experience

For many, the most useful way to customize a LISTSERV list is to get a *digest*. The automatic availability of a digest mode is a great advantage of LISTSERV. A digest

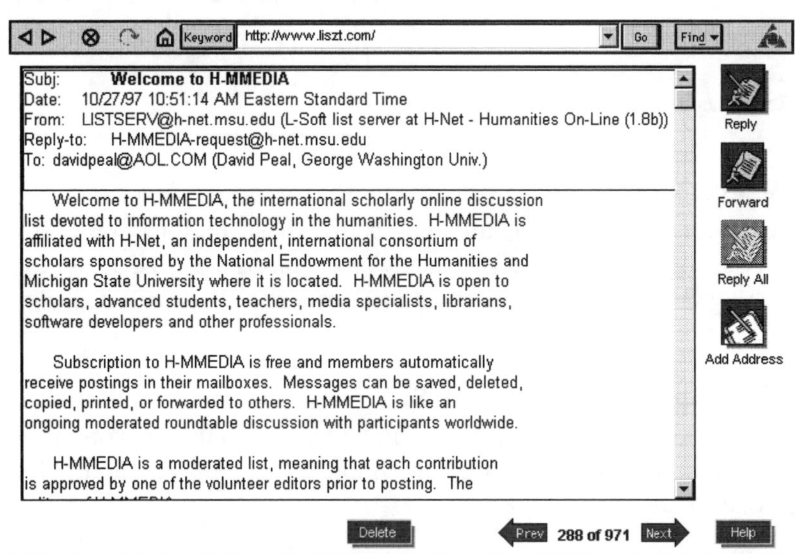

FIGURE 4-7 A typical Welcome message, which you receive when you join a list. Keep it for future reference

is a single message you receive in which all the day's messages are assembled. The benefits? If you belong to a high-volume list, your mailbox will soon be overrun with messages, but a digest packages the day's traffic in one tidy message. Having the day's messages in a single message makes it easy to skim the list and follow *threads*—discussions about the same topic. Usually, each digest is preceded by a numbered list of the day's topics, so you can jump to messages of likely interest, especially if the digest is so big that it arrives as an attached file that you must read in a word processor.

To get a digest of a list, you must first subscribe to that list. Once you've requested the digest, the individual messages will stop coming to your mailbox.

The downside? Digests usually exceed the size limit AOL sets on messages, so they're automatically turned into attachments that you must download. Since digests often arrive as attachments to e-mail messages and each day's digest will have an attachment with the same filename, you'll have to rename each attached digest if you want to save it; otherwise it will be overwritten by the next day's digest. Also, it's a bit more difficult to respond to messages if you're reading a message within a word processor, which is how you read attachments.

To get the daily digest of a list to which you are subscribed, send a message to **listserv@*domain.name***, leave the Subject line blank, and put the following in the body of the message:

```
set listname digest
```

Other LISTSERV commands let you turn off digest mode, retrieve files (archived messages, usually), and get help. These options for customizing LISTSERV are outlined in Table 4-2. At any time, you can get a list of all LISTSERV commands by sending a message saying **info refcard** to **listserv@*domain.name***.

Leaving a LISTSERV Mailing List

To leave any LISTSERV mailing list, send a message to **listserv@*domain.name***, putting a period or something else in the Subject Line and writing the following message in the body:

```
signoff listname
```

That's it. You don't have to provide your name or any other information. Unless there's a typo, you will be unsubscribed and your unsubscription request will be confirmed.

Tip *LISTSERV automatically makes a note of the e-mail address when you ask to subscribe to a list. Make sure to leave the list using the same address! Using different accounts, different service providers, or different screen names can confuse LISTSERV.*

To...	Send this message to listserv@*domain.name*
Get help	help
Subscribe to list	subscribe *listname [your name]*
Unsubscribe to list	signoff *listname*
Get a copy of messages you send to the list (as a record and to verify that the list is distributing messages appropriately)	set *listname* repro
Don't get a copy of your own messages	set *listname* norepro
Temporarily turn off the list (when you go on vacation, for example)	set *listname* nomail
Turn a list back on—after you get back from vacation	set *listname* mail
Get the list in digest form	set *listname* digest
Return to regular form (lots of mail)	set *listname* nodigest
Get a brief acknowledgement of messages you send the list	set *listname ack* norepro
Turn off acknowledgement	set *listname* noack norepro
Get a list of files associated with the list (usually archived messages, organized by day)	index *listname*
Get a complete, long list of all the things you can do with LISTSERV	info refcard

TABLE 4-2 Major ways of customizing a LISTSERV List

Basics of Listproc Lists

Listproc, a popular variant of LISTSERV, is another program used to administer many mailing lists. In other words, to join, customize, and leave a Listproc list, you must send messages to the Listproc software (not to the people on the list). The basic Listproc commands are summarized in Table 4-3. Sometimes the Listproc administrative address is *listserv* or *listserver*, which can be confusing, since the commands for LISTSERV and Listproc differ in slight ways.

Basics of Majordomo Lists

If you're familiar with other types of list software, Majordomo won't present any shocking departures from your experience. Majordomo is a popular type of list software for smaller lists. To join, customize, and leave a Majordomo list, you send messages to the Majordomo software. Table 4-4 summarizes the stuff you can do with Majordomo. As with Listproc, Majordomo's options are limited relative to the myriad LISTSERV options. Note that the digest is a whole new mailing list, not a version of the regular mailing list, so to request the digest you must first subscribe to the regular list, then request ***listname*-digest**, and then unsubscribe from the regular list.

To...	Send this message to listproc@*domain.name*
Join	subscribe *listname your real name* —or— join *listname your real name*
Leave	unsubscribe *listname* —or— signoff *listname*
Get digest	set *listname* mail digest
Get a list of people on the list	review *listname*
Get help	help

TABLE 4-3 Most important Listproc commands

Tip *Once you've taken part in (or at least subscribed to) a mailing list for a long time, it is quite easy to forget what kind of list it is (LISTSERV, Listproc, etc.). If you study the* headers *of your messages, you will find lots of useful information about the list's address, the owner's address, the type of list software being used, and even information about how to unsubscribe. If you receive a digest, the header will tell you the e-mail address of the original sender and of the list itself, so you can reply to an individual or to the group, as appropriate.*

Finding Out Who "Owns" a List

Every mailing list has at least one "owner"—the person who sets up the software and makes sure that it's working, that messages don't bounce, and that inappropriate

To...	Send this message to majordomo@*domain.name*
Join	subscribe *listname* [*your e-mail address*]
Leave	unsubscribe *listname* [*your e-mail address*]
Get digest	subscribe *listname-digest* unsubscribe *listname* (note that not all lists have digests)
Find out what files are available for the list	index *listname*
Get files related to the list	get *listname filename*
Find out who's on the list	who *listname*
Get the Welcome message again	intro *listname*
Get help	help

TABLE 4-4 Helpful Majordomo commands

messages don't find their way onto the list and into subscribers' mailboxes. It's useful to know this person's e-mail address, just in case you have problems *using* the list—posting messages or accessing archives, for example. Such administrative problems should be shared with the list's owner and *not* with all the actual subscribers. Before asking the owner a question, it's wise to consult the Help file that's available for every kind of major list software.

How do you find out who owns a list? When you first subscribe to a list, chances are good that you will receive a Welcome message. This message will often include the name of the list owner and his or her e-mail address. In general, it's always a good idea to read and save this message. AOL's LISTSERV software has the address **listserv@listserv.aol.com** (or just **listserv@list**), and you can write that address for automated help (put anything in the Subject line and the word **help** in the message body, then click Send Now).

Here is advice from AOL's Postmaster General, David O'Donnell, about finding out who owns a list if it's not obvious from the Welcome message:

"First, determine the type of software that's administering the list by sending the Help command to the software administering the list. For example, send a message to **listserv@listserv.aol.com**, leaving the Subject line blank and putting **help** in the body. In the reply, there may be a line in the headers that indicates what particular server software is being used—LISTSERV, Listproc, Majordomo, and so on."

- For a LISTSERV list, you can contact the list owner by writing to ***listname-request@domain.name***. For example, the owner of **belief-l@listserv.aol**.com can be reached at **belief-l-request@ listserv.aol.com**.

- For a Majordomo list, you can typically contact the list owner by writing to ***listname*-approval**, although a number of sites are now adopting **owner-*listname*** or ***listname*-owner**. For example, to contact the list owner of **2020WORLD@seatimes.com**, you could write to **2020world-approval@seatimes.com** or, if that doesn't work, **owner-2020world@seatimes.com**.

- As a last resort, you can attempt to write to the *Hostmaster* at the site where the list is hosted. The Hostmaster (if one exists) may choose to forward the message to the list owner, provide you with an address, or ignore the request. If there isn't a Hostmaster, try the site's *Postmaster*, who may take any one of those steps. If you choose to write to either of these accounts, provide the details of how you've already tried to contact the list owner and a brief description of why you are doing so; it may just make the difference between being ignored and getting a response, especially at larger sites.

FROM HERE...

Without special software beyond AOL's built-in e-mail program, mailing lists let you join any of tens of thousands of communities and receive information about anything you're likely to be interested in. Useful mail on every subject from like-minded people located anywhere in the U.S. and the world comes reliably, securely, and in great volume to your mailbox. Join a mailing list today, and you'll learn something new every day.

The next chapter introduces newsgroups, which are more public, less cozy places than mailing lists. While mailing lists can be private, newsgroups tend to be noisy and raucous. Mailing lists and newsgroups are at the heart of the traditional community experience on the Internet.

Chapter 5

Discovering Newsgroups

If you want to tell your neighbors about your garage sale, you might put a notice in the local newspaper or attach a sign to the phone poles in your neighborhood. If you want to announce something to attendees at a large conference, you could thumbtack a scrap of paper on a bulletin board designated for the purpose. And if you are selling something at work, you'd probably post a notice where everyone would see it—on the bathroom doors, the bulletin boards, the candy machines.

On the Internet, you can reach a public audience by using *Usenet News* or just *News* as it's called. News is like a big bulletin board insofar as it's (1) public, (2) usually not controlled by anyone, and (3) a little wild at times. Instead of a single bulletin board serving a single public, however, News consists of thousands of *newsgroups*, organized by subject and serving thousands of small communities—groups of people with the same belief, passion, or interest. It's a big world with many passions, so whether you have a taste for Indonesian music, a particular TV show, or a certain Mexican fast-food chain, you're likely to find a newsgroup devoted to it. The best newsgroup communities can become tightly knit social groups with their own cultures and traditions.

Message Boards and Newsgroups: More and More Alike

The AOL feature that's most similar to newsgroups is the message board, where members can ask questions, provide help, and just mingle. On AOL you'll find two kinds of message boards. The older sort (Figure 5-1) allowed any member to post messages and respond to other members' messages. These message boards listed postings chronologically (from the earliest posting to the latest) and didn't keep track of which messages you had read. Nor were they "threaded" to make it easy to find messages about the same subject.

Newer AOL message boards (shown in Figure 5-2) are patterned after Internet-style newsgroups, with "threading" (organization of messages by topic) and the ability to keep track of what you've read. A benefit of the new newsgroup-like message boards is that they can be read offline, which wasn't true of the older variety of message boards. Nonetheless, habits die hard and many AOL members prefer the simplicity of the old message boards. Like the old message boards, these new ones are available only to members of AOL.

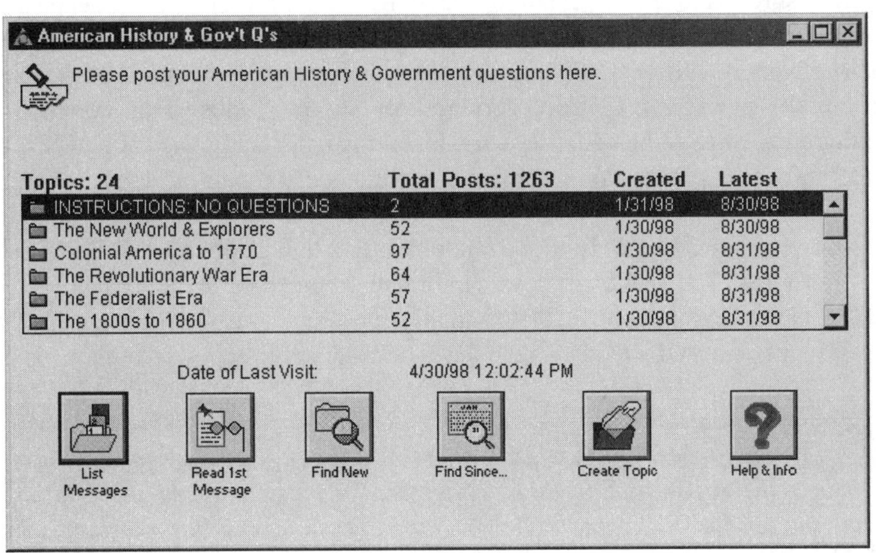

FIGURE 5-1 AOL message boards (old-style) in the Ask a Teacher area

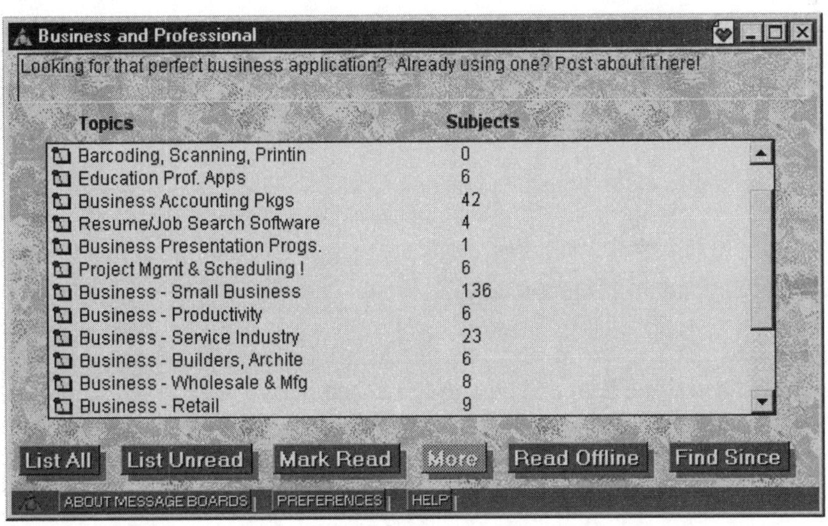

FIGURE 5-2 Message boards morphing into Internet-style newsgroups (the Computing channel)

Newsgroups were invented in 1979 by several graduate students at the University of North Carolina as a way of sending and receiving messages between their university and Duke. Using the same technology, a network of discussion groups, or newsgroups, grew very rapidly in the 1980s. This collection of newsgroups came to be called *Usenet*. Usenet is not a real physical network. The "real" network is made up of computer servers based on an old Internet standard called the Network News Transport Protocol (NNTP). Every News server in the global network receives messages from and sends messages to "neighboring" servers, keeping each other up to date with a vast flow of information composed of millions of messages. AOL's News servers receive half a million postings a day in more than 30,000 newsgroups, and AOL members send out about 20,000 messages a day.

Tip *There's News and there's news. Usenet News has nothing to do with the* daily *news. For that, AOL offers a wide range of ways to stay informed, including the ABC news feeds available in the News channel and the custom "clipping service" delivered right to your electronic mailbox* (keyword: News Profile). *On the Web, you will find numerous news sources such as Crayon (http://crayon.net), plus the superb resources in the News Web channel at AOL.com. See the "News" section of Chapter 11.*

With so many newsgroups, it's hard to know where to start. America Online can make it easy. This chapter tells you all you need to know about the workings of newsgroups as a global system for sharing information among millions of people. Among other things, you'll discover ways of :

- Finding newsgroups of interest to you
- Keeping track of your favorite newsgroups
- Taking part in newsgroups
- Saving and printing postings

First, let's get a better idea of what newsgroups are by looking at how they're different from mailing lists and how they're organized.

HOW NEWSGROUPS AND MAILING LISTS ARE DIFFERENT

Mailing lists and newsgroups are often lumped together as "discussion groups." It is true that they both involve groups of people discussing topics of shared interest—sometimes, mailing lists even find their way onto Usenet and become available as newsgroups (see "Mailing Lists That Masquerade as Newsgroups"). And they're both great ways to meet people who share an interest. I have a friend who met her husband on a newsgroup.

Mailing lists and newsgroups are different animals, however, and it's good to keep the differences in mind, especially if you'll be using both. For one thing, mailing lists aren't really public; they're semiprivate. You must take the effort to subscribe to them. Newsgroups, on the other hand, can be read by anyone; no subscription is necessary. Because they're public, it is easy to browse newsgroups. There is no good way to browse mailing lists.

Note *AOL allows you to keep a list called Read My Newsgroups (described in detail in a few pages) to make it easy for you to access the newsgroups you like best and to keep track of the articles you've read in those newsgroups. You do not formally "subscribe" to newsgroups the way you do with mailing lists.*

Newsgroups are rarely moderated; no one guarantees that they are kept civil or even that they remain on topic. Larger and more popular newsgroups can get wild, while smaller newsgroups on more obscure topics can be every bit as informative and intimate as good mailing lists.

What's distinctive about newsgroups is the absolutely uniform way you use them. While mailing lists require that you learn to subscribe and unsubscribe in a slightly different way for each type of mailing list (LISTSERV, Listproc, etc.), on Usenet you access **alt.gothic.fashion** in just the same way as you access **sci.chem.analytical**.

A final difference is that newsgroup articles can contain files. While mailing lists are used primarily to send text, newsgroups can contain both text and files, including software, sounds, and images. All these files are available to anyone with full access to newsgroups, and America Online's unique FileGrabber service makes it simple to retrieve certain types of files.

Mailing Lists That Masquerade as Newsgroups

Several hundred mailing lists are also available as newsgroups, simplifying access and reducing the volume of incoming mail for those who take part. Unlike mailing list messages, newsgroup postings (also called *articles* or *messages*) have to be retrieved—but only when you want, on the specific subjects you want. The *bit* hierarchy (see the next section for more information on hierarchies) contains hundreds of mailing lists in newsgroup form.

A list of mailing lists available over Usenet is also available via FTP at **ftp://rtfm.mit.edu/pub/usenet-by-hierarchy/news/groups/Mailing_Lists_Available_in_Usenet**. (Chapter 8 covers FTP, which you use to send long documents and other files over the Internet.) Lists available as newsgroups accept messages from both Usenet and mailing lists.

HOW NEWSGROUPS ARE ORGANIZED

Here are a few newsgroups you might find some evening while you're signed onto America Online:

- **alt.fishing**
- **misc.taxes**
- **rec.autos.antique**
- **comp.infosystems.net-happenings**

At first glance, these newsgroup names look like the addresses you see in e-mail messages (such as **dpeal@aol.com**) and on Web pages (such as **http://www.aol.com**). Actually, newsgroups are organized and named in a way that's unique to Usenet (see "Which Is It: Internet Address or Newsgroup Address?").

Which Is It: Internet Address or Newsgroup Address?

Unsure whether you're looking at an Internet address or a Usenet newsgroup address? Both kinds of addresses consist of elements separated by periods, and the period is pronounced "dot" when spoken. But here's how they differ.

In an Internet address, or URL (Uniform Resource Locator), the most general element (*com, edu, gov,* etc.) is the *last* part: **http://www.aol.com,** for example. See Chapter 3 on domain names and Chapter 6 on URLs, which are based on domain names. In a newsgroup address, the most general element (*sci, comp, news, alt,* etc.) is the *first* part: **biz**.jobs.offered, for example.

There's another "behind the scenes" difference: Internet addresses identify actual computers or banks of computers, together with the networks to which they belong. That's why URLs begin with *protocols,* such as *http://* and *ftp://* and *news:*, which govern how physical machines "talk" to each other over the Internet. Newsgroup names, by contrast, don't identify any particular computer but are human categories used to classify and keep track of people's postings. Newsgroup names are intended to convey their content; a URL by itself won't necessarily indicate its content.

Newsgroups are organized in big categories called *hierarchies*. The two big hierarchies on Usenet are called *standard* and *alternative*. Each contains subhierarchies, abbreviated in such a way as to indicate their subject matter. At the lowest level are thousands of individual newsgroups. In the standard hierarchies, for example, you'll find the **misc** subhierarchy, which has *miscellaneous* personal finance newsgroups such as **misc.taxes**. The **misc.taxes.moderated** newsgroup is even more focused, thanks to the presence of a human moderator who keeps conversations on topic.

Tip *Newsgroups are the best place to learn about newsgroups, and the most useful hierarchy for beginners is* **news** *(devoted to newsgroups, not the evening news). The* **news.newusers.questions** *and* **news.answers** *newsgroups, in particular, have a wealth of information if you're just setting foot in the wilds of Usenet.*

A Matter for the Name Police

On the Internet, newsgroup messages—the documents written by individuals—are called *articles* or *postings*. On AOL they're usually called *messages*, even though e-mail messages and News messages are different. In this book, I'll be saying *article*, to make it clear that I'm not talking about e-mail.

On the Internet, people refer to clusters of messages devoted to the same topic as *threads*; on AOL, threads are called *subjects*. And while Internet folks are used to speaking of *hierarchies* and *subhierarchies* of newsgroups, on AOL you'll usually see *categories* and *topics*. I'll be using *threads* and *hierarchies*, for the most part.

The Standard Hierarchies

Newsgroups were originally organized into the standard hierarchies—sometimes called the Big Seven or "traditional" hierarchies—listed in Table 5-1. Think of a hierarchy as a sort of bucket in which newsgroups about a certain large theme are stored. Newsgroups in the **sci** hierarchy all have to do with science, and serious, academic science at that. Newsgroups in the standard hierarchies have general circulation via News servers around the world. These newsgroups are created according to strict guidelines (see the "Creating a Newsgroup" box) and tend to be more serious than alternative newsgroups. The need for a new newsgroup must be established and accepted by other members of the Usenet community, and then it's formally voted upon. On America Online, you can readily find all of the standard newsgroups.

Creating a Newsgroup

If you want to create a standard newsgroup, you'll first want to read "Guidelines for Usenet Group Creation," which is regularly posted to the **news.answers** newsgroup. If you want to create an alternative newsgroup, there's a document called "So You Want to Create an Alt Newsgroup," which is regularly posted to the same newsgroup. You can get a sense of the cultures of the standard and alternative hierarchies by reading these documents. The standard hierarchies' "Guidelines" document has a rigorous protocol that must be followed. In the instructions for creating alt newsgroups, however, you will read: "Votes? Did someone say votes? Let me repeat. There are _no votes_ in alt. Period." Voting or no voting, both types of hierarchy are democratic in process; no individual or organization controls them.

Standard Hierarchies	Subject Matter
comp	Computers, networks, hardware, operating systems, multimedia, and the Internet
misc	Taxes, kids, investing, education, family matters
news	Usenet news-related topics (*not* the evening news)
rec	Sports, books, movies, the arts, entertainment, and other leisure-time pursuits
sci	Serious science—archaeology, biology, chemistry, physics, etc.
soc	Social issues, foreign cultures, current events
talk	Controversial issues—gun control, abortion, etc.

TABLE 5-1 Standard newsgroups hierarchies

The Alternative Hierarchies

The distinguishing thing about alternative hierarchies is that they are relatively easy to form, and for this reason they are growing faster and contain more newsgroups than the standard hierarchies. If they seem less serious, it's partly because they often pop up before a need for them has been established and then fade away before a community has been able to form; they are formed more by individual whim than through the formal workings of community.

Because of their small number of readers, many alternative newsgroups are not carried by the entire network of News computers, which means that some ISPs do not carry all newsgroups. Some alternative newsgroups, however, are devoted to exactly the sort of topics you find in the standard hierarchy, and were in fact created to accommodate the volume of a popular standard newsgroup or to handle a fundamental subject-matter disagreement. Others were created because they weren't approved by the Usenet community.

AOL makes a good effort to carry a full "feed" of alternative newsgroups, that is, they try to carry all the newsgroups and all their postings. One result of this openness is that some newsgroups available on AOL contain no articles; these newsgroups are extinct. You can post to them if you really want, but it's unlikely anyone will respond. AOL can't do anything about extinct groups. Another result of the vast scope of the newsgroups carried by AOL is that some alternative newsgroups may be highly objectionable to some AOL members, especially parents. For this

reason, AOL offers members a powerful set of Parental Controls for limiting children's access to newsgroups, which you can read about in Appendix C. Finally, a big and growing problem with the alternative newsgroups results, again, from the fact that they're public and unchaperoned. You will quickly learn that countless off-topic, irrelevant, rude, and unsolicited commercial messages are posted to even the most serious-looking newsgroups.

The Regional Hierarchies

Regional newsgroups are considered part of the alternative hierarchies. They're easy to form, but instead of being focused on some subject, they're focused on a geographical area (a city, university, or region). For that area, newsgroups can be devoted to all subjects. Like other alternative newsgroups, the regional newsgroups are not universally carried by the globe's News computers. These alternative newsgroups reside primarily on News servers in the region to which they are devoted.

Because America Online is available throughout the U.S. and, increasingly, throughout the world, AOL's News feed includes many regional hierarchies such as **bermuda.***, **boulder.***, **ca.*** (for California), **utah.*** and **utexas.***.

Note: *An asterisk (*), as in* **bermuda.***, refers to the entire family of newsgroups in a hierarchy, such as **bermuda.jobs.offered**, **bermuda.general**, **bermuda.politics**, and **bermuda.sports.**

Specialized Alternative Hierarchies

Many alternative newsgroups focus on topics of somewhat limited interest and are every bit as serious as the standard newsgroups. At *keyword: Newsgroups* (or Internet | Newsgroups), click Add Newsgroups to get a list of the dozens of alternative hierarchies carried by America Online, which fall neither into the **alt.*** hierarchy nor into the regional hierarchies: **bionet.*** is for biologists, **k12.*** for school teachers, and **hepnet.*** for high-energy physicists to name just a few.

FINDING NEWSGROUPS

Where do you start? How do you find newsgroups devoted to your hobby? The standard approach is to either to do a search for relevant newsgroups, if you know just what you're looking for, or to browse, if you're curious about what's available. (Similarly, on the Web, you can browse or do highly specific searches.) For searching and browsing, the place to start is the AOL Newsgroups window shown in Figure 5-3. To get there, either use *keyword: Newsgroups* or select Internet | Newsgroups.

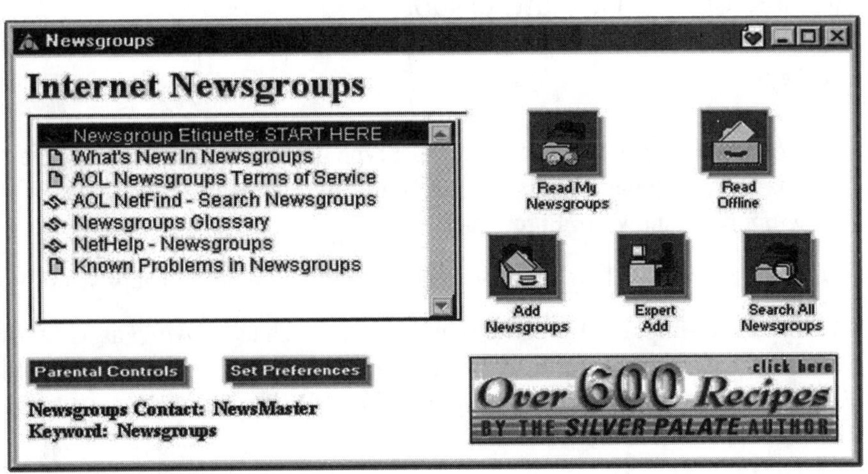

FIGURE 5-3 The AOL Newsgroups window. Start here whether you're searching or browsing

Searching Newsgroups

You can search newsgroups in three ways.

First, you can *search for a specific newsgroup*. The easiest way to do this is by using the Search All Newsgroups feature, available from the main Newsgroups window (Figure 5-3).

Second, with a newsgroup displayed, you can *search for an article about a specific subject* (see the "Searching a Long List for Something Specific" box). These two types of search are easy with AOL.

Finally, you can *search the body of articles for specific words*. Because there's so much *noise* (irrelevancy) in newsgroups, a search for highly specific information can be your best bet—and it's a good way to discover the best newsgroups for your purposes. To do a search for specific information in newsgroup messages, you need to start with one of the general search services discussed in Chapter 9: AOL NetFind, AltaVista, Excite, HotBot, or InfoSeek. Three of them (NetFind, Excite, and InfoSeek) use the DejaNews search service; the other two have their own tools. For more information about these powerful tools for weeding through billions of words in thousands of newsgroups in seconds, see Chapter 9 and especially the box called "Searching for Newsgroup Postings—From the Web."

Searching for Specific Newsgroups

If you're looking for a newsgroup dedicated to a specific subject, follow these simple steps:

1. Go to *keyword: Newsgroups* (or, just type **newsgroups** into the Address box on the navigational bar). This brings up the main Newsgroups window, as shown in Figure 5-3.
2. Click Search All Newsgroups to go to the Search Newsgroups window.
3. Type in a simple but specific search phrase such as *cooking*, as shown here. You can type multiple words or phrases separated by AND (if both items must be in the newsgroup name) or OR (if *either* item must be in the name). Click List Articles.

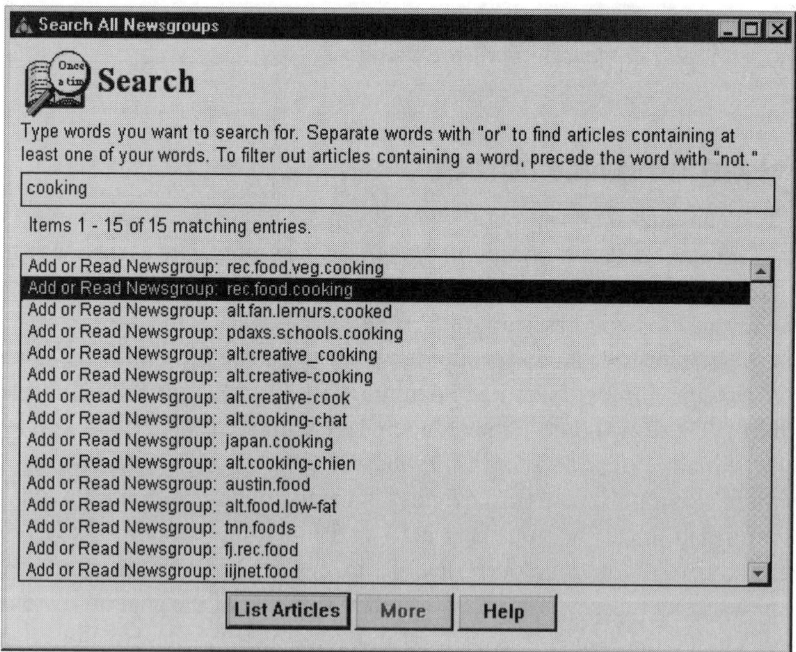

4. If your search had results, they'll appear in the bottom part of the window. Double-click any newsgroup to see the window shown here:

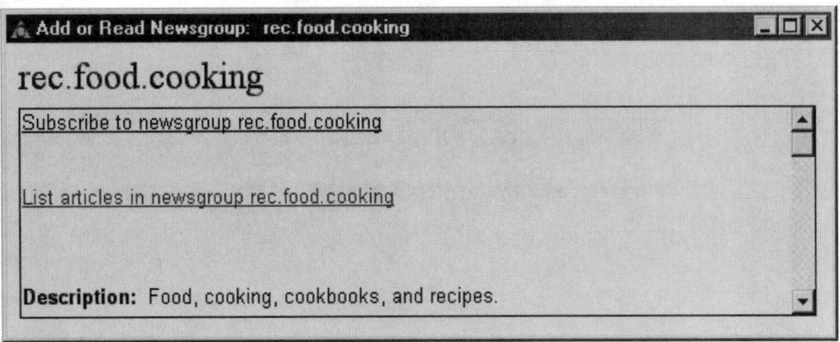

5. Click Subscribe to add the newsgroup to Read My Newsgroups, or click List Articles to read the newsgroup without adding it to your newsgroup list.

Newsgroup Scoop

The World Wide Web is all the rage, but how do you find out about other Internet resources, such as newsgroups? *Harley Hahn's Internet and Web Yellow Pages* (Osborne/McGraw-Hill, 1998) is an excellent place to start if you're looking for groovy newsgroups about obscure subjects. The AOL Book Shop *(keyword: AOLstore*, click Books) carries the *Yellow Pages*—and every Webhead (or aspiring Webhead) should have a copy handy.

Browsing for Newsgroups

You can also *browse* for newsgroups that interest you. Browsing is a more top-down approach that takes you through hierarchies and subhierarchies to specific newsgroups. Browsing lets you discover newsgroups that interest you by starting you off with a hierarchy of the appropriate subject and seriousness (standard or alternative).

1. From the main Newsgroup window shown in Figure 5-3, click *Add Newsgroups.*
2. A list of categories comes up, beginning with the standard hierarchies and proceeding through a long alphabetical list of dozens and dozens of alternative hierarchies.

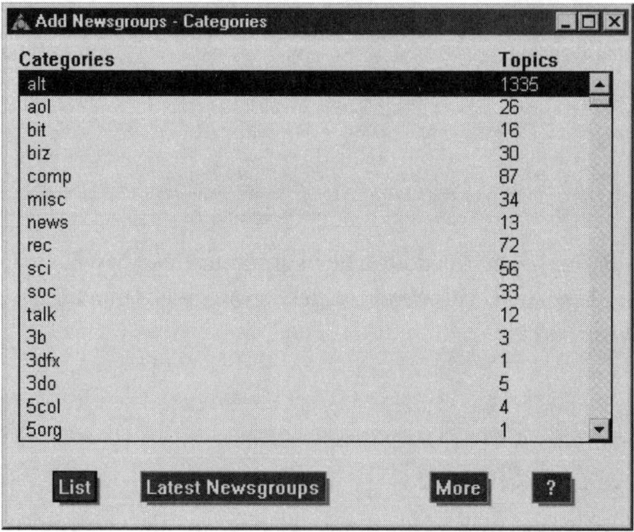

3. Select a category by double-clicking. The Topics window for that hierarchy comes up (see Figure 5-4). For each topic, or subhierarchy, you'll see how many newsgroups are associated with it. If there's only one newsgroup, the topic is itself a newsgroup.
4. Double-click a topic to see a list of one or more newsgroup(s).
5. To add a newsgroup to your Read My Newsgroups list, select the newsgroup and click Subscribe. You can also double-click a newsgroup and browse it—that is, read it without being able to post to it. Just click List Subjects, then Read Messages

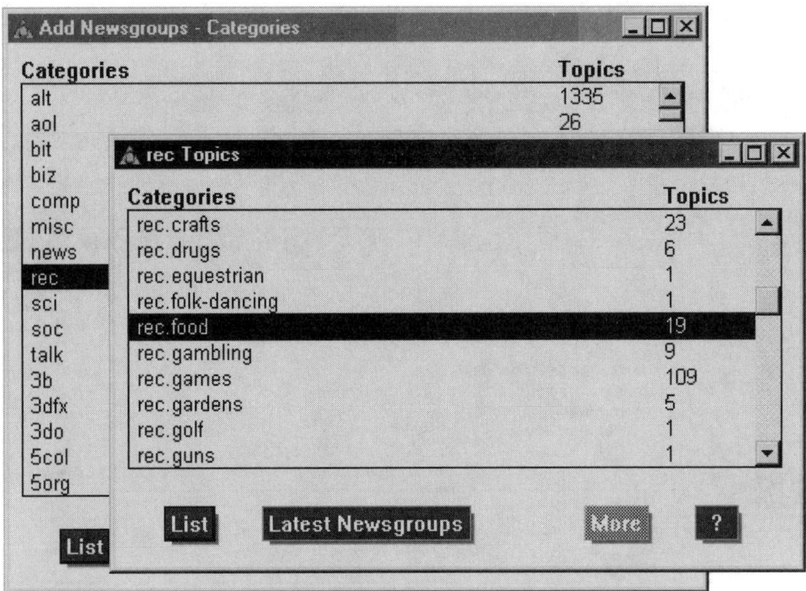

FIGURE 5-4 A list of recreational topics in the **rec** hierarchy

Keywording to a Newsgroup

If you know a specific newsgroup's name—from the newspaper, a book, a friend, or a search of newsgroups, as explained in the previous section—you can go *directly* to the newsgroup using the Keyword window or the Address box in the navigational bar. This useful and direct way to read newsgroups doesn't, however, give you the option of adding a newsgroup to your Read My Newsgroups list.

To keyword to a specific newsgroup, go to the Address box or the Keyword window. Type in **news** and a colon (**:**) and the name of the newsgroup (for example, **news:comp.internet.net-happenings**).

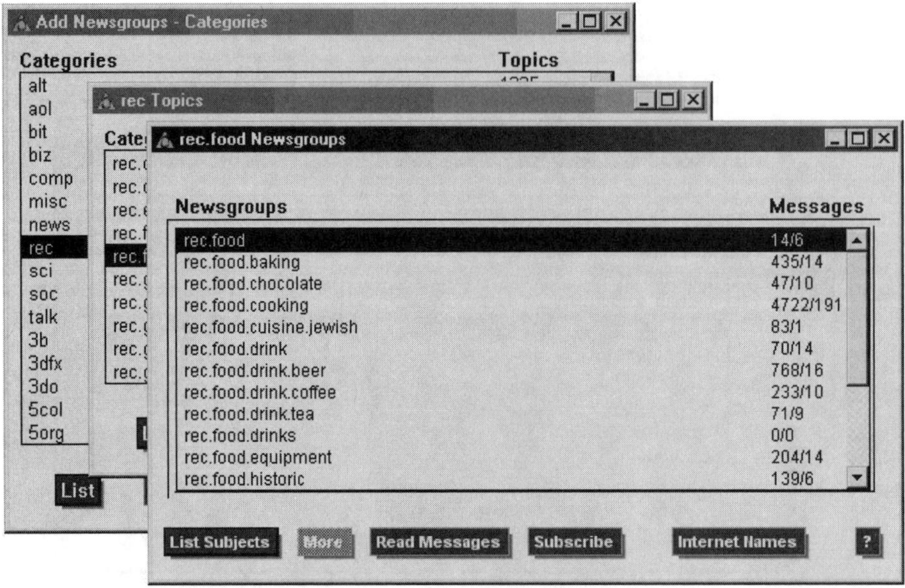

FIGURE 5-5 Some of the newsgroups devoted to the **rec.food** topic. Select a newsgroup and click Add to include it in your Read My Newsgroups list

KEEPING TRACK OF NEWSGROUPS

With so many newsgroups to read, how do you keep track of the ones you like? America Online lets you do just that in the Read My Newsgroups list. When you register as an AOL member, you will find several newsgroups already in this list. You can add and remove newsgroups to and from this list as you please, making it easy to return and read your favorites whenever you like.

Adding newsgroups to Read My Newsgroups doesn't really subscribe you in any formal way; you can read newsgroups without subscribing, and there are times when you want to do just that.

The Read My Newsgroups list has three benefits for you:

- It's a convenient way of quickly getting to the newsgroups you like.
- It's a way of keeping track of articles you have read *within* a newsgroup.

- You can read offline any newsgroups you have included in Read My Newsgroups (and can't read offline newsgroups you haven't included).

There's another good way of keeping track of your favorite newsgroups—see the "Favorite Place It!" box.

Adding to Read My Newsgroups

The main reason for keeping track of newsgroups you like is pretty obvious—it makes it easier to return in the future, even when you're offline. If you *don't* know the exact newsgroup name you want to add, start by clicking Add Newsgroups. Burrow through the hierarchy to the particular newsgroup, and browse the newsgroup (scan the postings) if you're not sure whether you want to add it. If you are sure, click Add to put the newsgroup in Read My Newsgroups.

If you know the exact name of a newsgroup you want to add to Read My Newsgroups, you needn't burrow but can instead use AOL's *Expert Add* feature:

1. Go to the main Newsgroup window and click Expert Add to bring up the Expert Add window.
2. In the Internet Name field, type the newsgroup's name and click Add (in fact you're using the Usenet name). Your choice will be confirmed; click Add.

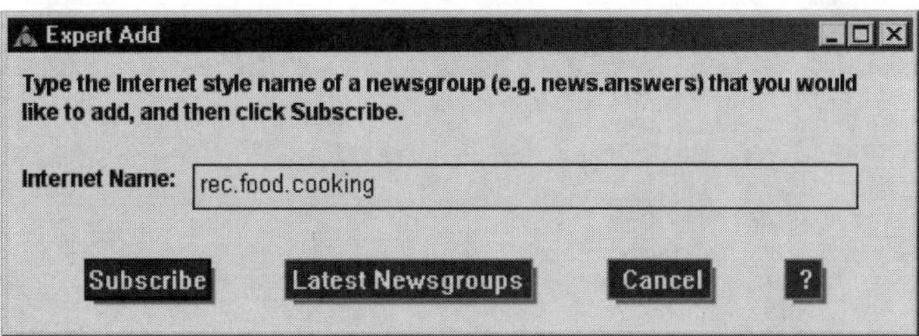

3. Close the Expert Add window.
4. To go to the newsgroup you've just added, click on Read My Newsgroups in the main Newsgroups window (Figure 5-6).
5. To open any newsgroup you've ever added to Read My Newsgroups, double-click the newsgroup to bring up the screen shown in Figure 5-7. To delete a newsgroup from Read My Newsgroups, select it and click Remove. Next time you open the list, the newsgroup will not appear.

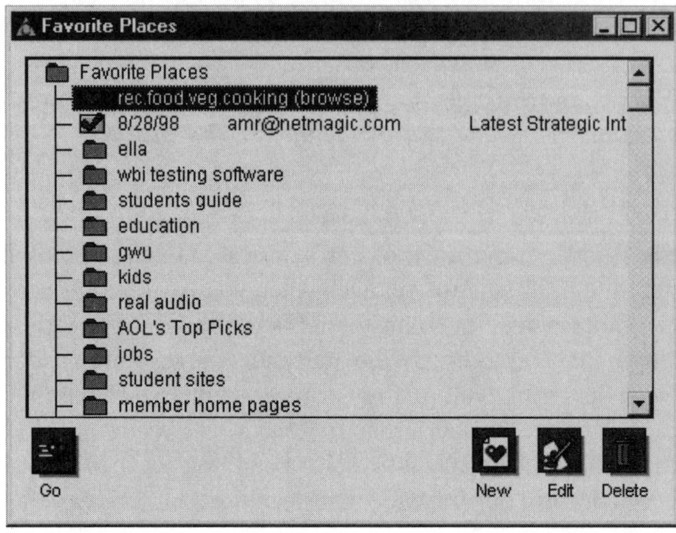

FIGURE 5-6 Read My Newsgroups—a list of newsgroups you want to visit and revisit

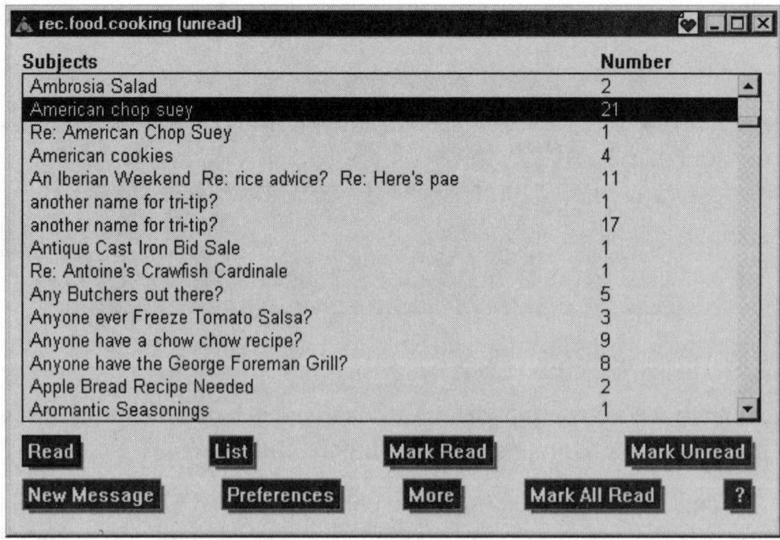

FIGURE 5-7 Working with a newsgroup: **rec.food.cooking**, one of AOL members' favorites

Tip *From time to time, you'll get an Invalid Group message using* Expert Add. *You've either incorrectly entered the newsgroup's name, or the newsgroup is not carried by America Online. Double-check the name, and re-enter it. If you're having persistent problems and you feel the newsgroup should be carried, send e-mail to screen name* newsmaster.

Favorite Place It!

Using AOL 4.0 for Windows you can add a newsgroup to your Favorite Places folder (available by clicking Favorites on the AOL tool bar). With Favorite Places, you can store links to every kind of site you like on both AOL and the Internet—individual e-mail messages, AOL forums, Web pages, and newsgroups. By creating customized folders, you can compile newsgroups, Web pages, and AOL forums all dealing with the same subject.

Here's how to add a newsgroup to your Favorite Places folder: With the main window of a newsgroup displayed (as in Figure 5-7), click on the heart on the far-right end of title bar. Then select Add to Favorites.

To access the newsgroup, open the Favorite Places folder and double-click the entry for the newsgroup. The "(unread)" label indicates that this Favorite Place is a newsgroup:

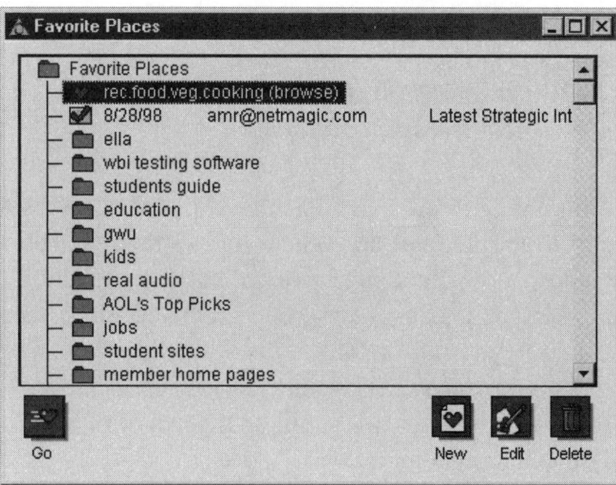

To add a folder, click the New button. In Add New Folder/Favorite Place, click the New Folder button, enter a name in the box, and click OK. In the main Favorite Places folder, use your mouse to move the folder to the place where you want it relative to other folders and Favorite Place items.

What's the difference between Read My Newsgroups and Favorite Places? Read My Newsgroups consists only of newsgroups, while Favorite Places can be any Internet or AOL destination. Favorite Places is available offline but requires you to sign on if you want to take part (while offline, open Favorite Places; double-click a newsgroup to sign onto AOL and open that newsgroup). With Read My Newsgroups, however, the individual newsgroups are available for offline use with Automatic AOL. Finally, with Favorite Places you can keep track of individual articles. Unlike e-mail messages, however, the articles won't be available once AOL has "expired" them (removed them from the list of current articles for a newsgroup) after about two weeks.

Using the Browser to Go to a Newsgroup

Every newsgroup has a URL, or Internet address (see Chapter 6 on URLs). This means that a World Wide Web page can have a link pointing to a newsgroup; click on the link and you go directly to the newsgroup.

Note *A newsgroup's URL consists of* ***news:*** *plus the newsgroup name, without any spaces and also without the customary double forward slashes (//). You are using a URL when you use the Keyword window or Address box to go directly to a newsgroup, as in* ***news:rec.autos.antique****.*

While browsing the Web on AOL, clicking a link that points to a newsgroup takes you directly to the newsgroup. When you do this, you bring up the AOL Newsgroups window, so you don't have to master an additional method of navigating hierarchies and using newsgroups. On the other hand, when using newsgroups in this way you can't return to the Web with something as simple as a click on the Back button; you must close the newsgroup windows. Still, you do get a taste of a future in which the browser will be the center of everything you do on the Internet and on your computer as well.

Note *AOL does not yet give members the option of using third-party newsreaders such as Trumpet, WinVN, and Agent, but you can use such programs if you take advantage of the Bring Your Own Access billing plan and access AOL over a TCP/IP connection, as described in Appendix A. If you use a third-party newsreader over your other connection, you won't be using AOL's News servers, and you must make the appropriate settings for that reader (NNTP server, signature, organizational information, etc.); your ISP or your newsreader's Help menu should be able to provide the guidance you need.*

SCANNING NEWSGROUP ARTICLES FOR THE GOOD ONES

Figure 5-7 shows a listing of articles and threads in the **rec.autos.antique** newsgroup. Whenever the More button is active (can be clicked), you can click it once or several times until all messages are listed. Until they've been listed, you can't search them for specific subjects (see "Searching a Long List for Something Specific").

You can control this listing in three ways:

- Mark articles read or unread
- List articles from the earliest to the most recent, or vice versa
- List articles alphabetically

Searching a Long List for Something Specific

With newsgroup articles displayed, you can search for articles of special interest by searching for a specific word in their headers.

1. From AOL's Edit menu, select Find in Top Window.
2. In the little window, type in the words of interest, and click Search.

You can use this neat feature to search your e-mail mailboxes and Personal Filing Cabinet as well.

Marking Messages Read and Unread—What's the Difference?

Your New Mail box, when you're reading e-mail, displays only unread messages and messages you have kept as new. Similarly, when you read a newsgroup message (article), it's automatically defined as *read*, and it won't display next time you open the newsgroup unless you decide to mark it as *unread*. Thus, every message you can read is either unread or marked as *unread*.

With AOL, you can mark articles as *read* or *unread* one at a time or a bunch at a time. To do so, select the article(s) and click the appropriate button. You can mark all of them *read* by just clicking the Mark All Read button.

Why would you want to mark a message as *read* without even reading it? Some newsgroups have a good deal of *noise*—off-topic, obnoxious, useless, argumentative, and offensive postings. Marking such postings *read* can get them out of the way and help you focus on the articles you're really interested in. Or, if you've just returned from vacation and don't have the time to plow through thousands of articles, just mark them all *read*.

Note *From Read My Newsgroups, you get an overview of the number of unread messages and the total messages for each of your newsgroups. You can click a button at this window to mark* all newsgroups read*, thereby setting the Unread column (Figure 5-6) to 0. Or, select a single newsgroup and mark just those articles read.*

Why mark articles *unread* after you've read them? For one thing, it gives you the time to draft a well-thought-out response to the group (after reading subsequent articles on the same subject). Also, marking an article *unread* lets you download it for offline reading since only unread articles can be downloaded, as explained later in "Reading and Posting Offline."

Listing Articles Oldest to Newest, or Vice Versa—What's the Difference?

AOL also gives you the choice of listing articles from most recent to least recent, or vice versa. Here's how:

- From the main Newsgroup window, click Set Preferences, and click the appropriate button indicating whether you wish to see Oldest or Newest articles first.

Following a newsgroup in chronological order (with the oldest articles posted first) gives you a sense of how discussions evolve and interrelate. Following in reverse order (from most recent to oldest) brings you up to date more quickly; most people are interested in the most recent articles, even though these articles may lack the context of the previous days' articles. First-to-last (to see how discussions evolve) or last-to-first (to see what's new)—it's your choice.

Listing Articles Alphabetically

Finally, you can set your preferences at the main Newsgroups window to sort all threads and messages alphabetically instead of chronologically, which can help you sort through especially long lists of articles, especially for newsgroups like **comp.internet.net-happenings**, whose standard Subject lines (BOOK, K12, etc.) can speed access to the information you want.

WORKING WITH ARTICLES

Figure 5-7 shows you what you see when you "drill down" to a specific newsgroup on AOL. Each line is either a single article or a *thread* consisting of several articles with the same subject line (and usually the same subject). If you want an overview of a specific thread, select the thread and click List to bring up a little window showing the individual messages in the thread, including their authors' e-mail addresses, the size of the messages, and the times they were posted.

Figure 5-8 shows a single article.

All newsgroup articles contain *headers* and *bodies*. They can, optionally, contain *files* and *signatures*. The *header* contains a little information about who sent the article and what the article is about (cars, in this case). Like an e-mail message header, a newsgroup article header can also provide a time and date. The Subject line provides the hook used to catch the attention of other people. When an article's Subject line is preceded by "re:" the article is a reply to another article, and the two form a part of a thread. Some newsgroup programs offers a range of other optional headers, including e-mail addresses to use for responding.

Tip *With AOL you can choose whether to have headers appear at the beginning of articles or at the end. Placing them at the end makes it easier to get to the article but harder to see essential information such as the sender's name and the message's date. To place headers at the end of messages, click Set Preferences from the Newsgroups window, click the Headers at Bottom button, and click OK.*

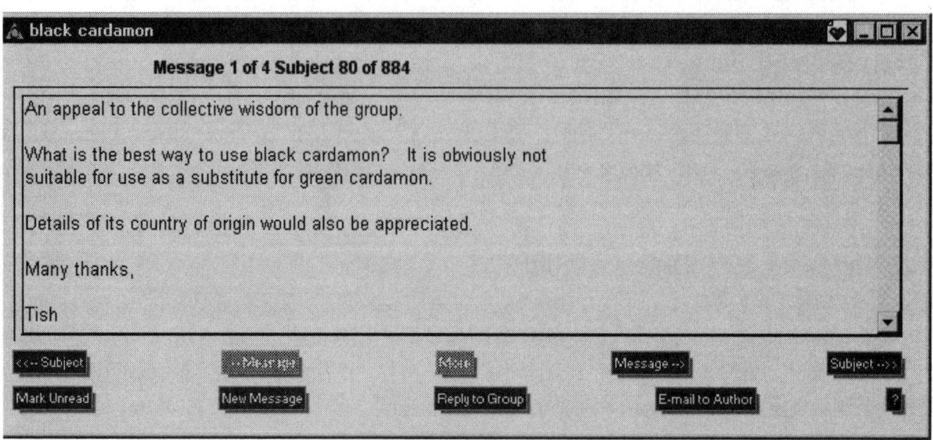

black cardamon
Message 1 of 4 Subject 80 of 884
An appeal to the collective wisdom of the group.
What is the best way to use black cardamon? It is obviously not suitable for use as a substitute for green cardamon.
Details of its country of origin would also be appreciated.
Many thanks,
Tish
<<-- Subject
Message -->
Subject -->>
Mark Unread
New Message
Reply to Group
E-mail to Author
?

FIGURE 5-8 A message posted to rec.food.cooking. Click Message –> to see the response, or Subject –>> to see the next thread

The *body* of the article is, of course, its content. If an article is part of a thread, content from earlier articles will probably be quoted, with each quoted line "spaced in" from the left or preceded by a particular character (as you can see Figure 5-9).

Note *With newsgroups, as with e-mail, you can quote only the pertinent parts of the original in order to frame your response when you reply to it. Just use a little program called QCLIP, available in the Software Center at* keyword: Filesearch. *This is not an AOL utility but was designed to work with the AOL for Windows software.*

Messages can contain *files*—anything from image and sound files to Windows utilities. Using other Internet providers, it can be a time-consuming and technical matter to download, convert, and use files. Using AOL's unique FileGrabber feature,

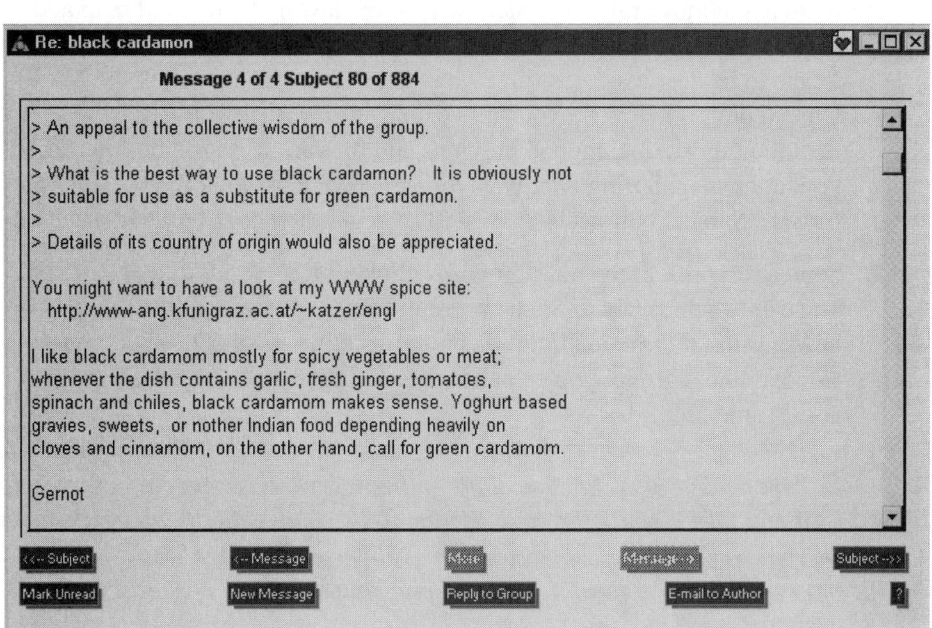

Re: black cardamon
Message 4 of 4 Subject 80 of 884
> An appeal to the collective wisdom of the group.
>
> What is the best way to use black cardamon? It is obviously not
> suitable for use as a substitute for green cardamon.
>
> Details of its country of origin would also be appreciated.
You might want to have a look at my WWW spice site:
http://www-ang.kfunigraz.ac.at/~katzer/engl
I like black cardamom mostly for spicy vegetables or meat;
whenever the dish contains garlic, fresh ginger, tomatoes,
spinach and chiles, black cardamom makes sense. Yoghurt based
gravies, sweets, or nother Indian food depending heavily on
cloves and cinnamom, on the other hand, call for green cardamom.
Gernot
<<-- Subject
<-- Message
Subject -->>
Mark Unread
New Message
Reply to Group
E-mail to Author
?

FIGURE 5-9 Part of the body of the reply to the message in Figure 5-8, from a person in Austria

however, you can extract a file with a point and click of your mouse, as you'll see in "Getting Files from Newsgroups Is a Breeze."

A final and optional article element is the *signature*. If you choose to use it, this bit of text is automatically added to the end of your postings. If you want to create a signature file, get the lowdown in the "Personalizing Your Response by Adding a Signature" section.

RESPONDING TO AN ARTICLE

So, you've read an article. Now what? With an article open (as in Figure 5-9), there are several of things you can do:

- Read it and move on. The article will automatically be marked *read* and won't be displayed next time you visit the newsgroup. (If you want the article to be displayed next time you visit the newsgroup, click the Mark Unread button.) How do you "move on"? If the article you've just read is part of a thread, clicking the previous and forward Message buttons takes you to the neighboring articles in the thread, and clicking the previous and forward Subject buttons takes you to adjacent threads (Figure 5-9).
- Send a response to the newsgroup by clicking Reply to Group. Note that you can respond only to the newsgroup you are reading, not to other newsgroups at the same time (this is called cross-posting). When you respond to the group, you can choose to CC the author by e-mail message at the same time.

Note *With newsgroups, your postings go from News server to News server, so it can take a while for your posting to become available to everyone in the world with News access. Because of the volume of postings worldwide, most News servers get rid of (expire) postings after a couple of days or weeks.*

- Respond only to the author, using e-mail, instead of responding to the entire newsgroup. Just click E-mail to Author.

Tip *Responding to the author is appropriate for personal, heated, and off-topic responses to an author's posting to the newsgroup. It's the right choice, in general, if what you have to say would not be of likely interest to the group at large.*

- Start an entirely new thread, or at least send an article to the newsgroup on a new topic, by clicking Send New Message from the newsgroup's main window, as in Figure 5-7 (see "Threads of Your Own: Starting a New Subject").

Personalizing Your Response by Adding a Signature

If you plan on sending articles to a newsgroup, it's a good idea to add a signature. A *signature* is a bit of text that will be automatically added to every posting you make to any newsgroup. It's a way of tacking on a joke, a motto, or some contact information. You can also advertise a Web site or feature information that promotes your business. You can even add elaborate ASCII (text) drawings of dragons, cows, and other pictures.

To add a signature:

1. From the main Newsgroups window, click Set Preferences to get the Preferences window shown in Figure 5-10. Note that these general preferences differ from the ones you get by pressing the Preferences button on the individual newsgroup window.
2. In the Signature box at the bottom of the window, type in the text you want to use. Click OK.

Tip *Before you share your signature with the world, you might want to post a test article to one of the newsgroups devoted exclusively to this purpose, such as* ***alt.test*** *or* ***misc.test****.*

Threads of Your Own: Starting a New Subject

If you don't want to respond to another person's posting but do have something to say, start your own thread! From a newsgroup's main window (like the one displayed in Figure 5-7), click the Send New Message button to send an article.

The Post New Message window asks you for only two things: a Subject line and a Message, and lets you make the choice of whether to include a signature file as well (see the "Personalizing Your Response by Adding a Signature" section). Click

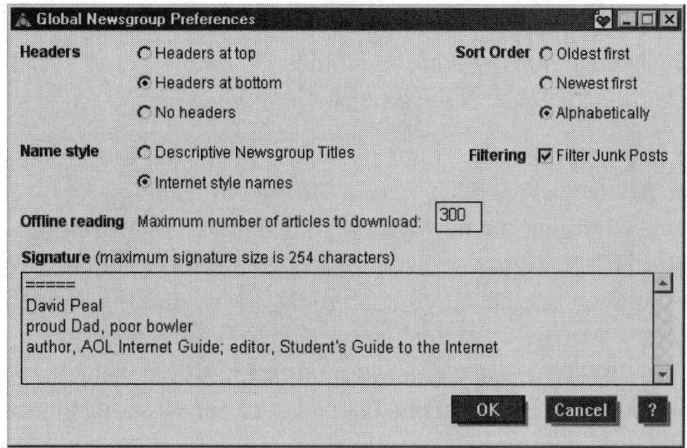

FIGURE 5-10 Supply a signature to automatically add a personalized message to every article you post to any newsgroup

in the Use Signature box to include your signature file, if you have one. (The window appears very similar if you are *replying* to an article, except the Subject line is filled in, and you have the choice of sending the message as an e-mail message to the author of the original.) When you've polished your article, click Send. Your article will join a global flow of information that reaches every continent and is accessible to more people than you might imagine.

READING AND POSTING OFFLINE

Automatic AOL is an AOL feature that lets you take care of some Net chores even when you are not signed on. For communication such as e-mail and newsgroups, where people aren't communicating in *real time* (at the same time), working offline makes perfect sense. The beauty of the Net, however, is not so much real time communication as communication when you want, on your terms, and after you've had a chance to think about what you want to say. With Automatic AOL you won't tie up the phone and you don't have to worry about being disconnected from AOL while reading a newsgroup.

Here's how it works: your computer signs on automatically at times you specify, performs a task such as reading newsgroup messages and posting any messages you have written, then signs off again. This way, you can download all your newsgroup postings at regular intervals, then browse them at your leisure. They'll be available in your Personal Filing Cabinet (in the Newsgroups folder's Incoming/Saved Postings subfolder).

To read your newsgroups offline:

1. In the Newsgroups window (you must be online), click Read Offline to bring up the Choose Newsgroups window (see Figure 5-11).

2. The Subscribed Newsgroups list shows the newsgroups you've put in the Read My Newsgroup list—*these are the only newsgroups you can read offline.* Highlight the newsgroup you want to read offline in the Subscribed Newsgroups list and click the Add button. You can quickly select all newsgroups in your personal list by clicking the Add All button. Any newsgroups you select are moved to the "Newsgroups to read offline" list. To remove a newsgroup from this list, select its name in the Newsgroups to Read Offline list and click the Remove button. Click *Remove All* if you don't want to read any newsgroups offline. *You must click* OK *to save any changes you have made.* Or, click Cancel if you change your mind.

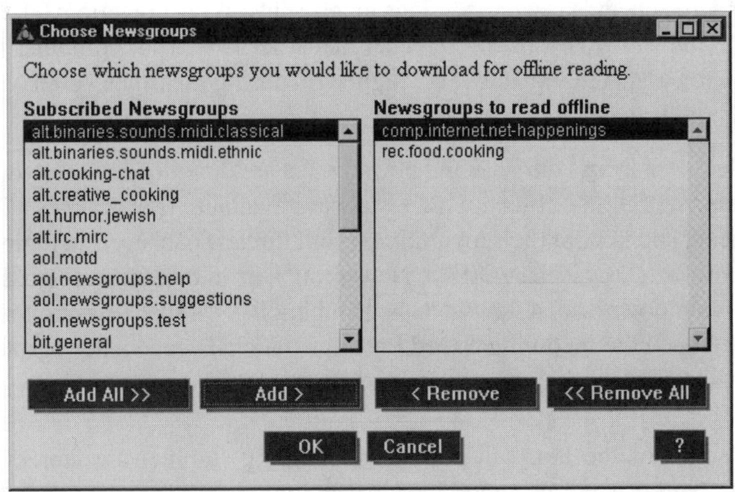

FIGURE 5-11 Add newsgroups from Read My Newsgroups to a list of newsgroups to read offline

Offline or online, here is how you set up an Automatic AOL session:

1. From the toolbar's Mail Center menu, select Set Up Automatic AOL. The fourth and fifth check boxes allow you to send postings and retrieve unread postings. Place checks in one box or both.
2. Click Select Names and provide both a screen name and password for that screen name. Click OK.

Tip *If you check "Copy author of original message by e-mail" when replying to a newsgroup posting and then set up an offline session to send your posting, you must also check Automatic AOL's "Send mail from the 'Mail waiting to be sent' folder" box in order to send your e-mail responses.*

3. You have a choice:
   - To get and send postings now, click the Run Automatic AOL Now button. If you're offline, AOL signs you on, then either retrieves postings or sends postings (or both). If you're online, AOL downloads the postings. In both cases, you'll be asked whether you want to stay online after the postings have been sent or downloaded.

- To schedule regular sessions, click Schedule Automatic AOL, indicate your time preferences, and click OK. Your computer must be on and AOL open, but not signed on during the times you have indicated.

4. Messages from your selected newsgroups are downloaded into your Personal Filing Cabinet, which is always available from the My Files menu, and kept in their own folder (with threads packaged in their own subfolders). Or, select Offline Newsgroups from that menu to go directly to your downloaded newsgroups. Double-click on the Newsgroups folder, then open the Incoming/Saved Postings folder. To read a newsgroup article, double-click it.

Because all of the items in the Personal Filing Cabinet are stored on your computer's hard drive, it is a good idea to regularly delete any articles that you've read and don't want to keep. An overflowing Personal Filing Cabinet can slow down AOL!

DON'T BE A JERK!

In your private e-mail, netiquette is important because it's easy to be misunderstood online. E-mail is so ubiquitous that good netiquette can make a big difference in how you get along with others. On mailing lists, netiquette becomes more important than in one-to-one e-mail, because you're dealing with people you probably don't know—people who can't be counted on to extend you the benefit of the doubt. And in newsgroups, netiquette is even *more* important, because you are communicating with people you are even less likely to know; unlike mailing lists, no one really knows who reads newsgroups. Your words can get you in trouble in countless ways. They can make the wrong impression, convey a meaning that you hadn't intended, or simply rub people the wrong way.

What follows are some guidelines, distilled from Chuq Rosbach's classic *Primer on How to Work with the Usenet Community.* If you're serious about newsgroups, read this document from beginning to end; it's regularly posted to the **news.answers** newsgroup. If you're a glutton for this admonishment, check out the Netiquette section of AOL NetFind's Newsgroup area (**http://www.aol.com/netfind/scoop/newsgroup_etiquette.html**).

- Lurk before you leap. (In other words, hang out and read the postings on a newsgroup for a while before participating.)

- Respect your reader.
- Respect people who *might* be your readers.
- Be brief.
- Use clear and descriptive subject lines.
- Post to the correct newsgroup.
- Avoid sarcasm and irony.
- When responding, summarize.
- Do not use a newsgroup to sell something.

5

GETTING FILES FROM NEWSGROUPS IS A BREEZE

Newsgroups are a source of more than text articles. They are also a source of software, images, and sounds. You can use the Search All Newsgroups button on the main Newsgroups window to find newsgroups that offer all sorts of useful files.

In e-mail, you can get files *attached* to articles. With newsgroups, files are *inserted* inside articles. How? The files are encoded by means of a technique called UUE (*UNIX to UNIX Encoding*, if you really want to know). Encoding articles is a way of taking *binary* files (programs or the documents used by programs) and turning them into text files. To the eye, these files look like gibberish—but rest assured, they're meant to be understood by computers, not people:

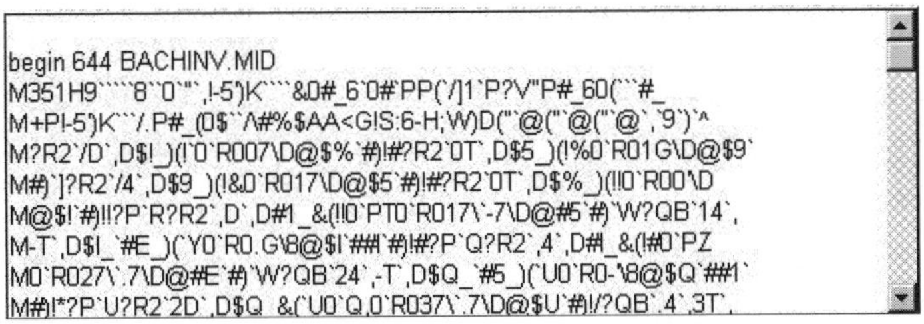

```
begin 644 BACHINV.MID
M351H9`````8``0`"`,!-5')K````&0#_6`0#PP(`/]1`P?V"P#_60(```#_
M+P!-5')K```/.P#_(0$``A#%$AA<G!S:6-H;W)D("`@("`@("`@`,`9`)`^
M?R2`/D`,D$!_)(!`0`R007\D@$%`#)!#?R2`0T`,D$5_)(!%0`R01G\D@$9`
M#)`]?R2`/4`,D$9_)(!&0`R017\D@$5`#)!#?R2`0T`,D$%_)(!!0`R00\D
M@$!`#)!!?P`R?R2`,D`,D#1_&(!!0`PT0`R017\`-7\D@#5`#)`W?QB`14`,
M-T`,D$I_`#E_)(`Y0`R0.G\8@$I`##I`#)!#?P`Q?R2`,4`,D#1_&(!#0`PZ
M0`R027\`.7\D@#E`#)`W?QB`24`,-T`,D$Q_`#5_)(`U0`R0-\8@$Q`##1`
M#)!*?P`U?R2`2D`,D$Q_&(`U0`Q,0`R037\`.7\D@$U`#)!/?QB`.4`,3T`,
```


The great virtue of these files is that they can be transmitted the same way simple text is transmitted. The resulting text files can be very long, so files encoded as text

are often automatically divided by the encoding program into several articles. This helps ensure that the data is transmitted smoothly and completely.

In the olden days, decoding UUE files took work, luck, and time: you'd consolidate many files into one file, then run that one file through a special *de*coding program (programs that encode usually decode, too). The result: the same file (an image, a sound, a program, whatever).

AOL's FileGrabber tool makes it easy to extract and use files that have been UUEncoded. Here's an article that contains a file (actually, a part of a file), a MIDI version of the Blue Danube Waltz:

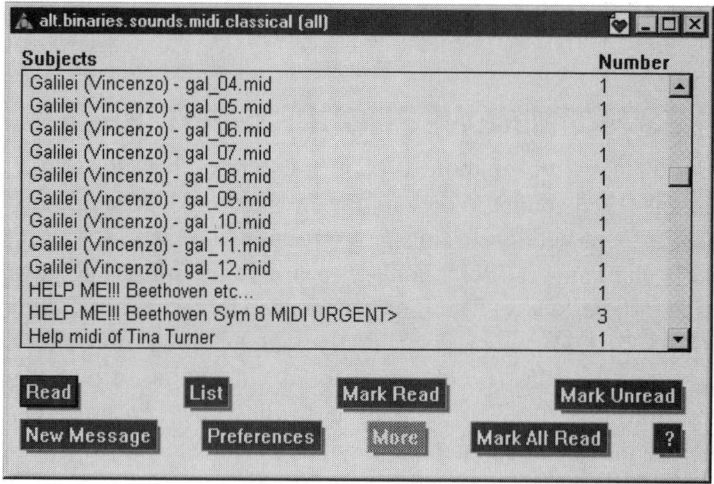

1. Double-click an article with a file inserted into it. Unlike e-mail (which automatically shows attached files with a special icon), with articles you'll have to rely on the accuracy of Subject lines to determine whether a file is present.

   If a file is present, you'll see the following window when you double-click the article.

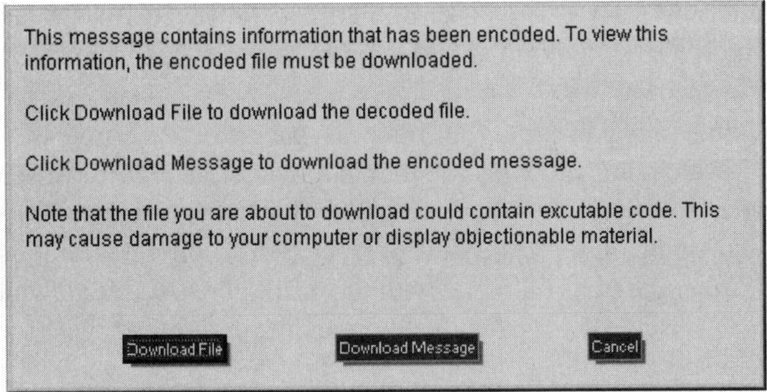

This message contains information that has been encoded. To view this information, the encoded file must be downloaded.
Click Download File to download the decoded file.
Click Download Message to download the encoded message.
Note that the file you are about to download could contain excutable code. This may cause damage to your computer or display objectionable material.
Download File
Download Message
Cancel

2. Click Download File. (Downloading the *article* provides you a copy of the human message, if there is one, plus the "gibberish"—the encoded music.)

3. Indicate where to put the file on your hard disk, what you want to name the file (if you want to change its name), and click OK. A progress bar tracks the download, letting you know approximately how long the download will take. If the file is spread out over a couple of articles, FileGrabber automatically finds all the articles and puts them together before downloading and decoding.

If you're downloading an image file (GIF, PCX, JPG format), you will see the file gradually being decoded as it's downloaded. If it's a sound file (WAV, MIDI format), AOL displays or plays the file automatically. Chapter 8 covers the world of files and file types and includes tips for handling types of downloaded files that aren't automatically played or displayed.

Note *Make sure to download your files to a place where you can readily retrieve them. Using the c:/America Online 4.0/download directory is the default, and it's a handy way to keep track of all your downloads.*

When Files Aren't Immediately Usable

FileGrabber is a neat feature when it works, and it almost always does. If you've ever decoded a UUEncoded file, you will be instantly impressed by FileGrabber's

power and how easy it is to use. Sometimes, however, FileGrabber is unable to handle the files inserted into articles, for the following reasons:

- Some files you extract from newsgroups will be compressed for quicker downloading, or *zipped* up to make it possible to retrieve several files at the same time. You'll need additional software for decompressing or unzipping these files. WinZip, from AOL's software libraries (*keyword: Filesearch*), can help you with most files, and AOL's Download Manager can be set to automatically unzip many compressed files (see Chapter 8).
- Some files won't be usable because they are spread out over several articles and at least one article is missing. There is nothing you can do about this except to send e-mail to the poster of the file and request a reposting.
- Some files are in an unusual format or are "MIME-encoded" and can't be handled by FileGrabber. You may have better luck decoding the file manually using software available in AOL's software libraries. The article itself will usually indicate the format clearly at the top. At *keyword: FileSearch*, do a search for that format to retrieve software for *handling* the format. Double-click a likely-seeming program and read the accompanying information file. Download and install the software as instructed in the information file.

Sending Files in Newsgroups

AOL makes it very easy to retrieve files from articles, but you'll need extra software to post files to newsgroups because you'll need to convert them into text files you may also need to split each text file into several smaller files. At *keyword: Filesearch*, you can search for programs such as Fcode that handle this encoding. Follow the instructions for any of these programs for converting binary files. Once a file has been converted, it's a simple matter to paste an article into the Post New Message window and to send it to the appropriate newsgroup.

ESSENTIAL READING: FAQS

Many claims are made about the Internet as a source of information about everything under the sun. Much of this supposed treasure, especially on the Web, is neither systematic nor reliable. For many newsgroups, however, information has been systematically collected and, more important, *collaboratively* reviewed and refined, sometimes over many years. The result is a large collection of Frequently Asked Question documents, or FAQs. These FAQs address questions about either individual newsgroups or the topics to which the newsgroups are devoted. Often they look at both.

What's special about FAQs is that they are written and commented on by many members of a newsgroup's community. Over time, they become widely accepted as authoritative within the community and genuinely useful beyond it. In theory, everybody can recommend changes to the maintainer of the FAQ, who is usually prominently identified in the FAQ.

Tip *The assumption behind FAQs is that it's a waste of people's time and of network bandwidth for old-timers to repeatedly answer beginners' routine questions. The idea that the Net has lots of people ready and eager to answer your questions is not always true. An AOL message board can be a friendlier place to go for help. At* keyword: On the Net, *you will find a large set of Internet-related message boards.*

Some FAQs make for good reads and serve as useful introductions to difficult topics. Some provide great sources for self-instruction if you want to learn more about anything Internet-related, for example, MIME, graphics formats such as JPG, access forms such as ISDN, and Usenet itself. Look for FAQs on nontechnical subjects such as dogs, puzzles, specific disabilities, Lego, running, medicine, model rockets, and on and on.

FAQs are routinely published in the newsgroups they grow out of, as well as in the **news.answers** newsgroup. The FAQ archives of **news.answers** are available in a famous collection called **rtfm.mit.edu**, an FTP site. (Think of an FTP site as a big public hard disk on someone else's computer—a collection of files arranged into folders containing more folders. Chapter 8 goes into more detail about FTP.) Several Web sites have mirror versions of this FAQ archive, including **http://www.cis.ohio-state.edu/hypertext/faq/usenet/**. Using FTP, you get quick access to a mirror of the MIT site:

1. Use Internet | FTP to go to AOL's FTP area. Once there, click the Go To FTP button.

2. From the listbox of FTP sites, double-click on **rtfm.mit.edu:/pub**. Information about the site comes up. Click OK.

3. Navigate the site by double-clicking the **usenet-by-hierarchy** folder, then the **news** folder, and finally the **news.answers** folder—the archives of the **news.answers** newsgroup.

4. Browse the list for topics of interest. Note that topics are alphabetically arranged, and that topics with capital letters precede topics with small letters. Using FTP on AOL, you can view a text file (and most FAQs are text) without downloading it. First double-click on the file, then select View File Now.

SAVING AND PRINTING NEWSGROUP ARTICLES

Newsgroups, especially FAQs, are extraordinary repositories of information and knowledge. Saving and printing them is a way of extending their value by making them easily available when you're not online. As always on the Internet, do not incorporate any content from FAQs in your own writing without explicit reference to the source and without permission from the writer of the original material.

To save an article:

1. Display the article, then select File | Save.

2. Give the file a name and folder, then click *OK*.

To print an article or FAQ, display it and click the Printer icon on the toolbar.

FROM HERE...

Community is what draws people to the global Internet. Traditionally, community on the Internet can be found in 100,000 newsgroups-plus-mailing lists, in which you are likely to learn something new and meet other people with similar interests. From AOL, you have full access to these planet-circling communities.

The next chapters focus on *information* on the Internet. The World Wide Web, the driving force in today's Internet, is the focus of the next two chapters. Chapter 6 is about using the Web more or less passively—browsing it for information. Chapter 7 shows you how to publish your own Web pages.

Chapter 6

Exploring the Web with America Online

If it's human, it's on the World Wide Web. People use the Web to advertise their products, market their services, celebrate their ideas, amuse their friends, *make* friends, vent their frustrations, publish their magazines without cutting down trees or paying postage, and teach children how to discern stars and dissect frogs. The Web has been called a publishing revolution comparable to the invention of movable type. Maybe it is, maybe it's not, but it *has* produced well over 100 million globally distributed and publicly available pages of information, on every subject, in an amazingly short period of time, with 100,000 new pages going up every day. The entire experience of exploring the Web and creating Web pages is available to you through America Online.

What *is* the Web?

In its origins, the Web was just a way of getting at information available through *other* Internet services; it was a common interface to newsgroups, Telnet, and FTP (all of which you can read about elsewhere in this book). The physicists and computer scientists who launched the WWW Project in 1989 had a vision of linking related information located on networks anywhere in the world into a seamless and easy-to-navigate web of information.

What happened next made the Web the white-hot center of the Internet. Thanks to a simple "scripting" language called HTML (short for Hypertext Markup Language), the Web quickly evolved into a way for people, and not only scientists, to both access and *publish* information, thereby creating even more information.

Then came a major change in the software you use to navigate the Web—called *browsers*. The first browsers were meant for reading text. In 1993, a browser called Mosaic, with a "graphical" interface, displayed images as well as text and allowed users to get around by the click of a mouse. In 1994, Mosaic went commercial and was refined and marketed by a new company called Netscape Communications Corp. In a brilliant marketing ploy, Netscape distributed *free* Macintosh, Windows, and Unix versions of their browser.

In 1995, Microsoft got into the act with a competing browser called Internet Explorer, also free. Thanks to these free products and a swelling sea of information, the Web went mainstream in 1995. In 1996, the Microsoft browser was integrated into the AOL software, and a customized version of Netscape was made available at *keyword: Netscape*.

Where Is the Web on AOL?

Eager to get started? You can get the hang of the Web yourself by "surfing," or browsing from site to site. For all the fine points, you can use this chapter as a reference.

The Web's always a click away when you're on AOL:

- From the Welcome screen, click Go to the Web. You'll go directly to the AOL Web site, AOL.com, one of the globe's busiest and most useful sites.

- If the Welcome screen is not viewable, use the Internet menu on the toolbar and select Go to the Web, which spirits you, again, to AOL's Web site.
- Whenever you see one of the following icons in an AOL area, double-click it to go directly to a specific Web site that was specially selected for its relevance to the area's theme.

If you know a Web site's address, or URL (such as **http://www.aol.com**), just type or paste it into the Address box, and press Go. Chapter 11 provides hundreds of starting places for your Web adventures.

America Online gives you everything you need to enjoy the World Wide Web's multimedia feast of sounds, pictures, and animations. This chapter provides everything you need to get started. You'll learn how to:

- Use the AOL browser
- Make the most of AOL's revamped Web site, AOL.com
- Get from place to place on the Web
- Search for information on the Web (a subject treated more thoroughly in Chapter 9)
- Enjoy multimedia files
- Use non-Web Internet services with the browser—Gopher, FTP, e-mail, Telnet, and newsgroups

Note *AOL 3.0 for Windows came in two versions, with different browsers. With AOL 4.0, both Windows 3.1 and Windows 95 users can enjoy the powerful Microsoft Internet Explorer browser. This chapter focuses on AOL 4.0 for Windows 95 but applies to AOL 4.0 for Windows 3.1 and AOL 4.0 for the Macintosh.*

How the Web Works

A *page* is the Web's basic element. In computer terms, a page is a simple text file, usually with a file extension of HTM or HTML. A collection of linked pages is a *Web site.*

When you visit a Web site on America Online, your browser begins by requesting a single page. Your request goes to one of AOL's big computers, or *servers*, which opens up a connection over a very fast communications line to the Internet computer (also called a server) where the page is located. AOL then requests a copy of the page. When it arrives, the page is transferred to your computer and your browser displays it. When you browse the Web, you're really bringing the Web to yourself, page by page.

If the page you're requesting has graphics—as AOL.com does—the image files come to your computer, too, along with any links. These are the bits of text or pictures you can click to get more information on additional pages. Click a link and presto, another page comes to you, taking the place of the one you were just visiting.

TERMS THAT CHANGED THE WORLD: URL AND HTML

A Web page is the basic unit of the World Wide Web (see "How the Web Works"). Every Web page has its own unique address, or URL (Uniform Resource Locator). The page itself is a simple text file created in HTML, which your browser turns into a more or less polished document. Let's look closer at these two fundamental aspects of every Web page.

Where Is That Page? URLs

A URL is simply an Internet address. Every page, or file, on a Web server has its own separate URL. You use URLs to get the information you want.

A URL such as **http://www/aol.com/netfind** has three parts:

1. The first bit, *http*, specifies a *protocol*, or set of rules for exchanging information between two computers. That may sound complicated, but it merely indicates which Internet service is being used: the *Web* (the Hypertext Transfer Protocol, or **http**), *e-mail* (**mailto**), *file transfer* (the File Transfer Protocol, or **ftp**), or *newsgroups* (**news**), to name the most common services.

Note *You can learn about the non-hypertext protocols in "Your All-Purpose Browser," toward the end of this chapter. For a complete glossary, see Appendix B.*

2. The next bit, **www.aol.com**, is the domain name, which tells you a little more about the site—whether it's a company or other entity, and perhaps where it's located (if its domain name ends in *au*, for example, the server is probably in Australia). The domain name scheme used for Web domains is the same as that used for e-mail messages (see "What Is an E-Mail Address?" in Chapter 3).
3. The final bit of the URL, */netfind*, is the specific page, or path to the page, you are requesting. On an Internet computer, a path is a series of folders and subfolders, each level separated by a forward slash (/), such as */mycomputer/myfamily/mykids/ella/circus.jpg*. You can tell an actual file because it usually ends in a file extension such as .HTML, .JPG, or .GIF.

Tip *URLs always take you to a specific page, or file, on the Web. If you type in a URL without a file name such as index.html or main.html (**http://www.aol.com/netfind/**, for example), a specific filename is assumed. In typing URLs in the address box, you can leave off **http://**.*

How Is That Page Put Together? HTML

Web pages are created using something called the *Hypertext Markup Language* (HTML). Often called a publishing tool, HTML is just a way of describing the

The Microsoft Internet Explorer Browser: Two for the Price of One

When you install AOL 4.0 for Windows, you simultaneously install the Microsoft Internet Explorer (MSIE) browser as a completely separate (or *stand-alone*) application. Its icon is placed on your Windows desktop and modestly labeled "The Internet." The integrated browser that opens *within* AOL 4.0—when you select, for example, Go to the Web from the Internet menu—is based on the same software as the stand-alone browser. Both the integrated browser and the stand-alone browser are, in fact, two heads on a single body: Microsoft's Internet Explorer browser. This chapter focuses on the integrated browser, not the stand-alone one, but it helps to be aware of the stand-alone browser, especially since its preferences apply to both browsers.

Note *If you have MSIE 4 installed on your computer, AOL will use it as both the integrated and stand-alone browser. Otherwise, it will install MSIE 3.02 or (if your system permits) MSIE 4. I used MSIE 4 in this book, and as a result the preferences window shown in Figure 6-8 may differ from the one you see if you have MSIE 3.*

There are advantages to having two browsers. You can run both browsers at the same time if, for example, a large page or file is downloading and you want to do something else, or if you need a full-screen browser (the stand-alone version). You must be signed onto AOL to use the stand-alone Microsoft browser.

content of a document. Using HTML, the Web designer uses simple tags (like <h1> for a header or <b> for bold) to identify the parts of a document and the way they should be presented. Each browser determines how the tags will actually appear. So, while traditional magazine and book publishers have great control over how their publications look, the Web designer can't do much better than saying "this is a header" or "that bit of text should be bold." The browser determines exactly how a header appears or how bold that bit of text is. Chapter 7 goes into these matters in greater depth.

Figure 6-1 shows a page of HTML, and Figure 6-2 shows the corresponding page as the AOL browser displays it.

How does the HTML shown in Figure 6-1 turn into something as intelligible and fun as Figure 6-2? The text and images you see are tagged with little instructions that tell browsers what to display and how to display it. Your browser looks at these tags and displays text and pictures accordingly. If your browser sees a "strong" tag (<strong>), it displays text in heavy bold until it's told to turn the tag off (</strong>).

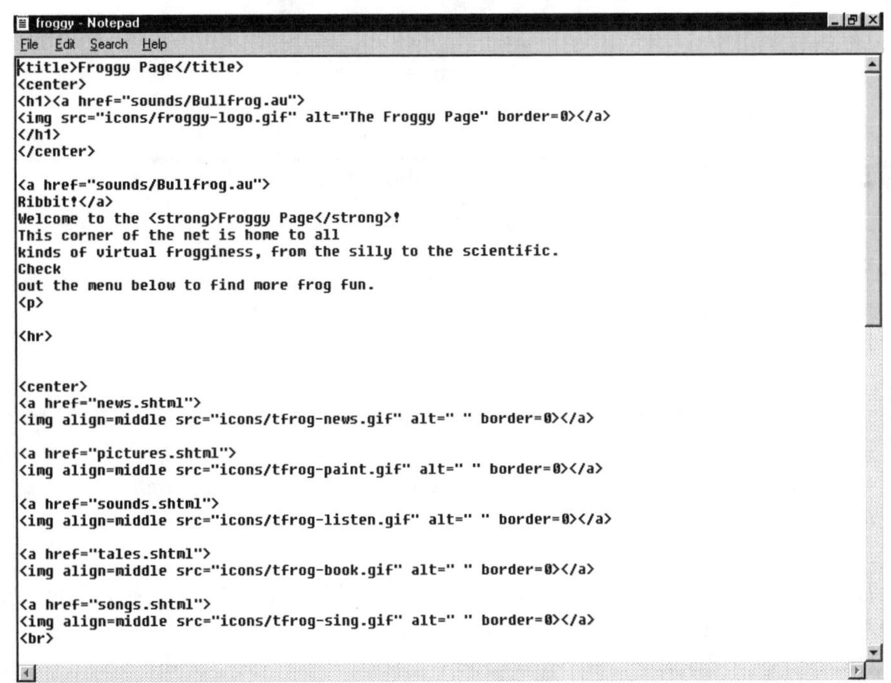


```
<title>Froggy Page</title>
<center>
<h1><a href="sounds/Bullfrog.au">
<img src="icons/froggy-logo.gif" alt="The Froggy Page" border=0></a>
</h1>
</center>

<a href="sounds/Bullfrog.au">
Ribbit!</a>
Welcome to the <strong>Froggy Page</strong>!
This corner of the net is home to all
kinds of virtual frogginess, from the silly to the scientific.
Check
out the menu below to find more frog fun.
<p>

<hr>


<center>
<a href="news.shtml">
<img align=middle src="icons/tfrog-news.gif" alt=" " border=0></a>

<a href="pictures.shtml">
<img align=middle src="icons/tfrog-paint.gif" alt=" " border=0></a>

<a href="sounds.shtml">
<img align=middle src="icons/tfrog-listen.gif" alt=" " border=0></a>

<a href="tales.shtml">
<img align=middle src="icons/tfrog-book.gif" alt=" " border=0></a>

<a href="songs.shtml">
<img align=middle src="icons/tfrog-sing.gif" alt=" " border=0></a>
<br>
```

FIGURE 6-1 Surfing the Web means fetching HTML files like this one, which your browser knows how to display

6

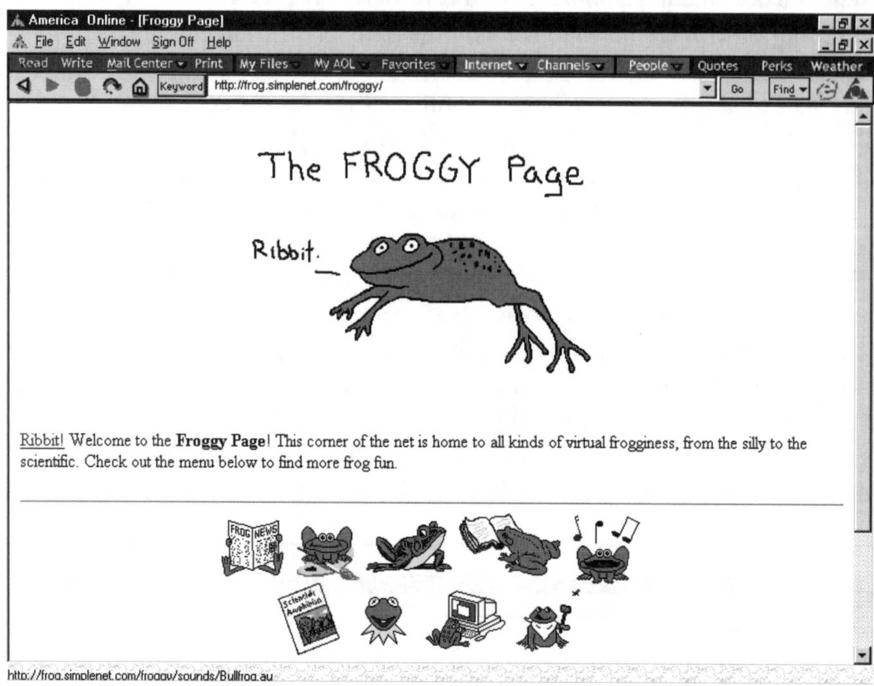

FIGURE 6-2 The Web page created by the HTML shown in Figure 6-1

If it sees a link tag, it displays some blue (or some other color) underlined text that can be clicked to request another Web page from an Internet computer. If it sees a tag for a graphic, it fetches the image and displays it *inline*. And so on.

Tip Inline *means part of the page, not displayed separately. Graphics are the most important inline elements of a Web page, but more and more you will see video, Java, and other inline files as well. The more inline elements on a page, the longer it takes to download.*

Different browsers present the same Web page differently. Netscape and Internet Explorer will take the same tag and render it slightly differently. Some tags or Web content can't be displayed by all browsers. AOL's browser, built by Microsoft, displays just about everything, and good sites are designed in such a way that if your browser can't display something, you see the next best image and usually won't be aware that something is not working.

HTML is easy to learn, and AOL makes creating your own Web pages a fill-in-the-blank process. AOL's Personal Publisher, covered in Chapter 7, creates the HTML for you automatically. If you know even a little HTML, you can then tweak your page into a thing of beauty.

A PAGE AND ITS ELEMENTS

Once, not long ago, when you viewed a Web page you got one thing: words. Then, people started adding pictures—graphics files—to brighten up their pages and to illustrate their words. In the last few years, Web designers have added a vast array of multimedia elements to enliven their creations with animations, video, and interactive features. It's worth understanding these elements, especially if you plan to create pages of your own. Knowing even a little about how pages are put together can also help you understand what to click, why certain pages are "slow," and what's going on as you browse the Web.

A Web page can consist of any or all of the following HTML elements. These are the various parts of a Web page that you see (or hear or otherwise experience), which together convey some content or message:

- Text
- Graphics
- Links
- Forms
- Tables
- Frames
- Multimedia (plug-ins, Java and ActiveX, and dynamic HTML)

Text

Thanks to its origins in academia, the Internet was built on words, and words make the Net a feast for the mind. HTML offers many ways to present *text* for maximum effect. Your AOL browser, like any good browser, can display many text effects, including:

- Several levels of headers. Like the word *Text* in this section, a header on a Web page shows you how a document is organized.

- Numbered and bulleted lists, as well as lists within lists; you're reading a bulleted list now.
- Text of different sizes, colors, and fonts.
- Emphasis such as bold and italics.
- Alignment of text (and other elements) along the right margin or the left margin or centered between the margins, both within a page or within other elements (such as tables and frames, discussed below).
- Text links (or *hyperlinks*) to other pages.

Graphics

Pictures make the Web a feast for the eyes as well as the mind. You'll encounter several types of images on the Web:

- *Backgrounds (wallpapers)* are the colors or repeating images (*tiles*) that create a certain feeling and mood, usually to reinforce the actual content or message being conveyed by the text. Backgrounds can consist of either colors or images.
- *Inline images* are graphics files that are downloaded along with any HTML pages you fetch. Since it can take a while to download and display these images and since they don't always provide a lot of information, you can choose to turn images off. See "Turn Down the Picture!"
- *Animated GIFs* look like simple movies. Each file contains several images, with each image different enough from the previous image to create the impression of simple movement (like those little picture books whose pages you flip to see Cupid shooting an arrow or Mickey Mouse running from a tornado). You'll see animated GIFs all over the Web; they're the easiest way to add movement to a Web page.
- Images can contain *links*; click the image and you're linked to another page. Hyperlinked images can take the form of an *image map*, or visual tables of contents. Click a *part* of the image and you'll go to a specific section at a site; click another part and you go to a different section. In the increasingly commercial Web, you'll see clickable banners everywhere—they're like billboards for site sponsors; click Amazon's banner at AOL.com and you're taken to Amazon.com, the Web bookseller.

- Text captured as a graphic file to create an effect, like "Froggy Page" in Figure 6-2. The new version of HTML gives designers so much additional control of text that it is less important to include GIF images of text headline. Such pages download faster as a result of their using dynamic HTML instead of inline images to create styled text.

Images add pizzazz to a page but can also slow down the time it takes to use it. AOL offers a patented technology for compressing graphics files and hence speeding up their download times. On AOL you always have the choice of turning off images altogether, though it makes the Web a less interesting place (see "Turn Down the Picture!").

Turn Down the Picture!

Browsers, including AOL's, allow you to prevent inline images from downloading in order to reduce the time it takes for the browser to present a page. These days, with faster modems, better graphics, and image-compression technologies, turning off the images isn't necessarily a good idea; you lose too much information. If you have a 14.4K or slower modem, however, you still might want to do so, as follows. Make sure you're signed on, then open the stand-alone browser by double clicking its icon (on the Windows 95 desktop or Windows 3.1 program window):

1. Select Internet Options from the View menu.
2. In the Multimedia section on the Advanced tab, make sure there's no check in the Show Pictures button. Click OK.

Note *With some versions of Microsoft Explorer, this preference can be set by using the integrated browser (My AOL | Preferences, click WWW). In the General tab's Multimedia section, remove the check from the Show Pictures box. You can also turn off videos and sounds.*

If you will be viewing Web graphics, make sure to use AOL's patented technology, which speeds up their transfer. Open up the preferences window: using the integrated browser (My AOL | Preferences) click the WWW button. In the Web Graphics tab, make sure there's a check in the "Use compressed graphics" check box. Click OK.

Links, Also Known as Hyperlinks

A link is something you click to get a Web page or other file with related content. Links are often called *hyper*links, because they make hypertext possible—the transparent linking of related information, regardless of location. Hypertext uses clickable images as well as text links, and links to any kind of file (click on the big frog picture in Figure 6-2, for example, and you link to a file that plays a "ribbit" sound). You can spot linked text because it is underlined and generally in blue.

Tip *To tell whether a word or a picture is hyperlinked, pass your mouse over the item. If it's a link, you'll see the pointed-to URL in the status bar at the bottom of your browser. Your mouse pointer (arrow) turns into a pointing finger, which means you can click the link. That's the way things work on AOL, too: try passing your mouse slowly over any tool on the toolbar—the arrow turns into a pointing finger.*

Forms

A form makes a Web page into a mini-application, as in Home Fair (**http://www.homefair.com**), an indispensable information service for anyone thinking of buying or renting a new home. Here you'll find mortgage, salary, and qualification calculators, as well as the Relocation Wizard™ shown in Figure 6-3.

Forms give you all the standard Windows features you may know from other applications: radio buttons, check boxes, entry fields, drop-down listboxes, and buttons for processing or canceling your entries. You see forms in many places on the Web: when you register to use a site to buy something, when you customize a site, and when you take a poll or enter a contest. Forms make the Web a more interactive, less static place. With forms you're giving information to a Web site, not just passively receiving it.

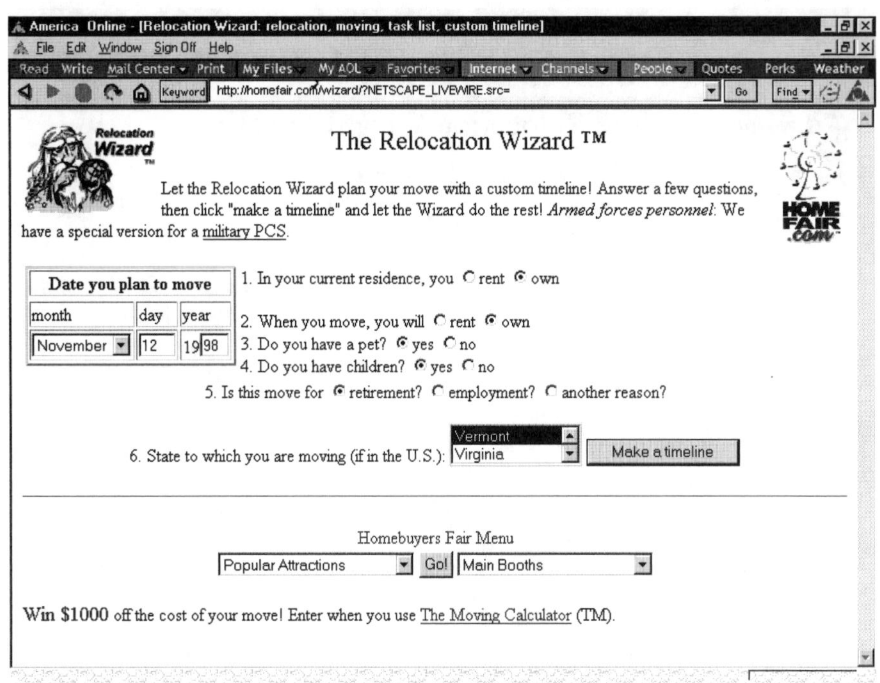

FIGURE 6-3 The Home Fair's Relocation Wizard ™ provides a *form* to gather information about a planned move, and creates a detailed custom timeline (Figure 6-4)

Tables

Tables allow for the formatting of text and images (and anything else) in rows and columns (Figure 6-4). The value of tables is best appreciated when viewing a table through a browser that doesn't support them: the text is often a mess. Probably the most common use of tables is to present text in columns of different width, magazine style. By giving designers control over margins, tables allow for shorter line lengths and text that's easier to read.

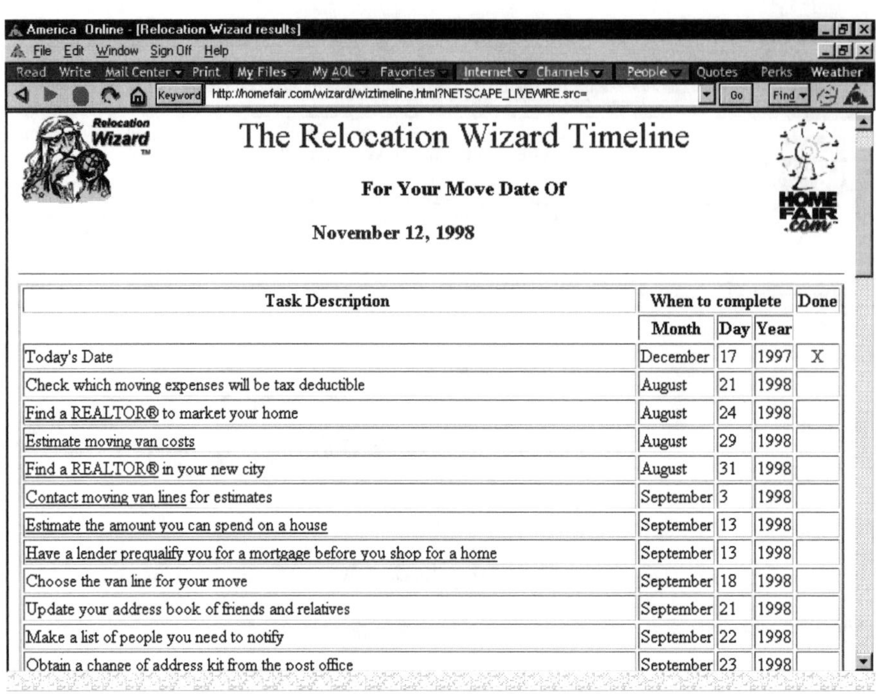

FIGURE 6-4 An HTML table that shows a timeline based on the information in Figure 6-3

Buying Things on the Web: It's Safe, with the AOL Browser

It's a short step from being about to fill out a form that supplies a Web server with personal data to filling out an *order form* with your name, address, phone number, and credit card number. More and more companies sell products and services in this way. If the products are electronic (any publication or piece of software that can be digitized and sent over the phone lines), they can be delivered as well as purchased on the Web. All other products must use the postal or overnight services.

It's safe to buy things on AOL's Shopping channel, but is it safe to buy things on the World Wide Web? The AOL browser supports an Internet security standard called Secure Sockets Layer (SSL). SSL protects your entire transaction, not just confidential data such as your credit card number. First, SSL *confirms the identity* of the company Web server from which you buy (this is called *authentication*). It also *encrypts the data* sent back and forth between you and the company Web server—scrambling the data packets so they are practically impossible to reconstruct.

As a result, you can have confidence that your transaction is safe on the Internet. *Completely* safe? No, but nothing is. Consider that very big companies such as Apple, Dell, Cisco, and of course AOL are beginning to do a considerable share of their overall business on the Internet, not to mention companies like Amazon.com and CDNow that do business *only* over the Web. Your "real-life" transactions are subject to risks such as phone tampering, lost credit cards, and mislaid credit card slips. Virtual transactions are subject to fewer risks, and technologies are getting dramatically better as companies seek better and lower-cost channels through which to sell to a greater number of customers.

Tip *At AOL.com, AOL's Web site, the Shopping Web channel links you to dozens of companies that do business on the Web, including Eddie Bauer, Lillian Vernon, Gap, Virtual Vineyard, and many others. Chapter 11 lists a few of these companies.*

There's another aspect to your security on the Web: the *confidentiality* of what you do and where you browse. See the "Cookies" text box later in this chapter for more information.

6

Frames

Netscape Communication Corp. pioneered the use of frames, which AOL's browser fully supports. A frame is a way of dividing your browser into separate windows, each capable of displaying a different page (Figure 6-5).

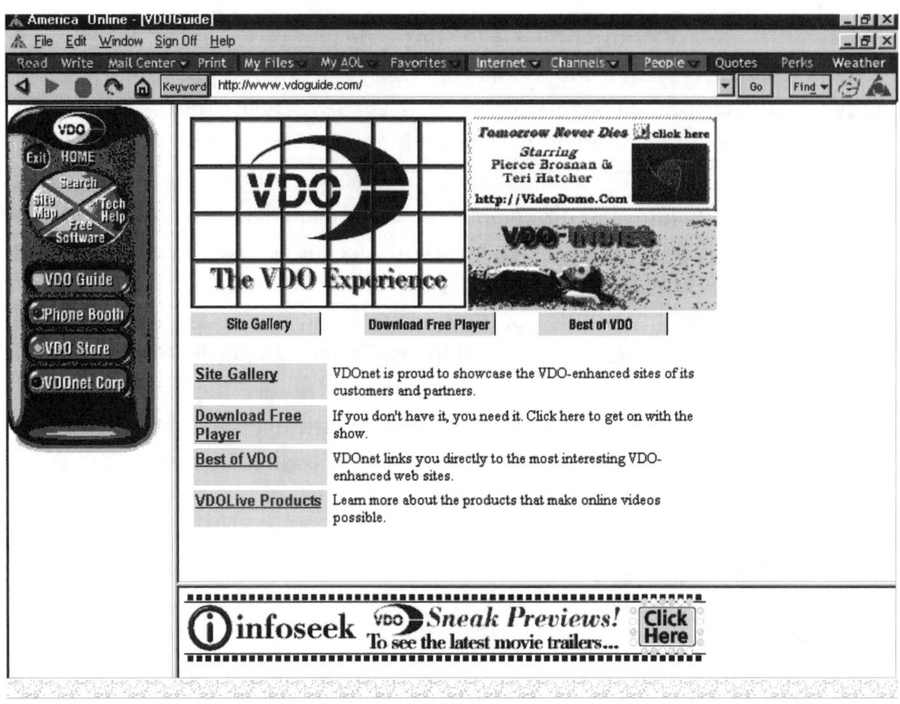

FIGURE 6-5 Frames used by VDOnet Corp., makers of "plug-in" software described later in this chapter

Why do you need frames? Sites can be complex, and pages can be long—longer at least than the vertical space available in a browser. With frames, a site's "table of contents" (navigational bar) can be made available at all times, so that it is easier to jump back and forth between different parts of a site. They can also present advertisements in such a way that the advertisement is always present in one frame even if you navigate somewhere else in another frame. Frames can also present the site's title as a constant feature, so you'll always know which site you're visiting. Some title frames remain visible even after you've left the site altogether, by linking to another site that's displayed in another frame.

Frames can take up a lot of space, sometimes leaving too little room to read the actual content; sometimes, as a result, you must resize them.

Tip *To resize a frame, slowly pass your mouse over the frame border. When the mouse cursor turns into a double arrow, click and drag the border to resize the two adjoining frames. Not all frames are resizable.*

Another problem with frames is that sometimes they don't give you an idea of your current location within a site, because they instead always display the URL for the top-level page.

Note *With the Microsoft browser that's built into AOL, you can now print the frame you want (or all frames) when you select File | Print or click the Print icon. See "Printing Web Pages" at the end of this chapter.*

Multimedia Gumdrops

You don't need any technical expertise to enjoy today's multimedia creations; pages (some pages, at least) move, change, react, interact, and make noises all by themselves. Multimedia effects are being created in three major ways (ordered from most to least intrusive):

- **Plug-ins** A Web page can play home to multimedia elements such as "streaming" sound, video, and animation. More and more of these elements play right inside the browser using a technology called "plug-ins," programs that are *automatically* summoned whenever you click certain files. Some of the powerful and cool plug-ins planned for AOL 4.0 are RealAudio (for hearing music and the latest news while you work) and Shockwave (for delivering large animations, displays, and games). The "Sights, Sounds, Moving Pictures: Working with Multimedia Files" section later in this chapter provides a compact guide to making the most of multimedia Web pages.
- **Java and ActiveX** These small programs used by a Web page to achieve a specific interactive effect usually don't require their own "player." Instead, they download when you open certain pages or click certain files. See "Java, JavaScript, and ActiveX."
- **Dynamic HTML** A new way of presenting complex effects using text and graphics *without* special software (either plug-in or Java) and *within* HTML. Designers are beginning to move away from Java, ActiveX, and even plug-ins, and toward dynamic HTML. Only version 4 of the Microsoft Internet Explorer browser fully supports dynamic HTML (Figure 6-6).

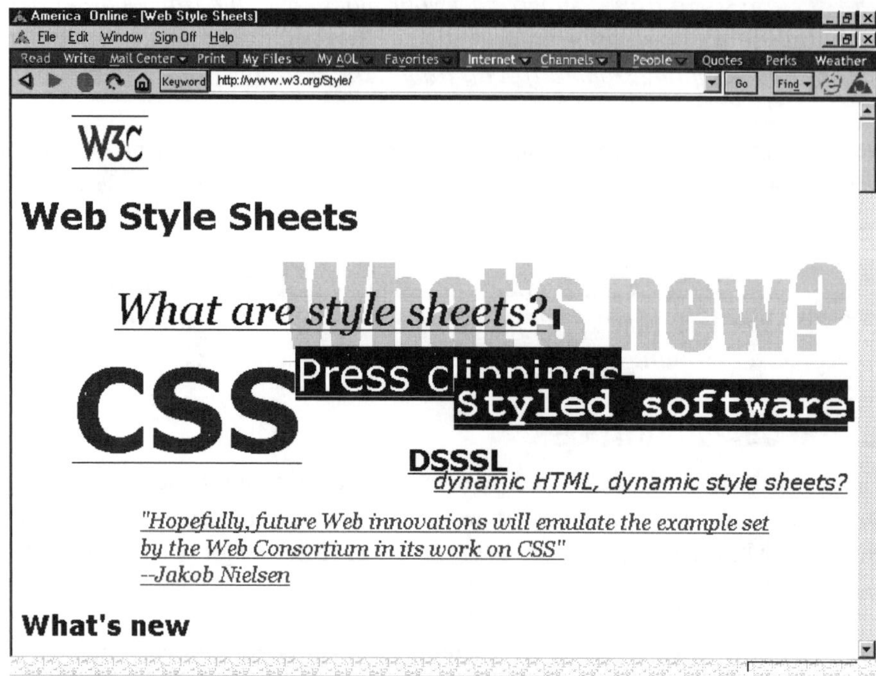

FIGURE 6-6 The latest version of HTML gives the Web publisher more precise control over how a page will look, including font types, sizes, styles, positions, and colors

For you as Web surfer, things have never looked better on the Web. The downside is that for Web developers, creating Web sites requires the thinking style and logical skills of the programmer; HTML isn't as easy as it used to be! Another downside is the continuing discrepancy between the two major browsers, Microsoft's and Netscape's. Not all the cool things you can do with one are available with the other.

Java, JavaScript, and ActiveX

The traditional Web is static: you request a page of HTML, and your browser downloads and presents it. A page just sits there till you download another page. Since around 1994, Web developers have added active and interactive elements to Web pages, but all the processing takes place at one central computer serving pages to countless people.

When you request a Web page with a Java element, you bring life to the Web experience. The experience not only becomes more interactive, but it all takes place at your computer—which is good for you (performance is better) and good for the Internet (you're not using scarce computing and networking resources).

A Java applet is a little program that downloads and plays on your computer when you click a link. These applets *do* something. They can let you simulate the Bay Area Rapid Transit system, play ping pong or Chinese checkers or snakes and ladders, view a scrolling ticker tape, or twist the parts of a 3D Rubik's cube. With Java, you can even chat across the Web. Sometimes applets open in a separate window, sometimes in a little gray box within the normal Web page. Over a modem connection, Java applets can take a couple of minutes to load and play.

You'll also encounter JavaScript, a computer scripting language that can be integrated into a page's HTML. The effect of JavaScript is less jarring than the experience of applets. Whenever you see a Web page that displays pop-up bits of balloon text when you pass your mouse over a link or an image, or that has scrolling text in the status bar, you're watching JavaScript in action. JavaScript gives the Web developer the power to create Web pages that respond to where you move your mouse and what you click.

The Gamelan Web site (http://www.gamelan.com) links to the sites that make innovative use of Java and other advanced Web technologies.

ActiveX is a technique for creating similar effects as Java but for Windows 95 only. For programmers and developers, there's a bit of religion in the choice between Java and ActiveX, but if you're a Windows user (especially if you've got Windows 95), it doesn't much matter since you can run Java and ActiveX with AOL. ActiveX "controls" are downloaded to your computer, where they present an animation, a video, or otherwise do something. The beauty of both ActiveX and Java is that neither requires special plug-in software, unlike RealAudio, Shockwave, and QuickTime. They take place within the Web page, not in a separate player or other piece of software. These little programs can, however, be very slow to download and do their thing, and AOL 4.0 for the Mac users will not be able to experience all of them.

YOUR DASHBOARD: A CLOSER LOOK AT YOUR BROWSER

The Web's the same the world over—text, pictures, and any additional elements, packaged up as HTML pages. Browsers, however, behave differently, that is, they display Web pages differently. Let's take a moment to look more closely at the AOL

browser, which sports ease of use and an AOL look, while under the hood is Microsoft's powerful Internet Explorer.

Browsers are becoming mainstream applications, like word processors and spreadsheets, with the difference that the documents they use aren't located on your own computer and could be anywhere on the globe. More and more you'll find that your Internet applications and your standard desktop applications work closely together.

Opening Your Browser

The fastest way to get from AOL to the Web is to click Go to the Web from the Welcome screen or to select Go to the Web from the Internet menu. In either case you're whisked off to AOL.com, the AOL Web site (**http://www.aol.com**), described in detail in "Your Home on the Web: AOL.com." Figure 6-7 shows the AOL Web site's opening page.

Naming of Parts

In Figure 6-7, you will notice that the integrated AOL browser is a window *within* the larger AOL window; you must be logged onto AOL to use the browser.

Tip *While you're using the browser, it's a good idea to maximize both the AOL window and the browser window by clicking their respective Maximize buttons in the upper right-hand corner. Maximizing the browser will help you see as much of a Web page as possible without scrolling. Wait until a page has downloaded before maximizing the browser.*

The integrated browser is composed of the standard windows elements (see Figure 6-7).

- The *title bar* shows the name of the Web site (picked up from its Title tag in the underlying HTML code, in case you were wondering). If the browser is maximized, the Web site's title appears in the main AOL title bar, at the very top of your screen. Until a page has completely downloaded, you see *World Wide Web* instead of the page's name.

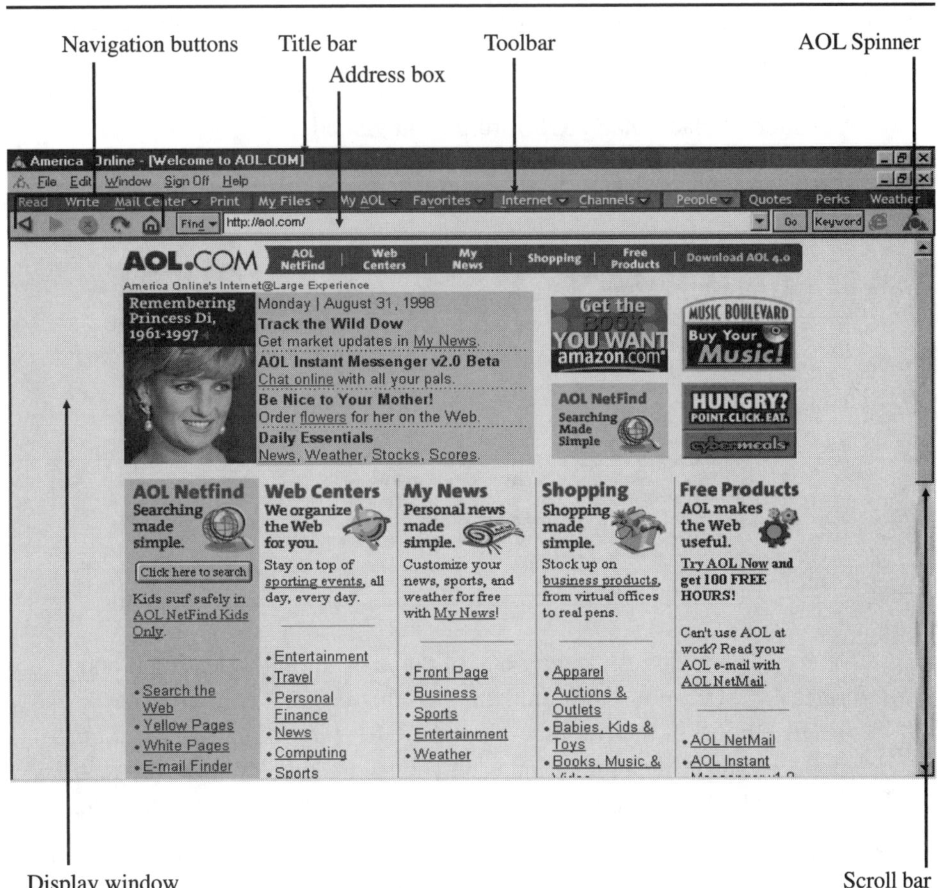

FIGURE 6-7 AOL.com is indispensable. Check back regularly to see what's new

Note *In earlier versions of AOL, the browser's navigational buttons (for going forward, backward, and so on) were part of the browser's window. With AOL 4.0 for Windows they're part of the general AOL toolbar, where one set of buttons applies to all open browsers as well as to any open AOL windows (forums, your mailbox and Buddy List, and so on).*

- The *Address box*, which displays the URL of the current Web page, is now part of the main AOL toolbar, too. Click the little downward-pointing arrow to see a drop-down list, or menu, listing your *History Trail*: the last 25 Internet places *and* AOL forums you visited.

  Here's an example:

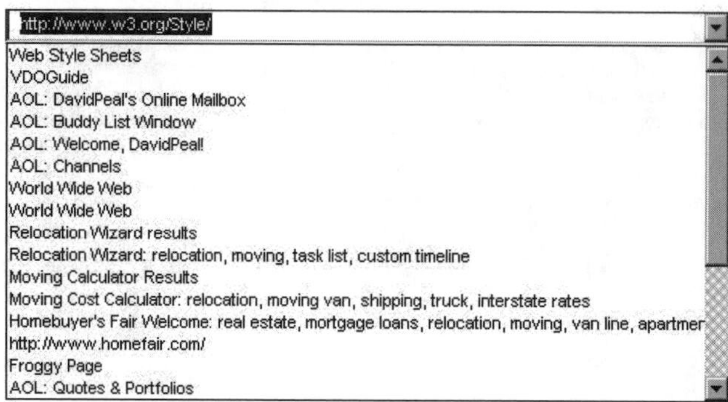

  You can jump directly to any one of those by simply selecting it and releasing your mouse button. Note that this History Trail gives the English name of the resource—not the URL (*http://*, etc.). The English name can make it easier to find what you are looking for. AOL destinations begin with *AOL:*, while Internet destinations just have the site's title.

- The five *navigation buttons* w(Table 6-1) work much as you'd expect if you've used the Microsoft Internet Explorer (or any other) browser. The Previous and Next buttons can be tricky, however; see "Going Back and Forth between Pages."

Tip *With the latest version of Microsoft Explorer, you can now move backward and forward while browsing the Web by pressing* ALT-LEFT ARROW *and* ALT-RIGHT ARROW. *Pressing* ESC *stops a page from downloading, and pressing the* F5 *key refreshes it (causes it to download again).*

What You See	Button's Name	What It Does
	Previous	AOL keeps a History Trail of the last 25 places on AOL and sites on the Internet you've visited (see "Going Back and Forth between Pages"). *Also available by right-clicking any part of the Web page (except a link), then selecting Back.*
	Next	If you've backtracked to a site (using the Previous button), Next takes you to the site from which you backtracked. You can use the drop-down list in the Address box, which displays your History Trail, to visit any site you visited recently. *Also available by right-clicking, then selecting Forward.*
	Stop	Stops a page from downloading if you change your mind, or if you make a mistake, or if it's taking too long for all of the elements of the page to arrive.
	Refresh	If a page was only partially displayed, or if it's frequently updated, or if you've changed your preferences, Refresh fetches a new copy of the same page. *Also available by right-clicking, and selecting Refresh.*
	Home	Returns you to the home page, which is AOL.com, unless you choose a different home page (see "Changing Your Home Page").

TABLE 6-1 The AOL browser's buttons and what they do

- The *spinner,* the blue AOL icon on the far right of the toolbar, no longer really spins. Instead, with AOL 4.0, it gyrates and sparkles while a Web page (or *anything* on the Internet or AOL) is downloading. It stops gyrating and sparkling when a page or AOL window is either successfully downloaded or the download got interrupted for some reason. (If it got stuck, just click the Refresh button to attempt to download it again, or try again later.)
- The largest part of the browser is the *display* window, which is where you actually look at and respond to Web pages. If a Web page is either too long or too wide to fit nicely in this window, horizontal or vertical scroll bars (or both) appear. Click the appropriate ends of the scroll bars to see content that doesn't fit. Thanks to the removal of the navigation buttons from the browser and the modifiable AOL toolbar, there is more room to view the Web in AOL 4.0.

Tip *Set your screen resolution to 800 × 600 or higher to see more of the Web (by making everything on your monitor a little smaller). In Windows 95, from Start menu | Settings, open your Control Panel, then double-click on Display. Click on the Settings tab and, in the Desktop area section, drag the lever to the right (toward More). You'll have to restart your computer for the setting to take effect.*

- Finally, there's the status bar at the bottom of the browser. Move your mouse over a link (word or image), and the URL of the page it's pointing to will appear in the left part of the status bar. The status bar also registers what's going on as the Web server is contacted, a connection is made, and the elements of a page are downloaded. You'll be notified in the status bar as each page element is downloaded, until all elements of the page have arrived and you can start clicking and browsing.

Note *Sometimes, when a page is downloading, you'll notice a series of numbers (like http://101.29.90.22) in the status bar, instead of the URL. This is the IP address, the series of numbers used by computers to route data around the world to specific computers. Behind the scenes, URLs are translated into these unique numbers. See Appendix B for more information.*

Fish and Fowl: AOL's Hybrid Browser

Across the AOL service you will encounter a customized version of the AOL browser (called a *hybrid* because it's part AOL screen and part Web browser). Hybrids are used to display Web sites specially chosen for a particular channel. In the Kids channel, for example, *all* the Web sites appear in hybrids, like this one:

Hybrids ensure the best performance, though sometimes they lack one or another of the basic AOL browser features, such as the status bar. Hybrids have been customized for a specific purpose, sometimes to display a specific Web site. Often they have their own controls for going backward, forward, stopping, and so on. Sometimes they have extra features, such as message boards and buttons pointing to related content.

Setting Your Preferences

Microsoft's Internet Explorer offers many ways to tweak your browser to your liking. Using the integrated browser, the Internet Options (preferences) window is

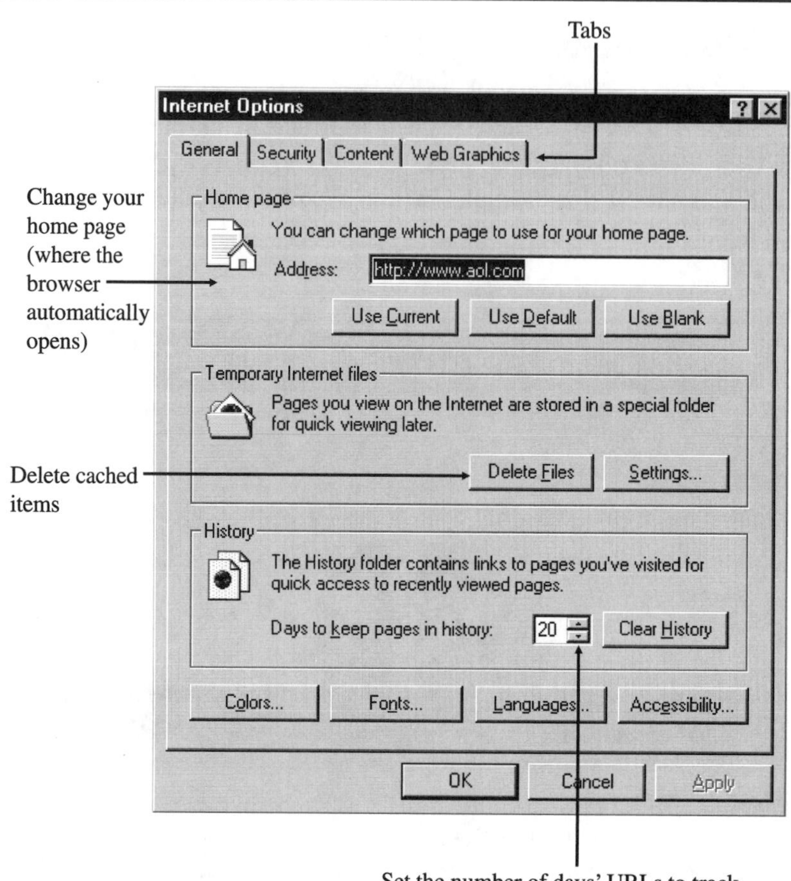

FIGURE 6-8 The Web, your way (setting your preferences)

available by selecting My AOL | Preferences and clicking WWW. Preferences are arranged in four tabs ranged along the top of the window (Figure 6-8). Click a tab to see a different set of preferences.

Note *Your exact preferences may differ from the ones shown in Figure 6-8, because preferences vary with the specific version of the Microsoft browser on which the AOL browser is based. The most important preferences (for turning off graphics, setting your home page, and adjusting your cache) are described in context in this chapter.*

Your Home on the Web: AOL.com

AOL does a lot more than select and integrate other Web sites into its service. With AOL.com, shown in Figure 6-7, AOL is creating one of the most popular and useful sites on the Web. AOL.com sets standards, selects sites, and simplifies Internet navigation. While in the past nonmembers could not view the entire site, AOL.com is now open to the world.

By now you should be familiar with the many ways of getting to AOL.com:

- Click Go to the Web on the Welcome screen.
- Select Go to the Web from the Internet menu.
- Live dangerously and type either **http://www.aol.com** (URL) or **aol.com** (keyword) directly into the Address box, and click Go.

When you first install AOL 4.0 for Windows, AOL.com is your *home page*, the page that comes up automatically when you use *keyword:* ***WWW*** or *keyword:* ***Web*** or press the toolbar's Home button.

AOL has simplified the design and vastly expanded the content of AOL.com since the first edition of this book, and like everything on the Web, you can count on continued evolution. I find the site brighter and more useful than its predecessor, and worth repeat visits. Here are some of the revamped site's outstanding features:

QUICK ACCESS TO AOL NETFIND From the opening page of AOL.com, you have direct access to AOL NetFind, the centerpiece of AOL's Web presence. This vast search engine is the focus of Chapter 9. For now, it's enough to say that AOL NetFind is the place to start whether you're looking for people or information on the Internet.

WEB CENTERS An AOL Web Center is a collection of Web sites devoted to the same subject, with a sprinkling of AOL content as well. In the Travel Web Center, for instance, you'll find "Our Favorites" (like Preview Travel and Fodor Travel Online); "Shortcuts" (quick information about cheap fares and weather around the world); "More Great Sites" (a dozen selected Web sites devoted to business travel, bargains, and tourist guides); and links to sites about different parts of the world. Web Centers don't aim to provide everything, just the best. Figure 6-9 shows part of the Travel Web Center.

NET MAIL This new service is available if you subscribe to another Internet provider (at work, for example). It provides access to e-mail from the Web

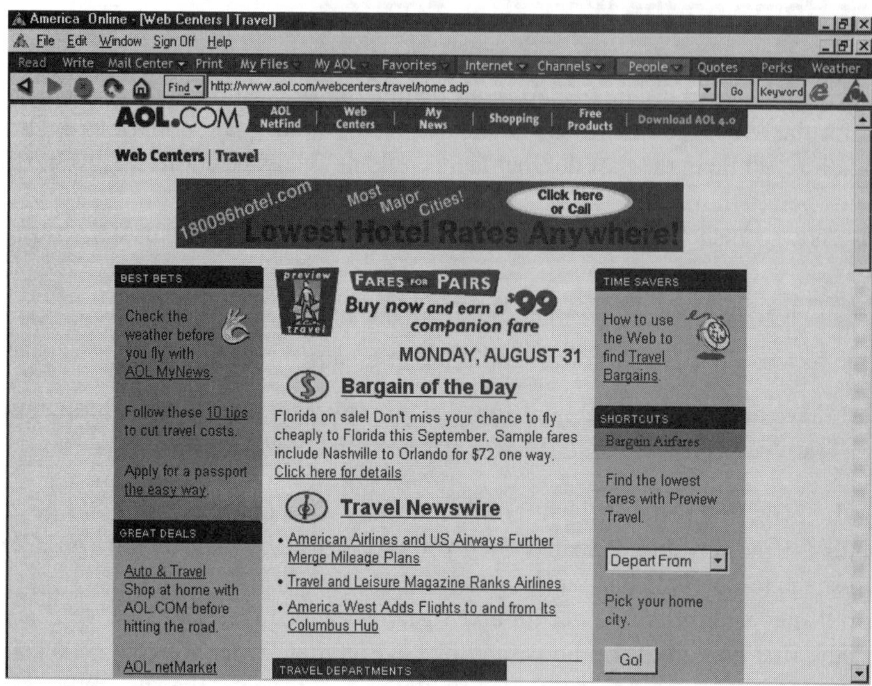

FIGURE 6-9 The Travel Web Center, the complete resource for planning your next trip

whenever you're not signed onto AOL but are using another Internet service. NetMail, a click away from the opening page of the AOL.com site, lets you send mail, read mail, reply and forward mail, and take part in your mailing lists. It won't, of course, save your messages in your Personal Filing Cabinet or provide access to your Address Book, since some features can only be provided while signed onto AOL.

MY NEWS This new service allows members and nonmembers the ability to create a custom newspaper composed of news stories about the subjects and places they care about.

AOL GOODIES As AOL's official Web site, AOL.com has some unique advantages over other sites. From the AOL Web site, for example, you can link into the service itself if you're a member; no other Web site can provide access to AOL itself. Or, you can get company information about AOL, including AOL job listings

itself if you're a member; no other Web site can provide access to AOL itself. Or, you can get company information about AOL, including AOL job listings (something else no one else offers). Throughout the Web channels you'll find the Web version of selected AOL content—providing a taste of what's available on AOL, though not a full meal. Finally, from the top page you can find out more about AOL's Instant Messenger software, which now gives people on the Net the ability to send each other Instant Messages, as described in Chapter 1.

Changing Your Home Page

A good home page is one of intrinsic interest or general usefulness—like AOL.com. It's the place from which you choose to start your wanderings on the Web and to which you can usefully return again and again. If you frequently use a search engine such as AOL NetFind, then **http://www.aol.com/netfind** is a good place to call home.

Just in case you want to use another Web site as your home page:

1. With the browser open, select Preferences from the MyAOL menu, then click WWW. The Internet Options window comes up. Open to the General tab, the first section of which is *Home page*.
2. In the Address box, type in the URL you wish to use as your home page. You can use anything under the sun: a Gopher menu or FTP directory (if you really want), a search engine such as AOL NetFind, or your company's Web site.
3. Click OK.

Tip Keyword: Web *and* keyword: WWW *both take you to your home page, whether it's the default* (***http://www.aol.com***) *or your own preference. Clicking Go to the Web from the Internet menu and Welcome screen always takes you to AOL.com. Or, of course, click the Home button on the navigation bar.*

GETTING FROM A TO B: HOW TO VISIT A WEB SITE USING AOL'S BROWSER

The comforts of home are necessarily fleeting on the Web, unable to compete with the pull of favorite haunts and the lure of new places to discover. America Online's browser gives you many ways to get to any site on the Web.

Tip *The easiest way to get from one Web site to another is to click a link. With the AOL browser you can open a link in a new browser window while keeping open the page you're linking from. To do this, right-click on the link, then select Open in New Window. Use AOL's Window menu to go back and forth between multiple open browser windows.*

Here are three ways to proceed directly to any page you please:

- Hopping with keywords or the Address box: Gives you the most freedom; even if a site doesn't have a keyword, you can type its URL into the Address box or Keyword window.
- Skipping to Favorite Places: Allows you to revisit sites you've already seen.
- Jumping after channel selections: Lets you go directly from your favorite channel to sites related to the channel's theme.

Keeping Up with New Sites

The Web is growing so fast that you cannot possibly keep up with all the latest Web sites. How do you keep up with the ones of likely interest to you? Here are a few suggestions. In general, the mailing lists devoted to the subjects of closest interest to you are probably the best source of new Web resources, since people who share your specific interests are most likely to know of new sites.

- Two mailing lists described in Chapter 4 provide good reviews of new Web resources: **Scout-Report** (for serious content) and **Yahoo!'s Picks of the Week** (for fun content).
- **Net-happenings**, Gleason Sackman's classic newsgroup (**comp.internet.net-happenings**). This is a good one to download with Automatic AOL and read at your leisure (see Appendix E for Mac/Windows procedures).

Hop with the Keyword Window or Address Box

If you know a site's URL, you can type it in the Address box or Keyword window and click Go. If you already have a page open (such as your home page, or anything else), you'll open a *new* browser window. The most popular Web sites have their own keywords, so you don't have to use the URLs. In the Keyword window or Address box (in the toolbar), you can type in **Liszt** to go directly to the great Web-based searchable directory of mailing lists, or **Slate** to read the Web's review of politics, or **Four11** to search for an e-mail address.

Tip

At keyword: Web keywords *(click Web Keywords) you get a list of keywords that take you directly to Web sites. Even better, just leave off the http:// of* any *URL entered in the Address box.*

With a browser open, you can use your mouse to select the current URL in the Address box and type a new one over it. Click Go (to the right of the Address box), and the site you've selected is contacted, downloaded, and then takes the place of the current one.

Tip

Typing in the URL box can be tricky. Click once on the URL of the currently displayed Web page, and the whole address is selected, so that typing anything replaces the entire current URL. Click again to move the typing insertion point to any specific point of the current URL, to edit it. Thus, to jump to a new site, click once on the current URL and type a new URL. To remain within the current site but move to a different part of the site, click a second time and edit the current URL (from ***http://www.aol.com/netfind*** *to* ***http://www.aol.com/*** *for example). Backing up a directory path in this way can be a good way to explore a Web site, especially if you've linked to a low-level page in a large site and need some additional context.*

6

Skip to a Favorite Place

Favorite Places give you quick access to your favorite online destinations, whether they're on AOL or the Internet. You can save any kind of content—an individual e-mail message, your personal AOL stock portfolio, your local weather forecast for your Zip code, any AOL forum, any newsgroup, and any Web site—as long as its window has a little heart on the right side of its title bar:

When you click this heart, you'll get a choice of things to do with the favorite place—insert a link in an Instant Message or mail message, or include it in your folder of Favorite Places, which is saved on your hard drive. (You can also add a Favorite Place by simultaneously pressing the CTRL-SHIFT-+ keys.)

You can also drag the heart (click on it and move it) to the Favorites button on the AOL tool bar to add it directly to Favorite Places, bypassing the e-mail/Instant Message/Favorite Places choice.

After you've saved a number of places in your Favorite Places folder, you can organize them any way you want—in any order and with as many levels as you want. To get to your Favorite Places folder, click the Favorites button in the toolbar and select Favorite Places.

The window in Figure 6-10 shows AOL's recommended favorites; you can customize them as you wish. The first 15 or so of your Favorite Places are also

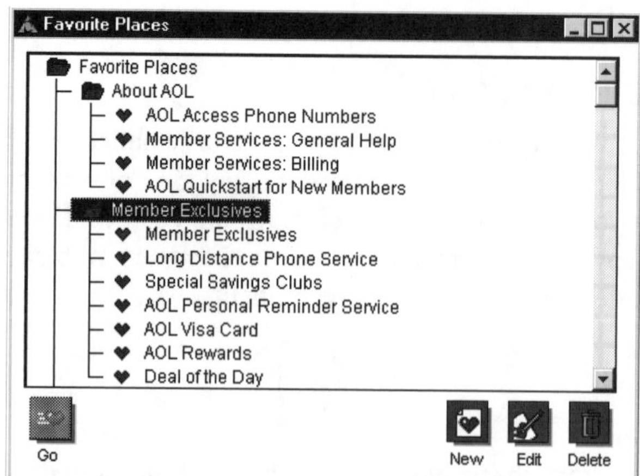

FIGURE 6-10 Your Favorite Places folder includes these links to useful places; you can add your own Web sites, newsgroups, AOL areas, and more

available directly from the Favorites menu on the toolbar; for the remainder, select More Favorites to bring up your Favorite Places folder.

- *To jump to a Favorite Place*, just open the Favorite Places folder and double-click any item. If a browser is already open, double-clicking a Favorite Place opens up a *new* browser window. On AOL you can keep as many browser windows open as you want, though the more browsers you open, the slower your computer works.
- *To create a new folder* for related Favorite Places, open Favorite Places and click the New button. In the window that comes up, click in the New Folder radio button, enter the folder's name, and click OK.

- *To move a Favorite Place into the folder*, just click and drag the item into the folder. Note that if a folder is the first item in your Favorite Places, you can't move anything before it (the thing you're moving falls into the folder), and likewise you can't add an item between adjacent folders (it drops into one folder or the other).
- *To change a folder's name*, select the folder and right-click. Select Rename, type in a new name, and click OK.
- *To change the name of a Favorite Place* (to better indicate its subject, for example, or to remind you why you put it in a particular folder), select the item and right-click. Select Rename, type in a new name, and click OK.
- *To delete a folder or Favorite Place*, select it and click Delete (or right-click and select Delete). You may find that today's favorites are tomorrow's dead wood; it's not a bad idea to prune your favorites from time to time.

Tip *If you use AOL on several machines or if you use more than one version of AOL on the same machine, each version on each machine will have a separate Favorite Places folder. On your hard drive, the actual folder is kept in a file based on your screen name (for example, dpeal for the screen name dpeal) in the America Online 4.0 /Organize folder. This file holds all your preferences, so you may want to back it up on a floppy for safekeeping, and you can also move it to a newly created /Organize folder in order to use your old preferences.*

Yet Another Way to Keep Track of Places You Like

Microsoft's Internet Explorer browser (the stand-alone version) offers an alternative to AOL's Favorite Places: a separate collection of your favorite Web sites.

- With a page displayed in AOL using the *integrated* browser, right-click and select Add to Favorites. After you confirm, the name of the page and its URL will be stored in the Favorites subfolder of your Windows folder (**c:/windows/favorites**). (In the latest version of Windows 95—available if you install Internet Explorer 4.0 separately—your favorites are directly available from the Start menu.)
- With a page displayed in the stand-alone browser, select Add to Favorites from the Favorites menu. You'll see the following window. Usually you'll just want to keep the first selection, "No, just add the page to my favorites," and click OK.

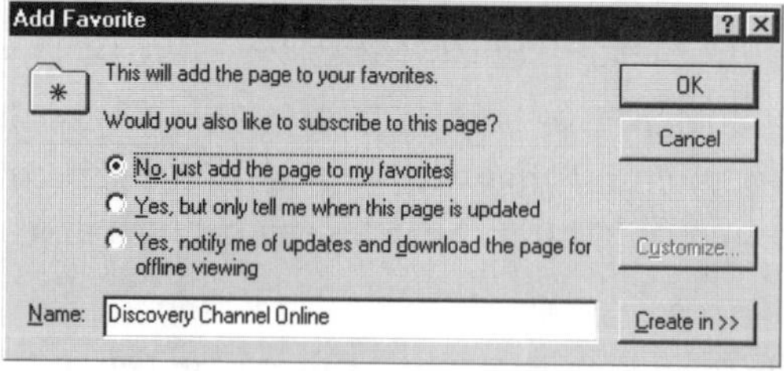

How do you use these favorites? First, you must be signed onto AOL or an ISP. Whenever you use the stand-alone Internet Explorer browser, these favorites—not

AOL's Favorite Places—are available to you by clicking Favorites on the toolbar and selecting the site. Unlike AOL's Favorite Places, Microsoft's Favorites include only Internet resources. If you use Netscape (see Chapter 10) with AOL, you will generate yet another set of favorite Internet sites, in the form of Netscape's bookmarks.

Tip *For that extra-special Web site you discover on AOL: make the site a Favorite Place, then drag it from the Favorite Places folder to your Windows 95 desktop. In the future, clicking the icon of the Favorite Place on the desktop will prompt you to sign onto AOL. Once signed on, you go directly to that Web site! You can do something similar by right-clicking on the Web site and selecting Create Shortcut, and an icon for the site will be placed on your desktop. For this to work, you must be signed onto AOL. When you double-click the shortcut icon on your desktop, it's the stand-alone Microsoft browser that comes up, not the integrated browser.*

Cookies

A cookie is a little file that a Web site creates to track your visits to the site: the pages you visited, the login or password you used, the items you placed in your "shopping cart" but didn't purchase, and so on. The marketing uses of such a file are obvious: sites get a clear idea of your browsing preferences. The positive aspects, from your perspective, are clear, too: you never have to remember your login and your custom view may present material more pertinent to your interests.

Many people consider cookies a violation of their privacy. After all, it's personal information whose use you don't sanction and can't control. The AOL browser gives you the option of being warned when a cookie file is being created and having the choice of not allowing it to be made. With the *stand-alone* browser open, select Options from the View menu. On the Advanced tab, scroll down to the Cookies section. Click in the "Warn before accepting cookies" radio button. Now, every time a site tries to create a cookie, you'll be given a choice of *not* allowing a cookie to be created for you. At *keyword: Filesearch* you can search for programs for cleaning up all the crumbs left on your hard drive by cookie files.

Leap to a Specific Web Site from an AOL Channel

All AOL channels integrate Web sites into channel content. You'll find these sites arranged in list boxes, and behind buttons in your favorite channels. In the Health channel, for example, there's a well-chosen selection of valuable Web sites at *keyword: Medical reference*:

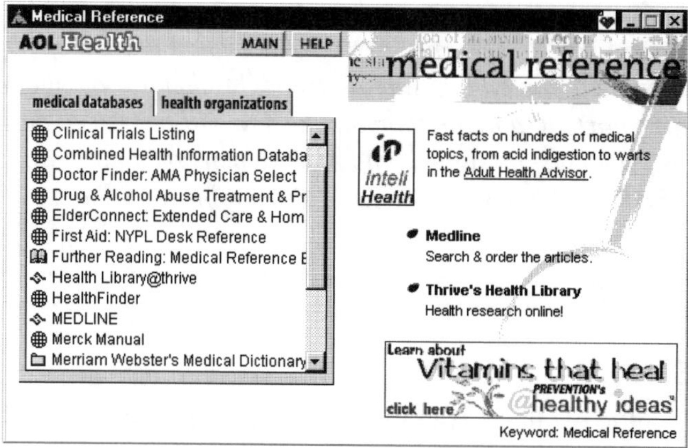

Do You Know What Your Children Are Viewing?

"If it's human, it's on the Web." This means that there may be sites, pictures, and sounds that parents might not want children to experience. AOL does not censor the Web; it *can't* censor the Web. But it does give parents two things: (1) The tools to limit what members of their household see and do on the Web (*keyword: Parental controls*). You'll find the procedures for using these controls in Appendix C. (2) A family-friendly selection of sites in the Kids Only channel and AOL.com's Kids Web channel.

MANAGING YOUR WEB SESSION

Once you start visiting Web sites, you'll invariably start visiting *other* Web sites. That's the nature of the Web and of browsing. Clicking a hyperlink—underlined text, or part of a clickable image, or image map—takes you to another page or a completely different site. With more than 100 million pages out there, the linking never stops. You can tell if something's a link if a URL appears in the status bar when you pass your mouse cursor over it or if the mouse pointer (arrow) turns into a pointing finger. At any point in any session, you can return home by clicking the Home button.

Moving Around within a Page

A Web page rarely fits within the browser window. To help you get around long or wide pages, vertical or horizontal scroll bars, or both, appear automatically when a page is too big.

Tip *The UP ARROW and DOWN ARROW keys and the PAGEUP and PAGEDOWN keys are also available to help you navigate up and down, but to use these keys you must first click anywhere on the Web page (except on a link!) and make it your active window.*

The current versions of both the Netscape browser and the stand-alone Microsoft browser (which is automatically set up for you when you install AOL) include a Find feature, allowing you to search for a specific word on a Web page. Use CTRL+F in either browser (Netscape or MSIE) to search for a word on a page. You can read about the customized Netscape browser in Chapter 10.

Managing the Slow Page

Sometimes a page can take too long to download. This can happen because it's badly built, because it's in great demand, because network traffic is too heavy, or because the page has lots of images or text or multimedia files. If you ever suspect a page has gotten stuck somewhere between the Internet and your PC, click Stop (or give the ESC key a good poke).

Sometimes the text (the part of the HTML file that downloads the fastest) will already have been downloaded, but the pictures won't have yet arrived. In this case, clicking Stop may cause just the text to appear on your screen—and it may be what you were trying to get in the first place. Sometimes, nothing will have arrived, and

your browser will be blank. If that's the case, you can click Refresh (or poke the F5 key a couple of times) to retrieve the page again.

You would also use the Refresh button if you change your preferences while displaying a page. For example, you're viewing a site with very big, very slow images, and you turn them off as explained later in Table 6-2. You'll see the picture-less page only when you refresh it.

Going Back and Forth between Pages

Using the Previous and Next buttons *seems* straightforward. "Previous" is relative to the current page, and a list of the last 25 pages (and AOL areas) you visited is available in the History Trail (click the down arrow by the Address box to see this list). The most recent items are at the top, so clicking Previous takes you *down* the list:

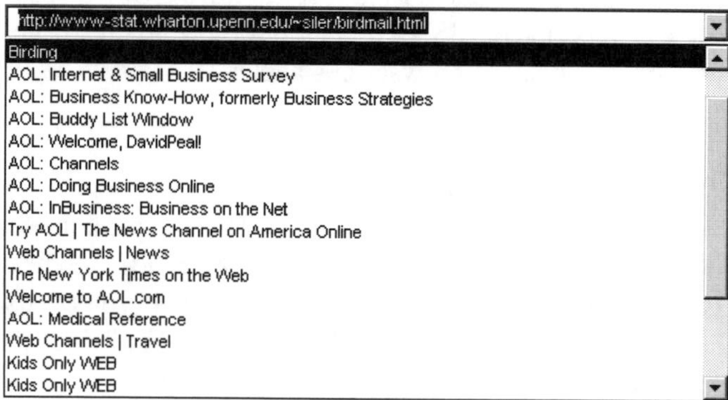

Tip

To simplify matters, you can set Next and Previous to apply to open windows only—rather than all the places you visited recently, open or not. From My AOL, select Preferences and click on Toolbar. In the Navigation section of the Toolbar preferences window, put a check mark in the "Use Previous and Next navigation arrows to track open windows only" box. Click OK.

You can jump to any of the pages on your History Trail by simply selecting it, which moves it to the top of the list. When an item is at the top of the list, there is no "forward," and clicking Previous moves you *down* the list one item at a time.

With AOL 4.0 you can determine whether your History Trail will be made up of sites from the current session only or from previous sessions. For the History Trail to apply to the current session's sites, use the Toolbar preferences (My AOL | Preferences) and put a check mark in the box that reads "Clear History Trail after Each Sign Off or Switch Screen Name."

Tip *It's a standard Windows trick to bring a window to the front of your display by clicking part of the window. Say you click a corner of a browser window in order to make the window active. The Address box will **not** display the page's title, so you may not know where you are. It is thus a good idea to bring up a Web page you viewed earlier in the current AOL session by selecting it from the History Trail rather than clicking on the page's window.*

THE 15-SECOND WEB SEARCH

Suppose you need a source of tulip bulbs, want to learn about beekeeping, or have the itch to plan an outing in Wyoming. Where do you start? Much of your experience on the Web will probably begin with a quest for specific information. The tools for

Get Cache Fast

Going forward and backward can be a lot faster than downloading a page again and again, since with AOL the pages you visit are automatically *cached*. A cache is a place on a computer where something is stored for fast retrieval. Next time you want to visit a page you've already visited, you don't have to request it again from some distant Internet computer.

AOL uses caches at two points while you're browsing the Web; one of these is under AOL's control and the other is under yours. First, copies of pages that AOL members visit are stored on AOL's computers, so that members who subsequently want to visit the same pages can download directly from the cache instead of going out to the Internet for a new copy of the page. These

caches are frequently cleared to ensure that pages are as up to date as possible. Old pages are constantly reviewed, and pages that are no longer accessed are removed.

Second, there's a cache on your hard disk that keeps track of the pages you visit most frequently during a session. Loading the page or elements of the page from the cache can be quicker than getting the whole thing off the Internet.

You can set the size of the cache on your hard disk by selecting Preferences from the My AOL menu and clicking WWW. In the AOL Internet Properties box, click the General tab. In the Temporary Internet Files section click Settings (see Figure 6-8). Now, using your mouse, slide the "lever" right or left to tell AOL how much of your hard disk to dedicate to copies of Web objects (GIFs and the like).

Your cache can eat up large gobs of your hard drive. Microsoft's (AOL's) browser gets rid of cached material frequently and automatically, but if you're short on disk space you can delete your cached files at any time. Just click Delete Files in the Temporary Internet Files section of the General tab.

The History section of the General tab works a little differently. It keeps track of the URLs you visit each day, for any number of days (from zero days to 999 days). To see and use the listing, you must use Microsoft Windows Explorer, and open up the c:\windows\history file. Signed onto AOL, you can link to any site you've visited in the last 999 (or fewer) days! Unlike your History Trail, this history list keeps track of Web sites only.

searching have improved further since this book's first edition, and changes are in store that will make for radically simpler custom-searching in the future. Chapter 9 helps you perform effective searches, regardless of where the information you need is located or how it's made available. For now, it's enough to introduce AOL NetFind, AOL's exclusive search service and perhaps the only such find-it service you'll need. In addition to helping you find stuff on the Web, AOL NetFind helps you find street addresses for people and businesses and lets you search newsgroups. AOL NetFind is always available at **http://www.aol.com/netfind**, even when you're not signed onto AOL. If you are signed on, use *keyword: Netfind.*

To go to AOL NetFind, click the Find button on the AOL toolbar and select Find It on the Web. To search for information about tulips or bees or Wyoming, enter key words such as *tulip bulbs* or *Wyoming backpacking* in the box and click Find. You can add more specific key words joined by words such as *AND* and *OR*. In general it's a good idea to conduct as specific a search as possible to avoid being swamped by tens of thousands of less-than-useful pages. NetFind makes it easy to zero in on the truly useful pages, even if your search returns a zillion pages. After NetFind has finished looking through its huge index of Internet addresses, it displays a list of pages that contain the word or words you've entered (see Figure 6-11). To visit a site from the list, just click it! Chapter 9 introduces the rapidly changing world of searching for information on the Net.

SIGHTS, SOUNDS, MOVING PICTURES: WORKING WITH MULTIMEDIA FILES

The Net's File Transfer Protocol (FTP) was once the major way to transfer software, images, and other files across the Internet. Using FTP is like navigating someone else's hard disk, finding a file, then copying it over the Net to your computer. With

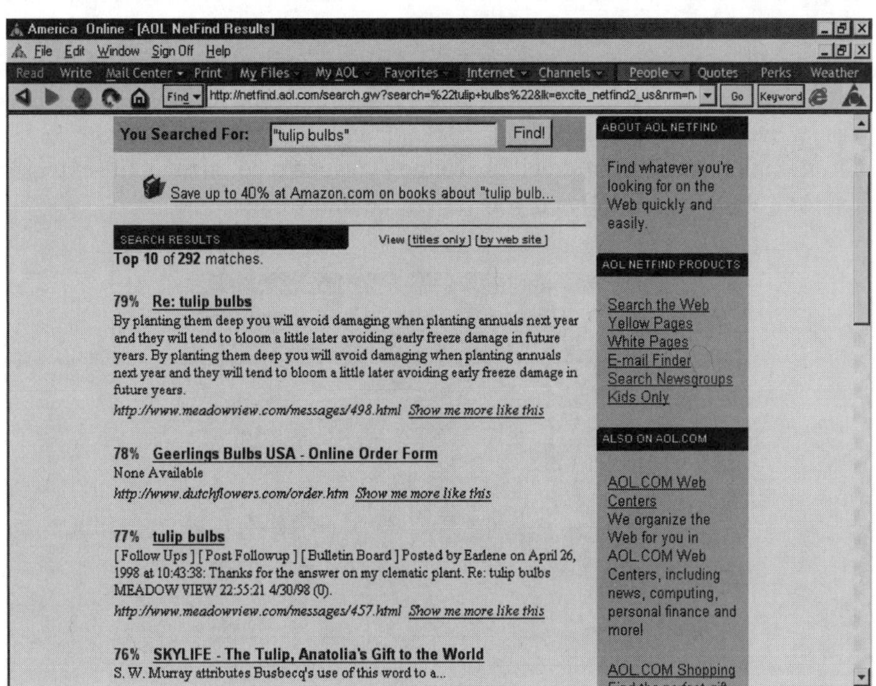

FIGURE 6-11 May I help you find something? Start with AOL NetFind...

FTP, you then have to find a word processor, or graphics viewer, or other program that can play the file. All you get with FTP is files—no context, no discussion, no links to related files.

Because of its ease of use and because you experience sounds and sights directly, the Web has now become the preferred way of delivering files over the Internet. Using your browser you experience multimedia in two ways:

- The most common image and sound files are displayed automatically by your browser.
- Other files require special players that are more or less well-integrated into Web pages, so the *content* of the files—the music, the video, whatever—is more or less smoothly integrated into the content of the Web page. All you have to do is click.

Common Multimedia Files

Some types of files can be automatically presented by your browser, a built-in Windows program, or by AOL itself. Common image files (called GIFs and JPGs) appear directly in the browser without requiring any special program. With the file displayed, you can save it on your hard disk, print it, or delete it. Table 8-1 in Chapter 8 gives an overview of common image, sound, and video files.

Click a link to a common sound file (which you can recognize by file extensions such as AU, WAV, and MID) and you'll first see this window:

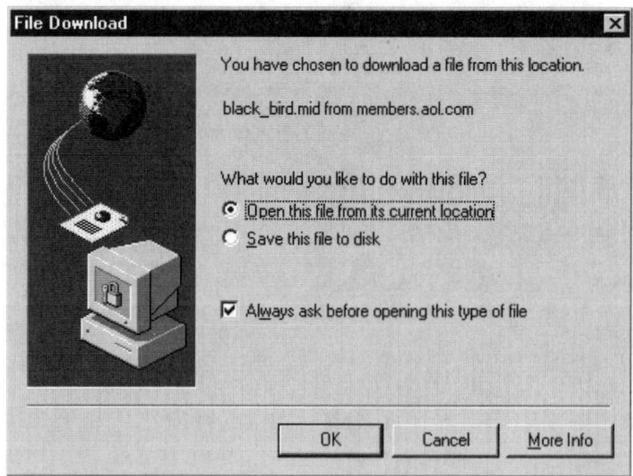

If you choose to open (play) the file, instead of saving it directly to your hard drive, you will experience it more directly. When your file's downloading, you'll see a little player, and when the file has completely downloaded you can play it by clicking the triangle (forward) button:

Likewise, you get *video files* in the same way: downloading and running them. The common video file formats are MPEG, MOV (QuickTime), and AVI. Windows' built-in Media Player can handle AVIs as well as some types of MPEG. Other types of MPEG files require special "helper" applications (see Chapter 8, and especially Table 8-2, for AOL areas where you can learn all the tricks of finding and using various types of files).

Note *Many software companies make* programs *available over the Web; this is how Microsoft and Netscape make their browsers available to the world, for example. These programs can be downloaded to your hard disk, then installed and run as separate programs. Using the AOL browser, you will be asked, when downloading such files, whether to open them or save them to disk. You'll want to save them instead of opening them (as you do with sound files). While a file is downloading, you don't have to remain parked at the Web page from which you're downloading it, but you do have to remain signed onto AOL.*

6

Uncommon Multimedia Plug-ins

More and more Web sites are delivering video and audio directly to your browser. For example, instead of MPG/MPEG and AVI video files, you are likely to find VDO and RealVideo files, which require a *plug-in* program that is smoothly integrated with your browser; click a link and the file plays by itself, thanks to plug-ins. Plug-ins also go beyond simple files in what they can do. Shockwave, for example, delivers sound, video, and animation entertainments and can create some amazing effects, as you can see at AOL's Asylum (**http://www.asylum.com**).

With AOL 4.0 for Windows, the mostly widely used plug-ins are installed for you when you install AOL: QuickTime, RealAudio, VDO, and Shockwave. Where do you find other plug-ins and more information about these plug-ins? The best place to start is at the Web sites of the companies that create them (Table 6-2). The Netscape browser (covered in Chapter 10) makes it especially easy to use plug-ins and experience 3D Web sites (VRML) and other innovations.

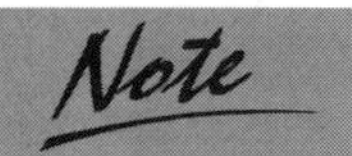

The list of plug-ins included with AOL 4.0 is subject to change.

If you ever encounter a type of plug-in that's not supported by AOL (and there are well over 100 plug-ins on the market), you will probably be given the opportunity (via a link) to download the plug-in software using the Web. Installing a plug-in is like installing any program these days: run the downloaded file, follow any prompts, and restart your computer if required.

Plug-ins of the Rich and Famous

In the future, you'll have access to a broad range of automatically installed plug-ins on both Windows 95 and Windows 3.1. Over a modem, the experience of Shockwave and RealAudio can be less than instantaneous, but the excitement of hearing music or watching a more or less live broadcast must come close to the feeling of tuning into a scratchy radio broadcast in the early days of this century. The taste of the future

Plug-in	What It Lets You Do	Where You Can Get More Information and Sample Files
Acrobat	View complex formatted non-HTML documents	*keyword: Adobe*
Macromedia Flash	Get mini-applications with interactive buttons, drawings, and cartoons	**http://www.macromedia.com/futurewave/**
QuickTime	Experience music, audio, and video	*keyword: AppleComputer*
RealAudio and RealVideo	Play "streaming" audio and video clips, get live news and music any time of the day	**http://www.real.com/**
Shockwave	Run full-screen interactive animations and games	**http://www.macromedia.com/**
VDOLive	View streaming video	**http://www.vdo.net/**

TABLE 6-2 Plugging in to the Multimedia Internet with Plug-ins

and sense of connection with other people and places is more tangible here than perhaps than anything on the Web.

Tip

*AOL's new Web site, Multimedia Showcase (**http://multimedia.aol.com**), is a good place to start if you want to have fun with RealAudio, Shockwave, Quicktime, and VDO. You'll find links to the plug-in software, plus links to all the coolest Web sites.*

RealAudio

Real Audio is currently the most satisfying plug-in because of its ease of use, its adoption by myriad sites, its relatively good sound quality, and its sheer usefulness. What's special about Real Audio is *streaming*: the sound starts playing while the file is still downloading, no matter what modem speed you're using. The Real Audio player, shown below, runs automatically whenever you click a link to a Real Audio sound. Right-click on the Real Audio player and you can pause, stop, and skip to a specific point in the sound clip.

*Yet another reason to buy the fastest modem you can afford! The AOL Store (*keyword: Bookstore*) offers a good selection at the best prices.*

The potential for integrating sound into Web content is enormous. Interviews, news commentaries, sports reporting, music—all are being delivered via RealAudio. Progressive Networks, makers of RealAudio, also offers something new called streaming video (called RealVideo, of course), which works the same way. Both audio and video can be played through the RealPlayer, which you get automatically when you install AOL 4.0.

Unlike other plug-ins, the RealPlayer gives you links from the player itself to dozens of news, business, entertainment, and other resources. You can also create a set of custom buttons (like a programmable TV), so you can hear the news you want from sources like Fox News, BBC World Service, and National Public Radio.

From the Progressive Networks site (**http://www.real.com**) you can also get to directory services such as WebActive, an extensive collection of RealAudio content related to social causes (**http://www.webactive.com/**), and TimeCast (**http://www.timecast.com**), a *TV Guide*-style directory of RealMedia sites. For music, you'll find numerous RealAudio sound clips at LiveConcerts (**http://www.liveconcerts.com**) and CDNow (**http://www.cdnow.com**). Finally, AudioNet (**http://www.audionet.com**) offers a broad selection of high-quality links for you to enjoy. And here's a final tip: once the RealAudio player's running, it maintains a link to the server, so you can do something else and play RealAudio in the background. Using RealAudio is like having the radio on while you're using at your computer.

VDO

What RealAudio does for sound, VDO does for video: compressed images, streaming, and about a dozen frames per second, all presented in its own player, with its own controls. This clip, produced by the France 3 television network, shows a newscaster delivering a breaking story about a big snowfall in central France (VDOnet Corp. has made a strong effort to assemble international content):

The plug-in is not in broad use yet, but some pioneering sites such as the Nightly Business Report have put VDO to good use. These sites and others are available from AOL's Multimedia Showcase (**http://multimedia.aol.com/external/vdoliveg.htm**) and from VDOLive's own Gallery (**http://www.vdoguide.com**).

Shockwave

The coolest plug-in, Shockwave, comes from San Francisco-based Macromedia. When you click a Shockwave file, the Director program is launched automatically and plays interactive animations, with sound. Figure 6-12 shows a Shockwave application you can use to happily squander what's left of your free time.

Links to "shocked" pages are available in the Shockwave gallery at AOL's Multimedia Showcase (**http://multimedia.aol.com/external/dshckg.htm**), as well as Macromedia's own "shockzone" (**http://www.macromedia.com/shockwave/epicenter/**).

Adobe Acrobat

"Cool" it's not, but it's probably the most useful plug-in on the Net. Adobe Acrobat gives you access to highly formatted documents that don't lend themselves to

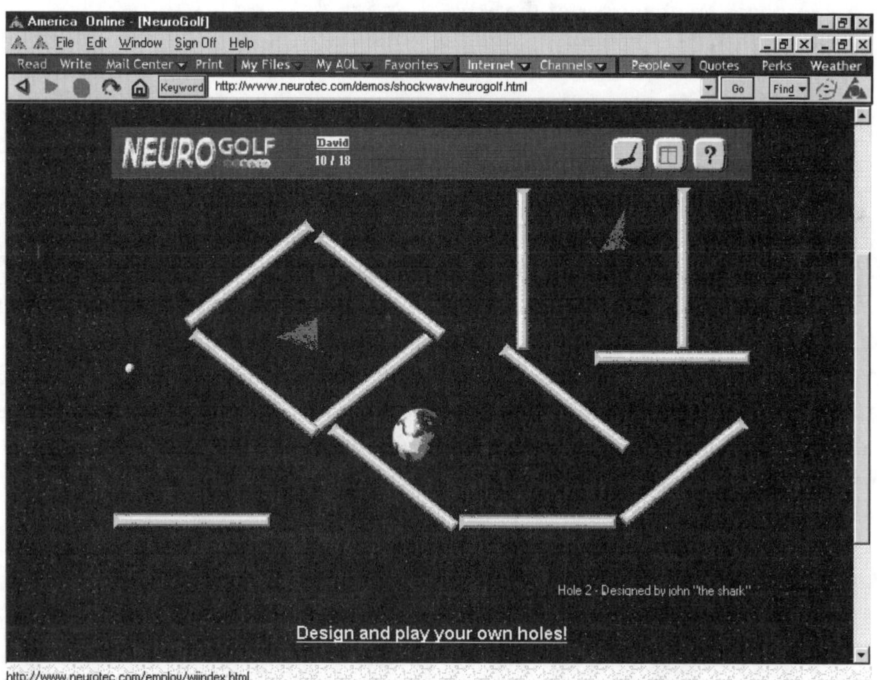

FIGURE 6-12 A Shockwave golf game designed to burn away those early-morning hours

formatting in HTML. Usually these documents begin life as print documents: newsletters, newspapers, policy statements or white papers, and the like. The Adobe plug-in gives people on different computer platforms (Mac, Windows, etc.) access to attractively formatted documents without requiring use of any word processor. You can recognize Acrobat files by their extension (PDF, for portable document format). Clicking a link to a PDF file opens the plug-in, downloads the file, and presents the document. You won't be able to edit or alter the document, but you will be able to print it.

YOUR ALL-PURPOSE BROWSER

Links beginning *http://...* (Web pages) aren't the only ones you can use with the AOL browser. In fact, the Web was originally designed to create a uniform way of viewing diverse information, not just (or even primarily) Web pages. With your browser you can access:

- Gopher, the precursor of the Web
- FTP, thousands of sites with millions of files to download
- Newsgroups, public, global bulletin boards
- Telnet: Use the computing resources of a remote Internet computer

When you visit a Gopher or FTP site, everything takes place within the browser window; you use the browser's controls to get around. However, when you read a newsgroup, send a mail message, and access a library catalog via Telnet, everything takes place in a separate application window, and you must use the controls of these separate applications; there's no Previous or Stop button. The trend in the next few years will be to integrate more and more in the browser, but for now it's good to get used to a mix: some Internet services are directly supported by the browser; others launch a separate program.

Gopher's Swan Song

In 1991, after the Web was invented but before it became hugely popular, Mark McCahill and others at the University of Minnesota invented Gopher. This tool had a similar purpose to the Web—to provide easy access to different types of information located around the globe. However, while the Web used hypertext as the model for how to find and link information, Gopher used simple menus to provide access (Figure 6-13).

A *menu* is just a list. Click a menu item and you either go to another menu (directory) or to actual content (a text file, usually). While the Web integrates text, sounds, and video into a new type of publication, Gopher was designed and is still used mostly as a way of accessing information one file at a time, particularly textual information such as statistics, government reports, books, magazines, current temperatures, earthquake reports, and the like.

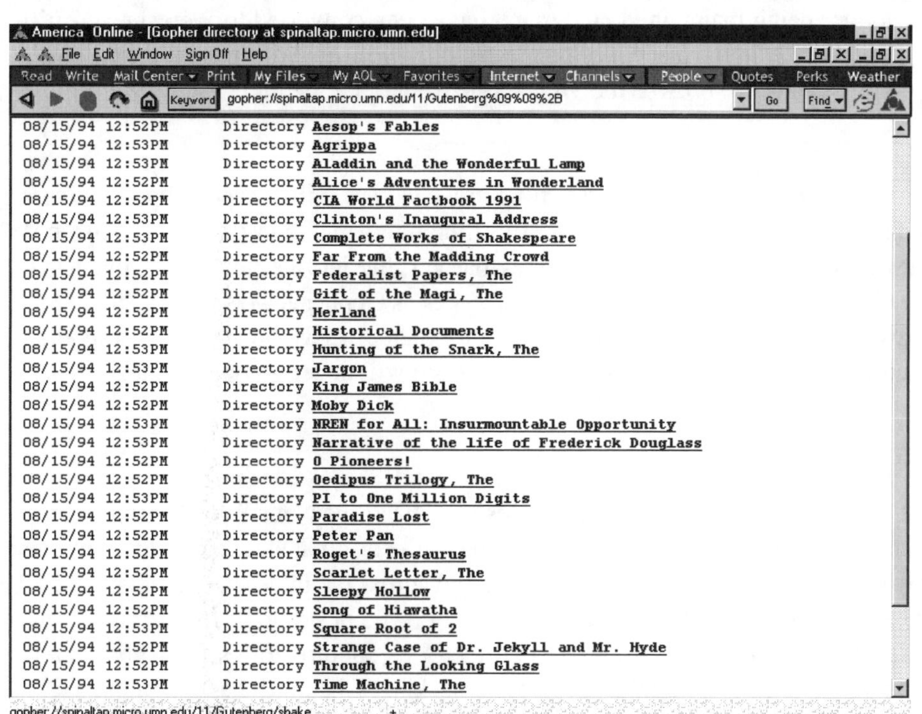

FIGURE 6-13 Gopher via the AOL browser. The Gutenberg Project has published electronic versions of hundreds of classics in the public domain

Gopher It on the Web

Going to a Gopher site is easy when you use the AOL browser. Just enter the full URL, beginning *gopher://,* in the keyword window. For instance, **gopher://spinaltap.micro.umn.edu** takes you to a big collection of public domain books, reference works, and classics available at Gopher's birthplace, the University of Minnesota (Figure 6-13).

Gopher URLs, like all URLs, have several parts separated by periods. On AOL, at *keyword: Gopher*, you will find a list of Gopher Treasures that provide access to goodies ranging from the Congressional Record to 35 years of speeches by Fidel Castro. Be forewarned, however, that many Gophers are no longer being maintained, and many have been converted to Web sites. You'll find increasingly that Gopher menus point you to Web pages, from which you're likely to browse the Web and leave Gopher behind.

In 1994-95, information was still published via Gopher, especially on university campuses; the NIH Gopher served 1 million files a month in 1995. But soon the Web absorbed all of the energy and resources that had gone into the creation and maintenance of Gopher sites. Today, even such classic sites as Gopher Jewels and the NIH Gopher have been retired. If you have serious information needs, however, it's important to know about Gopher, since some of its treasure will never go out of date.

File This: FTP on the Web

In contrast to Gopher, transferring files with FTP (the Net's File Transfer Protocol) remains a fundamental part of the Internet—the original and still significant means by which files are stored on and transmitted across the Internet. When you use FTP, you log onto a distant computer in search of a file or group of files. You search for files in directories, going in and out of directories, subdirectories, sub-subdirectories, and so on, until you find the files you're seeking. Chapter 8 has the full story.

With AOL's browser, you can visit any FTP site by entering its full URL into the Keyword window or the Address box. An FTP site's URL consists of *ftp://* plus the domain name, for example, **ftp://ftp.aol.com**. Using the browser to access FTP is an alternative to using AOL's FTP gateway at *keyword: FTP*. Chapter 8 makes a case for the browser being a better way to search FTP than to actually download files from an FTP site. For that, go to *keyword: FTP*.

E-Mail and Newsgroups over the Web

Some Web sites link to newsgroups. Clicking such a link brings up AOL's Newsgroup area with the specific newsgroup displayed (Chapter 5 is all about newsgroups).

The URL for a newsgroup is *news:* (without the forward slashes) and the name of the newsgroup. If you know a newsgroup name, such as **comp.internet.net-happenings**, you can type **news:comp.internet.net-happenings** directly into the Address box or Keyword window and click Go.

Some Web sites have hyperlinks that, when you click them, allow you to send an e-mail message to someone (the Webmaster, or person who runs the site, for example). Clicking such a link on AOL calls up the Write Mail window and inserts an e-mail address (for the Webmaster or whomever) into the Send To window. Finish the message by supplying a Subject line and writing the message, then clicking Send Now. You will return to the Web site (actually you never left the page from which you linked to the Write Mail window) so you can continue to browse.

Telnet

Telnet lets you log onto and use remote computer resources. Just as FTP gives you access to a remote computer's *hard disk*, Telnet gives you access to the *actual computer,* where you can run programs that reside on that computer. You use Telnet to access a university account where you might have an e-mail account, to search through a library card catalog, to play role-playing games such as MUDs and MOOs, to use community networks (Free-nets), and to use information databases of many types. Using the AOL browser you automatically get Telnet access: click a link and you're transported to the Telnet site.

A Telnet link on a Web page begins **telnet://**. That's what you see in the status bar when your mouse passes over a Telnet link. To go to the actual Telnet resource, just click. Note that you will usually need a log-in and a password to use the site, and finding out those things can take some effort. One site from which hundreds of Telnet sites are available is Hytelnet (**http://library.usask.ca/hytelnet**). With the Hytelnet Web site, you'll find log-in and password information for many Telnet sites, as well as loads of information about using Telnet. Another Web site that links you to hundreds of simulated environments available via Telnet is MudConnector (**http://www.mudconnect.com**). For more on Hytelnet and MudConnector, see Chapter 10.

SAVING WEB PAGES

In the world of old-fashioned computing, "saving" meant keeping a copy of something (a program, a word processing document, an image file, or any file) for yourself, on your own hard disk, for later use or archival purposes. On the Web, *saving* a page has a broader meaning and can refer to one of three things:

- Saving a *link* to the page with Favorite Places
- Saving the page's underlying *HTML*
- Saving content—some or all of the text or multimedia elements

Saving a Link to the Page with Favorite Places

With Favorite Places, you can save *links* to the places you like. Instead of saving the actual Web page, you're saving the URL and title of the page, thus making it as easy as possible to return there. In addition to Favorite Places, you can save a link as a favorite using the stand-alone browser. See "Skip to a Favorite Place" earlier in this chapter.

Saving a Page's Underlying HTML

You've seen what HTML is all about ("How Is That Page Put Together? HTML," at the start of this chapter). Why would you want to save the HTML file such as the one shown in Figure 6-1? Simply put, it's an excellent way to learn HTML, especially the fancier extensions to basic HTML such as Cascading Style Sheets.

To save a page's HTML:

1. Display the page. Right-click and select View Source. From the File menu, select Save As. Make sure the extension is TXT.

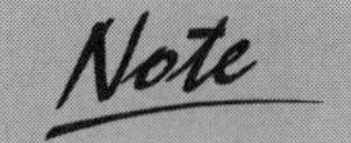

If there are any inline graphics, they won't be saved, since they're not actually part of the HTML file. See "Saving a Page's Elements."

2. To look at the text file with the HTML script, open it up in any text editor or word processor, or in the editor built into AOL (select the file using File | Open).

Saving a Page's Elements

More interested in the text or the art than the HTML tags? You can save part of the text of a Web page by simply selecting it with your mouse and using the copy (CTRL-C) and paste (CTRL-V) functions. To select *all* the text on a page, right-click and choose Select All. Copy (CTRL-C) the selected text, paste (CTRL-V) it into a new document in a word processor, and save it.

Note *To save an inline image, move your mouse over it, click the right mouse button, select Save Picture As, then give the image a filename and find a folder in which to save it.*

PRINTING WEB PAGES

Printing's a snap with AOL's Web browser, and AOL 4.0 offers some new capabilities. With a page displayed, just click the Print icon on the toolbar at the top of your display. Of course, you'll need a printer with paper, and the printer must be plugged in and properly set up. Graphics will print, as well as text. Note that you can't print a page until all its elements have downloaded.

Tip *With AOL 4.0, you can now print background images and patterns. Using the stand-alone browser (the Internet icon on your Windows desktop), select Internet Options from the View menu. In the Advanced tab, scroll down to the Printing section and make sure there's a check mark in the "Print background colors and images" box.*

To print an HTML file, just open it and either click the Print icon or select File | Print. You'll see the Print dialog box shown in Figure 6-14:

If you are printing a Web site with frames, the Print frames section offers the following choices:

As laid out on screen	What you see is what you print. For example, a framed page with static logo and navigational bar will print showing these elements, plus any content, just as they appear in the entire browser display.
Only the selected frame	With this option, only the one, selected frame prints. (To select a new frame, just click it.) A good way to print just the content and not the navigational elements or the ads.
All frames individually	Prints each frame on a separate page.

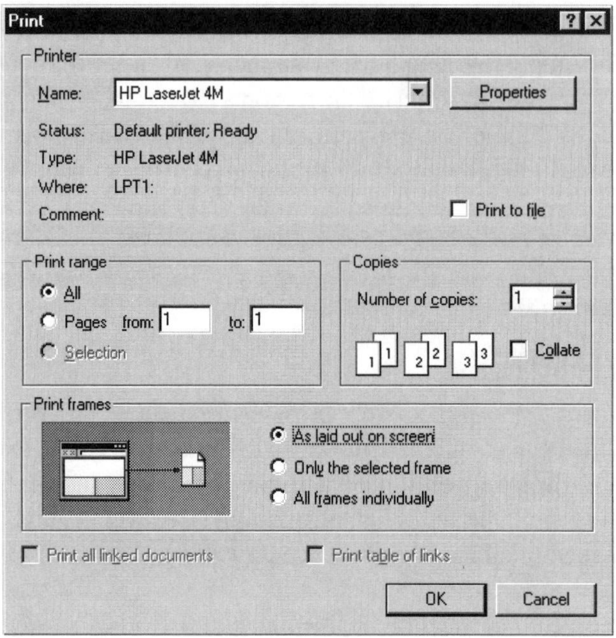

FIGURE 6-14 You can now print individual frames and tables of links

At the bottom of the Print dialog box are two check boxes available whenever you print a Web site, regardless of whether it uses frames. Choose either or both:

Print all linked documents	Every page linked-to will be printed in turn. A "tree killing" option, but if you're designing a Web site, a good way to ensure the appropriateness of your links.
Print table of links	An extremely useful compact table containing the URLs and titles of all places to which a Web page is pointing.

WHEN THINGS DON'T WORK

It is a miracle the Web works as well as it does. It's also a miracle how much better the Web experience gets from month to month. Still, things go wrong. Some sites won't be available, and you will encounter the occasional dreaded message:

Cannot retrieve http://134.84.105.26/Cookbook/

or

File not found

or

404-File Not Found

What happened? Perhaps you've mistyped the URL (which is easy with all those complex names) or the site is not available because it has changed its URL, or it has literally gone away, or too many people want to see it right now and the server is busy, or the server is down for maintenance, or someone tripped over the plug. For another type of problem, there is no solution: not all browsers support all HTML and multimedia effects. Whenever you see a JavaScript "error" or a blank (or "broken") element on a page, it is likely that the browser does not yet support some fancy new technology (or the technology is badly implemented at the site). Notwithstanding such nuisances, it's amazing that the HTML-based Web remains as open and as accessible as it is!

Note *Sites will never be unavailable because AOL is censoring them. If you're ever unable to visit a site, it is not because AOL is blocking it. If, however, you want to block sites (from your kids, say), you can use filtering software such as the packages mentioned in Appendix C.*

So, if things go awry, try again, checking your spelling, punctuation, and capitalization (just like in school). If that doesn't work, try again later.

Tip *At* keyword: Help, *click Error Messages, then Internet Error Messages, then Internet Error Messages, for a great list of all Web errors and what to do about them.*

Reality Check: Are You Ready for the Web?

When you open the integrated AOL browser, you are revving up a powerful piece of software that demands its share of your system's memory and processing power. Once you start surfing, Java applets, Shockwave programs, and multimedia files can be S-L-O-W to download, especially with an older modem.

Using AOL forums and Web pages at the same time can be frustrating. Until a page has downloaded, the browser may want to be front and center in your display (or at least will slow everything down). Unless you have a really fast computer and lots of memory, it can be difficult to run the browser in the background while you're doing something else.

The moral is, if you're thinking of upgrading your PC or buying a new one, get the most powerful chip, the most RAM, and quickest hard disk, and the fastest modem you can afford. You don't need this hardware to use AOL, but you will get more out of the Internet (the Web, at least) if you do. Of all these items, a modem is perhaps the easiest and cheapest to upgrade, and at *keyword: AOLstore* (click Modems) you can shop for a new one.

FROM HERE...

This chapter covered a lot of ground, but so does the Web! The best way to get comfortable with the Web is to start browsing. It's easy, fun, fairly intuitive, and you can't break anything. You can get tangled up in it, but it will never tear. The AOL Web site is a good place to start exploring. The next chapter shows you how to create your own Web page using AOL's Personal Publisher.

Chapter 7

Publishing on the Web with Personal Publisher

America Online's Personal Publisher provides everything you need to create, publish, and refine a single Web page or an entire Web site. Publishing for the world does not get any easier.

Why would you want to create a Web page?

- If you own a small business, you could probably benefit from your own Web presence. The tens of thousands of American businesses with Web sites range from the smallest one-person outfits to giants like Dell and Apple. Some businesses, like the bookseller Amazon.com, exist only on the Web (see the "Shopping" section of Chapter 11).
- If you have a large and wired family and want to post the latest batch of pictures for everyone to see, a Web page may be the easiest way to stay in touch with loved ones.
- If you're a parent, you can help your kids share an interest or hobby with other kids.
- If you want to promote your church or community association or need to keep others informed of group gossip and events, a Web page may be just the ticket.
- If you recently bicycled cross-country, why not share your adventures, pictures, and links with the world?
- If you breed hybrid tulips or raise cocker spaniels, a Web page may be the best way to display your expertise and discover exactly who in the world shares your specific passion.

Tip *For large, professional, and commercial sites, AOL also offers a Web-hosting service called PrimeHost, described later in the section called "In Business? Let PrimeHost Maintain Your Site."*

A Web page consists merely of a simple text (ASCII) file saved in a format called HTML (Hypertext Markup Language). (See "How Is that Page Put Together? HTML" in Chapter 6.) In the last chapter, Figure 6-1 shows a page of HTML consisting of text (the words you see on a Web page) and tags (the formatting—such as <b> for bold and <i> for italics—applied to the words you see when you browse the Web). Your browser's job is to turn tags into an informative and attractive page, with live links to other pages as shown in Figure 6-2. In this chapter, you'll learn to create a Web page that anyone on the Internet can visit. Using AOL's Personal Publisher, the HTML is generated automatically for you. All you have to think about is what you want to say and show.

Let's begin with a discussion of My Place, the free disk space AOL makes available on its computers to every member. When you use Personal Publisher, you're using My Place. Even when you're not using Personal Publisher you can use this free disk space to make files available to others. Next, you'll learn the nuts and bolts of Personal Publisher, a simple but very capable tool for making a Web page or Web site. If you used Personal Publisher with AOL 3.0, you'll want to read these sections closely, since the new Personal Publisher adds many features. Then you'll find out how to refine Personal Publisher pages using both Personal Publisher and an HTML editor, such as AOLPress.

THREE WAYS TO MAKE A WEB PAGE

On America Online you basically have three ways to create a Web page:

- By hand, using a text editor such as Windows Notepad.
- Using an HTML visual editor such as AOLPress. An HTML editor is like a point-and-click word processor used to make Web pages instead of ordinary documents.
- Using Personal Publisher, which focuses on the content you want to convey and not the HTML methods to convey it (these are automatically handled for you). Pages created with Personal Publisher can be refined using an HTML editor.

Making Web Pages by Hand

Many Web pages are created with nothing more than Windows Notepad, the program included with every version of Windows. On the Mac, many Web creators use BBedit. In fact, you can create an HTML file with *any* text editor or word processor, then upload it to My Place or another Internet computer to which other people have access (see "Publishing and Maintaining Your Web Pages in My Place"). Because of the intensely visual nature of the Web, it's becoming more and more important to use an HTML editor so you can see what you're doing, as described in the next section.

Using an HTML Editor

A much easier way to make a Web page is to use an HTML editor, many of which are available at *keyword: Software* (open the Internet folder). Popular commercial HTML editors include Microsoft FrontPage, Adobe PageMill, and AOL's own AOLPress (see "Editing Your Page with AOLPress"). These graphical tools work in much the same way as your word processor. You simply type in the text, highlight it with your mouse, and apply formatting effects by clicking buttons on a toolbar or selecting items from a menu. The editing tools create the HTML tags for you, make sure they're correct, and usually let you view the results as others will see them *before* you actually publish your page. Such software makes it possible to generate a page using visual methods such as menus and buttons, but you still need to know HTML to use the tools effectively.

Point and Click with Personal Publisher

The easiest way to make a Web page on America Online is with AOL's Personal Publisher, a complete publishing solution that allows you to create and edit pages, as well as make them available for people on the Internet to see. The next few sections look at My Place, the publishing area on AOL's computers that makes Personal Publisher possible. The heart of this chapter is devoted to Personal Publisher (see "Using Personal Publisher").

Tip *With the new version of Personal Publisher, unlike the previous version, you can make a page with an HTML editor and edit with Personal Publisher. You can also make one with Personal Publisher and edit it with AOLPress or another HTML editor.*

PUBLISHING AND MAINTAINING YOUR WEB PAGES IN MY PLACE

My Place is the free Internet-accessible disk space available to every AOL member. Each AOL screen name automatically receives 2 Mb of storage space on an AOL computer called **members.aol.com**, in a directory called */screen name* (for example, **members.aol.com/stevecase**). Since every Master Account can have four additional screen names, that makes a total of 10 Mb per account. With this much disk space to store your files, you can create an awesome multimedia Web site.

Tip *With My Place you can publish any Web page, whether you've made it with Personal Publisher, with an HTML editor, or by hand. You can also use My Place to share files with people. Many AOL members create and publish Web sites in My Place without even using Personal Publisher. If you'll be using Personal Publisher and not editing your pages extensively with other tools, you probably won't have to make much direct use of My Place, and you can now skip to "Using Personal Publisher."*

To use My Place, go to *keyword: My Place*. You will see the My Place window (Figure 7-1), from which you get access to both Personal Publisher and My Place.

Click My FTP Space to use the 2 Mb of disk space for your screen name (Figure 7-2). If you'll be using this area often, you might want to save it as a Favorite Place by clicking the heart in the title bar. Now My Place will be available in your Favorite Places folder, available from the Favorites menu.

My Place is based on something called *File Transfer Protocol* (*FTP*), for many years the most important way to store and copy files on the Internet. (Chapter 8 offers a complete introduction to FTP.) While you ordinarily use FTP to *download* (retrieve) files from public FTP sites, My Place is mostly used for *uploading*

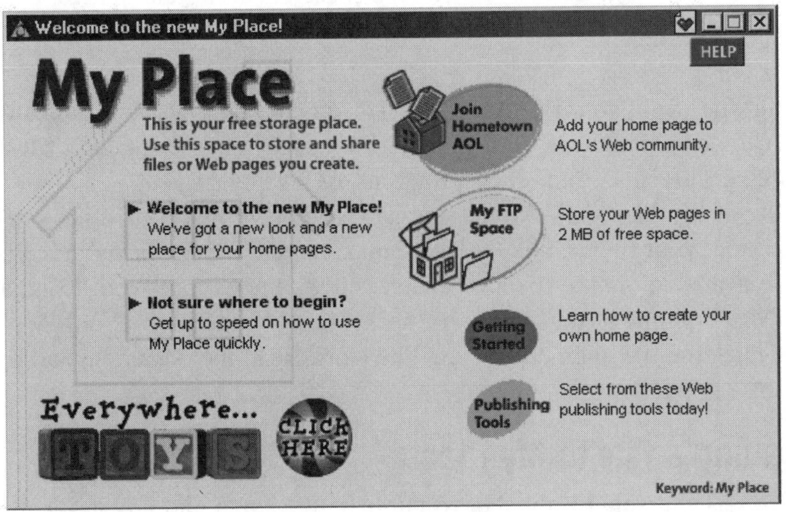

FIGURE 7-1 Start here to access both My Place and Personal Publisher

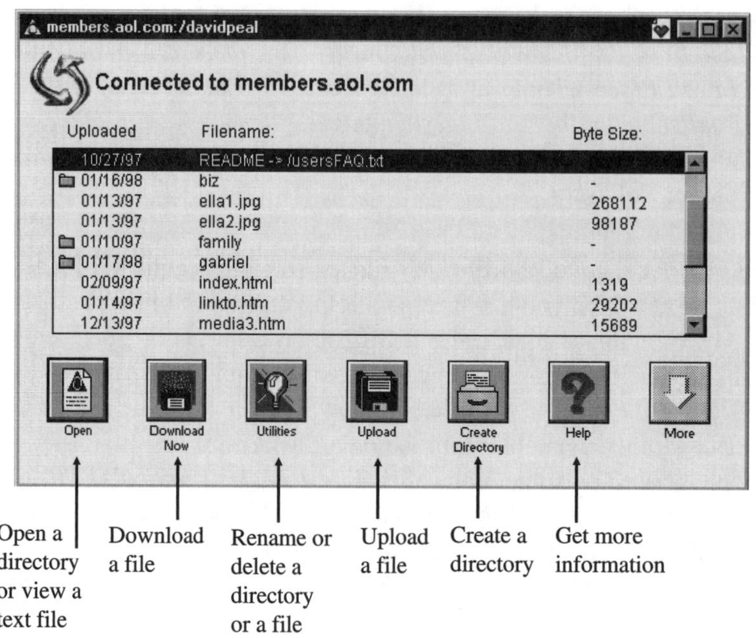

FIGURE 7-2 My Place is your storage space on AOL's computers; it's the physical place where you publish your Web pages

(copying) files from your PC to AOL's FTP computer at **members.aol.com**. Other people can download these files as either Web pages or free-standing files (word-processed documents, sound files, programs, or whatever).

Think of My Place as 2 Mb of storage space on AOL's computers where only you can store your files. Unlike the hard disk on your PC, however, My Place can be made available to *other* people. When you visit My Place, you'll find a handy README document that answers some basic questions about My Place. Double-click the file, then click View File Now. Read the document and print it if you want.

Uploading a File to My Place

When you use Personal Publisher to publish your page and any associated files (such as image files), your work is automatically uploaded—copied from your hard disk—to My Place. You can also upload your files one at a time, when, for example, you change an image or add a sound file. If you will be using AOLPress or another HTML editor, you may want to get comfortable with the process of moving files to My Place.

Before you begin uploading a file, you must know the name and type of the file you want to upload, as well as its location on your hard drive.

1. Go to *keyword: My Place*, and click Go To My Place. Or, use Favorite Places if you've already saved My Place in your Favorite Places folder.
2. Open (double-click) the directory *into which you want to upload a file*. (If you want the file to go in your top-level directory, don't do anything.) Click the Upload button. The following window comes up:

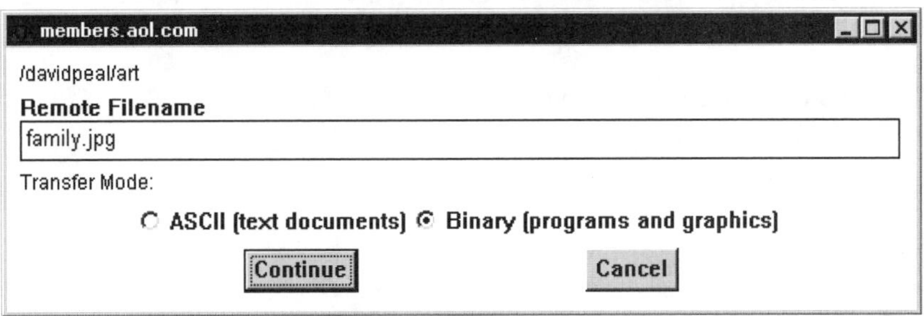

3. Type in the name that you want the file to have in My Place (yes, you provide the *target* name before the *source* name). If the file is for your Web page, note that HTML files must end in *.HTM* or *.HTML* and that graphics files must end in *.GIF*, *.BMP*, or *.JPG*. You must also select a Transfer Mode. Select ASCII for your HTML or other plain text files, and Binary for everything else.

Tip *Keep all of your filenames short and memorable. To avoid confusion and simplify management, use the same name in My Place that you use on your hard disk. If you upload a file with the same filename as an existing My Place file, the existing file will be replaced by the new one.*

4. Click Continue to bring up the Upload File window.

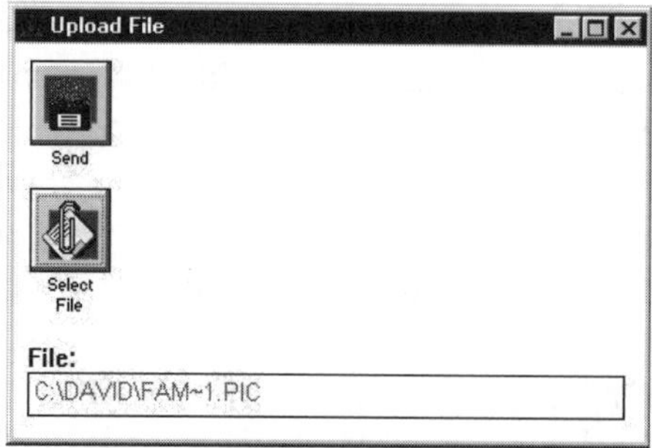

5. Click Select File, and browse your hard drive to select the file you want to upload. Click OK.
6. In the same window, click Send. The File Transfer window comes up and tracks the progress of the upload. When the transfer is complete, your directory window (Figure 7-2) is updated to display the file you just uploaded.

You can now view the file you've uploaded. Its URL is

http://members.aol.com/*screenname*/*filename*

or

ftp://members.aol.com/*screenname*/*filename*

Using My Place, you can't upload to Internet-accessible disk space ("FTPspace") other than ***members.aol.com.***

Managing My Place

Like your own hard drive, your space on My Place can easily get cluttered. If you're using large multimedia files or working on several projects, it can also fill up. Just as you do with your hard drive, you manage My Place by creating directories, moving files around, and deleting files and directories when you no longer need them. In fact, you'll probably find it easier to manage My Place than your hard disk!

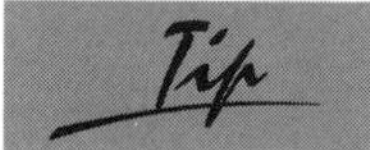

Using Personal Publisher, you can do some of the work of maintaining My Place by clicking View/Edit My Pages. See "Managing Your Pages."

Creating a directory is useful if you want to either make individual files available to people or allow people to upload files to you. If you want to *make files available* to anyone over the Internet, you create a **/pub** directory in your top directory. To *accept* files, you'll need to create an **/incoming** directory. Bear in mind that a well-publicized **/incoming** directory can become clogged with files and eat up the 2 Mb of hard disk space available to you.

Tip *The "/" symbol separates folders from each other.* ***/incoming*** *is shorthand for* ***http://members.aol.com/screename/incoming****, and* ***/pub*** *is shorthand for* ***http://members.aol.com/screename/pub****.*

Creating a Directory

Revisit the My Place screen shown in Figure 7-2. (Yours will look different, of course, since it will have *your* screen name and will contain your files.)

1. Click Create Directory to bring up the following window:

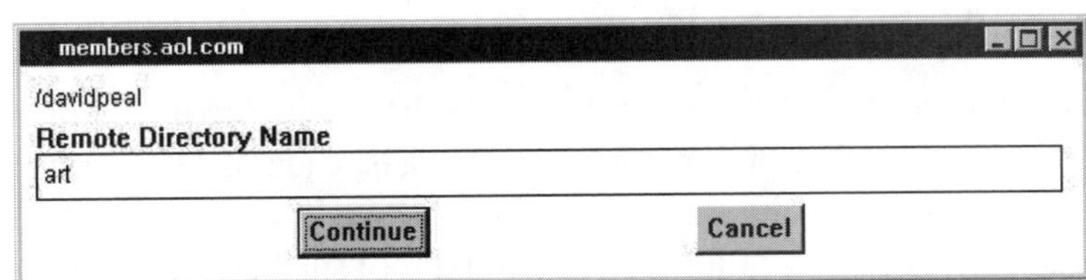

2. Type in a directory name (in this case, *art,* because it's for graphics files), and click Continue. A message confirms the creation of the directory. Click OK. If you want, you can create additional directories, including directories within directories. Close the little window when you're done.

Tip *My Place (like FTP) is case sensitive, and uppercase letters precede lowercase letters, so within any list, the* ***Art*** *directory would come before the* ***art*** *directory.*

Deleting a Directory (or File)

Select the directory (or file) you want to delete, click Utilities, and click the Delete button. Be sure you want to delete it, because you cannot undelete using CTRL-Z or any other keystroke. All files must be individually deleted before a folder containing them can be deleted.

Renaming a Directory (or File)

What if you've incorrectly entered the filename at My Place or uploaded a file to the wrong directory? You can change it as follows: simply select the file, click

Utilities, click Rename, type in the correct name and click OK. If you've put a file in the wrong directory, you can move it by renaming its *directory* path, as in the following example, changing

```
/aardvarks/arthur.jpg
```

to

```
/art/arthur.jpg
```

In other words, in My Place a file's full name includes its directory path. Changing its name from one path to another removes it from one directory and *moves* it to another directory. Or, just delete the file and upload it again to the correct directory.

USING PERSONAL PUBLISHER

Personal Publisher makes it easy to create a Web page in a couple of minutes, adding images, fancy text effects, background colors, lists, and links to your favorite places using point-and-click techniques. It's also easy to edit and refine your page, using either Personal Publisher or an HTML editing tool such as AOLPress.

Note *The following sections are based on a pre-release version of Personal Publisher. As a result, some of the screen captures and specific procedures may differ slightly from what you will find in the final version. You may encounter additional elements and a greater variety of templates.*

Personal Publisher 3: What's New?

The new version of Personal Publisher (Version 3) is just as easy to use as Personal Publisher 2 but offers additional features, including the ability to create lists, links, image maps, counters, e-mail links, and formatted text. Many more templates are available as well, making it easier to create pages ranging from subdued résumés to celebrations of your parakeets. The Manage Your Pages Feature in Personal Publisher gives you control of all the Web-related resources on both your hard drive and My Place, so you can create complex sites consisting of several pages.

At keyword: Hometown, *AOL members can create communities around the themes developed in their Web pages.*

Using Templates

Templates are what make Personal Publisher a breeze to use. Think of a template as a complete Web page that you personalize and make your own by simply filling in the blanks or changing elements to suit your needs. Figures 7-3 shows the kind of template you find in Personal Publisher, and in "Creating the One-Minute Web Page (Give or Take)" you'll learn how to turn this particular template into a personal page

Here are the *kinds* of templates you get with Personal Publisher. AOL plans to expand and refine this list:

- Résumés
- Photo albums
- Business brochures
- Team sports
- Personal sports
- Blank, for maximum flexibility

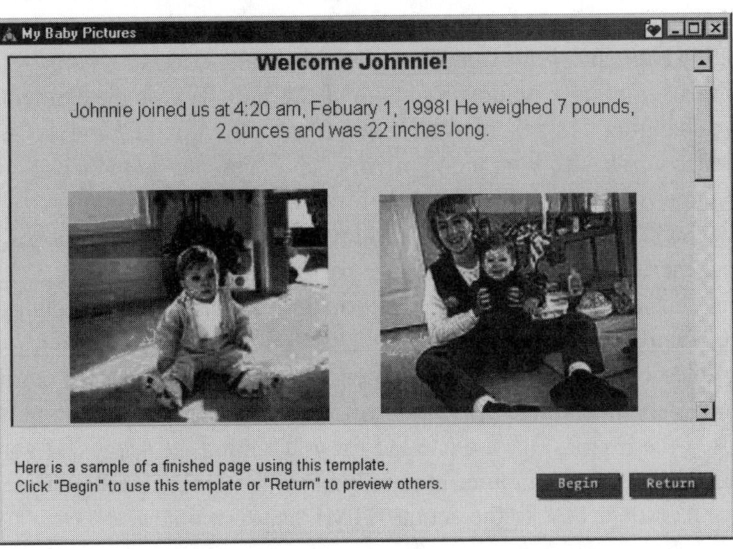

FIGURE 7-3 A Personal Publisher template. Add your own pictures and fill in the blanks to make it your own

The Blank template offers the greatest flexibility. You can add any element, or the same element any number of times, in any order. (see "Editing Your Personal Page").

Most templates consist of the same basic elements:

- Title
- Text, including headings and text links
- Color schemes, for backgrounds, text, and links
- Images, including hyperlinked images and image maps
- Lists
- Extras, such as a counter to keep track of visitors to your page

Tip *For a more complete overview of the page elements you'll experience when you browse the Web, see "A Page and Its Elements" in Chapter 6. You can't create every Web element with Personal Publisher, but it's a good place to start, and you can add fancier elements later, using AOLPress or another HTML editor (see "Editing Your Page with AOLPress").*

Templates vary in the elements they employ, in the ordering of elements, and in the properties assigned to elements. When you customize a template you're really just tweaking elements. For example, a résumé usually consists of lots of text, often arranged in lists of jobs, achievements, and the like. Text is an element that you modify by changing its size, color, alignment, and style. In a résumé, large bold text can be used to emphasize your name or your achievements, and you can create links from the names of your employers to their company Web sites.

In this chapter I'll first identify the elements used in all the templates, and then provide a generic step-by-step procedure for personalizing a template. If it seems like all the decisions are being made for you, don't worry; you can always modify your page, even after it's been published. (*Published* is a fancy word for copying a file from your computer to My Place, where it remains available for editing.)

Just as in Personal Publisher 2, when you create an element in Personal Publisher for AOL 4.0, the HTML tags are created for you behind the scenes. If you do want to create or edit your page, either manually or with an HTML editor, you can have as much or as little access to the actual HTML as you want.

The Elements of a Template

No matter what template you choose, you'll be dealing with the same elements. If a template lacks an element you want, or if you want to use the same element several times, it's all possible when you edit your page (see "Editing Your Personal Page").

- **Title** *A title* is the phrase that appears in the browser's title bar when someone looks at your Web page.

Tip *When you search for something on the Web using AOL NetFind, the search engine often weighs words in titles more heavily than words used elsewhere. Thus, in naming your own page, be as precise as possible (while keeping the wording as interesting as possible to your readers), so that your page will be found when people are searching for information about a particular subject.*

- **Text** You use text in many places in Personal Publisher, but mostly you use it for headers and body text. As with the enhanced AOL e-mail program, in Personal Publisher you can add styles (bold and italics) to text and you can align it relative to the margins (right, left, center). You can also turn your text into a hyperlink, alter its color, and change its size.
- **Color Schemes** With Personal Publisher you choose AOL's preselected color schemes, assigning them to the background, to the text, and to any links you use in your page. A *background* is the color or patterns against which all text, links, and images appear.

Tip *Nothing is more annoying than an overdesigned Web page whose loud background makes it impossible to read the text. Personal Publisher gives you the ability to choose type color as well as background color and pattern. If you choose* ***any*** *colored background or any repeating image for your page, make sure to choose a legible type color. Going with AOL's color schemes ensures legible, attractive designs. Also, if you use a background on one page, you may want to use it on all pages—to give your site (collection of pages) a common look and feel.*

- **Images** Personal Publisher lets you choose a graphics file from either its own library of clip art or your own hard disk. When you add an image by clicking Get My Pictures, as described in the next section, Personal Publisher takes you directly to your Picture Gallery. Using your own digitized images, you use Picture Gallery (always available from the File

menu) to *edit* your images in many ways: brightening them, enhancing their contrast, rotating them, distorting them to create an effect, enlarging them, and even making them black and white. For more about using image files, see the section called "Images on the Web: What You Need to Know." New to Personal Publisher is the ability to attach a link to an image or part of an image, allowing your viewers to visit related places by simply clicking the image or image part.

- **Lists** New to this version of Personal Publisher is the ability to make bulleted lists and other simple lists. Both can contain regular text as well as links that your readers can click to visit new places.
- **Extras** It's now easy to automatically add (1) an e-mail link on your page, so people can send you e-mail, (2) a counter, so you can tell how many visitors you have, and (3) in some templates, a Personal Publisher logo, to let people know how you made your page. These finishing touches are available at the end of the process of creating a page.

Images on the Web: What You Need to Know

Your Web pages can incorporate any graphics files of the common formats. In practice, you'll just be using mostly GIFs and JPGs. How do you *get* such files?

- **For clip art and generic art on AOL** Start at one of the AOL image archives such as the PC Graphics Art Forum (*keyword: PGR*) .
- **Graphics resources on AOL** *Keyword: PPGraphics* collects a range of links of interest to people using Personal Publisher. *Always make sure to check the copyright status of any borrowed image you intend to use on your own page.*
- **To turn photos into files** Turning a photo that you can view into a file on the Net requires a *scanner*—a piece of hardware that works like a photocopier, but produces a file instead of a paper copy of an image. For more information about scanners and scanning, visit AOL's Digital Resource Center (*keyword: Digital Imaging*). Many photo processors scan photos and make files for a fee. Digital

cameras create digital files that can be brought directly into your Web page using a serial cable. Digital photography promises in the near future to become the easiest way of creating digital images for your Web pages. Scanners and digital cameras for all budgets, as well as imaging software, can be purchased at the AOL Store's Digital Imaging Shop (*keyword: AOL store*).

- **To learn about making your own images** If you're proficient using a tool such as Adobe PhotoShop, CorelDRAW, Fractal Design Painter, or a similar program, you can make your own graphics and backgrounds and save them as GIFs or JPGs for use in your Web page. Visit the Web Art Resource Center (*keyword: Webart*).

Creating the One-Minute Web Page (Give or Take)

Let's see how easy it can be to make a personal page. In this exercise I'll be using one of the Photo Album templates in order to keep the page simple, but you can get as ambitious as you want. Remember that other templates use the same elements but with different "properties" (e.g., different colored backgrounds) and in a different order. The process is pretty much the same from template to template.

1. At *keyword: Personal Publishing* click the big Create a Page button.

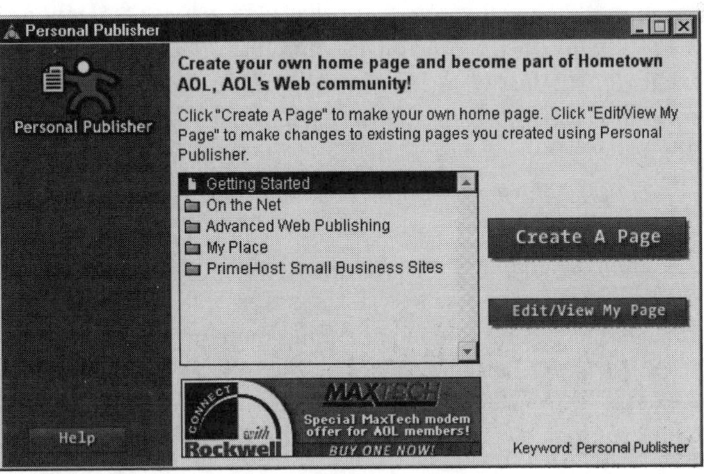

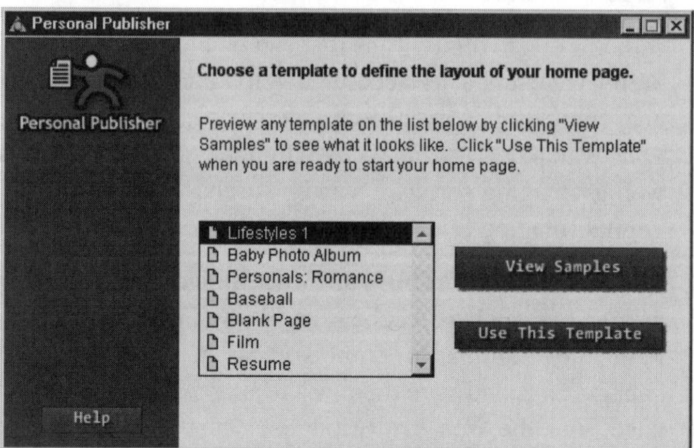

2. Select a template. To see what a sample template looks like, select it and click View Samples. If you like the looks of a sample, close the preview page (click Return) and click Use This Template. If you have ever made a page or started to make a page using this template, you're first asked whether you want to use an existing copy or make a new page. Let's say you click the button to create a new one. The template now downloads to your computer. When the template is ready, click Next and you'll see the template window—in this case, the My Photo Album window.

Tip *When you use a template, it is downloaded to your computer and saved there. When you create your own page using the template, the template elements are replaced with your own work. You should get in the habit of saving your work regularly. Just click Save, and you'll be prompted to save your page as* ***index.htm*** *in your America Online directory (MbrFiles\pp3\[*your screen name*]\[*template*]). You can save an HTM file with a different name if you have another Web page you want to use as your default (****index****) page.*

3. A common element of every template is its title. A title provides important context, in a few choice and specific words, to anyone viewing your page. Change the general title to something more personal, like *Ella Looks Back, Birth to Five*. Click Next.

4. You're next prompted to choose a design for your background, text, and links. A *design* consists of a background color or background pattern, a color for your text, and a color for your links (including a special color to show your readers which links they've clicked).

   Click a design from the list box on the left to see how the choice looks in the box on the right. In the text box, give a name to the combination of custom text and background colors you want to use.

Don't know what to pick? Just play around. You can always edit your page later.

5. Click Next.

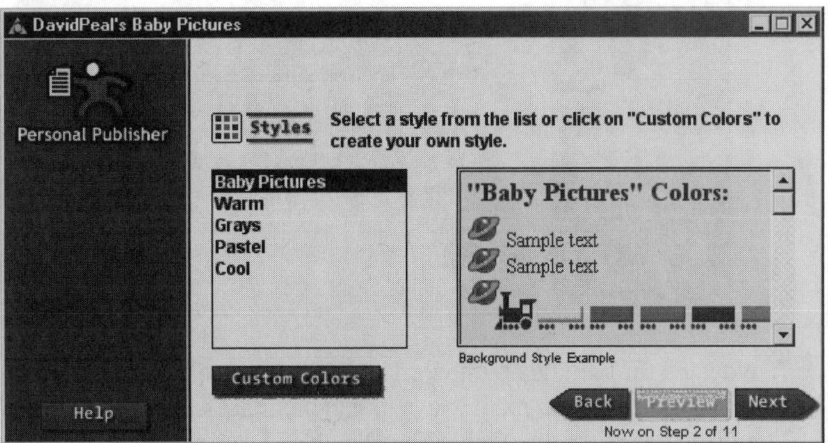

*In the lower right-hand corner of the Personal Publisher window, you see the navigational arrows for proceeding forward from element to element, or backward to revisit an element already created. Below the arrows is an indication of how many elements the template uses (**Now on Step 2 of 9**).*

As you proceed from element to element within a template, you can always return to an earlier element in order to tweak it. At any point, click Preview to see how your page is shaping up.

6. Time to add a heading for your creation. Type in the text, then apply any formatting you wish, just as you would in an e-mail message on AOL. To add effects, select some or all of the words or individual letters you typed, and press the appropriate buttons.

   The first three buttons let you control the size of your heading; the next three buttons control the alignment of your heading; **B** makes your heading bold, ***I*** italicizes it, and the last button lets you apply color to your text. In this example I've centered the text and applied boldface, but not attached a link (an advanced option). Play around, and click Next.

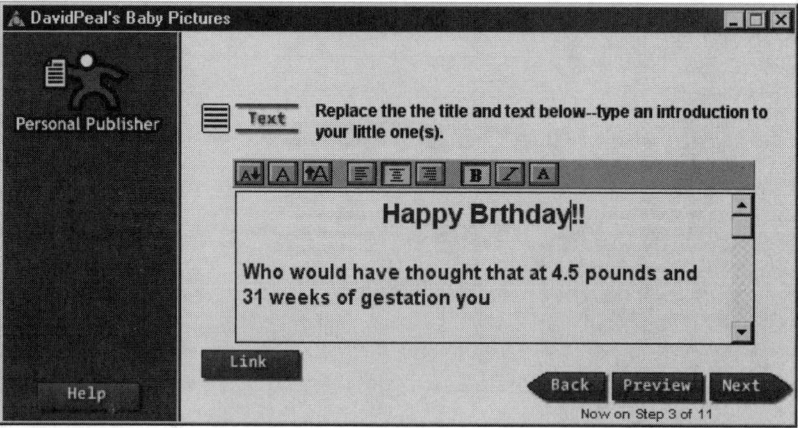

7. Now it's time to add an image. The Web's a visual place, and Personal Publisher gives you many ways to handle images. See the earlier box called "Images on the Web: What You Need to Know" for some tips about how to get images onto the Web.

   - Select an image from your own collection (click Get My Picture) or from Personal Publisher's clip art collection (click Get Clip Art). If you use your own images, you must first navigate to the picture on your hard drive. Once you find it, select it and click Open Gallery to view your picture in AOL's Picture Gallery, which will actually display all the available images in that directory. Click the image you want to use, and it will appear in Personal Publisher's sample window.

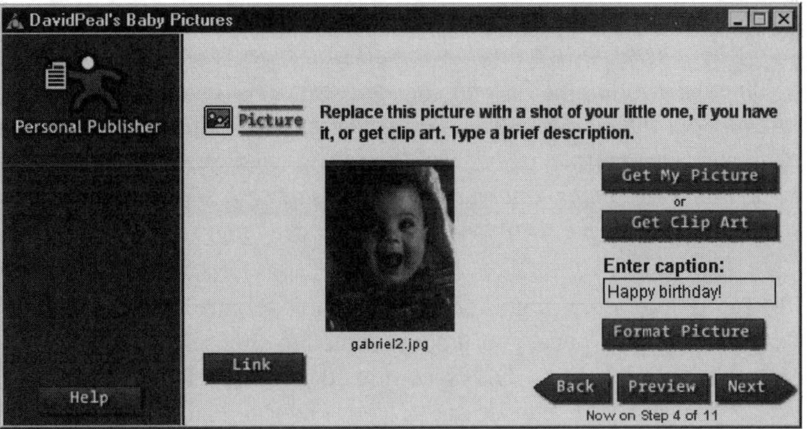

- Type a few words about the image in the Caption box. These words are *not* an actual caption; they merely appear in people's browsers before the page has completely downloaded. Also, any time a mouse cursor passes over the image, the text from the Caption box appears briefly.

- Click Format Picture to specify exactly how you want your image to be aligned (right, center, left) and scaled (in percentage of the picture's original size). Don't align the image if you're planning to indent it from the left margin. (To do this, select one of the Indent options.) Click OK when you're done.

- Click Link to make your image a hyperlink. A user clicking the image will go to another Web page or AOL area. Click OK when you're done.

You can link the *entire picture* to any online destination (click Whole Picture) or parts of the picture to several destinations (click Sections of the Picture). Linking several sections of the pictures to several destinations creates what is known as an *image map*.

Tip *You'll want to use an image map if you have a complex image with discrete parts (like a map showing 50 states, or a compass with four arrows)* and *if you have meaningful links for each part of the image. Some people use image maps as tables of contents, which they place on every page in order to help people get around their sites. The right metaphor (like a compass) can give a site identity and bring people back. For image maps, you must define the part of the image to link, then label it and link it. The onscreen instructions simplify this seemingly complex task.*

In this case, I'm going to select Whole Picture and click OK. When you make your page, you'll be prompted to choose from several types of links, including AOL's recommended Hot Spots (the choice will vary by template). Or, choose one of your Favorite Places or *any* URL. Or, choose another Web page you've built (a useful option if you're creating a complex site) or a particular element on this page (useful for long, complex individual pages). I'd like to keep the attention of my audience, so I'll put off linking people to another destination for now and click Cancel.

8. This might be a good time to click Preview to see how your page is looking. You will see the elements you have added up to this point, and you have the chance to change anything you don't like. Click Close when you're done, then Next to move on to the next element.
9. Time for the text that's accompanying the picture you just added. Type in a line, formatting as necessary. Click Next.
10. For some templates, you may be prompted to write more text, a couple of paragraphs even—about anything. This is different from the text used in Step 3 in that here you can create links. Select the text that you want to be clickable, and click Link. As when you linked images in Step 7, you can link text to an AOL Hot Spot, a Favorite Place, or any URL of your choice. You can also make a "mailto" link, giving your readers a chance to send you fan mail or other useful feedback. Click Next.
11. Now's the chance to add a list of places to visit, using your Favorite Places. If you want to add something not included in your favorites, click New and type in the name and URL of the resource (Internet resources only). Double-click those places you wish to be linked from your Web page, and click Next.

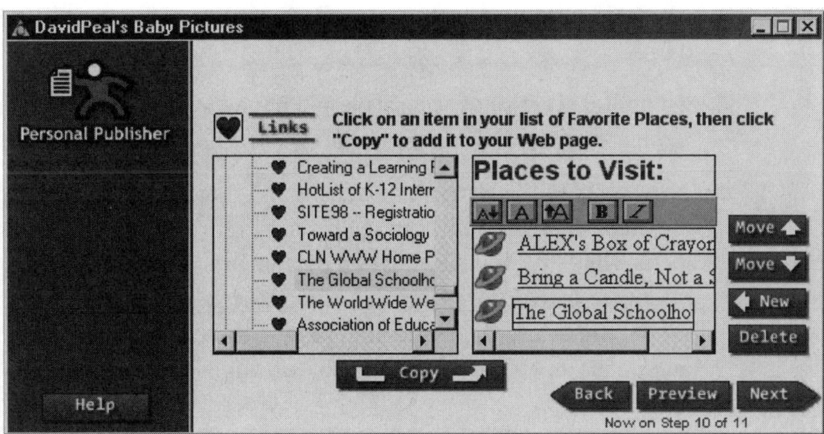

Tip *In some templates at this point, Personal Publisher lets you create bulleted lists. For additional effects, such as numbered lists and nested lists (lists within lists), you may need to use AOLPress or another HTML editor to modify the HTML.*

7

12. Now add those finishing touches—called Extras—that can separate your Web page from the crowd. All these Extras are available only if you clicked Advanced and placed a check mark in the appropriate box. The extras available to you vary by template.

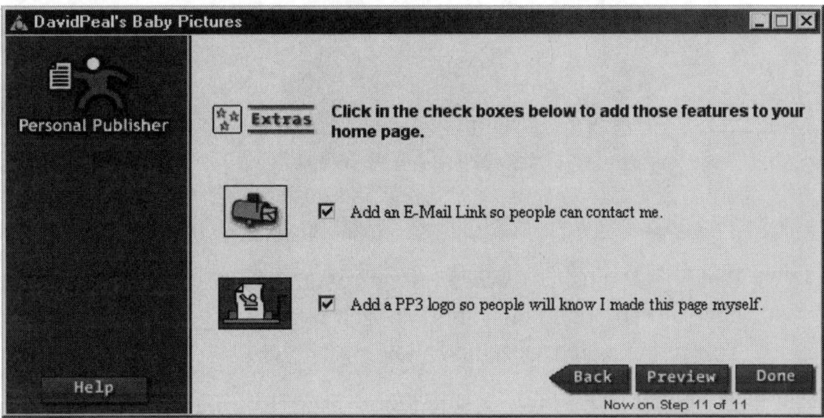

- An e-mail link lets someone send you an e-mail message by clicking a link.
- A counter shows how many people have visited your page (not all templates provide for this option).
- A Personal Publisher logo tells the world how you made the page. If you are creating a specialized page for a "ring" of sites about the same theme (like the Preemie ring that parents use to celebrate their premature infants at **http://members.aol.com/liznick1/ preemiering.htm**), make sure to use the associated logo if there is one. Of course, if your page wins any awards, use the contest logos too.

13. Click Done to see your work.

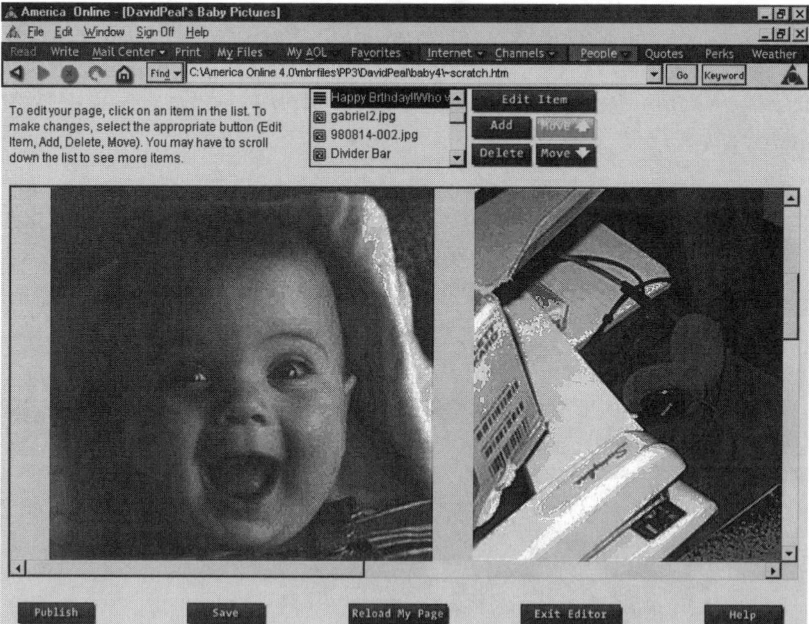

Personal Publisher now saves your work as index.htm (change it if you have already published another Web page in My Place using that name). You're presented with the following choice:

- Click Edit to tweak some more (see "Editing Your Personal Page").
- Click Publish to upload your page and all its elements to My Place, where it's available to the world (see "What's My URL?"). Don't

despair if you decide to publish but later want to make a change. You can always add to your page later, republishing your page when you're done. Your associated files will be copied to My Place, where a new directory (named after the template) will be created. Before publishing, you'll be prompted again to accept index.htm as your page's filename (use that name, unless you've already changed it to another name). You're also informed of its file size, to help you keep track of your use of the 2 Mb at your disposal in My Place.

What's My URL?

When you create a page using Personal Publisher, this page and all associated files are kept in My Place, as described earlier in "Publishing and Maintaining Your Web Pages in My Place." *Anyone* who knows your screen name can view this page at the following URL: **http://members.aol.com/[*screenname*]/[*template*]/**. In place of *screenname*, your friends should type your actual screen name. It's not necessary to specify a file in the ***/screenname*** directory, since browsers automatically attempt to open the file called *index* if a page is not specified in a URL.

Sharing Your URL

On AOL, you can mail someone a hyperlink to your home page. The recipient must also be using AOL 3.0 or AOL 4.0 to use the hyperlink.

1. Click the Write button on the toolbar.
2. Address your message, then write it. In the body of the message, highlight the word or phrase related to your page.
3. Right-click the highlighted text, and select Insert a Hyperlink.
4. In the Edit Hyperlink window, type in your URL (**http://members.aol.com**, etc.)

7

EDITING YOUR PERSONAL PAGE

Editing before you publish gives you a chance to find typos or improve the way something looks or reads. If you're at all dissatisfied with any page you have created,

click Edit in Step 13 of the previous section. Read the window that explains the purposes and techniques of editing, then click OK to go to a window like the one shown in Figure 7-4.

Tip *If you have more than one version of AOL on your computer, or if you used another computer to make your page, you must edit your page using the same computer and same version of AOL that you used to create it.*

When you edit a page, you can change the wording, the images, and the links, and even reverse the order of elements. As a result, you can get similar effects no matter which template you originally used, though special color schemes and list options vary from template to template.

Editing a page is simple:

1. Select an element from the list at the top of the window shown in Figure 7-4.

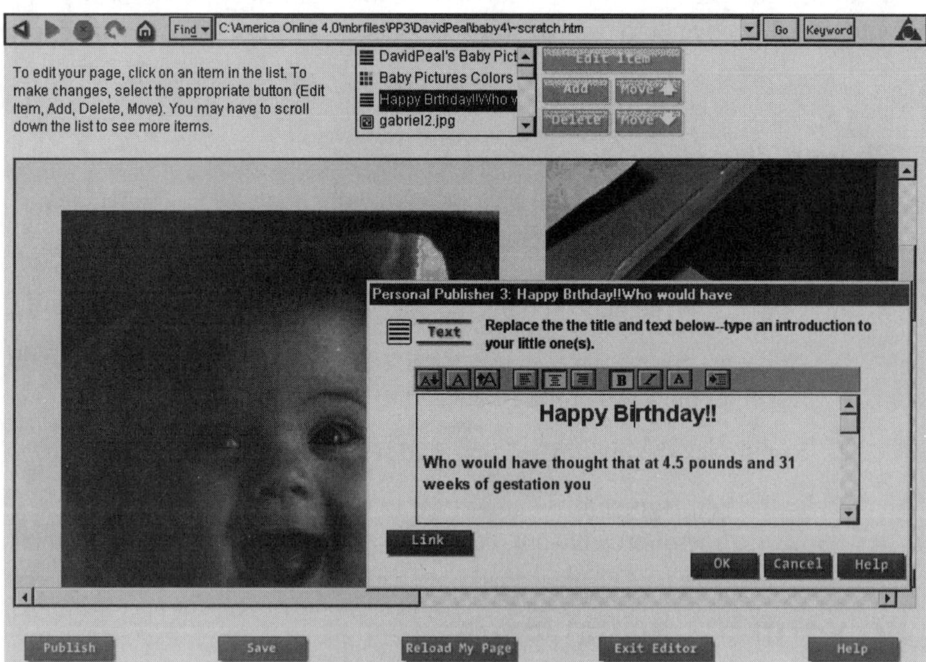

FIGURE 7-4 Edit your page before strangers find typos

2. Tell Personal Publisher what you want to do to the selected element by clicking the appropriate button: edit it, delete it, or move it up or down relative to other elements on the page. You can also *add* elements such as pictures, lists, text, and Favorite Places. With the flexibility of being able to add elements in any order, you can create pages as complex and informative as you want.
3. Save your page, then click Publish when you're happy with it. Remember, publishing just means copying your page to My Place, where anyone who knows about it can find it. Personal Publish now makes a connection with My Place and uploads your files. Just as when you downloaded a template at the beginning of the process, you may need to be patient at the end of the process.

When you edit an element, you work with boxes very similar to the ones you used to make the element in the first place. You can realign images, reselect background colors, and add to lists. Any links you use will be clickable in the editing window, so you can ensure that they work and make sense for your page.

Tip *When you edit with Personal Publisher, you're looking at your page inside a miniature browser. Click the Refresh button on the navigation bar to see the effects of your edits.*

A Notable Site: Geography World

Brad Bowerman teaches geography at Lakeland High School in Jermyn, Pennsylvania. Using an earlier version of Personal Publisher, he created Geography World (**http://members.aol.com/bowermanb/101.html**). This huge catalog is conveniently arranged in categories like weather, plate tectonics, population, maps, cultures, and ecosystems. He refined his site with custom backgrounds, tables, anchors, and animated GIFs. For kids with geography homework, it can save the day.

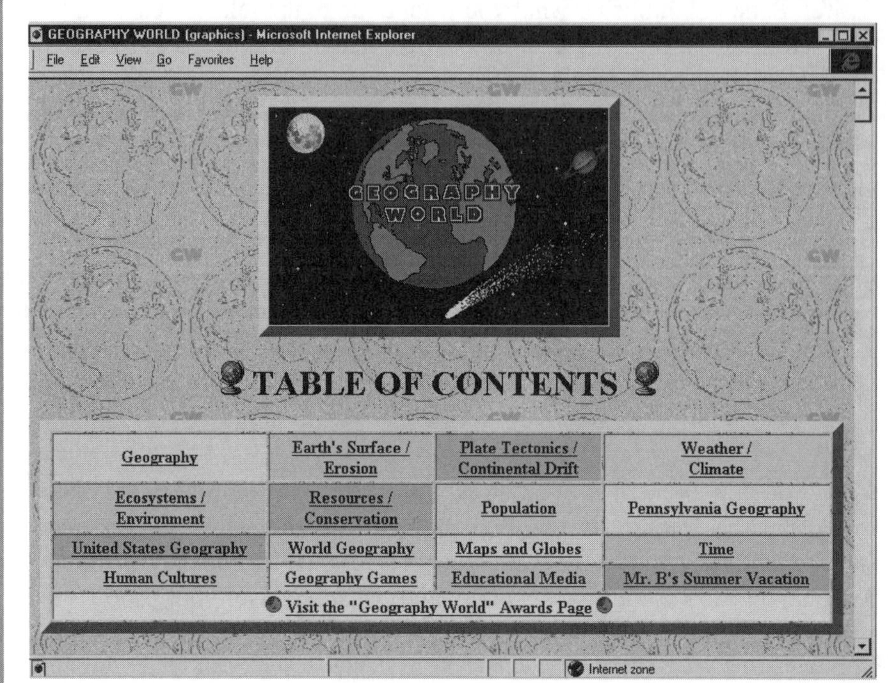

Geography World has won numerous awards, and was named by *Education World* as one of the 20 Best Web educational sites of 1997.

MANAGING YOUR PAGES

If you want to edit a page you have already published, go to *keyword: Personal Publisher* and click View/Edit My Pages to display the window shown in Figure 7-5. You'll see a list of all your Personal Publisher files in My Place (left-hand column) and on your hard drive (right-hand column). Select a file from either column, and click Edit.

Tip *When you first click View/Edit My Pages, Personal Publisher has to connect to My Place and create a list of your editable files there. This can take a moment, so be patient!*

Managing your pages means much more than merely fiddling with their elements. It includes coordinating sites consisting of pages spread over many directories.

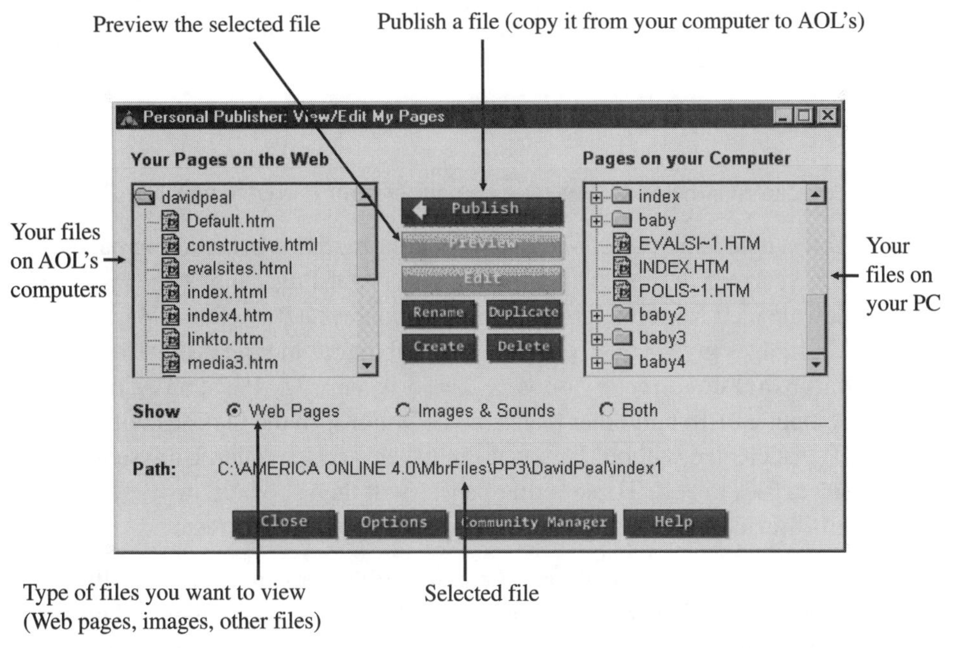

FIGURE 7-5 View/Edit My Pages gives an overview of your Web files on your hard drive and AOL's computers

Tip *When you manage your pages, you're dealing with files. Before you can edit a page or manage a set of pages, you must be able to recognize their filenames and know where to find them. When you save an index.htm file using Personal Publisher, for example, it is kept in your* ***c:\America Online 4.0\MbrFiles\PP3\screen name\template*** *directory.*

From the View/Edit My Pages window, you can select and edit any file, either on your own hard drive or in My Place. Note that Personal Publisher lets you edit *all* Web pages, whether you made them with Personal Publisher or with another editor. When you edit a page, you see the window shown in Figure 7-4, which gives you the ability to refine, add, delete, and reposition elements. Once you're happy with an HTM file stored on your hard drive, you can publish it—make it available at My Place—by clicking Publish.

You can use this window to move non-HTM files (such as GIFs and JPGs) from your hard drive to My Place. Just select the file and click Publish.

The View/Edit My Pages window offers other useful features:

- You can rename and delete files on either your hard drive or My Place.
- You can add any other Web pages on your hard drive, including pages you've saved or made using tools such as AOLPress, plus pages you've downloaded from mailing lists or other sources. (By default, Manage Your Pages gives you a view only of Web pages in your **America Online 4.0\ MbrFiles** directory on your hard drive and My Place on AOL's computers.) To add other pages, click Options. In the Options window's "Pages created without Personal Publisher" section, click Browse and select files to edit. These "other pages" will then show up in your **c:\America Online 4.0\ MbrFiles\pp3*screenname*** directory.
- You can create a navigational menu if you've constructed a site with several pages. The menu appears at the bottom of your pages and makes it easy to move from page to page within your mini-site. To create this kind of a menu, click Options (see Figure 7-5) and fill out the Menu screen.

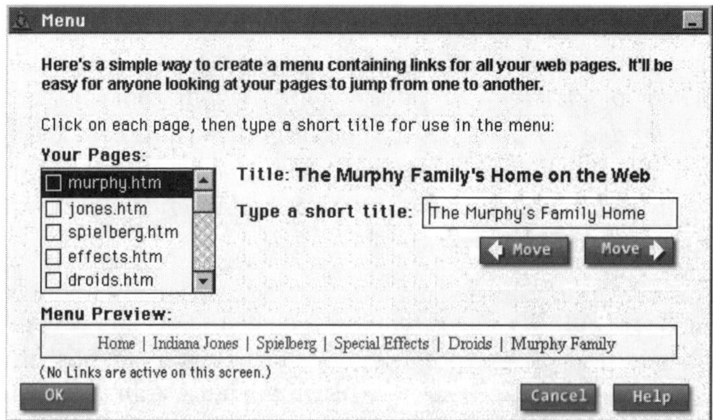

Use this menu feature to help your readers avoid pages that take too long to download and are difficult to navigate.

In Business? Let PrimeHost Maintain Your Site.

AOLPress can be used as a stand-alone application, but it also forms part of the more complete business service offered by AOL's PrimeHost (*keyword: PrimeHost*). *Hosting* allows a business to lease the technology required for an Internet presence, so it can focus on business while the hosting provider focuses on the technology—running the server, installing the software, leasing fast connections to the Internet, and ensuring security.

AOL's PrimeHost service offers companies fully supported publishing software (AOLPress), AOLserver software with a fully integrated database, and simple Web-based methods of gaining access to your site. Customer service and technical support staff can assist you with any questions along the way. PrimeHost also facilitates domain name registration in case you want your own Internet address, such as **sunnyprospects.com**.

For more information, visit *keyword: PrimeHost* or *keyword: Online Business.*

EDITING YOUR PAGE WITH AOLPRESS

Amazing things are possible on the Web these days—animation (from animated GIFs to Shockwave and beyond), high-quality audio, streaming video, dynamic HTML, and more—but most of these effects require that you learn some HTML and related scripting languages. The easiest way to do that today is with a graphical HTML editor like AOLPress.

Using an HTML editor does not make your page unusable in Personal Publisher. Using Manage Your Pages you have access to all your Web work.

At *keyword: AOLPress*, you come to information about both PrimeHost (AOL's Web-hosting service for commercial Web sites) and AOLPress. To use AOLPress, download and install the program following the online instructions. Free versions for the Macintosh, Windows 3.1, and Windows 95 are available at **http://www.aolpress.com/download.html**. Double-click the downloaded file, and it will install itself.

AOLPress has a simple interface that quickly lets you get working. You can even open up a complete Personal Publisher template and edit it from scratch, as shown in Figure 7-6.

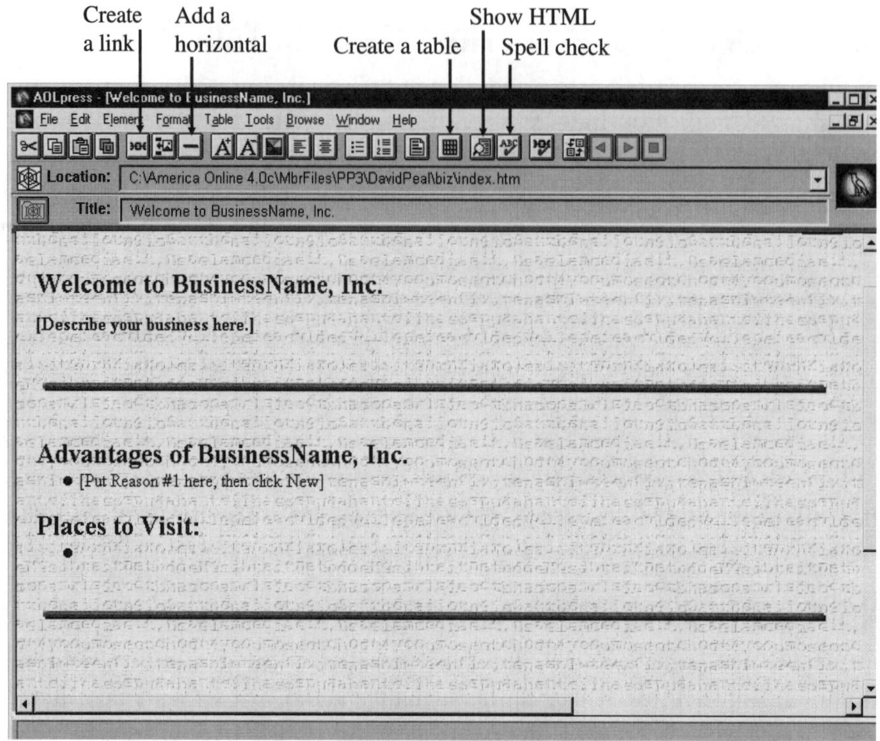

FIGURE 7-6 AOLPress lets you edit pages visually or using HTML, then publish them

With AOLPress, you can edit your Personal Publisher pages by simply opening up an index.htm or other HTM file and editing it. Unlike other editors, AOLPress doesn't force you to go back and forth between HTML and the "real" page that people will see. However, if you are comfortable with HTML, you can view it and change it any way you want. AOLPress has a very helpful feature that prevents you from closing a page of HTML if you've made any changes that don't conform with standard HTML.

You start AOLPress as you do most any program. To open a page, use File | Open and navigate to index.htm, then double-click. The page will be displayed in AOLPress. Note that the file is stored as index.html on **members.aol.com** but as index.htm on your computer, since Windows does not handle file extensions with four letters, such as .HTML.

Publishing your AOLPress files means copying them from your hard drive to AOL's computers: Choose File | Save As from the AOLpress menu, then

http://members.aol.com/[*screenname*]/[*filename*].html. If you wish this page to be the default page returned in My Place when people request **http://members.aol.com/[*screenname*]/**, you will need to name it **index.html** or **index.htm**.

Tip *AOLPress help is available on AOL. To access this feature, at* keyword: AOLPress, *click AOLPress Help Station. For a low price, you can purchase the AOLPress documentation at* keyword: AOLPress.

Here are some features of AOLPress that you might want to explore:

- *A graphical tool for making multicolumn, multirow structured tables, without the hassle of coding them in HTML* To add certain effects like background color, you'll need to play with the underlying HTML. Just click the Show HTML button (see Figure 7-6).
- *Ability to edit in either graphical or HTML mode* If graphical edits on the page itself don't produce the effect you're intending, check the HTML.
- *A spell checker*
- *An easy way to link to other pages and anchors* Just highlight text, click the Link button, and type in or navigate to a URL. A *link* takes you to the top of a page, and an *anchor* to some point you specify within a page. AOLPress makes it easy to create, link, and edit the links between pages in a complex site.
- *Simple tools for making bulleted and numbered lists* Just select the text and click the appropriate button.
- *Complete control of type style, size, and color*

NEXT STEP: REFINING YOUR PAGE'S HTML

When you use Personal Publisher, you are generating HTML behind the scenes. To edit HTML, you must use a product like AOLPress, introduced in the previous section. You can use Manage Your Pages to publish any page created with any editor in My Place.

The following sections barely begin to show how far you can go in building and refining a Web page. For more ideas, read the section "Learning HTML on AOL," and spend time in the Desktop and Web Publishers forum (*keyword: DWP*).

7

Tip *With AOL for Windows 4.0 and Personal Publisher, it's easy to get a behind-the-scenes view of the HTML you've generated. Just display your page in the AOL browser, right-click, and select View Source. Your HTML script appears in Notepad. You can save it and study it.*

Learning HTML on AOL

HTML is simple in concept but more and more difficult to master because of a continuous stream of improvements that enable increasingly complex and fancy effects. Here are some places to start if you want to learn HTML on AOL.

- Start with the Computing channel's new On the Net area (*keyword: On the Net*) for pointers to the best AOL resources for learning HTML.
- For a selection of books about HTML, go to *keyword: My Place*, where you can click a button to go directly to a selection of the AOL Book Store's tutorials and reference guides.
- On the Web itself, many tutorials and references are available. A classic place to learn correct HTML is the *Beginners' Guide to HTML* at **http://www.ncsa.uiuc.edu/General/Internet/WWW/HTMLPrimer.html**.
- Tim Berners-Lee, one of the inventors of the World Wide Web, wrote the *Style Guide for Online Hypertext* to help you write *good* HTML—tags that convey your content as effectively as possible. You'll find it at **http://www.w3.org/pub/WWW/Provider/Style/Overview.html**.

For a longer list of books and Web sites devoted to HTML, see **http://members.aol.com/DavidPeal/recommend.htm**.

Adding Multimedia Files

Want your visitors to *hear* a cool sound as part of your Web page? You can either require them to click a link to the file (giving them the choice of whether to hear it) or make it play automatically in the background.

Let's say you have a WAV file on your hard drive called **tiffanys.wav**. To add this file to your page as a clickable link, you type in the following bit of HTML in the appropriate spot of your page:

```
<a href="tiffanys.wav">Moon River (700k)</a>
```

You've just used HTML's link tag (<a>), the standard tool for linking elements on the World Wide Web. *Href* stands for hypertext reference—it's just the name of the linked file. What the reader sees and clicks is:

```
Moon River (700k)
```

In order for the link to work, you must publish the page again in My Place and upload the audio file (**tiffanys.wav** or whatever) to the same directory.

Tip: *On AOL you'll find loads of audio files, which you can use without violating any copyright, at* keyword: Midi *(click Software Libraries). MIDI files tend to be much smaller than WAV files.*

Background Sound

A variation on the theme of the clickable sound link is the *background* sound, which plays automatically when someone merely visits the page. How? The file downloads in the background and AOL plays it automatically (if the person browsing is an AOL member or otherwise has a helper application set up to play sound files).

To add a background sound file to your Web page, use AOLPress to add this HTML:

```
<EMBED SRC="mySound.wav" height=2 width=2 autostart=true hidden=true>
```

In place of *mySound.wav,* put the actual filename of your WAV or MIDI file. Users whose systems can't play these sounds for some reason won't get an error message; the sound just won't play.

Learning Web Design on AOL

Mastery of HTML in itself doesn't make for good design. Here are some places on AOL where you can learn the fine points of Web design:

- The Desktop and Web Publishers' forum (*keyword: DWP*) brings together design-minded desktop publishers and Web builders.
- To take a chat-based lesson on HTML or Web design, check out the Online Classroom's schedule at *keyword: Online Classroom* (click Web & Internet).
- At *keyword: AOL Store*, click Books to visit the AOL Book Store. You'll find the latest books from top Web designers like David Siegel and Lynda Weinman.

Adding Animation

The simplest way to add animation to your Web page is to use an animated GIF, which is a file that contains several images shown in sequence when someone views the page, creating the impression of simple animation. There are other more advanced types of animation you could use—those which can be viewed with plug-ins such as Shockwave and VDO—but they require more advanced software to create, and users around the world may not have the required plug-in software. (For more on plug-ins, see Chapter 6.) Since animated GIF files have a GIF extension, like static images, you can add them to pages directly using Personal Publisher.

Tip *An excellent guide to animated GIFs has been published by an AOL member at* ***http://members.aol.com/royalef/gifanim.htm****. For sample GIFs, animated GIF software, and resources, visit* keyword: Animated GIF.

TELLING THE WORLD ABOUT YOUR SITE

What good is a page if no one knows it exists? There are search engines and directories that collect Web addresses (URLs); for others to find your page, it has to be available on one of these search engines. Chapter 9 is devoted to the whole topic of searching. Some search engines regularly "crawl" the Web looking for sites, and most also accept URLs sent to them by Web builders eager for promotion. At AOL NetFind, for example, just click Add a Site to submit your URL.

The Submit-it service lets you provide information about your site to hundreds of search engines at the same time, including the hugely popular, general purpose sites like AOL NetFind. You can get more information about this service at **http://www.submit-it.com**.

Letting the World Sign Your Guestbook

A guestbook gives you a way of collecting information about people who visit your site. It also makes your site interactive, which people increasingly expect. You can find out what they think of the site, for example, or what they'd like to see you add. Making a guestbook requires the use of forms, with fields and other Windows elements. AOL supports the *CGI* (*Common Gateway Interface*) capability required if you want to add a guestbook on your site. For instructions and samples, see **http://members.aol.com/wwwadmin/guestbook/guestbook.htm**. You'll have to use AOLPress or another editor, rather than Personal Publisher, to add this and similar interactive features.

FROM HERE...

Browsing gives you somewhat passive access to Web sites. With Personal Publisher, My Place, and all the HTML tools and resources at your disposal on AOL, the Web comes alive. FTP, the subject of the next chapter, is the final Internet feature covered in this book. While My Place lets you upload to a single site (**members.aol.com**), FTP lets you download millions of files from thousands of Internet sites. Again, AOL has everything you need to use this essential Internet service.

Chapter 8

Downloading Software from AOL and the Internet

In personal terms, the work you do at the computer can consist of the messages you send people and the reports you prepare for work. Or, perhaps you use your PC to keep track of your recipes and addresses. Maybe you play games and do your bills on your PC. *Files* are the way your PC stores all this information. In fact, everything you do on a computer requires files: discrete pieces of software, each with a name and a location on a hard drive or other kind of storage medium. Even the AOL for Windows software is just a bunch of files.

The Internet gives you access to millions of files of every type, thanks to one of the oldest and most popular Internet services, FTP, short for File Transfer Protocol. It sounds complex, perhaps, but using FTP is about as complex as using your own hard drive. The amount of software and the simple tools AOL provides for retrieving this software make it worth getting familiar with FTP. America Online provides everything you need to search for FTP files and download them.

Note *Copying a file from a distant Internet computer to your own PC is called downloading. Uploading means moving a file from one computer to another, usually from a PC to a larger computer. On AOL you won't do much uploading, unless you create a Web page using Personal Publisher (Chapter 7).*

America Online has a built-in FTP program, or *client*, that enables you to go quickly and easily to any public FTP site on the Net. AOL's World Wide Web *browser* gives you an alternative way of going to FTP sites. Which do you use? This chapter makes a case for the browser as the better way to *find* files, and the built-in client as the better way to actually download them. It begins with an introduction to filenames and types, and ends with an overview of the vast software libraries available on America Online itself.

UNDERSTANDING FILES AND FILE TYPES

Every file has a filename and a file type.

A *filename* is the name that a person gives a file so that others know what is *in* the file. Naming files is in fact a subjective matter and does not always clarify a file's contents. Sometimes, naming files is an exercise in shoe-horning. In the old DOS and Windows 3.1 file-naming system, filenames had to be eight characters or less and were followed by a period and an *extension* of no more than three characters. Windows 95 allows longer filenames.

A file's *type*, or format, on the other hand, can give you a good deal of reliable information. How do you tell a file's type? The file's *extension* is the best guide, since it is usually assigned automatically by the program that created it. The extension is the part of a file's name after the period (usually called a "dot"). In *chapter8.doc*, *doc* is the file extension (a *doc* file is Microsoft Word's extension for all of its DOS and Windows versions). Not all files have extensions, but even the absence of an extension can be informative—such files are likely to be for the Macintosh or Unix operating system (and are probably not usable on a Windows computer). Table 8-1 provides an overview of the most common file extensions of PC files you'll encounter on FTP. Here's what you can learn from a file's type:

- Which operating system you must have to use the file. Unix, Macintosh, and Windows are the primary operating systems for which files are available on the Net. Generally speaking, as a Windows user you won't have much use for non-Windows programs, although text files (see the next item) can be read on any platform.
- Whether the file is *binary* or *text*. Computers read binary files; people read text files. Basically, all files are binary except pure text files (ASCII). A text file can be read with any program and easily printed out. With a binary file, you must use a specific program, and programs themselves are binary. It used to be that when you downloaded a file using FTP, you had to specify whether it was binary or text. AOL's built-in FTP program takes care of that for you. Table 8-1 provides some guidance, as does the "Using the Files You Download: Graphics, Sounds, and Beyond" section.
- Whether the file is compressed or zipped (archived). A *compressed* file has been run through a special program to reduce its size and thus decrease the download time. A *zipped* file usually consists of several files that have been run through a program to make it possible to download all the files at the same time.
- What the file contains. Reading a file's extension can tell you whether the file contains a program or raw program code, whether it's an image or a

8

video file, whether it's a Word or Excel document or something else. To name the most common extensions, image files have extensions such as GIF and JPG; video files use AVI, MOV, and MPG; and audio files use RAM, WAV, AU, and MID.

Tip *The excellent Web page Common Internet File Formats is available at* ***http://www.matisse.net/files/format.html*** *and includes software tips for using files of each major format. On AOL,* keyword: Nethelp *(click FTP) has an excellent article called File Types and Extensions.*

File Extension	Platform	How to Use
	Image Files	
ART	Windows, Macintosh	Compressed image file; can be viewed only on AOL.
BMP	Windows	Bitmapped picture file; can be viewed on AOL.
GIF	Windows, Macintosh	Stands for Graphics Interchange Format, an Internet standard; can be viewed on AOL or using browser.
JPG, JPEG	Windows, Macintosh	Stands for Joint Photographic Experts Graphic; can be viewed on AOL or using browser.
PCX	Windows	Can be viewed on AOL.
PDF	Windows, Macintosh	Delivers highly formatted documents; requires Adobe Acrobat (freeware) available at *keyword: Adobe*. See Chapter 6 (on plug-ins).
	Sound Files	
AU	Windows, Macintosh	Internet audio file; can be heard on AOL.
MID	Windows, Macintosh	MIDI (Musical Instrument Digital Interface) sound file; can be heard on AOL.

TABLE 8-1 Standard file types

File Extension	Platform	How to Use
RAM	Windows, Macintosh	Real Audio streaming audio file; requires the RealAudio plug-in (**http://www.real.com**); see Chapter 6.
SND	Macintosh	Macintosh System 7 sound file; AOL for the Macintosh can play, but Windows requires conversion software (*keyword: Filesearch*).
WAV	Windows	Windows sound file; AOL for Windows can play, but Mac requires special conversion software (*keyword: Filesearch*).
	Video Files	
AVI	Windows	Audiovisual file, a Windows standard; can be played on AOL for Windows (Mac requires converter).
MOV, QT, MOVIE	Windows, Macintosh	QuickTime; requires a player, available for both platforms at *keyword: Mac video* (QuickTime Virtual Toolbox).
MPEG, MPG	Windows	Windows standard, runs in Microsoft Media Player but some versions require special software.
	Text Files	
HTM, HTML	All	Text file with formatting instructions for a Web page; can be used with any browser.
TXT	All	Text file; open in any word processor or AOL's text editor (if under 16K).

TABLE 8-1 Standard file types (*continued*)

File Extension	Platform	How to Use
Compressed, Archived, and Other Binary Files		
EXE	Windows	Executable file; may also be a self-extracting file that you can run from the Windows 95 Start menu or Windows 3.1 File Manager.
HQX (BinHex)	Macintosh	A binary file that's been encoded and converted into a text file; automatically decoded on AOL for the Mac by opening from File menu.
SEA	Macintosh	Self-Extracting Archive: run a SEA file and its parts are automatically decompressed in a new folder.
SIT	Windows, Macintosh	A zipped file produced by the StuffIT program, originally for Mac only; unstuff on Mac by opening from File menu; Windows version of StuffIT allows decompressing but not compressing, but not all uncompressed files will necessarily run on Windows.
Z, GZ	Unix	Compressed file.
ZIP	Windows	Zipped file (very common); unzip with WinZip or PKZip, or automatically using Download Manager.

TABLE 8-1 Standard file types (*continued*)

Where's It At? Files and Directories

A full filename consists of a name of the actual file and the *path* to that file. A path is the exact directory (*directory* is another name for *folder*) where the file is located, including any directory to which it belongs, any directory to which that directory belongs, and so on up to the computer's *root* directory. A path starts at the top (root) level of a site, which is similar to the root of your hard drive; it's the directory that contains all other directories.

For example, here is the path at an FTP site (igc.org) to WinZip, a Windows program for decompressing files:

```
igc.org/pub/Internet/windows/Misc/winzip.exe
```

The file is contained in the Misc directory, which is contained in the windows directory, which is contained in the Internet directory, which is contained in the pub directory, which is in this site's top level, or root, directory. Note that FTP directory and file names are case sensitive. *ACME* comes before *Acme*, which comes before *acme*.

Why Use FTP?

FTP is perhaps most useful as a way of making available a specific file or set of files that many people want—software or a group of sound files, for example. In projects where people live in different places, FTP can be an excellent way to allow limited access to files while keeping files secure by password-restricting access to them. In addition, FTP is the most practical way of *uploading* files to a place from which they can be referenced by a Web site you are building (see Chapter 7). Finally, it's easier to publish a single file (a program, say) by uploading it than to design and maintain a Web page just to make the file available. More than five million files are available by FTP. The Web may seem like the center of things on the Internet, but in fact FTP is used by hundreds of major Web sites (like Netscape's) when you download files.

Ways of Retrieving Files over the Internet

FTP may be the most efficient way of transferring files, but it's only one of many. You can also get files in the following ways:

- **Files via newsgroups** Using a technique called UUEncoding, many people insert binary files into newsgroup messages by converting them to encoded text files (strings of characters that only a computer can understand). As an AOL member, you can use FileGrabber to automatically decode and use these files, as explained in Chapter 5.
- **Files via the World Wide Web** The Web has become a popular way of making files available to a broad audience—not just as files to download to your own computer, but in *context*. A NASA Web site, for example, lets you view images based on photographs taken by the Hubble Spacecraft, together with information about the Hubble mission (**http://spacelink.msfc.nasa.gov/**). Web pages today are loaded with files—Real Audio, Shockwave, image, video, and more (Chapter 6).
- **Files via e-mail** If you need to send a file to a single person or a small group of people, attaching it to e-mail can be easier than using FTP, because your recipients are more likely to have (and know how to use) an e-mail reader than an FTP client.

If you're ever in desperate need of a file, start with AOL's file libraries, which are available all over the service. The files can be searched at keyword: Filesearch *(see "Downloading Files from America Online" later in this chapter).*

FINDING FTP FILES

Unlike the Web or newsgroups, FTP was not meant for browsing. With FTP, browsing makes little sense, since you cannot automatically tell what's in a file from its name. Moreover, almost all FTP sites limit the number of incoming connections—the number of people who can use that site at the same time.

Tip *Browsing an FTP site (going up and down the directories in search of interesting files) is considered bad netiquette because it ties up limited FTP resources and can prevent access to people who require specific files and know exactly what they are looking for.*

On AOL, you have two ways of finding the FTP sites with the files you need:

- Using AOL's Search for FTP Sites button at *keyword: FTP*

Note *FTP is now available from AOL's new Internet menu on the AOL toolbar (see Chapter 2).*

- Using an Internet program called Archie

Anonymous and Non-anonymous FTP

When you use AOL or Archie to search for files, you're really searching only for publicly accessible files (of which there are "only" a couple of million). These public files are available by a method called *anonymous FTP*. All this means is that you log on to these sites with the user name *anonymous* and the password set to your e-mail address. Don't worry, though. Logging on is handled automatically by AOL if you use the FTP client (*keyword: FTP* or select FTP from the Internet menu).

Need to access a password-protected (non-anonymous) FTP site? First, make sure your friend gives you a user name and password for the site. Then, select FTP from the Internet menu, click Go To FTP, then click Other Site. You'll see a check box, "Ask for login name and password." If you need to use a password-protected (non-anonymous) FTP site, put a check in the box. When you arrive at the FTP site, you'll be asked for a user name and password.

AOL's Search FTP Service

At *keyword: FTP* (or select FTP from the Internet menu), you can search FTP sites by clicking the button labeled Search for FTP Sites. This search looks through a gigantic text document consisting of a list of FTP sites. This valuable list provides

information on every known anonymous and non-anonymous FTP site in the world: its address, location, and date last modified. It is posted in two dozen long parts to the **news.answers** newsgroup, and it's also available by FTP at **rtfm.mit.edu/pub** (one of the Favorite Sites available at *keyword: FTP* when you click Go to FTP).

This list of FTP *sites* does not, however, provide a list of the *files* actually available at these sites—only a characterization of the kind of files available and the names of some of the most popular publicly available directories. So, you can search by subject with AOL's FTP Search service, but you also have to assume that the people who run FTP sites make the same assumptions you do about characterizing files.

Here's how to go to an FTP site that you find using AOL's FTP Search service:

1. Write down the FTP site name (see the sample illustration showing a site description and address in "Where Do You Find Images on FTP?" later in this chapter). Close the Search window.
2. From the main FTP window, click the Go To FTP button.
3. Click the Other Site button. In the Site Address box, type in the FTP address you wrote down in Step 1, and click Connect. An information window usually appears (scope of site, number of connections, etc.); skim it and click OK. For help getting around an FTP site, see "Navigating an FTP Site Using the AOL FTP Client."

FTP Site Names

FTP site names are a type of *domain name.* (For more on domain names see Appendix B.) They consist of little bits of text separated by periods, or *dots.* For instance, the FTP site **ftp.aol.com** is the domain name for AOL's FTP servers. Sometimes you'll find FTP sites beginning *ftp* (such as **ftp.zdnet.com**), just as you'll find Web sites beginning *www* (such as **www.zdnet.com**). Other times, you'll see sites like **igc.org** or **sunsite.unc.edu**, whose names don't reveal that they're FTP sites.

FTP sites have their own URLs, making them accessible by the AOL Web browser. To create the URL, simply tack ftp:// *onto the beginning of an FTP site name. Type the URL into the AOL Address box to access the site using the browser.*

Searching with Archie on the Web

Archie is an Internet search service that goes further than the AOL Search FTP Sites option. It searches a list of actual files and directories available on anonymous FTP sites around the world. The list is updated approximately weekly, and is the industry standard method for searching FTP.

Archie was created by Bunyip Information Systems, Inc., a Canadian firm whose Web site provides good background information about Archie (**http://www.bunyip.com/ products/archie/**). According to Bunyip, Archie today indexes about 5.7 million files on some 1,500 anonymous FTP sites, plus some Web-based file archives.

Today, the easiest way to use Archie is over the World Wide Web, using a Web-based Archie search. All you do is type a keyword (part or all of a file's name) and click the Search button. The Web site contacts the Archie server, asks Archie to search its list of files, and presents the answers back to you as *hypertext* links; to go to an FTP site and get the specific file at that site, just click a link. See "Searching FTP on the Web: a Few Starting Places."

Figure 8-1 shows a search for the **ws_ftp** program using Archie, and Figure 8-2 shows the results (from a list of 50 sites). For each return I got the name of the FTP site, a link to the directory containing the file I'm seeking (if I want to see what else is available there, including similar files and other versions of the file I'm seeking), and a link to the file itself.

What I didn't get is an estimate of how long it would take to download the file, useful information that's always available when you download a file directly from AOL (see "A Word about File Size").

Note *With earlier methods of using Archie (via Telnet and e-mail), you had to know some rudimentary commands, then type them in accurately. The commands have now been embedded into easy-to-use Web forms, though only a few of Archie's many commands have been implemented in most of these Web sites. Lists of Archie servers and key Archie commands are available at the Bunyip Web site mentioned earlier in this section.*

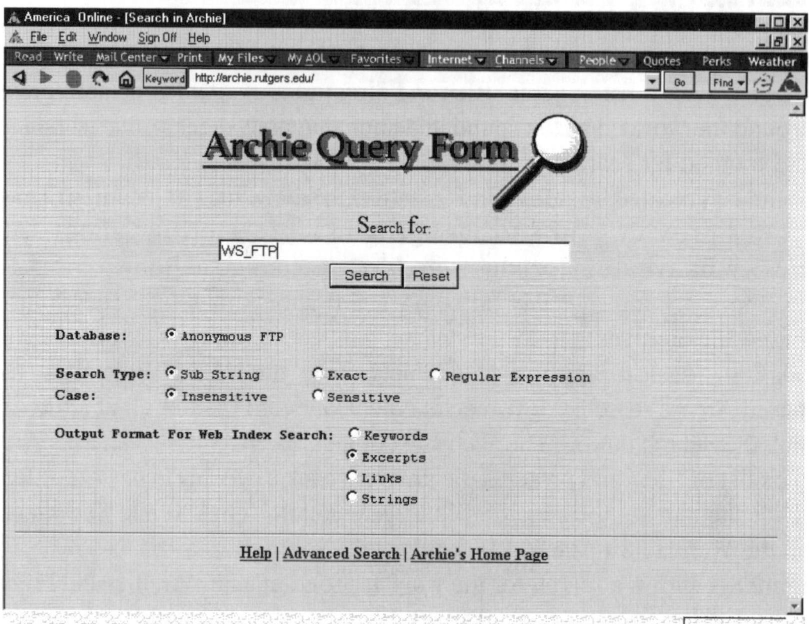

FIGURE 8-1 The new Archie service at Rutgers

Searching FTP on the Web: a Few Starting Places

The following World Wide Web sites give you a simple, point-and-click interface to Archie. All of them are very busy, and it's good netiquette to begin with servers in your own country (the first three are in the U.S.):

- **http://archie.rutgers.edu/archie.html**
- **http://www.lerc.nasa.gov/archieplex/doc/form.html**
- **http://www.amdahl.com/internet/archieplex/form.html**
- **http://www.nexor.com/public/archie/archieplex/doc/form.html**
- **http://cuiwww.unige.ch/archieplexform.html**

If you're not familiar with the Web, all you have to do is type any of these Web addresses into the Address box on the AOL navigation bar, and then click Go.

To use these Archie sites, all you have to do is enter a filename or part of one in a text box, and click Search (or Submit, or something similar).

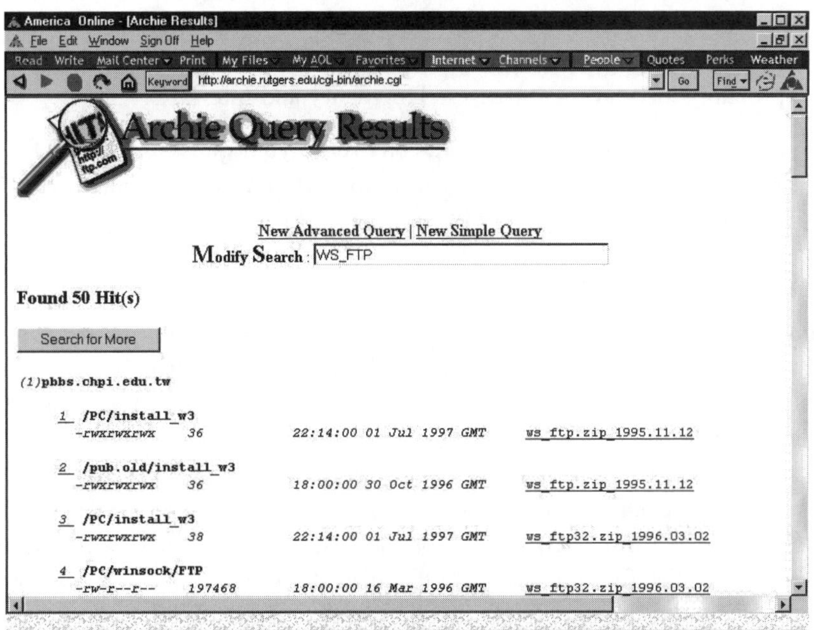

FIGURE 8-2 The first four results of an Archie search shown in Figure 8-1

Archie on the Web: Common Options

As easy as it is to do an Archie search over the Web, Archie *forms* (windows with text boxes, radio boxes, check boxes, and other Windows elements) can still present some fairly obscure choices, such as:

- **What type of search** The basic choice is *exact* versus *substring* (don't worry about "regular expressions" unless you know the Unix operating system). If you do an exact search, Archie searches only for the exact characters you type in, paying attention to uppercase and lowercase. If you do a substring search, you're really doing a search for a part of a name, which makes sense if you're not exactly sure of the full filename. If you do a *case*-insensitive *substring* search (Figure 8-1), Archie ignores whether the actual filename has uppercase or lowercase letters.

In general, FTP is case sensitive, so when you are searching for a specific file, pay attention to its pattern of capitalization.

- **Which server to search** There aren't all that many Archie servers in the world—only about two dozen—to handle the entire Internet's file-searching needs. Try to search the Archie server closest to you—probably the servers at Rutgers University and InterNIC.
- **How many hits** A *hit* is just an answer to your question—an FTP site with the file for which you are searching. If you've chosen a server close to you, you can safely keep the number of hits low (under 50).

USING FTP THE AOL WAY

When you search FTP using Archie-over-the-Web, search results are presented in a clickable list of FTP sites that contain the file (Figure 8-2). Usually, you'll be able to click either on the directory containing the file or on the file itself. Just click to download the file.

What could be easier? In fact, it's not always a good idea to use the browser to access FTP sites, even if you're using a Web-based search. For one thing, FTP sites don't always accept browser requests for files. Also, it's slower as a rule using the browser to download files than using AOL's specialized FTP client (the one you get at *keyword: FTP* or by selecting FTP from the Internet menu). Finally, a browser wasn't made to access FTP; it was made to access the Web. As a result, when you use the browser, you don't get all the options you get when you use *keyword: FTP* (Figure 8-3).

Here are some reasons to use AOL's built-in FTP software (*keyword: FTP*) rather than the browser to download files:

- AOL's FTP client gives you the ability to explicitly request non-anonymous FTP (see the "Anonymous and Non-anonymous FTP" box). The browser does not always gracefully handle anonymous and non-anonymous FTP log-ins, and sometimes you'll even be prompted to supply a username and password for anonymous FTP sites.
- The browser can be slow in connecting to and navigating FTP sites, and even slower in downloading files; connections can time out if they take too long.
- With Download Manager (available only if you use AOL to download files), you can (a) keep track of files you've downloaded using AOL's FTP client, (b) decompress them by clicking a button, and (c) jog your memory when you forget where you've downloaded them (see "AOL's Download Manager" later in this chapter).
- AOL's My Place service (Chapter 7), also lets you *upload* files—something you can't do using the AOL browser.

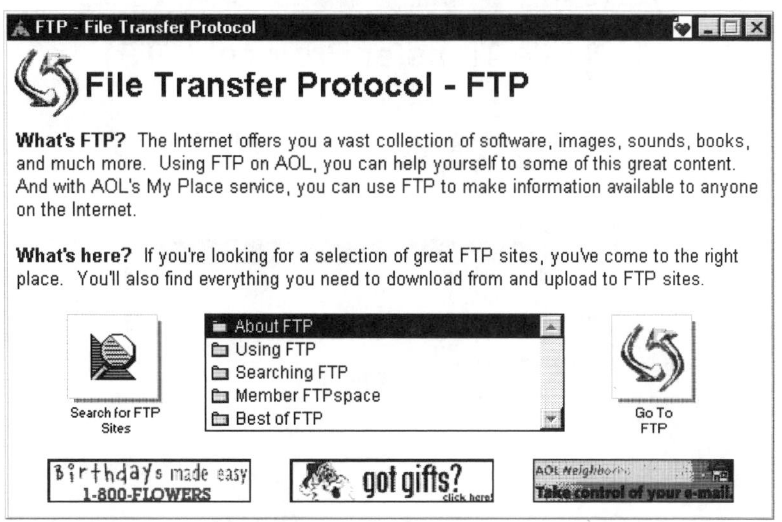

FIGURE 8-3 AOL's starting point for downloading files from the Internet (*keyword: FTP*)

Before using AOL's FTP client to download a file, make sure you have the file's exact directory path. Here's a useful exercise: search and retrieve **WinZip.exe**, a great program for both creating compressed Windows files and unzipping them. An Archie search reveals that the file is available at many FTP sites, including one of my favorite nonprofits (**igc.org**).

Follow these four numbered steps below to retrieve *any* file.

Note *The following example is merely illustrative. Since the number of incoming connections on FTP sites is limited, you should visit a site only when you need a file.*

1. **Connect to the site.**
   - Select FTP from the Internet menu to go the FTP area (Figure 8-3).
   - Click on the Go to FTP button. The Anonymous FTP screen comes up.

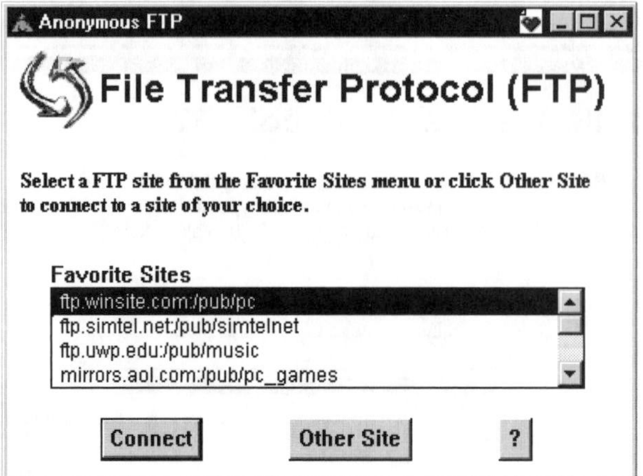

- Click on Other Site.
- In the Other Site screen, type the FTP address into the Site Address box. Do *not* put a checkmark in the "Ask for login name and password" box. Click Connect.

Tip *If you know the entire file path, enter it (see "Avoiding Window Clutter"). If you enter a full path to a specific file, you can skip to the last step.*

When you connect successfully with the FTP site, a message comes up from the FTP site itself. The welcoming message sometimes includes the name of someone at the site (the FTP administrator) to contact if there's a problem. This message can also provide the names of mirror sites. Read the message, and then click OK (see "Great FTP Sites Mirrored on AOL" later in this chapter).

Avoiding Window Clutter

Here's a great tip for avoiding window clutter from Bob Hirsh, who administers AOL's FTP service: In the FTP window, you can download a specific file using its file URL (**file://**) in the Site Address box of the Other Site window.

For example, typing **file://ftp.cdrom.com/.2/games/windows/jokes/fish3.zip** in the Site Address box grabs the file without opening a single window! This command navigates directly through the **ftp.cdrom.com** FTP site, follows a path down through several directories, and then finds a file called fish3.zip. (You will find many games here if this one's not available for downloading!) Note the inclusion of the host name, **ftp.cdrom.com**, as part of the entire address, separated from the directory path by a forward slash and no space.

Navigating directly to a specific directory such as **ftp://ftp.cdrom.com/.2/games/windows/jokes/** is also a good way to minimize the number of open windows, but it doesn't itself download the file. (For that, select the file and click Download Now.)

2. **Navigate to the directory that holds the file you're seeking.**

   After getting past the welcome message, you'll find yourself looking at the top level of the FTP site—something like the root directory of your hard disk, the point at which you start looking for a file on your local computer. Where to start? In general, it's best to start in the *pub* directory—the publicly accessible directory of files available by anonymous FTP. Within pub, double-click the subdirectory and keep clicking until you come to your file. In this case, the path leads through the following subdirectories:

   - INTERNET
   - windows
   - Misc

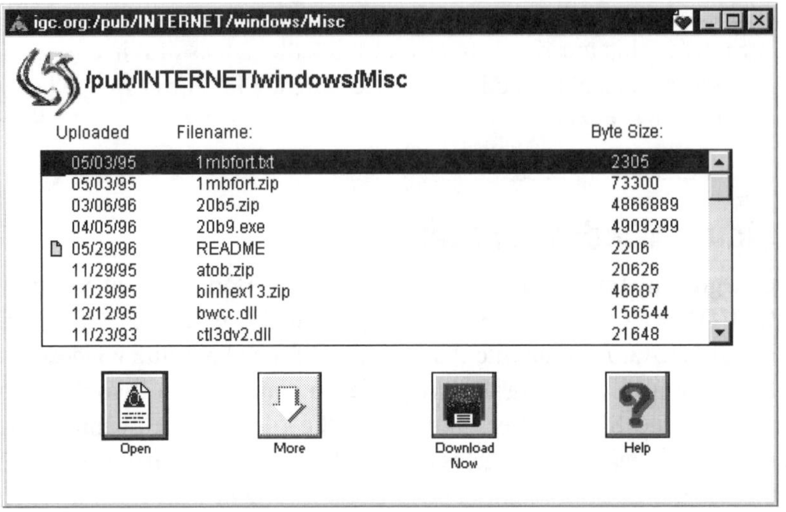

3. **Locate the file.**

Identify the file you're seeking in the directory you've opened. You'll see three pieces of information for the file: the date it was uploaded, its filename, and its size in bytes (without commas—so look closely to make sure it's 40,000 and not 400,000). For more information about file size, see the "A Word about File Size" box. Note that capitalized filenames precede filenames in lowercase, and names beginning with numbers precede both.

Note *Throughout an FTP site, you'll notice the dates when a file or directory was last modified (uploaded). Just because a folder was last modified on one date doesn't mean it won't contain files with more recent dates, so don't be put off by old dates. Likewise, if a site's README file is really old, the individual files at the site may still be more recent; it's just that no one's updated the README file. Finally, the file least likely to be changed—the opening message—can make a site seem old, even if many individual files are up to date.*

To see how long it will take to download a file, select it and click the Open button (note that you're not actually opening the file, just getting some information about it).

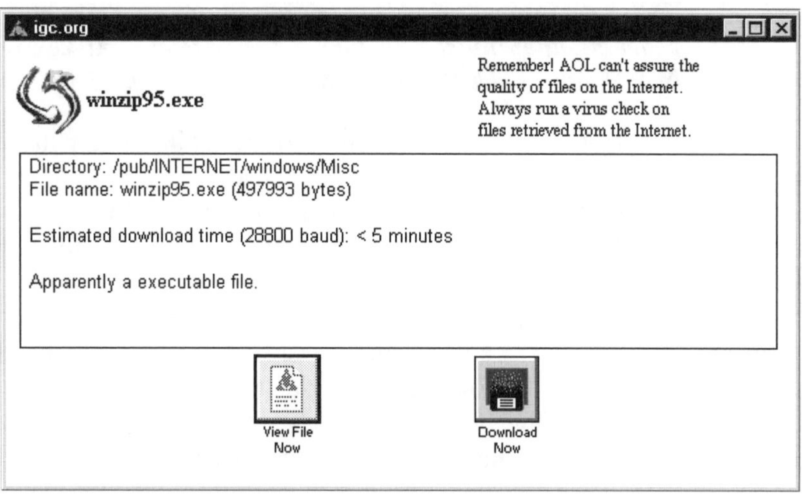

For text files, you'll be able to read the text without downloading the file; just click View File Now.

Tip *Many FTP sites have README and INDEX files that can provide valuable information. A README file usually provides advice about choosing and using files. An INDEX file usually provides a listing of files in a directory. Using AOL's FTP client (*keyword: FTP*), you can read both types of file right on your screen without downloading the files to your hard disk. Just select the file and click View File Now.*

A Word about File Size

A file's size, together with your modem speed, determines how long it will take to download. File size is also important because files take up space on your hard drive, and even a huge hard drive can be eaten up if you do enough downloading.

Files are measured in *kilobytes* (1,024 *bytes*, an important unit for measuring data); 1,024 kilobytes is a *megabyte*.

On AOL, when you double-click a file at an FTP site to download the file, you first get a window that estimates how long it will take for the file to download. With a 28.8 modem, the estimated download for a 2 Mb file is *<18 minutes,* or under 18 minutes, while for a 40K file it's under a minute.

Yet another reason to buy a fast modem! At keyword: AOLstore, *click Modems if you want to shop for one.*

It's a good idea to weigh how much content you're getting against the time it takes to download a file. Take sound files. A 1 Mb WAV file might, for example, play for under a minute, but so will a standard 15K MIDI file (1-2 percent as big as that WAV file). A huge graphics file can take forever to download and convey little information.

Using Windows 95's Explorer (or Windows 3.1's File Manager), you can learn the size of every file on your system; you can even arrange files by their size in order to find out which ones are taking up the most space. That's the place to start if you're running out of hard drive space and need to make some room by getting rid of those "indispensable" downloaded files.

4. **Download the file.**

   If you want a copy of the file, click Download Now. You'll be prompted by AOL's Download Manager to give the file a filename and directory on your hard drive. The only time to change a filename is when there's already a file with the same name in the directory where you are downloading it. After you've selected a directory on your computer and clicked OK in the Download Manager, you'll see AOL's thermometer box telling you how much of the file has downloaded and how many minutes are left:

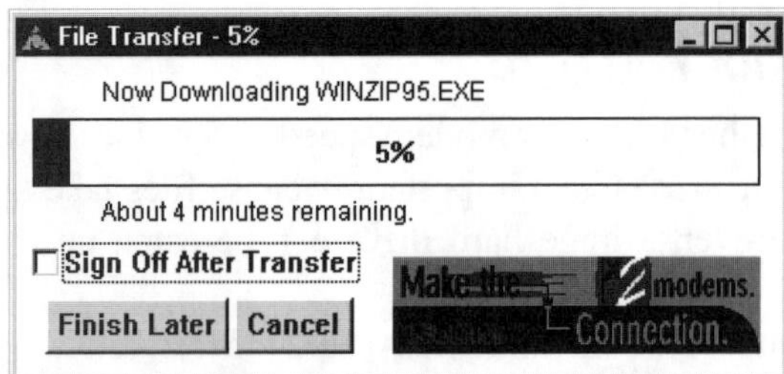

   Using AOL's Download Manager, you cannot create a list of several FTP files you want to download later, in order to download them all at a convenient time (at the end of your session, for example). One reason for this is that FTP connections are limited: there is no guarantee that a site with a file you want will be available when you want to do a "batch"

download (when you connect with a site, you'll usually see a message indicating that you are the twelfth person of a possible total of 20, or something similar). So you've got to download now. You can do something else while you're downloading a single file (like read your mail or browse the Web), but if your computer seems a little sluggish, it's because downloading files is a fairly demanding task for your PC.

Note *With Download Manager you can download only one file at a time, but if you're using the Web to download files, you can download several at a time (it might be slow, but it's possible). See the box "AOL's Download Manager" for more information.*

AOL's Download Manager

On AOL, downloading is downloading—whether it's from one of AOL's many software libraries, an Internet newsgroup, an e-mail message, or an FTP site. The one exception is downloading over the Web, which is handled separately. (Using Windows 95, Start menu | Documents gives you a list of files you've most recently downloaded from the Web.)

AOL offers a series of options to adjust the way you use FTP with Download Manager:

- Whether image files you download (GIF, JPG, PCX format) are automatically displayed as they're downloaded
- Whether a downloaded ZIP file is automatically unzipped when you log off
- Whether a downloaded ZIP file is kept on your hard disk after it's unzipped
- How many downloaded files are recorded in Download Manager. For every file, you get information such as where you downloaded files *from* and where you downloaded them *to*

To see your Download options, select My AOL | Preferences and click Download. Check and uncheck the following boxes as appropriate.

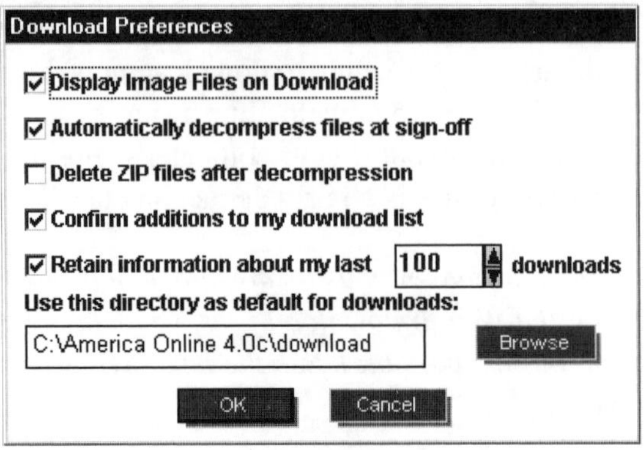

Download Preferences

- [x] Display Image Files on Download
- [x] Automatically decompress files at sign-off
- [ ] Delete ZIP files after decompression
- [x] Confirm additions to my download list
- [x] Retain information about my last 100 downloads

Use this directory as default for downloads:

C:\America Online 4.0c\download — Browse

OK — Cancel

What happens if you can't remember where you've downloaded something? Choose Download Manager from My Files menu, then click the Show Files Downloaded button. Find the file you've downloaded, select it, and click Show Status. Information about the file will be displayed, including its name, size, and where you downloaded it.

How can I unzip something right away, instead of waiting until I sign off? In Download Manager, select the ZIP file and click Decompress.

Where can I get more information? A large set of frequently asked questions is available in the Download Info Center (*keyword: Download Info*).

Navigating an FTP Site Using the AOL FTP Client

Navigating an FTP site usually means going up and down a directory path, from the top (or root) level to lower-level directories and any subdirectories. When you double-click a folder to open it, you open up a new window and go down a level. Close a window to go back up.

If you find yourself at an FTP site in search of a specific file and the file does not appear to be where you expected, the best bet is to start with the pub directory and to browse downward through appropriate subdirectories. A pub directory is usually accessible from the root when you're using anonymous FTP.

Tip *Many FTP sites are maintained as public services to the Internet (as are Archie servers), and most can support only a limited number of incoming connections. In general, it's a good idea to access an FTP site at an after-hours time, bearing in mind that the FTP site is probably in a different time zone from yours. How do you know where a site is? Do a search for the specific site from the main FTP window (Search for FTP Sites). Double-click the name of the site to read a description of the site and scan for a mention of its location.*

Navigating FTP with Your Browser

When you use the AOL browser to navigate FTP, the browser's the only window that's open; it's a good way to avoid window clutter! Another reason to use the browser is that it can actually *play* files, as described in Chapter 6.

Note *When using an FTP site from the browser, you may at some point—or perhaps at many points in a single session—be asked to supply your username and password. If you are, type* **anonymous** *as the username and your full e-mail address (screenname@aol.com), then press* ENTER.

To use the browser, you need to know an FTP site's address and just tack on **ftp://** at the beginning. For instance, typing **ftp://ftp.aol.com** in the Address box (on the AOL toolbar) and clicking GO takes you to the FTP site visited in the previous exercise. Figure 8-4 shows the directory at the AOL site where the AOL software (SETUP.EXE) can also be downloaded.

Using the browser you will see two types of items at an FTP site: files and directories. A directory is labeled as such in the third column (after date and time), while files have a file size associated with them. Clicking a hyperlinked directory name (fourth column) opens up a new directory.

To download a file, just click! If the file is text (AOL30.TXT in Figure 8-4), clicking displays the text. If the file is a binary, clicking brings up a Download File box, which Microsoft Internet Explorer displays while it's figuring out the size and type of file you're about to download. The next box you see gives you the chance to either save the file or to open it, that is, to play it if it's a multimedia file of some

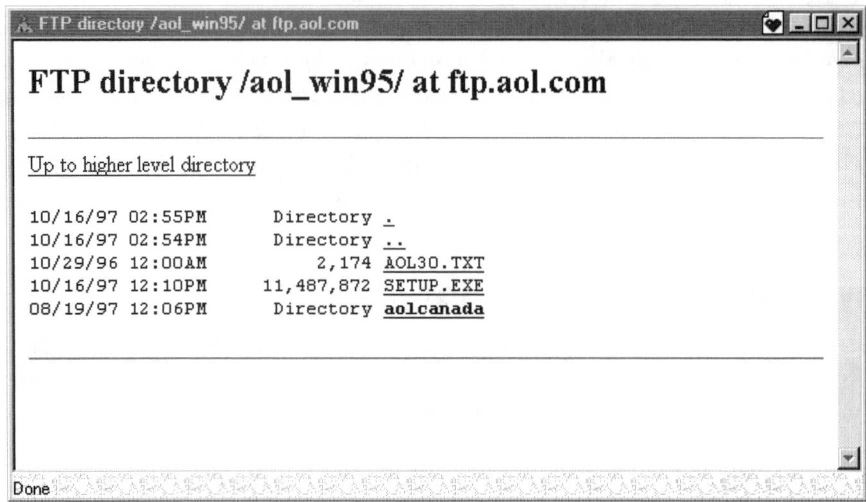

FIGURE 8-4 The Browser's view of AOL's FTP site, showing directories and files

sort. In Figure 8-4, you would want to save the setup.exe file and then run it, because it is a program.

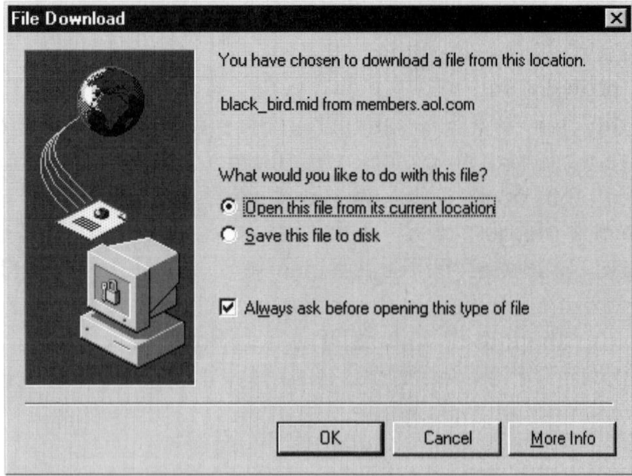

If you'll be saving the file, give it a name and place on your hard disk, and click OK. A new window displays the progress of the download, estimating the amount of time left based on the size of the file and your modem's speed. Because you're not using Download Manager in this case, any ZIP file you download with the browser won't be automatically unzipped when you sign off, so you'll have to use WinZip or a similar utility, readily available at *keyword: Filesearch.*

You can close the browser by clicking the Close box (the X in the upper right-hand corner) in Windows 95 or double-clicking the Control box (the little box in the upper left-hand corner) in Windows 3.1 or Windows 95.

Virus Alert

However you download a file, whether it's using the FTP client or the browser, you need to be careful about viruses—nasty little programs that can harm your programs, your data, or your hard disk. Every file you download from AOL has been checked for viruses. But no file you get from the Internet using FTP has necessarily been checked for viruses. You need to check them yourself.

For the most part, the files that can spread a virus are *programs* (executable files). *Documents* can be infected, but infected documents will not ordinarily hurt other files. Macro viruses, however, or *prank* viruses as they are often called, work by replacing the existing global template in applications like Microsoft Word with a new global template. *Any* document you create or open that is normally dependent on the global template will become infected (difficult to open and use). In addition, these macro viruses can be shared unwittingly simply by anyone else opening the document or spreadsheet. In AOL's software libraries (*keyword: Filesearch*), you can find disinfectant programs such as Scanprot to clean the affected files and replace the global templates.

AOL has excellent information in the AOL Computer Protection Center (*keyword: Virus*), where you'll also find software such as Dr. Solomon's Anti-Virus for detecting and rooting out the nasty critters.

USING THE FILES YOU DOWNLOAD: GRAPHICS, SOUNDS, AND BEYOND

Files you download using AOL's FTP client require an additional piece of software if you want to *use* them. Sounds require a sound player so you can hear them, videos require a video player to watch them, and so on. There's one exception: images. When you download standard image files using FTP, they'll display on your screen. Even so, you may want a more sophisticated program for viewing and editing your downloaded image files.

Note *Chapter 6 looks at how the AOL browser handles multimedia files displayed within Web pages. More and more, the browser itself plays multimedia files, and it's quickly becoming the tool of choice for playing multimedia files of every type.*

Working with Image Files

When you download an image file in one of the common formats, it displays automatically as it's being downloaded. (GIF and JPEG formats make up the overwhelming majority of the image files for PCs available by FTP.) Actually, it's progressively rendered, which means you gradually see more of the file until the whole thing is downloaded and the entire image is visible.

AOL offers built-in editing software to help you tweak your downloaded images. From the File menu, select Open Picture Gallery. Specify the directory where your image file or files are located. Here's a file I found on AOL and opened in AOL's Picture Gallery. Note the controls for adjusting the color, for flipping and rotating the image, and for viewing it in black and white. One button even lets you insert the edited image into an e-mail message and send it to someone.

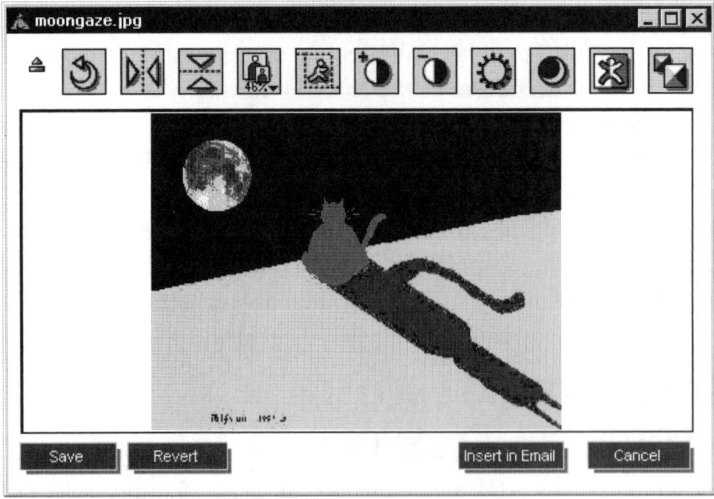

See keyword: Viewers *for popular editing utilities such as PaintShop Pro and LView Pro.*

Where Do You Find Images on FTP?

AOL itself has great and easy-to-search image file libraries, some of which are listed in Table 8-2. If you get adventuresome, FTP has software treasures as well. Since Archie doesn't allow searches for file types (only for filenames), you must use AOL's Search for FTP sites if you're doing a broad search for types of a certain format.

1. From the main FTP screen, click Search FTP Sites and enter any keyword(s) you wish, such as *space gifs*.
2. Double-click any FTP site retrieved by your search, and skim the entry. *Write down the FTP address* and as much file and directory information as you can gather from the site description. If in the URL field you see ***ftp://ames.arc.nasa.gov/***, then the FTP address is just **ames.arc.nasa.gov**. Write down the URL (or select it and copy it using, Edit | Copy).

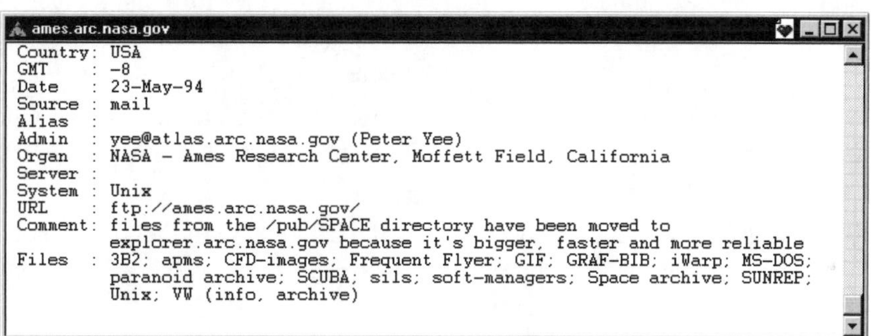

Tip *Resize the AOL window describing a particular FTP site so the text displays normally. To resize a window, pass your mouse cursor over the window's border until the cursor turns into a double arrow. Now click and drag the border and release the mouse button when the window is the size you want.*

3. Return to the Anonymous FTP window by closing the Search window. Click Go To FTP, then click Other Site to enter (or paste) the URL and connect to the site.

Where Do You Find Images on AOL?

If you want sophisticated display and editing capabilities, head for AOL's Multimedia Zone (see Table 8-2). Also, at *keyword: Viewers,* you'll find a bushelful of recommended viewers. Like all AOL software, viewers are guaranteed to be virus-free.

Tip *Using any stand-alone graphics utility or sound player, you can view images or play sounds when you're not online. Just open the program, go to its File menu, choose Open, and select the file you want to use.*

Forum (Keyword)	Software Library & Other Features
Animation & Video (*keyword: Software,* click Animation & Video)	Video files and utilities for QuickTime, AVI, and other formats; includes some animations and animated GIFs; good source of plug-ins
Mac Graphic Arts & Animation (*keyword: MGR*)	Fractals, stereograms, clip art, and utilities, plus FAQs on all these things
PC Multimedia Zone, also known as the PC Animation & Video Forum (*keyword: MMZone*); from here, visit the Video Zone for links to companies and files on the Web	Staffed area, with message boards and software libraries
PC Music and Sound Forum (*keyword: PC Music*)	File libraries, Web links, message boards, a very useful FAQ about playing music on AOL, large libraries of MIDI and WAV files by type of music
Mac Music and Sound Forum (*keyword: Mac Music*)	MIDI, MOD, WAV and other files, and much more, with sound-playing utilities and operating instructions

TABLE 8-2 AOL forums devoted to multimedia

Working with Sound Files

Sound files are a bit more complex than image files. For one thing, you can hear them only if you have a sound card and speakers. For another, if you do have this stuff, Download Manager does not give you the chance to hear sounds automatically as they are downloaded from an FTP site. You must find a player—a separate program—if you want to hear a sound file. You may also need a different player for different types of sound files! Luckily, all the additional software you need is available on AOL.

Most common sound-file formats, such as AU, MIDI, and WAV, can be played using the Media Player, a little program that is built right into Windows. In Windows 95, this program is available from the Start menu by clicking the following menus: Programs, then Accessories, then Multimedia, and then selecting Media Player.

*Huge libraries of sound clips as well as utilities for playing every kind of sound clip are available in the PC Music and Sound Forum (*keyword: PC Music).

MIDI files simulate musical instruments digitally and squeeze a great deal of content into some very small packages. A 15K file can run for a minute and delight any child within earshot. You play it *within AOL* by going to the File menu and selecting Open, then choosing the file. MIDI files can also be played with the Microsoft Media Player.

Tip *Looking for good MIDI sites? Try the Ultimate MIDI Page (**http://www.netrunner.net/~jshlackm/**). A dozen newsgroups have encoded MIDI files, too; check out the **alt.binaries.sounds.midi.*** hierarchy.*

Setting Up a Helper Application

You can set up Windows 95 to automatically open the browser (or any other program, such as PaintShop Pro or LView Pro) when you open a particular file type (sound, image, or video). From the Windows 95 Explorer, select View | Folder Options, and then click on the File Types tab.

Using the File Type Details section, you indicate what program you want to open with a specific file type, and a file's type is indicated by its extension, as explained at the beginning of the chapter. To associate a specific file type with a specific program:

1. Select the file type from the list of Registered file types, and click Edit to bring up the window shown above.
   - If you see the word *open* in the Actions box, click Edit. In the "Editing action for type…" box, click Browse.
   - If you don't see the word *open* in the Actions box, click New. In the New Action box, type Open in the Action field, then click Browse.
2. Navigate to the place on your hard drive where Internet Explorer (or another viewing application) is installed (c:/program files/Microsoft Internet, or wherever the viewing application is located). Select the **Iexplore** (or other) program, then click Open.
3. Close the three open windows: Click OK to close the Edit Action or New Action window. Click Close to leave the Edit File Type window (shown above). Click Close to leave the Folder Options window.

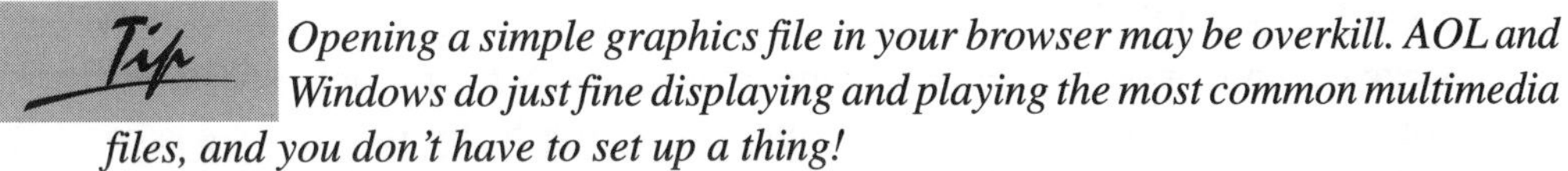

Opening a simple graphics file in your browser may be overkill. AOL and Windows do just fine displaying and playing the most common multimedia files, and you don't have to set up a thing!

Working with Video Files

Video files don't quite stack up to the quality of the video on VCR. The images are jumpy, the box in which you see them is tiny (an inch or two square), and the experience is quickly over. What Hobbes said of life—that it's poor, nasty, brutish, and short—applies to video over the Internet as well. The streaming effect on the Web, which lets you experience multimedia without special software, is much better, but streaming video files such as **RealVideo** aren't widely available by FTP.

The common video file types available by FTP are MPEG, MOV, and AVI. AVI can be played with Microsoft's **Media Player** (included with Windows 95), which can usually play MPEG as well. MPEG, however, comes in many varieties, and you may need to visit *keyword: Viewers* if you can't run a specific MPEG file using the **Media Player**; many viewers can be downloaded from this place. The **Nettoob** program, for example, is an excellent piece of shareware for playing MPEGs and AVIs as well as common sound files. For QuickTime (MOV) videos, you'll need a QuickTime player, available on AOL at *keyword: VZ.*

Tip

*If you use Windows 3.1, make sure to download the 16-bit version of the QuickTime player; for Windows 95, use the 32-bit version. Chapter 10 goes into the difference between 16-bit and 32-bit. AOL has a special forum called the Video Zone (*keyword: VZ*) where you'll find answers to all your video questions, as well as players and files.*

GRAPPLING WITH COMPRESSED AND ZIPPED FILES

One common characteristic of multimedia files—sounds, images, videos—is that they're often *big*—500K, 1 Mb, and more. (See "A Word about File Size" earlier in this chapter.)

As a result of their size, they take up more and more space on Internet computers, they can take a long time to download, and they can take up a lot of space on your computer. To deal with these issues, site administrators and designers often shrink, or *compress*, multimedia files before making them available via FTP. This reduces storage space at the FTP or Web site and reduces download time. You can't, however, use compressed files until you've uncompressed them, which is another thing AOL can handle automatically for you if you want.

Often compressed files will be *zipped*, as well, meaning that several files have been packaged up in a single file to streamline the downloading process. With PC files, you can spot a file that's been compressed or zipped by its ZIP extension (*chap1.zip*, for example). With Macintosh files, these files usually have an extension of *SIT* or *SEA*. Zipping files also compresses them to some extent, so you'll often see individual files that are zipped to reduce their size.

There are two ways to deal with zipped files:

- Unzip them yourself, right after they're downloaded.
- Let AOL do it for you when you sign off.

UNZIP THEM AS SOON AS THEY HAVE BEEN DOWNLOADED To do so, you'll need a program such as PKZIP (for DOS) or WinZip (for Windows). Both are available on America Online (*keyword: Filesearch*) as well as on the Internet (see the downloading exercise earlier in this chapter). You'll need to download the program (itself compressed and zipped) and install it. To install, just run the file (File | Run in Windows 3.1 or Start menu | Run in Windows 95). Browse to where the file is located, select it, and press ENTER. Follow the onscreen prompts.

It's useful to have a program such as WinZip especially if you'll be compressing your own files for transfer via e-mail. An even easier way to unzip a file is to let Download Manager do it.

1. From the My Files menu on the toolbar, select Download Manager.
2. Click Show Files Downloaded, then select the file you've downloaded and click Decompress. The files zipped up together will be kept together in a new subdirectory (with the same name as the unzipped file) under the directory where the file was downloaded.

LET AOL UNZIP COMPRESSED FILES AUTOMATICALLY WHEN YOU LOG OFF You can set your preferences to automatically unzip files when you sign off and even to delete the zipped file afterwards (thereby saving space on your hard disk). As when you do it yourself, all the unzipped files are placed in a subdirectory with the same name as the ZIP file itself. So, if you download a file named SCOOTER.ZIP to c:\America Online 4.0\Download and AOL unzips it, the component files will appear in your system in a new C:\America Online 4.0\Download\Scooter directory.

DOWNLOADING FILES FROM AMERICA ONLINE

On the face of it, America Online's collection of a hundred thousand or so files is modest in comparison to the Internet's *millions* of files available via anonymous FTP. But several things make AOL's software libraries indispensable:

- FTP files are frequently available *in many versions on multiple sites*. The redundancy reduces the number of unique files available over FTP. More important, the redundancy can be confusing, since it's not always possible to know which version of a file is the best or the most recent. Many of the best FTP files are available on AOL as well and can be downloaded more quickly from there. If several versions are available, you can tell by filename or upload date which version is the most current.

Great FTP Sites Mirrored on AOL

Why are the same files available in so many places on the Internet? The Net is a decentralized and distributed network. In part there's redundancy because there's no central control, but there's also intentional redundancy in order to make sure important files will always be available in case one site is unavailable. For the latter reason, you'll find mirror sites of the most popular FTP resources.

AOL maintains such mirrors at *keyword: FTP* (or select FTP from the Internet menu). Click on Go To FTP. At the Anonymous FTP window, you'll see a list of Favorite Sites. The mirrors are the first ones listed, and you can tell a mirror because it has a site name *and directory path* (that is, only part of a larger site is being mirrored). One such site is **rtfm.mit.edu/pub**, a mirror of MIT's wonderful FAQ archive, described at the end of Chapter 5. Another is **ftp.simtel.net/pub/simtelnet**, a vast archive of DOS and Windows software. (In Simtelnet, open the directory for your operating system, either *win95* or *win3*; open the *Winsock* subdirectory for a big collection of Internet utilities, described in the 00_index file.) Between the sheer amount of information locked in the newsgroup FAQs and the cool stuff at Simtel, you'll fill up your hard disk in no time.

- All of AOL's files have been subjected to virus checks. You can't be sure that the Net's files have been virus checked.
- Downloading files via FTP, especially when you use the browser, can be painfully slow. Using AOL's FTP client (*keyword: FTP*), downloading is reliably fast, since it opens a dedicated connection with the FTP site. (However, with FTP you can download only one file at a time, and your computer's performance can slow down as the processor handles the download.)
- Searching with Archie requires that you know a filename, or at least part of its name. On AOL's software libraries, your search is not restricted to filenames. You can also search by subject, author, date, file type, or other criteria.

WHERE TO FIND THE GREAT FILES ON AOL

Software, images, videos, and all the utilities you need to run these files are available throughout the AOL service.

Computing Channel

The starting point in any search for files on AOL is the Computing channel, available from the main Channels screen or the Channels menu on the toolbar.

- Daily Download, featured in the channel, gives you the chance to read in detail about a new file every day and to download it, a useful feature if you have one of those new, large hard drives (four gigabytes or bigger).
- Download Software, a Computing department, links you to big software libraries, arranged in categories like Business & Finance, Fun & Games, Internet, and Tools & Utilities.

Table 8-2 lists other AOL forums where you'll find files, utilities, and, in many cases, someone to turn to if you have questions about finding and using software.

Note *The ZDNet software library is now available on the Web (go to* keyword: ZDNet *and click* Download*). Sites are rated by Ziff Davis's editors and nicely categorized. Another magazine publisher with a huge software library on the Web is CMP (*keyword: CMP*).*

Software Search

It's hard to avoid AOL's Software Search window (Figure 8-5), which lets you search an archive of more than 100,000 files. It's available in many ways:

- In the Computing channel, click Download Software, then click Software Search, then click Shareware. (If you click Brand Name instead of Shareware, you will have the opportunity to purchase commercial software packages.)
- Use *keyword: Filesearch* from anywhere.
- On the main AOL toolbar, click the small Find button and select Software; click Shareware.

To narrow your search for specific software at *keyword: FileSearch*:

1. Choose a file release date: All Dates, Past Month, or Past Week. Click the appropriate radio button. Searching for last week's or last month's files can filter out files that may be outdated or may not run on your operating system.
2. Choose several categories of files to search for by clicking the check boxes. Choosing more than one can usefully narrow the search results—checking both Games and Windows launches a search for game files that run under Windows, for instance. Choosing Applications will keep you from retrieving text files.
3. Type in any qualifying text in the box at the bottom. If you do know a filename, enter it here.
4. Click Search to run the search. The results of the search in Figure 8-5 are shown in Figure 8-6. Double-click any result to get information about the file. You will get information about the file's upload date, what the file does, and any requirements for using it. If it's a program, you will get instructions for installing it. From the information window, you can choose to download the file now or download it later using Download Manager.

Note that the files in Figure 8-6 are arranged by category. In some AOL software libraries listed in Table 8-2, you will have the option of sorting files by the date they were uploaded and by subject.

Software Search
1. Select a Timeframe: Choose only one
All Dates Past Month Past Week
Today in the Superstore...
Computing Superstore
2. Select a Category: Choose the categories you wish to search:
Applications Games OS/2
Development Graphics & Animation Telecommunications
DOS Hardware Windows
Education Music & Sound
3. Enter a Search Definition: Narrow search by typing in key words.
avi
SEARCH
COMPUTERS & SOFTWARE MAC SEARCH HELP Keyword: FileSearch

FIGURE 8-5 AOL's software library: the more information you provide, the better the results

Tip *To search for a specific word in a long list of files, go to the Edit menu and choose Find in Top Window. Enter some text to search for and click Find. This technique searches headers (what you see in Figure 8-6), not the full text of the file descriptions.*

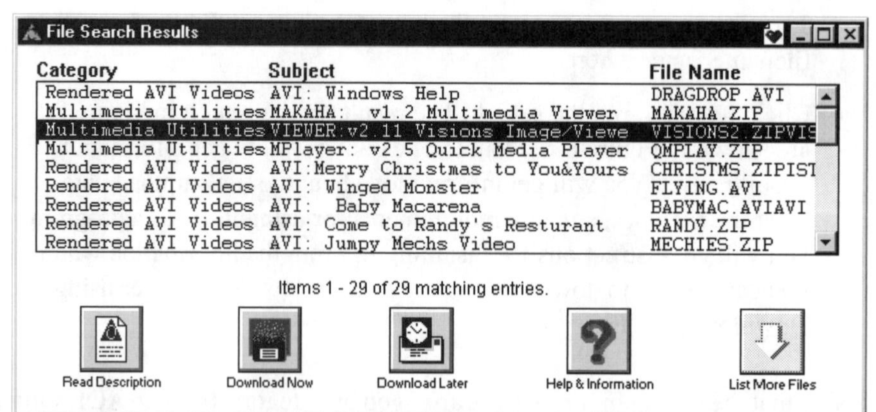

FIGURE 8-6 Results of the search shown in Figure 8-5

Using Shareware

It should be pretty obvious that the software available via FTP and on AOL differs in an important way from the software available in shrink-wrapped boxes that you buy at your computer store: it's distributed directly to you, and it doesn't cost anything (at least, there's no monetary outlay). Otherwise, commercial software doesn't necessarily differ in quality from the software available online.

Many software creators prefer to distribute software directly to users, since it reduces their distribution costs and creates the opportunity for valuable customer feedback. However, much of this software is *shareware*, meaning that the creator expects a nominal payment of $10 to $30 or even more. Sometimes the "free" software will lack some features until you pony up the cash. Sometimes it will expire 30 or 45 days after it's installed. And sometimes the creator will rely on the honor system or forego payment altogether, in the hopes of creating a big group of enthusiastic users. Netscape (the company) got its start by giving away browser software and establishing a huge market, then selling other products to companies. They recently returned to the "free software" concept. Some of the best software on AOL is shareware, and many software creators both request and deserve your support (read: through payment). A rule of thumb: if you use shareware on AOL, please respect the people whose hard work makes shareware possible.

If you prefer your bits in boxes, you can buy excellent commercial software at *keyword: Computer Superstore,* which is prominently available from the Computing channel (*keyword: Computing Superstore*). Or, go to *keyword: AOLstore* and click Software. Some of the commercial software can be downloaded directly from AOL after you've paid for it, saving the packaging costs and ensuring the fastest delivery to you.

No Internet service is as closely integrated into America Online as FTP. In many cases, AOL's features for working with files—Download Manager, FileGrabber, myriad software libraries, software forums—*duplicate* what's available on the Internet via FTP. The real value of AOL's file-related features is that they *complement* what you'll find on FTP by making it easier to use the incredibly rich, globally scattered files available on the Internet. Since files affect everything you do on the Internet, the services you find on AOL—from the forums, to the software libraries, to the help resources—can enrich everything you do on the Internet.

FROM HERE...

This chapter wraps up the discussion of the Internet programs and services that are built into the AOL service. The next chapter takes a look at how to find information and people on the Internet. It moves away from *how* you use the tools to *what you do with them*, which is probably your reason for being on the Net in the first place.

Chapter 9

Finding What *You* Want on the Internet

Browsing the globe is fun, but not everyone has unlimited time to read about things they're not that interested in. When you really need information—whether it's a recipe for pie crust, a guide to raising terriers, a phone number in Iowa City, Babe Ruth's birthday, or today's showings at a local movie theater—how do you find it? There's yet another challenge: some of the information is not all that great. Unlike AOL, on the Internet there's an abundance of less than useful information; at any rate, it can be difficult to find information of direct use to you.

This chapter provides a complete guide to getting what you need from the Internet, whether you're searching for raw information or for knowledgeable people with information at their fingertips. You'll read about:

- A quick and easy search strategy ("Better Living Through Good Searching")
- Using AOL's NetFind to meet your searching needs
- Finding information on the World Wide Web using the major Web search services
- Finding mailing lists, so you can get information from *people*
- Finding people's and businesses' e-mail and street addresses
- Doing many searches at the same time

WHAT'S ON THE INTERNET AND WHAT'S NOT?

With so much information on the Net, many people assume everything is on the Net. It's not true, at least not yet. Here are some things you *won't* find on the Internet:

- **Books** You *won't* find whole libraries or books that are still in print, and if you want easily accessible online encyclopedias, you're better off starting with AOL (*keyword: CCE*). On the Internet you *will* find more than a thousand public-domain books electronically published under the auspices of Project Gutenberg (**http://www.promo.net/pg/**). Kevin Savetz has created a valuable directory of this and many other public-domain resources at **http://www.savetz.com/pd** (no longer being updated but unlikely ever to be out of date!). On the Internet you will find superb resources *about* current books and publishers (starting with BookWire at **http://www.bookwire.com**). Finally, you can buy any of millions of in-print and out-of-print books at Barnes and Noble (*keyword: Barnes*) and Amazon.com (**http://www.amazon.com**). Searching the B&N or Amazon.com catalog is a good way to do a literature review for any research project.
- **Really private information** You *won't* find lists of Social Security and credit-card numbers on the Internet, nor will you find tax records and employment information. You will find mega-reams of information *about* companies. You will also find street addresses and e-mail addresses for more than 100 million people and businesses.
- **Legal materials** If you do legal research, you should probably still use a proprietary service such as Lexis-Nexis to get current case law, local statutes, federal regulations, and the like. The Internet is catching up, however, and you may be able to find what you need at the searchable legal directory **http://www.findlaw.com**. One of the best ways to stay informed on laws-in-the-making is the Thomas site (named after Thomas Jefferson), run by the Library of Congress, which lets you read selected House committee transcripts and find out how well your congress-folk are representing you (**http://thomas.loc.gov**).
- **Searchable multimedia files** The Web is much touted for its sounds and other multimedia effects, but for technical reasons the myriad GIF, AVI, and other files are not yet readily searchable. This, too, is changing, and later in this chapter I'll mention a few sites such as Hotbot and Lycos that help you find Beatles sound clips, or pictures of sailboats, or whatever you please.

Better Living Through Good Searching

Sure it's easy to search the Net. It's even easier *not* to find what you're looking for. Here is a procedure for finding what you want as quickly and effectively as possible:

Step One: Be as Clear as Possible about What You Need to Find Out.

Does it have to be authoritative or hold up in court? The Web might not be the best place to start, but people on the Internet might have advice and useful information. Ask someone in a mailing list. Chapter 4 provides a complete introduction to mailing lists.

- Do you need software? Try FTP (see Chapter 8) or AOL's huge software library at *keyword: Filesearch*. Looking for image or sound files, or a *type* of file? Try Lycos or Hotbot, with their special file-searching features (see "Search Arsenal: The Best of the Rest" later in this chapter).
- Is the information discrete (the number of car washes in Houston)? Search the Web. Or are you at the start of deeper research (for a school paper, for instance)? Start with a directory such as AOL.com's Web Center.
- Are others likely to be interested in your question? Check out newsgroups and mailing lists, especially if your interest is long-term rather than a one-time need for a fact.

Step Two: Choose the Best Tool for Your Needs.

With so many search services, it's sometimes hard to know where to start. You need to choose between an index and a directory, as explained a little later in this chapter, and you then choose between individual directories and indexes.

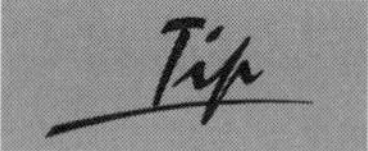

Get as much mileage as you can from AOL NetFind, described in a few pages, but understand the benefits of the other tools and use them when your standby doesn't give you the results you need.

Step Three: Turn Your Question into a Query.

You have questions; computers understand only *queries* (a word or words in a deliberate order and, optionally, joined by important words like *AND*). How do you get from one to the other? Some sites (Lycos and InfoSeek) let you put queries in your own terms (called *natural language*). For others, you must think of one or more *keywords* that convey your search needs. With keywords it helps to be explicit (using *terriers* rather than *dogs*) and to use several keywords from most specific to least (*+terriers +breeding +clubs*). The plus sign tells the search engine that you have to find Web pages with those particular words.

Step Four: Evaluate Your Results and, If Necessary, Refine Your Query.

If your query was specific, you can usually limit yourself to the top 10 or 20 sites returned by it. If any particular site looks especially good, click the More Like This link by the site (as in AOL NetFind). If the results aren't useful, refine your query by making your query more specific. If *terriers* didn't work, for example, try *short-haired terriers*.

FINDING INFORMATION ON THE WORLD WIDE WEB

The sheer size of the Web makes it a good place to start for many searches. Where exactly do you start your Web search? The first choice to make is between an *index* and a *directory*. Then, choose a specific index or directory (this chapter provides a mini-guide to the best services in "Search Arsenal: The Best of the Rest").

As you'll see in a few pages, AOL NetFind offers an excellent index *and* an excellent directory. Before using NetFind, it helps to have a sense of when to use an index and when to use a directory.

Index or Directory?

Think of a book. Nonfiction books usually have a table of contents and an index. The table of contents takes you to chapters, big clumps of related information about a particular subject (for example, "Plants of North America"). The index takes you to highly specific references (such as "kudzu, diseases of, in the Southern states"), no matter what chapter they're in. Or, think of AOL: the Channels menu takes you

to specific channels, huge groupings of information and interactive opportunities around a big theme such as sports or entertainment. AOL Find (*keyword: AOL Find*) lets you seek out specific forums of the hundreds available, no matter what channel they're in.

On the Web you have a similar choice:

- *Directories* give you access to groupings of Web sites about some large subject, such as Business or, within Business, Marketing. Directories are meant to be *browsed*, which means you start with a general category and drill down to subtopics and sub-subtopics until you find something of interest. Directories often rate and annotate sites.
- *Indexes* on the Web give you the same kind of targeted results you get with an index in a book. They are useful when you have a clear idea of what you want—clear enough to ask a specific query.

The general process of using any index is similar: First you choose what you are searching (the Web or Usenet newsgroups, for example). Then you specify what you are searching for (your query). Finally, you click a button (Find, Go Get It, Search, or something similar) or press the ENTER key. You get back a list of matches, and clicking any result whisks you off to a particular site. If your query was off-target or too broad, refine it.

Here's an important difference between the two ways of looking for information. Indexes such as AOL NetFind are created by *computers* and are useful if you know exactly what you are looking for. Directories are compiled by *people* and can be excellent starting places if you need general information or are just starting to learn about something. Indexes are as a rule much bigger than directories, but directories such as NetFind's TimeSavers tend to be more reliable than indexes—every site was chosen for a reason, while in an index sites are chosen by computer programs that crawl the entire World Wide Web collecting URLs.

Search Terms and What They Mean

Here are some terms you may see on the Web when you do searches:

Boolean operators These are terms like AND and OR, which you use to join your *keywords* and indicate exactly what you are seeking. See the sidebar "The No Bull Guide to Boolean Operators."

Browse In a *directory*, you browse categories of sites such as Business or Recreation, instead of doing a highly focused search for specific information. The approach is usually top-down, from a general category to less general subtopics.

Database A structured list. Each row in the list contains related information, for example a URL for a Web page and the words appearing on that Web page. A database stores information and makes it searchable.

Directory A catalog of selected sites, often with ratings and descriptions, arranged into topics for easy *browsing*. A good place to get an overview of a subject.

Engine A geeky word that usually means *searchable index* plus the Web "crawlers" and similar tools used to create it. Excite is an engine, but Yahoo is a directory. Engines are a good place to start a search for specific information.

Hit A single item returned by a query. Hits are also known as *returns.*

Index A listing of URLs and associated words (that is, you enter words, and it *returns* URLs). Indexes make it easy to quickly find a specific URL. Search for *wild roses*, and you bring up a whole bunch of URLs for the Web pages containing that phrase.

Keyword The word or words you type at a search site to indicate what you are looking for. (When you use AOL, a *keyword* is the word assigned to an AOL area that you type into the Keyword window or Address box in order to go there.)

Phrase Two or more words that together have a special meaning, such as "League of Nations" or "home run" or "Murphy's law." To indicate that you are searching for a bunch of words in a certain order, you surround the phrase with quotes.

Query What you are searching for, in terms the computer can work with. Queries can be simple *keywords*, optionally linked by *Boolean operators*. A *natural language* query is one that is expressed in *your own, conversational* terms, not computerese.

Relevance The computer's best guess about whether a Web page will meet your needs. Most search engines list the most relevant sites first. Relevancy takes into consideration such factors as how many times your keywords appear on a page, how many of the words you entered are found (if you entered several words), and where the words appear on a page (the closer to the top, the more relevant).

Returns An *engine's* answer to your *query*: a list of clickable pages with a reasonable likelihood of containing the information you are searching. Returned sites are often ranked by *relevancy*. Returns are also known as *hits*.

Spider The technology used by Web search *engines* to collect URLs. Spiders vary in how they travel from page to page on the World Wide Web and how much information they gather about each page, as well as how often they make their global rounds.

URL Stands for Uniform Resource Locator. The standard way of specifying the actual location of an Internet resource, such as a Web page or Gopher menu. See Chapter 6 ("Exploring the Web with America Online").

FIRST STOP: AOL NETFIND

Think of AOL NetFind (Figure 9-1) as a huge information booth that AOL has created on the Web—like one of those kiosks where someone answers visitors' questions when they just arrive at the airport or train station. It's the place where you ask questions like "Where's the best place to stay?" or "With just three days, what's the best way to use my time?" or "I'm looking for so-and-so; how do I find him?" or "I need new soles; where do I get them?" Most of the time, you're likely to find what you're looking for. Similarly, AOL NetFind makes it easy to quickly find what you need on the Net. Usually, on the Web you'll be amazed by how much you find. Later in the chapter I'll review additional Web find-it venues if you're one of those visitors whose questions stump the folks in the kiosk.

AOL NetFind is available in many ways:

- Select Find It on the Web from the toolbar's Find menu (to see that menu, click the Find button).
- Go to *keyword: Netfind.*
- Enter the URL **http://www.aol.com/netfind** directly into the Address box or Keyword window.
- Click the prominent link at AOL.com (which itself is available by selecting Go to the Web from AOL's Internet menu or from the Welcome screen).

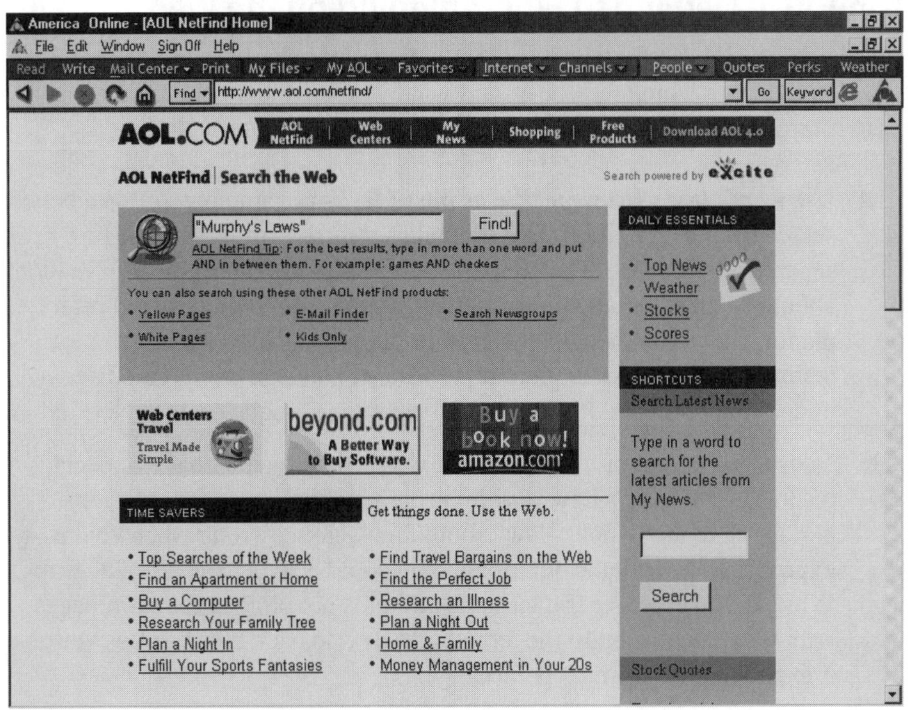

FIGURE 9-1 AOL NetFind, your information kiosk on the Web. Here you see an AOL NetFind search for sites about Murphy's Laws

AOL NetFind offers rich and diverse tools for finding what you need:

- A searchable index, for finding specific information on the World Wide Web
- Directories for finding the best Web sites
- A newsgroup search tool, whether you're looking for newsgroups that focus on a certain topic or individual postings in any newsgroup about that topic
- A people finder, coupled with a business finder, to track down and get driving directions to just about any street address in the U.S.

Using AOL NetFind to Find Anything on the Web

At the heart of AOL NetFind is the little box for entering your search terms (Figure 9-1). NetFind can't guarantee you'll find what you need, but here are three simple tips to improve your odds, based on the sage advice available at NetFind:

- ***Use words that are as specific as possible.*** For example, *tulips* is a better search term than *flowers*. Use several specific terms in the same box, separated by a space. The query *tulips bulbs planting* returns information about when and how to plant, plus companies that sell bulbs and offer planting advice. When you enter multiple terms, NetFind uses a technology that lets it explore relationships between words and discover underlying concepts. It's a powerful technique unique to AOL NetFind.
- ***Use phrases.*** A phrase is a group of words that together have a special meaning. "Murphy's Law" (with the quotes) fetches URLs of pages pertaining to the famous "law" about things going wrong when you least expect it. Leave out the quotes and you could also get sites for *law* firms. Why? If you enter several terms, NetFind is not obliged to return pages with *all* the terms, or all the terms right next to each other, unless you ask it explicitly (see the next point).
- ***Use symbols and Boolean operators to clarify your information needs.*** Joining two search terms with AND tells NetFind to find only pages containing both terms. Joining with OR tells NetFind to find pages containing either term. (*Make sure to place the terms AND and OR in all capital letters.*) Placing a plus sign (+) directly before a word instructs NetFind to make sure that every returned page includes that word, while placing a negative sign (-) before a term tells NetFind to return only pages not including it. Note that NetFind won't let you use a Boolean term like AND and a sign like + in the same query.

Tip *Experiment if you don't find what you need.* ***League of Nations*** *returns sites about the League of Nations and the Native American "League of Five Nations." Here's the query I used to retrieve only the sites I wanted:* ***"League of Nations" -Five****. Adding* ***-Five*** *got rid of the non-League of Nations sites and reduced the number of sites by 50 percent.*

Figure 9-2 shows pages returned for the search in Figure 9-1. AOL NetFind returns ten items per page, ordering them according to its best guess of their relevance to your query. If your fishing expedition yields any old tires, it may be necessary to refine it by adding terms, and by using plus signs (+) before words that must be included and the minus sign (-) by terms that must by excluded. For each item returned, you get the following information and options:

- **Show me more like this** If the site has what you want, click the More Like This link to do an additional search based on the words contained at the site you like. This technique can improve your results.
- **Title** The name of the page with a live link to that page, preceded by a percentage. "100%" denotes a perfect match as far as NetFind is concerned, but you may still need to do some searching.
- **URL** Lets you see how deep the page is at its Web site (the lower the link, the more detailed the information, in general). If you see the same URL for several returns, you've come across a site that may be worth exploring more closely.
- **Summary** Short description of the site to which the page belongs, often based on the first few words on a page.

Don't be put off by the many thousands of sites your search will likely return; it's a result of the size of the Web and the imperfection of search technologies. I generally find what I need within two to three pages of returned sites. To see the next ten sites, click the appropriate link at the bottom of the page.

You can see your results in several views by clicking the appropriate viewing option (Figure 9-2). Viewing *titles only* lets you see twice as many sites per page, but without the helpful descriptions. Viewing *by Web site* means grouping all your URLs by Web site, which is sometimes a good way of identifying particular Web sites with a sizable collection of pages about a subject of interest to you.

Using AOL NetFind to Find the *Best Sites* on the Web

AOL NetFind is more than an index. It also offers an indispensable directory called *TimeSavers,* with collections of Web sites chosen to simplify your life. Topics relate to such concerns of daily life as buying a computer or a car, watching your finances, planning a trip, finding a job, and maintaining your health (see Figure 9-3). In both

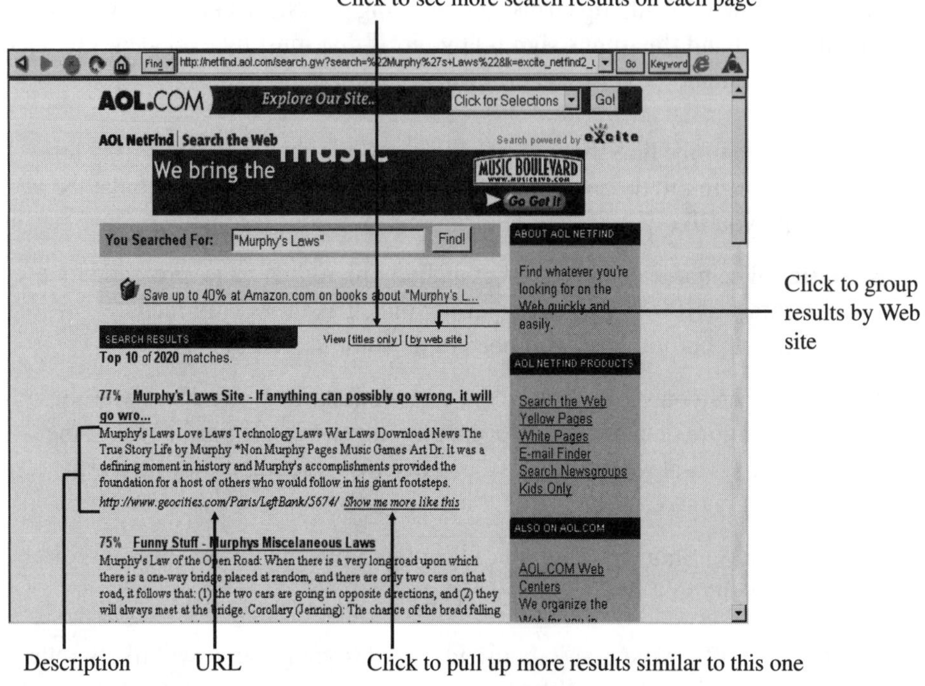

FIGURE 9-2 Results of the search for "Murphy's Laws"

TimeSavers and AOL.com's Web Centers, some links take you back to AOL content, if you're signed onto AOL.

Using AOL NetFind to Find Kid Stuff

AOL NetFind Kids Only is a good-sized directory of kid-friendly sites. This database is searchable, making for a mini-index. My search for *Mars Pathfinder* uncovered 552 sites for kids! Click Fun Stuff for a mini-directory of safe sites like the Exploratorium, Sports Illustrated for Kids, the Smithsonian Air & Space Museum, and the Why Files (cool science facts). In Chapter 11, the Kids Only section provides a sampling of excellent sites for kids, all of which should be available from AOL NetFind Kids Only. Appendix C, on Parental Controls, includes a table with a dozen or so sites for parents seeking guidance as their kids start exploring the Internet.

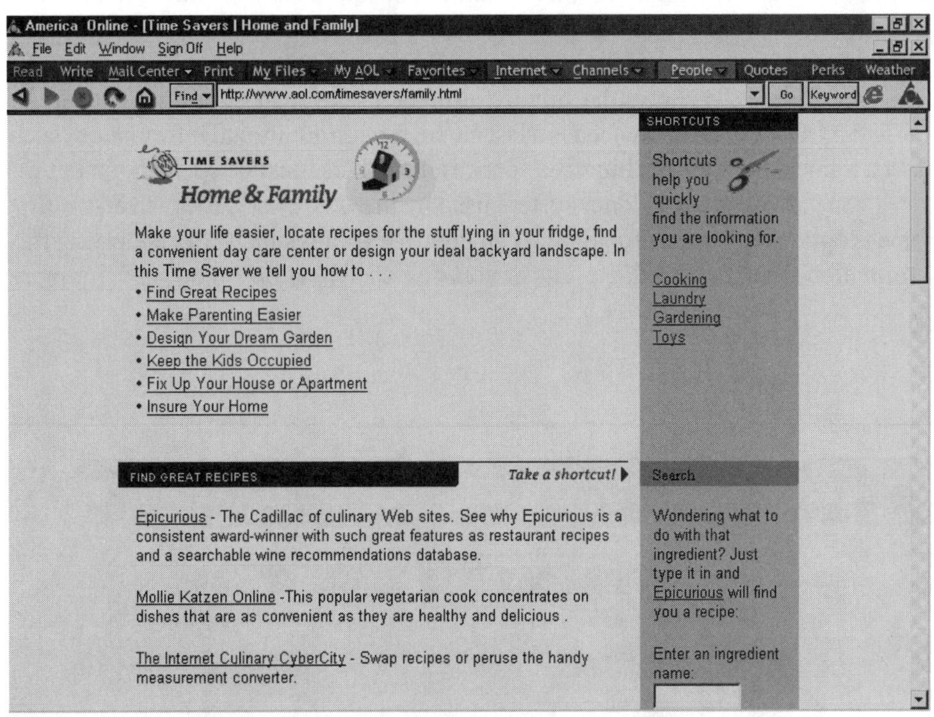

FIGURE 9-3 TimeSavers: life is too short to waste time searching for indispensable information

Using AOL NetFind to Find People and Businesses

Everyone is familiar with the white pages (residential phone and street listings) and yellow pages (business listings). The Internet has made it possible to create white and yellow pages listings for the entire country, and they're both available on AOL NetFind.

These two searches can be lumped together here because the searches are conducted similarly and because they are based on the same powerful search service. How to get there? The NetFind "table of contents" (Figure 9-3) is always available in the upper-left corner of your display. Just click Find a Person or Find a Business.

Finding a Person

Finding a person and finding a business mean finding a street address. If you're looking for an e-mail address, see "Finding People One at a Time: E-Mail Searches,"

later in this chapter. With more than 10 million business listings and more than 100 million residential listings, AOL NetFind will almost certainly retrieve most people's street address; I even found my parents' address, neither of whom has ever used a computer. Figure 9-4 shows the simple form you use to search for a street address.

To find a *person*, all you need is a last name, though additional information (such as first name and city) will improve your results. Cities must be spelled out, but for states you can use the two-letter system used by the U.S. Post Office. Even the first name is optional, though a first initial can improve your results. After supplying this information, just click Find! Results of your search appear on a new page; for more

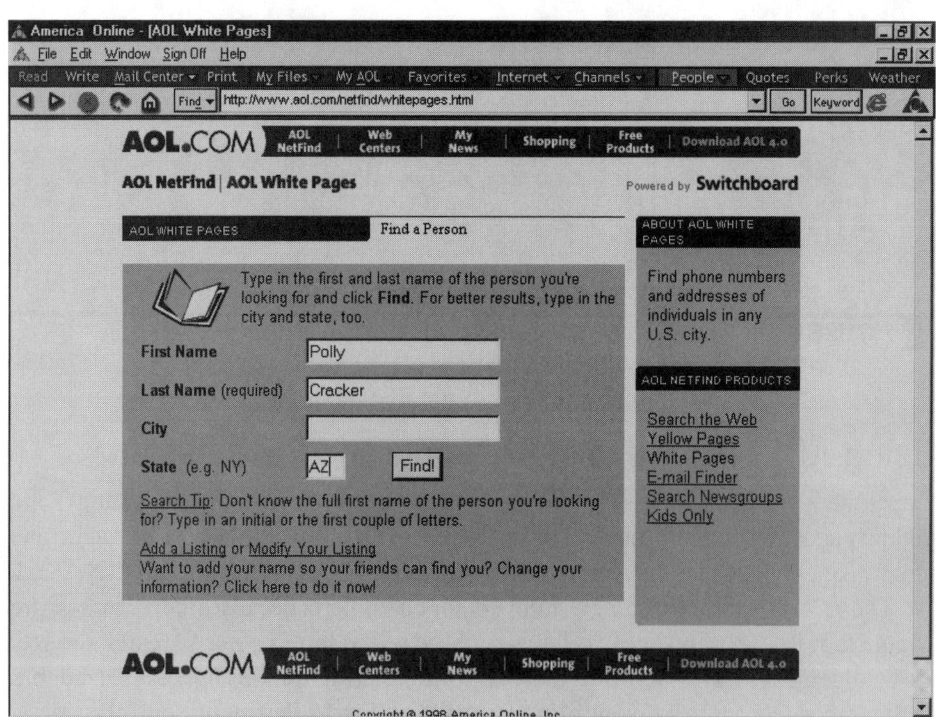

FIGURE 9-4 AOL NetFind: the Net's white pages

than about ten answers, you'll see multiple pages (click Next if necessary). If your search has too many answers because it is too broad, just add more information to the search form and click Find again. As with a Web search, the more information (and the more specific information) you add, the better your results.

Tip *AOL NetFind bases its personal information on publicly available white page listings that are updated every four to six months. What if your listing is out of date or duplicated, or if you don't want to be listed? For free, the creators of this service, Switchboard, Inc., allow you to modify your listing from their home page,* ***http://www.switchboard.com/****. You'll find information about modifying your listing and making it invisible to others. Switchboard itself is directly available from both the People menu and the toolbar's Find button (just select Internet White Pages).*

Finally, make sure to visit the links at the bottom of the Find a Person page. If you're currently signed onto AOL, you can link to the AOL Members Directory (see the "Looking for Someone on AOL?" box); and if you're not, you'll still have access to Classmates Online and the Congressional E-mail Directory, two useful and fun people finders.

Looking for Someone on AOL?

Think of the AOL Members Directory as a white pages directory with an attitude. It's the place where AOL members can choose to make personal information about themselves available to other members—their birthday, hobbies, marital status, favorite music, and so on. Unlike the white pages, you're only included in the Members Directory if you want to be included (rather than being automatically included unless you ask to be unlisted, as in the white pages).

From the People menu, select Search AOL Member Directory (or, from the Find button, select AOL Members). Click the Advanced Search tab to search for members with the same interests and professions as you, even members with the same interests who live in your community! I know of someone who found a handyman in her community using the AOL Member Directory.

This particular search for Maryland bowlers returned more than 250 AOL members. Nonmembers don't have access to this directory. If you do want the AOL community to know about you, just click Create or Modify My Profile and tell them who you are.

Tip *Use care in providing any personal information, such as your phone number and street address. Many members avoid providing contact information altogether. Children with their own screen names should never provide such information (see Appendix C).*

Finding a Business

For any business, the Internet has drastically cut the costs and simplified the methods of doing competitive research. It's also easier for consumers to get contact information for both local stores and mail-order companies *anywhere*. When you're looking for business information you can use either a directory or an index; the best tools combine the two. AOL NetFind's useful service will help you get where you're going in *real* space, not cyberspace.

Looking for a business is much like looking for a person on AOL NetFind. From anywhere at AOL NetFind click Yellow Pages, available on the right side of the page.

1. Type in the city and state where you are searching a business, plus the type of business you wish to search for. Click Find!

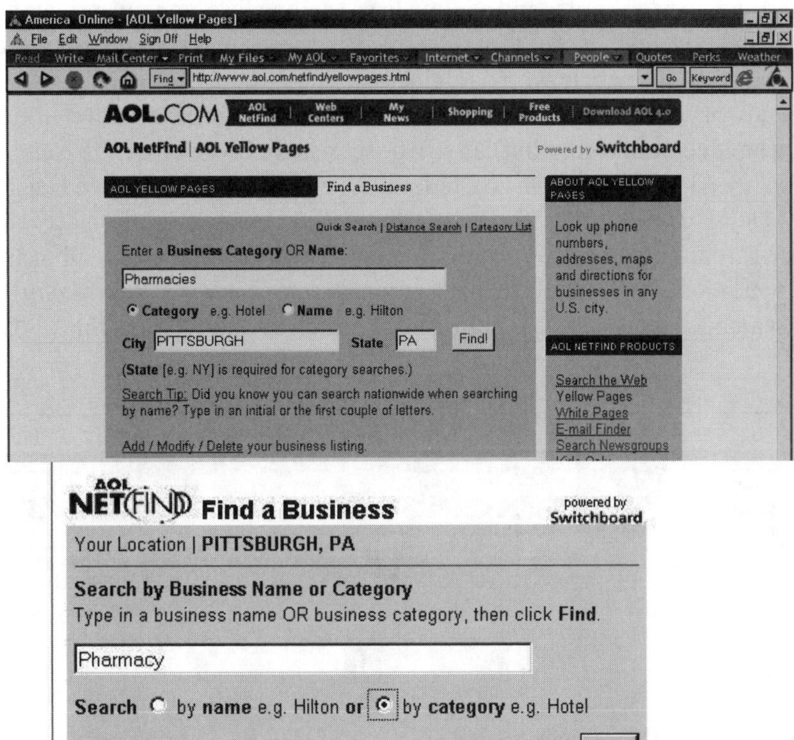

instructions (after you've entered your starting point).

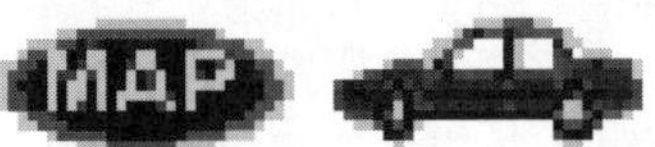

Tip *If you still can't find that business address, you might want to try the BigYellow service from NYNEX at* **http://www.bigyellow.com**. *It has its own white pages as well as business-related links. For more information about businesses, start at AOL's Hoovers Online (*keyword: Hoovers*) or* keyword: Company research.

Using AOL NetFind to Find Newsgroups and Postings

Much of the most informative content on the Internet is locked away in millions of messages to newsgroups and mailing lists. Mailing lists are semi-private and difficult to search, but you *can* tap the collective experience and knowledge of the hundreds of thousands of people who participate in newsgroups. To search newsgroups, you use a wonderful site called DejaNews (referring, I guess, to newsgroup messages that have come and gone but can still be searched). If you're new to News, you might want to skim Chapter 5. If you're familiar with News, you'll love DejaNews.

DejaNews (Figure 9-5), available by clicking AOL NetFind's Search Newsgroups link, lets you search for newsgroups about specific subjects of interest to you. While AOL's built-in Newsgroup feature (*keyword: Newsgroup*) allows you to search for specific newsgroups and to search through subject lines, AOL NetFind

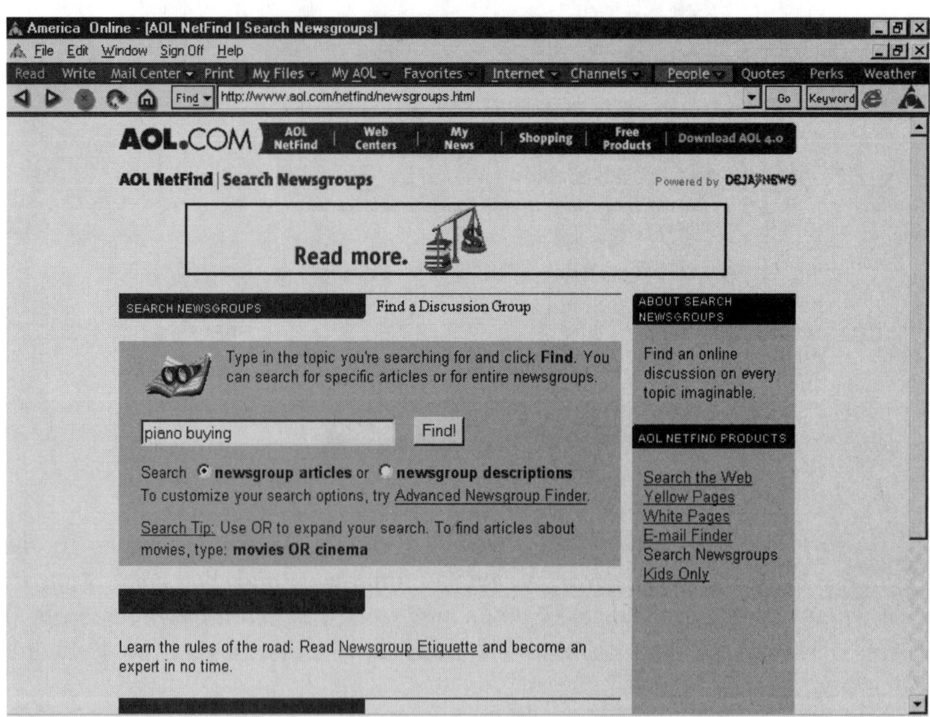

FIGURE 9-5 DejaNews helps you find newsgroups whose messages contain specific words—a good way to identify newsgroups worth following

(DejaNews) gives you the additional capability of searching through actual messages for specific words. DejaNews boasts a database that is growing by 500 Mb a day, with more than100 million messages from just about every newsgroup, stretching back to March 1995. Despite its size, it's very fast.

Click the Newsgroup Articles radio button to search for newsgroup *articles* (messages) containing a particular word or phrase, no matter what newsgroup it's in. Click Newsgroup Descriptions to get a *list of newsgroups* containing messages with a keyword of interest to you; the newsgroups having the highest concentration of messages with the keyword are rated highest. These are the newsgroups you may want to follow on AOL over time.

Tip *Like other find-it services, with DejaNews you can use* OR *and* NOT *to broaden or restrict your search respectively, but you needn't use* AND*—it's implicit if you just use a series of words separated by spaces. Phrases (putting several words in quotes) indicate that words must appear together and in a particular order. You can also use wild cards:* moon* *might return postings containing* moonstruck, moonbeam, moonie, moonbus, moonshine, moon.jpg, *and more. Use wildcards when you're unsure of a word's spelling or when you want to conduct a broad search for different kinds of information.*

DejaNews' advanced options let you restrict your search to older or more recent messages, view them by relevance, and view them in threads (to see all the messages with the same subject line).

Your results (Figure 9-6) are linked to actual postings, with the subject of the posting in bold. You read the postings from within DejaNews, not in AOL's Newsgroups window. Buttons let you see the next and previous messages (of the messages returned by your search), as well as the other messages in any threads within a newsgroup.

For every message, you can get an author profile, to find out how many messages a poster has sent to which newsgroups. Sending e-mail to the author of the posting is often more appropriate than responding to the newsgroup. With AOL NetFind's DejaNews you can post your own messages to the newsgroup. (To post, however, you must first register, which is free.) Posting a response to an old (expired) message is not possible, but using NetFind you can post a brand-new message, perhaps starting a thread of your own. To do so, click Post Message instead of Post Reply.

Tip *AOL NetFind offers newsgroup fans more than a way of finding stuff. You'll also find links to AOL's newsgroup netiquette tips and its home-grown Newsgroup Scoop, an excellent way to learn about the best newsgroups.*

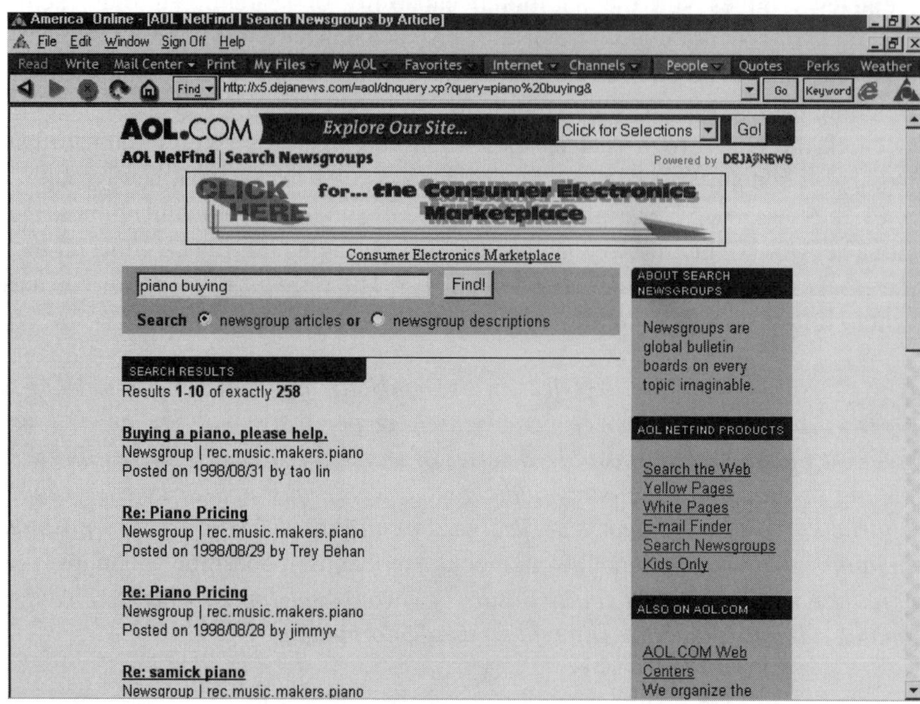

FIGURE 9-6 Messages about buying a piano. You can read them, reply to them, and send e-mail to their authors

SEARCH ARSENAL: THE BEST OF THE REST

AOL NetFind will likely meet most of your needs, whether you are searching the Web or searching newsgroups, whether you need a friend's address or a company's phone number. It's worth learning about other Web search engines, however, since some have specific strengths to help you meet special needs, and if you're searching for something other than Web pages—such as e-mail addresses or mailing lists—you'll have to resort to another service (Table 9-1). Using AOL, all these Internet services are readily available.

On the next few pages you'll find short reviews of several major search indexes and directories. The reviews compare their reliability and ease of use. I'll be using some search jargon like *query* and *relevance*, explained in the "Search Terms and What They Mean" box.

When you compare search services, remember that they vary in several important ways:

- The number of URLs they track.
- Their graphical tools for creating queries. Some (like HotBot) give you menus and other graphical aids; others (like AltaVista) require you to know the correct syntax. The trend is toward ease of use through graphical aids, however, since no one really *likes* Boolean operators.
- Their ability to rank URLs according to likely relevance to you.
- Their tools for helping you refine your query.
- Their additional bells and whistles—site reviews and home-grown content such as Excite's City.Net, InfoSeek's Web Guides, and Lycos's 5% catalog.

Bear in mind that engines with the best interfaces don't always produce the best results. Similarly, a large index is not necessarily a good one, and a small but well-chosen directory can contain more useful information than the myriad Web pages kept in the largest index. Likewise, the services with the most bells and whistles don't necessarily offer the best underlying search technology. Skimming the following reviews should give you a sense where to start. For in-depth research projects, using multiple services is almost a requirement. See "Pulling It All Together" toward the end of this chapter.

Tip *Think of something you need to find out (the more specific the better), and try the various search engines described below. Which one best meets your needs?*

Altavista

http://www.altavista.digital.com/

This powerful search engine created by Digital Equipment recently expanded its index to include more than 100 million pages. The service is fast as well as huge, and it does full-text searches. AltaVista is the site favored by the Yahoo directory (Figure 9-7).

Tip *One of the special new features of AltaVista is NetShepherd, a searchable directory of family-friendly, screened Web sites appropriate for younger children. NetShepherd consists of more than **1.5 million Web pages** collected by librarians and concerned adults. The site (**http://family.netshepherd.com/**) is available from the AltaVista opening page.*

Engine/Directory (URL)	Strengths
AltaVista (**http://altavista.digital.com**)	Full-text searches of 100 million Web pages; speed; ability to search by Web element (such as images, applets, titles); excellent foreign-language support and promising translation service; sophisticated tool for refining a query. *A huge, reliable, and fast service, with new features that set it apart.*
Argus Clearinghouse (**http://www.clearinghouse.net**)	Contextual essays on serious subjects; access to all Internet resources, not just Web sites; ratings by experts and librarians.
Excite (**http://www.excite.com**)	Directory of reviewed and ranked sites; concept searching; More Like This feature; customization (My Channel); home-grown content (City.Net).
HotBot (**http://www.hotbot.com**)	Bright, simple, fun interface, minimizes input errors and increases quality of query through filtering; searches by file type (images, Java, particular extensions); directory of searchable Web resources from Wired.com. *Particularly good for recent information and specific multimedia files.*
InfoSeek (**http://www.infoseek.com**)	Usenet searching and browsing within the browser; natural language queries; speed; simple interface; good content channels and many information utilities (people finders). *Reliable and fast, Infoseek lets you do a search within the set of URLs returned by your first query.*
Lycos (**http://www.lycos.com**)	Strong directory and channels, with ratings (Lycos 5%); large database; search for sounds and images; support for natural language queries.
Virtual Library (**http://www.w3.org/vl/**)	A high-quality, serious, international directory, with 200 listings of resources, maintained by scholars and experts around the world; not restricted to Web sites.

TABLE 9-1 Web search services: how they differ

Engine/Directory (URL)	Strengths
Yahoo (**http://www.yahoo.com**)	Dynamic but small directory of under one million pages, selected and arranged in a multilevel hierarchy; directory is searchable, and searches can broaden into AltaVista searches; specialized Yahoos (My Yahoo, Yahoo for kids, metropolitan Yahoos, and national Yahoos); weekly e-mail newsletter with the most interesting new listings. *A good place to start a search.*

TABLE 9-1 Web search services: how they differ (*continued*)

FIGURE 9-7 Alta Vista: big, fast, and getting simpler

AltaVista offers a simple search and an advanced one. Since the first edition of this book, the simple search has gotten dramatically better, while the advanced one is no longer required to get good results. Here are key tips for using the AltaVista simple search:

- ***Use natural language.*** Instead of obscure Boolean terms and easy-to-forget symbols, a natural language query lets you ask a question in your own, conversational terms, not computerese. I got excellent results from the query, "What's the weather today in Chicago?"
- ***Specify language of results.*** You can specify a language so that for a particular search you will retrieve only pages in languages you can read (a valuable feature if your first language is not English). AltaVista also is developing a translation service, so you can translate into English any pages whose language you can't read. When I tried translating pages from a language I know (German) into English, this experimental service did a somewhat mechanical word-for-word translation, but the potential for this service is enormous on the global Internet.
- ***Zero in on most relevant sites.*** AltaVista assigns a relevancy rating, so the sites most likely to meet your needs are listed first. At the bottom of each page of results is a graphical index that lets you jump ahead to the twentieth page of results (for example) to get a sense of the number of good sites retrieved by your search.

- ***Use wildcards.*** Like DejaNews, described earlier, AltaVista lets you use a wildcard (that is, an asterisk) to stand for one or more characters. This technique lets you broaden your results or do a query even if you're uncertain of the correct spelling of your keywords.
- ***Search for specific content.*** AltaVista lets you search for specific elements of a Web page, for example, you can search for images of (former President) Nixon (**image:nixon.gif**), Java applets with maze games (**applet:maze**), or pages devoted to North Korea's prospects (**title:North Korea 1998**). It's a good idea to keep such searches for specific elements simple and to refine the results (instead of writing complex queries), as described next.

- ***Refine your results.*** AltaVista has recently added a powerful tool for refining your results, an especially useful feature if your query returned tens of thousands of results. With the results displayed, click Refine. You will see a list of topics that AltaVista found to be associated with the keywords in your query. For each topic, use the drop-down list to exclude or require the topic. Click Search to rerun the original query, requiring or ignoring the topics you specified. Serious researchers will appreciate this powerful tool. A graphical Java-based version of the Refine tool is available, and it offers even more features. To use it, click Refine and then click Graphic.

Search Tips: For Any Search Service

The following tips apply to all the Web search engines discussed in this "Search Arsenal," though for some you may have to use the advanced search to take advantage of them.

Always read the online help.

- Put phrases in quotes if you want to fetch pages containing words that must be adjacent like "home run".
- Capitalize with care: Most services interpret small letters as either lowercase or uppercase, but any word you *do* capitalize returns *only* pages containing the capitalized word. As a rule, you should capitalize names of people (*Babe Ruth*).
- Precede words that must be included in your list of returned sites with a plus sign (+), as in *Babe Ruth +Yankees,* and words you definitely are not looking for with a minus sign (–), as in *"film noir"* -*"pinot noir"* (to use AltaVista's example). A plus or minus sign can be used before an entire phrase to ensure its inclusion or exclusion.

If you want to use Boolean operators (AND, OR…), then you'll have to use AltaVista's advanced search, which gives you precise control of the proximity of keywords on a page and lets you specify a range of dates during which the pages you are seeking were last updated. Click Help if you need help with AltaVista's sometimes daunting advanced syntax.

9

The No Bull Guide to Boolean Operators

Boolean operators were named after George Boole (1815-1864), an Irish professor of mathematics who contributed fundamental concepts to modern logic and algebra. Basically, in the Web context, *operators* are the terms AND, OR, and NOT, which, when placed between words in a search, change the way a search is conducted. In actual searches, make sure to capitalize these words, since they may otherwise be automatically excluded.

These terms have two effects:

- ***AND and NOT limit a search.*** If you search for *bread AND wine*, you're searching for Web pages that contain both words. If you search for *bread NOT wine*, you're searching for only those pages with *bread* that don't include *wine*. You can use these operators to get fewer irrelevant sites.
- ***OR expands a search.*** If you search for *bread OR wine*, you're searching for pages that contain either word: pages that contain *bread* and pages that contain *wine*, a much broader search than using AND.

Not all uses of the words *AND* and *OR* are Boolean. Sometimes you are actually searching for the words *and* and *or*. Suppose you're looking for pages with information about the book called *Bread and Wine*, by Ignazio Silone. You'd want to package up these three words and look only for that particular phrase. You do this by simply enclosing the phrase in quotation marks: *"Bread and Wine."*

Excite

http://www.excite.com

Excite's underlying search technology is the same as AOL NetFind's. When you click Newsgroups at the bottom of the Excite window, you're using DejaNews technology, just as with AOL NetFind.

The stand-alone Excite service offers a few benefits and some original content, but in general does not offer a compelling alternative to AOL NetFind:

- **Content** Excite offers a strong directory of rated and reviewed Web sites. The directory can be reached from the main page. Like AOL and AOL.com, Excite's content is arranged in channels. Perhaps the most notable channel is Travel, based on *City.Net*, a vast collection of Web sites having to do with 5,000 places around the world, with the associated maps required to plan any trip, anywhere.
- **Customizability** *MyChannel* lets you create your own starting point for using Excite to stay informed about the subjects of interest to you, as well as your weather, stocks, etc.
- **Viewing options** The List by Web Site option lets you view your results by domain, so you can identify sites with notable concentrations of pages about the subject you are researching. Unfortunately, Excite requires you to review your results sequentially, one page at a time.
- **Easy-to-refine queries** Clicking More Like This reruns your original query, searching for pages that also contain some of the terms found at that particular site. Excite boasts a concept extraction technology that searches for relationships between keywords instead of mere matches. However, unlike AltaVista, Excite doesn't allow for refinement based on additional keywords you want to associate with your original query.
- **Newsgroup searching** Like AOL NetFind, Excite lets you search newsgroups using DejaNews.

Unlike AOL NetFind, Excite offers both simple and advanced searches, and for some important features, such as wildcards and the use of the plus (+) and minus (-) signs, you are *required* to use the advanced search option.

HotBot

http://www.hotbot.com/

HotBot, run by the folks who bring you *Wired* magazine and the HotWired Web site, sports a bright and easy-to-use interface (see "Center of the Wired World"). The underlying technology, called *Inktomi,* is the brainchild of a Berkeley professor who is trying to devise databases big enough to track the entire Web but fast enough to enable access by the entire Web community. By and large he has succeeded: HotBot is very easy to use, but not as fast as competitors such as AltaVista.

The HotBot people understand that different types of Internet content require different kinds of searches, and they also understand the complexity of turning

Center of the Wired World

If you have a speedy modem and late-model Pentium or Macintosh, you'll want to explore HotBot's sibling sites, all a click away from the HotBot opening page. Like HotBot itself, each of these Web creations grew out of the publishing revolution that began five years ago with the launch of *Wired* magazine.

- *Wired News* offers analysis of the very latest events in business, technology, culture, and politics. It comes in an e-mail version that you can sign up for.
- *Wired Magazine* on the Web presents selected articles from the famous print magazine, with searchable archives and, of course, an easy way to subscribe. The Web message boards, called "Threads," provide a forum in which to debate strategy in the digital revolution and also to respond to Wired articles.
- *HotWired* does on the Web what the magazine tries to do in print: shake up conventions and evangelize on behalf of a wired future. Its design changes all the time, sometimes while you're watching. Don't miss HotWired's excellent WebMonkey feature, which provides tutorials for Web creators of all levels and excels at introducing more demanding subjects such as JavaScript. HotWired's RGB Gallery shows off innovative Web artistry and ingenuity.

human questions into computer queries. The first step in using HotBot is choosing what to search: the Web, newsgroups, the news, discussion groups (Web-based interactive forums), stocks, businesses, or shareware. These choices are available along the left-hand side of the HotBot opening page. These miscellaneous search services vary in quality, but the Web search stands out, and it does so for one reason: graphical filters.

Say you want to search the Web. Searching the Web has a simple option and an advanced one (click SuperSearch), but the beauty of both is that they can be entirely managed with graphical elements like drop-down lists and check boxes. Instead of Boolean operators, you use a drop-down list to choose whether all of your keywords are to appear on the same page (the same as using AND) or *any* of your keywords are to appear on a page (the same as using OR). You can also define your keywords as a phrase without using quotes.

HotBot's filters make it easy to choose

- The *locations* where you want to focus your search (and from which you want to retrieve Web pages); for example, search European sites for information about the new European currency.
- The *dates* as of when you want your pages to be current. HotBot excels in retrieving the most up-to-date information on the Internet, and it lets you filter out old information. This is a great way to get the latest information on breaking news stories.
- The *kind of file* you want to retrieve: image, video, audio, and Shockwave (click SuperSearch for more choices).

Results in HotBot are ranked numerically (starting with 1) and by percentage, with the best results (in HotBot's estimation) at the top of the list.

The advanced option expands on the simple option but doesn't add needless complexity (as Lycos and AltaVista do in their advanced options). It offers boxes for the addition of search terms, additional media types to search (such as Java or file types that you specify, such as GIF), and the ability to specify page depth. You would increase page depth to broaden your search.

Unfortunately, HotBot returns sites sequentially (you can't jump to the two hundredth site or the tenth page of results), and it lacks a specialized way to refine results using different criteria from the ones used in the original query. Also somewhat disappointing, the search-newsgroup tool lacks the ability to browse messages and newsgroups. That is, it lacks the power of DejaNews. On balance, however, HotBot has the simplest interface and most up-to-date databases. It's the place to start if you're looking for information about something that happened last week or in the last 24 hours.

InfoSeek

http://www.infoseek.com/

InfoSeek, shown in Figure 9-8, offers a simple interface and powerful underlying search technology. It comes close to AOL NetFind in simplicity and in combining search and directory services. InfoSeek doesn't, of course, provide links to the AOL service.

InfoSeek makes it easy to phrase a good query, and in fact the service pioneered the use of natural language queries. (AltaVista and HotBot are now catching up,

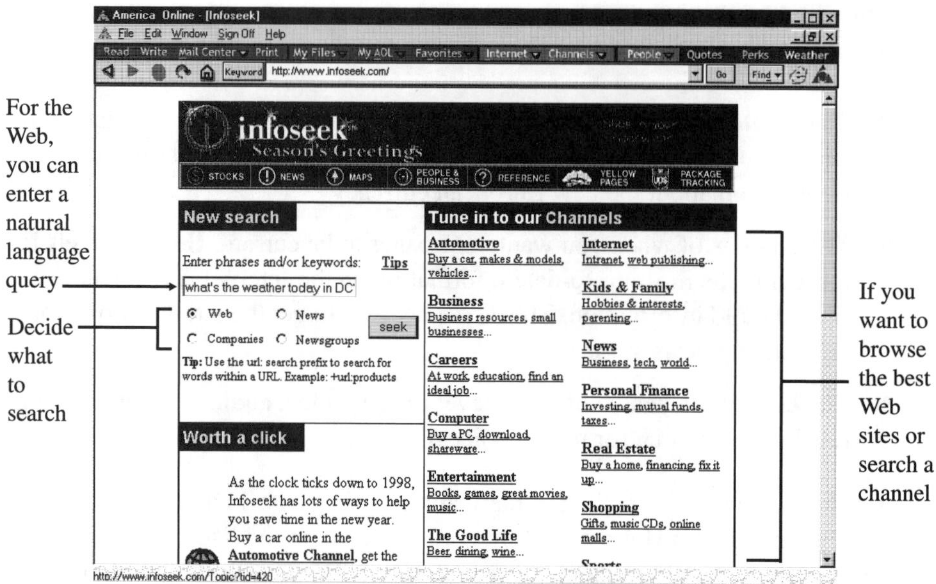

FIGURE 9-8 InfoSeek lets you search or browse, and provides an information mall to help you along the way

though.) The "Search Tips: For Any Search Service" box, earlier in this chapter, provides pretty much all you need to use InfoSeek. For simple searches, it's a good idea to use a natural language query. For more precision, you can string together multiple specific keywords, use phrases as required, use the plus and minus signs to require and exclude terms, and capitalize names. Advanced search options can be entered in the same text box as the simple ones, and they include the techniques for searching for parts of a page. For example, title:Oz (InfoSeek's example) searches for pages whose title contains *Oz*.

InfoSeek returns results quickly—in a rough comparison, faster than HotBot and almost as fast as AltaVista. Simple queries and natural language queries fetched good results, in my experience. To refine a search, you can narrow it as follows. A Search More box at the bottom of the page gives you the option of doing a search *within* your answer set. Click the radio button, type in a keyword, and click Seek for a new and refined set of results.

InfoSeek conveniently puts many additional listings and services at your disposal:

- 12 million e-mail addresses
- Personal and business listings
- Image files, using ImageSeek, available in the Shareware & Chat area
- DejaNews
- Company information provided by Hoover Online, which is also available on AOL at *keyword: Hoover*
- News, updated every 15 minutes
- Channels. InfoSeek's channels include the big subjects you'd expect (Kids, Computers, Business, Entertainment, etc.), and all are individually searchable
- Miscellaneous indispensable information: Zip codes, area codes, toll-free listings, government listings, and more

A final note about Infoseek: like AltaVista and Yahoo, Infoseek is building up international content, in the form of German, Japanese, and other national Infoseeks. Look for all the search services to create international versions.

Lycos

http://www.lycos.com

Lycos has been around for a while, at least in "Web time," though its interface is thoroughly up to date (Figure 9-9). The search engine, developed at Carnegie-Mellon University, was the Net's favored Web engine for a while, and its success paved the way for more powerful services such as AltaVista, Excite, HotBot, and InfoSeek.

A Lycos search requires two steps. First, select what kind of content to search, then type a query. The "what" part has some unique features: you can search the Web, Lycos's Web *reviews*, Lycos's multimedia catalog of sounds and images, books (from Barnes & Noble's catalog of more than one million titles), and stocks and other financial securities. Then, enter your query. For your Web queries, you can keep it simple, using specific terms, selective capitalization, and phrases as required.

AltaVista and InfoSeek make it *possible* to search individual domains and sites, but Lycos makes it really easy to do so: from the opening page, click Search Features.

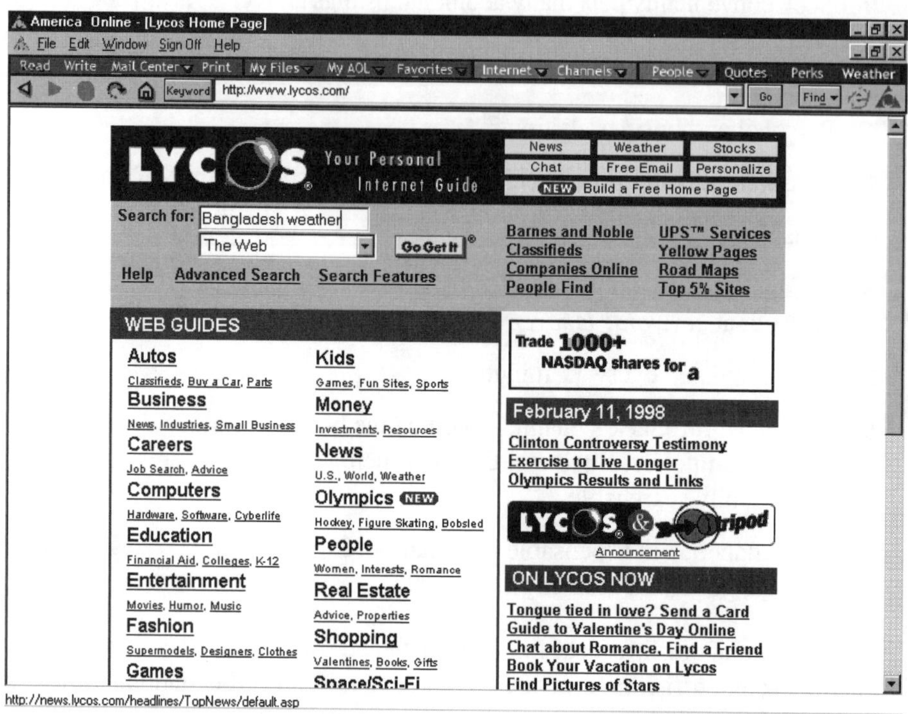

FIGURE 9-9 Lycos offers simple searching and Web Guides (channels), plus Lycos's Top 5%

You can now choose to search within a specific Web site. Or, search for text that appears in URLs—a sure sign that a site is devoted to a certain subject. I did a search for *autism* occurring in URLs and retrieved an excellent resource at Yale.

Like all the search services, Lycos has an advanced search; it's called Lycos Pro. Lycos Pro has a menu that lets you define a string of keywords as an AND construction or a phrase. You can even specify how strong a relationship you want to exist between your keywords.

Click Power Panel on the Advanced Search page to gain precise control over how you want your results to be listed: how close together your keywords should be, whether they should appear in the title or the text, and whether they should appear early in the text. Natural language queries (like "who was stranded on Gilligan's island," in Lycos's example) are now supported, but you must (1) click Lycos Pro and (2) select Natural Language from the drop-down list. You'll also need Lycos Pro to use Boolean operators.

As for refining results, Lycos, like Infoseek, lets you refine a query *within the set of sites* returned by the original query, filtering for sites containing additional keywords—a powerful way to reduce the number of useless URLs.

Lycos offers channels (called *Web Guides*) with selected sites, plus a catalog of the Top 5%, based on Lycos's catalog of sites notable for their design and content. When you choose a Web Guide such as Education, Lycos does a nice job adding editorial value. Web sites aren't just listed but are actually described and grouped. In each channel, you get the pertinent top 5% sites and the latest news.

Searching for Multimedia Files

Sometimes it's hard to know where to start a search. In the case of multimedia files, do you start on FTP or on the Web? More and more, the answer is the Web. If you don't find a file using FTP's Archie service (see Chapter 8), you're likely to find it on the Web.

AltaVista, HotBot, Infoseek, and Lycos let you do searches for files of a certain type, that is, image files or even files with a certain file extension (such as MIDI or WAV). In AltaVista, you can currently search only for image files, using the syntax **image:nixon.gif** (or whatever you want a picture of; leave off gif if you want an image of any format). In HotBot, just click the type of file you want. Infoseek's comparable ImageSeek service is based on Interpix's cool Image Surfer technology (**http://isurf.interpix.com**). In Lycos, you can search Lycos's multimedia catalog by selecting Sounds or Pictures from the drop-down list on the main page. I found some terrific whale cries using Lycos.

Yahoo

http://www.yahoo.com

Yahoo is a large and popular directory (Figure 9-10). In number of pages indexed, it's much smaller than AOL NetFind and the other service indexes. As with any directory, however, it's the quality that counts. Yahoo arranges sites in big categories such as Business and Education. Although all the search engines discussed so far have their own directories, Yahoo offers a directory with many levels of subtopics and sub-subtopics for every category.

Using Yahoo is simple: you either browse Yahoo for specific sites, drilling down from categories to subtopics until you find what you want. Or, you search Yahoo for pages that may be in more than one category. Sites are handpicked, so in general

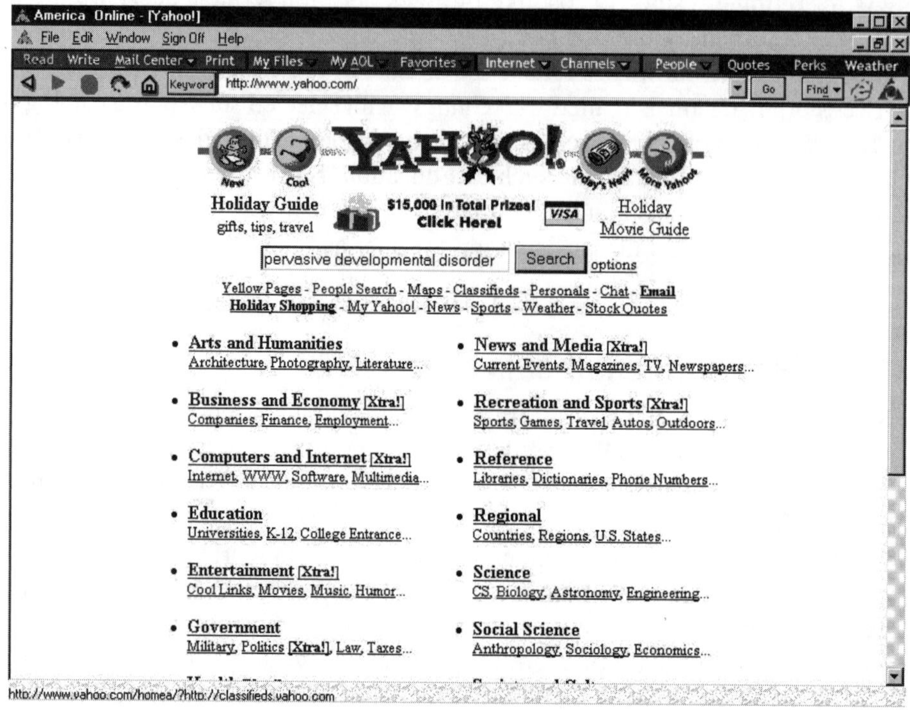

FIGURE 9-10 Just curious? A good place to start a general search

you can count on the links working. However, unlike AOL NetFind or Lycos's 5% directory, sites are neither described nor rated, although for some sites you'll find a short descriptive phrase.

Compiling a directory of Web sites is like building a sand castle during high tide. It is futile because of the rate at which new sites are created. Yahoo confronts the problem by offering visitors easy access to AltaVista: any search of Yahoo's directory can be expanded into an AltaVista search of 100 million machine-gathered URLs by clicking Go to AltaVista. In addition, Yahoo adds value to its directory with:

- **Flexible searching** Some of the Yahoo subtopics pages can be quite long and slow to load. You'll appreciate searchability, especially if you know what you are looking for or if you want to find resources scattered across several categories. Within a category or subtopic (such as Biology in the Science category), you can choose to search only that group of sites.

- **Navigational aids** (1) For each subtopic, the number of sites is available in parentheses—a useful measure of the depth of Yahoo's contents for any area and of the length of time it will take for the page to download. (2) New sites have a special little picture by them (*New*), as do especially cool sites (a pair of glasses). Indices (mini-directories) are separately listed in every category and subtopic.
- **Kid stuff** Yahooligans is a large directory of kid-appropriate sites.
- **Newsletter** Unlike the other search sites, Yahoo offers an e-mail newsletter to keep you apprised of the week's top picks (with a fun slant). It's available by clicking Weekly Picks (at the bottom of the opening page) and looking for a subscription link. Online, you can get the same information, but getting it by e-mail is a major convenience if you use e-mail more often than you use the Web.
- **Custom, local, and international Yahoos** In addition to Yahooligans (for kids), there's MyYahoo, a free, personalized Yahoo service. Yahoos are also available for a dozen major countries and continents (including Australia, Korea, Japan, Germany, and Canada) and a dozen major metropolitan areas in the U.S.

Essential Directories for the Serious Researcher

The **Argus Clearinghouse** (formerly the Clearinghouse for Subject-Oriented Internet Resource Guides, now available at **http://www.clearinghouse.net/**) consists of hundreds of hypertext essays, each reviewing the best Internet resources for a specific subject. The essays were written by trained librarians. The Clearinghouse can be browsed or searched. Some of the essays are dated, but all are rated for their overall usefulness.

The **Virtual Library**, launched by the Web's creator, Tim Berners-Lee, is a labor of love. The listings in this library are written and maintained by scholars around the world. Launched in Switzerland in 1991, it moved to the World Wide Web Consortium in 1996, and has since moved to several mirror sites in the U.S. and Europe (the U.S. site is **http://www.ugems.psu.edu/~owens/VL**).

The Virtual Library consists of approximately 200 essays and annotated listings, each devoted to the Internet resources dealing with a specific topic. Many of the topics are of strictly academic interest (Mycology and Cognitive

Science, for example), but others have broad appeal (Recipes, Men's Issues, Games, Gardening, and so on). The Virtual Library sites are separately maintained by experts throughout the world, not just in the U.S., so you will get an international perspective on many subjects—something that's surprisingly rare on the global Internet. You'll also find in-depth information *about* the rest of the world, and not merely travel tips. Special listings are devoted to Taiwan, Singapore, India, and many other non-Western places.

The Virtual Library will link you to *all* the pertinent information for a subject, not just Web sites. You can find out about Telnet resources, FTP sites, newsgroups, mailing lists, and more. It's not systematic or fancy, but it makes for a true information feast.

Less imposing than the Virtual Library, but great for students of every age, is the Internet Public Library (**http://www.ipl.org**), with links to reference books, newspapers, and other valuable reference material.

FINDING *PEOPLE* WITH INFORMATION: MAILING LISTS

Mailing lists and newsgroups form the basis of tens of thousands of communities of interest. They provide myriad forums for learning from other people and providing information to them. They mix sociability and information in a way that's unique to the Net. So, if you raise terriers for a living, a good first stop may well be the Internet discussion group that lives and breathes the subject (and there is one). Getting to know the people who frequent a mailing list or newsgroup, you can often find better answers more quickly, and you can stay more current about any topic, than if you just used a passive resource like the Web.

Note *Newsgroups are public and tend to be more open and a bit noisier than mailing lists, which require that you join. See "How Newsgroups and Mailing Lists Are Different" in Chapter 5.*

For newsgroups, AOL NetFind's Newsgroup Finder gives you the best search service on the Internet (see the earlier section "Using AOL NetFind to Find Newsgroups and Postings"). For mailing lists, the comprehensive service has the strange name Liszt (that's *Liszt* as in the composer, not *List* as in laundry list or mailing list).

Searching for Newsgroup Postings—from the Web

With the amount of spam, noise, and irrelevancy you get in newsgroups, doing targeted searches for specific information has become the required first step if you need to find information in newsgroups.

All major search engines except Lycos let you do newsgroup as well as Web searches. When you do such a search, your answers and your access to newsgroups will come in two different forms:

- For AOL NetFind, Excite, and InfoSeek, you're using DejaNews. After you do a search, you can read postings, view the thread to which the message belongs, and post a reply or a new message. All this takes place in the browser itself using DejaNews.
- With AltaVista, you are presented with a list of individual postings containing the word or words you want. Click a link to read the posting. Once the posting appears, you'll see a link to the newsgroup to which the posting belongs (e.g., **bit.listserv.autism**). Click that link to bring up AOL's Newsgroup window, where you can read, browse, and post, as spelled out in detail in Chapter 5. Likewise, HotBot uses the AOL newsgroup program, not a Web-based service like DejaNews.

If you're doing a search for specific information, you'll be starting from the Web, so it's a good idea to become familiar with DejaNews, using AOL NetFind. If you'll be reading the same newsgroup regularly, use *keyword: Newsgroups*.

Liszt: Searching for Mailing Lists

Keyword: Liszt

http://www.liszt.com

Over the years, some great mailing list *directories* have been created and manually maintained by individuals such as AOL's own David O'Donnell. The Liszt database is the first true searchable index of mailing lists—currently more than 80,000 of them. At Liszt, you enter a search keyword, and Liszt searches an index

for mailing lists whose name or description matches the keyword. Liszt searches only through the names (and, where available, short descriptions) of mailing lists; *it does not (and cannot) search through messages posted to lists.* See Chapter 4 for a complete introduction to mailing lists.

To use Liszt to find a mailing list about a specific topic, you enter a term as you do in any index, then click Search (see Figure 9-11).

You need to be explicit about what you want. If you want a phrase, enclose it in quotes (*"home run"*). Otherwise, *home run* returns all mailing lists with either *home* or *run* in their title or in the short descriptions lists sometimes provide about themselves. Not only that, Liszt will return the names of mailing lists with the words *run*, *run*ning, and b*run*ch in them! Specificity can rescue any search, and not just on Liszt. The Liszt database consists merely of the names of mailing lists, so you won't get the voluminous responses you'd expect from a Web search with AOL

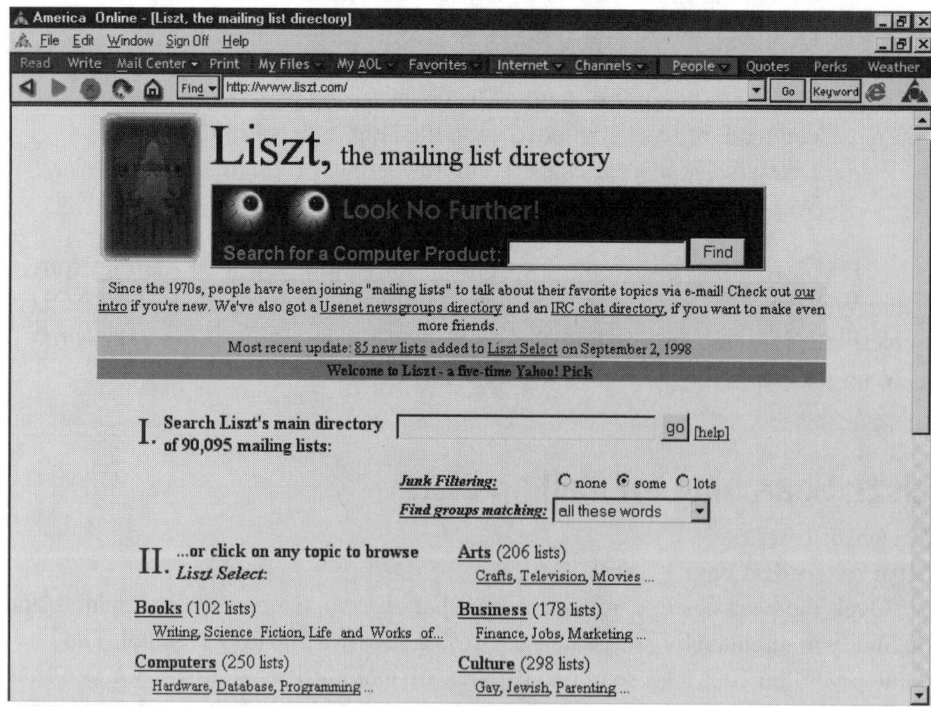

FIGURE 9-11 Search Liszt for a mailing list about your hobby, profession, or obsession

NetFind. As a result, it pays to cast your queries a little more broadly than you would with AOL NetFind or AltaVista.

Liszt searches both its database of all mailing lists and its database of about 1,000 popular lists (Liszt Select). The result of your query is a list of hyperlinks to mailing lists with Liszt Select lists highlighted.

Click one to bring up a description of the list. Don't expect detailed substantive information from Liszt. At best, you'll get subscription instructions based on your list's *type* (for example, LISTSERV).

Newsgroup and IRC Searching with Liszt

Despite its focus on mailing lists, Liszt also lets you do Usenet searches (click Newsgroup Directory at the opening page). Currently this search looks through the *names* of newsgroups, not the actual postings; AOL's newsreader does much the same thing and searches through a longer list of newsgroups. This Liszt feature does allow you to do all your searching for good discussion groups—newsgroups and mailing lists—in one place. When you find a newsgroup that looks interesting on Liszt, click it (it will be hyperlinked) to go directly to the newsgroup on AOL (if you are signed onto AOL and not using the Bring Your Own Access plan at the time).

New in Liszt is the ability to search the names and titles of current Internet Relay Chat (IRC) channels. You get a select list of the most popular IRC channels by IRC network, with current usage statistics. Good help and background information make it easy to use the IRC search and to use IRC itself.

IRC channels are the Internet's chat rooms. You can read all about IRC in Chapter 10.

9

In short, with Liszt you can identify all the mailing lists, IRC channels, and newsgroups of likely interest to you.

FINDING PEOPLE ONE AT A TIME: E-MAIL SEARCHES

Newsgroups and mailing lists plug you into active discussions that take place over the Internet. If you're looking for a single person or certain Susan, you need to use a people finder. All of the Web search services (Excite and the rest of them) offer a link to one or another of the major *people finders*—searchable white pages and e-mail directories.

What follows are short descriptions of leading e-mail search services available over the Web; they're not the only ones, but they're probably the biggest. AOL

NetFind offers an e-mail service, but just in case it doesn't retrieve the address you're seeking, try one of the services described below.

Note *Searches for street addresses are likely to be a lot more successful than searches for e-mail addresses because they're based on existing white pages and other printed directories. E-mail addresses cannot easily be systematically collected or maintained, so e-mail searches are less successful. Why? For one thing, people change e-mail addresses faster than they change real addresses, so e-mail addresses can be out of date. Also, they are more likely to have multiple e-mail addresses than to have multiple real addresses. Thus, the e-mail address finders would love for you to add your e-mail address to their database, and they make it easy for you to do so! Another caveat: E-mail services have a hard time with duplicate entries, since there is no sure way of determining whether the David Peal who lived in San Francisco is different from the one who lives where he currently lives. If the computers can't tell the difference, you probably won't be able to either! If you haven't seen Harry Housebound in 20 years, there is no way to tell whether the Harry in Phoenix is different from the one in Piscataway. You may be surprised how many people have the same name as you.*

Four11

Keyword: Four11
http://www.four11.com/

Four11, one of the oldest Web-based directory services, claims complete and constantly updated Web access to U.S. white pages and more than 15 million e-mail addresses (Figure 9-12). When you use Yahoo's People Search service you're using Four11's technology and listings (which is not surprising—Yahoo now owns Four11). Special Four11 features include directories of celebrities.

Tip *In searching for an e-mail address or a street address with* any *of the services, it's best to start your search broad and then to narrow it (with Web searches, it's best to start narrow and narrow further). You can use just the last name, adding the first initial if you're uncertain of the full name. To narrow a search, add a country, then a state, then a city (in that order). Remember, calling the person and asking for an address is sometimes the best way to get it.*

Four11 lets you register for free, then add or modify your personal information as you wish. Registering also gives you the privilege of keeping your e-mail address out of your listing and of using Four11 as an intermediary to intercept and forward

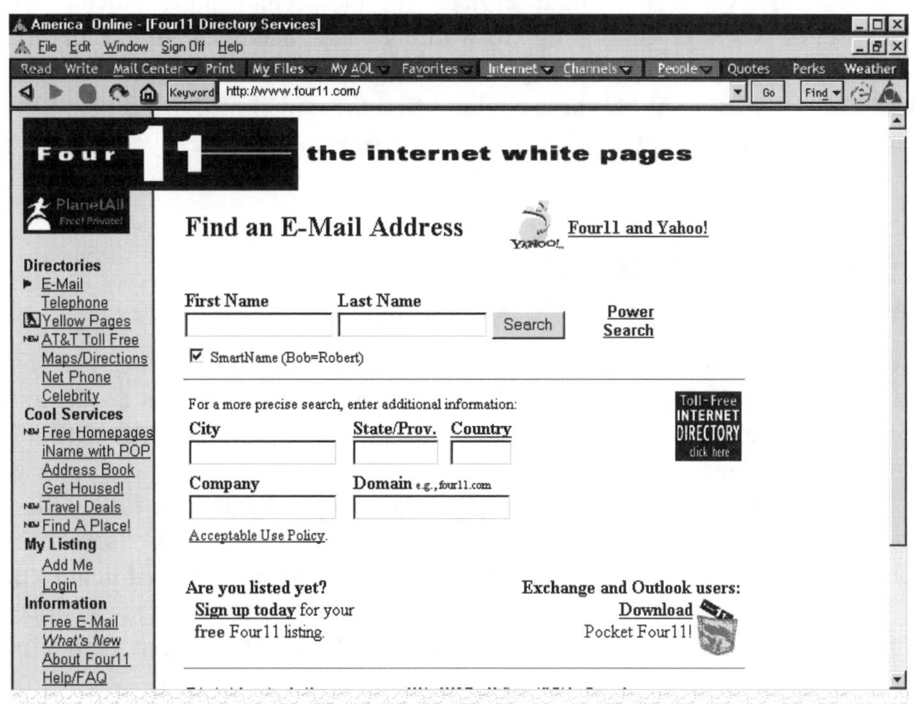

FIGURE 9-12 Four11, the Net's leading way to find an e-mail address

mail to you. Four11 provides e-mail and white page listings for BigYellow, the data source behind InfoSeek and other services.

Other E-mail Services

Bigfoot (not to be confused with BigYellow, with its business listings) has about eight million e-mail addresses (**http://www.bigfoot.com**). Like Four11, Bigfoot lets you edit your personal information when you move or change your preferred e-mail address. Bigfoot also lets you hide all or part of your personal information, to ensure your privacy. Unlike Four11, with Bigfoot you get a single box in which to enter your search information. So, if you're looking for John Smith in New York, you enter: **John Smith, NY** (the comma is mandatory).

The value of Bigfoot is based on the depth of its e-mail services, which include a searchable database of e-mail addresses. If you use AOL's Bring Your Own Access

service and use your ISP's e-mail services, you may want to look into Bigfoot's many services for consolidating, forwarding, and managing your e-mail. A competing service, WhoWhere (**http://www.whowhere.com**), features breadth, not depth, of information. WhoWhere couldn't find the e-mail of a friend of mine at Fermi Lab, while Bigfoot could. However, WhoWhere does offer special features such as a searchable list of personal Web pages.

SEARCHING THE MEGASITES: FINDING SPECIALIZED INFORMATION

More and more, you'll find search tools being adapted to narrower and narrower subjects; InfoSeek, Excite, and AltaVista even make their services available to individual organizations and corporate intranets with sites consisting of tens of thousands of documents.

If you need specific information, consider finding and searching a megasite: a specific, content-rich site devoted to sports, law, medicine, computers, or some other subject. These megasites often seek to be meccas, the best sites for their field. What follows are short descriptions of several such sites of the hundreds of massive sites you can find on your own. Many additional megasites are available at the Internet Sleuth (**http://www.isleuth.com/**), described later in this chapter.

Finding Medical Information

HealthAtoZ.com, a creation of the Medical Network Inc., offers a searchable directory of more than 20,000 pages of health information arranged in some 25 categories (**http://www.healthatoz.com**). The site meets the needs of both healthcare consumers and medical professionals. You can either search across categories for specific information or browse one category at a time. Every item returned by its search has clearly formatted descriptive information, including a rating, a live link, a review, and a link to a pertinent category in which similar sites can be found. All sites in its own directory are reviewed by medical professionals and rated in such a way that their appropriateness for professionals or consumers is clear.

For authoritative information and the latest research, turn to *Medline,* available at *keyword: Medline* (a link is also available from HealthAtoZ). This database of medical journal abstracts, started in 1990, grows by some 30,000 abstracts a month. It is published by the National Library of Medicine in Bethesda, Maryland. You can search for an article by author, author's affiliation, title, publication date, and journal. AOL adds value to Medline in many ways. You can share your Medline findings with others (or have them interpreted) in the Disabilities Forum (*keyword: Dis*) or on the Better Health and Medical Network (*keyword: Better Health*). AOL has created online help for Medline and maintains Medline message boards. A fee-based document delivery service is now available over AOL, if you want complete articles in addition to abstracts.

Learning About Other Places: City.Net

Mecca is the right metaphor for **City.Net (http://city.net)**, a comprehensive directory of place-related Internet content for travelers and students, owned by Excite and now part of the Excite Travel channel (Figure 9-13).

With City.Net you can search for a specific location on any continent. I've done searches of places where I've lived in Germany (Marburg) and Canada (Halifax), and retrieved abundant local information about these towns. Maps and people finders were also available.

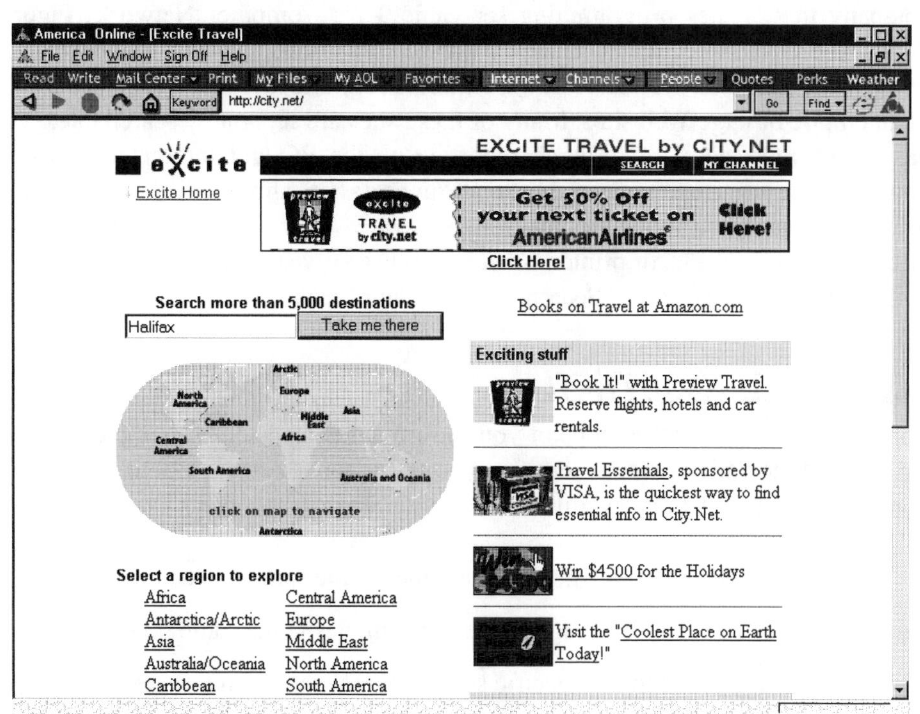

FIGURE 9-13 Don't leave home without consulting City.Net

Suffering from *Wanderlust*? On City.Net you can choose a continent and wend your way through countries, states, and provinces to local communities that interest you. Armchair travelers never had it so good. If you are planning a trip, you can book plane tickets, make hotel reservations, get local maps, look up local numbers and addresses, and find out about hostelling. Of course, if you want to make reservations, you'll have to register and provide some personal information.

CNET: The World of PCs

Everyone on the Internet has access to a computer, so it's not surprising that some of the best resources on the Internet are computer-related. Publishers of computer magazines such as CMP (**http://www.cmp.com**), Meckler (**http://www.internet.com**), and Ziff-Davis (**http://www.zdnet.com**) have put together huge sites based on the content of their print publications, with frequently changing and interactive material.

One of the leading computing megasites is **CNET**, from the same-named company that creates programming for cable TV's Computer Network (Figure 9-14). The CNET megasite (**http://www.cnet.com**) brings you computer-related news, feature articles, product reviews, editorials, and site reviews. CNET is the hub of an empire of large Web sites. Many of these sites are separately searchable: you can search **news.com** for in-depth reporting on the PC and Internet industries; **shareware.com** for "hundreds of thousands of shareware" programs; **download.com** for demos of commercial software; and **computers.com** for good prices on a modem, PC, or printer. Search.com is a very special case, being itself a collection of megasites (see "Searching Individual Megasites").

PULLING IT ALL TOGETHER

Sometimes, because of the scope of your information needs or the complementary strengths of the various search services, you need more than one tool to get the job done. Sites bring together several search services in different ways by:

- Gathering several general search engines in the same place
- Letting you run a query against several engines at the same time
- Collecting hundreds of specific searchable megasites in one place

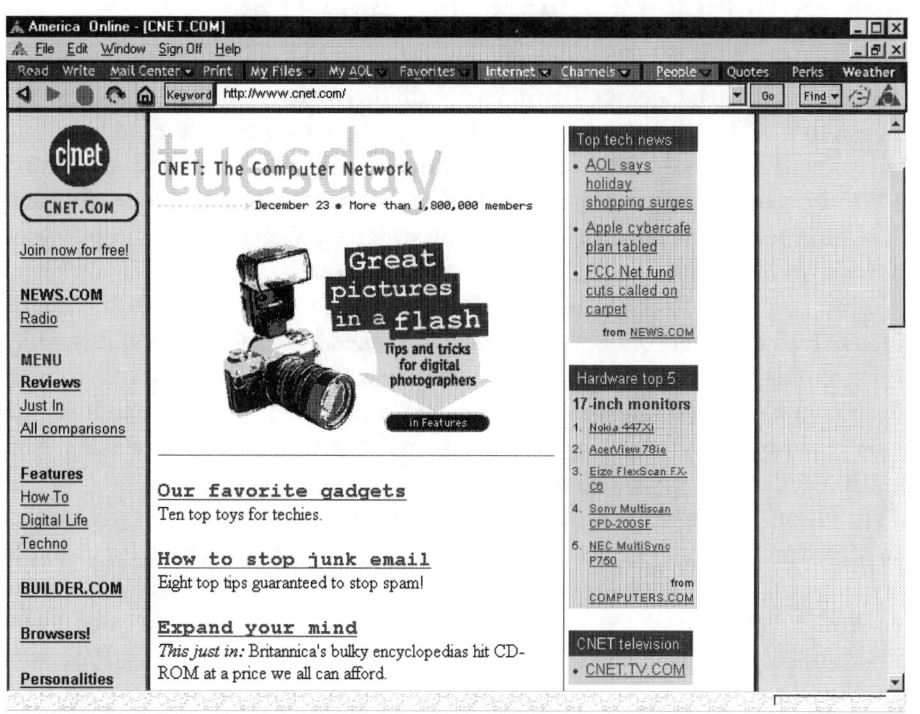

FIGURE 9-14 Heart of the CNET empire, whose satellite sites can be searched for news, files, and prices

Linking to Multiple Search Engines

A simple resource of this type is InterNIC's **Internet Search Engines** page, which takes you to dozens of search engines grouped into categories such as Web, mailing lists, FTP, metasearch, libraries, Usenet, and others (**http://www.internic.net/tools**). The **All in One Page** (**http://www.albany.net/ allinone/**) goes even further in bringing together hundreds of search services, including all the sites in this chapter, in one place. Perhaps simplest of all, Netscape's home page (Figure 10-1) gives you direct access to most of the major search sites discussed in this chapter.

Running Multiple Queries at the Same Time

Some services go a step further and run multiple searches using different engines *at the same time.* MetaCrawler (**http://www.metacrawler.com**) is the oldest and simplest to use of such services. You write a query, indicate whether to treat your words as a phrase or a Boolean series, tell MetaCrawler whether you want to search the Web or newsgroups, or search for files, and then click Search. Your one query will be run through several search sites. If you search the Web you'll be hitting Lycos, InfoSeek, WebCrawler, Excite, AltaVista, and Yahoo at the same time. If you search newsgroups, you're likely to use just DejaNews, however, since it's the engine preferred by most other services. Each result is ranked by relevancy no matter which service returned it. PowerSearch lets you specify where you want to search for sites (which continents) and how many returns you want to get for each search engine. If you're nosey, click MetaSpy to find out what other people are seeking from MetaCrawler at this very moment.

ProFusion (**http://www.designlab.ukans.edu/profusion**) is a newer service than MetaCrawler, and it offers more features (Figure 9-15). Up front, for example, you can select the engines against which you want to run your query at the same time. You can also choose the three search engines that are currently responding the fastest. Or, keep it simple: write a query and choose all search engines. ProFusion gives you the power (and complexity) of Boolean operators if you want to write specific queries.

Tip *ProFusion's Check Links option test whether links returned by your query actually work—an intelligent feature used by no major search service. Like MetaCrawler, ProFusion ranks results, but using any of the ProFusion options (especially Check Links) can slow things down.*

Searching Individual Megasites

Need results? Depth? Sites like **Internet Sleuth** (**http://www.isleuth.com/**) and **Search.com** (**http://www.search.com**) give you a single place from which you can do many focused searches *within* individual Web sites.

Internet Sleuth (Figure 9-16) currently lets you search any of 2,000 such megasites. Searching Internet Sleuth is a two-step process. First, search Internet Sleuth itself for one of its databases. Then, use the database itself to search for the information you need. Say you're looking for a recipe. First type **recipes** into Search the Sleuth box on the opening page, and press ENTER. Then, choose from more than 30 searchable databases, ranging from Bar-None Drink Recipes and FlavorWeb to HomeArts Recipe Finder and Healthy Choice. Each of these databases searches a

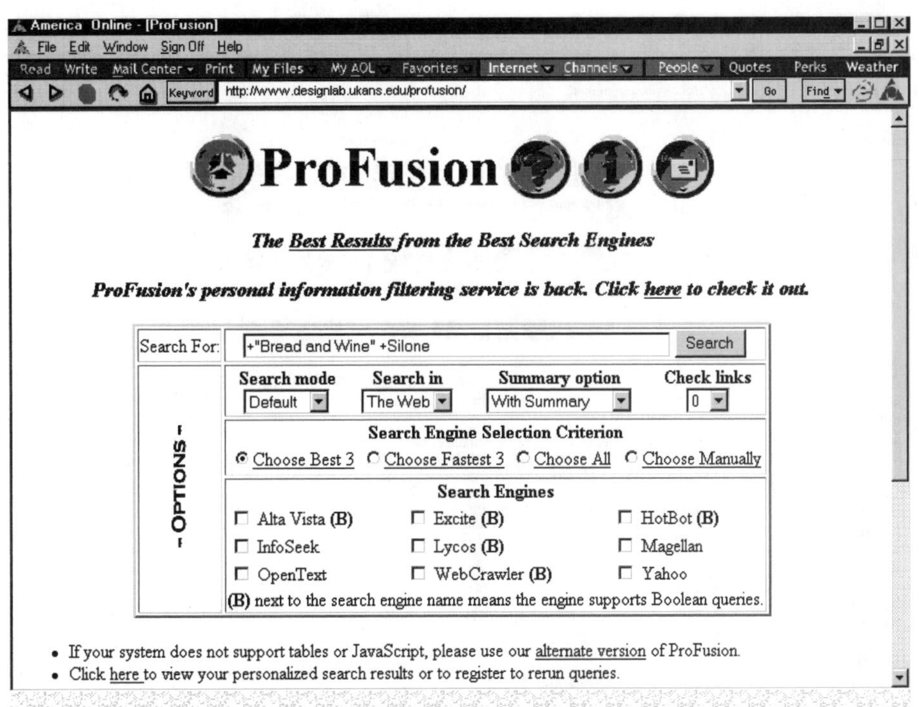

FIGURE 9-15 ProFusion, a newer meta-service with many options, runs a single query through many engines, returning a single set of results

9

particular food-related Web site. You can also browse Internet Sleuth, which is a great way to kill time hunting for trivia.

Tip *Internet Sleuth also provides links to dozens of individual search engines—for searching the Web, newsgroups, mailing lists, and more—and it offers limited metasearches (so you can use several engines at the same time).*

Search.com, part of the CNET empire discussed a little earlier, is another place to do a specialized search. Search.com collects several hundred searchable Web databases. It lets you browse them (they're arranged in familiar categories) and then search them one at a time. Smaller than Internet Sleuth, Search.com offers a better

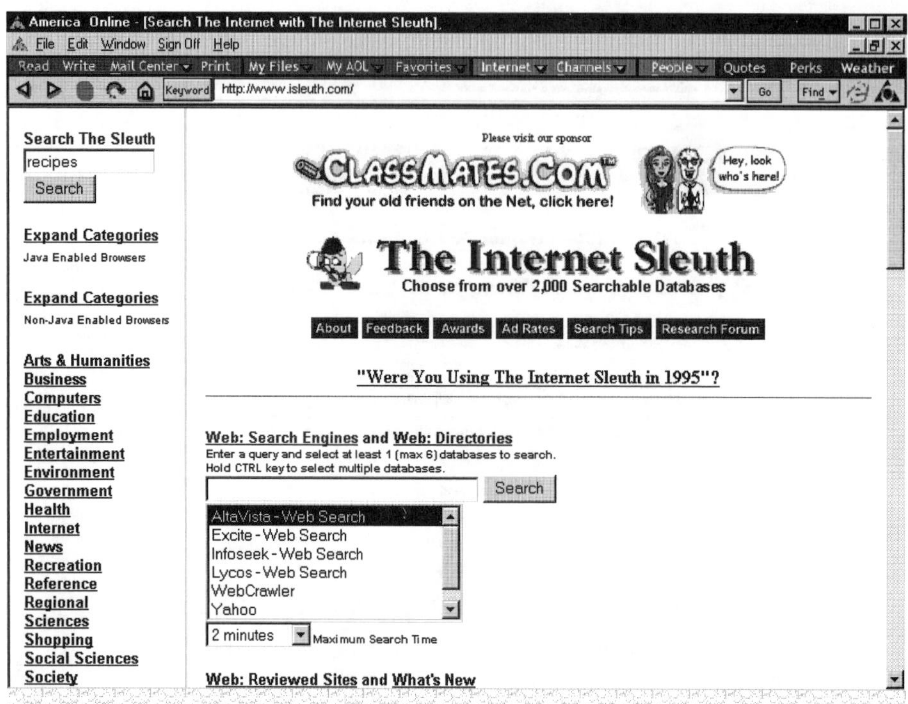

FIGURE 9-16 Internet Sleuth makes short work of finding that needle in the haystack

interface and more value-added services, and InfoSeek is always available for those broad sweeps of the whole Web.

FROM HERE...

With these search tools and this chapter, you can use AOL to make the Internet a part of your life. It's easier than ever to learn something new, do some armchair traveling, research your family's history, find out the capital of North Dakota, or search for the whereabouts of your favorite high school teacher.

Everything up to this point in the book is possible with the AOL software and AOL browser. The next chapter looks beyond, to all the non-AOL software you can use with AOL, such as Netscape, Internet Relay Chat, and Telnet. It's not just about software, though. In the next chapter you'll learn to find community on the global Internet.

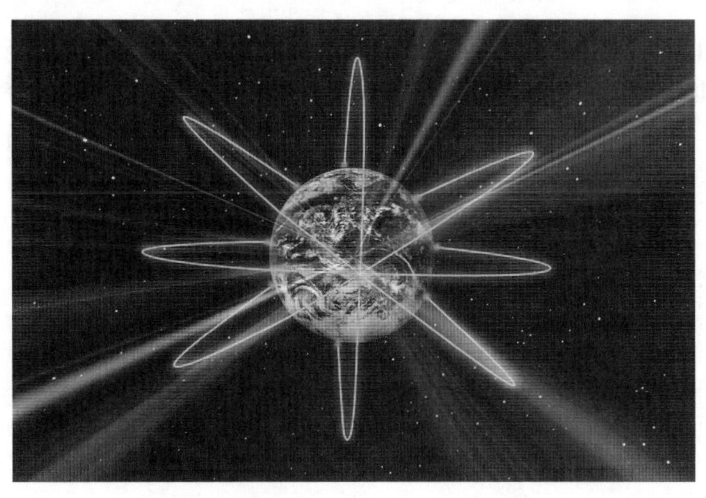

Chapter 10

Netscape and Beyond: Using Internet Applications with AOL

America Online provides everything you need to browse the Web, download files with FTP, read newsgroups, manage your e-mail, and take part in mailing lists. But AOL's Internet access doesn't stop there. A little file called Winsock, which is automatically included with AOL 4.0 for Windows and AOL 4.0 for Windows 95, opens an even broader world of possibilities on AOL.

This chapter begins with a look at Netscape Navigator 4 and concludes with two Internet applications that let you take part in virtual communities on the Internet:

- Internet Relay Chat—for chat rooms on the global Internet
- Telnet—for collaborative learning, simulated role-playing, and accessing library catalogs

The browsing, IRC, and Telnet programs described in this chapter are only a few of the Winsock applications available to you on AOL and the Net. See "Where Do I Find Winsock Applications?" for places where you can find truckloads of Internet software.

ALL YOU NEED TO KNOW ABOUT WINSOCK

A single small file (winsock.dll) makes it possible for you to use Internet programs such as Netscape Navigator with AOL. The beauty of AOL 4.0 for Windows is that you don't have to think, much less worry, about Winsock; you can run virtually any Windows Internet software without a second thought.

There are two basic types of Winsock: 16-bit for Windows 3.1 and 32-bit for Windows 95. Just as there are two types of Winsock, there are two types of Winsock *applications*: 16-bit and 32-bit. The 32-bit software written for Windows 95 theoretically processes more data at the same time than the 16-bit software written predominantly for Windows 3.1, but the difference isn't always perceptible. The 32-bit Winsock applications can do more ambitious things such as let you browse 3D Web sites (VRML). Many programs (like Netscape) do, however, come in two versions. When you download such programs, make sure to specify the 16-bit version if you will be using AOL 4.0 for Windows 3.1 and the 32-bit version if you'll be using AOL 4.0 for Windows 95.

The type of Winsock you have depends on the version of AOL you use, and it determines which Winsock applications you can use:

- If you use AOL 2.5 for Windows, you must manually download the 16-bit Winsock file to your windows directory, renaming other Winsocks that might be on your computer already. The instructions for downloading Winsock and renaming other Winsocks can be found at *keyword: Winsock*. With this software, you can use only 16-bit Winsock applications.
- If you use AOL 3.0 for Windows (3.1) or AOL 4.0 for Windows (3.1), you automatically have Winsock but can use only 16-bit Winsock applications.
- If you use AOL 4.0 for Windows 95, you automatically get Winsock and can use either 16-bit or 32-bit applications.

Tip *So you've upgraded to AOL 4.0 but don't know which version you have? Choose* About America Online *from the Help menu. You will see either America Online 4.0 for Windows (in which case you have 16-bit Winsock) or America Online 4.0 for Windows 95 (in which case you have 32-bit Winsock).*

The good thing about 32-bit Winsock—what you get in AOL 4.0 for Windows 95—is that it runs *either* 32-bit *or* 16-bit Winsock applications, while 16-bit Winsock won't run 32-bit Winsock applications.

With AOL 4.0 (for Windows or Windows 95), Winsock loads automatically when you sign onto AOL. You don't have to do anything! Don't move or rename your winsock.dll file! If you use the Bring Your Own Access plan, AOL's Winsock won't load if your other ISP's Winsock is loaded.

Where Do I Find Winsock Applications?

Hundreds of Winsock applications are available to download from AOL and the Internet: HTML editors and browsers; FTP, Gopher, and IRC clients; cool Internet telephone and teleconferencing programs; and (for your ISP connection) myriad mail and News programs. Wherever you download such software, be careful to download the appropriate version—16-bit or 32-bit, depending on the version of Winsock you have (see "All You Need to Know About Winsock"). You can't go too far wrong with 16-bit applications, since they'll work with both AOL Winsocks.

On the Internet, several megasites provide thousands of applications of every kind. Most of these sites highlight new arrivals and popular downloads.

The following two sites focus on Winsock software and have mirror (identical) sites around the world to make it easier to access:

- CWSA, the Consummate Winsock Applications list (**http://www.stroud.com**)
- The Tucows (as in "two cows") Ultimate Collection of Winsock Software (**http://www.tucows.com**)

The following sites have enormous software collections that include substantial software archives, organized by platform (Mac or Windows) and topic (business, education, etc.):

- CNET's Shareware.com (**http://www.shareware.com**)
- Jumbo (**http://www.jumbo.com**)
- ZDNet (**http://www.hotfiles.com**)
- If you have AOL 4.0 for Windows 95, there's a Web site with nothing but 32-bit software to download: **http://www.32bit.com**.

Note *With AOL you cannot yet use separate mail or News clients, but if you're using the Bring Your Own Access billing plan, you can use programs such as WinVN (News) and Eudora (mail). However, you'll be using your ISP's mail and News computers, and you'll be using the e-mail address you use with that other account—not your AOL screen name.*

How Do I Use a Winsock Application?

Using a Winsock program is like using any program—you must install it, run it, and learn what it does. The only hitch is that you must be signed onto AOL or logged onto your ISP if you have the Bring Your Own Access plan.

To install a Winsock application, first download the file, then run it—using either File | Run (Windows 3.1) or Start menu | Run (Windows 95). During installation you'll be asked where you want to put the program's files (it's usually fine to accept the recommended folders). After installation, you have a program window with a clickable icon (Windows 3.1) or a new addition to your Start menu or desktop (Windows 95).

You can use more than one Winsock application at the same time. You could, if you wanted, run an IRC program (such as mIRC, described a little later), the Netscape Navigator browser, and a Telnet client all at the same time. You could browse the World Wide Web using more than one browser at the same time (AOL's and Netscape's, for example). You could even run more than one AOL browser and several Netscapes at the same time! Of course, your system will slow down and your eyes will glaze over, but that's another matter.

If you exit from AOL or your AOL connection is broken for any reason, all your Winsock applications will disconnect from the Internet as well. What's new in AOL 4.0 is that if you sign onto AOL again, you *don't* have to close and re-open any Winsock applications before using them again. You'll appreciate this with a slow-loading program such as Netscape.

NETSCAPE NAVIGATOR

America Online members can use the most current version of Netscape Navigator. Netscape is fast and easy to use and, like the AOL browser, it supports Java, Javascript, and dozens of plug-ins (discussed in Chapter 6). Netscape Navigator now forms part of Netscape Communicator, a complete Internet suite consisting of a mail and News program, Web design software, push technology, and collaborative tools for networks, as well as the Navigator browser. This chapter looks only at the browser, not the complete suite.

If you want to use all of Communicator, start with Christian Crumlish's Netscape Communicator for Busy People *(Osborne/McGraw-Hill, 1997).*

Although AOL includes a strong, integrated browser, some members may want to use Netscape as well. Why? If you use Netscape at school or work, you may want to use Netscape at home on AOL as well. Netscape also offers a few features not available in the AOL browser. Perhaps the best reason to use Netscape is to test Web pages you are creating.

When you use Netscape, AOL-only features are not available. It may, for example, be less convenient to read your mail while browsing with Netscape.

Downloading and Installing Netscape

The latest version of Netscape can be downloaded directly from Netscape's Web site (**http://home.netscape.com**).

Note *In the near future, AOL plans to offer a version of Netscape Navigator 4 directly to AOL members, just as it offered Netscape 3 (*keyword: Netscape*). AOL's version of Netscape is likely to be customized to recognize AOL.com as its home page and AOL NetFind as its Search page. Keep checking back at* keyword: Netscape, *using the following instructions in the interim.*

1. Starting at Netscape's Download area (**http://home.netscape.com/products/download**), click a link indicating which products you want to download in the Communicator/Navigator and Accessories section—for example, Communicator. Be aware that the whole Communicator package can take hours to download over a modem connection.

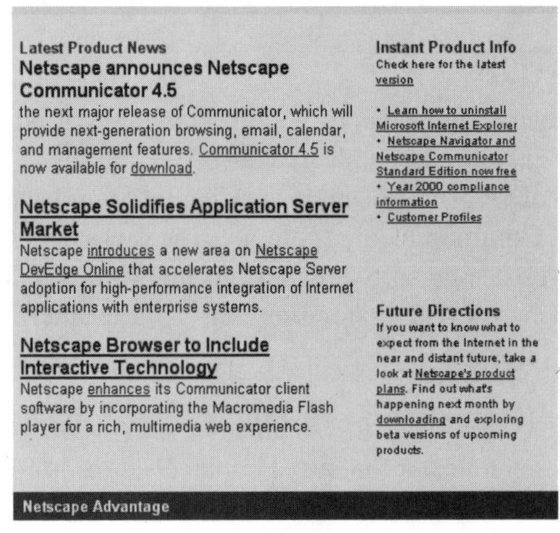

2. On the page for the product you chose to download, click the Download button.

3. Use the forms to indicate which version you want, in which language, and for which operating system. You also have the option of purchasing the product if you want documentation and support. Downloading is free for noncommercial users, however, and downloading from the Web is the best way to get the specific version you need, with the latest bug fixes. Press ENTER to start the process, indicate where you want the Netscape file to be stored on your hard drive.

To install Netscape, run the file you downloaded, answering any questions along the way. Make a note of where Netscape is installed, and if you're prompted to put Netscape on your Windows 95 Start menu, do so.

Note *With Netscape Navigator for Windows 3.1, you will be asked whether you want to continue using your netscape.ini file. Answer Yes only if you used Netscape in the past and want to use your existing bookmarks and preferences. Answer No to create a new netscape.ini file and lose your existing settings.*

Using Netscape Navigator on AOL

When you click on a Web link while using America Online (a link integrated into a forum or elsewhere in a channel) or when you type a URL into the AOL Address box, the integrated Microsoft AOL browser comes up. Follow these simple steps to use Netscape:

1. Sign on to AOL as usual. It's OK to be signed on using the Bring Your Own Access plan.

Tip *If you do have your own ISP and want to use Netscape, your Netscape browsing won't be disconnected if you get automatically logged off AOL during times of the day when the AOL service is especially busy. If Netscape is the default browser for your ISP, you can use it with AOL and avoid the bother of downloading it!*

2. In Windows 3.1, go to the Program Manager and find the directory where Netscape was installed; double-click its icon.

   In Windows 95, from the Start menu, select the Programs menu, navigate to the place where you've installed Netscape, and select it; if it's on your Start menu, just select it from there.

Grand Central Netscape

Netscape's home page (**http://home.netscape.com**), shown in Figure 10-1, is one of the world's busiest Web destinations—and starting points. At the center of this site is the search area, available from the opening page. Choose any search engine (including AOL NetFind), type a query, and click Search. Or, start here to download the latest version of Navigator, including any preview versions of upcoming versions. Tell your friends who aren't AOL members that they can get a copy of Instant Messenger here, too. Finally, if you're brave and have a fast connection, learn about Netscape's channels, consisting of information that is "pushed" to your desktop at regular intervals without your having to click a thing.

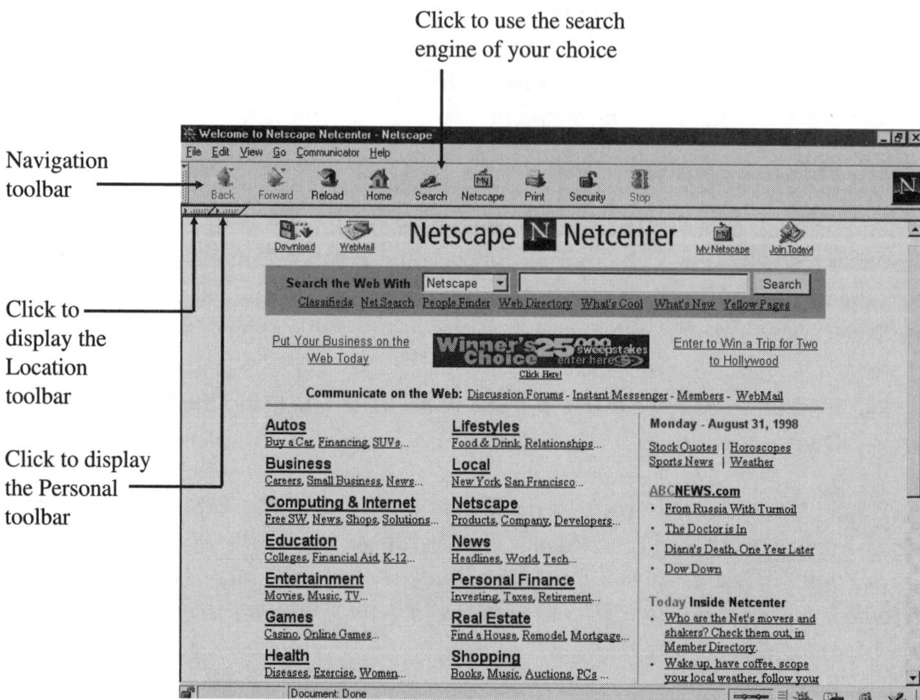

FIGURE 10-1 Netscape Home, a mansion that's always getting a new addition or paint job. This figure shows the latest beta version.

NETSCAPE NAVIGATOR 4: THE LEAST YOU NEED TO KNOW

Whole books have been written on Netscape, but browsing the Web with Netscape really doesn't take much explanation. If you're familiar with the basics of clicking, going backward, and jumping to a new Web page, then you'll pick up Netscape in a few minutes. See Figure 10-1 for a quick tour of the Netscape browser.

Getting Used to the Netscape Look

Like AOL, Netscape now puts different types of controls on different toolbars. To free up space so you can see more of a Web page, you can minimize any or all three Netscape toolbars by clicking the knobby handle with the triangle on it on the far left of the toolbar. Here's what the toolbars look like when minimized:

With the toolbars minimized, there's no telling which is which, so pass your cursor over the handle to see its name.

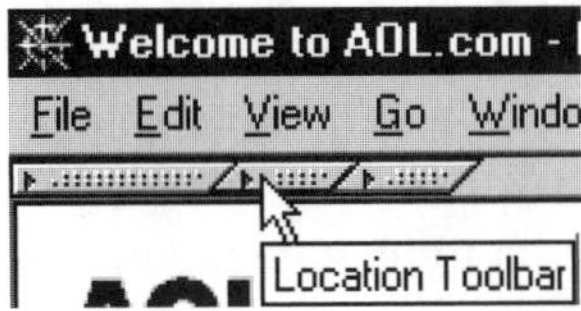

Click again to restore the toolbar.

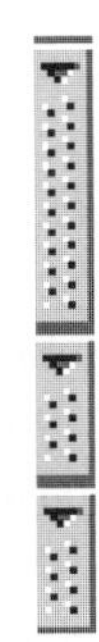

- The *Navigation* toolbar does the basic work of helping you move back and forth between pages and stopping a page while it's downloading. Click Print to print the current page (with helpful inclusion of URL, title, and page number on the header and footer of the printout). Some navigation buttons are hardwired to specific pages: Search takes you to the NetSearch area of the Netscape Web site, and Guide takes you to a directory of Web destinations created especially for Netscape by Yahoo. Security gives you more information than you're likely to want to have about the security status of the page you're viewing (it's an experts-only thing).

Tip *The standard Back and Forward buttons have drop-down lists showing you what the next few pages are going backward and forward: just click the Back or Forward button and keep the mouse pressed down until the list appears (it's like having additional, one-way history trails).*

Finding Information with Netscape Navigator

- Click the Search button and choose an index to search the Web (one will come up automatically, but you don't have to use it).
- Click Guide for a mini-Yahoo, customized for Netscape.
- Click Find to look for a word within a page. This feature is a lifesaver if you do a Web search, click a link, and then get a long page that doesn't seem to include the keyword.

- The *Location* toolbar looks innocent enough, but it offers a great deal of power. Netsite remembers URLs you've visited, so instead of typing **http://www.amazon.com**, all you have to type is **http://www.a** or **http://www.am** and Netscape attempts to fill in the rest. Or, let Netscape read your mind and just type **amazon** into the Netsite box; it'll do its best to figure out what you want, especially if you've already visited the site. The Location box, just below the toolbar, is a drop-down list of sites you've visited in the current and past sessions. Click the down arrow at the right side of the field to see all Web sites you've recently visited in the order you've visited them; select a site from this list to visit the site. Note that only the top-level sites are recorded, not the many pages you may have visited within a site. Unlike AOL, Netscape records URLs (*http://…*) and not titles (*Birding*), making the list slightly harder to use. Most important, there's the Bookmarks button on the left of the Location toolbar, discussed in "Using Bookmarks to Keep Track of Your Favorite Web Destinations."
- The *Personal* toolbar lets you add your own buttons, taking you directly to the sites you most frequently visit. To do so, you must add one or more bookmarks to the Personal Toolbar Folder in your Bookmarks window, as explained in the next section.

Using Bookmarks to Keep Track of Your Favorite Web Destinations

Bookmarks, like AOL's Favorite Places, hold your favorite Web sites. With Netscape you can keep track only of Internet sites—not AOL content, e-mail messages, and the like. When you discover a good site while using Netscape:

1. Click and hold down the Netsite button on the Location toolbar.
2. Drag left to the Bookmark button and release the mouse button to drop the site into your Bookmarks file.

Before long, you'll have lots of sites in a tangled mess. To hold related bookmarks, you can create folders and even folders within folders:

1. With Netscape open (offline or online), click the Bookmark button.
2. Click Edit Bookmarks, and you'll see the Bookmarks window, shown in Figure 10-2. (A keyboard shortcut, CTRL-B, takes you right to the Bookmarks window.)
3. Select File | New Folder, and give the new folder a name. Click and drag individual bookmarks into the folders you've created (in addition to the folders included with Navigator). Repeat whenever you need to make a folder. Close the Bookmarks window.

Next time you want to save a site you're visiting, click the Netsite button and drag to the Bookmarks button. *Keep the mouse button clicked* as the Bookmarks list opens. Drop your site into a folder or place it in a specific spot in the list of bookmarks.

Tip *Netscape's bookmarks are kept in a separate file called bookmark.htm in your Netscape directory. You can use this file on other computers with other copies of Netscape Navigator 4.*

FUN WITH BOOKMARKS Here are some useful housecleaning chores you can do in the Bookmarks window:

- Are you the tidy sort? To create a dividing line (*separator*) between groups of adjacent folders and bookmarks, use File | New Separator.

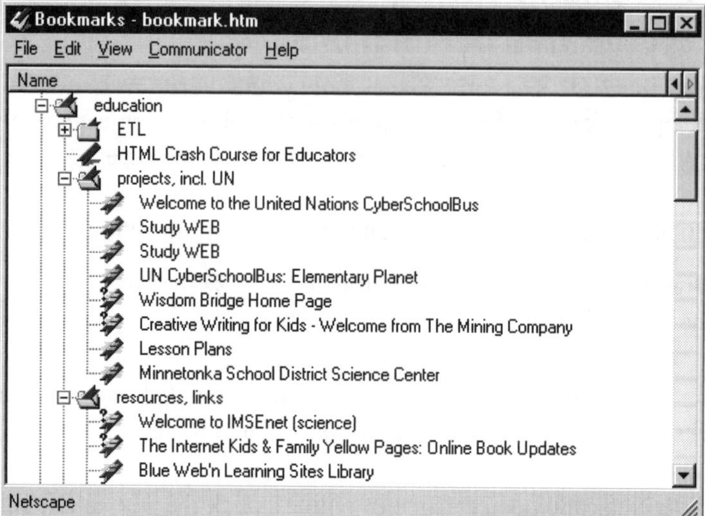

FIGURE 10-2 Netscape's Bookmarks window lets you keep tabs on the places you've been

- Has a favorite place fallen out of favor with you? To delete a bookmark or folder, click it and select Edit | Delete.
- Can't find that bookmark? Use CTRL-F (then CTRL-G to find the next match).
- Losing touch? To see which of your bookmarked pages has changed through the addition of new content, open the Bookmarks window, select a bookmarked item, and select View | Update Bookmarks. Netscape checks the date the Web page's file was last changed, compares it to the date your bookmark was last updated, and indicates whether the site has changed. It doesn't, however, tell you which content has been updated.

To add a bookmark to your Personal toolbar, select the bookmark, click File | Add Selection to Toolbar.

Netscape Preferences

Take a minute to explore the preferences available to you at Edit | Preferences (Figure 10-3). These preferences are less elaborate than Internet Explorer's but are easier to

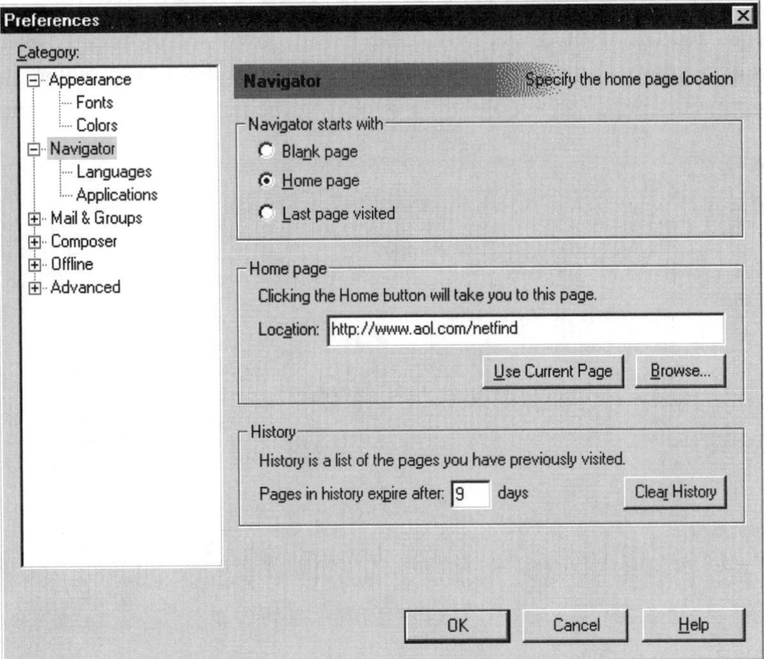

FIGURE 10-3 Netscape's Preferences window: click a category on the left to see and set up a panel of choices on right

use and understand. Preferences are grouped in panels; to see different panels, click one of the items on the left-hand side of the window.

- Set up the plug-ins and helper applications you want to use with Netscape (Applications panel).
- Set up a new home page (main Navigator panel).
- Turn off graphics by removing the check from the Automatically Loads Images box (main Advanced panel).
- Reject (or accept) cookies (main Advanced panel).
- Set your cache (explained in Chapter 6, "Get Cache Fast"). (Advanced/Cache panel, use Disk Cache box.)

Using the Keyboard for Common Netscape Tasks

As a freestanding application, Netscape has its own set of menus and assigns keystrokes to many common menu tasks. For other keyboard equivalents, visit the Netscape menus; when available, they appear to the right of command names.

Task	Keystroke
Go forward	ALT-→
Go backward	ALT-←
Refresh (reload) page	CTRL-R
Stop a page from downloading	ESC
Find a word on a page	CTRL-F
Select all the text on a page	CTRL-A
Increase font	CTRL-]
Decrease font	CTRL-[
View HTML for a page	CTRL-U
View bookmarks	CTRL-B
Add a bookmark	CTRL-D

Netscape Supports Plug-ins (Integrated File Players)

What's a plug-in? Basically, a plug-in is a well-integrated helper application, which means that when you click on a link to a Real Audio sound file or VDO video file, for example, the appropriate player appears within Netscape (or within a new Netscape window) and plays the sound or video or whatever it is. Plug-ins bring Web pages to life. From the Help menu, a special selection called About Plug-ins takes you to a page that keeps track of which plug-ins you have, what file types they support, and how you can get new plug-ins (just click the conspicuous link to more information about plug-ins). Installing a new plug-in is simple. Just download the plug-in, and Navigator sets everything up for you.

Leaving Netscape

To close down the Navigator program, File | Exit does the trick in any version of Windows; in Windows 95, click once in the X box in the far upper-right corner.

CHATTING ON THE INTERNET WITH mIRC

Chatting on the Internet is like chatting on AOL—or at the checkout counter or anywhere else, for that matter. It's informal, lively, sociable, and often has no purpose beyond itself.

The most popular way to chat on the Net, Internet Relay Chat (IRC), differs from chat on AOL primarily in its global reach. IRC also differs from AOL's chat in that it requires special software, and the software is a bit more complex than AOL's. There are many IRC programs available for the PC, and one of the best of them, mIRC, is conveniently located (with installation instructions) in AOL's download library. A large community of mIRC users has created a big body of help resources (and IRC channels) devoted to the software (see "Finding Out More about mIRC and IRC").

At *keyword: Filesearch* (then click Shareware), search for mIRC, then download the most current version of the software (version 5 or greater). Run that file using Windows 3.1 or Windows 95, following the prompts.

Note *If you're using Windows 3.1, download the 16-bit version of mIRC; for Windows 95, download the 32-bit version. The interface is the same; in this chapter I'll be using the 32-bit version.*

Setting up mIRC and Starting an mIRC Session

With mIRC downloaded and installed, you have to provide mIRC enough information for it to connect to an IRC computer at AOL.

1. Start mIRC by double-clicking the program's icon. You might be prompted to register; this program is shareware, which means that if you use the software frequently and find value in it, you should register and pay the nominal fee requested by the program's creator, Khaled Mardam-Bey.
2. From the mIRC File menu, select Setup to bring up the mIRC Setup window (if it doesn't appear automatically).

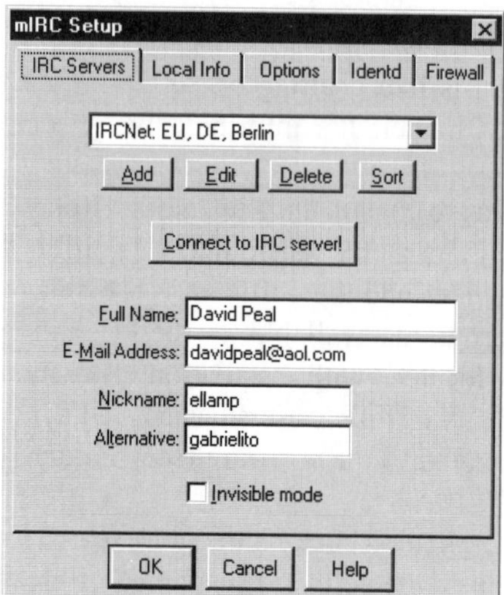

3. Click Add to get the mIRC Add Server window:

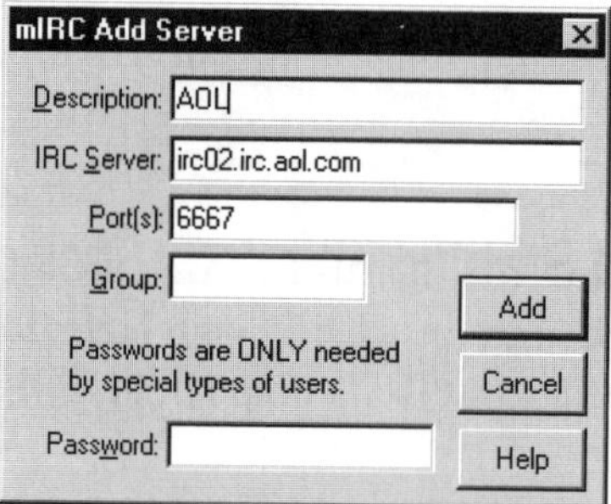

For the best chance of reliably getting onto IRC, use one of AOL's servers. Type **AOL** in the Description field, type **irc02.irc.aol.com** in the IRC Server field, and type **6667** in the Port field. Click Add to return to the Setup window, and click OK.

Tip *AOL runs many IRC servers, named* irc01.irc.aol.com *through irc07.irc.aol.com. Different servers connect you to different IRC networks, as explained in "IRC Networks." For the latest information, check out* **http://irc.web.aol.com/**.

4. Supply your real name (your AOL screen name will do) in the Full Name box and your real e-mail address (***screenname*@aol.com**) in the E-Mail Address box.
5. Supply a nickname in the Nickname box. A nickname is your IRC *persona* (like *bluemoon* or *hounddog* or *scarecrow*); it's how you want others to see you in an IRC channel (chat room). Unlike e-mail addresses, nicknames are not unique, so you can't prevent someone else from using the same nickname. That's why you must supply a second choice in the Alternative box. If the first one is in use when you sign onto IRC, you will automatically be assigned the alternate name. You can also change them whenever you want, using Commands | Change Nickname.

Connect to IRC now by selecting the server you just added and clicking Connect to IRC Server (or File | Connect). With any luck, the main mIRC window (Table 10-1) comes up. From now on, when you start mIRC all you have to do is click the Connect button (the lightning bolt icon on the far left-hand side of the mIRC toolbar). You'll connect to whatever server is selected in the Setup window.

The mIRC Status window registers what's happening as you're signing on and using various channels. If for some reason you can't use the AOL server, either try another server in the Setup window (select from the drop-down list) or try again later.

Note *To use the AOL IRC server, you must sign onto AOL directly, not using your ISP under the Bring Your Own Access plan. Once on IRC, if you ever need to change your nickname, use Commands | Change nickname.*

Connect to IRC server
Disconnect
Setup info
General options (preferences)
Channels folder (favorites)
List channels (search)
Colors (apply colors and effects to different kinds of text)
DCC Send (send a file to someone)
DCC Chat (have a direct conversation with another person on IRC)
Help

TABLE 10-1 Essential buttons on the Main mIRC Toolbar

IRC Networks

IRC is made up of channels, and channels are arranged in networks, each of which has its own set of servers—physical computers connecting IRC users to each other. AOL's main server is on EFnet, one of the largest networks. The other top networks are Undernet, IRCnet, DALnet, and GalaxyNet. Channels differ in their channel offerings, and a good place to get an overview of what's on a channel at any moment is Liszt, the mailing list/newsgroup IRC search site described in Chapter 9 (**http://www.liszt.com/chat/**).

You can use mIRC to join any major network using one of the AOL servers listed at **http://irc.web.aol.com/**. From the mIRC Setup window, simply set up and choose a new server whenever you want to use a new network. One reason to use a different network is to take part in specific dedicated chat channels or to take part in a foreign language channel. To disconnect from a network, use File | Disconnect. You'll remain within mIRC, so you can now connect to a new network.

Choosing a Channel to Join

OK, you've connected to a network. An IRC channel may remind you of an AOL chat room. Unlike an AOL chat room, however, an IRC channel can grow to be very big; there's no 23-person limit or self-replicating feature, whereby an AOL chat room conveniently spawns a new chat room if it gets too big. On average, however, IRC channels are pretty small. You will find thousands of one- and two-person chat rooms consisting of people waiting for the party to start; sometimes it never does.

Note *IRC channels are denoted by a pound sign (#) and the name of the channel. For example,* **#irchelp**, **#ircnewbies**, *and* **#mIRC** *are the channels where you can get help with your basic and not-so-basic questions about IRC. Channel names sometimes start with an additional pound sign or exclamation mark (!) or percentage sign (%) in order to be listed first in the channels list.*

Choose a channel to join from the mIRC Channel Folders window, which pops up automatically as soon as you connect to a network server:

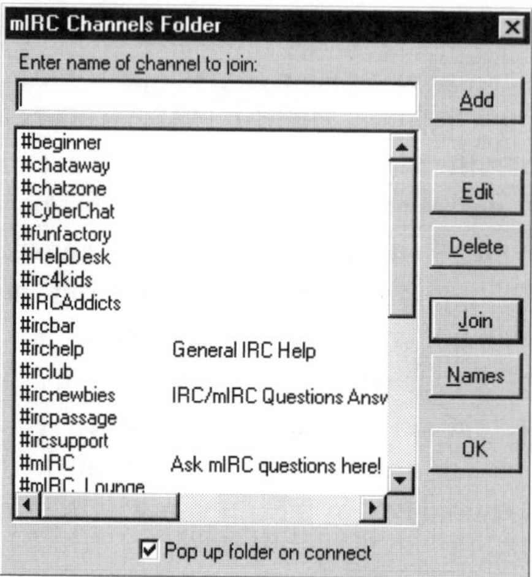

You can return to this window at any time by clicking its toolbar icon (a folder with a pound sign [#] on it), and you can both add channels and delete them. Several of the most popular channels on the network you're using are automatically included in the list in the Channels folder. Think of this list as the IRC equivalent of your Favorite Places on AOL (note that IRC channels can't be Favorite-Placed, however).

With the Channels folder open:

- To join a channel on the list, double-click it.
- To add a channel to the folder, type in the name (for example, **#irchelp**) in the text box at the top of the window and click Add. How do you know which channels are available? Either check Liszt (see "IRC Networks" above) or use the List Channels window (see "Getting a List of Available Channels" below).
- To create a channel, enter its name preceded by a # and click OK. See "Running a Channel." Yes, you create a channel by just giving it a name. You'll want to use the IRC Invite command (read on) to tell any buddies who are on the network at the moment to join your new channel.

To get the hang of IRC, join a channel such as **#beginner** *(Figure 10-4). It's like using the* **misc.test** *newsgroup if you're learning to use a newsgroup.*

Getting a List of Available Channels

Which channel to join of the thousands available? To find out, click the List Channels button on the mIRC toolbar (see Table 10-1).

Tip *The buttons on the toolbar are small and not always self-explanatory. You can tell a button's purpose by passing your mouse arrow over it slowly until a text description (a* balloon*) appears. If another window is active (such as the Channels folder), you won't see the balloon text.*

The List Channels window comes up:

List Channels
List channels which match these criteria:
Match text:
IRC
Apply
Match text in topics
Get List!
Do not sort channel list
Number of people on a channel:
OK
min: 20 max: 999
Lock
Hide channels which match these criteria:
Hide non-alphanumeric channels

Use this window to search for channels on topics that interest you. You can restrict the topic by typing in some text that must be contained in a channel's name. Also, you'll probably want to screen out the smallest channels by specifying a minimum number of people you want to find in a channel (using the min box). Obviously, a minimum number is required for *any* conversation.

My search for IRC-related channels in the current network with at least 20 people in each one yielded more than a dozen, including many devoted to the popular mIRC program. A broader search, for smaller channels or for all channels available on your server, will amaze and possibly offend you with the variety of channels available on IRC. Double-click any channel to go there directly.

Elements of a Channel Window

Channel windows have three basic elements: a place for input, a place for output, and a place to list the people taking part (Figure 10-4).

- To the right, a *list of participants* appears in alphabetical order, beginning with the channel's operators (note that the symbol @ comes before the letter *a*). Operators are the ones who create and run channels (see "Running a Channel").
- To the left appears the *chat window*, where chat text is displayed.
- At the bottom appears the *entry field*, where you enter either chat messages (text) or commands (preceded by a forward slash, /). Commands are discussed a little later.

When you're using a channel, you should be aware of a window that never goes away: the Status window. To keep it out of the way, you might want to minimize it.

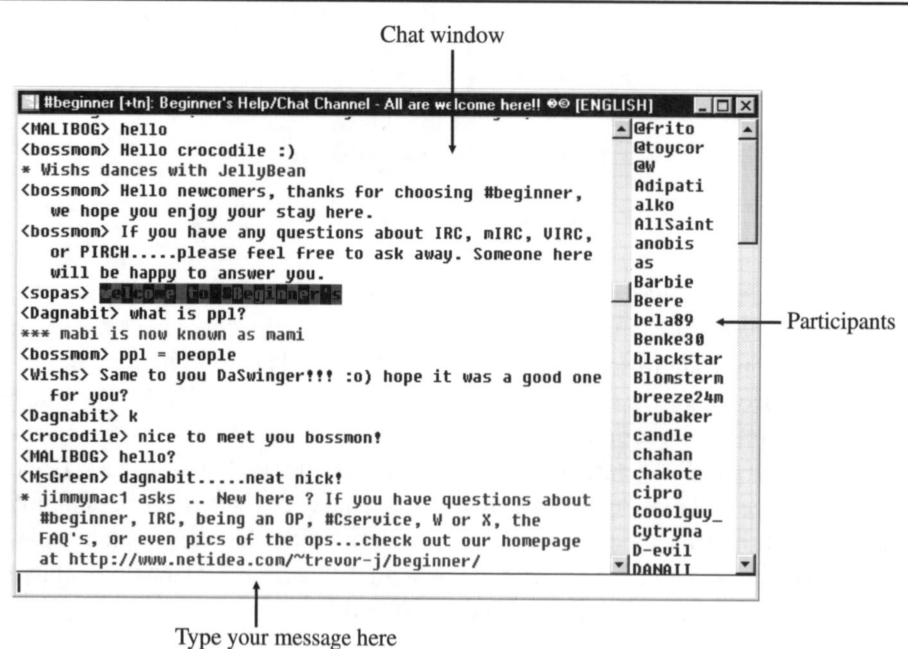

FIGURE 10-4 Anatomy of a virtual IRC community, the popular **#beginner** channel

Tip *If it ever appears that something you did or information you requested got no results, check the Status window. Or, if you suspect that nothing's happening, it could be that you've been disconnected from the server for some reason. The Status window will read "Disconnected" if this is the case. Click the first icon on the toolbar (the lightning bolt) to log on again.*

Taking Part

As on AOL, in an IRC channel you can either communicate with a group or with an individual. To chat with a group, type a message in the text box at the bottom of a channel window and press ENTER. Your message appears in colored text, *not* preceded by your nickname.

Tip *Your messages don't have to be in color and can be preceded by your nickname. mIRC offers dozens of ways to customize the program. To see the options available to you, choose File | Options, or click the toolbar button. One very useful preference lets you remove all the messages about people coming and going: in the Show section of the IRC Switches tab, remove checks from the boxes indicating information you don't want displayed in your chat window.*

If you want, you can make your text appear in different fonts, styles, and colors, for people whose IRC software supports such effects. These effects are available using Tools | Fonts and Tools | Colors.

ONE-TO-ONE CONVERSATIONS VIA IRC To communicate with an individual in a chat room, just double-click the appropriate name in the list of participants to start an Instant Message-type exchange. This is the same thing as selecting a nickname from the participants list (on the right-hand side of the window), right-clicking, and selecting Query. When someone queries you, a chat window pops up, just like an Instant Message.

Tip *You can keep a list of people (a sort of IRC Buddy List) so you can be automatically notified when any of them logs onto the network. Select File | Options and use the Notify List tab to enter the nicknames whose comings and goings you want to know about.*

Something called DCC (Direct Client to Client) communication is also available on mIRC. With DCC, you're communicating directly with the other person and not using the IRC server. Just right-click a participant's name and select DCC | Chat. Using DCC you can also exchange files with someone on IRC (DCC | Send). In both chatting and file-exchanging, the other person must first agree to take part.

Tip *Don't accept DCC messages from people you don't know. In sending such messages, use the /whois command to find out if someone is on IRC (on your IRC network, at least) and what that person's e-mail address is. In the Status window's text box (at the bottom of the window), type **/whois nickname** and press ENTER. The response will appear in the Status window.*

Using Simple Commands

Commands give you the flexibility to customize mIRC and to create the equivalent of macros (chains of commands you'd like to carry out routinely). You enter a command by typing it into the chat window's text box preceded by a slash (/), then pressing ENTER. For example, if you want to type a message saying you're stepping away for a moment, the command is **/away back in a sec** (actually, */away* is the command and *back in a sec* is what others see in the chat window).

The most popular commands are also available from the Commands menu. Table 10-2 explains what each command does.

Running a Channel

Like an AOL chat room, an IRC channel exists as long as someone is in it; the last person who leaves a channel also kills the channel automatically. If you try to join a channel that doesn't exist, you don't get an error message; you get a new channel! You've also appointed yourself channel *operator* of this new channel.

Every channel has at least one operator. Relations between a channel's operator and everyone else can make an IRC channel a different environment from an AOL chat room. For one thing, an operator has considerable power in this small world and can name other operators, kick people out of a channel for any reason, ban certain people or certain domains from admittance, and define a channel's topic—the bit of optional text that accompanies a channel's description when you search for channels. Operators can have the power to limit the number of people in a channel, declare the channel invitation-only, and define the channel as either private (it won't appear in the list of all channels on the network) or secret (a person in the channel won't be revealed by a whois query).

Command	To Do the Following
Join channel	Join a channel. In the window that comes up, type ***#channel name***.
Part channel	Leave a channel. In the window that comes up, type ***#channel name***. See also the Set Away command.
Query user *	Send a message to someone on the channel using a special query window. In the window that comes up, type in that user's nickname, leave a space, and type a private message. Click OK.
Send notice	Send a message to a nickname, but have the message appear in the chat window and not in a special interactive window.
Whois user *	Find out the e-mail address and other information (such as channels currently joined) for a nickname. Results appear in Status window.
Send CTCP *	Get information about a nickname, such as how long messages take to reach that person (Ping) and the IRC software they are using (Version). Results appear in the Status window.
Set Away	To present a message to the group saying that you'll be temporarily away and can't respond to queries and messages, etc. From the pop-up menu, select On, and type a message. Select Off when you come back.
Invite user	Invite another user (nickname) to a channel. In the window, provide both the user's name and the ***#channel name***.
Ban user	For channel operators only (see "Running a Channel").
Kick user	For channel operators only (see "Running a Channel").
Ignore user	For channel operators only (see "Running a Channel").
Change nickname	Change your nickname on the fly, for any reason (if you're being bothered by someone or someone else has the same nickname, for example).
Quit IRC	Same as File | Exit.

* These commands are also available by right-clicking a name in the list of participants on the right-hand side of any channel window.

TABLE 10-2 mIRC's command menu commands and what they mean

Tip *The best way to learn about running a channel is to create a channel (simply create one that doesn't exist yet) and double-click on its window. In the window that comes up you can define the channel's attributes: its size, whether it's private, how big it can get, and so on. For a normal channel you join, double-clicking on the channel window brings up the same window, with the settings used by the operators listed at the top of the participants window. You can't alter these settings unless you're an operator.*

Leaving a Channel and Quitting IRC

The *easiest* way to leave a channel is to close its window: in Windows 95, just click the X in the far upper-right corner. The *preferred* way to leave is to inform everyone else, as follows: from the Commands window, select Part channel, type in the channel name preceded by #, and click OK.

Leaving mIRC is like quitting any program: File | Exit does the trick.

Finding Out More about mIRC and IRC

Here are some resources for getting more information about IRC:

- The easiest way to get your questions answered is on IRC itself. Click the List Channels button on the toolbar and search for channels with *mirc* in the name. The **#mirc** channel is excellent, as is the more generic and much larger **#beginner** channel.
- From the mIRC Help menu, take advantage of the excellent and complete help.
- Informative Web sites are devoted to mIRC, such as the mIRC creator's site, **http://www.mirc.co.uk/mirc.html**, with links to many related sites.
- A general IRC FAQ is available at **http://www.mirc.co.uk/ircintro.html**.
- Check out the **alt.irc.mirc** newsgroup, as well as the family of newsgroups in the **alt.irc.*** hierarchy, such as **alt.irc.games** and **alt.irc.questions**. (At *keyword: Newsgroups*, click Search All Newsgroups and do a search for **irc**.)

TELNET

What is Telnet? When you access a Telnet site on an Internet computer, your PC becomes the terminal—a mere keyboard and display—for that computer. You type in commands and respond to prompts at your terminal, while all the computer processing takes place at the distant computer where the computing work actually happens. The results are displayed on your monitor as old fashioned and not very attractive courier text.

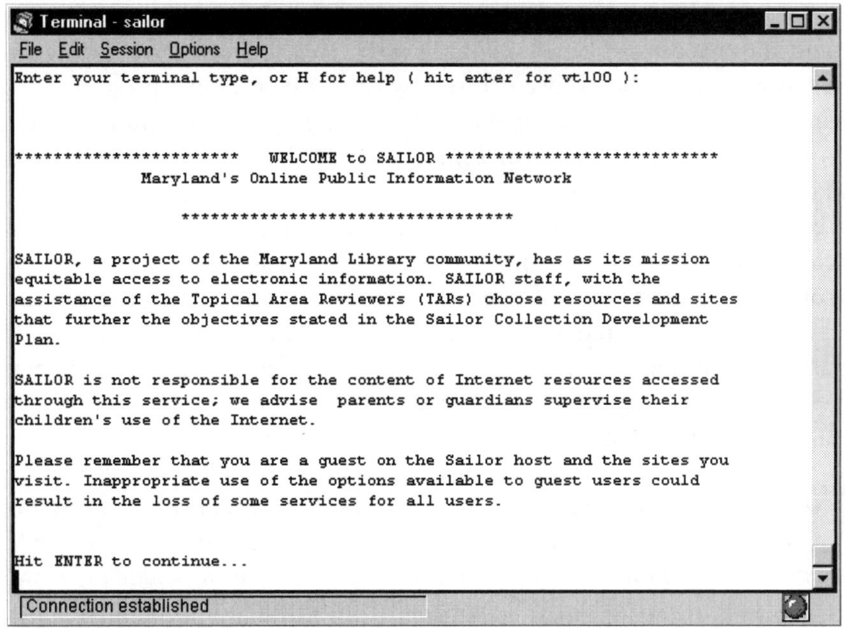

It may not be very sexy, but Telnet is useful and versatile precisely because of its lowest-common-denominator display. For parts of the world with low bandwidth connections to the Internet, Telnet is of even greater value. And if you do any kind of research, Telnet is an indispensable tool because it is widely used in libraries and universities.

AOL provides you with a choice of ways to use Telnet. If you're using AOL 4.0 and are browsing a Web page that links to a Telnet site, you can click the link and go automatically to the Telnet site. A very simple terminal program opens in a separate window, where you can enter commands and otherwise interact with the remote computer.

Tip *Because AOL's browser provides this Telnet support, if you know a Telnet address, you can enter it directly into the Address box in the toolbar, tacking on* **telnet://** *before the actual address (for example,* **telnet://moo.du.org:8888**).

If you want to access a Telnet site that's *not* linked to from a Web site, or if you want more features than those offered by the built-in Telnet program, you can run any one of the many Telnet Winsock programs, such as Ewan. This chapter deals with Ewan 1.5, a powerful Telnet program that is easy to use and readily available at *keyword: Filesearch.*

Telnet gives access to two essential Internet resources. First, Telnet lets you search hundreds of library card catalogs, which can save time and money in any kind of research. Every kind of Internet-accessible library catalog can be searched: law, medical, public, community, university, and K-12 (see "Gateway to a Thousand Libraries"). Unfortunately, many of these sites are being phased out and converted to Web-based searching. Others are simply very busy, so you'll need some patience to make the most of Telnet.

Tip *If you're a college student or the spouse or parent of one, chances are good that you will have a free or low-cost e-mail account using a text-only shell account. With Telnet you can access the e-mail account from anywhere in the world.*

Second, Telnet also enables people to create collaborative games and simulated environments. Hundreds of such environments have grown up since the 1980s, thanks to Telnet, and they are collectively known as MUDs—multi-user dimensions (or dungeons). See "Garden of MUD." While libraries are getting harder to access by Telnet, MUDs are alive and well.

Downloading and Installing Ewan

If you'll be visiting libraries, I recommend Ewan, a Windows program, with many useful features. Ewan lets you keep a directory of sites you like—your own Telnet hotlist (Telnet places are not Favorite-Place-able on AOL because, like IRC channels, they take place inside of a non-AOL program). You can adjust the background color, screen font, and printer font, and there's full online help. This Swedish program costs nothing and can be freely used and distributed for noncommercial purposes. To get this useful software:

1. Go to *keyword: Filesearch*. Click the Shareware button. In the Software Search window, type **Ewan** into the Search box at the bottom and click Search. In the File Search Results box, select the file whose subject is Ewan 1.5 (or later version) and click Download Now. Tell AOL where you want to put the file, and click OK.
2. From the My Files menu, select Download Manager; click Show Downloaded Files; select ewan105.zip (or whatever you downloaded) and click Decompress. A new directory, ewan, will be created in the directory where you downloaded the file.
3. Install the program by running the install program (it's in the Ewan directory) using the File Manager's File | Run command (Windows 3.1) or Start menu | Run (Windows 95). The installation program creates a new directory, c:\Ewan, containing the necessary files.
4. To run Ewan, make sure you're signed onto AOL, then double-click the new icon you just created. To make Ewan your browser's default, see the instructions for setting up a program to launch automatically in "Working with Sound Files" in Chapter 8; you'll want *URL: Telnet Protocol* (registered file type) to open with Ewan.

10

Gateway to a Thousand Libraries

Have you noticed that card catalogs have disappeared from your public library? Several years ago, those inefficient and difficult-to-maintain space-wasters gave way to the electronic catalog, which can be easily searched by anyone, anywhere, using simple computer terminals. Electronic searches allow you to search for books by title, author, year of publication, and other standard criteria.

Telnet makes it possible to do such searches from a distance and to do several such searches at a sitting. (The books themselves are not available by Telnet. For that, you'll need to get in the car or on the phone.) Hytelnet (**http://moondog.usask.ca/hytelnet/**) is the service to use to find out which libraries have which books—whether, for example, the Hong Kong Institute of Education and the Chinese University of Hong Kong libraries have books on the Tiananmen massacre (they do).

When you use Telnet, as when you use FTP, you establish a dedicated connection with a particular computer (server). Telnet servers, unlike Web servers, can only support a fixed number of such connections. If you ever get the Ewan message "couldn't assign an address," it is probably due to fact that the site is temporarily down or the maximum number of people are already signed on. Try again later, or try a different library in the same subject or same locality.

Caution *Hytelnet's creator, Peter Scott, has announced that he will no longer support Hytelnet, but will replace it with something "better." In fact, when you use Hytelnet, you may find that many library Telnet sites are not available for one reason or another.*

Libraries are increasingly available directly on the Web, both because of the Web's popularity and because of the improvements in the technologies that enable a Web page to act as interface to large databases, so users can fill in simple forms and get clickable results. (That's also what makes a search engine like AOL NetFind possible, after all.) Peter Scott, who did so much to make Telnet library sites accessible on the Internet, now makes available many Web-based library sites at webCAT (**http://library.usask.ca/hywebcat/**). Berkeley's LibWeb (**http://sunsite.berkeley.edu/Libweb/**) is another directory of library Web sites, currently linking to approximately 2,000 library sites. Like webCAT, LibWeb includes some informational sites that don't yet include searchable catalogs.

More over, many libraries' Web sites still take you to Telnet links, from which you can search the catalog, so for now, it's good to be comfortable with both Telnet and the Web. In the future, the strong trend is toward Web-based library searching.

Telnet 101

Logging onto a distant computer often requires that you know a password and log-in name. Hytelnet usefully provides you such information for libraries, but other kinds of Telnet sites may require that you first contact an administrator. Other sites provide sign-on information for guests when you first log on.

A key setting you may need to adjust in your software—or set at the site—is your terminal emulation type, which makes your keyboard behave in a way that makes sense to the distant computer. The most common terminal emulation type for PC-compatible keyboards is VT-100, though you will also see VT-102.

Once you're signed on, you'll find that navigation differs from site to site. As a rule of thumb, you use the arrow keys on your keyboard to get around; the mouse is useless at a Telnet site. When in doubt, try to get help at the distant computer by typing **H**, **?**, or **help**. To end a Telnet session, you can simply close the Telnet window or (more gracefully) end the session from Ewan's Session menu (choose Disconnect) or with a similar command using another Telnet program. Pressing CTRL-] or typing **logoff** will often get you out as well—it depends on the specific computer you've accessed remotely. To leave Ewan, use ALT-F4 or File | Exit or just close its window.

Garden of MUD

Community has come a long way on the Internet. Graphical communities based on Java or other fancy technology are still too slow and experimental to support virtual communities. Dig a little, and you come to IRC, a real community builder, with its graphically simple but fully mature environment for chatting with people around the world. Dig a litter deeper and you'll find (appropriately, with all that digging) MUDs, which have primitive graphics and consist of nothing but text but which offer what some people consider the most creative environment for interacting with others on the Internet. MUDs require an active imagination and good typing skills. Subsequent innovations have not replaced MUDs but have emulated and supplemented them.

Tip *If you're serious about MUDding, use a Winsock program like zMUD. It offers a much easier-to-use interface than "vanilla" Telnet, it makes it very easy to join any MUD, and it gives you a level of control over your display that programs like Ewan don't provide. zMUD and other such MUD clients are available at* keyword: Filesearch. *zMUD is a Telnet client customized for use with MUDs. If you use Windows 3.1, use the 16-bit version; for Windows 95, use the 32-bit version. zMUD is shareware, so remember to register.*

Depending on whom you ask, MUD stands for *multi-user dungeon* (after the Dungeons and Dragons games that were popular in the seventies) or *multi-user dimension*. Unlike an IRC channel, a MUD is a structured environment in which people assume and develop online identities other than their real identities. In *Life on the Screen*, MIT professor Sherry Turkle argues that MUDs are a profound tool for exploring the parts of one's self that aren't fully expressed in day-to-day life. Some people find this liberating and self-expanding, others find it an escape. At any

rate, there are enough MUDs—hundreds of them—for just about anyone to find a comfortable MUD in which to try on a new persona or just to chat. Variants of MUDs called MOOs (MUDS that are Object-Oriented) have been used by instructional designers to create virtual classrooms.

Tip *At the excellent MudConnector Web site (***http://www.mudconnect.com***), you will find a huge amount of information about MUDs, as well as direct links to just about all of them. Its list of MUDs includes every variety, from aggressive galaxies to peaceable kingdoms, from Age of Dragons to New Age. Particularly useful are the plain-English MUD categories, which allow you to link to MUDs that are Educational, Safe for Children, Research Oriented, or Newbie Friendly, for example. Or, choose a theme such as Cyberpunk, Medieval Fantasy, Science Fiction, Star Wars, or Tolkien.*

MUDs tend to fall into two big classes. Some MUDs (with names like AberMUD and LPMUD) are devoted to adventure. You assume an often elaborate identity, defined by a set of traits you can choose. You name your character and join a specific clan or guild. You're now ready to interact with other personas, developing the characters and story in the process, in pursuit of giants, the Grail, evil, whatever. With practice comes recognition, advanced levels of play, and prestige. Characters engage in activities such as whispering, walking, fighting, and flying, and action unfolds in elaborate imaginary places, with rooms and neighborhoods. Bored with what's going on in one room? Try another.

The social MUDs—the "talkers," with names like Mush, Muck, and TinyMUD—have more in common with an AOL chat room than with Dungeons and Dragons. They're sheerly for socializing, although with their role-playing and invented spaces they have more structure than a chat room.

Learning about MUDs

Each MUD has its own culture. Where do you start? Harley Hahn's chapter on MUDs in the *Internet Complete Reference, Second Edition* (Osborne/McGraw-Hill, 1996) gives an excellent overview. The best place to start exploring actual MUDs is the Web's MudConnector (**http://www.mudconnect.com**). The MUDConnector has excellent information for beginners, including how to get started, how to pick a client, and how to figure out the various flavors of MUD. It's the place to find descriptions of more than 1,000 MUDs (almost double the number available when the first edition of this book was published). MudConnector's links take you directly to any MUD you want to explore, as well as to the many Web sites created as communal hearths for particular MUD communities. Newsgroups devoted to MUDs abound, including the **alt.mud.*** and **rec.games.mud.*** families (where the * stands for *announce*, *diku*, *tiny*, and many other individual newsgroups).

The best way to learn about MUDs—like anything on the Net—is to jump right in. You can't break anything, and you will never be alone. Welcome to the Internet community!

Chapter 11

Taking in the Sites: A Guided Tour of the World Wide Web

If you're ready to explore the Internet, you can use the Internet sites on the following pages as starting places. They range from the indispensable to the bizarre. In short, they are typical of what you will find on the Internet.

These sites are arranged by channel and come from many sources. Some come from the new Web Channels at AOL.com (click Go to the Web at the Welcome screen). Others come directly from AOL's online channels, where they're woven into channel content. Still others I just liked. People's Connection and AOL Today aren't included here because they're not "content" channels. The Internet is included here because there is no better place to find out about the Internet than on the Internet itself.

New sites are cropping up daily, some, no doubt, as good as what you'll find here. Begin with sites of personal or professional interest, and see where they lead you. If you're looking for something that's not here, Chapter 9 provides plenty of guidance in finding exactly what you're seeking.

When you use the Address box to access a Web site, you can leave off http://. *For example, just put* **www.cmp.com** *to go to http://www.cmp.com.*

This guide brings you *Web* sites because they're fun and easy to use. But remember from Chapter 1 that the Web is not the Net. In your exploration, don't forget the other core Internet services: FTP, newsgroups, and especially mailing lists.

Tip

Osborne/McGraw-Hill publishes several books for your reading and Net-browsing pleasure: Harley Hahn's Internet & Web Yellow Pages *(1997 Edition) and Jean Polly's* Internet Kids & Family Yellow Pages *(Second Edition, 1997). Osborne's new* America Online Yellow Pages *(First Edition, 1998) is a guide to resources you'll find only on AOL. All of these books are available through the AOL store.*

How Channels Use Internet Resources

Some of the Web sites in this chapter are siblings to AOL forums. Motley Fool, for example, has both a big Web site and a spectacularly popular AOL forum in the **Personal Finance** channel. And AOL's Entertainment Asylum (*keyword: Asylum*) is joined at the hip with the Asylum Web site (**http://www.asylum.com**).

What's the difference between a Web site and an AOL forum? Usually there's quite a bit of overlap in actual content, but the presentation differs somewhat. The Web sites tend be weighed down with multimedia effects, but as a rule the AOL forums will download *much* faster and offer more and simpler ways to interact with other people. AOL forums have the additional advantage of linking you directly to the *most useful* parts of the Web sites, as you'll discover in the Personal Finance forums run by the major financial services and mutual fund companies.

Feedback

If you ever encounter problems with a site—because its address changes or the site disappears or anything else—please send a message to me at screen name **dpeal**. Please use the same address to recommend sites to include in the next edition of this book. Thank you!

COMPUTING

CMPnet

http://www.cmp.com/

Like ZDnet (**http://www.zdnet.com**), CMPnet is a Web empire that reflects the content and structure of a magazine empire. Like ZDnet, it goes well beyond the limits of print publications. It's a vast site with many large parts, all of which can be reached from the CMPnet main page. One of the features available here is NetGuide, which grew out of the now-extinct *NetGuide* magazine, a directory of reviewed Web sites, written with personality (like the AOL area at *keyword: NetGuide*); TechWeb offers authoritative news from the computer and online industry; and the Tech Encyclopedia cuts through difficult topics with clarity and precision. Plus, link to CMP publications-on-the-Web such as *Windows Magazine* and *Information Week.*

Computer Virus Help Desk

http://www.indyweb.net/~cvhd

The Computer Virus Research Center in Indianapolis, Indiana has one of the most comprehensive Web sites dedicated to keeping the public informed about computer viruses. In their own words, they try to provide "the very latest in information and utilities in the detection, prevention, and eradication of computer viruses." It also offers many links to anti-virus software, cryptographic software, and law enforcement Web sites. Visit this site early in your Internet explorations, and surf safely.

Design & Publishing Center

http://www.graphic-design.com/

The Design & Publishing Center is a gold mine of information and resources for those involved in typography, graphics, advertising, and any of the visual communications fields. There are links to Photoshop Tips and Tricks, the most recent issue of *DT&G* magazine, marketing resources, Web chat on graphic design, news on the latest graphics-related software, and lots more. You can even submit samples of your own work for display in their online gallery.

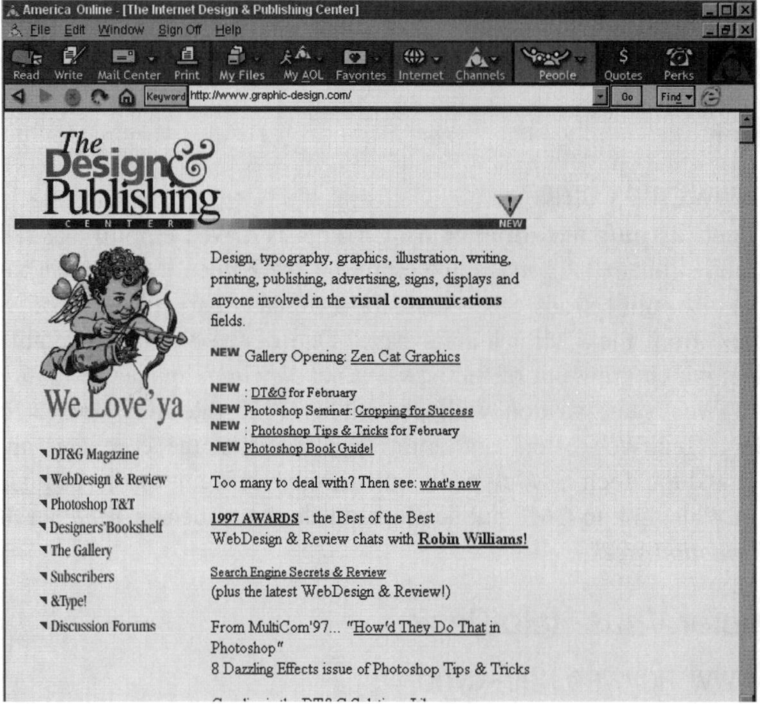

Modems, Modems, Modems

http://www.rosenet.net/~costmo

Just about everyone on AOL relies on a modem, but most AOL members rightly find the subject of modems boring, and very few know how to buy one. However, a good, fast modem can make all the difference in your online experience. Start with the FAQs section to teach yourself something about those noisy boxes that connect you to AOL and the Internet. Here you can also find links to over 50 modem manufacturers, links to sites about modems, and "initialization strings" for all occasions. If you're in the market for a modem, start here to make an informed choice, then make your purchase at the AOL Store (*keyword: AOLStore*, then click Modems).

Online Today

http://www.online-today.com/

Take one radio personality, add a little—no, a *lot* of—experience in both Mac and PC computing, plus a dash of Comedy Central, and you have "Online Today with David Lawrence." This syndicated radio talk show provides reviews of hardware and software, takes calls from novices and power-users on a variety of problems and questions, and presents entertaining interviews with newsmakers and personalities. You can also subscribe to the Personal Netcast mailing list, which delivers a 3–4 minute RealAudio slice o' Online Today segment every morning to your e-mailbox. (You'll need to download a copy of RealAudio 5.0 to listen to it: go to **http://www.real.com** for the latest version.)

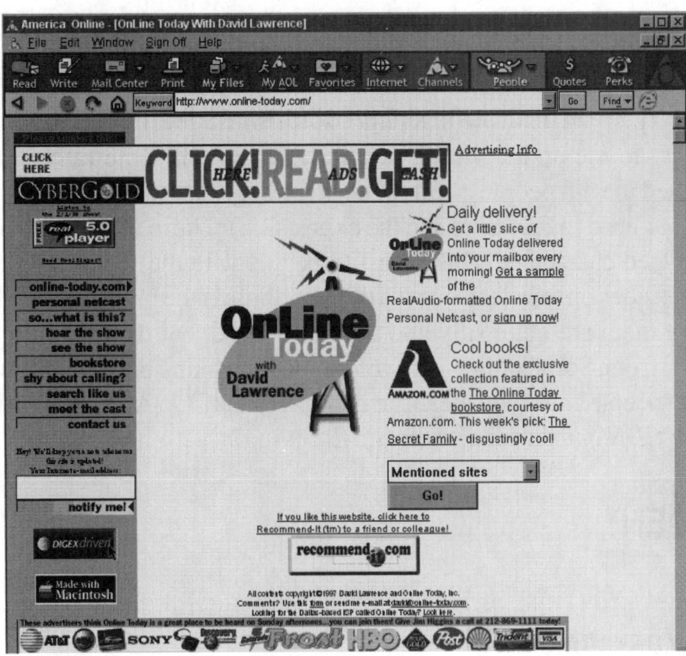

PC Magazine Online

http://www.pcmag.com/

The big Ziff-Davis biweekly comes to the Web, without quite so many ads. The best of the authoritative magazine is here, including the mammoth product reviews, the trenchant editorials by Michael Miller and John Dvorak, and the industry news briefs. Plus, you can help yourself to bushels of freeware and shareware, even if you don't subscribe. PCMag.com also brings you breaking news and feature stories, plus links to the universe of ZD magazines on the Web. Whatever you're in the market for, start your product research here, then go to *keyword: AOLstore* and click on either Hardware or Software.

PRINT Magazine

http://www.printmag.com/

PRINTmag.com is a site for the surfer tired of squinting at ugly, noisy Web sites with no regard for design integrity, aesthetics, or structure. Beautiful images abound, with indexes searchable by designer, design firm, client, region, and other categories. Study this site carefully if you hope to create your own site, or if you just want to understand the elements of a great Web site.

Smilies, Smilies, Smilies

http://galway.informatik.uni-kl.de/rec/smilies.html

If you're new to the online world, you may have seen some rather odd-looking symbols tossed in with people's comments in newsgroups or Instant Messages, such as :^} (tilt your head to the left to see the expression). These *smilies* convey emotion using only typed characters. This Web site begins with the Webster's definition of *smile* (n), then goes on to list the dozens of variations on the industry-standard smiley :-) . Many of them are quite silly and are rarely used, but this site is fun to browse and to borrow from. So, next time you write something biting but don't mean any harm, just grin to let people know you meant no harm ;-) (wink). On AOL, make sure to check out *keyword: CDNSmileys* for another fun list.

ENTERTAINMENT

Asylum

http://www.asylum.com

What *Seinfeld* did for TV, this site does for the Web: it's the Web site about nothing! Actually, Asylum is the Web site about the entire world of entertainment, from action movies to *Melrose Place*. It's *not* for couch potatoes, though. Web-based message boards and chat rooms bring the experience of Tinsel Town home, literally. In Studio-I you can even mingle with the stars. This multimedia extravaganza takes full advantage of plug-ins such as Shockwave Flash and I-Chat.

Cafe Utne

http://www.utne.com/cafe

The *Utne Reader* magazine is a progressive version of *Reader's Digest*. Café Utne has taken the concerns and interests of *Utne* readers and created a Web site with over 40 conferences with hundreds of topics. As they say of their site, it is "a fun, relaxing...community where ideas and issues are discussed in a thoughtful and respectful manner." Although it is free, you must register to use this service, and, because of Utne's concern about the male/female ratio of contributors, the gender balance in the membership is monitored. Currently, equal numbers of men and women are registering, so there is no waiting period.

Celebrities On-Line

http://www.mgal.com/links/celeb.html

Subtitled "Cool Links to Celebrity Sites," Celebrities On-Line delivers the goods, with more than 225 links to celebrities from the worlds of movies, TV, and political activism. There are also links to other celebrity lists, *People* magazine's Web site, and the Official Interactive Guide to the Academy Awards.

Country Music Row on the Web

http://www.evansville.net/~jazzyjen/cmr/cmrow.html

Jazzy Jenny has created a clever compendium of links to a wide variety of country-related sites. She has decorated it with engaging animations that add to the country flavor of the site, which is well researched and maintained. Spend time here with the bands and artists you like best. Link to fan clubs, find song lyrics, and hang out in discussion groups. Just take your hat and boots off, and make yourself comfortable!

Jokes

http://www.jokes.com

Collecting jokes is a venerable Internet pastime, so with a little work you can uncover countless joke sites on the Web. This one features funky typefaces and silly monkey

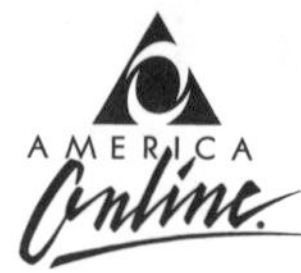

graphics (banana peels make up the background image). You can check out the Joke du Jour, search the database for old faves, play with digital fingerpaints in the Goo Gallery, and ask advice of Dr. Monkeylove (although making major life decisions based on his suggestions is not necessarily wise). Submit your favorite lightbulb or knock-knock joke, and allow your humor to live on for eternity.

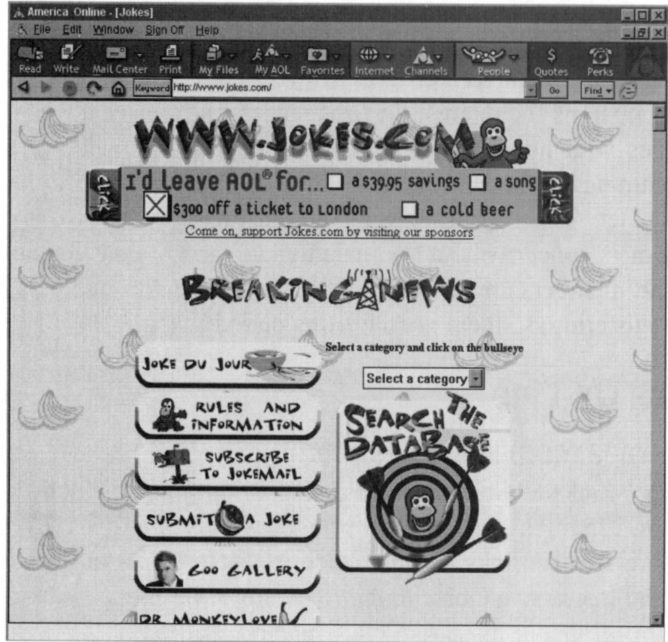

Internet Movie Database Search: Over 116,000 Movies

http://us.imdb.com/search.html

The Internet makes available vast searchable databases, enabling you to quickly locate just about any atom of information. Take this hugely popular destination: it's got information about just about every movie you can imagine, with details about cast members, crew, directors, even Best Boys (yes, credit-watchers, you can finally learn what a Best Boy is). Search out just about any film, and you'll get the plot summary, director, cast, trivia questions, and a chance to rate the movie. Many of the cast and crew are cross-indexed, so you can read biographies and follow other links. Bring along some Jujubes, since popcorn can mess up your keyboard something fierce.

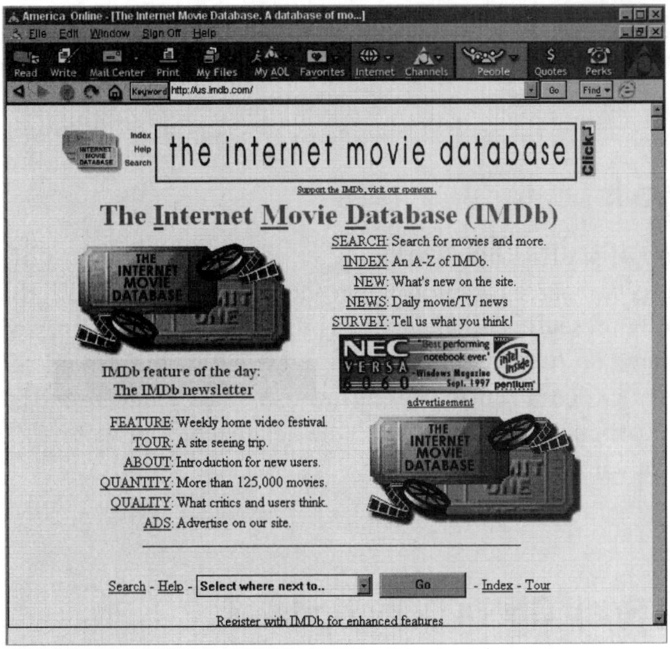

Matrix Gallery Music Links

http://www.mgal.com/links/music.html

If you thought Celebrities On-Line was fun, wait until you get to the Matrix Gallery's Music Links page. Like Celebrities On-Line, it has a vast number of links to general interest music sites as well as to specific sites like Discoweb, Broadway, and the Rock & Roll Hall of Fame and Museum. And *then* you get into the approximately 400 artist/band links from Bing Crosby to Megadeth to Zappa. You will surely find someone here to rock your world!

Playbill On-Line

http://www1.playbill.com/playbill/

Do you yearn for the stage? The smell of the greasepaint, the roar of the crowd? Or, if you're not the performing type, the roar of the greasepaint, the smell of the crowd? If theater is your first choice for an evening's (or afternoon's) entertainment, then Playbill On-line should be your first choice for Web exploration. With show listings for on- and off-Broadway, regional productions, national touring companies, London performances, even summer stock, you could schedule yourself for a show every week into the next millennium. Playbill On-Line also has industry information

regarding casting, college productions, reference areas with lists of awards, theater art, and audio clips from your favorite shows.

Rocktropolis

http://www1.rocktropolis.com/

Rocktropolis is *the* source for information about your favorite rock groups, past and present (mostly present). The site contains daily news and gossip, reviews of new albums, features on rock culture, and an overview of the evolution of music. If reading about rock doesn't cut it, you can link to Music Boulevard and buy the hottest CDs. If it's experience you want, search the detailed database of rock concerts and other events into the foreseeable future.

TV Guide Soap Opera Daily Updates

http://www.tvguide.com/soaps/episodes/index.htm

Find out what all your favorite villains and angels are up to this week at the TV Guide Soap update page. If you miss an episode, their daily recaps will bring you up to speed. They're updated every afternoon after all the soaps have aired and include synopses of the last five installments, so you don't ever have to worry about missing anything really important.

Ultimate TV—Your Source for Everything Television

http://www.ultimatetv.com/

The name says it all: Ultimate TV gives you listings by time zone, interactive polls on your favorite shows and characters, features on the newest additions to and departures from the Thursday night lineup, ratings reports on all the networks, even quick thumbs-up/thumbs-down polls on shows that aired the night before. It doesn't get any fresher than this, so grab the Doritos and come channel-surf like you've never surfed before!

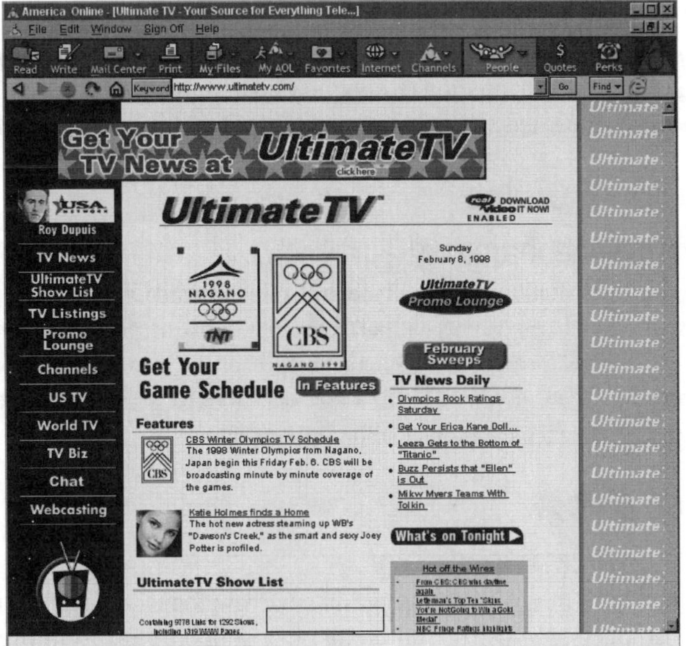

VIBE Magazine, Online ,TV

http://www.vibe.com/

VIBE online is described as "the living breathing companion" to the late night TV show *Vibe*, hosted by comic Sinbad. This site takes the show much further than the TV format can allow, telling you all you'd ever want to know about fashion, urban culture, and the hottest videos and audio recordings. Read backstage interviews with guests from the show and get the chance to chat with fans and stars alike.

FAMILIES

Adopting.com—Internet Adoption Resources

http://www.adopting.com/

Adopting.com is one of the largest adoption resources on the Internet, providing prospective adoptive parents with all they need to know about adoption, including:

photolistings; links to hundreds of agencies, facilitators, support groups, and adoptees' rights organizations; sample letters to send birthparents; newsgroups; and international adoption information (by country). There is also a large area with links to organizations concerned with special-needs children waiting to be adopted.

College Board Online

http://www.collegeboard.org/

SAT...PSAT...FAS...BMOC...what's it all mean? College Board Online can help graduating high school students and their parents with all their admissions questions. This comprehensive site provides schedules for upcoming standardized exams, financial aid information and advice, college search databases, and even sample questions for practice purposes. This Web site is a fine place to begin the journey into higher education.

The Divorce Page

http://www.divorcesupport.com/

Although the title of this Web site suggests a narrow focus, the site actually brings many subjects together under the umbrella of "a support page for those in divorce or in the loss of a relationship." This thoughtfully constructed site covers everything: parenting, legal matters, resources for both men and women, support groups (including the Straight Spouse Support Network), spirituality, child support and custody, and steps toward recovery. The creator of the Divorce Page invites visitors to share their experiences and describe the pain and assures them that they can look forward to happier times.

Eldercare Web—WWW Center for Eldercare Information

http://www.elderweb.com/

As the population of our country ages, elder care becomes a bigger issue for all members of our society, especially in these days when members of extended families may live hundreds or thousands of miles apart. The Eldercare Web is the creation of Karen Stevenson Brown, a CPA with over 11 years as elder-care provider, advisor, consumer, and advocate. She has brought together an impressive array of resources on the financial, legal, social, and health issues of long-term care for elderly loved ones. As a community focal point, this site itself provides a partial solution, and both providers and consumers of these services will find valuable advice.

Family.com

http://www.family.com/

Family.com is a wonderful online resource for families everywhere, with suggestions for family activities, recipes, Internet resources, crafts, as well as advice on more pressing matters such as education, stress, learning disabilities, and more. Need advice on how to calm a crying baby? Go to the Parent Adviser's column for a new approach. Learn how to entertain your infant in a way that will help her learn at the same time. Talk to other parents about your difficulties with step-parenting. And all before sitting down to dinner together!

Genealogy—Ancestry Hometown

http://www.ancestry.com/

Who do you *really* take after? Ancestry Hometown is the first place you should visit when you decide to trace your family history. This Web site was created by Ancestry, Inc., an established publisher of print and electronic products for the study of genealogy, and it is one of the most thorough resources you can find on the subject. The site continually adds new sources from around the world. Its databases are searchable, for free when they are first added, and by subscription as the databases are archived.

Kids' Camps—Camp Directory

http://www.kidscamps.com/

Need to make plans for the kids' summer vacation? How about a family camp where you can experience the great outdoors together? Kids' Camps bills itself as the Internet's most comprehensive directory of camps and "summer experience," and it certainly covers the spectrum of opportunities. From residential and day camps to arts and sports camps to academic programs and family rental sites, Kids' Camps slices and dices its listings by region, gender, religion, and session length.

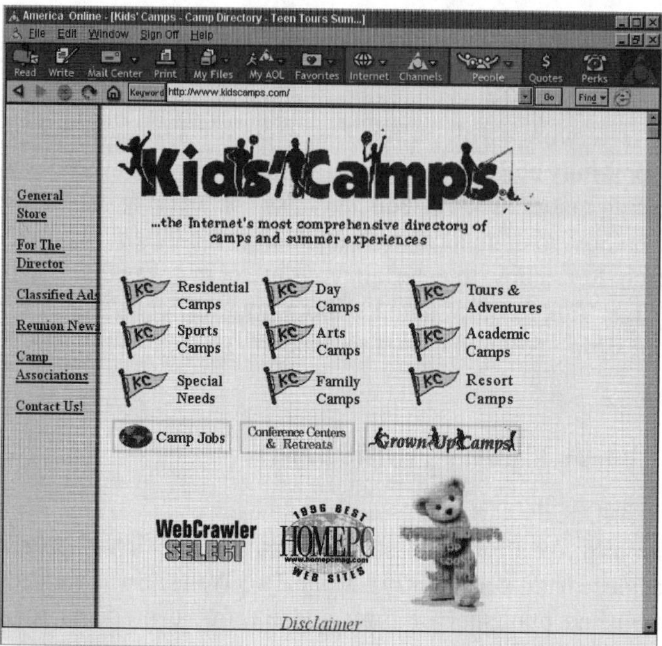

KidSource OnLine

http://www.kidsource.com/

Whether your child is eight days, eight years, or eighteen years old, KidSource OnLine has become known as an excellent source of information on education and healthcare for children and their families. Features about school readiness and infant dermatology are provided alongside lists of product recalls of toys, garments, and other items. The educational resources set the site apart. You can choose articles on specific topics such as food poisoning, spanking, and developmental milestones.

The Knot: Weddings For The Real World

http://www.theknot.com/

Unless you're marrying into royalty, chances are that if you're engaged, you need to plan your Big Day very carefully, searching out all the possible resources so you still have enough money to buy that first house someday. The Knot is just the Web site for the couple that works hard for what they want but just hasn't hit the executive office quite yet. Inexpensive but romantic honeymoon ideas, china sources, bridesmaid fashion and management...even 6,000 pictures of wedding gowns, all here to help you make it the best-planned day of your life!

Our Kids

http://rdz.stjohns.edu/library/support/our-kids/

The Net at its best, this site grew out of a mailing list (see Chapter 4 on mailing lists) for parents of kids with cerebral palsy, epilepsy, Down syndrome, autism, and a broad variety of undiagnosed disorders. The site forms the center of the mailing list community (currently 700 members in 35 countries) whose members share their kids' pictures and their own home pages at this Web site. A clickable map shows exactly where the mailing list's subscribers live. The directory of Internet resources is exceptional, linking to many comprehensive Internet resources dealing with disabilities, the law, and specific disorders.

Parent Soup: Baby Name Finder

http://bnf.parentsoup.com/babyname/

Soooo, just how many Emilys are there out there already? How about Michaels? It turns out the Popularity Finder at Parent Soup's Baby Name Finder shows these two names to be the current number one choices for girls and boys. Use Find-O-Matic to produce lists of names by gender, number of syllables, religion, and ethnicity. Or just look up what your great-aunt Bertha's name means (of Saxon-Germanic origin, it means "glorious, learning, beautiful").

SeniorNet

http://www.seniornet.com/

keyword: SeniorNet

Long a popular area and vibrant community on AOL, SeniorNet has taken root on the Web as well. While Third Age (described next) is for seniors who see 65 as a green light, SeniorNet is more for people who want to pursue reflective activities such as learning, reading, and computing. SeniorNet's interactive Round Tables cover a huge variety of topics, including ebonics, HTML, great books, memory, recent history, and making ends meet.

Third Age

http://www.thirdage.com

You'd never know this happening site had anything to do with "senior citizens"—it's too much fun! Sociable seniors can chat, get the current news, take part in discussion boards, make their own personal pages, schmooze with guests like Peter Max, and find

out everything they ever wanted to know about sex after 60. Their weekly newsletter keeps them up to date on the site's many events and latest additions. And, for graying technophobes, here's the place to get over any hang-ups about the Internet.

GAMES

The AMD Professional Gamers' League

http://www.pgl.net/

Remember playing computer and video games as a kid and hearing people say, "What a waste! Why don't you do something worthwhile with your spare time instead of throwing it away on something so pointless?" Well, it turns out you were in training for the AMD Professional Gamers' League: the first pro league specifically catering to the computer gaming crowd. Delivered to your PC by The Total Entertainment Network and sponsored by AMD and other top technology manufacturers, the PGL offers cash prizes.

Bridge World

http://www.bridgeworld.com/

Bridge World.com brings to the Internet all of the features and information of its print publication, *Bridge World Magazine*, along with many other resources for experienced bridge players and novices alike. There is a thorough introduction to bridge, with five detailed lessons on the mechanics of the game, an intermediate-level practice area, a place to buy books, software and supplies, details on tournaments and scoring, and more. This is an excellent place to experience the intellectual competition, challenge, variety, and teamwork inherent in the game.

CNN: Games—Daily Crossword

http://cnn.com/games/crossword/index.html

Has someone stolen your paper from the apartment lobby again? Or clipped a coupon from the back of your daily crossword before you got your Across and Down fix for the morning? Then come to the CNN Daily Crossword online, where you can select either a Master or Regular level puzzle and test your vocabulary skills. This online puzzle makes good use of Java. The page's direct access to the rest of CNN Interactive also makes for a great way to get your minimum daily information requirement.

Computer Gaming World

http://cgw.gamespot.com

If you enjoy playing games on your computer, you've come to the right place. This is an excellent resource for getting insider information on good gaming computers, peripherals, and networking connectivity. Here you can find news and features; reviews; sneak previews; strategies, tips and cheats; worthy opponents; and interactive discussions on all sorts of games from role-playing to simulations to blood-and-guts war games. Go to the Ultimate Game Machine for reviews of the best hardware to maximize your gaming experience.

Demoland: Favorite Game Demos

http://www.demoland.com/faves

Do you have limited funds but unlimited desire to play all the hottest games? Then test out all the latest releases at Demoland before you lay out that hard-earned cash. You can grab demos from over 400 titles in categories like Today's Pick, What's New, Favorites, and the Big List. Be sure to dig through the archive files, too, for other hidden gems.

GameSpot

http://www.gamespot.com/

GameSpot is home to a mountain of computer games of every type—action, adventure, role-playing, sports, simulations, and strategy. Each page provides in-depth reviews and test results according to game play, graphics, sound, learning curve, and difficulty. Shopping for a 14-year-old or a closet gamer? Check out the GameSpot Top 10—or jump directly to GameSpot's Product Index to find an extensive alphabetized list of computer games.

Internet Chess Club

http://www.chessclub.com/

If you want to match wits and endurance with some of the best chess players in the world without getting out of your red-and-black checkered PJ's, come visit the Internet Chess Club. Here you can play with over 10,000 regular members, watch broadcasts of tournaments and championship matches, improve your own game through study of online help files, and win prizes. Don't be just a pawn on the Internet—take charge at the ICC.

Macintosh Gaming League

http://www.magleague.com/

The Macintosh Gaming League (MaG) is one of the best places for Macintosh gamers who love fierce online competition. Warcraft II, Command and Conquer, Duke Nukem 3D, Net Mech, and Quake are some of the games for which the MaG has set up competitive arenas, with many more planned for the near future. Once you have joined the MaG, choose your games and begin climbing the ladder to glory!

Monopoly.com

http://www.monopoly.com/

C'mon, admit it: when you were a kid, you may have *slightly* miscounted the cash when you were the banker, or maybe you tried to distract your kid sister while you moved your game piece around the board. Which was *your* favorite game piece, the shoe or the race car? When you play Monopoly online, there's no cheating the bank or picking two cards at once from the Chance deck, but there *is* terrific animation, great graphics, and a soundtrack. Do not pass GO, do not collect $200...go directly to Monopoly.com! (Game software on CD-ROM required to participate in online play.)

The MUD Resource Collection

http://www.godlike.com/muds/

This site provides an impressive index of Multi-User Dungeon (MUD)-related informational and gaming links. Both MUD users (which the site describes as "normal" users) and researchers studying MUDs and related forms of communications will find many useful resources here. You'll find a huge list of FAQs and Usenet newsgroups. Students and teachers may want to explore Research-Oriented Links first. Other resources you can find here include MUDlists and MudWHO, Web interfaces to games, and FTP archives.

Riddler

http://www.riddler.com

Riddler has long been considered one of the best gaming sites on the Web. You will find endless stores of gaming opportunities here, from word games to trivia, all free and all presented with the promise of major prizes available to those who triumph.

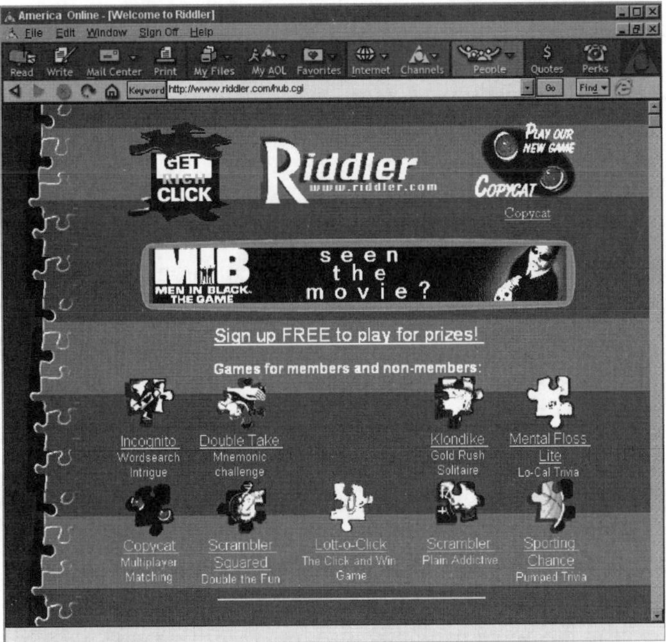

HEALTH

Addictions and Life Page

http://www.addictions.com/index.htm

A wonderful resource for people struggling with addictions of all sorts, such as alcohol, drugs, sex, gambling, and many others. Written with kindness, humor, and sensitivity, it provides a wealth of information, including suggestions for new paths to choose. Best of all, it provides the fellowship of kindred spirits.

American Cancer Society

http://www.cancer.org/

The site map alone will impress you with the sheer number of topics covered. Winner of many awards, this site offers information on almost every type of cancer, from the best known to the very rare. The segment on patient and family information contains, among many other things, fact sheets, suggestions on how to talk with a cancer patient, and guidelines for detection and especially prevention. Alternative therapies are covered honestly and openly. The list of ACS programs, events, offices, meetings, and associated links to Net cancer resources grows weekly.

Electra

http://www.electra.com/

"Real women...real life...Electra" is the first graphic you see as you load the Web site for Electra.com. This Web version of *keyword: Electra* reflects the many facets of women's lives today, covering careers, money, mind and body, style, time off, and relationships. There is a link to Moms.online (also available on AOL at *keyword: Moms Online*) and an area dedicated to honoring (and nominating your own) Electra women—powerful women who have overcome obstacles and made a success of their lives, regardless of the paths they chose. Electra recognizes that beauty comes in all shapes and sizes and that health and stamina are often the highest goals.

First Aid Online

http://www.prairienet.org/~autumn/firstaid/

"What seems to be the problem?" First Aid Online's friendly 1950s-style nurse asks you as you arrive at the home page. She then provides you with a list of aches, pains, and problems such as burns, poisoning, bites, sprains/fractures, choking, and more. When you click on a topic, you are brought to a page with clearly written instructions on how to handle a variety of situations, with helpful graphics to illustrate these techniques. There is also an extensive list of links to other online medical resources for more information. First Aid Online should be at the top of every household's bookmark list, right next to the ipecac syrup.

KidsHealth—Children's Health and Parenting Information

http://kidshealth.org/

What should you tell a child who is going to the hospital for surgery? Read an article written by parents for parents. What's it like to be a kid who has an illness? Find out when you check out My Journal, a collection of interactive stories written by kids who have different conditions or illnesses. The Nemour's Children's Clinic at the duPont Hospital for Children presents a wonderful site devoted to the health of children and teens, with games, articles, Shockwave animations, and kids' activities. One area even covers kids' health questions, such as "What makes you sneeze?"

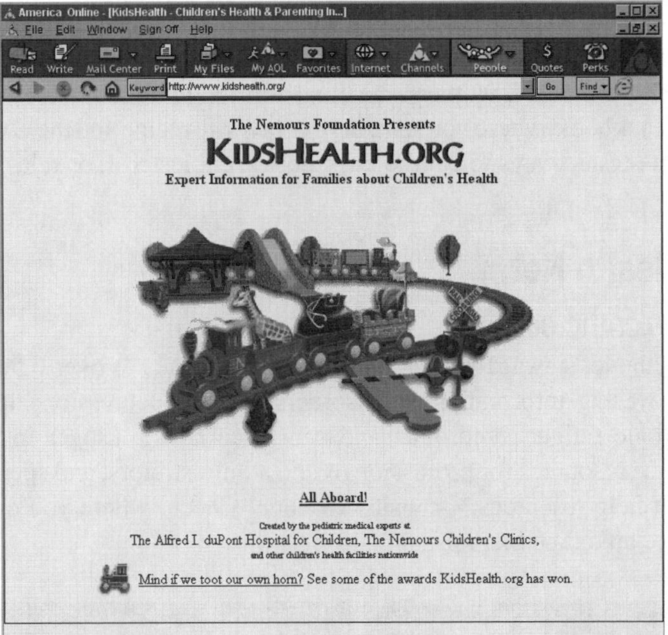

Male Health Center

http://www.malehealthcenter.com/

Bold graphics, intelligent writing, and well-organized link lists combine to make this an excellent resource for information on men's health. The home page states, "Men need an OB/GYN…too," reflecting the fact that men don't have a single specialist whom they can consult on male health matters. The real Male Health Center, located in Dallas, brings its resources to men everywhere. Its holistic approach to health care looks at the whole man, not just his symptoms, and stresses prevention as the key to a healthy life.

Mayo Clinic Health O@sis— daily news on diseases, treatments, drugs, diet

http://www.mayohealth.org/mayo/common/htm/index.htm

Thirsting for more information than your local newspaper's Health and Science section can provide? Then welcome to the O@sis, brought to you by the

world-famous Mayo Clinic. Its resources include a substantial library covering the gamut of health topics, a cancer center, areas focusing on diet and nutrition, pregnancy and pediatrics, women's health, and cardiac disease. You can even visit the Virtual Cookbook, where you send in your favorite recipe and the O@sis dietitian provides taste-tested ways to cut the fat, calories, cholesterol, or salt.

Mental Health Net

http://www.cmhc.com/

Mental Health Net's award-winning site now offers links to over 6,500 individual resources covering information on disorders such as depression, anxiety, panic attacks, chronic fatigue syndrome, and substance abuse. Linger in the Reading Room, browse resources for professionals and administrators, and spend some time with the self-help resources. Or visit Credential Check, where you can verify the credentials of an online therapist.

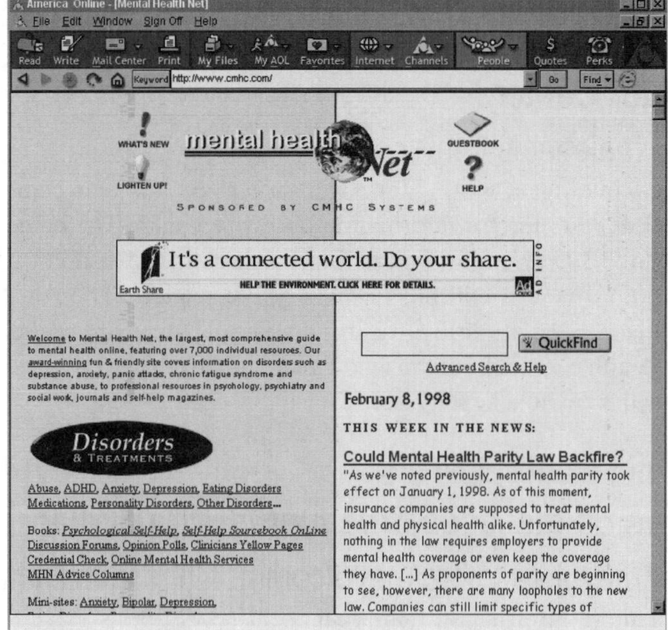

RxList—The Internet Drug Index

http://www.rxlist.com/

RxList is a database of over 4,000 U.S. pharmaceutical products available for searching by name, symptom, side effect, drug interaction, and more. Although it reminds all users that RxList is not intended as a substitute for seeking necessary professional medical advice, it is a useful tool for collecting information on various drugs and medications available to the public either over the counter or by prescription.

Shape Up America!

http://www2.shapeup.org/sua/

Shape Up America's goal is to provide the public with the latest info about safe weight management and physical fitness, with an emphasis on understanding one's Body Mass Index (BMI). The Cyberkitchen helps you choose customized meal plans, and the Health and Fitness area takes you through an assessment of your fitness level and how to improve it. Now reach for that mouse and click! click! click!

U.S. National Library of Medicine (NLM)

http://www.nlm.nih.gov/

The resources of the world's largest biomedical library have been put online at the NLM Web site, with free access to MEDLINE (the database of over 9 million references to articles published in 3,800 biomedical journals described in Chapter 9) and information on 40 other online databases. You can read Clinical Alerts from the National Institutes of Health (NIH) and visit the Visible Human Project, which is creating complete, anatomically detailed, 3-D representations of the male and female human body for educational purposes.

WellnessWeb

http://www.wellweb.com/

WellnessWeb was created by a community of patients who were frustrated at the difficulty of getting the information they wanted from their doctors. Here you'll find information about clinical trials, community health, alternative treatments, healthy lifestyles, and much more. It does not take the approach of some alternative sites, which refute all traditional medicine, but rather recommends that *all* resources be recognized as worthy of consideration and discussion.

INFLUENCE

Cigar Aficionado

http://www.cigaraficianado.com/

No meek apologies are forthcoming from this Web site. The Cigar Aficionado is confident, proud, and bold in its statement that the cigar is *in*! This site is elegant yet comfortable, with clever links and graphics connecting users to areas for cigar ratings, retailers, restaurants, library resources, plus links to other elements of "the good life," like travel, sports, and drinks. You can even research the stocks of cigar makers.

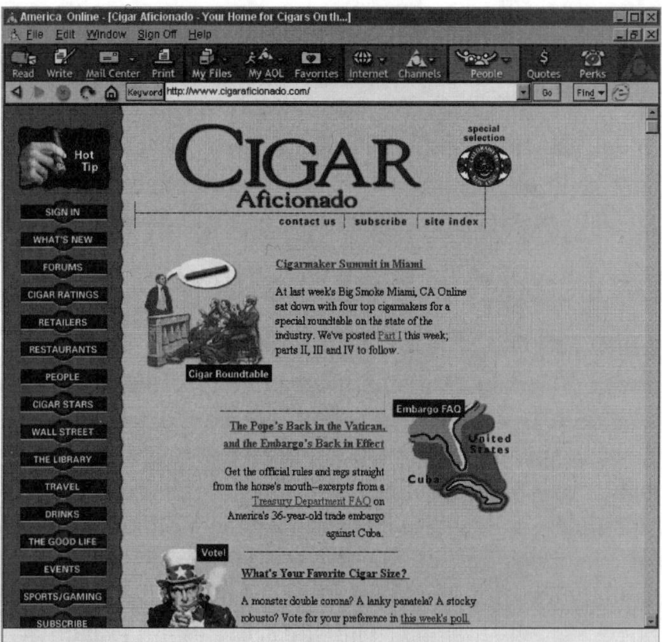

CultureFinder

http://www.culturefinder.com/

CultureFinder.com rightfully describes itself as the Online Address for the Arts. It offers CityGuides for over a dozen metropolitan areas in the U.S., with listings for a wide variety of arts events. You can participate in live chats with celebrities and artists from all fields. CF Tribune offers weekly arts news reports on galleries, the stage, the cinema, and the CD-store aisle. The CultureFinder Dictionary is an extensive online resource of basic arts terms. Start here to plan your vacation, using the listings of summer arts festivals.

The Hollywood Reporter

http://www.hollywoodreporter.com/

If you're not a doctor but you play one on TV, or even if you don't, the Hollywood Reporter is the source for the inside news on entertainment happenings in and around Hollywood. Film, television, music, and all the places where these three intersect are reviewed and reported upon in this snazzy Web site. News reports on industry happenings come in from all around the world, as do full listings of the nominees for all the big award shows (Grammy, Oscar, Globe, Emmy).

The New York Observer

http://www1.observer.com/

This witty weekly once the province of New Yorkers is now available to readers everywhere who find themselves drawn to New York City. Politics, business, the media, society, culture (both pop and high)—all angles of life in New York are examined from an independent perspective.

The New York Times Book Review

http://www.nytimes.com/books/home/contents.html

Long considered the final word on literary review and commentary, The Book Review is part of the larger Web site for the *New York Times*. Registration is required to access articles within the NYT site, but there is no charge for this service for U.S. users. The current and back editions are available here (without the ads), as well as Web-only interviews, reviews, and excerpts.

Salon

http://www.salon.com

Salon.com is the online manifestation of Salon Magazine, a passionate meeting place for authors, artists, and thinkers akin to the salon communities of Paris and New York in the 1920s. Salon, also available at *keyword: Salon*, uses the Web to offer an alternative to the blandness of many print magazines, providing its visitors with a place to engage in radical thought and civic discussion.

Slate

http://www.slate.com

Conviction is the game played at Slate (easily accessible by AOL members at *keyword: Slate*), a waggish and contrary collection of opinion pieces on politics, society, and trends in American culture today. At the end of every article in Slate, readers have the opportunity to jump in the fray and match wits with other Fraygrants on issues of the day.

Wine Spectator On-Line

http://www.winespectator.com/

You'll be able to experience wine in almost every way except actually tasting it at Wine Spectator On-Line. Search the database of over 55,000 wine ratings to learn more about the Chardonnay you had at dinner yesterday, or to choose a highly rated wine for your dinner tonight. You can also locate top wine retailers and research stylish restaurants all over the world. Join in discussions about this year's Beaujolais Nouveau, or just learn more about the drink that makes any occasion special.

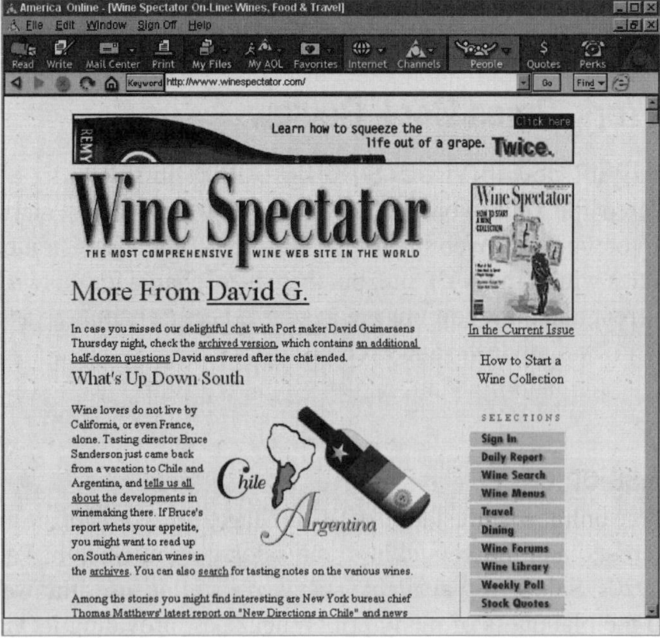

INTERESTS

212.net

http://212.net/

212.net is one of those Web sites that's difficult to describe, yet a blast to visit, with its funky 1950s-style graphics, wildly busy home page, and major attitude. Describing itself as a melting pot of information, 212.net devotes areas to all manner of issues, physical, social, intellectual, financial, personal, and practical. You can even listen to the Barry Z show, Manhattan's leading TV news and entertainment resource for theater, television, and film. All this comes with its own soundtrack, too—you can pick out rock, funk, or techno tunes for continuous play while you're here.

Astronet

http://www.astronet.com/

The first thing to load on this Web page is a counter showing the number of days until the new millennium. Get the idea? Astronet is also the premier astrology site on America Online, with over 50 professional astrologers and 200 part-time hosts (*keyword: Astronet*). Both the AOL area and Web site offer interactive horoscopes and readings. You can participate in chat rooms on astrology or get a complimentary mini-reading from world-renowned astrologers. There are areas to delve into your dreams, have your tarot cards read, and even play the world's only online astrology trivia game. If you believe the answers are all in the stars, you'll feel at home here.

Biography.com

http://www.biography.com/

Are you one of the millions of fans of AandE's Biography? Then you'll love this online version, Biography.com. In the Biography database, you can search for information in more than 20,000 notable people, past and present. Find out who they were, what they did, and why. You can take the Biography Quiz to test your knowledge of famous lives, search for names in Biography Anagrams, or win your own copy of a Biography video. Or just go to the Speak area and search the message boards for a Biography topic that interests you, from Artists to Cops and Criminals to Historic Leaders.

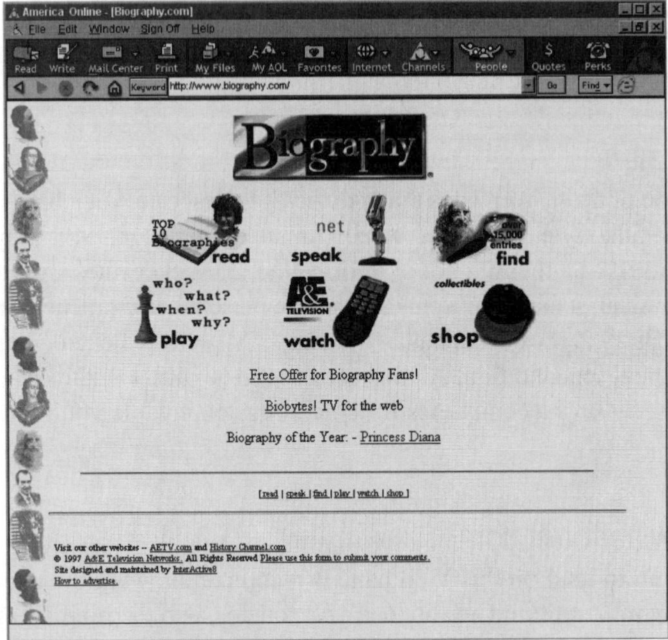

Blind Spot Home on the Web

http://www.blindspot.com/

Say cheese? Well, maybe not here. On this photography Web site, the focus is on art photography. *Blind Spot* magazine is among the most highly regarded periodicals on the subject, and this site brings the magazine's resources online. Sign in the guest book, then read the current issue or flip through back issues. You can review Editions for Sale, a gallery of magnificent images caught on film and available for purchase, or see an even wider variety of photographs in the Artists A-Z section.

The Callboard

http://www.thecallboard.com/

Itching to feel the stage boards under your feet? The CallBoard provides actors and actresses with casting information from all over North America, and The Open Call is the largest online publication of job postings and casting calls in the country. Check out the extensive lists of agents, casting directors, LORT (League of Regional Theater) listings, and film resources. Get tips on auditioning or take classes that will help you get the big break you've been looking for!

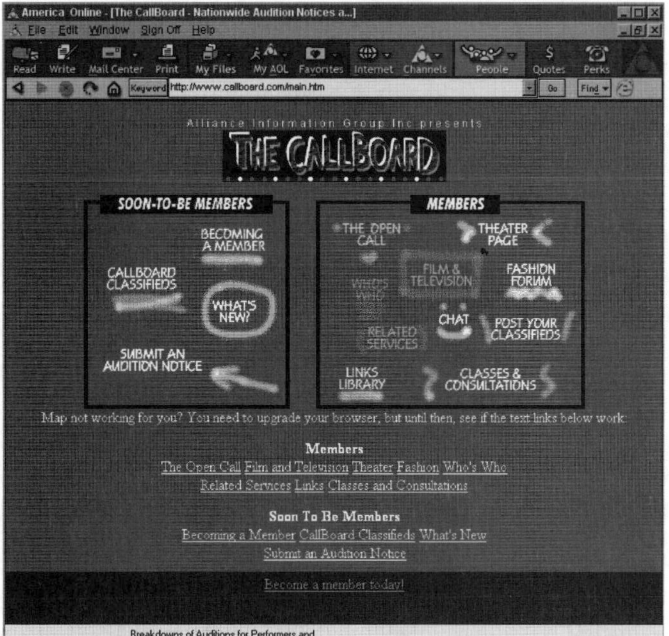

CarTalk

http://www.cartalk.com

If you haven't discovered it already, CarTalk is one of the best things to happen to talk radio in, well, forever. Tom and Ray Magliozzi, otherwise known as Click and Clack, the Tappet Brothers, dispense jokes, puzzlers, occasional car advice, and a Dodge Ram pickup's cargo load of silliness every week on National Public Radio. This Web site captures the essence of their show: smart, funny, and more entertaining than anything purportedly about automobiles ought to be. From any page in the site you can click on the Boss Button, which displays an official-looking memo, so you can look like you're working when you're actually frittering away a perfectly good workday looking at this site.

Catholic Online Saints

http://www.catholic.org/saints/stsindex.html

Catholic Online Saints is a godsend to anyone researching information on a particular saint. You can look up a list of saints' feast days, patron saints for an amazing variety of events and subjects, ethnic saints, and Doctors of the Church.

Go to the Catholic Online homepage, which serves as a center for the exchange of information about the Roman Catholic church. There's also an area called Angels, the Magnificent Servants of God, where you can learn more about angels than you thought possible. You might even get the feeling that someone is watching over you while you do.

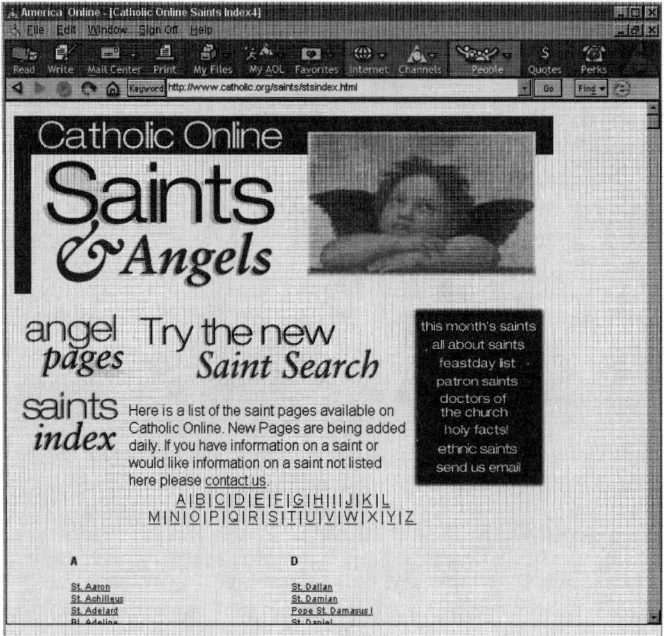

The Food Network's CyberKitchen

http://www.foodtv.com/

The CyberKitchen is brought to you by the people at the Food Network, a cable TV channel dedicated to preparing and enjoying food. This virtual cornucopia of resources for the gourmet chef and kitchen novice alike includes browsable recipes, lists of upcoming live events sponsored by FoodTV, and wine and restaurant reviews. Ask Cyberchef Georgia Downard your questions about shopping for and storing ingredients, and about general cooking issues. *Bon appetit*!

Genealogy Home Page

http://www.genhomepage.com

Looking for your roots can lead nowhere—unless you visit the Genealogy Home Page. This resource includes help files, guides, libraries, maps, deeds and photographs, lists of associated newsgroups and mailing lists, and links to other online genealogical resources. You will find commercial services, software, and lists of genealogical societies, too. Come here directly after visiting AOL's Genealogy Forum (*keyword: Genealogy*).

North American Cockatiel Society (NACS) Web Site

http://www2.upatsix.com/nacs/

This Web site is a terrific resource for all bird lovers but especially for those who enjoy the company of a cockatiel. These intelligent, sociable birds are longer-lived than parakeets, averaging a ten-year lifespan, and they are easy to train to speak and whistle. The NACS Web site has numerous sections covering cockatiel care and genetics, with discussion groups, chat rooms, and lists of mutations for breeding purposes. One fun area to visit is the Pet Tiel of the Month, in which NACS members share photos and stories about their favorite feathered friends.

Rock and Roll Hall of Fame and Museum

http://www.rockhall.com

You can visit the House That Rock Built even if you aren't anywhere near Cleveland. Each year, half a dozen new inductees (artists, songwriters, and producers) are enshrined in this museum of rock. At this Web site, you can see featured exhibits on different eras in rock and roll, check out the cool artifacts collected by the curator, or get a virtual tour of the museum with Eddie the Elevator Man. Every inductee is represented at this site by a biography with pics and audio clips. You can order t-shirts, caps, and other rock and roll related souvenirs in the Gift Shop, of course, or just speak your mind in the Forums area.

WebLit

http://www.rust.net/~rothfder/weblit.html

WebLit is just what it says: Literature on the Web. This Web site, created by a high school student, is a great place to go for information on a wide variety of authors.

The Authors and Poets page is a list of links to Web sites on hundreds of authors, many of them ranked by the Webmaster for graphics, information, format, and quality of other links. There is also a huge list of downloadable texts by an equally impressive list of authors as well as a Java search engine you can use to find specific writers by gender, style (prose or poetry), and rating.

INTERNATIONAL

Welcome to Berlitz World!

http://www.berlitz.com/

Going someplace where you don't speak the language? Make Berlitz World your first stop, even before you buy that travel insurance. You can take a quick course in about 15 different languages at LanguageExpress and pick up tips on culture differences and etiquette for over 20 destinations at the GlobeTrotter. Visit Café Berlitz to chat with other travelers, test your knowledge, and hear the current news from around the world. Of course, you can also order books, tapes, and CD-ROMs from Berlitz's famous educational programs.

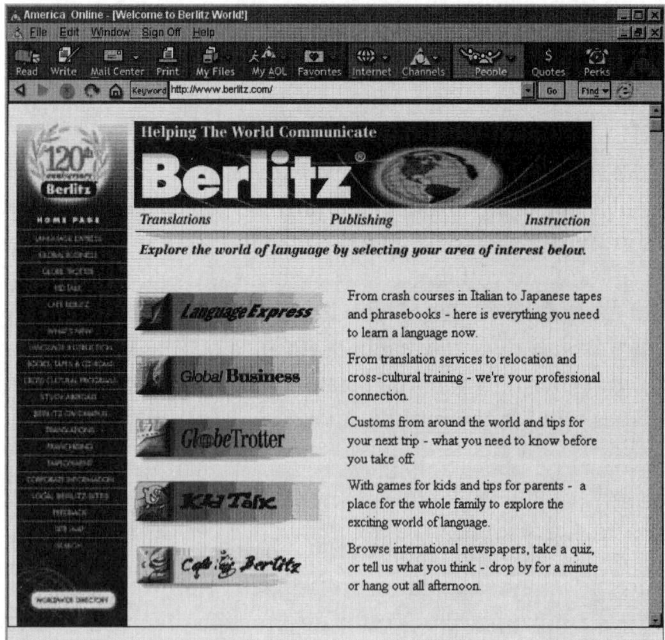

Caribbean Online Directory

http://www.caribbeanonline.com/

The Caribbean is one of the most popular travel destinations in the world, and this Web site gives you an idea why that is true. There is a section for each of over two dozen islands or groups of islands in the Caribbean, each with subsections providing information on hotels and resorts, real estate, business services, travel (getting there), and tourism/leisure (what to do once you've arrived). Don't forget your sunscreen!

The Hindu

http://www.webpage.com/hindu/index.html

The Hindu is the first complete Indian Newspaper on the Web. On this site you can read about daily events and domestic politics in India, regional reports, entertainment, sports happenings, quotes from the Bombay stock exchange, Asian travel, classified ads, and more.

infoXenios: G.N.T.O.—Greece—Tourism—Travel—Vacation

http://www.areianet.gr/infoxenios/intro.html

infoXenios is ranked among the top tourism Web sites in Europe. It provides travelers to the Balkan Peninsula a sea of information on geography, history, culture, accommodations, and entertainment. An extensive area provides details on camping in Greece, with locations, rates, and seasonal schedules. Look up the hours for a wide variety of museums, cultural centers, and archaeological sites.

International Chamber of Commerce World Business Organization

http://www.iccwbo.org/

The International Chamber of Commerce serves as the only representative organization that speaks with authority on behalf of international companies in all sectors. At this Web site, you can read articles on the latest developments in international business, finance, and trade issues. You can also participate in the ICC's Global Business Exchange, inquire into international arbitration, and initiate commercial crime investigation services.

International Herald Tribune

http://www.iht.com/

The International Herald Tribune brings the intelligent reporting, commentary, and insight of the New York Times and the Washington Post to an even broader audience. With its online version, users all over the globe can access this concise digest and analysis of the world's most important news.

The Irish Tourist Board

http://www.ireland.travel.ie/

The Irish Tourist Board wants you to see Ireland, and to entice you there it has created this inviting site. Search their database of recreational activities, browse through lists of dining and nightlife options, arrange your transport around the island, or trace your family roots through the genealogy center. First, make sure to register in the Personal Brochure, where you can collect specific information and print it out for later review.

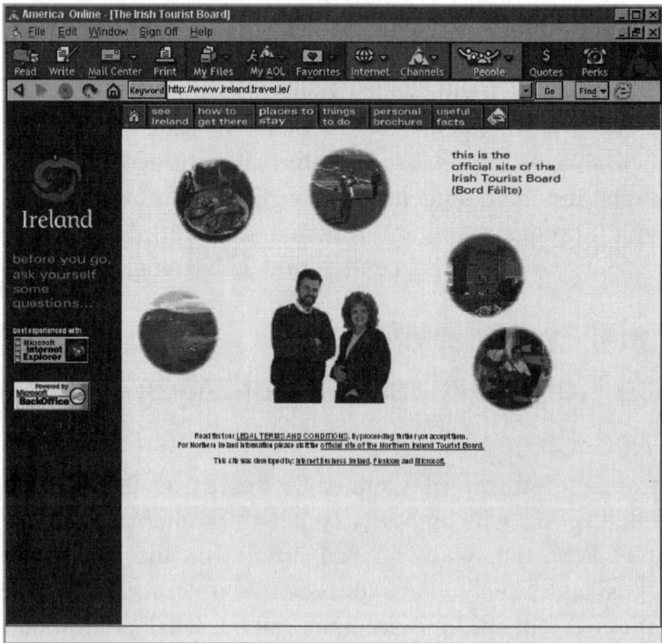

Nikkei Net

http://www.nikkei.co.jp/enews/index.html

Nikkei Net is the premiere source for business news and information for top corporate executives and decision-makers in Japan. Nikkei produces five different publications, and sponsors a wide variety of cultural events in art, music, and theater, all of which are detailed on Nikkei Net. The Business Browser lists Asia-Pacific and Japan-based companies with English-language pages on the Web, company ranking data and market share reports, and of course, the latest stock reports from the Tokyo market.

Queensland, Australia—Holiday and Vacation Information for Australia Travel

http://sunzine.net

SunZine presents Interactive Queensland, as close as you can get to Australia without enduring the 30-hour flight! This Web site promoting tourism in Queensland, the northeastern province of Australia, has detailed maps, long lists of entertainment ideas, accommodations, organized tours, real estate opportunities, transportation options, and more. Lose yourself in the brilliant photographs of the landscape, flora, and fauna.

World Health Organization

http://www.who.ch/

The World Health Organization (WHO) is the branch of the United Nations dedicated to ensuring the physical health and social well-being of people everywhere. Headquartered in Geneva, Switzerland, WHO, through its Web site, makes available its research, policies, statistical studies, and educational programs. The International Travel and Health area gives country lists with vaccination requirements and health advice for travelers, details on health risks and their avoidance, maps of hazardous regions, and relevant WHO publications.

INTERNET

Beginner's Guide to HTML

http://www.ncsa.uiuc.edu/General/Internet/WWW/HTMLPrimer.html

NCSA (The National Center for Supercomputing Applications) presents this excellent tutorial and reference for learning HTML. Although the presentation is

simple and straightforward, the guide contains everything you need to know to write your own Web pages. Start by learning what HTML is and isn't; how you use head, title, and body tags; when it's appropriate to use headings and preformatted text; how to create links, forms, and tables; and much more. It also provides you with a number of instructional links on working SGML and Java. *Note: Marc Andreessen, one of the creators of the Netscape browser, wrote the original version.*

Cyberatlas

http://www.cyberatlas.com/

CyberAtlas's goal is to provide accurate information about the Internet's dimensions—how big it is, how it is used, how fast it is growing, and *where* it is growing, plus trends in each of these areas. Visit CyberAtlas's Tools area to learn more about the software and hardware you use to access the Net everyday, and find out everything you should know about intranets, retail Web sites, and E-commerce in general. For anyone doing research about the Internet or doing business on the Internet, CyberAtlas is indispensable.

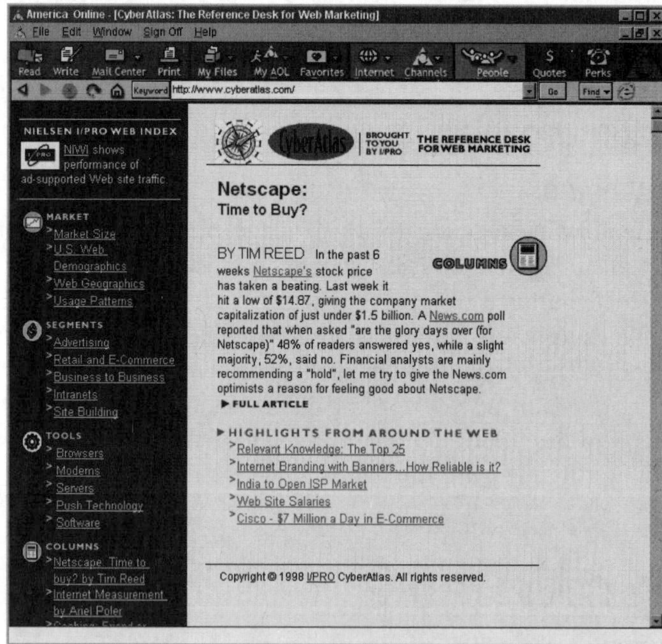

Gamelan

http://www.gamelan.com

Gamelan is considered the comprehensive site for people who want to experience and learn about the latest technologies: Java, JavaScript, and ActiveX—especially Java. This site provides thousands of useful and fun Java applets in a wide array of categories, from arts and entertainment to business and finance and education. There are also links to publications about Java and comprehensive information about Java-related tools and utilities.

Internet Access Providers

http://www.loc.gov/global/internet/access-providers.html

When your mom told you go to the library to get answers to your questions, she was probably not referring to the Library of Congress, that granddaddy of all resources. But now you can access many of the LOC's voluminous files online at **http://www.loc.gov**. Among the gems is The List (**http://www.thelist.com**), a comprehensive listing of Internet service providers.

Internet Society

http://www.isoc.org/

This is the official Web site of the Internet Society, an organization working to secure and improve the standards on which the Internet as a physical network depends. The site offers Internet news; information about ISOC conferences; links to educational sites promoting good Web design; online versions of its bimonthly publication, *On the Internet*; and places where you can learn more about the Internet and its history.

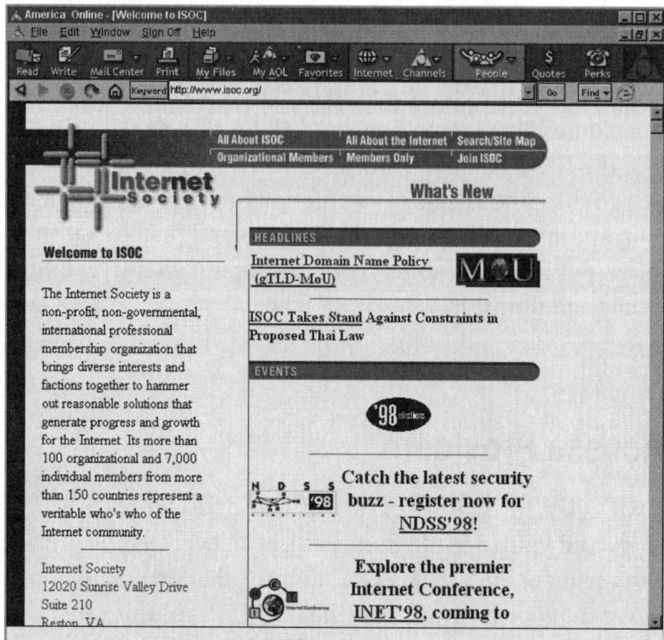

Net-happenings (newsgroup)

comp.internet.net-happenings

Every day's a feast on the Internet, and this is your menu. Net-happenings is an announcement service in which you can read recent postings about new Internet resources, so you can stay informed about the latest Web and Net information resources. Messages are categorized by type of resource (conferences, e-zines, educational, mailings lists, to name a few). Net-happenings will keep you apprised of the best new content on the Internet.

Web Developer's Virtual Library

http://www.stars.com

If you're involved in any way in creating Web content, bookmark this site, a one-stop compendium of information and tools for Web developers. It is insanely big, a Web developer's Library of Congress, with deep wells of information on every aspect of scripting, programming, graphics, VRML, style, tags—you name it! The Top 100 list will save you hours of online research, bringing you directly to the most influential sites for creators of Web content.

KIDS ONLY

AOL NetFind for Kids

http://www.aol.com/netfind/kids

A Web playground, with a catalog of selected sites for kids plus a searchable index of kid-appropriate places. For AOL members, this Web site, part of the bigger AOL NetFind service, has links to the best areas on the **Kids Only** channel, such as Blackberry Creek, ABC Kidzine, and Nickelodeon Online.

Bill Nye the Science Guy

http://nyelabs.kcts.org/

You don't need to be a rocket scientist to figure out why Bill Nye the Science Guy (BNSG) is such a popular show with kids, you just need to visit Nye Labs Online. Download video clips from the show in the Screening Room, listen to WAV files from the Sounds of Science, and dress BNSG in various goofy outfits in the Costume Closet. You can also search episode guides by topic to refresh your memory of that wild demo BNSG did in your favorite episode.

Cyberkids

http://www.cyberkids.com/

CyberKids is a friendly site for kids with varied interests and ability levels. There is an extensive Art Gallery with paintings and drawings sent in by members; a CyberKids Connection chat area; games; reading room; contests; downloadable software; and the Launchpad, from which young surfers can pursue links to destinations like the Young Composers site (**www.youngcomposers.com**). Kids feeling a little too old for CyberKids can visit its companion site, CyberTeens, the hottest teen community on the Web.

Headbone Zone, Party Time for Your Brain Cells!

http://www.headbone.com/home.html

Headbone Zone is one of the brightest, funkiest Web sites out there for kids—and it *is* out there! With its wild lime-green and purple color scheme, flashy animations, and a huge assortment of areas where kids can stretch their gray matter without even noticing it, this is a site kids will want to add to their Favorite Places and revisit. Join the Derby to solve mysteries or learn how to find stuff on the Internet. Enter

the Prize Buzz area to get free stuff or just chat with the friends you'll make while you're here.

Homework Tools

http://www.zen.org/~brendan/kids-homework.html

The Kids on the Web: Homework Tools is just the place to go when you've put off that assignment until the library has closed and your bike has a flat tire. Links on the page will take you to electronic versions of Webster's Dictionary, Roget's Thesaurus, the Encyclopedia Britannica, Bartlett's Familiar Quotations, and more, but the electrons weigh a lot less than all those books! Other links such as "Agggh! Homework!", will bring you to even more resources in a wide variety of subjects such as science, math, language arts, social studies, and history.

Internet Kids and Family Yellow Pages' Top 100

http://www.netmom.com/ikyp/samples/hotlist.htm

Jean Armour Polly, aka NetMom, author of *Internet Kids' Yellow Pages* (Osborne/McGraw-Hill, 1997), created this Web site with her Top 100 sites for preschoolers, teachers, and kids. A special section provides emergency help for kids who forgot to do their homework. If you have the book, you'll find links here that will keep the book from ever going out of date.

Joseph Wu's Origami Page

http://www.datt.co.jp/Origami/

In Japanese, *oru* means "to fold" and *kami* means "paper." This beautifully designed Japanese site is devoted to the art of paper-folding. It links to the world's best origami resources, providing diagrams (with instructions) and a gallery of origami art. Joseph Wu himself is a master, and you can view here many pictures of his paper dragons, gryphons, and flying pigs.

MLB@BAT For Kids

http://www.majorleaguebaseball.com/special/kidindex.sml

Young baseball fans can visit this awesome site to absorb all they ever wanted to know about America's favorite pastime. There are profiles of favorite players, interviews, Major League Baseball (MLB) video games, tons of good information on collecting cards, and tips from the experts—the guys who play professional baseball! The main MLB site has a History and Records section with more stats than any baseball fanatic could swing a Louisville Slugger at, plus links to areas on Women and Girls in Baseball, the Negro Leagues, and more.

UNICEF's Voices of Youth

http://www.unicef.org/voy

What do kids around the world think *about* their world? Start here to find out and interact with kids everywhere. Special sections deal with some of the problems faced by children, including crowded cities, war, and child labor. The Whole Picture lets kids match wits with each other, viewing parts of photographs and guessing what's missing. Available in English, Spanish, and French, the site stands out for its attention to the problems faced by girls.

Warner Bros. Kids Page

http://www.kids.warnerbros.com/

You know all those crazy Warner Brothers characters that you like to watch on television—well, now you can enjoy them online, too, beginning with AOL's WBNet (*keyword: WB*) and this far out Web site. Play silly games with your favorite WB cartoon characters, send a Looney Tunes WeB card, or learn how to draw at WB Online's Animation 101 studio. You might even begin your singing career at Looney Tunes Karaoke!

Yuckiest Site on the Internet

http://www.nj.com/yucky/index.html

The Yuckiest Site on the Internet is exactly what its name says, and a great place for science information and generally disgusting stuff—just what kids like! Ask Wendell the Worm any question about gross science or learn all the icky details about your body. Best of all, you can send a Yucky E-card to a friend or your big sister. Pick a yucky picture, add an even yuckier sound effect, and write her the message you've been wanting to send to her in her computer class that she'll read in front of all her friends.

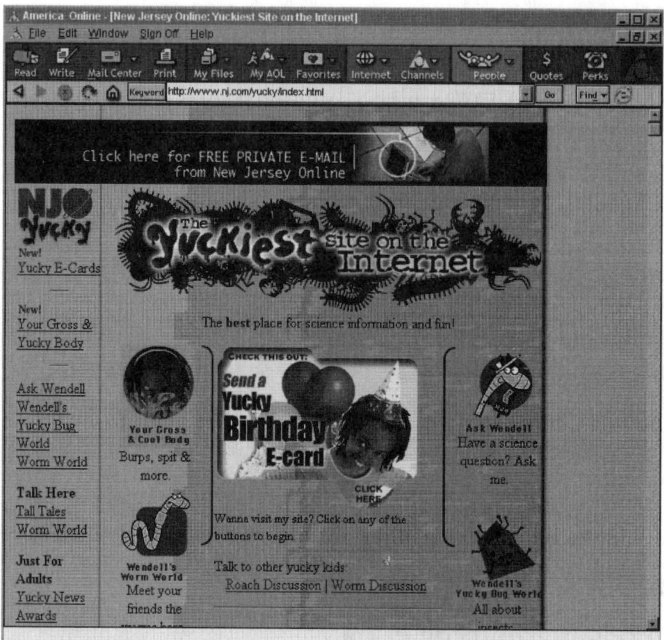

ZooNet—All About Zoos!

http://www.mindspring.com/~zoonet/

If you like animals, you will love ZooNet, a one-stop resource on zoos and animals on the Web. There is a long index of U.S. and international zoos, with links to the official Web pages of each individual zoo. Check out the ZooNet Gold Paw Awards page, where zoos and other organizations are commended for their educational efforts on the Web. Then go through the huge list of links for individual species (common and endangered), conservation organizations, and pet resources.

LIFESTYLES

2001: Journey to the Next Millennium

http://www.sun2001.com/index2.html

This site describes itself as "a full-service metaphysical site designed to provoke thought, be it silly or profound, about our journey toward the Third Millennium."

There are many possible destinations reachable from this gateway: Reincarnation, Planetary Purpose, Transformation, all explored from a variety of perspectives. Or seek the guidance via e-mail of one of the Empathic Counselors to learn if you have been on this strange planet before.

Black Voices

http://www.blackvoices.com/

Black Voices is a popular AOL news and information area of special interest to African-Americans, but most anyone would feel at home here (*keyword: Blackvoices*). Its corresponding Web site is also an area for open exchange of ideas and philosophies, with information and discussions on music, politics, culture, business, and more. Join chat rooms and message boards for live interchanges between persons of all colors and walks of life.

Channel A—Access to Asia: People, Products, and Lifestyle

http://www.channela.com/

One place to stay informed about Asian and Asian-American culture is this bright and elegant site, which has areas devoted to Health and Wellness, Food and Drink, Style and Design, Business, People and Culture, Entertainment, and more. Choose from a wide variety of products in the Channel A Shop, which you can access either directly or from within each of the subchannels. Or read the Daily A, where you'll see the latest newsflash and the featured product of the day.

Fitness Zone

http://www.fitnesszone.com/

Get wired for fitness at the Fitness Zone! This energetic Web site features an online health and fitness magazine, a nationwide gym and health club locator, and a library full of fitness resources. You can also order high quality fitness equipment for use at home. Go to the fitness profiler, where you fill out a questionnaire on your current condition, and Fitness Zone will provide you with a detailed fitness profile, including an overall fitness rating and a balanced nutritional and exercise plan.

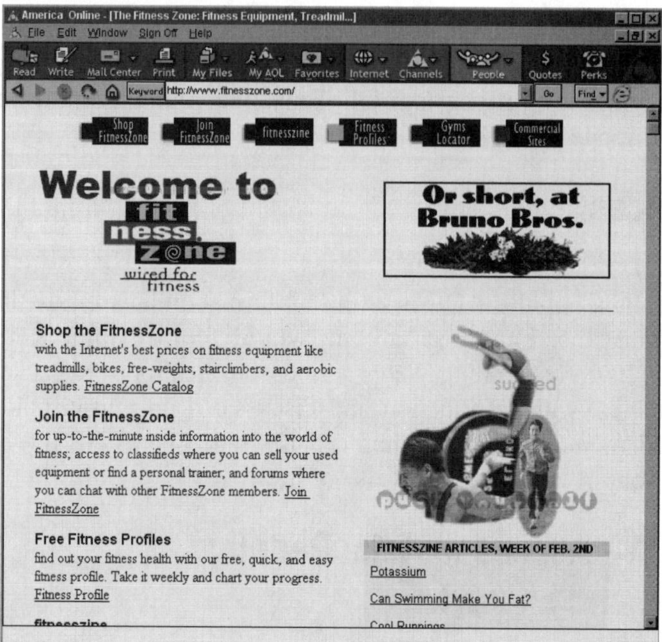

Hometime

http://hometime.com/

The popular TV show about home improvement has a wonderful Web site for both people who are handy and those who can't hammer a nail in straight. Click on one of the Phillips-head icon buttons to search a long list of topics, including everything from basement projects to roofing, and yes, even the kitchen sink. Log into the Users Forum, where you can share your home improvement questions, answers, and ideas or search the Forum archives. Check PBS and Learning Channel listings for the next broadcast in your area or just watch show bloopers that make you feel like the hosts are human. For a related area on AOL, check out *keyword: HouseNet.*

LatinoLink

http://www.latino.com/

LatinoLink is a fantastic resource on all facets of Latino life. The site's home page opens with headlines of the latest news, comments on community, and links to a wide variety of topics. There are sections on arts and entertainment, jobs, money, community, and even horoscopes, all fully bilingual. LatinoLink has recently added a section on its hometown (San Francisco) to supplement the news, commentary, and reviews of interest to a national audience. Read about the clubs, events, food, and people that link Latinos everywhere. For a related AOL area, visit *Keyword: Hispanic Online*.

National Gemstone's Home Page

http://www.preciousgemstones.com/index.html

Rubies and diamonds and pearls, oh my!! Talk about your Emerald City—visit National Gemstone's Web site and learn all you ever wanted to know about precious and semi-precious stones. Educate yourself about how gems are graded, so you can begin to collect them for fun and profit. You can study charts showing gem prices over the last 20 years. Add yourself to National Gemstone's e-mail list so you can receive the latest Gemstone Forecaster Newsletter to stay satisfied with your sapphires and on top of your tanzanites.

NativeWeb—an Internet Community

http://www.nativeweb.org/

This collective project combines ancient teachings with modern technology. There are two main regions, each with a Resource Center and Community Center. The former is a searchable database with hundreds of links to native, indigenous, and aboriginal Internet resources from all nations. The latter is a place to meet and communicate with other NativeWeb visitors, check out job listings and message boards, and post announcements and action notices.

Planet Cybergrrl

http://www.cybergrrl.com/planet/

Cybergrrl is a woman of many facets—counselor, best buddy, sister, mother, even superheroine! This witty Web site shouts out independence, strength, and humor in every link and icon. Through Femina, it links to many other female-friendly sites on the Web, all of them online communities for women and girls to share their experiences, fears, and joys.

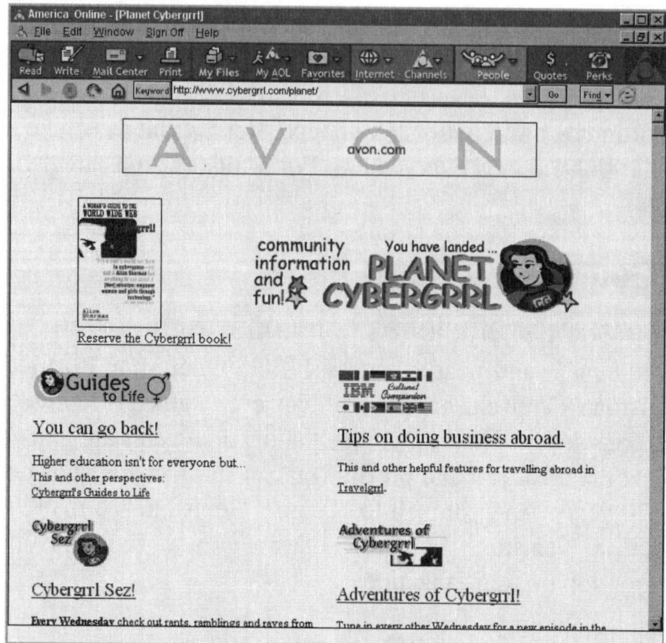

Religion and Philosophy Resources on the Internet

http://web.bu.edu/STH/Library/contents.html

From its beginnings, the Net has attracted individuals with a strong interest in religion and philosophy who have created discussion groups, electronic versions of all the great religious texts (both Eastern and Western), and searchable catalogs of theological libraries. To consolidate this information, the Boston University School of Theology offers an online guide to religion and philosophy resources. It includes sections on Judaism, Christianity, Islam, and Asian religions, as well as a broad range of resources on philosophy.

Shawna's Virtual Flower Shop

http://drew.netsua1.net/~shawna/virtual/

Shawna's slogan is "when you care enough to send the virtual best." In this virtual shop, you can pick out and send a virtual flower arrangement and a message to anyone with an e-mail address. Note the emphasis on "virtual": Shawna's doesn't send out *real* flowers, just an e-mail with a Web address to which your loved one can go to see a picture of the flowers you chose and read the message you wrote. You can even pick out a song to play (a MIDI file) when your recipient gets your message and virtual flowers! Your friends will be saying, "Aww, flowers? For *me*?"

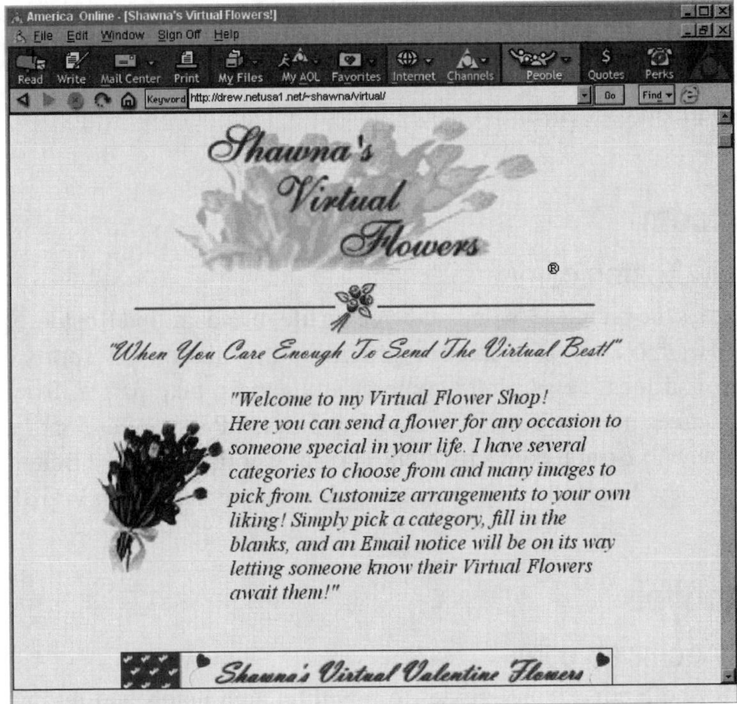

LOCAL

Digital City

http://www.digitalcity.com/

Everyone on AOL has been to Digital City or, at the very least, has seen the icon for it at the Welcome screen. What you may not know about Digital City is that there are dozens of them, each with its own dense mix of information about urban communities. New ones are forming monthly. In addition to local news and commentary, each Digital City also has its own MovieGuide, DiningGuide, and Real Estate Guide. For some 60 cities, you can even follow a chart tracking the daily stock-market performance of local companies.

Access Atlanta

http://www.accessatlanta.com/

Access Atlanta is where Atlanta goes online! Get the latest on news, community, sports, business, entertainment, even home improvement. You can look up scores for all the major sports leagues or check out the traffic report or the latest weather from local TV and radio stations. And check out the link to Y'all, the ultimate Southern online experience.

Boston.com

http://www.boston.com/

Boston.com is the premiere online resource on life in and around Boston. Sponsored by the *Boston Globe*, Boston.com provides information on sports, arts and diversions, and local news. Enter contests and games, take part in live chat, and review resources in Your Town, On Campus, Boston Passport, and more. A list of links takes you to Boston.com's partners, such as CarTalk.com, the Better Business Bureau, the New England Aquarium, and public television station WGBH.

Chicago Web

http://www.chiweb.com/

Yes, you'll find the usual city guides to nightlife, area hotels and restaurants, and detailed calendars of events over the next few months. But Chicago Web goes much further, offering links to the advertised sale specials at all the local supermarket chains (updated every Thursday); over 20 detailed street maps of different regions of Chicago; Lake Shore Drive (a Chicago soap opera on the Web); and even a collection of the best Dennis Rodman sites on the Web.

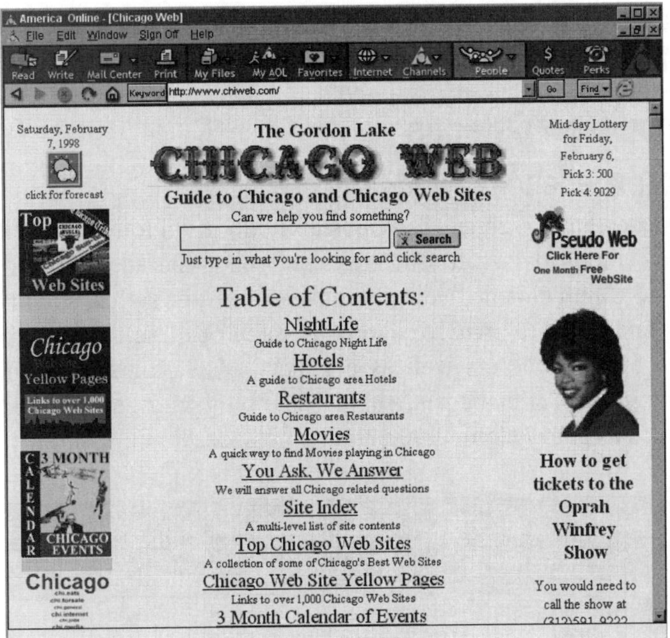

MN (Minnesota) Online

http://www.mnonline.org/

MN Online is the official list of Web sites and other online resources about everything Minnesotan. There are extensive links to such groups as arts and community organizations, government and health agencies, educational opportunities, business and commercial sites, and recreation opportunities. Visit Short Redhead Reel Reviews, with movie reviews by Wendy Schadewald, who is—you guessed it—a short redhead. Or go to Uffda!, where you can do a keyword search on any topic on any Minnesota Web site. ("Uffda!" is a Norwegian expression meaning "Oops!" or "Ouch!")

Pittsburgh.Net

http://www.pittsburgh.net/

This bright, witty Web site doesn't just provide all the information you could want about a booming metropolitan area. It also shines with the pride of a beautiful city that remains associated with smoke stacks long after it has ceased to rely on the mills. Learn about public art projects that represent community collaboration among Pittsburgh's neighborhoods. Review the latest rankings from *Fortune Magazine*

showing Pittsburgh as one of the most livable cities in the country. Or try to solve the Pittsburgh Puzzler, a regular trivia question about the city.

Experience New Orleans

http://www.experienceneworleans.com/

This newly redesigned Web site provides a vivid virtual tour of the city known as the Big Easy. Famous for jazz, Mardi Gras, the Orpheus Parade, cemeteries, swamps, the Saints, and Cajun cuisine, New Orleans is a feast of sights, sounds, tastes, and much more, and this site gives you some of each of these. It also provides a live netcast from Mardi Gras (as well as a gallery of photographs after the event), authentic Creole and Cajun recipes, a useful shopping guide, and info on "N'awlins" celebrities such as Harry Connick, Jr. and Anne Rice.

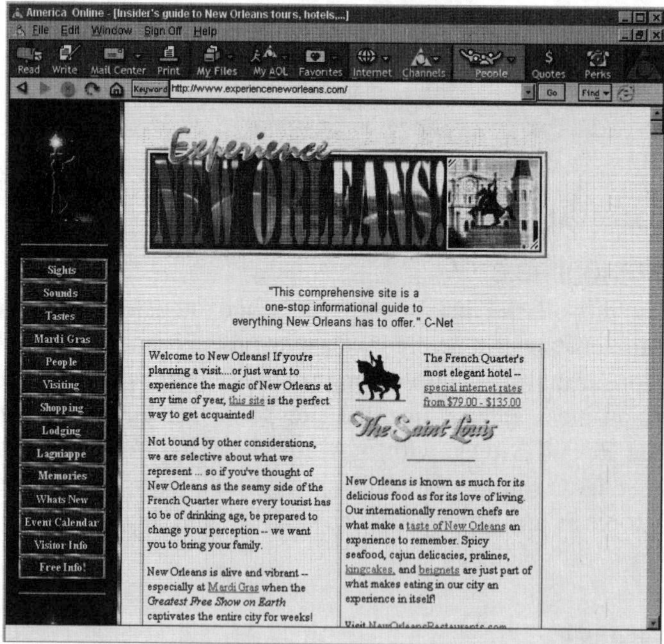

Inside San Francisco

http://www.insidesanfran.com/

Inside San Francisco is colorful and friendly, much like the city it represents, with vivid buttons for each of the subsections of the Web site, all displayed against a blue sky background. There are areas with information about weather and traffic, as well as detailed maps and full descriptions of 20 or so neighborhoods. Join in the Bay Area chat at Town Square or link to Match.com, an online matchmaking area and singles community.

Washingtonian Magazine Online

http://www.washingtonian.com/

Upscale residents of the D.C. area have relied upon *Washingtonian* magazine since 1965 for useful information, and now its online version brings the same resources to locals and folks outside the Beltway alike. Here you can find restaurant reviews, lists of things to do in and around Washington, weekend getaways, shopping and consumer info, and guides to private schools and continuing education in the area. Read articles about the latest developments in politics, the game that makes Washington what it is, or put in your two cents about sports teams such as the Redskins.

NEWS

CNN Interactive

http://www.cnn.com/

CNN Interactive has all the information, all the details, and all the news you have come to expect from the Cable News Network, and then some. The news reports are sorted by subject, with topics ranging from politics on the world stage to show biz to earth science, and everything in between. You can also link to other sites in the CNN empire, such as CNNfn, the Cable News Network Financial Network, and CNN/SI, with all the scoop on happenings in the sports world.

CRAYON

http://crayon.net/

CRAYON, which stands for CReAte Your Own Newspaper, is a tool for managing information overload, specifically the seemingly limitless news resources on the Internet. You choose the newspapers, magazines, and other publications you'd like to read every day, and CRAYON assembles a custom virtual newspaper, sent to you either on the Web or via e-mail, so you can read it at your leisure. Just follow the equation: "Newspaper minus the paper equals: just news."

The Daily Muse

http://www.cais.net/aschnedr/muse.htm

For biting sarcasm and sharp-witted irony mixed in with your morning reading, come to The Daily Muse, where you'll find a myriad of features, reviews, and observations on life, politics, the media, and the American dream...or nightmare. Just hold on tight to your coffee cup and let the slamming begin!

Editor and Publishers Directory of Online Newspapers

http://www.mediainfo.com/ephome/npaper/nphtm/online.htm

This is a phenomenal directory of online newspapers from all over the world, currently with links to over 2,500 newspapers. The statistics provide data on Internet publications by type (dailies, weeklies, business, alternatives, etc.) and by world region. If you want to attend journalism industry events, check the Conferences section.

National Public Radio Online

http://www.npr.org/

On this Web complement to National Public Radio, you can listen to new broadcasts of NPR news every hour with RealAudio and search station listings, program information, and transcripts. Jazz lovers will want to visit NPR's Jazz Profiles page to listen to a weekly one-hour jazz documentary series hosted by Nancy Wilson. You can also listen to other NPR shows, including "All Things Considered," "Morning Edition," "Talk of the Nation," "Performance Today," and "CarTalk." This is a great companion to the NPR forum on America Online (*keyword: NPR*).

The New York Times on the Web

http://www.nytimes.com/

The New York Times is one of the most influential newspapers in the world. The New York Times on the Web carries that tradition into the next millennium by publishing this online version of All the News That's Fit to Print. In addition to the excellent writing and intelligent insight woven through its articles, the New York Times on the Web also offers Web Specials, occasional projects showcased only on the Web site and not available in the newspaper.

The Wall Street Journal Interactive Edition

http://www.wsj.com/

The premiere business and financial newspaper on the Web parallels the print publication, with the Front Section, Marketplace, Money and Investing, and Sports. But there's much more online. You can customize your view of the WSJ Interactive Edition and search the listings of **Careers.wsj.com**. You can visit the Small Business Suite for news and advice. Be sure not to miss the award-winning Index to Market Data as well as the 14-Day Searchable Archive. And, if you subscribe to the WSJ Interactive, you can even check if your flight is on time.

The Weather Channel

http://www.weather.com/

Do you need an umbrella today? Don't leave the house (or the office) until you check the Weather Channel. Search the weather by state to check your city's five-day forecast and Doppler radar. Skiers can check the status of the slopes, and business travelers can check airport delays. At the Health and Allergies section where you can confirm the presence of common airborne allergens before you venture outside. You may not be able to *do* anything about the weather, but you can certainly get a better handle on it before you get offline and outside.

PERSONAL FINANCE

Bank Rate Monitor

http://www.bankrate.com/

If you're shopping around for a new bank or consumer financial institution, you can't afford to miss this site. Here you'll get easy access to up-to-date rates on mortgages, credit cards, home equity loans, auto loans, personal loans, bank fees, and more. Other services offered here include the automatic e-mail interest rate alert for mortgages, deposits, and federal discount rates, as well as the handy monitor for personal stock, bond, and mutual fund portfolios.

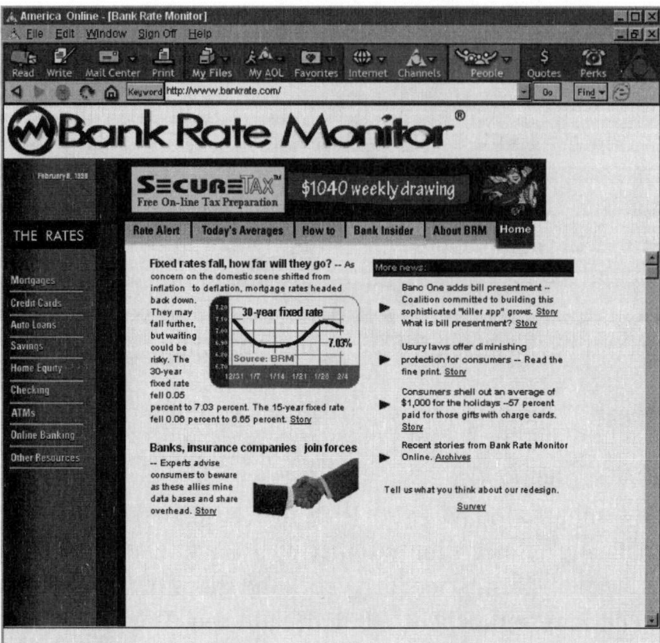

Cars.com

http://cars.com

keyword: cars.com

This new site provides access to a complete inventory of new and used vehicles for sale, as well as thousands of vehicle reviews. In addition, AOL members will be able to get new and used vehicle pricing and equipment information, calculate financing options, and review used car ratings and service advice. (This exciting area was under construction when this book went to press.)

CNNfn—the financial network

http://www.cnnfn.com/

"Business Unusual" reads the banner atop of CNNfn, but when you visit this Web site, it is clear what everyday business will look like in the near future. Investors can find a reliable source of updated stock quotes provided by Standard and Poor's ComStock. Any business person can keep abreast of the financial world by reading Breaking News and This Hour's Top Business Stories.

Hugh's Mortgage and Financial Calculators

http://alfredo.wustl.edu/mort/

This extensive compilation of financial calculators online was assembled by Hugh Chou from the Institute for Biomedical Computing at Washington University. Among many other things, you can calculate the amortization of your mortgage, figure out how much money you can borrow for a house, find out the APR of a loan (given points and other costs), and calculate the lease payments on that new car you've been eyeing. Don't forget to visit Hugh's Financial Common Sense Guide to managing your money.

IRS—The Digital Daily

http://www.irs.ustreas.gov/prod/cover.html

Faster than a speeding 1040-EZ! This free publication brought to you by the IRS shows that tax information doesn't need to be dry and boring: this publication is colorful, easy to read, and even fun. Here you can find tax information for both individuals and businesses, as well as tax forms, educational publications, and electronic services. If you're interested in how taxes work on a national scale, check out the proposed tax regulations and statistics.

Kelley Blue Book

http://www.kbb.com/

Anyone who has considered selling a car has heard of the Kelley Blue Book, the official resource for pricing new and used cars, from Audis to Yugos. Here you just fill out a form with your car's year, make, and model, as well as more specific data such as odometer reading and condition, and Kelley provides you with a current value. The online version of the Blue Book has recently been spruced up with lots of new areas, including a list of FAQs on new and used car values and Carfax, an independent service that will search its database to give you a detailed report on a car's history. You can also search listings of car dealerships in your area and investigate reviews of different vehicles on AutoVantage (*keyword: AutoWeb*).

Motley Fool: Finance and Folly

http://www.fool.com/

When you visit the Fool, you will see why it has become one of the most popular America Online forums (*keyword: Fool*). This online resource is devoted entirely

to stocks; you won't find information about any other type of investments here. Every day, the Fools entertainingly serve up their timely stock investment information and news. Every day, the burgeoning Fools community shares its ideas and experiences. Linger in The Fool's School, FoolWire, Lunchtime News, and The Fribble for up-to-the-minute news and advice. If you enjoy playing games, try your hand with Today's Pitch and Foolball.

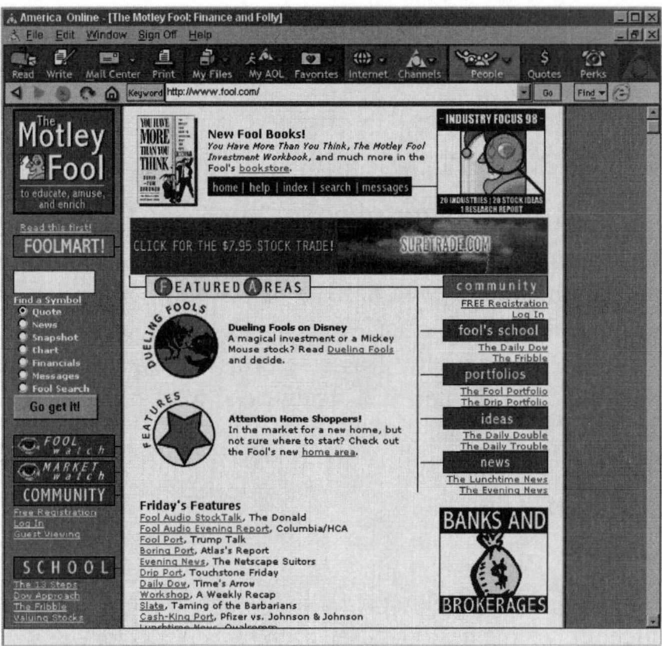

Realtor.com

http://www.realtor.com/

Begin your search for a new home from the computer in your current home with Realtor.com, the largest online database of residential real estate listings in the world. Every property listed with a real estate office affiliated with a Multiple Listing Service (MLS) is represented here. After you select Find a Home, click on the map to indicate the state and area within that state in which you hope to find a home. Enter basic data about the type of property you want to buy, such as town, number of bedrooms and baths, amount of land, style of house, and so on, and Realtor.com will bring up a list of properties that match your criteria, with descriptions, photos (in most cases), and the name and phone number of the listing real estate broker.

Social Security Online

http://www.ssa.gov/

Welcome to the official Web source of Social Security information. One unique application you'll find here is a Personal Earnings and Benefit Estimate Statements calculator, which incorporates the annual cost-of-living adjustment. You'll also find a compendium of government publications including everything you need to know about Social Security, plus forms, FAQs for various services, and Medicare information. Some publications are offered in Spanish.

U.S. News Colleges and Careers Center: .edu

http://www4.usnews.com/usnews/edu/home.htm

An indispensable resource for the college-bound, **.edu** provides four big clusters of information: Get into College, which offers school rankings (Rank-O-Rama), admissions test dates, and more; Beyond College, where you can find advice on job benefits, hot jobs and where they can be found, and graduate school rankings; Financial Aid, which gives advice on how most effectively to fill out the forms and negotiate aid offers; and Alt.Campus, where you'll find music and film reviews, political and social action discussions, study-abroad opportunities, and practical advice.

RESEARCH

Discovery Online

http://www.discovery.com/

Divided into five community areas (history, nature, science, exploration, and technology), this site features stories, contests, games, and conversations with experts, all exclusively produced for Discovery Online. You'll find Discovery Live!, a live weekly radio show and a list of any chats on the site. You can also access the television program listings for the Discovery Channel, Animal Planet, and the Learning Channel. Best of all, you can search the entire Discovery Online site for information on previous programs, features, and online specials.

FindLaw: Internet Legal Resources

http://www.findlaw.com/

Doing some legal research at FindLaw can help you make the most of your day in court or hour in a lawyer's office. FindLaw includes LawCrawler, a search engine

allowing focused searches for legal information; Cases and Codes, a growing library of case law and state codes, including Supreme Court decisions; Legal Minds, where you can discuss legal matters; FindLaw Online MCLE, which provides continuing legal education credits through interactive courses; and much more.

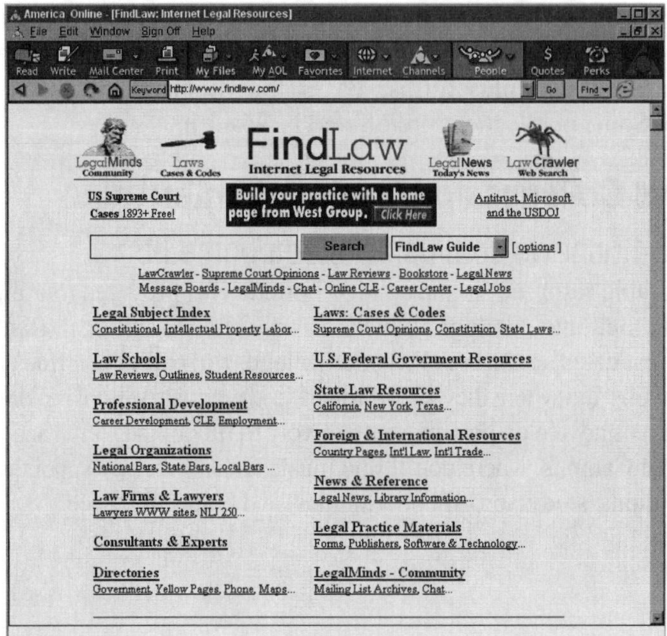

Library of Congress

http://www.loc.gov/

E pluribus unum might be the motto of the Library of Congress Web site: this site consists of many sites, each worth a visit. American Memory, for example, contains a collection of documents, photos, movies, and sound recordings that tell America's story. A dozen other virtual exhibitions can be browsed, too. Or, use Thomas to read the full text of any current legislation under consideration in the House and Senate. Under Research tools, search the Vietnam era POW/MIA Database. The holdings of the LOC itself can be searched, but you'll have to make a real visit to the spectacular reading room to pursue your studies.

MAGELLAN Geographix Maps—Interactive Atlas

http://www.maps.com/DOCS/atlas.html

Geography buffs will love this online interactive atlas, which begins with a clickable globe—just click on one of the regions of the Earth to get started. Then you are taken to a long list of options and can drill down to maps that are more and more detailed. These maps, excellently designed for either online or presentation use, may be purchased and downloaded. As GIF images, they are ready to use on a Web site. Since they are multilayered designs, you can edit and customize them by turning on or off layers such as land masses, city names, and rivers or by changing colors and fonts to meet your needs.

My Virtual Reference Desk— A One-Stop Site for All Things Internet

http://www.refdesk.com/

Here's a real timesaver for kids with homework. This well-organized jumpstation points to a vast array of useful Web resources. The most valuable features are First Things First, a list of recommended sites to visit first thing in the morning; My Favorite Applications and Utilities; My Search Engines, an organized compilation of over 150 search engines; My Virtual Encyclopedia; and My Virtual Newspaper. Here you can also find a huge list of computer and Internet links. Be sure to check out the current time, U.S. national debt, U.S. population clock, world population clock, and online calculator.

NationalGeographic.com

http://www.nationalgeographic.com/main.html

NationalGeographic.com gives you the world, from geography education to Collectors' Corner, from the Map Machine to the National Geographic Publications Index, where you can search some 108 years of National Geographic Society publications. The NG/kids area includes an online version of World magazine, Today's Amazing Facts, and chat areas where kids can talk with other kids from around the world.

On-line Dictionaries

http://www.bucknell.edu/~rbeard/diction.html

Ever taken two hours to look up a word? Be prepared to get lost in the 400-plus dictionaries of over 130 languages heroically assembled by Professor Robert Beard at Bucknell. Included are multilingual dictionaries (a tremendous resource for creators of international Web resources) and specialized dictionaries of banking, music, philosophy, and much, much more. Never again be stumped by that acronym or Latin phrase!

On-Line English Grammar

http://www.edunet.com/english/grammar/index.html

This wonderful resource serves students, writers, and all who have forgotten the finer rules of sentence construction, parts of speech, and all of those fun things your English teacher tried to fill your head with...oops—those things with which she tried to fill your head. Search the online grammar by topic, visit the Grammar Clinic discussion group, or try out your skills in the English Language Practice Pages.

Reference.com

http://www.reference.com/

Reference.com seeks to be the premier resource for Internet discussion groups: newsgroups, BBS's, and mailing lists. Reference.com simplifies the process of sifting through all of those sites and helps you find *just* the facts you need. Select the type of Internet forum you want to search, enter your keyword, and Reference.com returns a list of matches, sorted by relevance or alphabetically.

Today's Fun Fact

http://www.dreamsville.com/CSN/Wardo/fact.html

Trivia lovers, unite! If you always win Trivial Pursuit by a mile, if you're already forming your response in the form of a question before *Jeopardy*'s Alex Trebek has flipped over his own answer card, then this funky little Web site is just for you! If you have a burning desire to learn a new Fun Fact every day, subscribe to Today's Fun Fact by e-mail to receive tasty trivia nuggets in your mailbox five days a week!

The World Factbook Master Alphabetical Index

http://www.odci.gov/cia/publications/nsolo/factbook/global.htm

Whether you are traveling to Egypt or have a paper on Albania due, the *World Factbook* provides a digestible amount of useful facts, maps, and information on all the countries of the world. Country information includes a look at the economy, communication, defense, flags and maps, geography, people, and transportation.

WWWebster Dictionary

http://www.m-w.com/netdict.htm

Writing a term paper and finding yourself stuck mid-sentence? Looking for just the right turn of phrase? On AOL, start at Edit | Dictionary (the Merriam-Webster dictionary), or *keyword: Dictionary*. On the Internet, start at the WWWebster Dictionary, where you can do a simple search for a word or phrase and get a full dictionary entry on the word in question. If that word has multiple forms (i.e., it appears as different parts of speech), you can click on the version you prefer to get definitions for. Once you have those definitions, you can click on the Thesaurus button to find a variety of synonyms to your word, all of which are cross-referenced across the system. The Merriam-Webster Web site includes goodies like the Language Info Zone, Words from the Lighter Side, A Word for the Wise, and the Word Game of the Day.

SHOPPING

1-800-FLOWERS

http://www.1800flowers.com/

keyword: Flowers

1-800-FLOWERS has quickly grown to become one of the biggest online vendors, and its Web site now lets you place orders. On this site, you can see photos of the different options available so you'll know ahead of time just how your arrangement will appear. In the Quick Shop area, select an occasion (e.g., birthday, anniversary), a category of gift (e.g., flowers, gift basket, balloons), and your preferred price range.

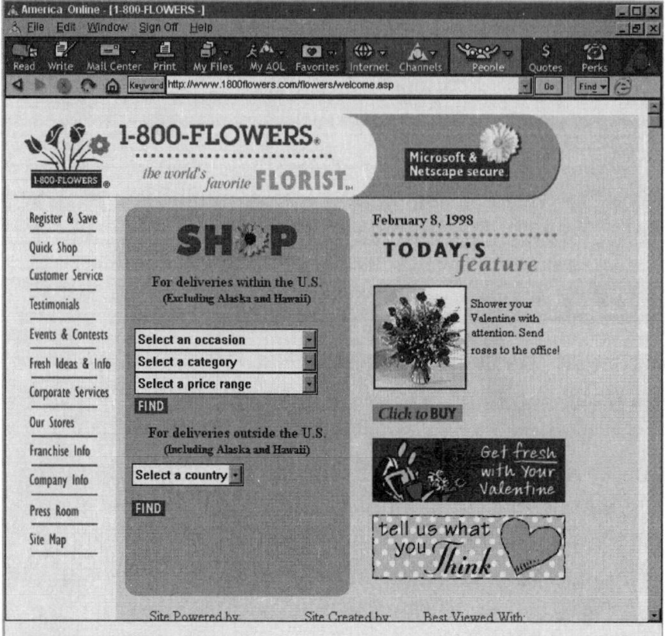

Getting There

All the vendors in this section have major Web sites at which you can make purchases. Some have AOL areas as well. And some of the Web sites have been customized for AOL members' ease of navigation.

The keywords in the Shopping section take you to either the AOL area, the Web site, or the AOL area that in turn makes it easy to access the Web. The information is all pretty much the same, however. Many more vendors would have been included here, were it not for space restrictions. The Shopping channel remains the best place to discover online shopping opportunities.

Amazon.com

http://www.amazon.com/

keyword: Amazon.com

This bookseller has inspired a generation of new businesses that exist only or primarily on the Internet. Amazon.com stands out by using the Internet to compete successfully with some very big competitors. Amazon does more than let you search for any book in print and hundreds of thousands of books not in print. You also get Editor's picks in many categories and the chance to rate books yourself. With a credit card handy, you can order anything and enjoy discounts on many popular and new titles.

Attention Shoppers

AOL has provided an alternative to crowded malls for years. In the Shopping channel you can choose from dozens of merchants selling hundreds of thousands of products in every major category—home, office, family, and leisure. Here's a sampling of the services available when you shop on AOL.

- *Comparison shopping.* Start with Consumer Reports (*keyword: Consumer Reports*) for unbiased and widely respected reviews that will help you decide which fax machine or car or anything else to buy.
- *Free reminder service.* At *keyword: Reminder* you can enter those birthdays and anniversaries you can't afford to forget, so you won't ever be caught empty-handed.
- *Order from print catalogs.* With a paper catalog in hand, order online by clicking Order from Print Catalogs at *keyword: Shopping Services.* Orders can be placed from almost 20 major catalogs, including L.L. Bean, Hammacher Schlemmer, and The Sharper Image.
- *The AOL Guarantee.* AOL guarantees your satisfaction and helps meet this goal by checking out all its merchants and maintaining the highest level of credit card security. *Keyword: Guarantee.*
- *Last-minute shopping services.* At *keyword: Quick Gifts*, find out how to get that Mad About You or Baby's Here basket in someone's hands as fast as possible.

- *The AOL Visa card.* Earn free AOL hours, pay no annual fee, and enjoy a low APR with AOL's own Visa card (*keyword: AOL Visa*).
- *Low price guarantee.* Join Shoppers Advantage for assurance that you will pay the lowest price on 250,000-plus products and enjoy a two-year warranty on most of them. Get the details about this AOL benefit at *keyword: SA*.
- *Perks.* With the size of AOL's community come some hefty material benefits for members. The new Perks menu on the AOL toolbar identifies many of these values, including the low-price AOL Long Distance plan, which allows you to check your bills online (*keyword: LD*).

American Greetings Online

http://www.greetingcard.com/
keyword: AG Cards

American Greetings Online has taken into the 21st century the age-old tradition of sending cards. On this Web site (whose design always reflects the next holiday), you can order traditional cards, e-mail postcards, even animated greetings to be sent to your loved ones. You can also register with PhotoNet in the Add-a-Photo area, which gives you an online source for photo reprints, enlargements, GIF files for Web use, and more (it requires that film be developed at a PhotoNet-participating dealer). The site also offers unique gifts that can be personalized with your photos.

Audiobooks.com

http://www.audiobooks.com/

If you commute or travel and have a cassette player in your car, be sure to visit Audiobooks.com. On this Web site, you can browse through a vast range of titles, from literary classics and language study to current bestsellers, from management gurus to philosophers, and much more. Listen to great thoughts read by the authors themselves or by talented actors and readers, such as Patrick Stewart reading Charles Dickens' *A Christmas Carol*.

Barnes and Noble

http://www.barnesandnoble.com/

keyword: barnesandnoble

The world's biggest bookseller is also among the world's biggest booksellers online. Do a book search through over one million titles, browse the long list of subjects available, or participate in live online events with authors. You can get personalized book recommendations or rate books in various categories, too. The database records your preferences based on what you buy and can then recommend new selections for you. Read and write Member Reviews of other books, or join a BN Book chat area. Join a preexisting group or design one of your own. It's easy to make a purchase, and discounts apply to many in-stock titles.

eToys.com

http://www.etoys.com/

keyword: etoys

eToys carries over 1,000 items, from Barbie to BRIO. You can browse their collection by age, level of development, or toy category. The Award Winners section gives a list of products recognized by the top parenting organizations and publications, so you know you're getting high quality toys for your child. eToys also carries a full line of children's software titles from companies such as Broderbund and Knowledge Adventure. Clear photos and colorful text make this Web site as much fun to play with as the toys you can order from eToys.

Garden Escape

http://www.garden.com

keyword: Garden Escape

Is your idea of happiness fresh soil under your fingernails? Do you know what the color green *smells* like? Then Garden Escape is the ultimate Web site for you. Ask the Garden Doctor why your daffodils look dejected or how to bring new vitality to your vegetable garden. The Garden Planner software can help you design the flowerbed or kitchen garden of your dreams. You can even enter your Zip code and the computer will help you choose plants that are right for your area of the country. The seeds of tomorrow are a click of the mouse away.

Lillian Vernon

http://www.lillianvernon.com/

keyword: Lillian

The famous catalog that occasionally shows up in your mailbox is now *always* available online. Lillian Vernon's online catalog has many of the same products she sells in her paper catalog: toys, home office products, household helpers, personalized gifts, sports and travel gear, kitchen equipment, and decorative items. Build your own Lillian Vernon catalog by specifying the types of items you are interested in so you can search for them later.

Music Boulevard

http://www.musicblvd.com/

keyword: MB

This popular music database can be searched by artist name, album name, or song title, and the classical listings can be searched by composer, conductor, orchestra, performer, album title, and catalog number. Order CDs even before they hit the stores. Visit the MTV CD Lounge to find CDs by the artists you have seen on MTV, or access e-mod singles, where you can buy and download CD-quality music right over the Internet. You can even listen to sound samples of many CDs before making a purchase.

Omaha Steaks

http://www.omahasteaks.com/

keyword: Omaha

The best place to buy the finest corn-fed midwestern beef is long-time AOL merchant Omaha Steaks. You can go shopping for various cuts in different combinations and find new cooking ideas in the Recipe Exchange. Make sure to check out the weekly specials, then sharpen those steak knives and plan a feast.

Onsale.Com

http://www.onsale.com/

keyword: Onsale

Onsale is a live, interactive auction house specializing in computers, peripherals, sporting goods, auction classifieds, and much more. Onsale "recreates in electronic form the fun and thrill of bidding at an auction, where prices and availability change in response to customers' actions." Going once, going twice…

SPORTS

College Sports News Daily

http://chili.collegesportsnews.com/

Whether you're a college athlete or just a big fan of college sports, be sure to visit College Sports News Daily. This Web site covers college football, basketball, soccer, golf, volleyball, baseball, and softball, as well as occasional features on other college-level athletic events. Get the latest scores, with updates every 15 minutes on game days. Read features and look up division scores and standings, daily game times, team stats, and individual stats. So go and visit this Web site for the Gipper!

Damn, We Suck!! A Cincinnati Bengals Homepage

http://acad.fandm.edu/~MB_Schuster/bengals/bengals.html

The creator of this Web site claims that he has one of the few sites devoted to the Cincinnati Bengals, and its title pretty much explains why no one else seems to be rushing to post a new one. In addition to being witty and entertaining, DWS is actually a well researched, thorough resource for information on the Bengals, with frequent updates on news reports, game recaps (posted within hours of the game's end), game previews, commentary, and stats. Also interesting are drive charts (a graphical representation of every ball possession of the game) and depth charts (depictions of the major offensive and defensive alignments in the coming game).

ESPN SportsZone

http://espnet.sportszone.com/editors/liveaudio/index.html

Live broadcasts of ESPN Radio, NBA basketball, and more can be heard from this Web site, which provides a full schedule of ESPN Radio broadcasts. You will need the latest version of the RealAudio Player to be able to listen to these programs, which you can download from the ESPN site, and you must also subscribe to ESPN SportsZone. Then you can listen to the latest edition of ESPN SportsBeat, ESPN Radio Weekend, and NBA games while you surf the Web.

Fantasy Sports Northwest

http://www.webcom.com/~fsnw/

Okay, so you think you're the big sports expert, eh? Well, prove it. Go to Fantasy Sports Northwest, the Internet's oldest company devoted to fantasy sports. What does this mean? You get a pile of play money to draft a football, baseball, basketball, or hockey team and follow it through weekly stats into the championships. Keep a foot in reality with links to real teams and other sports-related sites.

Golf.com

http://www.golf.com/

For those few hours spent *off* the links, Golf.com is the perfect Web site for the golfer. All topics are covered: the latest news reports, updates on current tours and player rankings, equipment features, playing tips, local events, travel suggestions, even articles on the big business of golf. You can register to take golf lessons online to improve your swing or your stance. Better yet, register for fantasy golf and avoid all that pesky walking and bag-carrying altogether!

Internet Waterway

http://www.iwol.com/

Internet Waterway is the premier resource for boating, fishing, and water sports. There are many rivulets at this Web site. The Yachting section, for example, has a tremendous chart giving detailed state-by-state towing laws for transporting large craft over state and interstate roads. When you're done, go to the Marina Finder to search for a place to store that shiny new boat. Get up-to-the-minute weather reports and nexrad radar graphics for any part of the country once you're ready to set sail.

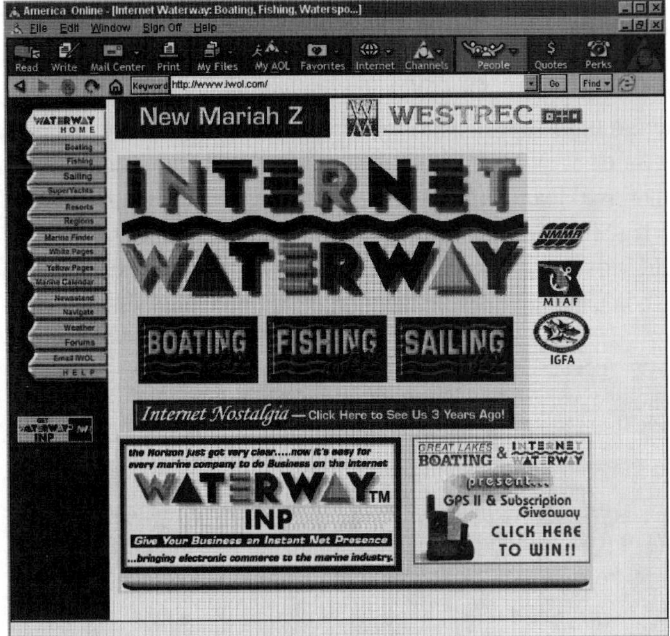

The Olympic Movement—Home Page

http://www.olympic.org/

This is the Web home of the International Olympic Committee. You can get Olympic news highlights, read the Olympic Charter, check the official IOC Medical Commission's medical code, and explore the Olympic Museum in Lausanne, Switzerland. If you're a devoted Olympics fan, you'll appreciate the International Olympic Federations section, where you can find a new page for each International Olympic Summer and Winter Federation. This site also hosts the official countdown clocks for Sydney 2000, Salt Lake 2002, and Athens 2004.

Planet Soccer

http://www.planet-soccer.com/

Can't get enough of the game outside? Then come in and blast off to Planet Soccer, where you won't believe the possibilities. You'll find coverage of U.S. soccer as well as international leagues, Major League Soccer, and youth soccer. Read up on the official FIFA (Fedération Internationale de Football Association) rules, learn about the history of soccer, and find the best soccer camp for next summer vacation. Hodgepodge consists of links to other soccer-related Web sites.

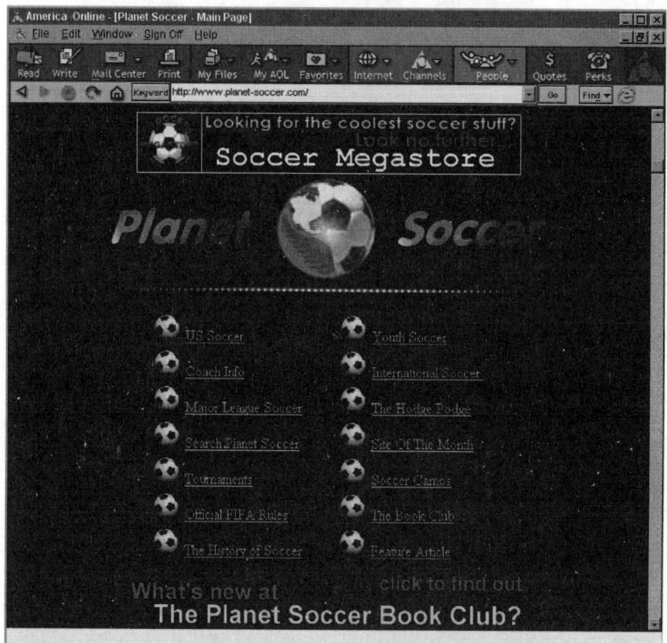

Real Fans Sports Network

http://www.realfans.com/

Real sports fans know what they like, and they're sure to love this Web site. It has a no-holds-barred approach to sports reporting that is refreshing and entertaining. You can check out the headlines in pro football, pro hoops, college hoops, and pro baseball. Look up the stats, slip into the press room, and exchange messages at the bulletin boards with other Real Fans.

SkiGate

http://www.skigate.com/

When you go to SkiGate, with its flashy angled graphics and fast-paced attitude, you'll feel like you've just pushed off the first ridge of the biggest black diamond of them all. Join in with the Powder Hounds, where you can post messages with other skiers from all over the country. The Warming Hut is an online magazine for the serious skier, with book reviews and features on technique and equipment. So what are you waiting for?! Step into your K2's and hit the moguls!

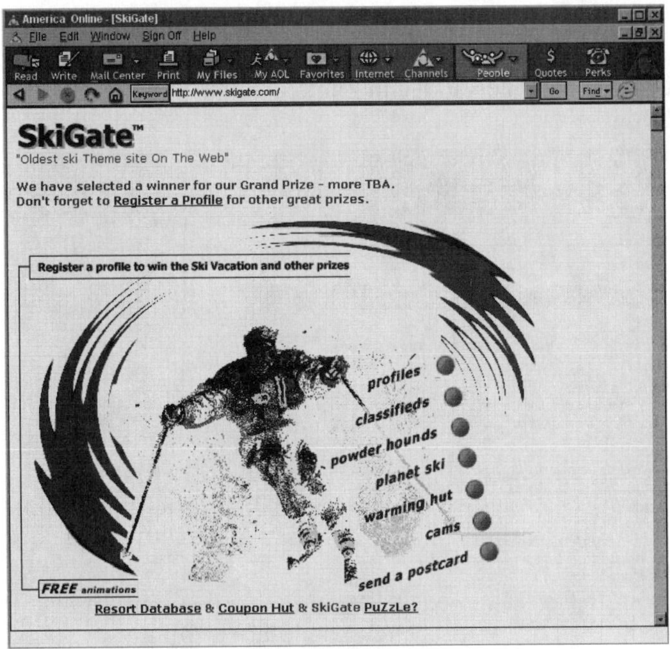

Sports Medicine and Orthopedic Surgery

http://www.sports-medicine.com/

Sports-Medicine.com was created by a board-certified orthopedic surgeon and team doctor for three different winning professional sports franchises. He knows his stuff, and he recognizes the Internet as a perfect medium for sharing his knowledge with professional and weekend athletes alike. This Web site has articles about some of the more common complaints (click on the "hot spots" of a picture of the human

body); you can also send e-mail to "Dr. Z" with more specific questions or for a second opinion. As the home page says, finally, a doctor you can talk to personally!

TRAVEL

Africanet

http://www.africanet.com/

Whether you're traveling to Africa or trying to understand the latest story in the newspaper, start at Africanet. For each of 30 countries, you can read about climate, economy, embassies, geography, history, and lodging options. Enter Africa Chat to discuss and share adventures with other travelers and get a peek at Tongabezi, considered by some the finest lodge in Zambia.

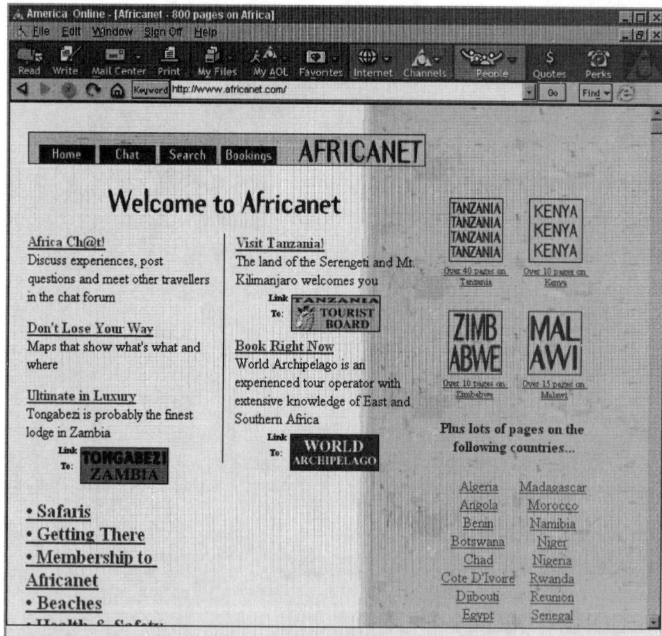

Budget Travel

http://www.budgettravel.com/

Budget Travel.com is for the world traveler who doesn't want to pay five-star prices. As a central location for budget travel information, it is definitely first-class, with resources on a multitude of locations and a wide variety of subjects. Check out the latest last-minute specials, search the budget travel pages for ideas, visit other countries and cities to get a taste of new locales, and scan lists of travel agents who can help you book it all.

City.net

http://www.city.net/

City.net is part of the Excite search service, focusing on travel information. This site is truly universal, with information on more than 5,000 destinations. For many of these, Travel Essentials provides a variety of tools: Fact Sheet, Where to Eat, Where to Stay, Calendar, Sightseeing, Shopping, and Transportation. Read the message boards and reservations areas. And don't forget to check out The Coolest Place on Earth Today.

The Cruise Ship Center

http://www.safari.net/~marketc/CruiseShipPage.html

The Cruise Ship Center and Cabin Exchange is a nonprofit Web site designed to bring to the public the most informative and unbiased material available on cruises and cruise ships. Over 85 destinations are presented, with profiles on the major cruise lines and ratings of over 150 ships. Cruise discounts are publicized here, along with the kind of details you want to know before sailing, like sample cabin floor plans, shipboard activities, and dinner menus from different cruise lines. The Cabin Exchange is a place where you can post your wish list, a kind of Help Wanted for cruises. Travel agents monitor these postings and get in touch with you if they can meet your price.

Family.com: Travel

http://www.family.com/Categories/Travel/

Family.com is an enormous Web site covering all aspects of parenting and family life, and the Travel area is just one fantastic resource contained within. Do a custom search in the Travel Archives by choosing a topic (such as Day Trip, Cities, or Camping), entering your child's age, then clicking Go. Road-Tested Vacations has

stories of other families' trips. Post your own or just take comfort from the fact that some family has an even worse travel horror story than yours.

Fodor's Travel Online

http://www.fodors.com/

Fodor's is one of those names that *means* travel—in many languages. The content of their thoroughly researched books on every travel destination worldwide has now been transformed into this excellent Web site. The Hotel Finder and Restaurant Finder give reviews on thousands of places to stay and eat worldwide. The Resource Center provides travel tips, language information, and more. Use the Personal Trip Planner to build your own travel guide for over 85 cities. Skiing USA gives you the scoop on 30 best resorts to visit. Before setting sail, stop at the Departure Lounge to chat with other travelers.

Lonely Planet On-line

http://www.lonelyplanet.com/

The well-known travel publisher has gone global with a Web site to use in planning your next adventure. Despite the funky graphics and typefaces, clever writing, and vast information resources, you won't get lost, thanks to the excellent navigation tools on every page. You might even visit this site for the beautiful travel photo gallery alone—you might not *get* to Istanbul, but it's still cool to *feel* like you were there. Once you have been somewhere else and lived to tell the tale, share it at the Thorn Tree, a gathering place "for travelers to share know-how and no-way."

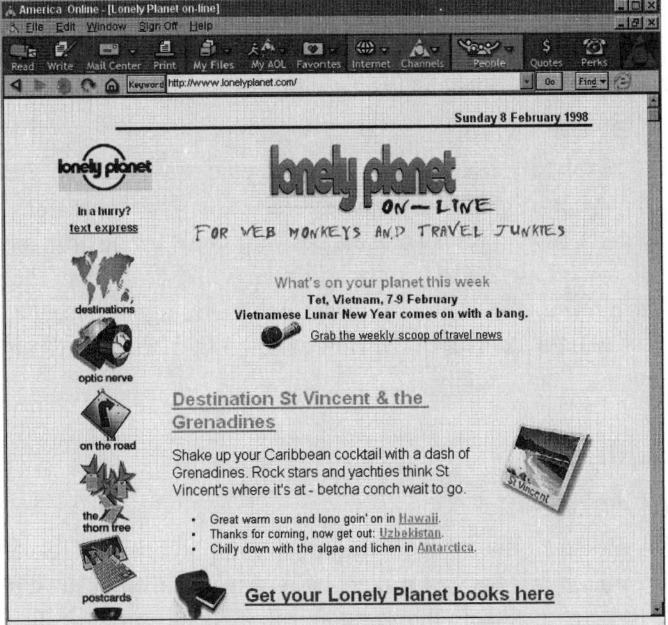

MapQuest! Interactive Atlas

http://www.mapquest.com/

It's clear to see why MapQuest! is the number one consumer travel site. With all its information and easy-to-use tools, all visitors feel welcome and comfortable. Plan a trip from top to bottom the easy way at TravelPlan USA, in conjunction with Mobil. Go to TripQuest to get clearly written driving directions and maps showing either door-to-door or city-to-city routes from and to locations of your choice. MapQuest can help you plan your move as well, with its link to MoveQuest.

Mexico Travel

http://mexico-travel.com/mex_eng.html

The official home page of the Ministry of Tourism for the government of Mexico, this site contains a national database of tourism information. It also offers a complete guide to beaches, architecture, archaeological sites, touring regions, fiestas, special events, business opportunities, and other travel-related services.

Preview Travel

http://www.previewtravel.com/

keyword: Preview Travel

As the perfect place to research and book all your travel plans, Preview Travel reminds you that your travel should be on your terms. There are many areas where you can research the lowest fares and best package deals for destinations around the world. Find the lowest airfare to your destination with Farefinder. The reservations system is connected to the same database that travel agents use, so you'll have real-time access to data for over 500 airlines and 13,000 hotels and rental cars from the major agencies. Start packing!

USA CityLink

http://usacitylink.com/

USA CityLink Project bills itself as the most comprehensive U.S. city and state listing on the Web today. This vast project helps American cities present themselves to the world, and it comes from the same marketing folks who created such classic Internet sites as Mardi Gras Madness, Santa Live, Cupid's Cove, and America's Birthday. Check out the City SpotLight every couple of weeks, when the CityLink Project spotlights one of the over 2,000 Web sites supporting different municipalities and regions. CityLink is an indispensable resource for travelers.

WORKPLACE

AboutWork

http://www.aboutwork.com/

AboutWork is *the* place to get help in dealing with today's workplace challenges. In Jobs, Jobs, Jobs, start with Know Yourself, with its self-assessment quizzes and career database. Then get tips on writing résumés and cover letters and acing interviews. Check out the Village/Work From Home area, and dig into the starter kit for your business plan, chatting with other freelancers and home-office workers. Small-business owners can get suggestions on making the right decisions and on choosing the right tools to make their enterprises successful. And take a break to jump into some live chat—ask questions, let off steam, learn to deal with this thing called Work.

Careerpath.com

http://www.careerpath.com

This popular service offers several novel and useful features: the ability to search job listings of more than 50 leading U.S. newspapers (you can search by type of position, and you can search several papers at once) and a single starting place for searching several Web sites for leading employers. You can also post your resume for employers to search when they're looking to fill certain positions. Additional features are available if you register, and registration is free.

CCH Business Owner's Toolkit

http://www.toolkit.cch.com/

Small business is not really all that small, making up the lion's share of the number of commercial enterprises in the U.S. That's why the CCH Business Owner's Toolkit is such a great resource for so many. The SOHO (Small Office/Home Office) Guidebook takes you through all the phases of a new business—planning your business, financing it, marketing your product, becoming an employer, and controlling your taxes. The Business Tools area has model letters, templates, and policies, plus forms and contracts you can easily customize, so you can spend your time making money instead of reinventing the wheel. Be sure to read the SOHO Daily News, with columns, commentary, tax updates, and other essential features.

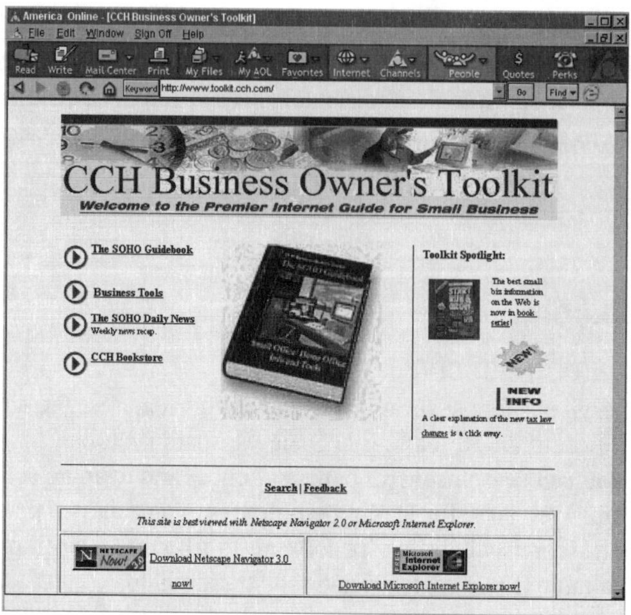

Ergonomics At Work

http://www.combo.com/ergo/

Did your mom ever nag you about your posture? Well, it turns out she was right all along. Sitting up straight and lifting heavy objects with your legs as opposed to your back are good for you. Ergonomics is the study of people's physical needs with respect to their working environment, and Ergonomics At Work is an excellent resource for information on staying fit at work, wherever you work, with a wide variety of articles and a list of Comfortable Solutions.

FTC ConsumerLine

http://www.ftc.gov/bcp/conline/conline.htm

ConsumerLine is the online presence of the Office of Consumer and Business Education of the U.S. Bureau of Consumer Protection. Here you can review the full text of consumer publications on topics that include autos, investments, health and fitness, and consumer credit. Learn about scams and fraud by reviewing the Consumer Alerts area and the Education Campaigns, a collection of consumer information initiatives. Copies of the publications are also posted in Spanish.

Monster Board: Jobs, Jobs, Jobs

http://www.aboutwork.com/AOL/jobsearch.htm

Get a job, pal!! No, seriously, you can get a job—any job—through the Monster Board. This Web site is one of the most complete job hunting resources on the Internet. For job seekers, there are over 50,000 jobs to choose from around the world, plus employer profiles, a résumé database where you can store a list of your achievements, and areas with career advice and relocation listings. Employers can recruit online with their job postings, search through the résumé pile, and learn more about recruiting on the Internet. Or, linger at the list of career events, from online open houses to career fairs. The trade show search utility puts you in touch with the major employers in your industry.

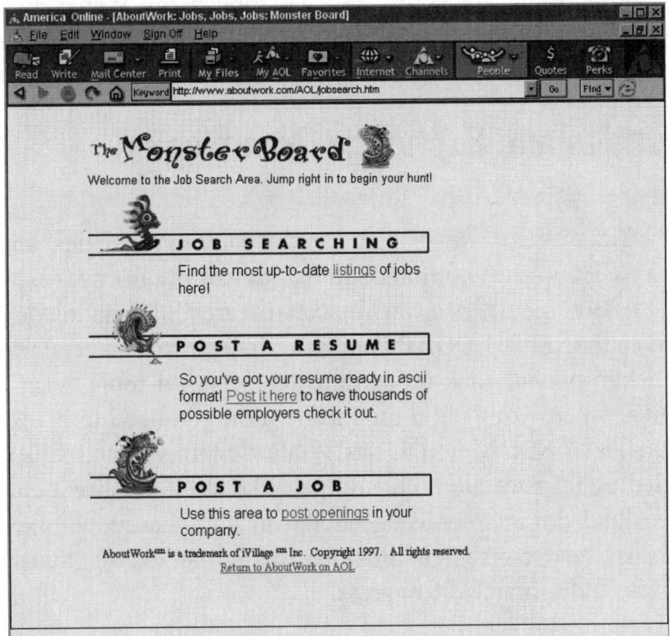

PrimeHost

http://www.primehost.com/

America Online's Web design and hosting service (*keyword: Primehost*) puts businesses on the Internet. If your business isn't already on the Web, you can learn more about PrimeHost here. By quickly getting you on the Internet, PrimeHost can give you

that competitive advantage. After following PrimeHost's four easy steps to a Web site, you can then communicate your product or service to the 10 million members of AOL, as well as to the rest of the Internet, for a very reasonable charge per month. PrimeHost also offers special services like free listings in dozens of search engines, discount pricing on Web design, listing in the AOL Business Directory, and more.

UPS Tracking Online

http://www.ups.com/tracking/tracking.html

Okay, take a deep breath...you *know* you shipped that package, but it hasn't arrived at its destination yet. Relax: UPS put its tracking software online for just this kind of emergency. (As did some of their competitors, such as FedEx, whom you can find at **http://www.fedex.com**.) Track any UPS bar-coded shipment, anytime, anywhere in the world by simply entering your tracking number at this Web page. You can also calculate the rate to send your next shipment with UPS or order UPS custom software solutions to help you better manage your shipping and receiving operations.

U.S. Securities and Exchange Commission

http://www.sec.gov/

This is the official Web site of the United States Securities and Exchange Commission (SEC), the nonpartisan regulatory agency responsible for administering federal securities laws. You can research information on any publicly held company in the SEC's EDGAR database of corporate financial filings, with its easy-to-use ticker symbol look-up and custom retrieval tools. Visit the Investor Assistance area, where you'll find the information you need to invest wisely and avoid securities fraud. SEC News Digests, Public Statements, and SEC Enforcement Actions (including investor alerts) are all posted here. An entire area dedicated to small business and the art of raising capital in compliance with securities law. Visitors will also find convenient links to the White House, Senate, House of Representatives, and Library of Congress.

America Online - [US Securities and Exchange Commission]
File Edit Window Sign Off Help
Read Write Mail Center Print My Files My AOL Favorites Internet Channels People Quotes Perks
Keyword http://www.sec.gov/
Go Find
About the SEC
Investor Assistance & Complaints
EDGAR Database
SEC Digest & Statements
Current SEC Rulemaking
Enforcement Division
Small Business Information
Other Sites to Visit
Text only | Search non-EDGAR documents | Search EDGAR Archives
SEC & Year 2000
U.S. SECURITIES AND EXCHANGE COMMISSION
"We are the investor's advocate."
Current News:
SEC Chairman Arthur Levitt, California Officials To Hold Investors' Town Meeting in Palo Alto
Staff Legal Bulletin No. 5 (Disclosure Obligations re: The Year 2000) Revised
First-Ever Hemisphere-Wide Investor Education Campaign Planned
SEC Website To Discontinue Gopher Service Temporarily
New Information Technology Employment Opportunities

Appendix A

Your AOL Connection

So, you have the AOL 4.0 CD or disk. Or you're using AOL 3.0 and want to move up to AOL 4.0 for Windows. Or you want to become an AOL member and start using AOL 4.0 right away. How do you get from here to the Internet? What do you do first?

- *Already a member?* If you have AOL 3.0, it's never been easier to *upgrade* to a new version of AOL, and you can start with your installed version of AOL; you don't need a disk. Your access numbers, Personal Filing Cabinet, and other personal belongings, including your password, will be automatically moved for you, if you wish. See the next section, "Existing AOL Members: Upgrading from an Earlier Version."
- *Want to join AOL?* If you're joining AOL and don't already have AOL installed, you will have to use the CD or disk for AOL 4.0. See the section "New AOL Members."

Note *You can access AOL using a local network or another Internet Service Provider (ISP), instead of by modem connection to AOL's network, as explained in "Using AOL with a Network or Internet Service Provider." However, you must still install the AOL 4.0 software as explained in the following sections for existing and new members.*

The balance of this chapter covers

- Signing on
- Using locations
- Modifying your setup
- Upgrading AOL 4.0 to any future versions of the software. Upgrading is free, sometimes automatic, and never requires putting another disk into your computer.

For all the factors involved—computer types, modem types, software versions, access numbers, service types, billing plans, and coexistence with earlier versions of AOL on the same machine—AOL has done an amazingly good job providing a simple and self-explanatory way of installing and setting up its software, regardless of your starting point and PC configuration. With AOL 4.0, installation and setup have gotten even easier. After the software is installed you can proceed directly and seamlessly to setting up your connection and (if necessary) your account.

However,

- If you have general questions, you'll find useful information in the Help menu, which is available even if you've installed AOL but haven't yet registered.
- If you need help using AOL, sign on and go to QuickStart: A Guide for New Members (*keyword: Quickstart*); or Learn to Use AOL (*keyword: Learnaol*); or Member Services (*keyword: Help*). For help with the Internet, go to *keyword: Nethelp*—or, use this book!
- If you can't install or register for some reason, call one of the phone numbers at the end of this appendix.
- If you've registered and have questions about your connection or your account, try *keyword: Help*, *keyword: Access*, or *keyword: Billing*.

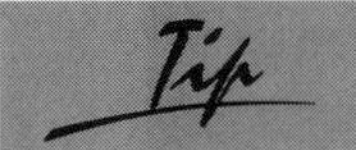

To use a keyword, just sign onto AOL and type it into the AOL Address box and click Go.

EXISTING AOL MEMBERS: UPGRADING FROM AN EARLIER VERSION

If you are already using AOL 3.0 for Windows, AOL has made it as easy as possible to move up to 4.0. You do not need a new disk or CD.

1. At *keyword: Upgrade*, click Get AOL 4.0 Now. If asked, confirm your desire to download the new software. If asked to choose which version of the new software you want, choose 16-bit if you have Windows 3.1, or 32-bit if you have Windows 95 or 98.
2. Follow the prompts, and click Agree when asked whether you accept the licensing agreement. (This agreement pertains to the powerful scrambling

technology AOL now uses in its browser; exporting such software is restricted by the U.S. government.) When you click Accept, then Download Now, you'll see the following window, which tracks the progress of your download.

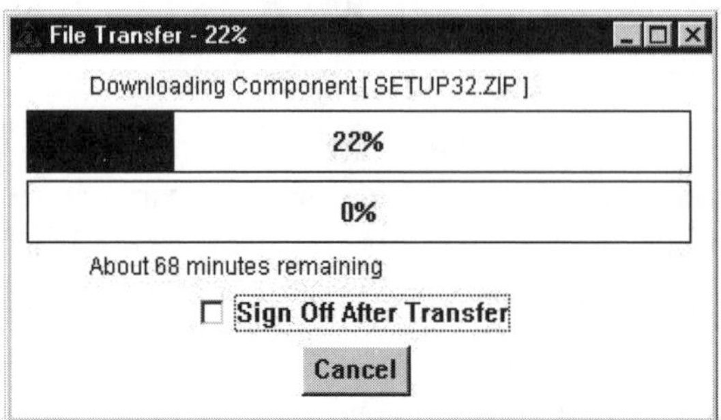

Note *If your download is interrupted for any reason, start back at Step 1. AOL will attempt to resume the download from the point at which it was discontinued.*

3. When the software has downloaded, installation starts automatically. You'll be automatically signed off AOL and will then be asked to close other Windows programs. Use ALT-TAB to switch to open Windows programs one at a time, closing each of them. Switch back to the AOL installation window, and click Yes to proceed to the Welcome to America Online window.

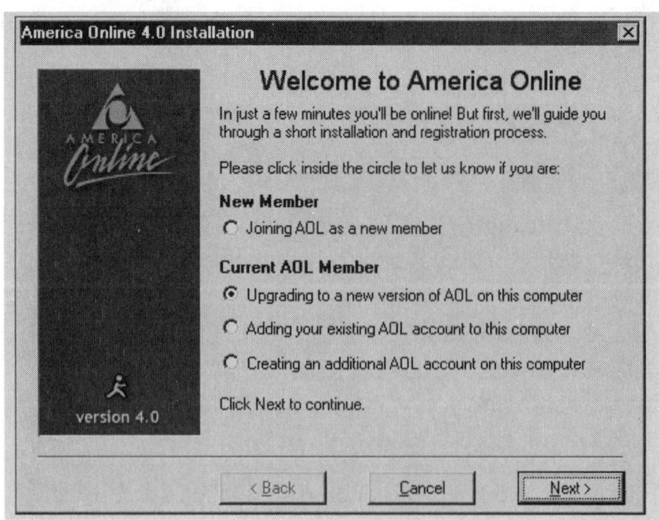

4. Select one of the following, then click Next.

   - **New member** You *are not currently an AOL member* (don't currently have an AOL account).
   - **Upgrading** You *are a member* and have installed an earlier version on this machine.
   - **Adding AOL account to this machine** You *are a member*, but there is no AOL software on this computer.
   - **Creating an additional AOL account** You *are a member*, and someone else has a copy of AOL on this machine—you don't want to sign on as a guest anymore!

Note *The following steps assume you* are *an AOL member and are* upgrading *from AOL 3.0. If you are just joining AOL (option one), the installation procedures are virtually the same, but when you sign onto AOL for the first time you will need to supply information about your connection as well as personal information, as described in "New AOL Members." For options three and four, see "Putting a New or Additional Copy of AOL on a PC."*

5. OK, you're going to *upgrade*. If there is more than one copy of AOL on your machine, you'll now be asked to indicate which one to upgrade (and from which to transfer your preferences). Generally, select the one whose "last used on" date is the most recent. Click Next.
6. You'll be asked where you want to install AOL. Note that on Windows 95, the AOL directory is **c:\America Online 4.0**, not **c:\AOL**. If there's an earlier copy of AOL 4.0, AOL will ask you to set up the new one in **c:\America Online 4.0*a*** or whichever letter is next. Click Next.
7. You're next presented with the Downloaded Files Action window. You have the option of *moving* files from the old AOL Download directory to the new America Online Download directory. Or, you can *copy* them, so you'll have the same files available from the old and new versions of AOL. Or, you can choose not to move them, creating an empty Download directory. Click Next.

8. When prompted with Launch Options, put a check in the box if you want to start AOL whenever you turn on your computer. Select this option if you use AOL all the time. Even if you don't select this option, AOL will be readily available from many places, especially if you're a Windows 95 or 98 user. You can launch AOL from the Windows 95/98 Quick Launch taskbar, from the Start menu, or from the desktop. Make a choice and click Next.

   AOL next checks how much disk space you have available. If you don't have enough, you can open the Windows Explorer or Windows 3.1 File Manager and do some deleting, returning to the installation program when you're done. (You'll need at least 70 megabytes of free hard drive space. See "Recommended System.")

   The Setup program then installs AOL, along the way displaying an overview of AOL 4.0's new features. The process shouldn't take more than a minute or so.

9. After installation, you're asked whether you want to print a detailed description of AOL 4.0's many new features. (You also get the chance to take a tour of AOL 4.0 when you sign on for the first time. Plus, from the Help menu there's a new option called What's New in AOL 4.0!) Click Finish when you're all done. You'll be given the opportunity of signing onto AOL immediately.

If you ever upgraded an earlier version of AOL, you may remember having to set up your connection and other preferences all over again for the new version. In moving up to 4.0 you will be happy to find that everything is transferred to the new version automatically when you upgrade: your phone numbers and other connection settings, your Personal Filing Cabinet, your Favorite Places, your Address Book (newly alphabetized), and (if you want) even the files you've downloaded using AOL 3.0. Also, your current icons for AOL will be updated, so you won't get confused about which icon to click. However, the old version of AOL will co-exist on your hard drive with the new one. Sometimes an older version can serve as a useful backup.

All you have to do to sign on is open AOL, type in your password, and click Sign On. You can jump ahead to the "Signing On" section just ahead:

Putting a New or Additional Copy of AOL on a PC

Say you are already a member but use AOL on a different computer, so you want to set up a *new copy* of the AOL software on a new or different computer.

Or, you are a member but want to set up an *additional copy* of AOL on a computer—instead of using someone else's account as a guest, for example.

You would choose option three or four, respectively, in Step 4 above. In either case, the process is *almost* identical to the steps in "Existing AOL Members" above, which you'd use if you were a member upgrading a copy of AOL and transferring all your earlier settings on the same machine.

However, you'll likely be starting from a CD and not from *keyword: Upgrade*.

Also, you will not be transferring any preferences or other personal information, because your preferences aren't on the new machine. This means that when you try to sign on for the first time, you'll have to supply information such as your modem speed and port (which you can let AOL figure out), your preferred access numbers, and the screen name and password you'll be using with this new/additional copy of AOL 4.0. Also, you won't have the option of transferring downloaded files or using your Personal Filing Cabinet with the new/additional copy.

Tip *To move your old preferences from one copy of AOL to another, go to the /Organize directory of your old copy of AOL. Look for a file with the same name as your screen name (so if your screen name is Sevenup, your preferences file is named Seven.up). Copy that file directly to the new /Organize file, using a floppy disk if the old and new versions are on different machines. Copying preferences in this way overwrites the new preferences file automatically created for you when you install AOL.*

NEW AOL MEMBERS

This section provides an overview of what you need to install AOL 4.0 and what information you must provide in setting up a new connection and new account. Joining AOL is a short trip, with three legs:

- *Installing AOL* means putting a copy of the AOL software on your computer's hard drive. If you just bought a new computer, AOL may be already installed for you.
- *Setting up your phone connection* means providing information about your modem (which AOL can usually figure out by itself) and choosing the local telephone numbers you want to use to access the AOL network.
- *Setting up your account,* or *registering,* means providing AOL with address and billing information

The whole process has been greatly simplified, so that the transition from one leg to the next is automatic, and you're provided with a great deal of information along the way.

What You Need

The CD or disk is the key to getting online, but it's not all you need to use AOL. You'll also need:

- A modem and phone line (even if you plan to access AOL over a network)
- An amply equipped PC (see the "Recommended System" box)
- A credit card or other payment means
- A password and screen name

Your Connection: Dial-up or Network

You can access America Online using AOL's network, AOLnet, which you'll use for normal dial-up access using a modem. You *don't* use AOL's network if you're

- Running AOL with a local TCP/IP network, such as you find in many organizations. If you have any questions about your network or need any help, ask your system administrator. If you can access the Internet over your work network, it's probably a TCP/IP network.

or

- Running AOL with a dial-up SLIP/PPP connection to an Internet Service Provider (ISP).

Note *You can use AOL with both a modem and a network, changing locations as required (see "Using AOL with a Network or Internet Service Provider"). Appendix B explains terms such as SLIP, ISP, and TCP/IP.*

CONNECTING OVER A MODEM *Dialing* into AOL requires a modem, a physical device that lets your computer send and receive data over the telephone lines. Your modem can be installed inside your computer (internal modem) or plugged into the back of the computer (external modem). It can be low-speed (9,600 bps or lower) or high-speed (28,800 bps or higher); AOL now supports 56,000 bps modems. Unlike ordinary Internet Service Providers, with AOL you will usually never need to worry about the details of your modem: parity, baud, hardware handshaking, and such issues. The AOL software figures out what modem you're using. If you are technically adept, however, you can tweak all you want.

Tip *If you don't yet have a modem, buy the fastest one you can afford. External modems are easier to install, but they do take up space on your desk. Once you're online, you can buy a better modem on AOL at* keyword: Modem Shop.

CONNECTING OVER A TCP/IP NETWORK OR ISP To use AOL over a TCP/IP local area network (LAN) or Internet Service Provider (ISP), you must have access to a local TCP/IP network or an account with an ISP such as AT&T's WorldNet, Netcom, Mindspring, or any of the hundreds of local ISPs. For a Web site that provides a complete directory of ISPs, see **http://www.thelist.com/**.

Recommended System

Packing a ton of features into a graphical user interface (GUI) requires what a couple of years ago would have been a mainframe computer to run the resulting program. The minimum recommended system for the AOL 4.0 program is just about average; however, for running a Windows application—and as with all Windows applications—the more, the better. Here's what you need:

- 16 megabytes of RAM
- A 486 or higher microprocessor (AOL for Windows); Pentium (AOL for Windows 95)

- 30 megabytes of hard drive space
- 640 × 480, 256 colors or better display
- 14.4 or faster modem

Your Means of Payment

In using an online service such as AOL, you incur two costs: one is your monthly phone bill from your phone company, which may reflect your calls to AOL if they are toll calls or local calls above your basic service. Even if you use the Bring Your Own Access plan with another ISP, you will have to pay the charges of connecting to the ISP by modem.

The other cost is the AOL bill. AOL bills you monthly or annually, and you must provide credit-card information (type, number, expiration date) when you register. AOL can also debit your checking account directly, but adds a fee to your bill in order to defray the costs of providing this service. Once you're online you'll find more information about such things at *keyword: Billing*. You must provide this information even if you'll be signing on via a network other than AOL's (that is, if you use an ISP or local area network). When you use an ISP or LAN, you will still be billed but at a lower monthly or annual rate (currently, $9.95 per month).

Way of Identifying Yourself

In registering with AOL, you'll be asked for a screen name and password. Your *screen name* is how other people on AOL and the Internet will recognize you; a *password* is how you keep your unique account confidential.

Note *If you have an AOL CD or disk, you start registration using the registration code and password provided on the AOL software package; during registration, you choose your own screen name and password, which uniquely define your Master Account. From then on, you use your own screen name and password, and can add up to four additional screen names for your Master Account.*

SCREEN NAME A screen name is how AOL members and people on the Internet will know who you are—it forms the personal part of your e-mail address (see Chapter 3), and it identifies you in chat rooms and Instant Messages. You can choose any combination of letters and numbers, using between three and ten characters, but you can't use punctuation marks. Screen names on AOL must be unique. They are not case sensitive, though AOL displays your screen name, in e-mail messages and elsewhere, with an initial capital letter and any other capital letters *you* use during registration. On the Internet you'll see the term *username* more than *screen name*, but they're the same thing.

Tip *When you register, you might not get your first choice, so be prepared with several alternatives. Many people use their first initial plus last name (VLenin) or first name plus last-name initial (LeonidB). Here's another tip: write down your screen names and associated passwords. On the Internet many Web sites ask you to choose passwords, logins, usernames and the like. I find it difficult to remember them all, so I started writing them in a notebook.*

PASSWORD A password ensures that only you can sign onto AOL with your screen name, and it can also prevent unauthorized access to your Personal Filing Cabinet. On AOL you'll need a password that is hard to guess if someone has any *other* information about you. So, it's a good idea to make your password different from your name and the name of anyone in your family. Nor should it contain your birthdate, mother's maiden name, or Social Security number. Creating a password that consists of arbitrary and alternating numbers and letters is a good way of making your password unguessable—and a good way of making it hard to remember, so write it down!

Caution *Never, in any circumstances, tell anyone your password, even (or especially) if someone claiming to work for AOL asks for it. As a policy, no one who really works for AOL will* ***ever*** *ask you for your password. If someone does ask for your password, say no, then write an e-mail message to AOL's Community Action Team (CAT): just go to* keyword: Notify AOL. *If the solicitation occurs in an e-mail message to you, forward the message as proof of the incident to TOSemail1 or TOSemail2. Display the message, click Forward, type* ***TOSemail1*** *or* ***TOSemail2*** *in the To box, and click Send. In Chapter 3 you'll learn everything you need to know to use e-mail.*

SETTING UP YOUR CONNECTION AND ACCOUNT

With a modem hooked up and turned on, with your computer powered up, with the phone line free, with a credit card at hand and a screen name and password in mind,

grab that disk and follow the instructions on the package. The Setup program guides you step by step, telling you what it's doing and informing you whenever *you* must do something. During installation you may have to make some choices; I recommend that you:

- Choose a full installation, so you can take advantage of all the goodies (such as plug-ins) AOL has packed into AOL 4.0.
- Place an AOL icon in your Windows 95 Start menu, so you can easily get to AOL 4.0 from the Windows 95 taskbar. An AOL 4.0 icon (shortcut to an icon, actually) will also be placed on your Windows 95 desktop, along with an icon labeled Internet, which you can use to open a stand-alone version of the Microsoft Internet Explorer browser. You can run this browser either when you're signed onto AOL or when you're using the connection of another Internet provider.

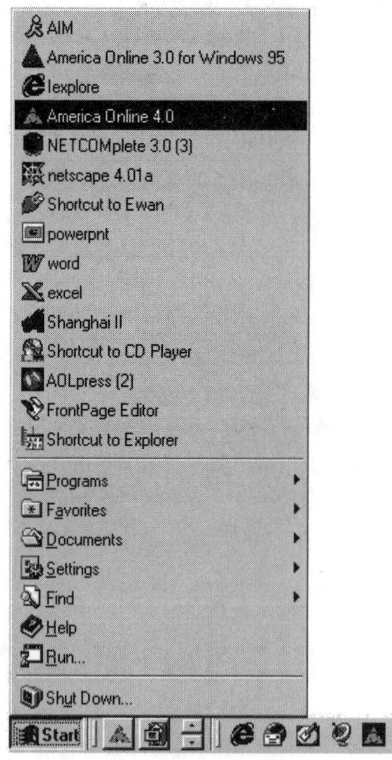

After installation, you'll be asked whether you want to sign onto AOL. I recommend that you do so. The Setup program will automatically search for your modem, then use the modem to dial a toll-free AOL number and retrieve the latest access numbers. Then you'll be prompted to choose an area code and access numbers within that area code. Next AOL hangs up, and connects using your local access numbers. At this point you'll be asked to set up your personal account, providing an address, credit card number, password, and screen name.

Note *The access numbers you choose create a* location. *To use AOL when you travel, you can create additional locations and access numbers within locations. (See "Signing on from Different Places.")*

SIGNING ON

Signing on, also known as logging on, means connecting to the AOL service (and, if you choose, from there to the Internet). Signing onto AOL is not like flipping a light switch. First of all, you have to open the AOL program, which is large, so it may take a moment or two between the time you double-click its icon and the time AOL displays on your screen.

Here's the ordinary way you sign onto AOL. Other ways, such as signing on as a guest, are discussed a little later.

1. Double-click the AOL icon, whether it's in a Windows 3.1 program window or on the Windows 95 desktop. (To start from the Windows 95 Start menu, move your mouse to the bottom of your screen or wherever your task bar is hidden; click Start and release the mouse button; at the top of the Start menu, select America Online 4.0 and release your mouse.) Of course, if you asked that AOL load automatically when you start your PC, you don't have to bother with this step.

   After the program comes up, the Welcome window appears, and the cursor (where you type something) should be blinking in the Enter Password box. If it's not, move the mouse arrow there, and click.

2. Type your password in the Enter Password box. Your screen name will already be entered for you (in the Select Screen Name box).

3. Click the Sign On button. AOL now looks for the modem, dials the local phone number you chose during registration, establishes a connection with the AOL network, verifies your password, and you're ready to navigate the Internet! If the phone number is busy, you can set it up to redial automatically, as explained later in "Editing Your Location."

Tip *The first time you sign on, AOL will ask you whether your software should remember your password. If you let it remember your password, you won't have to enter it again, and the Enter Password box will disappear from the Welcome screen.*

It's a good idea to weigh the convenience of storing your password against the risk that someone else can easily access your account.

Switching Screen Names

With AOL 4.0 for Windows, you no longer have to sign off in order to switch to a different screen name within the same Master Account. So, if you sign on to read your mail and check your portfolio, your child can then switch to the Games or Kids Only channel without your having to sign off first. This feature comes in especially handy at busy times of the day, when you may occasionally encounter busy signals in signing on again.

To switch screen names, select Switch Screen Name from the Sign Off menu, then choose a screen name and provide a password when prompted. For more information, select Screen Names under the My AOL menu.

USING AOL WITH A NETWORK OR INTERNET SERVICE PROVIDER

If you already have a SLIP or PPP connection with an Internet Service Provider (ISP), you can run AOL over that connection. If you regularly sign on in this way, you'll want to create a special location, as shown in Figure A-1.

How do you know if you have such an account? If you have Internet access through a commercial service such as AT&T's WorldNet and pay a monthly fee for dial-in access (using a modem), you probably have a SLIP or PPP connection. If you're using a modem and have a graphical Internet program such as Netscape or Eudora, you almost certainly have such a connection.

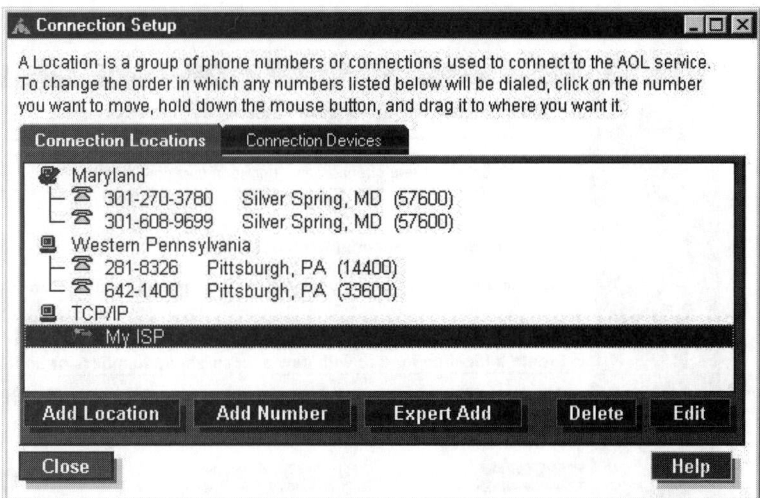

FIGURE A-1 AOL locations. Wherever you take your laptop, you'll be able to sign on by simply changing locations and clicking Sign On

AOL's Bring Your Own Access pricing plan makes it easy and cost-effective for subscribers of other services to use the content on the America Online service, but connect over *another* network. With an ISP, you may have access to (non-AOL) mail and News servers, and hence be able to use third-party programs such as Eudora or the mail and News readers built into the very latest versions of Netscape Communicator and Microsoft Internet Explorer.

Note *If you're using a stand-alone browser (one that's not integrated into AOL) and you click a news: or mailto: link, you'll be taken to your ISP's mail or News program, and will only be able to use the link if you've correctly set up your ISP's mail or News servers (that is, with your company's network or your Internet Service Provider).*

To set up AOL to work with your TCP/IP connection:

1. Open AOL but do not sign on. From the Welcome screen, click Setup. (If AOL is already open and you're not signed on, you'll see a Goodbye screen, which also has a Setup button; click it.)

2. In the America Online Setup window, click the last option, as shown here, and than click Next.

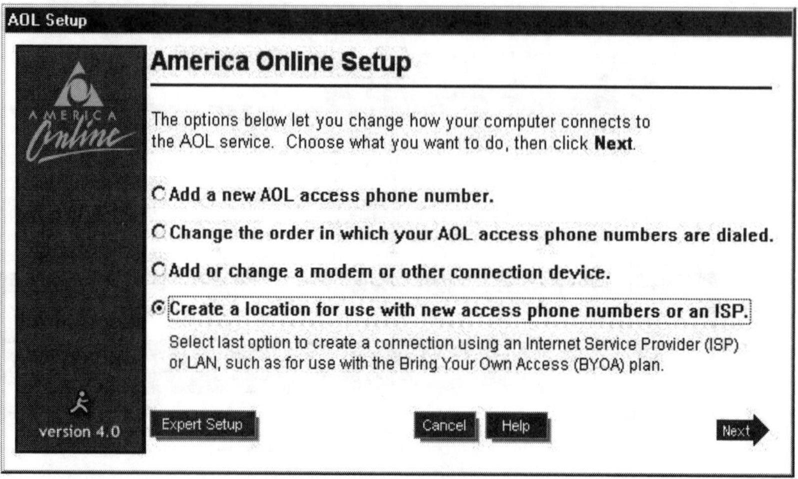

3. In the Add Location box, click the second option:

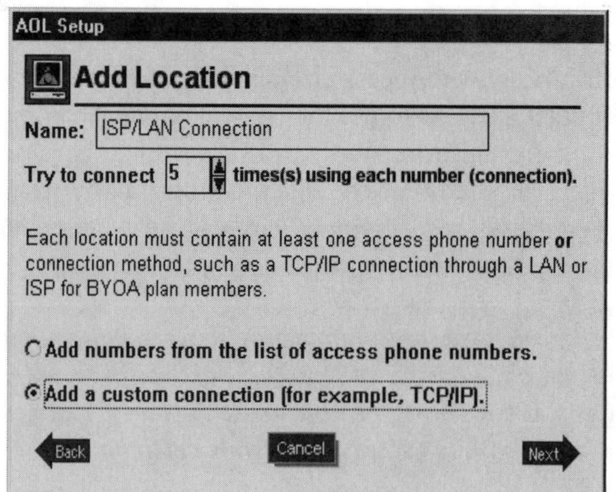

You don't have to give the new "location" a special name; it will be named automatically. Nor must you indicate the number of times to try to connect. (The connection is made, after all, using your other Internet Service). AOL names your connection ISP/LAN Connection, or something similar. Click Next, and your location is created.

4. Click the "Add a custom connection" radio button. Click Next.
5. In the Add Number (Connection) window:
    - Name your TCP/IP connection something like **My ISP** (Figure A-2).
    - In the Connect Using drop-down list, select "TCP/IP: LAN or ISP (Internet Service Provider)."
    - Place the TCP/IP connection in a location using the "Will be added to this location" drop-down list. In this case, do nothing to keep the connection inside the location just set up.
    - Click OK.

To use your TCP/IP connection:

1. Log onto your other (ISP or LAN) connection.
2. From AOL's Welcome (or Goodbye) screen, select the TCP/IP connection (ISP/LAN, or whatever it was named) from the drop-down Select Locations box.
3. Click Sign On if you have had AOL remember your password; otherwise, first type in your password and then click Sign On.

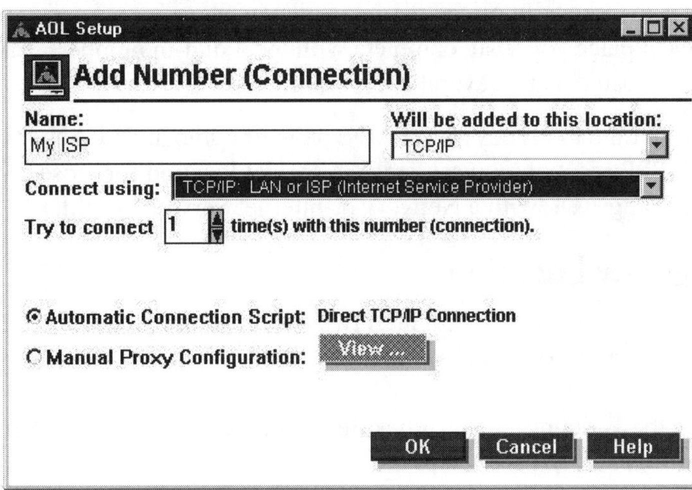

FIGURE A-2 Setting up a TCP/IP connection to use a network or an ISP

With TCP/IP selected as your network type, modem information becomes irrelevant to AOL. Even if you're using a modem to access WorldNet, for example, you're using TCP/IP to access AOL. Any problems with your modem or connection should be pursued with the Internet provider through whom you're getting access.

Caution *You can stay logged onto AOL only as long as your ISP or LAN connection is active; if you're disconnected from your ISP or LAN, you'll be disconnected from AOL as well. On the other hand, signing on through an ISP won't keep you from getting automatically disconnected from AOL* by AOL *if you are inactive for a long period. Getting logged off of AOL, however, won't disconnect your underlying ISP connection.*

SIGNING ON FROM DIFFERENT PLACES

If you access AOL from different places or by different methods (using a TCP/IP network or dialing into AOL's network), you may want to create different locations. With AOL 4.0, locations are conveniently selectable from a drop-down list on the Welcome screen. (You used to access them using the Setup button.)

Why create different locations?

- If you encounter a busy signal (in the evening, say), you can provide alternative access numbers and have AOL automatically redial your access numbers until one connects.
- If you're frequently on the road, you may want to keep a separate location for each place you visit, complete with local dial-in numbers. Each location can contain several access numbers.
- If, from time to time, you use AOL on your company's LAN or over a SLIP/PPP account, you can create a special location for those occasions. See "Using AOL with a Network or Internet Service Provider."

Adding a New Location

You can add a new location (with at least two access numbers) or add a new number to an existing location. Here's how to add a new location.

1. From the Welcome screen, click Setup. In the America Online Setup window, click Expert Setup.
2. In the Connection Setup window, click Add Location. Give the new location a name (such as *Western Pennsylvania* or *Delaware*). In the Try

to Connect box, indicate how many times you want AOL to redial each access number contained in the location. Click Next.

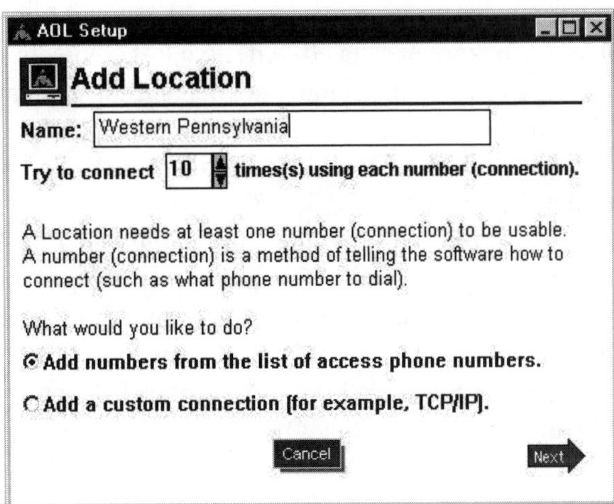

3. AOL now asks you for the new location's area code. Type one, and click Next.

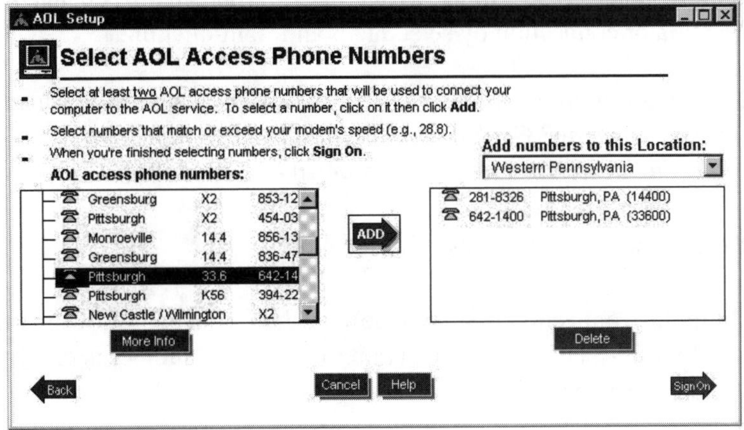

4. Pick at least two access numbers for the area code, selecting from the list on the left and clicking Add to move the number to the list on your right. For each, you'll be asked to edit the number, adding an area code if, for example, the area code is geographically so big that some calls in the same area can be considered toll calls. Click Done, then Sign On (or Sign On Again). AOL now automatically tries to dial the first new number in the new location. If it's busy, it dials the second.

Take Advantage of Automatic Redialing

Locations contain *connections* (access numbers). With AOL 4.0, you can set up your software to *cycle* between connections. When the first connection in a location is busy, the next one is dialed. After the last connection in a location is dialed, the second cycle begins, dialing the first and subsequent connections. To set the number of cycles per location, click Setup in the Welcome/Goodbye screen, select the Location (e.g., Maryland in Figure A-1), and adjust the "Try to connect" number from 1 to 25. Click OK.

Each of the connections in a location can be redialed 1 to 9 times during its turn in the cycle. So, if you know that a number in a location connects readily or supports faster modems, you could set it to redial up to nine times before the next number in the cycle is dialed. In the Connection Setup screen, select a Connection (e.g., Silver Spring in Figure A-1), click Edit, and adjust the "Try to connect" number from 1 to 9. Click OK.

Editing Your Location

From the Connection Setup window, you can drag an access number from one location to another (if it's in the wrong place). You can also change the details for any location or connection by selecting it and right-clicking.

Tip *Do you prefer silence to the grinding and whooshing sound of a modem connecting? Click the Connection Devices tab. Select your modem, then click Edit. In the Speaker Volume drop-down box, select Off. Click OK.*

To add a new access number to a location:

1. In the Connection Setup window, in the Connection Location tab (Figure A-1), select the location to which the number is to be added. Click Add Number.
2. Follow Steps 3 and 4 of the previous section ("Adding a New Location"). You can supply only one (instead of two) access numbers.

Signing On As a Guest

From time to time you may find yourself using America Online on someone else's computer. Your computer might be in the shop, or you might be traveling without your own computer.

From the Sign On screen's Select Screen Name drop-down list, select Guest and click Sign On. Select a location, then click Sign On. You'll connect as you do normally. What's different is that you'll be asked for your screen name and password *after* you connect. Once AOL verifies this information, you'll be able to see your Buddy List, send and receive e-mail, and use the core AOL features, but you won't be able to do things requiring access to the hard drive of the person whose machine you're using—you won't be able to use Favorite Places, Download Manager, or Personal Filing Cabinet.

With AOL 4.0, you can now add a new copy of AOL to a machine that already has AOL. Follow the steps in "Existing AOL Members: Upgrading from an Earlier Version," but in Step 4 indicate "additional copy of AOL."

Signing On While Traveling

If you take your portable on a business trip or vacation, you can still access AOL even if your ordinary local access number is halfway across the country. From the Welcome Screen, click Setup. Then add a location for the area code you are visiting. For parts of the U.S. without a local access number, you can use AOL's surcharged 1-800 numbers (1-888-245-0113 or 1-800-716-0023). These numbers currently carry a surcharge of ten cents a minute or $6.00 an hour.

If you're traveling abroad, you can still sign onto AOL using the AOLGlobalNet network, which carries a *variable surcharge* depending on the location from which you're calling. The current surcharges are available at *keyword: International Access* (click Access Surcharges). With this network, AOL is currently available in hundreds of cities around the world.

Note *AOLGlobalNet is quite a different thing from the international services available on AOL. Think of AOLGlobalNet as a physical network. Think of the new international services as communities much like AOL's channels, except that they serve the full range of needs of members in different countries. Currently, there are international services in Germany, France, the U.K, and Canada. Each has sports, entertainment, news, and more. These services are available free to AOL members by going to the Channels menu and clicking International.*

A

MODIFYING YOUR SETTINGS

What if you get a new modem, or change your address, or want to change your screen name? With America Online, it's easy to change the information you provided during set-up and registration.

IF YOU GET A NEW MODEM While *offline*, start the AOL program and select Setup at the Welcome screen. In the Connection Setup window, click the Connection Devices tab, where you'll see one line of information about your current modem and another about your TCP/IP connection (if you have one). If your new modem is already installed and ready to go, click Auto Detect to let AOL hunt for your modem and figure out what its settings are. If you want to do it manually, click Expert Add, then follow the prompts to indicate the type of modem you're installing, its speed, whether you use touch dialing and ordinarily dial 9 to get an outside number, the port you are using, and whether you want your modem to keep quiet when it dials. Click OK when you're done, then click OK in the Connection Setup window.

To change settings for your existing modem—to change port, for example, or turn off the sound—select the modem in the Connection Devices tab and click Edit; it's the same window as used in Expert Add.

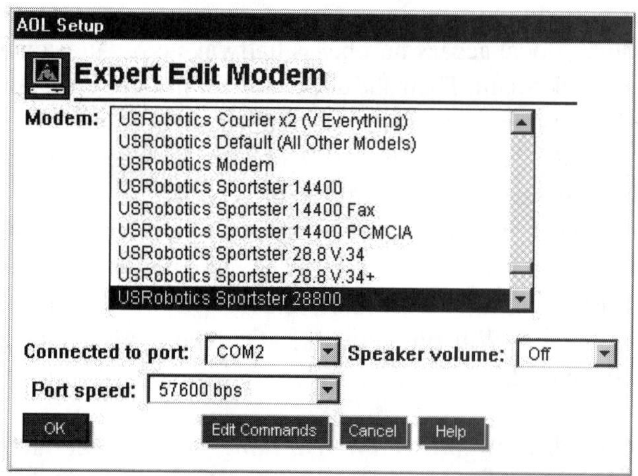

TO CHANGE YOUR PERSONAL INFORMATION (NAME, ADDRESS, ETC.) While online, go to *keyword: Billing*. Click Change Your Name or Address, or Change Billing Method or Price Plan, and follow the onscreen instructions. Or, use *keyword: Change* to change either your personal information or your billing information. To modify billing information, you will need to provide a password, and only Master Account holders can make this change.

IF YOU WANT TO CHANGE YOUR PASSWORD While online, go to *keyword: Password* and enter both your old password and the new one (twice, for verification). Write down your new password.

Note *My AOL|Preferences|Passwords is used to set a different kind of preference: whether your Personal Filing Cabinet is password protected and whether you store your password so you don't need it during Sign On.*

IF YOU WANT TO ADD A SCREEN NAME First off, you can't delete or change the main screen name for a Master Account (the one used to register with AOL). It's a unique identifier. Together with your password, it's how AOL knows who you are. You can, however, use up to four additional screen names in a Master Account and sign on using one of them instead. Each of these additional screen names gets its own password. *Keyword: Screen Name* (or *keyword: Names*—they're the same) has all the details; you can add screen names there too.

Why Would You Want Separate Screen Names?

If other people in your household use AOL, each person may want a separate screen name, in order to have his or her own mailboxes. Yes, each screen name gets its own set of three mailboxes (described in Chapter 3), and everybody gets their own storage space (2 Mb worth) using AOL's My Place, as described in Chapter 7.

- If you like to hang out in chat rooms, you may want different screen names for your various online personas.
- If you subscribe to many mailing lists (Chapter 4), you may be able to manage your mailboxes better by subscribing to lists from different screen names. If you ever delete a screen name, make sure to first unsubscribe from any mailing lists.

Parental Controls—which let parents control their children's access to the Web, e-mail, newsgroups, and other AOL or Internet features—can be set only by the Master Account holder for a particular screen name. See Appendix C.

If you do have several screen names, remember that only the computer where you established the names will be aware of them. So, if you set up a screen name at work, your home machine will be happily unaware of it. To update a computer so that it is aware of all the names you've added or deleted on other computers, go to *keyword: Names* and double-click Update Screen Names on My Computer.

A

Note *Only one screen name for an account can be used online at the same time and screen names must be unique, but with AOL 4.0, you can switch between screen names without signing off; just select Sign Off | Switch Screen Names.*

UPGRADING AOL

Upgrading AOL means getting a new version of AOL. For major upgrades, see the first part of this appendix. For incremental upgrades occasioned by new features, you will encounter more or less automatic upgrades. This is AOL's way of perfecting the current version of its software. If you don't have a CD but do have Internet access, you can always download the latest AOL software on the Web (**http://www.aol.com**) and by FTP (**ftp://ftp.aol.com**).

Minor Upgrades (Same Version Number, New Tool)

AOL has a powerful, simple, and free way of giving you incremental software releases. When a new service is added or an existing one enhanced, AOL automatically delivers the new software on the fly the first time you attempt to use it. Alternatively, when there's new software, you will be asked (in a little window) to update your AOL software automatically when you sign off. For example, if the browser's been spiffed up and you try to go to a Web site, you'll be asked to first wait for the new software to be downloaded. The beauty of such upgrades is that they both enable frequent essential changes and minimize the bother and abruptness of major upgrades.

While the software is downloading (in under a minute or two, usually), you may be presented with a New Features window describing why you are getting the software. After the software has been downloaded, you may be asked to allow the AOL software to restart itself (automatically). Click OK.

Numbers to Call If You Have Trouble

1-888-265-8001	To receive information on AOL products or services
1-888-265-8002	To upgrade to the current version or to order an AOL Membership Kit
1-888-265-8003	For billing information or to reactivate a canceled account
1-888-265-8004	For screen name or password assistance
1-888-265-8005	To obtain a new access number
1-888-265-8006	For AOL for Windows technical support
1-888-265-8007	For AOL for Macintosh or other technical assistance
1-888-265-8008	To cancel an account
1-888-265-8009	To request account credits

Appendix B

Indispensable Terms

For More Information

For an in-depth but easy-to-read technical encyclopedia, try magazine publisher CMP's **http://www.techweb.com:3040/encyclopedia**. *Matisse*, from the Internet Literacy Consultants, has clean and compact definitions of the most important Internet terms (**http://www.matisse.net/files/glossary.html**). Fuller definitions, with links to actual content, are available in the *Webopaedia*, from Sandy Bay Software (**http://www.sandybay.com/pc-web/index.html**). Finally, on AOL itself you will find quick definitions of important terms at *keyword: Glossary*.

address There are several kinds of addresses on the Internet. An e-mail address, such as **dpeal@aol.com**, is used by a person (me) to send mail to someone else. An Internet address, or *URL*, such as **http://www.aol.com** and **ftp://www.aol.com**, is used by people to request information from a computer. An *Internet Protocol (IP)* address, such as **206.139.24.100**, is used by computers on the Internet to send each other data. Gopher, Web, FTP, and e-mail addresses all follow the *domain name* system, and computers are set up on the Internet to "map" domain names to unique *IP addresses*.

Address Book On AOL, your Address Book lets you keep track of the people to whom you most frequently send *e-mail* messages. It lets you assign easy-to-remember names to those hard-to-remember Internet e-mail addresses. With your Address Book you can maintain simple mailing lists, assigning a single name to a series of e-mail addresses of people you frequently write at the same time. The new Address Book in AOL 4.0 can be alphabetized and edited, and personal information (and photos) can be maintained for each entry.

Address box On the AOL 4.0 *navigation bar*, the text box where you can type in either an AOL keyword or Internet URL, then click the Go button or press ENTER. Serves the same purpose as the old Keyword window, which is still available by typing CTRL-K or clicking the Keyword button to the right of the Address box.

agent Software used to perform some task automatically. Currently, many agents are being developed to automate the process of looking for information on the Internet. When you update your bookmarks in Netscape (as described in Chapter 10), you are using an agent.

Anonymous FTP *See* **FTP**.

ANS Stands for Advanced Network & Services, Inc., a company established as a nonprofit organization in 1990 to serve as the principle architect of the NSFnet, the U.S. network that was the immediate forerunner of today's Internet. Since 1991, ANS has been a pioneer in providing commercial access to the Internet. In 1995, AOL acquired ANS in order to provide reliable, fast, and affordable Internet access to a rapidly growing membership; in 1997 AOL sold the company to networking giant WorldCom. ANS provides private networking services to hundreds of American companies. For information about ANS's services and an overview of how the histories of ANS and the Internet are intertwined, go to *keyword: ANS.*

AOLnet America Online's high-speed, high-capacity data network, which provides modem access to millions of AOL members in hundreds of cities in the U.S. For more information, go to *keyword: Access.*

AOLpress Easy-to-use software for creating your own Web pages, described in Chapter 7. AOLpress lets you: create pages just as if you were using a word processor; edit your HTML; manage collections of pages or whole sites; publish pages on servers; and browse the Web. It's free and available at *keyword: AOLpress.*

Archie An Internet search service used for finding files available via anonymous (publicly accessible) *FTP*. Archie is a program that regularly visits known anonymous FTP sites, makes a list of files and directories at those sites, and makes the index available to people on the Internet to do file searches. Searches can be done by e-mail or Telnet, but the easiest way is over the World Wide Web. There are two dozen Archie sites around the world; all maintain the same index of files. *See* Chapter 8.

area, AOL *See* **forum**.

ASCII Stands for American Standard Code for Information Interchange; in practice, simple letters and numbers, unformatted so they can be read by computers

on any operating system (Mac, Windows, Unix, etc.). All *HTML* files are available in ASCII format, to make them as widely available as possible.

asynchronous vs. real-time communication Asynchronous is jargon for "not at the same time." Electronic mail and newsgroups are asynchronous types of electronic communication. You send a message to another person, or to a mailing list, or to a newsgroup for someone else to read later or not at all. *Synchronous* is the opposite of asynchronous; the more common term is *real time*. Chat, Instant Messages, Instant Messenger messages, and IRC all take place in real time, that is, with another person reading your message almost instantly after you've typed and sent it. Asynchronous communication is often more serious than real-time communication, which is more personal and direct. For more information, *see* Chapter 3 (e-mail), Chapter 4 (mailing lists), Chapter 5 (newsgroups), and Chapter 10 (IRC).

Automatic AOL Formerly known as FlashSessions. America Online gives you many options for quickly and automatically carrying out tasks online, so you can do the actual reading and composing offline. Many of these tasks can be done using Automatic AOL: reading and posting to newsgroups, reading and sending e-mail, and downloading files. With Automatic AOL (available from the Mail Center menu), you choose the activities you want to automate, then choose the times when you want these activities to occur (or you can do them *on demand,* that is, right now). With Automatic AOL, you could compose e-mail throughout the day but would only go online once a day to *send* all your messages at the same time. Similarly, you could *receive* mail and newsgroup postings either according to some regular schedule or on demand—go online once a day, say, and run an automatic session, then sign off. Once your mail or newsgroups have been downloaded, you can sign off and read everything offline, at your leisure and without online cost. For more information, *see* Chapter 4.

bandwidth The amount of data that can be transmitted over any communications medium (phone line or network) in a period of time, for example bits per second (bps).

BCC (blind carbon copy) In e-mail, a copy of a message sent to someone without the direct recipient's awareness. The direct recipient is the person whose e-mail address (screen name) is in the Send To field of the Write Mail window (if the message is sent from AOL). To send a BCC to someone, you put their e-mail address *in parentheses* in the Copy To field. You can send BCCs to more than one person by separating their e-mail addresses by commas. *See* Chapter 3.

binary A binary file is meant for a program to read; a text, or *ASCII*, file is meant for a person to read. In *FTP*, a mode used to transfer any *file* that requires a special program to use it. Basically, all files that aren't text are binary. AOL's FTP client doesn't require you to indicate whether a file is binary or text, but any *Winsock* FTP client you use, such as WS_FTP32, will require you to make this choice. When in doubt: use binary, since a text file can be transmitted in binary mode but a binary file can't be transmitted as text unless it's been encoded using a technique such as *MIME* (*see* Chapters 3 and 6).

bookmark Hot lists, bookmarks, Favorite Places, and Favorites all have the same purpose: to give you a means of keeping track of your favorite sites so you can easily return to them. *Bookmark* is Netscape's term for a list of favorite Web sites, while *Favorite Places* is AOL's term for your list of favorites available anywhere—on AOL, on the Web, in e-mail, newsgroups, etc. Microsoft's Internet Explorer browser, which is installed for you when you use AOL 4.0, refers to them as Favorites, and keeps them in the **c:/windows/favorites** folder. *See* Chapter 6.

bps *See* **bandwidth**.

browser Software used for displaying an HTML *page* on the *World Wide Web*. A browser takes a plain *HTML* page, which you download from the Web, and presents any images, formatting, and links contained on that page. AOL 4.0's browser is a customized version of the Microsoft Internet Explorer browser. Your browser is always available at *keyword: Web* or *keyword: WWW* (along with other ways discussed in Chapter 6). In addition, with *Winsock* you can run other browsers, such as Netscape Navigator. *See* Chapter 6 on using the integrated browser and Chapter 10 on using the Netscape browser.

Buddy List A list of your friends, colleagues, bosses, etc., who are currently signed onto AOL or (if they use Instant Messenger) logged onto their Internet service provider. You can send AOL buddies an Instant Message or invite them to a chat room, and you can similarly communicate with Internet buddies who use the free Instant Messenger service. You can edit your list by adding buddies on AOL or the Internet, and you can choose to be "invisible" to other people's Buddy Lists. More information at *keyword: Buddy*.

button A small graphic (picture) on AOL or the Web that can be clicked either to link to related information (that is, related to some information on the window where

the button is) or to *do* something (for example, print a Web page by clicking the Print button). The AOL toolbar consists of buttons.

CC (carbon copy, sometimes courtesy copy) In AOL's e-mail program, you send anyone a CC if you want the direct recipient to be aware of the CC. The direct recipient's e-mail address goes in the Send To field of the Compose Mail window, while people CC'ed go in the CC field. You can send CCs to any number of people by separating their e-mail addresses by commas. You can send CCs to people on AOL or on the Internet, or both. *See* Chapter 3.

channel **(1)** On AOL, communities and *forums* are organized into channels, based on either subject or the actual location of the communities. The subject-based channels are available in the Channels screen or from the Channels menu of the AOL toolbar. The best way to find specific content and forums is to click the Find button on the toolbar. **(2)** On *IRC*, a channel is the equivalent of a chat room, which can be formed by anyone and must have at least one person present to remain in existence. Unlike a chat room, a channel has an operator, who has broad powers to set the channel's topic, name other operators, and kick people out. *See* Chapter 10. **(3)** On the Web, a collection of the best Web sites about some big subject. AOL.com has Web Channels (parallel to the AOL channels), as do other search sites, such as Excite, Infoseek, and Lycos.

chat Chat is a form of real-time communication, meaning you communicate with a group of people by sending messages, which they can read almost as soon as you send them. On AOL, chat rooms are available in the People Connection channel and throughout the other channels. The closest thing to AOL chat on the Internet is *Internet Relay Chat (IRC)* (see Chapter 10).

check box In Windows programs such as AOL, the square check box gives you the ability to specify a choice (as at *keyword: Filesearch*). You can put a check mark in more than one check box (or no boxes). (With *radio buttons*, you can—and must—select only one choice.) You select a check box by clicking in the little square.

client Jargon for the software you run on your computer, such as an e-mail client or FTP client. On the Internet, client software interacts with *server* software. Clients receive, package, and transmit requests for information stored on servers. The whole Internet is built on client/server principles, with applications distributed across a network and millions of clients accessing the programs and data available on central and publicly accessible servers.

compress *See* **file compression.**

cookie A small text file created by a Web server and stored on *your* computer to keep track of the sorts of things you do on the server. Web designers create cookies in order to get information about users' browsing habits and to modify their site accordingly, or to present users with a customized view of the site. The cookie file can trace a user's "click path" through a site. Using AOL 4.0, you can set your preferences to be warned when a cookie is being created on your computer—you can then refuse to let the cookie be created. Some people consider cookies an invasion of their privacy. *See* Chapter 6.

DejaNews A search site (and the company that created it) used for searching for specific messages in tens of thousands of newsgroups. DejaNews has been incorporated into AOL NetFind (*keyword: Netfind*) and is available by clicking Search Newsgroups.

directory (1) The same thing as a folder—a named place on your computer, which you use to keep related files. Your computer has directories, as do FTP sites and Web servers. (2) In the context of Internet searches, a directory is a catalog of resources arranged into subjects such as Business and Medicine. A search directory is different from a search *index* in that it is created by people and hence it is selective, more or less subjective, and often annotated (with site descriptions, ratings, and comparisons). The major directories are Yahoo! and the Virtual Library. Some of the indexes, such as Infoseek, Lycos, and Excite, have their own directories, which are also known as *channels*. *See* "Search Terms and What They Mean" in Chapter 9.

domain name People use *domain names* to identify and communicate with computers connected to the Internet. Domain names consists of several parts, separated by periods (called "dots"), proceeding from specific to general. Your domain name as an AOL member is *aol.com*. The general part of the name (*com*, for example) identifies the domain *type*. The main domain types in the U.S. are *edu, com, mil, net, org,* and *gov*. Other countries usually have a top-level domain of two characters, such as *ca* for Canada and *nl* for the Netherlands. But you'll see three-letter non-U.S. domains (such as **www.corel.com**) and two-letter U.S. domains (such as **mcps.k12.md.us**). The domain name is the key part of every Internet address (URL). Every domain name maps to a unique numerical *IP address*.

B

download To retrieve a file from a generally accessible computer (*server*) in order to use it on a private computer (*client*), over networks such as AOL and the Internet.

You download files from the Internet in many ways: e-mail, FTP, newsgroups, and the Web. AOL's *Download Manager* queues files to download when you use e-mail or one of AOL's file libraries. AOL's browser handles Web downloads. *Uploading* is the opposite: it means copying a file from a PC to another computer, where it can be made available to others. On AOL some forums have software libraries into which you can upload files. Using Personal Publisher, you can upload files to your *My Place* area. Chapter 6 (on the Web browser), Chapter 7 (Personal Publisher), and Chapter 8 (on FTP) have information about downloading files with AOL.

Download Manager A program available only on AOL that manages files you download from newsgroups, files attached to e-mail messages, and files you download using FTP and AOL's dozens of software libraries. It *doesn't* keep track of Web site downloads. Using Download Manager you can download several files at a time (except via FTP), automatically decompress files you download, and keep track of when you downloaded them and where you saved them on your computer. Download Manager is available from the My Files menu even when you are offline, but offline use is limited to decompressing files and keeping track of where you downloaded files. Additional information about the Download Manager is available at *keyword: Download Info* and at *keyword: Download 101.*

drop-down box A window element that displays only the first item in a list. To see other items, click the downward-pointing triangle. To select, release the mouse, move your mouse arrow down the list, and click an item.

dynamic HTML Refers to the capabilities of HTML 4.0, the *HTML* standard, together with scripting languages such as JavaScript. Dynamic HTML gives Web designers much greater control of how a page looks to the user and how it responds to user actions such as mouse clicks. It requires more programming skill and planning, but frees the designer from the necessity of using *plug-ins*, *Java*, and other complex external files. The resulting pages are also smaller and download faster than pages linked to plug-ins and other large elements.

electronic mail Or *e-mail* or just *mail.* The main way to communicate with other people on the Internet. E-mail is an example of *asynchronous* communication, meaning it's not instantaneous; the other person may not see the message for days (or ever). AOL offers choices such as hyperlinks and highly formatted text when you send e-mail to someone else on AOL. Most of these features will be stripped out of mail sent to people on the Internet, however. Using AOL, you can send the same piece of mail to several people on AOL or the Internet at the same time, and you can choose to have one or more indirect recipients (*CCs* and *BCCs*). *Mailing lists* are a way of communicating with a group of people. For more information, *see* Chapter 3.

emoticon *See* **smiley**.

encryption A way of scrambling sensitive information to prevent others from accessing it. AOL's browser allows you to encrypt information like your credit-card number when you wish to purchase a product or service from a vendor on the Web. The integrated browser automatically uses an encryption technique called *SSL*, for Secure Sockets Layer, which not only encrypts data but can also guarantee the authenticity of the other party (to make sure the other party is the person he or she claims to be). *See* Chapter 6.

engine *See* "Search Terms and What They Mean" in Chapter 9.

Ewan A Telnet *client* described in Chapter 10. Windows software for using remote computers' databases, catalogs, games, and other services.

Explorer The file management program that comes with Windows 95 (it replaces Windows 3.1's File Manager). Internet Explorer is the name of the Microsoft Web browser, which has been customized for AOL and integrated into AOL 4.0. *See* Chapter 6.

extensions *See* **file extensions**.

e-zine Also known as a *'zine*, *zine*, and *Webzine*, an e-zine (short for electronic magazine) is a publication that appears exclusively on the Internet on a more or less regular publishing schedule, with its own editorial staff, writers, purpose, audience, and attitude. E-zines exist for every Internet service, including e-mail (where they're distributed by mailing lists), Gopher, and the Web (*Webzine*). E-zines have a reputation of being alternative, but some are devoted to mainstream topics as well. An excellent source of information is John Labovitz's searchable E-zine List of more than 2,500 e-zines at **http://www.meer.net/~johnl/e-zine-list/**.

FAQs Stands for Frequently Asked Questions. Sometimes pronounced as a word ("FAK") and sometimes spelled out ("F-A-Q"). In newsgroups, a classic format for answering questions about the scope of the topic and about the newsgroup itself (its

history, what's acceptable, etc.). The original idea was to get everyone up to speed and to keep newcomers from asking the same questions on a newsgroup. Usually, an individual maintains a FAQ, but everyone in a newsgroup can recommend modifications, giving many FAQs the status of authoritative, community-based documents. A FAQ is usually posted to the newsgroup in question as well as to **news.answers**. The **news.answers** archive, with hundreds of FAQs, is available at the **rtfm.mit.edu** FTP site, which is one of the FTP Favorite Sites available on America Online at *keyword: FTP* (click Go To FTP). The FAQ format has been adopted elsewhere on AOL and the Net. *See* Chapter 5.

Favorite Places An AOL-only feature that allows you to keep track of the places or content you like best, including AOL forums, Web sites, Internet newsgroups, and individual e-mail messages. With Favorite Places you can create folders to hold related content of different formats (e-mail messages and Web sites, for example). You access your Favorite Places folder by clicking the Favorites button on the AOL toolbar and selecting Favorite Places. *See* Chapters 2 and 6.

file PCs use files to store and make available programs and data. A file has a location (a specific directory or folder), a name (its filename), a type (or format, such as GIF), and a size (measured in bytes and kilobytes). Windows 95's *Explorer* lets you view the names, sizes, and dates of files and directories on your hard drive. *FTP* is the Internet service you use to *download* (retrieve) files from file archives located on FTP servers. AOL's many file libraries let you download files from AOL, including the programs you need to work with the files you download from the Internet. *See* Chapter 8.

file compression A technique for making a file smaller so it takes up less space on a computer and can be uploaded and downloaded more quickly. Compressing and decompressing files requires a special program such as WinZip. AOL's *Download Manager* can be used to automatically decompress some files. *See* Chapter 8.

file extensions In DOS and Windows, the part of a filename that follows the period, as with the **avi** in **vertigo.avi**. Extensions can tell you whether a file is compressed (*see* **file compression**), what operating system it's for (Macintosh or Windows), and what program you need to use the file. *See* Chapter 8.

FileGrabber Only on AOL! Newsgroups can be used to distribute files, such as software and sounds, but the files must first be converted from a *binary* format (readable by computers) into a text file (human-readable *ASCII text*). To decode the text and turn it back into a computer code (a usable file), the file must be decoded. AOL handles this for you automatically with a program called FileGrabber, which is accessed whenever you try to download a newsgroup posting containing such a file. *See* Chapter 5.

flame In Internet mailing lists and newsgroups, a heated and unproductive discussion. Flaming can be considered a form of hazing on the Internet. It can serve a rhetorical purpose, or it can be considered merely abusive and just plain obnoxious—a result of not respecting the other person because the communication seems anonymous. Flaming can be counterproductive insofar as it inhibits others from taking part in the communication or detracts from the subject. *See* Chapter 5.

FlashSession *See* **Automatic AOL**.

form In Web pages, a window giving you the opportunity to state your preferences or indicate a choice, as when you are taking a survey or buying a product. The standard elements of a form are a *text box* (where you type in something), *check boxes* or *radio buttons* (where you select from predetermined choices), and different kinds of lists. Forms help to make the Web interactive, not just a means of passively receiving information. *See* Chapter 2.

forum Information on AOL is organized into more than 1,500 topical forums, or areas, each with its own subject and community. Forums can have some or all of the following elements: message boards, dedicated chat rooms, links to related AOL and Web areas, a newsletter, events (with guests) and transcripts of events, libraries of software to download, and articles to read. Some forums have leaders, some don't. Most have their own keywords. Forums are organized in channels, and can be searched either across the entire AOL service (*keyword: AOL Find*) or using the AOL Channel Guide (*keyword: Channel Guide*).

forwarding e-mail Sending a message you've received to someone else. On America Online, if you select nothing in the original message to you, and then forward the message to someone else, you automatically forward the entire message. If you select any part of the message, you'll forward only what you've selected. In either case, you can precede the message with your own comments as well. When you forward a message on AOL, the Subject line is automatically picked up from the original message; all you have to do is supply an address in the Send To box. Any files attached to the message you received will be forwarded as well; you can't detach them.

frames Frames divide a Web browser into several windows, each of which displays a separate page. One benefit of frames is that they allow certain parts of a Web site to remain constant, such as the title, the table of contents, an ad, or the navigation bar. A drawback is that they can take up a lot of room. *See* Chapter 6.

freeware and shareware Freeware is software that doesn't cost anything—as opposed to shareware, for which you're expected (but usually not required) to pay if you continue using it. Freeware can be a limited version of full-blown commercial software, or it can be the older version of such software. Freeware and shareware are available on AOL (*keyword: Filesearch*), via FTP, and on the Web at sites such as **http://www.shareware.com** and **http://www.tucows.com**. *See* Chapter 8.

FTP The Internet's File Transfer Protocol service, the most efficient way of moving a file from one computer to another across a *TCP/IP* network. Using FTP is like having access to someone else's computer: you browse directories and you help yourself to (*download*) files you want, copying them to your own computer. Anonymous FTP sites are publicly available. (The word *anonymous* means that you automatically log in as **anonymous** and use your e-mail address as a password.) On AOL you can use both the *browser* and the built-in FTP *client* at *keyword: FTP* to search for and download files. Generally, the browser is better suited to searching, while the built-in client is better suited to downloading. The principle means for searching FTP for specific files is *Archie*. America Online offers excellent resources for using the files you download via FTP, and many of the files themselves are available on AOL. *See* Chapter 8.

Fwd: *See* **forwarding e-mail**.

Gopher An Internet service created in 1991 to permit easy access to Internet resources. Gopher simplified access in several ways. It organized resources in numbered lists, or menus, for easy selection. It provided English names instead of cryptic filenames, for clarity. It provided access to different types of resources, such as images, textual documents, Telnet sites, and FTP sites. The World Wide Web provides these same benefits, with the additional benefits of being able to directly display files of every kind and thus providing a better viewing and publishing platform. You search for Gopher resources using a program called *Veronica*. With AOL's browser you can access Gopher sites, and *keyword: Gopher* provides all the information and help you need to use Gopher on AOL, with a selection of the best sites. Most Gopher servers are not being maintained any longer, and few new ones are being created. *See* "Gopher's Swan Song" in Chapter 6.

helper application A small program, or utility, used to present an image or sound or video file. Before integrated *plug-ins*, AOL's browser used helper apps. With AOL 4.0, plug-ins have replaced helper apps, and most Web developers these days minimize the use of files requiring helper applications.

hierarchy *See* **newsgroup**.

home page (1) A home page, or personal page, is the creation of an individual, a way of publishing a resume or promoting a hobby via the World Wide Web. (2) A home page is also the opening page, or top page, of a Web site, the page from which you begin exploring a site or get an overview of its contents. (3) With AOL's browser (and with most browsers), your home page is also the page the browser opens to automatically when you start it (or go to *keyword: www* or *keyword: Web*)—unless you start at another page by typing a specific URL into the navigational bar. You can have the AOL browser open to any home page you wish. For information about the home page your browser opens to, *see* Chapter 6. For information about Personal Publisher, the free AOL feature that lets you create your own home page, *see* Chapter 7.

host (1) On the Internet, a computer that is addressable by (can exchange data with) another computer; it can accept and send *packets*. Sometimes (not quite correctly) used as a synonym for *server*. (2) To *host* a Web page means to make disk space available for it and to make it available to others on the Internet.

hot list *See* **Favorite Places**.

HTML Stands for Hypertext Markup Language. When you use the Web, you download HTML files from Web servers to your computer. HTML files are made up of text that has simple instructions telling a browser how to display text and other objects (centering, type size and type styles, and so on). HTML is the common language of the World Wide Web: all browsers understand how to read basic HTML, though they vary in their techniques of representing more advanced HTML. The HTML language is regulated in practice by the big software companies, such as Microsoft and Netscape, through the W3 Consortium (*see* Chapter 1). HTML is simple to learn, especially with editing tools such as AOLpress that create the tags automatically. AOL's Personal Publisher tool frees you from having to know any HTML to create a page, but for certain effects you may need to write HTML by hand. *See* Chapters 6 and 7.

http The *protocol* used on the World Wide Web governing the exchange of messages and files between Web *servers* and *clients* (*browsers*). When you enter a URL into your AOL browser, your browser first sends a message to a Web server asking it to send a specific Web page, then processes any return messages and displays the page itself.

hyperlink An image or piece of text on a Web page, e-mail message, AOL forum, or elsewhere that is linked to related content. On a Web page, you can tell a textual hyperlink because of its color and underlining. When you pass your mouse over any hyperlink (without clicking), the mouse arrow turns into a pointing finger, meaning you can click on it, and the address (*URL*) of the pointed-to resource appears in the status bar at the bottom of the AOL window. You link to that resource by clicking the hyperlink: move the mouse's pointer over the link and click once with the left mouse button. The browser lets you return to the place from which you linked using the Back button.

hypertext On the Web, a text document in which some phrases and individual words are hyperlinked to enable easy access to information related to the content of the document. Hypertext can function as a glossary linking to definitions of words; as a bibliography linking to related articles about the same subject; and as a way of getting related information that documents, qualifies, or amplifies a particular point. Writing hypertext is an art, requiring selection of the best words and phrases in a way that doesn't intrude on the reading experience.

Hytelnet A resource, available via Telnet, the Web, and in a stand-alone PC version, that provides access to more than 1,000 *Telnet* sites, particularly library catalogs. Hytelnet can be browsed or searched, and using AOL 3.0 for Windows 95, the Web version takes you to actual Telnet sites. As this book went to press, Hytelnet was being phased out, with its creator promising a new resource that would fulfill the same purpose. A more detailed discussion is found in Chapter 10.

icon In Windows, a small graphic that stands for, or links to, a program. Double-click the icon to run the program. In Windows 3.1 and Windows 95, icons are stored in program windows, which are created automatically during *installation*. In later versions of Windows 95 (if you've separately installed Internet Explorer 4.0), a Web view of the Windows desktop allows you to single-click icons.

installation Preparing a program for use on your computer. Installation usually involves "unzipping" a file consisting of many files and running a setup file, which creates a new directory for the program, changes any Windows settings as required, and makes an *icon* and program window so you can start the program by clicking on the icon. Installing usually means setting up a program for the first time. When installing AOL, you must also register—provide AOL with some billing information—before actually using the software and the service, as explained in Appendix A.

Instant Message An AOL-only feature that offers direct, one-to-one communication between two AOL members who are signed on at the same time. Similar to *chat*, which allows two or more people to communicate at the same time, but more like a conversation.

Instant Messenger A technology similar to the Instant Message, but designed for Windows 95 and Macintosh Internet users who don't have an AOL account but do want to communicate in real time with someone on AOL or the Internet. Includes a feature similar to AOL's *Buddy List*. Instant Messenger has been licensed to Netscape Communications Corp. for general use on the Internet, and is now available from the Netscape Navigator Personal toolbar (see Chapter 10).

Integrated browser The Microsoft Internet Explorer browser that comes up whenever you access a URL or click a Web link from within AOL. The browser's navigation controls are now part of the general AOL toolbar and apply to all AOL windows. The *stand-alone browser* is installed when you install AOL and can be accessed from a Windows desktop (Windows 95) or program window (Windows 95 and Windows 3.1).

Internet The world's newest and fastest-growing country, possessing neither borders nor immigration restrictions nor formal government nor regulatory apparatus; a self-governing entity with a strong but benign commercial sector and a disputatious population, yet no standing army or formal legal system. English is the most common language, but communication takes place in all major and many minor languages. A place to spend a vacation or a lunch hour, a place where privacy is as important as the right to assume another identity. A place to find information and to publish it. Home to millions of chatters and info junkies. Yes, it's also a *network* of networks. *See* Chapter 1.

IP Stands for Internet Protocol, a technical term. IP is the core of *TCP/IP*, the standard that specifies how files are turned into small packets and how these packets

are addressed so they can reach any other computer on the Internet. Every computer on a *TCP/IP* network is identified by a unique *IP address*.

IP address IP addresses provide instructions to packets as they travel to other computers on the Internet. IP addresses consist of four numbers separated by periods (called "dots"), each smaller than 255 (for example, 199.4.102.1). When you enter a *domain name* such as **www.aol.com**, it is converted behind the scenes into an IP address; you'll often see this number in the status bar at the bottom of the AOL window when you connect to a Web site.

IRC Stands for Internet Relay Chat. IRC offers the closest thing to chat rooms on the Internet. IRC is available on America Online through *Winsock* programs such as mIRC, which is available on AOL's file libraries (*keyword: Filesearch*). IRC is organized in channels, and channels are organized in networks (such as Undernet). Communication tends to be informal in IRC channels, as in chat rooms. *See* Chapter 10.

ISP Stands for Internet service provider. A company that provides access to the Internet, usually by modem, and provides little or no selection or programming of content, and (usually) no unique content. America Online is generally considered to be more than an ISP because it provides not only Internet access, but also its own tools, a huge amount of content, and its own community.

Java and JavaScript Two different technologies, created by Sun Microsystems and endorsed by most software makers (except Microsoft), that deliver interactive content over the Internet. Java is a programming language used to create small applications, or applets, for distribution over the Internet. The technology promises a high degree of security and platform independence (meaning it runs on any operating system, unlike competing technologies such as ActiveX). JavaScript is a computer scripting language that can be incorporated into HTML to allow a high degree of interactivity and responsiveness to what users do with the mouse and keyboard. JavaScript has become a fundamental part of *dynamic HTML*. A collection of sites that use all these technologies is available at **http://www.gamelan.com**. *See* Chapter 6.

Johnson-Grace An AOL company and the name of the technology created by the company for compressing (reducing the size of) sound and graphics files for faster distribution across the AOL network. To use this technology, make sure there is a check box in the Web Graphics tab of the Internet Options window (from the My AOL menu, click WWW to use the preferences window).

library On AOL, files and programs are available throughout the service, arranged in software libraries. You can search for files located in any library using *keyword: Filesearch. See* Chapter 8. A *virtual* library is a directory of links to high-quality sites, with descriptions of the sites and systematic arrangement of the links.

list box In a window, a box with a list of items that can be selected and linked to: programs, text articles, Web sites, AOL forums, etc.

listproc *See* **mailing list.**

LISTSERV *See* **mailing list.**

mailing list Refers to a group of people who communicate with each other about a shared interest by sending e-mail messages to a single e-mail address. Also the special software used to keep lists of people and distribute the message to everyone on the list. Lists range in size from a handful of subscribers to more than 100,000. Joining a list requires a subscription process that consists merely of sending an e-mail message to the software *administering* the list. The major varieties of software used to manage lists include LISTSERV, Listproc, and Majordomo. Lists can be *moderated* or *unmoderated.* Lists can also be distribution-only (newsletters) or true interactive discussion lists. *See* Chapter 5.

Majordomo *See* **mailing list**.

Master Account In AOL, the account belonging to the screen name set up during registration. This screen name has the ability to create up to four additional screen names. It's the screen name responsible for paying bills and empowered to restrict the account's other screen names' access to certain areas and features. *See also* **Parental Controls**.

menu A standard part of a Windows program, menus are usually arranged in a row at the top of an application's main window. A menu consists of a list of things you can do or places you can go. Most programs have File, Edit, Window, and Help menus. To use a menu, move your mouse over it and click to display the menu's commands. To select something, move the mouse down the menu and click on it. Many menu commands have keyboard equivalents—shortcuts to the same command using the keyboard. When there are equivalents, the keys are displayed

to the right of the name of the menu item (for example, in AOL's Edit menu the keyboard equivalent of Copy is CTRL-C); however, the menu commands tend to be more reliable than their keyboard equivalents (especially, for some reason, when using the Edit menu's copy and paste commands).

message A message is a unit of *electronic mail*. It originates from one person and is sent to one or more people or to *mailing list* software for distribution to a group. The elements of a message are (1) the Send To field and (optionally) the Copy To field, where you specify direct and (optionally) indirect recipients of the message; (2) the Subject field, where you indicate the content of the message; and (3) the body of the message—the content. Messages can contain attached files. In sending e-mail to someone on AOL, you can include clickable hyperlinks and formatted text (bold, centered, text of different sizes, etc.), as well as graphics files. On AOL, newsgroup postings are called messages, though on the Internet the term for a newsgroup message is *article*.

Message board An AOL-only feature available in many forums throughout the service; the AOL version of newsgroups, increasingly implemented *as* newsgroups. A place for members to ask questions and share information with each other and forum leaders. Newer AOL message boards have the same functionality as newsgroups, including threaded discussions. *See* Chapter 5.

MIME Stands for the Multipurpose Internet Mail Extension, designed to simplify the transfer of files through the gateways that separate different e-mail systems. AOL's e-mail program supports MIME. To send someone a file attachment over the Internet, your recipient must also be using an e-mail program that supports MIME. Simply put, MIME works by converting your *binary* document (a formatted word-processed file, for example) into a text document, then telling the recipient's e-mail program how to handle the attached file.

modem Not an acronym, but a shortening of MOdulator/DEModulator. A piece of hardware that takes your computer's (digital) signals and converts them into a form that can be sent over ordinary (analog) phone lines. Modems dial AOL when you want to sign on to the service, and transmit data in both directions when you want to use the service or the Internet. Internal modems go inside your computer; external ones go on your desk. They also differ in speed: a 14.4 modem is capable of sending data at the rate of 14,400 bits per second, or *bps* (a bit is a small unit of data); a 28.8 modem can transmit data at twice the speed or even more if a compression technique is used. Modems are important when you install the AOL software because AOL needs to know exactly what kind of modem you have, but the AOL installation software can detect this information automatically. More information is available online at *keyword: Modem.*

moderated A newsgroup or a mailing list that has a human moderator who keeps track of members and their messages. A moderator's responsibilities can range from deciding who can join a mailing list or newsgroup and what can be discussed there, to making sure that the mailing list software is working properly, to breaking up arguments or keeping the discussion on topic. An unmoderated mailing list has no one charged with monitoring people's messages. Most newsgroups are unmoderated; most mailing lists are moderated.

mouse The piece of plastic, molded to fit your hand, attached to the back of your computer with a cable, and used to control your computer. Your basic mouse usually has two mouse buttons, which you can press quickly, or *click*. The basic mouse actions are the click, the double-click, the right-click, and the drag-and-drop. The mouse lets you do everything involved in getting around Windows and Macintosh programs: selecting from lists (*menus*, *listboxes*, *drop-down lists*); clicking on buttons and icons; selecting radio buttons and check boxes; using a scroll bar; dragging things around the desktop; and highlighting (selecting) text in order to cut, copy, and paste it.

MUD A multi-user dungeon (or dimension), an electronic place where people assume fictional characters and interact with others to create identities and invent another social world. Some MUDs are peaceable, while others are more warlike. MUDs have applications in business and distance education (a type of learning in which students and teachers are in different places, and communicate via electronic media). Originally available only via *Telnet*, some MUDs are moving to the Web as that medium becomes more interactive. The Web has also become a good source of information about MUDs as well as a way of accessing them. An excellent source of information about MUDs is the MudConnector (**http://www.mudconnect.com**). *See* Chapter 10.

My Place An FTP-based service, available only on AOL, that allows you to *upload* files from your computer to one of AOL's FTP computers (**members.aol.com**), where they can be referenced by any Web pages you create using *Personal Publisher*. Every AOL screen name is allotted 2 Mb of space to store uploaded files. For information about My Place and Personal Publisher 2, *see* Chapter 7.

Navigational bar In AOL 4.0, the part of the toolbar that lets you (1) navigate windows (go backward and forward; stop and reload; go home); (2) type an AOL keyword or URL into the Address box; (3) use the Find menu to coordinate your searches for both people and information on both AOL and the Internet. *See* Chapter 2.

Net Same as the Internet, usually capitalized. *See* **Internet**.

AOL's Rules of the Road

From AOL's Rules of the Road: "The Internet is not owned, or operated by, or in any way affiliated with, AOL, Inc. or any of its affiliates; it is a separate, independent network of computers and is not part of AOL. Your use of the Internet is solely at your own risk. When using the Internet and all of its components, members must conduct themselves responsibly according to the Internet's own particular code of conduct. Participating successfully on the Internet is really a matter of common sense. Although AOL, Inc. does not control the Internet, your conduct on the Internet when using your AOL account is subject to the AOL Rules." These Rules of the Road can be read in their entirety at *keyword: Terms*.

netiquette A collection of guidelines for using Internet services and interacting with people on the Internet. Some netiquette guidelines are meant to promote a good, civil experience for everyone on the Internet—such as avoiding humor that could offend or be misunderstood on newsgroups. Other guidelines are meant to respect the physical, networking environment—such as the FTP customs of using nearby servers, logging on after hours, and not browsing or staying logged on too long. Every Internet service—e-mail, newsgroups, FTP, Telnet, and the Web—has netiquette guidelines. Breach of netiquette can have assorted negative consequences, from social disapproval, to getting kicked off your Internet service, to getting included on a black list or banned from an IRC channel. AOL's Terms of Service require members to respect netiquette or risk removal from the service. AOL's Terms of Service are available at *keyword: Terms* (Part II of Rules of the Road). For an AOL introduction to the subject, go to *keyword: Netiquette*. For an official Internet introduction, go to **ftp://ds.internic.net/rfc/rfc1855.txt.**

Netscape Navigator A *browser* made by Netscape Communications Corp., and available to AOL members (*keyword: Netscape*). Netscape pioneered Internet technologies such as *frames, plug-ins,* and *Java*. *See* Chapter 10.

network Two or more computers connected by cabling, telephone wire, radio wave, or other medium, so that they can exchange data. Networks need not be restricted to a specific location, and they can themselves be networked, creating a network of networks. In a way, the Internet is a radical extension of the idea of networking, because it could ultimately include all computers and enable communication among all people with access to a computer.

newbie Someone new to the Internet or to a specific Internet service, such as FTP, mailing lists, or MUDs. With the very rapid growth of the Internet, more than half of all people on the Internet in the last year or so have been newbies.

newsgroup An Internet discussion group, organized by topic and intended for broad public access and participation. AOL carries more than 20,000 newsgroups, which are arranged in categories, or *hierarchies*. The whole newsgroup system is called Usenet, which is not so much a *network* as a logical classification scheme. A newsgroup name indicates the hierarchy (category) and any subcategories to which it belongs, as well as the specific topic to which it is devoted (for example, **rec.sports.baseball** is about the topic of baseball, available in the sports subcategory, within the main *rec*reational category). You can search for newsgroups at *keyword: Newsgroups* (click Search All Newsgroups), and you can search for specific newsgroup postings using *DejaNews*. *See* Chapter 5 (newsgroups on AOL) and Chapter 9 (using DejaNews).

offline Otherwise know as RL (real life). AOL offers many ways for you to keep your online costs down by allowing you to do routine tasks while you're offline. For example, you can compose e-mail messages while offline, then click Send Later and send the message when you're online. Or, using *Automatic AOL*, you can read your incoming newsgroup postings and mail messages while you're offline.

online Traditionally, being online meant being signed onto a commercial online service such as America Online, as opposed to *both* offline and on the Internet. Today, there are plenty of activities that can be done offline as well as online. Signing

onto AOL makes it possible to use the Internet; nothing else is required, and no additional expense is incurred.

packet The unit of data transmitted over a *TCP/IP* network such as AOL or the Internet. Files, such as Web pages in the form of HTML files, must be broken up into tiny packets of data before they can be transmitted across networks. Every packet carries information about its source, its place in the sequence of all packets, and its destination. *See* Chapter 6.

page A Web page and the *HTML* file on which it is based. A collection of pages is a Web site. A *home page* is the top page of a site and also the page your browser automatically opens to. *See* Chapter 6.

Parental Controls America Online offers many ways for parents to shape the experience of children who share their account. (The *Master Account* is usually in the parents' name, while the associated screen names may belong to children in the household.) On AOL, parents can block kids' access to *chat rooms* and other features, as described in Appendix C. Parental Controls vary by Internet service. For *newsgroups,* parents can block access to specific newsgroups and downloads. For *e-mail*, parents can prohibit kids from receiving attachments or any e-mail. For the *Web*, kids can be restricted to sites deemed appropriate for children or for teenagers. Using Parental Controls, parents can also restrict children to the Kids Only channel. Parental Controls are available from the My AOL menu; click on Parental Controls.

password To sign on to AOL you must have a password and screen name, both of which you choose for the *Master Account* when you first register your AOL account. Once signed on, a Master Account holder can change, add, and delete up to four screen names, but the screen name used to register can't be changed. Your screen name and password identify you unmistakably to AOL's computers. It is vital to keep your password secret and to choose a password that others won't be able to guess. Tips for choosing a password and a form for actually changing it are available at *keyword: Password.* Many sites on the Internet require usernames and passwords (such as Medscape, Amazon.com, and the New York Times); it's a good idea to write down *all* your passwords because it's easy to forget them!.

Personal Filing Cabinet Using your Personal Filing Cabinet (PFC), you can automatically save a copy of every e-mail message you send and receive. You can also save copies of every newsgroup posting you send and receive using *Automatic*

AOL. E-mail messages you choose to send later are kept in your Personal Filing Cabinet, which is available from the My Files menu. To set up your preferences for this features, use the My AOL menu and select Preferences, clicking Personal Filing Cabinet.

Personal Publisher A free service available on America Online for creating your own Web *page*. Personal Publisher lets you upload files using My Place, then create a page and link the files without knowing any HTML. Chapter 7 is devoted to Personal Publisher.

plug-in Software that allows a browser to smoothly handle and present multimedia files so that video, audio, 3D, and other effects are a seamless part of the Web experience. Plug-ins were developed for the Netscape Navigator browser. The Microsoft Internet Explorer browser (which you get with AOL 4.0 for Windows 95) supports both plug-ins and a similar but Windows-only technology called ActiveX. Some of the major plug-ins you can use with AOL are Real Audio, VDO, and Shockwave. Real Audio and VDO are examples of streaming technology; they allow you to hear sounds and watch little video clips before the files have finished downloading. Other plug-ins can be downloaded from the Web and installed for either the Microsoft or Netscape browser. *See* Chapter 6.

PPP Point-to-Point Protocol, a standard way of accessing the Internet using a modem and the phone lines, preferred by many Internet service providers (ISPs). Connecting directly to AOL does not require a PPP connection, but AOL's new Bring Your Own Access pricing plan allows ISP subscribers to sign onto AOL using a PPP connection. *See also* **SLIP**.

protocol A set of rules that computers follow when exchanging data. The Internet is built on widely shared networking protocols called *TCP/IP* and a set of application protocols that underlie the basic Internet services (the protocols are in parentheses): the Web (*http*), Usenet News (nntp), e-mail (smtp), and FTP (ftp).

quoting In e-mail and newsgroups, the practice of selectively choosing bits of a person's message to provide context for your response. In responses, by Internet tradition, each line of a quoted passage is preceded by a vertical line (|) or greater-than sign (>). On AOL, you can choose to use this style in your e-mail responses (click on MyAOL | Preferences, click Mail, and set your e-mail preferences to Internet quoting). You cannot yet automatically quote when responding to a newsgroup article but must manually copy and paste.

radio button In Windows programs such as AOL, the round radio button gives you the ability to specify a single choice. With radio buttons you *must* click one (and only one) of the buttons. With (square) *check boxes* you can select as many as you want (or no choices). You select a radio button by clicking in the circle, and a check box by clicking in the square.

Re: Automatically tacked onto the beginning of the subject of an e-mail or newsgroup message when someone is responding to someone else's message. It can be edited out, but then the other people won't realize that your message is part of a *thread*—a collection of messages about the same theme or in response to the same original message.

real time *See* **asynchronous vs. real-time communication**.

Search Terms

Chapter 9 has a text box, "Search Terms and What They Mean," explaining the technical or technical-seeming terms you'll encounter while using search tools, such as *Boolean operator*, *directory*, *engine*, *hits*, *index*, *query*, *relevance*, and *returns*.

server A computer that makes a program, database, file, or other data available to other computers, called *clients*. The various Internet services—the Web, FTP, Gopher, e-mail—each use their own servers for controlling access to and distributing data to clients.

shareware *See* **freeware and shareware**.

SLIP Stands for Serial Line Internet Protocol. SLIP makes it possible for Internet service providers' subscribers to access the Internet using their modems. AOL does not provide a SLIP connection, but if you have a SLIP account with an *ISP*, you can log on to it, then run AOL. Similar to *PPP*. Instructions are provided in Appendix A.

smiley A way of indicating your intention or emotion by using characters requiring you to tilt your head to the left. Smileys save people the time of expressing their thoughts and feelings intelligibly ;-) If you want a big list of smileys, do a search for **smiley.txt** or **smiley.zip** at *keyword: FileSearch.* Want smileys? Visit *keyword: CDN Smileys.*

spam Unsolicited e-mail or newsgroup postings, generally considered to be a waste of time, *bandwidth*, and disk space. AOL has tools for blocking spam (Mail Controls and Preferred Mail, described in Chapter 3) and actively fights spammers in the courts.

Spinner, AOL In the new AOL 4.0 interface, the pulsating AOL logo to the right of the Address box (part of the AOL navigation bar). The spinner displays the progress of a page as it's downloading, stopping when a page has been downloaded.

SSL Stands for Secure Sockets Layer, an industry-standard method of securing Internet transactions by scrambling them so they can't be read. Implemented in the AOL browser.

Stand-alone browser Sometimes called the external browser, this is the Microsoft Internet Explorer browser that is automatically installed for you when you install AOL 4.0, available by clicking the Internet icon on your desktop (Windows 95) or program window (Windows 3.1). Whenever you are signed onto AOL or using an ISP, you can use this browser. It is based on the same technology as the *integrated browser*. The stand-alone browser has its own controls (for going forward, backward, home, etc.) and its own system for collecting favorite sites.

status bar In a Web browser or in the AOL window, the line of information at the very bottom of the window that gives you information about what you are doing. It indicates whether your mouse is pointing to a hyperlink; if it is, you'll see the URL of that link in the status bar. It also tells you what's going on while the elements of a Web page are downloading one at a time.

surf To browse the Web or the Net, jumping from link to link, page to page. The term was coined by Jean Polly, author of the *Internet Kids Yellow Pages, Second Edition* (Osborne/McGraw-Hill, 1997).

TCP/IP Stands for Transmission Control Protocol/Internet Protocol, the networking protocols on which the Internet is based. TCP/IP specifies how complex data is broken into little pieces (packets) of the same size and structure, sent across many networks, then reassembled at the other end. TCP/IP requires several layers

of protocols to carry out the various tasks of taking an application's data, breaking it into packets, addressing them, passing them off to physical networks, and (at the receiving end) reassembling the packets into a useful form.

Telnet The *protocol*, and the applications based on the protocol, that let you use programs, games, and databases on a distant computer. With Telnet, your keyboard and monitor allow you to communicate with the distant computer, where your program is running. Telnet makes it possible for people to play real-time simulation and adventure games on the Internet. Telnet also makes it possible to use electronic catalogs of libraries located all over the world. On AOL, the built-in (Microsoft) browser allows you to connect to a Telnet site. Or, with AOL's Winsock you can use a program such as *Ewan* to access Telnet sites. *See* Chapter 10.

text box In Windows, a box in which you type some text or numbers to tell a program your preferences or order a product or register at a Web site or enter your keyword when using a search service such as AOL NetFind.

thread In newsgroups, mailing lists, and e-mail, a set of messages about the same subject, or at least with the same Subject line. A thread is like a conversation where the people are talking about the same subject but at different times and places. AOL's newsreader lets you follow all the messages that comprise a thread, but AOL's e-mail program does not currently let you sort messages in this way. Whenever you see *re*: before a subject, you're looking at a response to another message, and thus part of a thread. AOL's newer message boards support threading.

upload To send a file from a PC or other *client* to a *server*, where it can be used by others or referenced by a Web page. On AOL, the My Place service allows members to upload 2Mb of files per screen name for use in Web pages or for other purposes. *See* Chapter 7. *See also* **download**.

URL Stands for Uniform Resource Locator. The standard Internet scheme for specifying the address, or location, of an Internet resource (such as a Web page or Gopher menu). A typical URL is **http://members.aol.com/**. URLs have three parts: the *protocol* (**http**), the *domain name* (**members.aol.com**), and the *filename* with full directory path (**stevecase**). File names are sometimes implicit; omitting a file name causes the browser to look for a default page, such as *index.html,main.html,* or something similar. *See* Chapter 6.

Usenet The organizational scheme for keeping track of *newsgroups*—widely accessible global bulletin boards devoted to specific topics. Newsgroups are arranged into categories (or *hierarchies*) such as rec (recreation) and sci (science). The two major hierarchies are the standard (or traditional) hierarchy and the alternative hierarchy. AOL's Newsgroup feature is available at *keyword: Newsgroups*. *See* Chapter 5.

Veronica The search engine used for finding information available by Gopher. Only a handful of Veronica servers are being maintained in the world today, and few if any are being updated. When you do a Veronica search, you can choose searching Gopherspace, which means to search an index consisting of all the files pointed to by all the world's public Gopher servers. You can also choose "search Gopher directories," which is similar to using a directory to find clusters of resources grouped under some subject head such as Business, Humor, or Recipes. *See* Chapter 9.

virus A small program intended to create unwanted changes to someone else's computer. Some effects can be destructive, others just annoying. Viruses work by latching onto programs or application templates, then causing programs to act in unexpected ways. The best way to avoid a virus is to scan all files downloaded from the Internet for viruses and never to download files from an unknown source. *Keyword: Virus* center has information, current alerts, and anti-virus programs you can use to prevent or eradicate viruses. All software available from AOL at *keyword: Filesearch* or any other software library on the service has been virus-checked.

WAIS Stands for Wide Area Information System, a standard and a protocol for indexing large collections of text documents to make them easier to search. WAIS is now rarely used because so few resources have been indexed and because other search tools have taken its place.

Webzine *See* **e-zine**.

Winsock Stands for *Win*dows *sock*ets. Winsock is a defacto standard for developing Windows programs that can communicate with other computers over a *TCP/IP* network like the Internet. To work, such programs require a small file called **winsock.dll**. Winsock applications let you browse the Web, search Archie, create Web pages, use FTP, and much more. For each Internet service built into AOL, several Winsock programs are available; Winsock makes it possible to use the Netscape browser, for example, and an FTP client such as WS_FTP32. In addition,

you can run Winsock applications (e.g., a Telnet client like Ewan) that have no equivalent on AOL. When you're using Winsock, it's important to know whether your version is 16 bit or 32 bit, as explained in Chapter 10. Since AOL 3.0, Winsock is automatically installed when you install AOL. When you use the Bring Your Own Access plan, you're using your ISP's version of **winsock.dll**, but in most cases, this will make no difference in how Winsock applications work, especially with Windows 95. *See* Chapter 10.

World Wide Web Often called just the *Web* and abbreviated *WWW*. The Web consists of millions of *pages* of information, arranged in more or less complex sites, on every subject, connected by *hyperlinks,* and navigated and viewed with a *browser*. The Web is often considered the graphical part of the Internet, but in fact it supports every type of multimedia including video, audio, *Java*, and animation. *See* Chapters 6, 7, and 10.

zine (or 'zine) *See* **e-zine**.

zipped file A file that contains several other files; the zipped files are simpler to send and receive over a network. Zipped files are usually *compressed* as well. Special utilities such as WinZip can be used to zip files, while AOL's *Download Manager* can be used to unzip them.

Appendix C

For Parents Only: Ensuring Your Child's Online Safety

Perhaps you've seen the newspaper and magazine articles about all the X-rated material and instances of child abuse on the Internet. Much of the negative commentary is sensational, cynical, and wrong-headed in its conclusion that the Net is for adults only. Yet the Internet *is* so big and so open that kids *can* meet unsavory strangers. It also contains documents and pictures to which most parents don't want children exposed. What's most alarming for some parents is that it's getting so easy to do a search that any older kid with a bit of ordinary curiosity can uncover inappropriate, illegal, or just plain scary stuff.

There's also the issue of the quality and viewpoints of what you find on the Internet. Since anyone can publish a Web site, the Internet can be considered more of an archive of daily life and opinion than a library of authoritative information. For example, the U.S. Holocaust Museum has a superb educational site, but Holocaust deniers have Web sites too. Kids are supposed to be streetwise these days, but I'm not convinced for a minute that even older kids can easily recognize the difference between Holocaust education and Holocaust revision, and a strong case can be made that children should not learn about the Holocaust from people who doubt its existence. This "strong case" applies to every serious and not-so-serious contemporary issue about which people publish on the Internet.

Yes, children run the risk of encountering nasty people and uncovering unsavory sites online. This risk must be seen in perspective, however. They run similar risks in the real world, and it's a lot easier to say "no" (or to click the Back button) online than in real life. If you have kids, are you more comfortable sending them alone on the bus into a big city or sitting in front of a computer monitor while you're in the room? The best defense in either case is to impart common sense and to work with your kids so that they'll make the best decisions for themselves (see "Safety Tips"). Until they're really independent, the next best defense is AOL's Parental Controls.

WHY KIDS *SHOULD* BE ONLINE

Simply put, kids can explore thousands of worthwhile, fun, and challenging sites, beginning with the Web sites available in AOL's **Kids Only** channel. Thanks to the Net, they can keep on learning after school. They can experience the blurring of fun and learning and find answers to their own questions. They can expand their horizons and follow their curiosity, meeting kids in different parts of the country and world. They can engage new ideas instead of passively taking in the latest unsavory offerings on TV—that other window to the outside world.

Where to start? Some of the sites in Table C-1 include directories of fun, kid-appropriate Internet resources. You'll also find some excellent kids' sites in Chapter 11 of this book. A vast collection of learning activities organized by curricular area, activity type, and grade level can be found at PacBell's Blue Web'n site (**http://www.kn.pacbell.com/wired/bluewebn**).

Site	Address	What's There
AOL NetFind: Kids Only	**http://www.aol.com/netfind/kids/**	The best Web sites for kids
A Parent's Guide to the Internet	**http://www.familyguidebook.com**	Text of an entire informative and well-regarded book by lawyer Parry Aftab; includes good sites, reviews of filters, and safety tips
American Library Association's Great Sites	**http://www.ala.org/parentspage/greatsites**	700+ safe, kid-friendly Web sites
Enough is Enough: Whitepaper	**http://www.enough.org/summit/whitepaper.htm**	Thorough review of the issue of online obscenity; the Safe Harbors section (**http://www.enough.org/safeharbors.htm**) has lots of kid-safe links
Family Education Network	**http://www.familyeducation.com/**	Content for kids of different ages, with a family slant and public school focus (FEN is in the business of creating school Web pages)

TABLE C-1 Indispensable sites for parents and kids

Site	Address	What's There
NetShepherd	**http://family.netshepherd.com/**	1.5 million screened, searchable family sites, created in conjunction with AltaVista (Chapter 9)
ParentSoup	Web: **http://www.parentsoup.com** AOL forum: *keyword: Parentsoup*	Tremendous resource on all aspects of parenting: fun, sickness, vacations, schooling, etc.
PEDINFO Parental Control of Internet Access	**http://www.uab.edu/pedinfo/Control.html**	List of links to the companies that sell filtering software; links to other useful parental guides
Technology Inventory	**http://www.research.att.com/projects/tech4kids/**	A detailed analysis from AT&T's research labs, reviewing the various Web filters and other technologies
Tools and Tips for Parents	**http://www.childrenspartnership.org/safety.html**	Solid, detailed advice for parents from the National PTA, National Urban League, and Children's Partnership
Yahooligans	**http://www.yahooligans.com**	Searchable directory of fun and otherwise worthy sites for kids; part of Yahoo (Chapter 9)

TABLE C-1 Indispensable sites for parents and kids (*continued*)

Tip *The Internet is so big and diffuse that a book can go a long way to making it manageable. A good place to start exploring is Jean Polly's wonderful **Internet Kids and Family Yellow Pages**, Second Edition (Osborne-McGraw-Hill, 1997). Seymour Papert makes the case for full-time, family-based learning in **Connected Family** (Longstreet Press, 1996). **Internet for Kids**, Second Edition, by Deneen Frazier, Barbara Kurshan, and Sara Armstrong (Sybex, 1996), includes many activities that parents can undertake with kids in the middle and upper grades.*

PARENTAL CONTROLS: WHAT ARE THEY?

Parental Controls allow you, as parent, to control whether and to what extent your children can use AOL features such as chat rooms, electronic mail, the Web, FTP, and newsgroups. Controls apply to screen names, so for AOL's Parental Controls to take effect, a child must sign onto the service using his or her own screen name. Each Master Account (the account registered with AOL) can create up to four screen names in addition to the one used to set up the account.

The general controls are often designated Parental Controls, and the specific controls are designated Custom Controls, but I look at them together as Parental Controls because Custom Controls pertain directly to kids' online experience.

There are two levels of control; procedures for both are provided below.

1. Assign a general designation (age bracket) to screen names: 18+ (unrestricted); Mature Teen; Young Teen; Kids Only. See "Step One: Setting the Screen Name Designation."
2. Assign custom controls to features such as e-mail and the Web. These controls take effect when a screen name uses those features, broadening or tightening the screen name designation. See "Step Two: Setting Custom Controls."

If you have complete trust in your children, considerable personal experience with the Internet (and know what's out there), and a PC that's placed where everyone can see it, then you can give older children general access and just work with them as they learn their way around the Internet.

All controls can be modified at any time by the Master Account holder.

Safety Tips

AOL's long-standing safety guidelines still apply:

"Remember that people online aren't always who they say they are. Stay safe by following these five rules:

1. Don't give your AOL password to anyone, even your best friend.
2. Never tell someone your home address, telephone number, or school name without asking a parent.
3. Never say you'll meet someone in person without asking a parent.
4. Always tell a parent about any threatening or bad language you see online.
5. If someone says something that makes you feel unsafe or funny, don't just sit there—take charge! Call a TOS Guide (*keyword: Guidepager*). If you're in a chat room, leave the room. Or just sign off."

Guidepagers are now available only *to kids using chat rooms.*

PARENTAL CONTROLS: WHERE ARE THEY?

AOL has made it easy for you to visit the Parental Controls area while online (you must be signed on to set these controls) by doing any of the following:

- Selecting Parental Controls from the My AOL menu on the AOL toolbar
- Clicking Parental Controls from the Welcome screen
- Setting up a new screen name (you will be prompted to set controls for that name)
- Going to the new *keyword: Neighborhood Watch*, which also has good ideas on how parents as well as kids can stay safe online

The main Parental Controls window is shown in Figure C-1. Click the big Set Parental Controls Now button to both set a screen name designation and adjust the

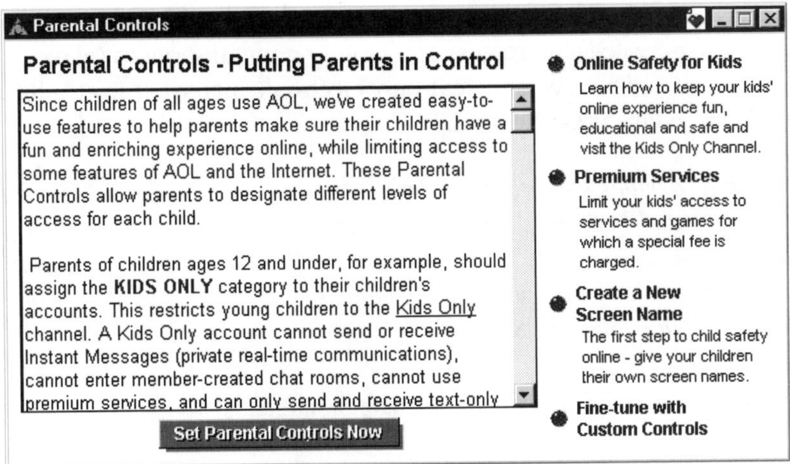

FIGURE C-1 Start here to keep your kids safe

custom controls. A smaller button on the main screen lets you set up screen names. Remember, without their own screen name, kids have no way of being protected. (Appendix A goes into screen names in more detail.)

STEP ONE: SETTING THE SCREEN NAME DESIGNATION

The first step in defining the kind of access and the quality of online experience you want for your children is to define an overall access level. You can choose from four levels:

- **18+** Not restricted in any way; appropriate for the Master Account and other adults
- **Mature Teen (ages 16-17)** Blocks inappropriate Web sites
- **Young Teen (ages 13-15)** May visit some chat rooms, but not member-created rooms or private rooms

Note: *Both teen groups are restricted to Web sites appropriate for their age categories. Both are also blocked from Internet newsgroups that allow file attachments, and users from this group cannot use premium services (games).*

- **Kids Only** Restricts kids 12 and under to AOL's **Kids Only** channel. A Kids Only account cannot send or receive Instant Messages, cannot enter member-created chat rooms, cannot use premium services (games), and can send and receive only text-only electronic mail (no file attachments or embedded pictures allowed).

Note *Who decides what's appropriate? Microsystems, Inc. (not AOL) rates Web sites and makes its listings available to AOL. Its lists are not publicly available. If you think a site isn't available for a category and should be (or is available and shouldn't be), go to Web Controls (see "Setting Custom Controls for the Web") and click Report a Site.*

To set general levels of control for a screen name:

1. For each screen name in the Parental Controls window (Figure C-2), click the appropriate radio button: 18+, Mature Teen, Young Teen, or Kids Only.

Tip *Make sure you are accessing Parental Controls using the screen name you used to open your account (the Master Account). This account always has general (18+) access. To prevent a child from using this account, make sure to choose a password for the Master Account different from the child's password.*

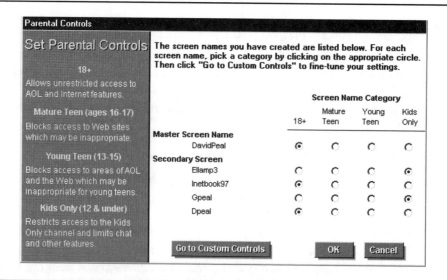

Parental Controls

Set Parental Controls

18+
Allows unrestricted access to AOL and Internet features.

Mature Teen (ages 16-17)
Blocks access to Web sites which may be inappropriate.

Young Teen (13-15)
Blocks access to areas of AOL and the Web which may be inappropriate for young teens.

Kids Only (12 & under)
Restricts access to the Kids Only channel and limits chat and other features.

The screen names you have created are listed below. For each screen name, pick a category by clicking on the appropriate circle. Then click "Go to Custom Controls" to fine-tune your settings.

Screen Name Category

	18+	Mature Teen	Young Teen	Kids Only
Master Screen Name				
DavidPeal	◉	○	○	○
Secondary Screen				
Ellamp3	○	○	○	◉
Inetbook97	◉	○	○	○
Gpeal	○	○	○	◉
Dpeal	◉	○	○	○

Go to Custom Controls OK Cancel

FIGURE C-2 Start by defining an age bracket for each screen name

2. Click OK to accept your choice.

The general restrictions imposed by these four grades of access can be loosened or tightened using Custom Controls. You can also set controls for e-mail, newsgroups, the Web, etc. (See "Step Two: Setting Custom Controls.")

Note *Only screen names with general (18+) access can create an AOL Member Profile that can be seen and searched by other AOL members. If your child wants to create a Member Profile to advertise hobbies and interests or to meet other kids, you'll have to turn off Parental Controls long enough for the child to fill in the form at* keyword: Member Profile. *Be mindful of what your child puts in a profile, making certain that it contains no contact information. Then turn Parental Controls back on for that screen name.*

STEP TWO: SETTING CUSTOM CONTROLS

Once you've assigned a screen name designation, you can adjust the way each child (that is, each screen name) uses interactive features: chat, Instant Messages, downloading, newsgroups, e-mail, and the Web. At *keyword:Parental*, click Fine-tune with Custom Controls to bring up the window in Figure C-3.

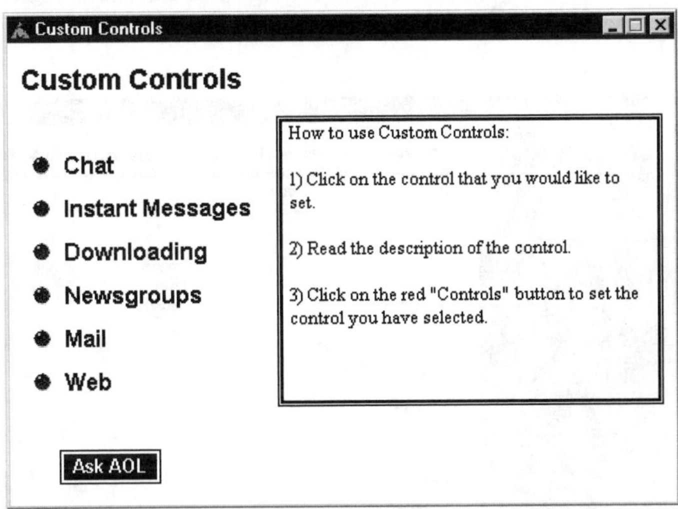

FIGURE C-3 Fine-tune the custom controls you want to assign to each screen name

Note *Chat and IMs apply only to AOL (you will find instructions for setting chat controls by clicking the Chat button shown in Figure C-3). The other features apply to your kids' use of the Internet and are discussed in the following sections.*

> ### Premium Services: Games
>
> AOL's new premium games service, which carries a surcharge, is automatically blocked to all screen names on an account except for the main screen name itself (Master Account). To unblock the service and give kids access, go to *keyword: Parental* and click on Premium Services. Remove the check mark from the box by the screen name, and click OK.

Setting Custom Controls for Downloading

It's easy to restrict what kids can download from either AOL's software libraries or (via FTP) the Net.

Note *For more on downloading, see Chapter 8. FTP is the Internet's File Transfer Protocol, which provides access to millions of files, including software and games.*

1. From *keyword: Parental*, click Fine-tune with Custom Controls. In the Custom Controls window, click Downloading to bring up an introductory screen. Read the text, then click Download Controls to bring up the following screen:

Parental Control- Downloading

Parental Control Downloading

"Downloading" is how you copy files to your computer from AOL or FTP sites.

Block AOL Software Library Downloads

Disables downloads from all AOL Software Libraries.

Block FTP Software Downloads

Disables downloads from Internet FTP sites accessed through Keyword FTP.

The screen names you have created are listed below. To restrict or block a screen name from using a feature, click on the appropriate box.

Screen Name	Block AOL Software Library Downloads	Block FTP Downloads
* DavidPeal	☐	☐
Ellamp3	☑	☑
Inetbook97	☐	☐
Gpeal	☑	☑
Dpeal	☐	☐

* Master screen name

OK Cancel

2. Screen names are listed to the left. For each one, click in either check box or both—or don't check anything to permit complete access.

   - Block AOL Software Downloads
   - Block FTP Downloads

3. Click OK when you're done.

To unblock access, return to the Downloading window and remove the check marks, making sure to click OK when you're done.

AOL's software libraries are screened for family appropriateness, and all files are checked for viruses. The dangers of these libraries are that they can waste time and fill up the hard drive on the family's PC. The danger from FTP downloads is more serious: the possibility of downloading virus-infected files. If you do provide FTP access to your kids, make sure they understand that viruses can't be seen and can cause damage to other software on the computer to which they are downloaded. *Keyword: Virus* has excellent information about viruses as well as programs you can use to check and disinfect files. When you're searching for a file it's a good idea (and faster) to look in AOL's file libraries (*keyword: Filesearch*) before proceeding to FTP.

Note *Files attached to e-mail messages can also be infected. "Setting Custom Controls for E-mail" shows how to block a child's ability to receive attached files.*

Setting Custom Controls for Newsgroups

America Online does not censor what you read in (or download from) newsgroups. It prevents access to only those newsgroups that are patent violations of AOL's community standards (if they have certain words in their name, for example) or if they are plainly illegal (if they deal in pirated software, for example). Thus, while many newsgroups are available on AOL because their titles do not break AOL's guidelines, they may still contain offensive messages and pictures, messages with obscene subject lines, or files that violate copyright laws and community standards.

Note *For more on newsgroups, see Chapter 5.*

AOL offers parents several sets of controls that make it more difficult for kids to access objectionable newsgroups or newsgroup messages. You can restrict newsgroup access in essentially three ways:

- Keep kids from accessing specific newsgroups (whose exact names they know) by blocking the Expert Add feature.
- Keep kids from accessing newsgroups using the Search feature or the Add feature by blocking newsgroups altogether.
- Keep kids from downloading obscene pictures by blocking their access to binary files.

To restrict newsgroup access by a specific screen name, follow these steps (note that you set these controls one screen name at a time):

1. From *keyword: Parental*, click Fine-tune with Custom Controls. In the Custom Controls window, click Newsgroups, then Newsgroup Controls. In the little Parental Controls window that comes up, click the screen name for which you want to set controls, then click Edit. The Blocking Criteria screen comes up (Figure C-4).

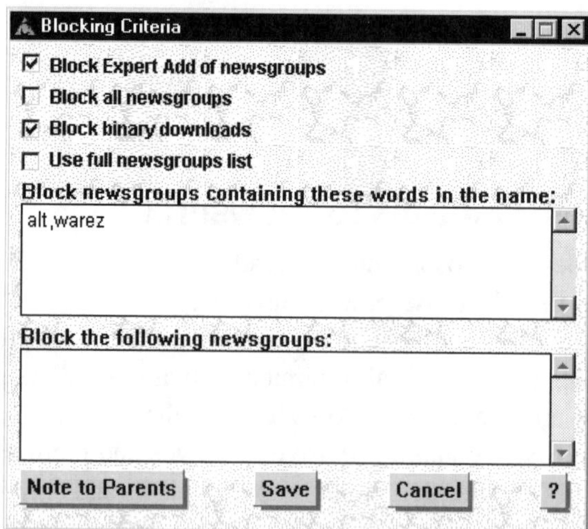

FIGURE C-4 Setting the Blocking Criteria allows you to restrict access to all newsgroups, to certain newsgroups, or to downloads

2. Set controls as appropriate, clicking in one or more of the following check boxes:

Block Expert Add of newsgroups	Prevents a screen name from accessing a specific newsgroup available on AOL (see Chapter 5).
Block all newsgroups	Even if Expert Add is unavailable, kids can still use the Add and Search buttons to find and see inappropriate material. Blocking all access is the most complete way to keep kids out of harm.
Block binary downloads	Much of the material people find objectionable in newsgroups is available in the form of *binary* files (pictures). Blocking downloads can keep a kid from seeing certain files and is probably the most effective way of blocking access to offensive material without keeping kids from taking part in worthwhile newsgroups on books, stars, physics, medicine, baseball, cars, and other subjects.
Use full newsgroups list	Unrestricted newsgroup access, unless you single out specific newsgroups for exclusion (see Step 3). Not recommended for children under 18.

3. To block specific newsgroups: In the first big text box, "Block newsgroups containing these words in their name," indicate which parts of newsgroup names, if any, you wish to block (*sex* or *binaries* or *alt* or *warez* [pirated software], for example). In the second big text box, "Block the following newsgroups," indicate which specific newsgroups you do not wish the screen name to use (you must, of course, know the exact newsgroup name yourself if you use this box).

4. Click Save to confirm and record your choices.

Setting Custom Controls for E-mail

If you don't want young children "talking to strangers" (or if you don't want strangers sending them unsolicited mail), you may want to restrict their access to e-mail. Again, the scope of restriction is fairly flexible: you can block access to messages from anyone or from people with specific addresses, or you can block just the files attached to messages—whether they're adult pictures, infected files, or completely inoffensive homework assignments.

For more on e-mail, see Chapter 3.

1. From *keyword: Parental*, click "Fine-tune with Custom Controls." In the Custom Controls window, click Mail, then Mail Controls. In the little Parental Controls window that comes up, click the screen name for which you want to set controls, then click Edit. The Mail Controls screen comes up (Figure C-5).
2. Using the radio buttons on the left side of the window, click the *one* button that best describes whom you want your child to communicate (or not communicate) with. You can allow all or block all mail exchanges. Or you can allow all mail from AOL members or allow or block mail from specific AOL and Internet addresses. Which choice do you make? See "What's a Parent to Do?"

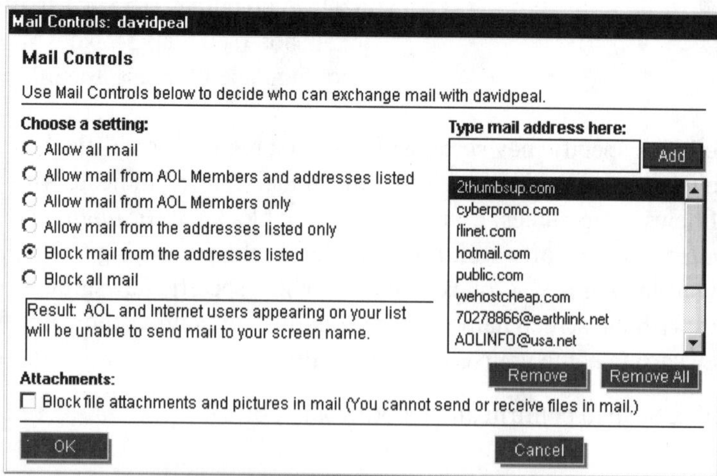

FIGURE C-5 Keep unsolicited messages and files out of kids' mailboxes

What's a Parent to Do?

The extent of access you allow your children depends on their age and the scope of their Internet use. For example, in the case of e-mail, if you want to prevent them from receiving unsolicited mail, including unsolicited X-rated mail, you may want to allow them to receive all AOL mail (thus blocking non-AOL Internet mail). On the other hand, AOL is waging a vigorous campaign in the courts against Internet "spammers" and already blocks incoming mail sent by the worst offenders. Also, your children may require Internet e-mail in order to take part in school projects, join valuable Net mailing lists, or correspond with international pen pals.

My advice?

- Take the time to discuss with your kids the opportunities and risks of e-mail and other Internet tools. Parental Controls offer one level of control but by themselves don't instill good judgment. That's a parent's job.
- Limit the time kids spend on the computer, just as many parents limit the amount of TV kids can watch. The difference between TV and the Internet, however, is that the Net can both help kids with their homework and motivate them to keep learning. (The Internet can also keep kids from watching TV, but that's a different story.)
- Put the computer in a part of the house where it's easy to monitor children's use or (even better) where it's possible to work together on activities of larger family interest.

3. Depending on the button you clicked, use the list on the right to list the e-mail addresses that are OK (or not OK) to receive mail from. You use the list on the right if you clicked one of the following buttons:

   - Allow mail from AOL Members and addresses listed
   - Allow mail from the addresses listed only
   - Block mail from the addresses listed

   To specify the addresses to block or accept: Type an e-mail address in the "Type mail address here" box and click Add. Repeat until you've entered

all the people you want (or don't want) your child to communicate with. To remove an address from the list, just select it and click Remove.

You can change this list at any time.

4. No matter which radio button you chose, you can use the "Block file attachments and pictures in mail" check box to indicate that you don't want your child to send or receive mail with attachments.
5. Click OK when you've made your selections. Repeat for each child's screen name.

Setting Custom Controls for the Web

"If it's human, it's on the Web" is the rough English paraphrase of a famous German maxim used at the beginning Chapter 6. This means that there may be sites and pictures that you, if you're a parent, might not want your child to see. AOL does not censor the Web—it *can't* censor the Web—but it does give you the tools to limit what members of your family do on the Web.

To use these controls:

1. From the Custom Controls window, click Web. Read the informative background information, then click Web Controls.

Parental Control - Web

Parental Control
Web

Kids Only Sites
Allow access only to Web sites recommended for children, aged 12 and under.

Young Teens Sites
Allow access only to Web sites recommended for young teens, aged 13-15.

Mature Teens Restricted Sites
Block Web sites that may be inappropriate for mature teens, aged 16-17.

All Web
Allow unrestricted access to the Web, recommended for adults.

For each of the screen names below, select the desired level of access and then click "OK" to save.

Screen Name	Access Kids Only Sites	Access Young Teen Sites	Block Mature Teen Restricted Sites	Access All Web
* DavidPeal	○	○	○	◉
Ellamp3	◉	○	○	○
Inetbook97	○	○	○	◉
Gpeal	◉	○	○	○
Dpeal	○	○	○	◉

* Master screen name

OK Cancel

2. Look familiar? When you set your general designation for a screen name in Step One above, you were directly affecting your Web controls as well. With Custom Controls, you can now modify those controls (you can modify them from the Parental Controls window as well). You get four levels of control for every screen name on the Master Account. These levels are described earlier, in "Step One: Setting the Screen Name Designation."
3. Click OK when you're done.

A WORD ABOUT INTERNET EXPLORER'S PARENTAL CONTROLS

AOL uses Microsoft's Internet Explorer browser. Both this built-in browser and the stand-alone version of this browser have an additional set of parental controls based on a system called RSAC (Recreational Software Advisory Council). If you use these controls, they will take effect alongside Parental Controls, at best reinforcing them but in no way weakening them. On the other hand, they're the only controls integrated into the stand-alone browser; Parental Controls don't apply to that browser.

Based on Web site owners' voluntary descriptions of their sites, the RSAC ratings are well-regarded but not yet widely used, so they should be used with care; objectionable sites might not have been identified as such by their creators.

To set controls for the stand-alone (and built-in) browser, you must use the browser's preferences:

1. Using the stand-alone browser (while signed onto AOL, click Internet on your Windows 95 desktop) select View | Options to bring up the Preferences window.
2. In the Security tab, click Enable Ratings. You'll need to choose a password. Don't forget to write it down and put it somewhere safe.
3. Click Settings to specify what kinds of content you want to screen out—how much nudity, violence, etc. is OK. Use the slidebar to make your settings.
4. Click OK.

Now when you go to a site, you won't be able to view it if it matches the criteria you set in Step 3. If the site's creators haven't specified any criteria, you'll be told

that, too. To turn off this filter, repeat these steps but choose Disable Settings in the Options window, providing a password when prompted.

Online documentation is not complete, and it's not a great idea to use RSAC preferences in place of AOL's Parental Controls since the standard is not widely used. It would be better to declare the stand-alone browser off limits for kids or to acquire filtering software, such as Surfwatch or Net Nanny, which works by blocking access to specific sites that are maintained in a list that you can modify.

Tip *For more information about the commercial filtering software designed to keep kids from seeing objectionable Web sites, visit the highly detailed and very useful Technology Inventory site and the simpler overview of technologies at PEDINFO: Parental Control of Internet Access (see Table C-1 for both sites' Internet addresses).*

Appendix D

AOL 4.0 for the Macintosh

The similarities between AOL 4.0 for the Macintosh and its Windows counterpart are striking. The menu bars and toolbars are identical, and only the navigation bar differs in one trivial respect (on the Mac, the drop-down list showing your History Trail is available to the left of the Address box, instead of the right as in Windows). For both, the toolbar contains room for additional buttons of your own choosing if you set your resolution to at least 800×600.

Still, a few general Mac features differ from Windows, beginning with the window in which AOL appears: in Windows, the AOL program fills the screen; on the Mac, you just see the menu bar and the toolbar while parts of your Finder (desktop) can be seen when AOL is active, giving you access to other programs and files. As a result, many screen captures in this book may look a little different from what you see when you use AOL 4.0 for the Macintosh.

AOL features differ in minor ways between the two platforms, and this appendix is devoted to those differences:

- Basic keystrokes
- Favorite Places
- Preferences
- Personal Filing Cabinet
- E-mail
- Newsgroups
- Browser
- Internet Software
- Getting Help

I'm going to assume you are comfortable with the basics of opening programs, saving files, closing and resizing windows, using control panels, and selecting from the Mac Chooser. I'm not going to assume you're using System 8 (which is why I'm leaving out the specifics of working with windows). Finally, I'm going to assume you are using Chapters 1 through 10 as your main reference. This appendix does not reintroduce the many topics covered in those chapters.

BASIC KEYSTROKES

Many of the Windows keystrokes and mouse actions in this book have Mac equivalents. The right-mouse-click, for example, gives Windows 95 users context-sensitive menus if they're writing e-mail messages or browsing the Web. With the Mac, you hold down the CTRL key while pressing the mouse button (and not releasing it) to see a menu of available options.

Tip *The hard-of-seeing can press the CTRL key and move the mouse cursor over Mac toolbar buttons and controls to hear spoken descriptions of these features.*

Keystroke commands work a little differently on the Mac:

- **Accessing menus** In AOL 4.0 for Windows, you use the ALT key plus the underlined letter to open a menu on the AOL (or any) menu bar. On the Mac you use the CTRL key plus the underlined letter.
- **Accessing commands** Mac menu items can be accessed by pressing the ⌘ key and the letter indicated by the menu item (for example, ⌘ -I to send an Instant Message).
- **Accessing shortcuts** Available from the My Files menu, your Shortcut gives you keyboard access to your favorite keywords on AOL and favorite URLs on the Internet (see Chapter 2). You edit your shortcuts on the Mac just as you do on Windows (the Shortcut areas vary only slightly), but use the Mac ⌘ key instead of the Windows CTRL key to access your shortcuts.

Tip *While using AOL message boards with a Mac, you can copy part of a message you're responding to and paste the text "as a quotation," in order to provide context for your reply. To do so, select text in a message and copy it, then use ⌘-OPTION-V to paste the quoted material into a new message.*

FAVORITE PLACES

AOL's Favorite Places feature gives you the chance to keep track of the areas you want to revisit, whether they're on the Net or AOL. Any window can be tracked in

your Favorite Places folder if the window has a heart in the far upper right-hand corner. You can access all your Favorite Places at any point by opening the Favorite Places folder, now available from the Favorites menu. Chapter 6 has the details.

On the Macintosh you'll notice a few slight differences.

- The Favorite Places heart on the Macintosh is in the upper right-hand corner of the window itself, not on the title bar. So, if you "roll up" the window by double-clicking its title bar (a feature built into System 8), the heart can't be seen. In this case, you can use the keyboard equivalent (⌘-+) to save the window. Though it's unlikely you'll want to save what you can't see, the ⌘-+ keystroke comes in handy if you prefer working at the keyboard. Note also that when you're browsing the Web, the heart appears only after the page has completely downloaded.
- When you click the heart, you get four choices on the Mac instead of three as in Windows. In addition to the options of saving the Favorite in your Favorite Places folder and inserting a link to it in an e-mail message or Instant Message, you can also copy the link to the clipboard. From there the name of the link can be pasted into a word processing document or anywhere else you please. If you paste it into e-mail, an IM, or a text file, it can be clicked on to display the site.
- The Favorite Places folder itself has a different look from the Windows folder, resembling what you see on your hard drive: the standard Mac tree with folders and files. (Your Personal Filing Cabinet also has more of a Mac look than an AOL look.) Whatever the look, you can drag files inside folders and folders inside folders, as well as create folders with equal ease and virtually identical techniques on both Windows and the Mac.

PREFERENCES

Well-done or medium? Sunny-side up or over? Some might argue that AOL 4.0 for the Macintosh offers a larger set of preferences in a more convenient format than does AOL 4.0 for Windows.

For starters, you can see the preference categories and actual choices in the same window, making it easier to switch categories and quicker to make choices. As in the Windows software, on the Mac you can set your preferences whether you're offline or online.

This book doesn't systematically discuss your AOL preferences but instead includes them wherever they're relevant (e.g., mail preferences in Chapter 3 and Web preferences in Chapter 6). In this appendix, I'll look at selected Mac preferences in one place, because it's so easy to manage all your preferences at once on the Mac.

Let's start with the **Web preferences**:

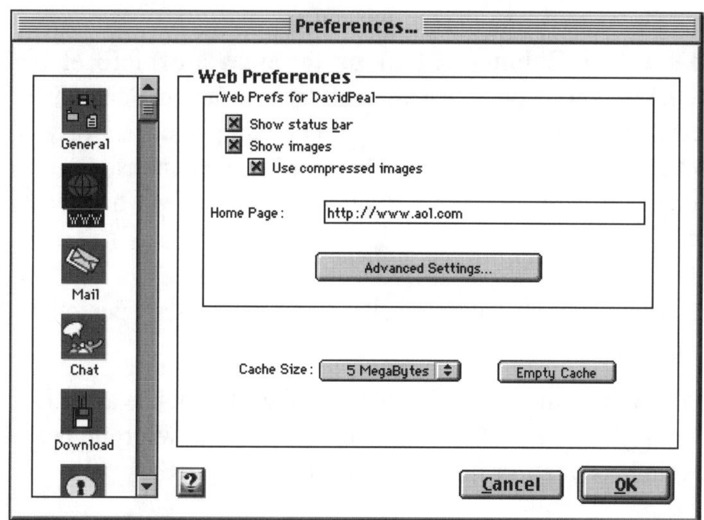

Your essential settings can be seen at a glance:

- Whether to show pictures (you can turn them off if you're visiting sites laden with graphics or if your connection is slow)
- What home page to use
- How big a cache you want

Chapter 6 discusses the purposes of these preferences, which are the same whether you're on a Mac or Windows platform. Click Advanced Settings to set options for adjusting things like type size, link color, and whether to automatically accept cookies (those little files used by Web site administrators to keep track of visitors' browsing preferences).

Mail preferences differ slightly on the Macintosh. Preferences available on Windows but not the Mac are the ability to display mail headers as white or gray and the ability to display header addresses as links. The important preferences (for

me, at least) are to keep all the mail I send and receive in my Personal Filing Cabinet and to use Internet quoting in my e-mail replies, preceding each line of the reply with the greater than sign (>). These key preferences are available on both Windows and the Mac.

Password preferences, too, are the same: you can now have AOL remember your password so you don't need to include it when signing on, and you can password-protect your Personal Filing Cabinet.

Personal Filing Cabinet (PFC) preferences are more elaborate on the Macintosh. In Windows, you get a warning if the size of your Personal Filing Cabinet reaches a certain number of megabytes or a certain percentage of your hard drive (you can set either or both numbers). On the Mac, by contrast, you can have PFC items automatically deleted after a certain amount of time (which you can specify) has elapsed.

1. Put a check in the "Automatically delete items in my personal filing cabinet" box.
2. Choose any of the following items you want to delete automatically: incoming/saved e-mail, sent e-mail, incoming newsgroup postings, outgoing postings, or downloaded files. Click OK.

Note *The list of downloaded files can quickly fill up your PFC, so you might want to limit the number of files you download to about one a month. On the Mac you limit the number of downloaded files you're tracking by age rather than by number (as you do in Windows). Doing this will keep your PFC from slowing down as it fills up.*

3. Click the double arrows for the type of item and choose from the pop-up window whether to have items deleted weekly; every two weeks; every one, two, or six months; annually; or never. Another preference lets you confirm any deletions before they take place. If you regularly download hundreds of newsgroup postings for offline reading, deleting these postings regularly keeps your PFC from getting bloated.

Toolbar preferences on the Mac differ in a few respects. First, unlike Windows, you can't have the toolbar appear at the bottom of your display, but you can "unanchor" it and place it where you please. Also, you cannot automatically clear your History Trail after switching screen names or signing off.

With AOL 4.0 for the Mac, you *can*, however, clear your History Trail at will (click the Clear History Trail Now button), and you *can* restore the toolbar buttons if you've customized your toolbar (click the Restore Original Buttons Now button).

AOL Link preferences are unique to the Macintosh, but you should not use them unless you have networking expertise and plan to connect via TCP/IP. See "Setting up a TCP/IP Connection and Editing Locations."

Helper preferences, which have disappeared from the AOL for Windows software, are still available on AOL 4.0 for the Mac. These preferences let you set up helper applications—programs that open automatically when you download a file using the AOL browser. (Chapter 8 shows how to set up a helper application using Windows 95, just in case you need one.) To use these preferences, (1) you must know *either* the MIME type or (something much easier to find out) the file extension of the files that should launch the helper application, and (2) you need to have the helper application on your hard drive. A list of the MIME types for common file formats is available at AOL.com's NetHelp (**http://www.aol.com/nethelp/error/errornohelper.html**).

Tip *Let AOL and the AOL browser handle multimedia files as best they can. When you encounter unusual file types, follow the instructions, if any, at the Web site. The Mac forums listed in Table D-1 at the end of this chapter contain software libraries with helper applications.*

Newsgroup preferences on the Mac, as on Windows, must be set at *keyword: Newsgroups*; there are no differences between Mac and Windows preferences.

PERSONAL FILING CABINET (PFC)

Both the Mac and Windows versions of AOL 4.0 give you the same capabilities for archiving your e-mail messages, newsgroup postings, and downloaded files, but they do so in a slightly different way.

As you can see here, the Mac uses a tray or drawer metaphor (like a drawer in a filing cabinet) rather than a folder metaphor (as in Windows):

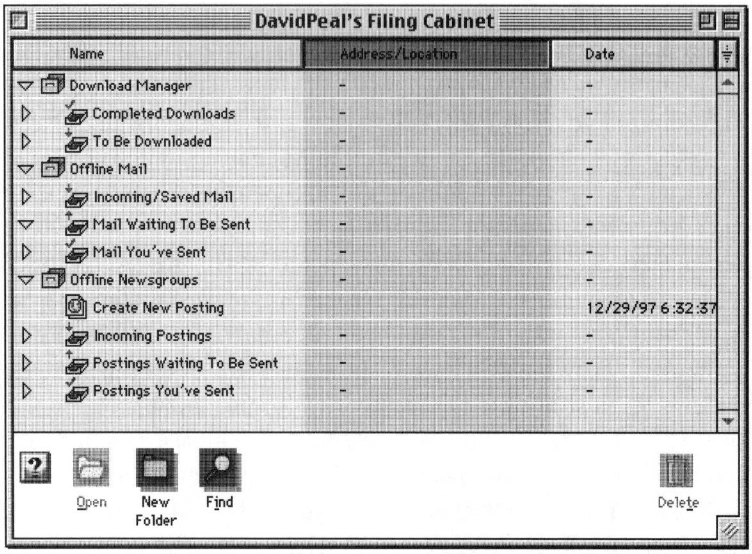

There's also a more substantive difference. On the Mac, you can sort your messages by name (that is, by subject, to see all messages on the same subject), by address (to see all messages from the same person), or by date (the default, to see messages ordered chronologically). This feature is an enormous help if you're searching for a specific old message. Next to Date is a button with a stylized arrow. Clicking the arrow reverses the order of the selected column from what is known as an ascending sort (*a* through *z*) to a descending one (*z* through *a*).

Tip *With AOL 4.0 for the Macintosh, you can arrange list items according to different fields by just clicking the column heads for the appropriate field. This feature is available using Download Manager, PFC, and the Address Book.*

The Find feature of the Macintosh PFC offers a compact format and enables you to find a specific message:

To look for a specific message, you can search message titles (i.e., subject lines and addresses) or actual content (what's in the messages). You can also search both at the same time.

Click the little arrow in the middle button to switch between AND and OR. Use AND if you are looking for messages from a particular person containing specific words in the body. Use OR if you want to search just message bodies (using the "whose contents contain" box). As in Windows, you can do a case-sensitive search or a case-insensitive search by adding a check or removing it from the check box.

E-MAIL

What's *not* different between Windows and the Mac is the most important thing: your mailbox. The AOL 4.0 for Windows software has now caught up with AOL 3.0 for the Macintosh. When you click Read on the AOL toolbar, you see all three mailboxes in a single window, whether you're on AOL 4.0 for Mac or Windows; each mailbox has its own tab.

The main difference can be found in the way you **write e-mail messages**. Click Write and you get a different sort of Write Mail window from the one described in Chapter 3.

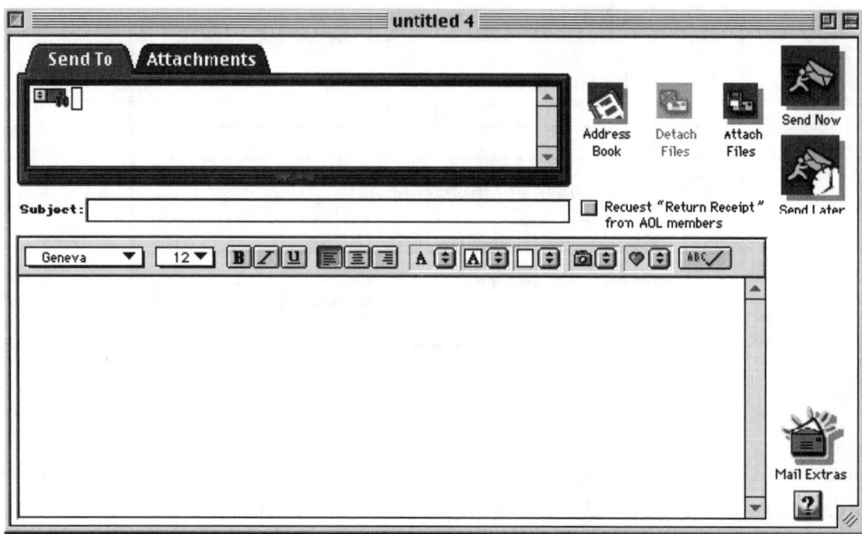

The good news is that all the features and functionality are all here; the window is just laid out a little differently.

Notice first that Send To and Attachments are tabs, not a box and a button respectively, as in AOL 4.0 for Windows (Chapter 3).

Tip *The amount of space used by the Send To and Attachments tabs can be reduced. Move your mouse over the lower border of this area until it turns into a double arrow. Click and drag upward to reduce the size of the Send To/Attachments tabs.*

To address a message to someone, you need two pieces of information: that person's address and whether the person is a direct recipient (To) or an indirect recipient (CC or BCC). Using the Send To tab, just type the address in the box. To indicate whether the recipient is direct or indirect, click the little box showing up and down arrows, then select To, CC, or BCC from the pop-up window.

Tip *By default, addresses are "To" addresses. If you're a touch typist, beginning an address with a square bracket ([) turns the address into a CC; beginning it with a left parenthesis [( ] turns it into a BCC. Typing either] or) at the end of a CC or BCC makes the next address a To.*

To send the same message to several people, you needn't cram the addresses in the same box as in Windows. Instead, press the ENTER key to create an additional address box in which to enter a new address and indicate whether the addressee should be designated To, CC, or BCC. As your list of recipients grows, a vertical scroll bar appears in the Send To box.

Attaching a file to a message is easy on the Macintosh. Switch to the Attachments tab. Click Attach files, then navigate to the folders on your hard drive or floppy where the files are kept. You can also drag files directly into the Attachments tab.

You can attach multiple files to a single message (this feature has been available longer on the Mac than on Windows), but they'll be *stuffed* instead of *zipped* when you send the message. On the Mac, unstuffing requires the StuffIT program, which is built into AOL for the Macintosh. If you download a StuffIT (SIT) file, it is automatically unstuffed when you open it from the File menu. BinHex files that you download using AOL 4.0 for the Mac will also be automatically decoded when you open them from the File menu.

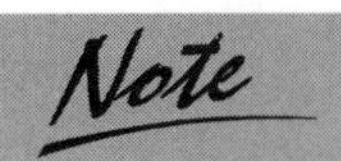

A StuffIT program exists for Windows, so your Windows friends will be able to use your stuffed files.

Unlike earlier versions of AOL, neither AOL 4.0 for Windows nor AOL 4.0 for the Mac require that you supply a Subject line and message.

All the formatting effects described in Chapter 3 are available to you on the Mac: bold, italics, underlining; center, left, and right alignment; variable fonts, font colors, and font sizes; and the ability to insert links, pictures, and background images and colors. If you used AOL 3.0 for the Mac, the spell-checking capability will be old hat.

Mail Extras are coming to the Mac, including pre-packaged images and designs, as well as online greeting cards.

The AOL 4.0 for the Macintosh Address Book differs in slight ways from the one described in Chapter 3. You can automatically place someone's address in your Address Book by opening a message from that person and clicking Remember Address (not Add Address). However, if you enter both a first name and a last name for the new person, the address will appear as Last Name, First Name in the Address Book window. So leave out the last name if you want to arrange addresses by first name.

Here's a more important difference: you can arrange your Address Book listings by either name or address just by clicking the appropriate column head in the Address Book window. Otherwise, all the power in the new Address Book is available in AOL 4.0 for the Macintosh. (Actually, most of it was available in AOL 3.0 for the Mac, but in a slightly different format and with a "notebook" look.)

NEWSGROUPS

As with AOL 4.0 for Windows, on AOL 4.0 for the Mac you can use Automatic AOL to download newsgroup postings for offline reading, then read the postings in your Personal Filing Cabinet at some later time (offline, if you wish). This procedure is roughly similar on both Windows and the Mac.

1. At *keyword: Newsgroups*, click Read Offline. In the Choose Newsgroups window, click and move newsgroups you're subscribed to from the left-hand window to the right-hand window. Click OK.
2. Run the Automatic AOL session. From the Mail Center menu, select Run Automatic AOL, then click Begin. Newsgroup postings are downloaded into your PFC.

Note *The Mac and Windows screens from which you start an Automatic AOL session differ slightly, but both have Begin buttons. To make sure you're downloading only postings (or only e-mail messages, or whatever you want), select the Mail Center menu's Set Up Automatic AOL before running an Automatic AOL session, and put check boxes only in the appropriate boxes.*

3. To read downloaded postings, select Offline Newsgroups from the My Files menu, whether you're offline or online. Postings for different newsgroups are downloaded to different folders in your Personal Filing Cabinet. Open a folder to read the postings in it. *Threads* (messages with the same subject line) have their own subfolders. Taking advantage of the Mac's ability to sort different fields, you can sort postings in different ways by clicking on the column heads. Also, you can use the PFC's Find capability to look for postings about specific subjects. These sorting features cannot be accessed online using *keyword: Newsgroups*; they are only available when you use postings downloaded with AOL 4.0 for the Mac and Automatic AOL.

THE WORLD WIDE WEB BROWSER

The browser integrated into AOL 4.0 for the Macintosh does not differ discernibly from the Windows browser. You can enter URLs either in the Address Box on the navigation bar or in the Keyword window. The same controls apply to both browsers: going forward, going back, stopping, reloading, and going home. Using either the

Internet menu or Welcome screen, click Go to the Web to go directly to the AOL.com Web site, where you can link to the AOL NetFind site. Web keywords are available on the Mac for the most popular sites (AOL.com, Liszt, Disney.com, Four11, and so on). If you want to make a Web page, the Mac version of AOLPress will serve you well. It's available at *keyword: AOLPress.*

Now for the (slight) differences:

- Press the mouse button down and keep it down to see a menu of available options. If you're pointing at a Web graphic, your options will include saving a copy of the graphic on your hard drive. If you're pointing at a link, you get several options, including opening the link in a new window. (This is like right-clicking with AOL 4.0 for Windows.)
- Preferences are simpler to set (see the "Preferences" section), but they are also more restricted in scope.
- The stand-alone MSIE browser is not automatically installed and placed on the Mac desktop.
- As far as plug-ins are concerned, Quicktime is automatically set up when you install AOL, and it lets you play many common audio, video, and animation files. All plug-ins are stored in the Plug-Ins subfolder of your America Online folder. For those other files you encounter, you'll need to download the plug-in or set up a helper application (see the paragraph on Helper preferences in "Preferences"). For Telnet, you can download NCSA Telnet from *keyword: Filesearch* and set it up as a helper application, with a MIME type of *URL: Telnet Protocol.*

USING INTERNET SOFTWARE ON THE MACINTOSH

Winsock (Chapter 10) lets you run a broad range of Internet software on AOL 4.0 for Windows. On the Mac, AOL Link does the same thing, and its file is installed for you in your Extensions folder when you install AOL.

Of the applications covered in Chapter 10 (Netscape, mIRC, and EWAN), only Netscape 4 runs on the Mac as well as in Windows. Netscape Navigator 4 for the Macintosh differs in small ways from the Windows version: there is no Personal toolbar, the Bookmark window (COMMAND-B) is not available on the navigation bar, and bookmarks can't be automatically updated.

While mIRC is a Windows-only product, other IRC clients such as IRCle enable you to take part on IRC using the Macintosh. The exact procedures for selecting a network, joining a channel, and taking part differ, of course, but the concepts

introduced in Chapter 10 fully apply. As for Telnet clients, NCSA Telnet is popular freeware that's more frequently updated than EWAN. For doing FTP, no program in the Windows world matches Fetch, which is available at *keyword: Filesearch.* With Fetch, downloading from an FTP site becomes as easy as using your Finder to retrieve a file from your hard drive. Anarchie for the Mac is a popular Archie-plus-FTP client for the Mac, also readily available on AOL.

On AOL, a big supply of Macintosh Internet software is available at *keyword: AOL Link*. Or, visit *keyword: Software* and open the Internet Kids folder (ignore the "Kids" part) for a big collections of Telnet, IRC, and other essential Internet software for the Macintosh.

Most of the Web mega-archives mentioned in Chapter 10 ("Where Do I Find Winsock Applications?") have Macintosh sections, including Tucows, Hotfiles, and Jumbo. A huge Mac-only Web archive, **http://www.macorchard.com**, is available from *keyword: AOL Link.*

SETTING UP A TCP/IP CONNECTION AND EDITING LOCATIONS

Setting up a TCP/IP connection is virtually the same on the Mac as described in Appendix A.

1. From the Welcome (or Goodbye) screen, click Setup. Select the third radio button, then click Next. In the Add Location window, give the new location a name. For TCP/IP, ignore the dialing options. Click Next.

Note *In the AOL Setup window you'll notice that there is no special tab for Connection Devices, as there is in Windows. Rather, a Modem Options button is available from most screens you'll use when setting up either a new location or a new access number within a location.*

2. In the Add Connections window (the title bar still reads AOL Setup), click the Add TCP connection radio button. Click OK to add this location.

   - To set up a TCP/IP connection, you must use your AOL Link preferences (available at My AOL | Preferences). Remove the check from the box in the Automatic Configuration section, and click OK.

- To actually use the TCP/IP connection, first sign on to your other service (ISP or LAN), then select the TCP/IP location in the Welcome/Goodbye screen, and finally, sign onto AOL. You will be asked whether you want to switch from AOL Link, and when you click OK, the switch will take effect.

To restore your dial-in connection after using TCP/IP, use the Welcome (or Goodbye) screen to change your location and confirm that you want to switch access types.

To set up a location for holding access numbers (as opposed to a location that consists of just a TCP connection), follow the steps in the preceding procedure, but in Step 2 select "Add numbers" (it's the default) from the list of access phone numbers. You'll then enter an area code and select phone numbers, exactly as in "Editing Your Location" in the section Appendix A.

GETTING HELP

Whenever you see a Question Mark button, click it to get context-sensitive help. Online help for Mac software tends to come in a more compact and systematic format than for Windows. All this great help is centrally available in the Help menu's America Online Guide, even when you're offline. You can find information using the general table of contents (Topics) or the more fine-grained Index.

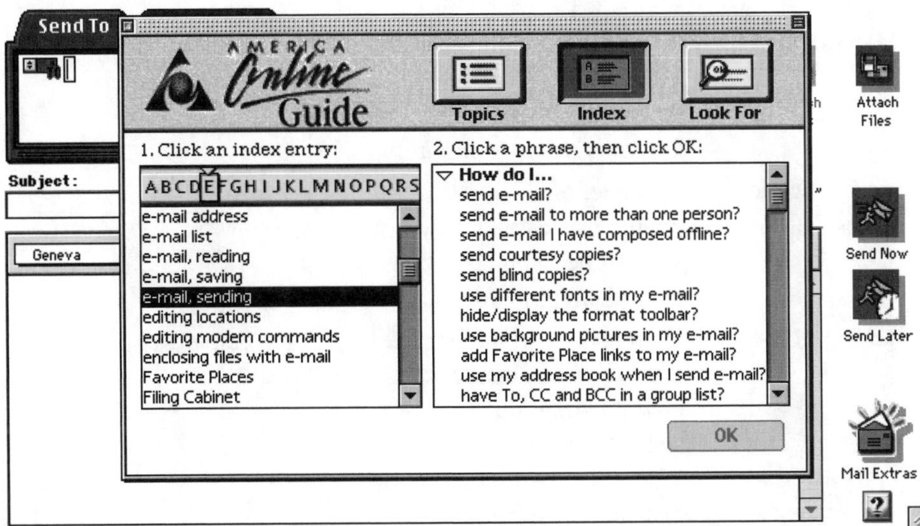

Macintosh users have always been close to the center of the AOL community, and Table D-1 lists some of the many Mac areas on AOL. If you have questions about

using the Mac, start with Mac Tips; for questions about using AOL as a Mac user, visit the Mac Help Desk; for non-AOL questions about using Mac applications, see one of the support forums, such as the Mac Utilities or Mac Applications forum.

Tip *For more technical users, the comp.sys.mac hierarchy includes many useful newsgroups dealing with Mac games, applications, programming, and hardware. At* keyword: Newsgroups, *click Search Newsgroups and do a search for* ***comp.sys.mac*** *to see a list of the many groups available. Chapter 5 has all the instructions for using newsgroups on AOL.*

Area or Forum	Content	Keyword
Apple Business Consortium	Promotes use of the Macintosh in business; a central source of information about Macintosh business solutions	Applebiz
Apple on AOL	Apple Computer: comprehensive product information, company news, user groups, chat, etc.	AppleAOL **http://www.apple.com**
BMUG Online	The Berkeley Macintosh Users Group, a great source of software, information (BMUG Glossary), and community	**http://www.bmug.org/homepage.html**
Mac Applications Forums	A collection of forums for people interested in specific word-processing, database, and other applications	Apps
Mac Help Desk	Help using and making the most of AOL; includes a downloading tutorial plus a central collection of all Mac-related message boards and support forums	Mac help desk

TABLE D-1 AOL areas for Macintosh loyalists

Area or Forum	Content	Keyword
Mac Tips	The basics of working with files, managing windows, printing, using the trash, formatting disks, and more	Mac tips, then click on same-named button
Mac Utilities Forum	A large collection of Mac software, including virus checkers, desktop decorators, and the like; message boards on INITS, CDEVs, and Mac system software	MUT
Mac Animation & Video Forum	The Macintosh multimedia forum, with loads of information and software for users of Quicktime and Director	Quicktime
Mac Communications and Networking Forum	A mixed bag of information relating to viruses, BBS's, and other networking issues	MCM
Mac Developers Forum	For programmers; a good place for information about Mac operating systems	MDV
Macintosh Games	Part of the Games channels; offers special interest groups, chat, software libraries, message boards, and help	Mac Games
Mac Music & Sound Forum	Message boards, software, and informational links relating to acoustics, composition, and working with various file types	MMS

TABLE D-1 AOL Areas for Macintosh Loyalists (*continued*)

Area or Forum	Content	Keyword
Macworld Online	AOL area for the leading Macintosh magazine with feature articles, columns, news, and product reviews; includes back issues through 1994	Macworld

TABLE D-1 AOL areas for Macintosh loyalists (*continued*)

A

INDEX

B

C

D

E

F

G

H

I

J

K

L

M

N

AMERICA
Online

O

P

Q

R

S

T

U

V

W

Y

Z